www.askwhisky.co.uk

C. ASK WHISKY

Distilled by
Rory Mhor Nicoll
and Peter Columbia

Foreword
by Big Peat

Edited by
John McKeever

Rory Nicoll

CONTENTS

FOREWORD BY BIG PEAT

Having been approached by the powers that be behind the production of this fine epistle of spiritual understanding to put pen to paper by way of an introductory commendation I had to consider well and long into the night for I am indeed possibly the most revered of all Whisky experts, having been created for this very purpose, and I turned to the alter of the cask for restitude and decided - Why Not? When one is steeped in the traditions of greatness a man and his wisdom can be seen as a Braggart but, be that as it may, I would have to accept my words are of the very essence and, for the life of me, I can think of no better man for the task.

If you're thinking in yir inner heart the braggart o' ma'sel ye ken little o the men o, Islay for, o' aw the isles aff the Western shores a' Caledonia, this is surely where the rain falls fairest and the waters flow clearest ower unsullied peat an provides the body o' the spirit o' Honest Men. So you can believe me when I tell you that, unlike some of our island neighbours, we men of Islay neffer fish on a Sunday', are renowned and sought after lovers and known as the ultimate word when the great god uisge tickles oor kilt, as is a given to describe the effect of the Wee Sensation, or, as you Sasenachs and Heathens wi the deep pockets and short arms prefer to call it - The Whisky.

Oh tae be sure there are Whisky's distilled in aw pairts o' god's world and, if the feelin has ye by the hied, there are no bad whiskies but, and I am no braggart, as my Auld Mither would vouch for, if ye wir tae produce a cask blended frae' the finest of every still ae the wide world ye widnae hiv onythin that could even match a reek o' an Islay man's keegch.

Whilst pride of Islay and the many misty moments of greatness I have experienced in the grip of the great god uisge gars me give forth the praise of my native spirit, I am honour bound to give praise to the many distillers far and near who, through the centuries, have sought to produce something akin to our Islay nectar and, whatever yir likin, if the Islay isn't available, may I hereby say ye can pay no greater compliment to freen or companion than to share a dram wi them wha indulge the grape in ignorance o' the grain and elighten and yet encourage them to produce the water of life, aye remembering that what they are seeking is tae Bottle Highland Hospitality when day is ower and fire in the belly when the battle has tae be fought and, whilst the world will never match the magic o' Scotlands' Cunning Chemists ae the past, we Men o' Islay graciously accept yir respect for oor superiority and wish ye weel in yir caskng.

Wi this wee bookie in yir possession ye will become gie near as knowledgeable as me an he lassies will fair fancy ye as their men fa' unner the spell o' yir wisdom, so here's tae ye ma worthie freen

Ony man worthie o' the name wid haud high that dram o' amber and marvel that surely frae he made that awsome discovery behind the closed door o' the wee hut in the gairden when he wis fourteen' there is nae ither thing as ye can find sae muckle guid feeling frae and yet haud it in the palm o' yin hand

May yir dram aye avour yir palette
May a' yir Bairns be Bonny
May a' yir eggs hiv double yolks and, maist o' a'

May your Giving Hand neffer fail you!
Big Peat

WHAT WOULD YOU C. AND ASK ABOUT WHISKY?

Whisky was the muse, the inspiration of Scotland's bard, the poet Robert Burns, at least on the occasion of his penning of the merry poem that follows:

"O thou, my Muse! guid, auld Scotch Drink!
Whether thro' wimplin worms thou jink,
Or, richly brown, ream owre the brink,
In glorious faem,
Inspire me, till I lisp an' wink,
To sing thy name!

C. Ask Whisky wants to bring you everything you ever wanted to know about the Auld Scotch Drink but were enjoying yourself too much to Ask, and beyond Auld Scotch Drink, the Whiskies of the world. Your appreciation for this luxurious pleasure created slowly over many a year, at least three years and a day and often much longer, should grow as your knowledge grows, and we trust that your thirst for both Whisky and all things about Whisky will be whetted.

The aim of this book is to bring the world's leading experts on Whisky all together in one tome to answer anything you would like to C. and Ask about Whisky!

We - as in Rory Nicoll and Peter Columbia, the authors - come from the Entertainment Industry. It was a pleasant surprise to find that the worldwide Whisky Industry and the Entertainment Industry have a lot in common - the most obvious common denominator is bringing you enjoyment. It was our intent to bring you an entertaining, thought provoking, humorous book to enhance the pleasure of your dram. The more you know about art or music or nature or - really anything - and in this case, Whisky! - the more you will appreciate it. Facts and figures alone can be tedious however. Quite honestly, we had trouble staying awake while sifting through some of the Whisky literature we looked at in our research for this book. Our goal was to be different and bring you a lot of solid, useful information while also keeping you interested and entertained. Our philosophy is that information doesn't have to induce yawns and so this book has been written in an approachable, use-friendly style.

Another approach we took was to bring in the smartest Whisky people on the planet together for your benefit. Instead of putting ourselves forward as experts, we wanted to bring in the experts and ask them the questions. We were very privileged to speak to some fantastic and fascinating people all around the world and interview them for this book.

THE PEOPLE BEHIND C. ASK WHISKY

Before we rightly disappear behind the scenes and become the invisible authors we should be, it is fitting that you should know a little something about the people that have Distilled this project for you. We've already said that we come from another Industry all together which gives us the vantage point of outside observers. Here are some of the details: Rory Nicoll is the author of the Music Industry books Hit Click and Hit Click Master Class. He collaborated with writer Peter Columbia on a novel about a Scottish legend known as the Fairy Flag and he collaborated again with Mr. Columbia on C. Ask Whisky. Rory grew up in the Music Industry. His parents, Watt Nicoll and Doreen Swan were well-known folk singers in their native Scotland and Rory started performing on stage at an early age, becoming a champion dancer in the process. While still a teenager, Rory started producing music and formed a Dance Music band (Colorscheme) that played the SECC in Glasgow and many of the biggest gigs in Europe. After signing his first publishing music contract at 17, Rory went with his solo RMN Project, which was signed with Sony Europe, Baby Records Europe and JVC -Victor in Japan and Asia selling hundreds of thousands of units. Rory continued in a career of producing records and staging shows and events. Rory has Produced and managed Hamish Imlach and Finbar Furey; their Whisky stories gave Rory an interest in the Auld Scotch Drink. Rory has also worked with Prince, Edwin Starr, Peter Joback, Kym Mazelle, Doug E Fresh and many other well known names from the Music Industry.

If you are from Scotland, you are never far from the Scotch Whisky Industry even if you work in another Industry. Rory's father, Watt Nicoll and Doreen Swan sang a number of Whisky songs as folk singers. Watt wrote many a Whisky song and toured with a play he had written called simply The Scotch Play. That play was sponsored by Grant's Whisky. These were some of the influences that inspired Rory to start his own Whisky collection and also start the C. Ask Whisky book and DVD project.

Peter Columbia had no connection whatsoever to the Whisky Industry prior to being brought in to the project. He comes from a comedy writing background and so a lot of humour was purposely injected into the book when and where appropriate - or inappropriate as it happens.

THE AGENDA

Our approach to this book was to be positive and talk up the Industry. There are all these amazing personalities who have invested their time, energy, money, interest and passion into bringing you a special Bottle of Whisky. Many Whiskies took a decade or more to reach you. We want to champion these people and their Whiskies.

If there was a negative to bring up, it was that we could C that there was an injustice to be addressed! Here is the injustice in a nutshell: There are people who don't make Whisky, didn't study the science of fermentation, don't operate the stills, don't compete in the worldwide Whisky marketplace and yet they come along and insult that long-aged, carefully made dram just because they put themselves forward as experts and critics.

C. Ask Whisky Asks "Why Ask self-proclaimed critics when you can Ask real experts!? Why not Ask these Masters of their craft who Make the Whisky, Blend the Whisky, Taste the Whisky and work day in and day out in the Industry?" C. Ask Whisky wanted to bring their stories, personalities, passion, enthusiasm, knowledge and expertise to you. From Scotland, Ireland, America, Canada, Japan, Taiwan, Australia, New Zealand, Europe - and even Mexico! - we whisk you around the whirld of Whisky to meet the people behind your favourite drams.

Here are the topics we will look at:

- WHISK-TORY:
- An entertaining history of Whisky.
- THE SIX REGIONS:
- Scotland takes aim at the world through its six Scotch producing regions.
- WHISKED AROUND THE WHIRLD:
- A round the world trip looking at Whisky all over the planet.
- THE NOSE KNOWS:
- The art of Whisky Tasting with wisdom from the Master Tasters.
- THE MAD SCIENTISTS OF MALT:
- We meet some of the world' greatest Master Blenders and take a look at their Blends.

- WHISKY GO-HOARD:
- We take a look at the pleasure of Whisky Collecting.
- TIPPLE TOURS?:
- We wanted to give you an overview of Distillery Tourism.
- WHISKY AND CULTURE:
- We discuss Whisky's impact on popular culture and look at Literature, Cinema, Music and the celebrities that have a connection with Whisky.
- THE WHISK- LISTS: Reference lists, ratings and awards.

SPELLING AND GRAMMAR

It should be noted that because this book is being written in Scotland, we are going to spell Whisky the Scottish way. That is not because the UK way to spell the word is better than any other way. It is simply a technical nightmare we wish to avoid by being uniform. Capitalising Whisky and all the Whisky words throughout was an artistic choice - so please don't call the grammar police. We also shorten "years old" to YO - Y, because its easier!

LEGAL WHISKY DEFINITIONS

We also know that there are different definitions of Whisky. To legally be called Scotch Whisky for instance, the following strict regulations must be adhered to, and I quote the following legalese:

"Produced at a Distillery in Scotland from water and malted

barley (to which only whole grains of other cereals may be added) all of which have been:

Processed at that Distillery into a mash.
Converted at that Distillery to a fermentable substrate only by endogenous enzyme systems.

Fermented at that Distillery only by adding yeast.

Distilled at an Alcoholic strength by volume of less than 94.8% (190 US proof)

Wholly matured in an excise warehouse in Scotland in oak casks of a capacity not exceeding 700 litres (185 US gal; 154 imp gal) for at least three years.

Retaining the colour, aroma, and taste of the raw materials used in, and the method of, its production and maturation

Containing no added substances, other than water and plain (E150A) caramel colouring
Comprising a minimum Alcoholic strength by volume of 40% (80 US proof)"

Ireland, Canada and USA will have variations of these particular rules to make them legally Irish Whisky, Canadian Whisky and American Whisky (with specific sub-divisions such as Bourbon, Tennessee Whisky and Moonshine).

C. Ask Whisky will take you to C them all. Thank you for joining us on this grand adventure!

THANKS AND DEDICATION

Rory Nicoll would like to thank Big Peat for his kind words in the Foreword.

I also thank Conny Forsgren for all the Whisky chats and welcome him as a honourable member of the C. Ask Whisky Members Club.

This book is dedicated to my Grandpa, George McGowan Swan who loved a rare Whisky - in fact any Whisky.

CHAPTER *one*

Whisk-Tory

YEAST MEETS WEST

The comedian W. C. Fields said, "Always carry a large flagon of Whisky in case of snakebite, and furthermore always carry a small snake."

Most people drink Whisky quite happily without the small snake in tow, but the story of Whisky would be no story at all without some living things much smaller than W.C. Fields' pet viper.

The story of Whisky begins with Saccharomyces Cerevisiae!

Forget the snake. We'll even ditch the tongue twister name in favour of a nickname. May I suggest Sac. C.? Yes, ladies and gentlemen, Sac C. almost single-handedly (and without hands) became a mass-producer of Alcohol and may just have inspired the video game Pac-Man. Sac. C. acts like and looks like a miniature Pac-Man, a globular sphere of a micro-organism that munches everything in sight (without the chewing sound effects, open and closing mouth, excitable eyes and plinky-plonky music). Unlike its video game counterpart, Sac. C. must excrete after it eats. Pac-Man the video game, would not have sold half as well if the kids all said, "Look Mom, Pac-Man is taking a dump!" Yes, Sac. C. dines upon the naturally occurring sugars in fruit or grains and excretes Alcohol. When someone claims to have gotten pissed or had a piss up, they are not far off the truth - though Sac. C. did the pissing first! All Sac. C. does is eat, excrete and reproduce. Millions of Sac C. pigging out on ever-ripening fruit (actually causing the ripening) or a type of grain will cause the desired fermentation - fermentation being the fancy word for Sac. C. eating the natural sugars/starches in fruit and grain before excreting Alcohol. Another name we have for Sac. C. is yeast, though Sac. C. is by far the most useful yeast and has helped us bake bread as well as produce Beer, Wine and Whisky.

How mankind buddied up with Sac. C. in the first place has been lost in the mists of time, but most think the meetings were accidental.

Science writer and biologist Rob Dunn argues that: "Humankind's Ascent took a path of yeast resistance." He says, "There's a strong case to be made that the first species cultivated by humankind was brewer's yeast, and a generation of researchers will drink to that."

Commenting on the theory of a scientist named Solomon Katz that the desire for Beer might have driven early man to forsake the hunter/gatherer lifestyle for an agricultural lifestyle, Robb Dunn paints this picture: "Imagine the scenario - an early Egyptian left wild wheat or some other grass seed in water. Maybe he had intended to make gruel, but he left it too long and the slurry sprouted (and happened to have fermented, as well). Yet, because he was hungry or thirsty or simply dissatisfied, he drank it anyway. When he did, voilà! With that little buzz was born the germ of the need for agriculture. Or at least this is part of Katz's idea. He also thinks that Beer is, or at least was, good for us. Beer, he has suggested, is healthy when compared to the raw products out of which it is typically made. Relative to raw wheat or barley, for example, Beer is enriched in some fats, vitamin B and the amino acid lysine. Relative to the water likely to have been found in early human settlements, the first Beer is also likely to have been less ridden with pathogens. Fermentation purifies. It may be a stretch to say that Beer does the body good, but relative to our early alternatives, it probably did the body better (as by some measures it continues to do today)."

Rob Dunn's story about the Egyptian discovering Beer is pure conjecture, but it is known that a nameless Egyptian of antiquity contaminated the dough for flatbread he was kneading with yeast from between his toes. Somehow, he got the idea to walk on the dough instead of work it with his hands. This idea was probably inspired by the Winemakers who walked over the grapes in big Winepresses. The point is, the yeast, the Sac. C. between his toes - YUCK! - caused the bread to rise.

Researchers from Mexico (Alba-Lois, L. & Segal-Kischinevzky, C.) tell the following imaginative story about how our ancestors may have discovered the Alcoholic beverage:

"Once upon a time, many, many years ago, a man found a closed fruit jar containing a honeybee. When he drank the contents, he tasted a new, strange flavour. Suddenly his head was spinning, he laughed for no reason, and he felt powerful. He drank all the liquid in the jar. The next day he experienced an awful feeling. He had a headache, pain, an unpleasant taste in his mouth, and dizziness — he had just discovered the hangover. You might think this is just a tale, but is it? Several archaeological excavations have discovered jars containing the remains of Wine that are 7,000 years old."

The Alcoholic beverage evolved as civilization evolved. It was with mankind before we could write, although discovering Alcoholic beverages before writing probably didn't help the skill of writing along! Perhaps we would have discovered writing a hundred years earlier than we did, but we had trouble scratching symbols that anyone could read after imbibing the drinks that preceded writing.

Alba-Lois & Segal-Kischinevzky continue the story of mankind's relationship with the Alcoholic beverage saying: "Over the course of human history, and using a system of trial, error, and careful observation, different cultures began producing fermented beverages. Mead, or honey Wine, was produced in Asia during the Vedic period (around 1700–1100 BC), and the Greeks, Celts, Saxons and Vikings also produced this beverage. In Egypt, Babylon, Rome, and China, people produced Wine from grapes and Beer from malted barley. In South America, people produced chicha from grains or fruits, mainly maize; while in North America, people made octli (now known as "pulque") from agave, a type of cactus. At the time, people knew that leaving fruits and grains in covered containers for a long time produced Wine and Beer, but no one fully understood why the recipe worked. The process was named fermentation, from the Latin word fervere, which means "to boil." The name came from the observation that mixtures of crushed grapes kept in large vessels produced bubbles, as though they were boiling. Producing fermented beverages was tricky. If the mixture did not stand long enough, the product contained no Alcohol; but if left for too long, the mixture rotted and was undrinkable. Through empirical observation, people learned that temperature and air exposure are key to the fermentation process."

How far back does the bevy-making go? It seems different findings keep pushing the dates back. Jars for Wine that were 7000-years-old have already been mentioned or in other words the Wine jars can be dated to around 5000 B.C. Then an even older date of 8000 B.C. came to light because evidence emerged of Wine making in ancient Turkey, but then stone-age Beer jugs were discovered that were as old as 10,000 B.C. giving scientific credibility to the phrase, "Yabba Dabba Doo!"

DISTILL MY HEART

There is an old children's joke that asks, "What do you get if you cross an elephant and a rhino?" One answer is to shrug your shoulders, swear and say, "Elifino!" but the alternative punch line is "a lot of strange people at the wedding."

Whisky does have a lot of strange relatives. We have already discovered that Whisky, like all Alcoholic beverages is related to the microscopic Pac-Men known as Sac. C. or yeast.

Whisky's is also related to perfume technology, the mystical, magical pseudo-science of alchemy and early forms of medicine.

The pursuit of perfume, alchemy and medicine eventually led to the technology that enabled us to Distill Whisky.

What does it mean to Distill? Most of us have never Distilled anything in our lives beyond watching steam come out of a kettle. The word Distillation is from the Latin de-stillare meaning drip or trickle down. A dictionary definition of Distillation is the "evaporation and subsequent collection of a liquid by condensation as a means of purification." That's a mouthful so let's slow that down and discuss an example. If you wanted to Distill seawater for instance, in order to separate the water from all the salt and produce drinking water, you would need to heat the seawater until it evaporates. The vapour is then funnelled into a cooler container where it will condense back into liquid water, leaving behind the salt in the heated container. Alcohol or ethanol can be separated from liquid water because it has a different boiling point. It will evaporate at 78.5 C while water's boiling point is 100 C. The Alcohol vapours are then collected and condensed back into a purified liquid form.

We might not know a lot about Distillation but most of us know our way around a computer and there is a computer analogy that can be made to help us understand Distillation. One computer connected to another can transfer information, whole computer files, pictures, sounds, even movies to another computer. We download information all the time to our PCs that are hooked up to the internet. Instead of two computers, Distillation in its simplest form involves two containers, one that's hot and one that's cold. The hot container will have a lid that traps all the vapours and leaves them no place to go but out through a narrow tube or spout leading to the other container where cooling condensation will cause the vapours to return to liquid form and collect in the cold container. The teapot and the still are very similar in design, though the spout device on an ancient still will curve downward only so gravity can help with all the draining and dripping. Distillation is a physical form of downloading, but instead of electronic bits of code, it is actual liquid that is being downloaded from one container to another, minus any unwanted liquid or impurities.

Simple Distillation methods enter the picture early on in our history - different dates are argued about - there is evidence of early stills as far back as 3500 B.C. that were dug up in Northern Iraq and 3000 B.C. stills in what is now India. Even with Distillation taking place this far back in time, we are still nearly 4 to 5 thousand years away from Distilled Whisky.

The writer for www.copper-alembic.com recounts the history of Distillation and says: "As far back as the fourth century B.C. Aristotle suggested the possibility of spirit Distillation when he wrote: "Seawater can be made potable by Distillation as well, and Wine and other liquids can be submitted to the same process."

We do know that early stills were being used by an old Mesopotamian King named Zimrilim in the making of perfume. By the way, who would name their kid Zimrilim? I wonder if he was beat up at school? He did like perfume. Hmmm? Anyway old sweet smelling Zimmy lived in what is now Iraq and the stills back in 1810 B.C. were not used to mass produce Whisky - we are still more than three thousand years away from Whisky. Rather these early deformed teapots were used to mass produce a whole lot of bombs - Sorry. Wrong homonym. It's Iraq and it was a Freudian slip - I mean, balms, perfumes, incense.

Back in the days before deodorant was invented, covering all the stinky b.o. with perfume was the need that drove the technology forward. A lot of fragrance was a status symbol back in the day like owning a Ferrari or a Porsche or a 70-year-old Mortlach. It was good for romance and all those royal mummies needed embalming. That is why the technology to Distill Whisky owes much to the technology related to making perfume. The Latin word 'Per fumum' became our word perfume and it originally meant "through the smoke." In the ancient world, good smelling stuff was a highly prized commodity. Two of the three very first Christmas presents consisted of very expensive fragrances called frankincense and myrrh. Perfume, balms and incense were big business and produced on an industrial scale for the time in places like Egypt and all over the Middle East.

A woman from 2000 BC from what is now Iraq had the honour of being the first chemist. Her name was Tapputi the Cutey. I added the cutey bit. I don't know if she was cute or not, but it rhymes! She was a perfume maker and we know about her because her legacy was recorded on an ancient cuneiform tablet - cuneiform being one of the earliest forms of writing with lots of picture symbols. The old tablet even reports how she made the perfume. She Distilled flowers and oil with other nice smelling ingredients and then filtered them again and Distilled them a further few times.

The world's oldest surviving perfumes were discovered by archaeologists in Cyprus around the same time that Tapputi the Cutey was making her perfumes in Mesopatamia. A whole perfume factory was uncovered with 60 stills, mixing bowls and perfume Bottles.

So the striving after perfume kept improving Distillation technology, but that is not to say that fermented drink Distillation wasn't being sought after from early on as well. The first evidence of any kind of primitive Alcohol Distillation happened a thousand years after the time of sweet smelling King Zimmy. In 800 B.C. the Japanese Distilled Shochu - a drink with a 25 % Alcohol kick Distilled from the rice Wine called Sake. Around this same time, a drink called Arrack was being Distilled from a mix of rice and molasses in India, and in what is now the country of Georgia (not the American state, but the Eastern European Georgia near Russia), horse milk was being Distilled to make a beverage called Skhou. I would imagine that after drinking fermented horse milk, the word Skhou would be the first word out of my mouth too followed by some foot stamping, a rear up and a loud whinny sound!

Fast forward to Alexandria, Egypt just before the time of Christ.

Alexandria is a scholarly centre in the ancient world with its famous library that was sadly burnt to the ground. Here, the technology of Distillation moves forward. Even Queen Cleopatra knew about Distillation and was said to have described the process though her original words were lost in that same damn library fire. You will recall that Cleopatra took W.C. Fields advice. She did keep the pet snake! She was bitten, but had no Whisky to treat the poisoned wound and so she snuffed it. A century after Cleopatra, alchemists in her hometown were performing lots of Distillation experiments.

Alchemy was a weird form of chemistry that became real scientific chemistry as time went on, but in ancient to Medieval times, it was mixed with all kinds of magical lingo and ideas. Alchemists were seeking the mystical 'philosopher's stone' thousands of years before Harry Potter was a twinkle in J.K. Rowling's eye. Alchemists wanted to turn other metals into gold, find magical healing and life prolonging elixirs. The great thing about alchemy though was that all the hocus-pocus led to some real scientific breakthroughs, and the early alchemists contributed to Distillation technology that would eventually bring you your prized shot of Single Malt Whisky. Raise a glass for perfume and alchemy!

A 4th century alchemist named Zosimos - which sounds like a great name for a stage magician (Ladies and Gentlemen, put your hands together for the marvellous, the mysterious, Zosimos the Magnificent!) - wrote about a mystical lady from a century or two earlier named Maria the Jewess. She was credited with inventing the Alembic Still. Just in case you ever go on a game show and this comes up as the million pound/dollar question, alembic is an Arabic word meaning deformed teapot. Actually, alembic comes from the Greek word 'ambix' meaning, a vase with a narrow opening, though today alembic is the word for a Distilling apparatus, now obsolete, consisting of a rounded, necked flask and a cap with a long beak for condensing and conveying the purified liquid. Zosimos credits Maria the Jewess with the Alembic Still along with the inventions of several other types of chemical apparatus. She was also said to have invented a kind of Alembic Still called the Tribikos - the tri in the word is a clue. It was a three armed still, an improvement on earlier stills, and more useful for collecting the desired substances from the Distillation process. According to Zosimos, Maria the Jewess recommended that the copper or bronze of the Tribikos Alembic Still be the thickness of a frying pan, and the joint between these tubes and the still-head be sealed with flour-paste. Maria the Jewess was behind the Kerotakis as well, a thingamajiggy used to heat up a substance and collect the vapours. It was a hermetically sealed (another Maria the Jewess innovation) container with a sheet of copper perched on the top, creating a vacuum.

With Maria's contribution of the Tribikos and Kerotakis, to other developments in early chemical and Distillation equipment, the technology kept marching on. Zosimos himself along with his sister invented many types of stills and condensers.

There is a legend that Saint Patrick learned about Distillation while visiting Egypt in the 5th century and brought this knowledge to Ireland. Whether this was true or not, a tradition of Alcohol Distillation became associated with monasteries in Ireland and then monasteries in Scotland and elsewhere. To quote the site, whisky.com: "The Distilling process was originally applied to perfume, then to Wine, and finally adapted to fermented mashes of cereals in countries where grapes were not plentiful. The spirit was universally termed Aqua Vitae ('water of life') and was commonly made in monasteries, and chiefly used for medicinal purposes, being prescribed for the preservation of health, the prolongation of life, and for the relief of colic, palsy and even smallpox." We still don't have proper Whisky at this point. We do start to get white spirit - un-aged, untreated, straight from the still, clear as water Alcohol that is closer to what Vodka is than what Whisky is.

Fast forward to the 9th century AD, and a book written by an Arabian chemist named Al-Kindi was published. His book was called The Book of the Chemistry of Perfume and Distillations and it included hundreds of recipes for making perfumes and many details about the Distillation process. Sharing the knowledge with the world in a book leads to even more improvements.

Distillation was becoming more advanced all the time, and took another step forward when a Persian chemist named Ibn Sina found a way to get the oils out of flowers through Distillation. Steam would be passed through the rose or daffodil or chrysanthemum or whatever it was. The heat of the steam would cause the oil in the flower to vaporise and this flower oil in gaseous form would then be siphoned off to the other container where it would condense as nice smelling flower oil. Perfumers of the present day, despite all our modern technology, still achieve the same basic effect using almost the same thousand-year-old methods.

A doctor, physician, surgeon named Abulcasis who was from Cordoba, Spain and lived from 936 - 1031 perfected the alembic and Distilled rose water and Wine, from which he obtained what was thought of as a magical elixir to guarantee immortality called "Aqua Vitae" an idea that spread, as we have heard, to the monasteries and then to the farmers of Ireland, Scotland, and the rest of the British Isles.

Using Alembic Distillation to obtain pure Alcohol for medicinal purposes takes us right up to a 1000 years AD. The next major step forward happens in the 11th century when the coiled cooling pipe was invented.

Henry the Second and his armies invaded Ireland in 1170 and found the Irish monks in their monasteries using Alembic Stills to Distill their version of holy water called Uisge Beatha. It is no coincidence that the word Uisge and Whisky sound alike because they are related words and Uisge Beatha evolved into the English word Whisky and means 'water of life'. Uisge Beatha, just like the original word, isn't quite Whisky just yet.

When the taxman starts coming, you know you're on to a winner and starting to make a profit. A hundred years later, the English began taxing the pre-industrial Irish Distilleries of the day making the white spirit Uisge Beatha.

The secrets of Distillation were largely Eastern and Mid-Eastern and the Europeans weren't quite as advanced in such matters. It is when the Turks invade Europe in the 13 and 14 hundreds that the secrets of Distillation become more widely known in Western Europe.

The Alembic Still eventually became more efficient. In 1526, a Swiss doctor, astrologer/occultist named Paracelsus used a water bath (called Balneal Mariae named in honour of Maria the Jewess) for the first time. This bath prevented the flask of the still from cracking while heating up, and brought stability to the temperature of the heated liquid. Paracelsus improved the vapour cooling system by running a tube through vessels of cold water. Thank you Paracelsus.

All the perfume, alchemy, and medicine, and the several thousand years of Distillation, finally took mankind to that crucial place where Distilled Spirits began to be used outside the field of medicine. In other words, the Distilled Alcoholic beverage finally went on sale in a big way, beginning in the 1400s and exploding in variety and in sales during the 1600s.

THE SCOTTISH - IRISH ARGUMENT

The history of Whisky in America, Canada and other countries around the globe such as Sweden, Japan and China will be discussed in a later chapter, but the centre of the Whisky universe is Scotland and Ireland.

The argument has raged for centuries. It has been the source of many a heated debate and probably a punch up or two. Both proud Celtic peoples claim that they were the first to come up with Whisky.

Leading up to the Whisky explosion was the art of Distilling that the monasteries had monopolised for medicinal purposes. There was then a dissolution of the monasteries by Henry the VIII and the suddenly unemployed monks needed work. They took their Distillation knowledge with them into the private sector. Whisky making went to the farming crofts and private individuals. To quote Katherine Macoll writing for the Answer Bank: "After the dissolution of the monasteries, Whisky-making became a people's art. It was practised by ex-monks who became apothecaries, barbers and surgeons. It was taken to the crofts and great houses in the Highlands. By the 16th century, triple Distillation was common practice in the Western Isles, and had spread to Ireland and France. By then Uisge Beatha (the Gaelic translation of Aquae Vitae, from which Whisky today is derived), was a central part of Highland life."

Many a monk and farmer in the two nations were Distilling the Vodka-like white spirits but it wasn't the amber, Cask-aged Whisky yet. This is believed to have happened accidentally on the Scottish Island of Islay, where White Spirit was left in a Cask, hidden away from the excise men and forgotten about for several years, and when the Cask was opened, a smooth tasty, first ever batch of real Whisky was the result. That is the legend.

Scotland's first recognized Distillery was in Fife mentioned in written records in 1494 and related to a receipt of 1500 Bottles.

The 1700s saw an explosion of production and Whisky Distilleries in both Ireland and Scotland. It was a neck and neck horse race as to who would dominate the world market. 2000 Distilleries, mostly small, Ma and Pa do-it-yourself Distilleries were in operation in Ireland.

There were legal, recognized Distilleries opening for business almost every year during the 1700s in Scotland. To take but one year as an example - the year 1795 - the following Distilleries opened their doors for business: Ardry, Barnshill, Boggs, Bonnytown, Cannongate, Coblebrae, Cowie, Craigend, Dumfries, Glasgow, Grange Burntisland, Greenock, Hamilton, Highland Park, House of Muir, Inverkeithing, Kepp, Kersebank, Kirkintilloch, Kirkliston, Littlecarse, Loanwells, Maines, Paisley, Richardtown, Shawend, Smallhills, Spynie, Torphichen, Tulliallan, Wallace Paw.

How did the Scots get the upper hand and run away with the lion's share of the Whisky industry? Here is one example of the Irish missing an opportunity that the Scots seized upon. An Irishman named Aeneas Coffey was behind a type of still that could continually churn out Distilled spirit instead of relying on the one batch at a time technique. This invention should have taken the Irish Whisky market into the stratosphere and leave the Scots behind in the dust. The irony would be complete if a Scotsman named Mr. Whisky had invented the modern coffee maker!

Felicity Cloake, writing for the Guardian newspaper states, "It was a Dublin man, Aeneas Coffey, who perfected the design of the modern Continuous Still, making Distillation cheaper and more efficient. Local Distillers pooh-poohed his idea, so he took his invention over to Scotland, where they seized upon its money-making potential immediately, enabling them to embark upon Grain Whisky production and to finally beat the Irish at their own game."

The Coffey Still ushered Whisky production into a new era of stability, and the taste was improved. In 1880 there was bad news for the Wine and Cognac producers in France, but their loss was Whisky's gain. The grapes of France were attacked by a plague of tiny grape-loving, sap-sucking insects called Phylloxera that wiped out the grape harvest that year. Whisky was there to console all the thirsty Wine-drinkers missing their Wine and so Whisky improved its international standing.

The story of Whisky would not be complete without the tax wars that ensued and its illegal trade. America's ban of Alcoholic beverages through the 1920s and early 30s - an event known as Prohibition is a major story in the history of Whisky and the illicit Alcohol made by the light of the moon or 'Moonshine' became well known during this period. America was not the only place to have 'Moonshiners,' however. Scotland and Ireland had their own version of the underground Whisky-makers as the powers that be attempted to bring regulation and taxation to the Whisky trade. The Scots called these men 'gaugers.' They were the despised excisemen. Robert Burns even wrote a humorous poem about an excise-man being carried off by the devil.

Burns wrote: "The deil cam fiddlin through the toun,
And danced awa wi th'Exciseman
And ilka wife cries "Auld Mahoun,
I wish ye luck of the prize, man."

The supreme irony is that Burns was an excise-man himself for a time in the quiet Scottish toun of Dumfries. He never experienced the pitch battles and community hatred that other excisemen endured in other parts of Scotland.

One such hated excise-man was Malcolm Gillespie who took on the illegal Whisky trade in the North East of Scotland, near Aberdeen. Ian Mitchell, writing for Whisky Magazine, wrote, "The 'King of the Gaugers', Gillespie enjoyed a lavish lifestyle on the proceeds of his enormous seizures." Mitchell goes on to say, "For more than a quarter of a century Gillespie harassed the smugglers of Aberdeenshire. In that time he impounded 6535 gallons of Whisky, 407 stills, 165 horses, 85 carts and 62,400 gallons of barley wash. Gillespie trained bulldogs to tumble the ponies carrying the Whisky, by biting their noses, and causing the spillage of their cargo. His own favourite dog suffered martyrdom by being shot dead by a smuggler. The ponies too suffered casualties. On one occasion Gillespie had been worsted by a superior number of foes, but as they fled, he shot one of the ponies carrying its wares and prevented them from triumphing. Gillespie and his men were armed with swords and pistols, which they unfailingly used. He himself sustained 42 wounds in his career and was battered near to death on frequent occasions."

Gillespie was so successful at putting people out of business that he put himself out of business! He turned to forgery to make up the lost income. The government he had served then hung him for his crimes.

On that cheery note, we conclude this chapter for now. In the Whisk-Lists chapter, there are more historical details for you to study should you so desire.

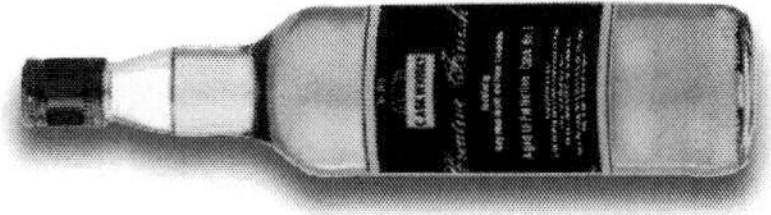

CHAPTER *two*

The Six Regions

Scotland has traditionally been carved up into six different Whisky producing regions. This chapter will therefore be broken into six micro-chapters as we investigate a sampling of Distilleries and Whiskies from each region, meeting some of the people from these Distilleries as we go. We shall therefore tour the following areas:

REGION ONE - ISLAY

REGIONTWO - ISLANDS

REGION THREE - CAMPBELTOWN

REGION FOUR - LOWLANDS

REGION FIVE - HIGHLAND

REGION SIX - SPEYSIDE

It is said that each region's Whisky contributes its own flavour emphasis, its own traits to the Whiskies. According to whiskiesofscotland.com the flavour traits that characterise the regions are as follows:

Speyside - Sweet, medium bodied, floral or big, rich fruity Sherry.

Islay - Big, powerful, very peaty, smoky, seaweed, medicinal.

Highland - Coastal air, peaty in the north or soft, fruity in the south.

Island - Soft, sweet, coastal air, seaweed, slightly peaty.

Lowland -Light, delicate, full of character.

Campbeltown - Rich, full-bodied, peaty.

How Whiskies can be so different from one another when all the processes and natural resources are virtually the same is part of the mystique of Whisky. They aren't the same of course, and variations that seem slight to an outside observer can bring a huge divergence in taste, even if the Whisky is being made down the street. It's like the snowflake mystery. They tell us that even though all snowflakes look alike, they are all different. I pity the scientist that had to look at all the snowflakes under a microscope to see if this was true. Sampling the Whiskies will be a much more interesting scientific investigation. Let's begin the investigation on the Scottish Island of Islay.

REGION ONE -ISLAY

Even though there is a whole region called Islands, Islay became a superstar among the Whisky producing islands. Just as Donny Osmond and Michael Jackson became more famous than their brothers so Islay became the superstar in the family. This relatively small place has become its own region with eight working Distilleries. At one time there were 23 Distilleries. The decaying layers of wetland peat bog covered many parts of the island while there was still enough land to grow grain crops. There was also sources of fresh water for Whisky production. The mighty eight Distilleries on Islay are Ardbeg, Bowmore, Bruichladdich, Bunnahabhain, Caol Ila, Kilchoman, Lagavulin and Laphroaig.

John Campbell, the Master Distiller of Laphroaig told us that everyone on the island knew each other and there were good relationships between the different Distilleries. John McLellen of Kilchoman added that the sales people might duke it out in the marketplace to promote the differences between the Whiskies but all the people working at the different Distilleries got on well with each other and supported each other. Often one Distillery would pitch in and help another if that was needed. Unlike football rivalries where the supporters of the different clubs would have a go bashing each other, there is apparently no such thing as Distillery hooliganism on Islay.

FROM CINDERELLA TO THE SEX PISTOLS OF SINGLE MALT

Jim McEwan always viewed the Bruichladdich Distillery as the Cinderella of the Islay Distilleries, an absolute beauty and yet neglected, forgotten and left in scullery maid rags. Jim told us his personal story and how it intersected with the Bruichladdich story:

JIM MCEWAN: I was raised in the town of Bowmore on the Island of Islay. When I was 15, I started to work at the Bowmore Distillery as an apprentice cooper. Coopering is the most amazing craft ever – second only to wheelwrights.

The guy who invented the wheel was good, but the fellow who invented the Barrel was even better. Egyptians were making Barrels 2000 years before Christ was born. Barrels were the universal vessel long before plastic, tin cans and all the cheap, disposable containers we have today. There used to be coopers everywhere. I think, today in Scotland there are a 150 coopers. I was very proud to be a cooper. I served my time at Bowmore Distillery, training under Scotland's number one cooper of the time, a gentleman by the name of Davy Bell. To be the number one cooper, you had to be in the business a long time because each cooper was given a number when they came into the craft and as people retired, they would move up a number. My teacher, Davy Bell, must have been in that number one position for well over two decades. He kept on working till he was 76.

I was very fortunate to be taught by him. When he retired, I became the head wares keeper, the cellar master looking after the stock at Bowmore. Once in the Distillery, you quickly pick up all the other jobs that others are doing, the Distilling, the mashing – sometimes I'd need to fill in for somebody else so I learned how to do all the various jobs inside the Distillery. I kept on working at Bowmore for another 13 years, quite content and happy with my lot in life. At 28, I got married and then one of the heads of Bowmore thought I should go away and train as a Master Blender – which would mean moving from the small town of Bowmore on Islay to the big city of Glasgow. I was enthusiastic and willing to have a crack at anything. So off I went to Glasgow and ended up living in a rough neighbourhood called Bridgeton.

I did my Master Blending training under a guy called George Fotheringham – a brilliant guy. He had come up through the ranks and hadn't come from an academic background, but he certainly knew his stuff. I trained under him for the next three years. I was then asked to run a Blending operation in Bellshill, Lanarkshire. I was there for a number of years and my two children were born at this time. After a long time in this position, I was asked to come back to the Bowmore Distillery and fill in for the general manager for a couple of months as he had to go away and have an operation.

After two months filling in, I was told I could stay on and I was offered the general manager position at Bowmore. Now, to someone who had started at Bowmore at age 15 as an apprentice cooper - and then to rise up and become the general manager - was in my mind the highest accolade one could achieve! It was a huge honour! My wife (who is from Port Charlotte) and I were delighted to move back to Islay. The timing of this move was lucky. When I arrived back in Bowmore, it was in bad shape and needing major investment. It was at this time that Suntory from Japan got involved with the company and it was their desire to make Bowmore a number one Distillery; they did make the investments needed to upgrade the Distillery. They bought new washbacks, new stills and much more. I was the lucky recipient of all that. Bowmore went on to win Distillery of the year 3 times over the next decade. A lot of requests came for me to travel out and educate the Japanese sales team. This snowballed and I became a global Ambassador for the company.

This meant uprooting yet again, moving to Glasgow so I could be near the airport. I was flying 33 weeks out of the year. At that time there were only four Global Brand Ambassadors representing Scotch Whisky – me and three others – There was John Grant from Glenfarclas, Jim Cryer for Glenlivet and Frank McHardy – we travelled the globe educating people about Single Malts. It was difficult at the time, especially with the Americans and Japanese - they were not used to the strong taste of peated Whisky; on several occasions people spat out the taste samples on offer – and yet we persevered. So much travelling and constantly performing became very wearing. I missed much of the early teen years of my children. I was missing Islay, missing production and the camaraderie that goes with it. It was then that the boys from Murray McDavid and Gordon

Wright at Springbank – they were part of a consortium to get the Bruichladdich Distillery back into production – approached me and asked if I would become the general manager for Bruichladdich. I knew Bruichladdich very well. In the past I had spent many a weekend at the Distillery because they didn't have a cooper of their own and so I would go fix the Barrels for them.

I knew the place. I knew the people. I knew the absolute quality of Bruichladdich Whisky. I decided to accept the offer and turned in my notice to Morrison-Bowmore. Some people thought I was crazy because I was two years away from a full pension after 38 years working for the company. The head would say, "Just stick it out another two years and retire," but my heart not only wanted to return to Islay but to see Bruichladdich restored to its former glory. It had been closed since 1994. As is often the case, particularly those of us from the West Coast of Scotland, my heart won out over my head, and I took on the challenge of getting Bruichladdich back on its feet. I remember walking through the gates of the Bruichladdich Distillery on January 6th 2001 and it was like looking at a bomb site. The Distillery had been left in a shambles and was in a bad state of decay.

"What have I done?" I thought. "I've just left Bowmore and the backing of a blue chip company like Suntory for a Distillery in ruins." After Bruichladdich's closure in 1994, two boys had been left behind, hired to look after the remaining stock. They were quite excited about the plans to re-open the Distillery and their enthusiasm was infectious. Nevertheless, I toured the site with a heavy heart. I thought, "Just sweeping the floor would be a hundred per cent improvement!" We had Victorian equipment that had been installed in 1881. The Distillery had changed hands six times over the century and yet not one of the owners had invested in the Distillery to improve it. And yet, as I toured around with the boys, they kept saying "Jim, we can do this and we can do that!" I started to get fired up about the big challenge ahead and put aside the gloomy thoughts I'd come in with. Among the islanders, Bruichladdich had been a popular Distillery and word quickly spread that I was coming back to take charge and Bruichladdich was going to go back into production. Almost immediately I started getting calls from the original crew that had lost their jobs in 94. A week later, almost all the original crew were back. It was like stepping back in time. Everyone hung up their coats on the same pegs and sat in the same places in the cafeteria. It was as if the intervening seven years of closure had not happened. On May 29th of that year, at 7:29 in the morning, we managed to get new Spirit running. I can honestly tell you that was the proudest moment in all my years in the Industry. Bruichladdich was back! You have to imagine how much it meant to the guys who had worked at the Distillery and then had been layed off. All of Islay had mourned the loss of the Bruichladdich Distillery and now new Spirit was flowing again. I can tell you that eyes teared-up and there was a hush brought on by the emotion of the moment. Big tough islanders - grown men were weeping. People tried to speak but could not find the words. That's how much it meant to these guys."

According to Jim, the Distillery lived from hand to mouth with real financial challenges as production re-started. The 1881 equipment turned out to be a blessing in disguise. There was a certain appeal to do things the old fashioned way without a computer in sight. It took three years to sort out the Cask and Barrel situation at the Distillery. Despite these troubles, there was a lot of invention, creativity and experimentation. Some had dismissed Bruichladdich as not a real Islay Whisky as it was traditionally not a very peated Whisky. Jim researched the history of the Brand and discovered that it actually had been a peated Whisky, but owners of the Distillery in the 1960s stopped the peated version in order to appeal to the Americans with a gentler version of the Whisky. Jim then started making some peated versions of Bruichladdich including Octomore, which is said to be the most heavily peated Whisky in the world. Trying to solve the cash flow problem, Jim had the idea of making Gin. He acquired some old stills from a Distillery that was closing down, including a battered old Lomond Still – probably one of the last of these in the world – that Jim dubbed Ugly Betty.

He also acquired a Gin recipe he thought would work, but was still after something more to make the Gin that much more special. He had an idea of using the local wild flowers and plants to flavour the Gin. As it happened, there were two botanists on the island of Islay, and Jim asked them to collect wild flowers and plants that could be dried and used in the flavour of the Gin. This happened and thus Botany Gin was born to great acclaim. This brought in ready cash flow while the Whisky continued to mature. Not only was Jim interested in doing things the old fashioned way, but he was interested in having everything from storage, to Bottling done on Islay and employing people from the island. He met with farmers on the island and encouraged them to produce barley for the Distillery. Most barley had come from elsewhere for the last century. The local, water, barley, and maturing there on the island makes Bruichladdich truly an Islay Malt in every sense of the word. In 2012, the Cognac company Remy Martin purchased Bruichladdich and Jim was thrilled to have such a company behind the Distillery. They liked the way Bruichladdich was being run and their ideas and so they have gotten behind the Distillery in a big way. The Cinderella of the Distilleries had been taken to the ball and was now appreciated for the beautiful princess she was. Cinderella maybe the image Jim had of the Distillery but one magazine described the Bruichladdich as the Sex Pistols of Single Malt because they were non-conformist, uncompromising and did things their own way.

THE NEWBIE

Kilchoman became the first new Distillery on Islay for 124 years - opening its doors in 2005. John McLellen's story mirrors that of Jim McEwan in several respects. He was on Islay boy made good becoming part of the Distilleries he had grown up around, and he went on to manage Bunnahabhain for 23 years, before taking on the challenge of seeing a Brand new Distillery through the choppy waters of start up. Under his leadership, Kilchoman has steadily increased production every year and the young Bottlings of Kilchoman - they don't have a 10 YO yet for instance - are garnering great reviews. John told us that there were some very Whisky-wise fellows out in Los Angeles who run a Wine/Spirits/Whiskies venture and they blogged that their two favourite Scotch Whiskies include the Bunnahabhain 12 YO and the new Kilchoman. John laughed and wanted to write to them and ask if they noticed a connection. In case anybody needs the connection spelled out, John was responsible for birthing both products.

ARDBEG YOUR PARDON

John McLellen said that in recent years, Ardbeg had acquired a cult following - becoming one of the prestige, must-have-Brands of Whisky. Mickey Head, like Jim and John was an Islay inhabitant who worked his way up into a management position he now holds at Ardbeg. He started working at Laphroaig in

1979 and after a good deal of quality time there, he went to the neighbouring Isle of Jura and managed the Distillery there before he was invited to manage Ardbeg. Glenmorangie owns Ardbeg and so the Distillery is in very good hands. Mickey told us that his father and grandfather before him had worked at the Port Ellen Distillery and you could say, Whisky was in his blood - at 63.5%.

FRIENDS OF LAPHROAIG

Laphroaig. It sounds like a French word - like what a French person says when they point to a small green amphibian. The original meaning is unknown - but it is thought to come from a mixture of Gaelic and Norse meaning the hollow of Broadbay. John Campbell is the fourth Islay resident to grow up to run one of the Isle's Distilleries and the world-wide Super Brand, Laphroaig ended up in his hands. One of the most clever marketing innovations that was started by the Brand was the Friends of Laphroaig Club. Usually it is the rock stars and movies stars that have fan clubs, but Laphroaig currently has 544,449 members of its club. Other Distilleries have taken this approach since, but it started with Laphroaig. Members get Bottling news before anyone else, Whiskies that only members can have and numerous other benefits. Laphroaig wants to be good to all its friends and reward them for their loyalty. The tour and Visitor Centre have a good reputation. That Laphroaig has survived the ups and downs of the Industry for two centuries speaks of the Brand's well deserved popularity.

FOR PEAT'S SAKE!

Mickey Head told us that all the Islay Whiskies are doing quite well and the market is steadily growing. Who would have thought all those swampy, waterlogged, sterile, stagnant, acidic piles of dead plants could add so much flavour to the Whiskies that characterise the Islay region! For Peat's sake!

REGION TWO – ISLANDS

The word 'Islands' conjures up images of hot tropical places with palm trees, crystal turquoise water, hot sandy beaches and Rum. The islands that surround mainland Scotland are anything but tropical and you will more likely suffer from windburn than sunburn. There is incredible beauty to be found on these Scottish islands though you might have to put up with some incredibly bad weather; seals and seabirds will pose for photos and even a bad photographer will get some decent snapshots of some of the gorgeous sights.

The islands that have Distilleries include the Orkneys with Highland Park and Scapa, the Isle of Lewis with Abhainn Dearg, The Isle of Skye's Talisker, Mull's Tobermory, The Isle of Arran and the Isle of Jura. We will sample a few Whiskies from the islands and meet some of the people behind three of these Distilleries.

WELCOME TO HIGHLAND PARK

If you visit Highland Park you will not be chased by giant Whisky Bottles that have escaped from their electrified enclosures, and nor will you see Richard Attenborough greeting you with the words, "Welcome to Highland Park!" The good people behind the Brand have come up with a much better story to associate with their Whisky. The Scandinavian and Viking presence is everywhere to be seen in the Orkneys and so it was only natural for Highland Park to launch a special series of Bottlings based on the Scandinavian gods and goddesses of lore and legend. Thor was the first in this series and in the opinion of C. Ask Whisky, it is one of the nicest presentations of a product we have seen. The Bottle comes in a wooden container that is carved like the dragon head at the bow of a Viking ship. We look forward in anticipation for the next few Bottlings in this series.

Distillery manager, Graham Manson, spoke to us about Highland Park. His background was in engineering and the way he tells it, he had two job offers on the table – he had just graduated from university and Britain was in a bit of recession at the time back in the 80s – in other words, there were few jobs on offer. Graham's choice of jobs came down to going to picturesque Pitlochry to work at Bell's Scotch Whisky as a Distillery trainee or to go to Scunthorpe and work in the blast furnace for British Steel...Whisky or steel? Pitlochry or Scunthorpe? What would you do? Graham chose Pitlochry and has been with Whisky ever since. After a number of years in Pitlochry and then Edinburgh, Graham was looking for a new challenge – he heard that the manager of Highland Park was leaving and so he approached the owners of the Distillery, the Edrington Group and asked, "What are you doing about that management position at Highland Park?" Edrington said, "Let's talk," and the result of that talk was a relocation for Graham and his family to Orkney. Graham came into a Distillery rich in history, dating back to the late 18th century.

The Distillery had the dubious honour of being started by a smuggler, a lovable rogue named Magnus Eunson. The tricks Magnus Eunson played on the authorities have gone down in history. He was like a Bugs Bunny who could outwit the Elmer Fudds of his day. Alfred Barnard recounted the following story in his 1887 book about Britain's Distilleries: "Hearing that the Church was to be searched for Whisky by a new party of excisemen, Eunson had all the kegs removed to his house, placed in the middle of an empty room and covered with a clean white cloth. As the officers approached after their unsuccessful search in the church, Eunson gathered all his people, including the maidservants, round the Whisky, which, with its covering of white, under which a coffin lid had been placed, looked like a bier. Eunson knelt at the head with the Bible in his hand and the others with their psalm books. As the door opened they set up a wail for the dead, and Eunson made a sign to the officers that it was a death and one of the attendants whispered 'smallpox'. Immediately the officer and his men made off as fast as they could and left the smuggler for some time in peace."

Today, Highland Park is completely legit. They don't get up to smuggling anymore or cheating the tax man. We asked Graham how it was that Highland Park had come to have such a good reputation around the world? The Brand is almost universally liked by Whisky connoisseurs and it is known as a prestigious, quality collectable Whisky. Graham attributes the success of Highland Park to the way the Whisky is made there on Orkney. The malting of Orkney barley takes place at the Distillery. The peat comes from Orkney as well. Careful Cask selection is a big part of the story and Spanish Oak Casks that have been used for Sherry contribute to the taste profile in the maturation process. The North Sea air also plays its part .

Do you feel that impact tremor? - do you hear that low rumble of the ground shaking? The Whiskies have truly escaped from Highland Park and are hunting you! Chances are you'll want to be consumed by the Whisky from Highland Park.

Highland Park ranges from ages 12 to 40 YO with ages 15, 16, 18, 21, 25 and 30 YO in between.

THE RED RIVER WHISKY OF LEWIS

There was no corporation behind the idea of starting a Whisky Distillery on the Isle of Lewis in the Outer Hebrides. It was one man on a mission. Mark Tayburn wanted to bring Whisky production back to the Isle after 170 years. This was not an easy undertaking. Many on the Isle would frown on Whisky drinking. The Outer Hebrides is one of the most religious parts of the UK with churches steeped in rigid traditions. There are four broken fractions of Scottish Presbyterianism. One of the denominations was formed after a prominent Presbyterian went to the funeral of a friend who had been a Catholic. Most of the churches won't allow the playing of music, and observing a Sunday shutdown of most services meant that ferries didn't run on that day for most of the 20th century. Against this cultural setting, Mark Tayburn persevered and founded what is now the most Westerly of the Scottish Distilleries, Abhainn Dearg, (pronounced Aveen Jarræk) or Red River Distillery. This can be found on Uig on the Western coast of the island. Mark has succeeded in producing a Whisky that is well worth the 170 year wait. The Bottle presentation is impressive and Mark's independent Spirit is impressive. Most Distilleries answer to corporate masters where as Abhainn Dearg answers to you, the consumer. Here is how the Abhainn Dearg website tells the story: "Abhainn Dearg Single Malt was launched at the Royal National Mod also known affectionately as the "Whisky Olympics". This festival of Scottish Gaelic song, arts and culture was held in Stornoway in 2011 and for the first time in history some participants were able to enjoy a Single Malt Distilled and Bottled on the Isle of Lewis.

Abhainn Dearg is a new Distillery we don't have any of the history, or grand old buildings associated with the famous Brands. You won't find a Visitor Centre or shop here; you might have a hard time just finding us, but if you do visit, you wont' be disappointed.

Whisky is Distilled in the traditional fashion using copper and wood and eventually home grown organic barley. Other ingredients are passion and commitment, old fashioned values of producing the finest Whisky we can, not just for commerce, but for the love of Distilling and taking a pride in what we do! For those who came before and our children who will hopefully carry it on for future generations."

THE JURA CAROL

Isle of Jura Whisky has its own version of the Christmas Carol. In the classic Charles Dickens' tale, miserly Ebeneezer Scrooge is warned by three ghosts to change his ways and heeding the dire warnings brings about a touching redemption of the man.
In 1781, Whisky-making was banned on the Isle of Jura. Jura's version of Scrooge, a landowning laird named Archibald Campbell was visited by a ghost some 29 years after the ban. As the story goes, Archibald was woken up in the dead of night by the apparition of a scary old hag floating above his bed. The phone hadn't been invented yet so the question "Who ya gonna call?" was not even taken into consideration. After the mandatory "BOO," Archibald's startled scream and the involuntary wetting of the bed, Archibald summoned the courage to say, "Why dost thou haunt me ugly hag? I tremble in thy presence and verily I say, I have seen highland coos better looking than you!"

"Whyyyyyyyyyyy?" wailed the banshee.

"W-W-Why what?" asked Archibald.

"Why has the golden liquid known as Whisky stopped flowing on the Isle of Jura?"

"Er...Because it was - er- b-b-banned."

"UN-BAN IT thou moron or I will haunt you and your children and your children's children!"

"I'm on it," Archibald assured the Spirit and then she disappeared. Archibald Campbell was therefore terrified out of being teetotal and re-instituted Whisky making in an old smuggler's cave. Maybe Archibald needed the story of the ghost to convince his wife that he should make Whisky? Usually nagging women, even ghostly ones, are all about getting rid of Whisky. This ghost nagged him into Whisky consumption – which is usually the result of nagging anyway no matter what the nag is about.

As superstition would have it, a Bottle, of Isle of Jura Whisky has been left in the cave so the Spirit won't come back. There was also a well known prophecy given hundreds of years ago when the Campbells were not a popular bunch on the island saying that the last Campbell to leave Jura would be a one-eyed Campbell with a white horse. The prophecy was remembered but laughed at until after World War 1, when a Campbell was injured, lost an eye, returned to the island to sell up, and left the island with all his belongings in a a cart drawn by a white horse. Such stories have given birth to the popular Isle of Jura Whisky Brands, Prophecy and Superstition.

We had a good talk about such stories and more with Isle of Jura's current manager, Willie Cochrane. Like Graham Manson, Willie came from an engineering background, and a visit to the island and the Distillery back in the 70s resulted in the offer of a position. Willie's wife fell in love with the island and so the Cochrane family made the move and have been there ever since. Though the population of Jura is only 190 people, 20,000 visitors come every year through the Distillery doors and get a very personal tour. Willie insisted that the tour be free because he reasoned that people had taken the trouble and paid for the ferry just to visit the isle so why should they be charged extra to visit the Distillery?

In addition to Superstition and Prophecy, the core range of Isle of Jura includes the popular 16 YO, and a 21 YO. There are also Boutique Barrels from 1999, 1995 and 1993. The website is excellent and the myths and legends are a fun read.

REGION THREE – CAMPBELTOWN HOPE SPRINGBANK'S ETERNAL

Paul McCartney and Wings had a hit with the song Mull of Kintyre. Campbeltown is the major municipality of the Mull of Kintyre and the name of the Whisky region. It used to be one of the biggest Scotch producing regions of Scotland and the home of a bunch of drunken pigs. The drunken pigs comment is not meant as a slight to the good people of Campbeltown. I mean there literally were a bunch of drunken pigs – swine that roamed free like so many stray dogs – There were 2000 pigs in the town itself back in the mid-19th century and they liked to partake in the excess pot ale and the debris from the many Distilleries that had emerged in the region - hence the drunken pigs comment. Some towns find pigeons a problem and all the poo they leave behind but there is a big difference between pigs and pigeons. You certainly would not have wanted your kids to go play in the mud. Fortunately, Campbeltown has since become a no-pig zone. The makeover was complete by the time Alfred Barnard arrived in the late 19th century.

Alfred was writing about the Distilleries of Great Britain and he doesn't mention the pigs. He speaks of prosperous Distillers and farmers. There was a fast shipping link to Glasgow and the Whisky trade was booming. Whisky Magazine said, "Campbeltown was in the right place at the right time. There was local barley, peat, a fast sea route, coal from the mine at Machrihanish and Whisky-making experience. Then it all went spectacularly wrong. Many Distillers, seeing a never ending boom, upped production and quality slumped. The Blenders turned their back on the town, already preferring the lighter flavours coming from Speyside. Prohibition spelled the end of the US market. From being Scotland's Whisky capital, Campbeltown's Distilleries were said to be making 'stinking fish', either because the Whisky was put into old herring Barrels (how long before someone does that as a finish?) or it was just badly made, peaty/medicinal, feinty Spirit. By the 1930s there were three Distilleries left: Springbank, Riechlachan and Glen Scotia."

Today Reichlachan is gone but Springbank and Glen Scotia remain. The owners of Springback have recently re-opened the Glengyle Distillery and started production there so three Distilleries represent the Campbeltown region.

We spoke to Frank McHardy of Springbank and asked him what made Springbank unique among the Whiskies of Scotland.

Frank has been making Whisky for 50 years and has worked at Invergordon Grain Distillery, Bruichladdich, Bushmills in Northern Ireland and he will finish his long career at Springbank, having been at the Campbeltown Distillery long enough to reinvigorate its production and products. Bringing back Glengyle from the dead is just one of the many contributions Frank has made to the world of Whisky.

In answer to our question, Frank said that Springbank was unique among the Distilleries of Scotland because it had been owned by the same family, the Mitchells since 1828 and the present owner is the great, great, great grandchild of the original Mitchell family that built the Springback Distillery. Springbank is unique in that it survived against the odds when every other Distillery apart from Glen Scotia had gone out of business. Springbank had survived the era when Campbeltown Whiskies came into disrepute and were looked upon as cheap, nasty Whiskies. Some of the Distillers of the day were indeed producing Whiskies that had a fishy taste and unfortunately Springbank had been tarred with the same fishy brush despite not being in the same league as the aquarium water Whiskies. Springbank is unique in that every part of the process from the malting to the Bottling is done on site in Campbeltown.

Here is how the Springbank Distillery Whiskies are described:

SPRINGBANK: Known and loved amongst Whisky enthusiasts the world over! Springbank is produced using lightly-peated barley and a unique two-and-a-half-times Distillation. This gives the Whisky a character all of its own, making it stand out as a must-have dram on anyone's shelf.

LONGROW: First Distilled in 1973, Longrow is a double Distilled, heavily peated Single Malt. The first Distillation was carried out as an experiment when the Springbank chairman set out to prove that it was possible to produce an Islay-style Single Malt Whisky on the mainland.

HAZELBURN: The newest addition to the range of Whiskies produced at Springbank, Hazelburn gains it's light, delicate character through being Distilled three times in the Distillery's old copper stills.

GLENGYLE DISTILLERY is also making Whiskies such as KILKERRAN: Kilkerran Work in Progress (2) 6y/o 70cl 46% Matured in Oak.

THE SPIRITS OF GLEN SCOTIA

Pity the night shift at Glen Scotia Distillery. It is then that the ghost of Duncan MacCallum is said to return to the Distillery from the depths of Campbeltown Loch where he drowned himself on a fateful day in 1930 after losing money in a shady business deal. There have been many sightings of Duncan by the Distillery workers over the years. He probably just wants a dram of delicious Glen Scotia. You can imagine him holding up a glass and saying, "From one Spirit to another! Doon you go!"

We didn't ask John Peterson about the Glen Scotia ghost. John is a scientist after all and I got the feeling he would find such a discussion irrelevant and somewhat silly. We were there to talk about more important things like the production of the two Distilleries he oversees. John is the man in charge of both Loch Lomond and Glen Scotia. In other words, he straddles two Whisky regions. Loch Lomond is technically in the Highland region a 119 miles from Cambeltown.

There are good people at both Distilleries that John speaks to about the daily production and so he more often than not is in the Mull of Kintyre rather than Loch Lomond's Dumbartonshire base of operation. John began his career as a chemical engineer and he still finds the chemical processes that go into making Whisky, the biology of fermentation a fascinating business. Even though he has had a long career, he is still learning about the intricate details of the science that goes into making your dram of Glen Scotia or Loch Lomond. John told us about his experimentation with different yeasts that were beyond our ability to pronounce, let alone understand. What we did understand was John's commendable passion for the science. Should the ghost of Duncan MacCallum ever appear to John while he is working late, John would most likely want to take measurements and scientific readings.

The Whiskies from Glen Scotia include a 5 YO, 12 YO, 14 YO, 15 YO, 31 YO, a heavily peated version and special Single Cask selections. We encourage you to go to the Loch Lomond Distillery website where the full list from the two Distilleries will be current and up to date.

REGION FOUR –LOWLANDS

Many people come to Scotland and are surprised to find that Edinburgh doesn't have its own Whisky Distillery. The nearest Distillery to Ediburgh is Glenkinchie and the tour they offer benefits from the close proximity to Scotland's capitol city. Truth be told there are only a handful of Distilleries in the lowlands despite the fact that most of the people in Scotland live in the lowland region. The Distilleries that are still alive and kicking include Auchentoshan, Glenkinchie and Bladnoch, although Bladnoch was shut before being recently revived. Closed Lowland Distilleries include Glen Fagler, Inverleven, Kinclaith, Ladyburn, Littlemill, Rosebank and St. Magdalene. Many of the independent Bottlers still have Casks and stock from these mothballed Distilleries. Annandale near Dumfries is being rebuilt, Cameron Bridge in Fife is a Grain Distillery and Daftmill in Fife is not a commercial Distillery at this point in time.

BLADNOCHIN ON HEAVEN'S DOOR

As previously mentioned, Bladnoch was mothballed but has since been brought back from the dead by the most unlikely of rescuers. Raymond Armstrong was not a third generation Scotch Whisky person who's father and grandfather and whole extended family worked for the local Distillery. Raymond didn't study Brewing, engineering or science. He was in the building trade with experience in surveying, construction and architecture. If he had applied for a job at any other Distillery, they would have told him he did not have the right experience or qualifications. He might have been able to start at an entry level position in the warehouse, but how to run a Distillery was not in his then skill-set. Not only did he have the disadvantage of no Distillery experience but he was not even Scottish. He was from Northern Ireland. His family did have roots in the Wigtown area of Scotland however and initially he took over the Bladnoch property as it had all kinds of tourist potential. Wigtown is a book Mecca with book fairs and a number of book shops in the town that draws in many tourists. It is also tucked into a remote gorgeous nook of Scotland near the English border. The Visitor Centre at the Distillery was quite attractive and so Raymond thought he could find a way to use the Visitor Centre and perhaps build some holiday homes on the site. Re-opening the Distillery for Whisky production wasn't part of the initial plan, but soon that was the only plan.

The people of the area wanted their Distillery back and Raymond wanted to give the people what they wanted. Not one to shy away from a challenge, Raymond took a crash course in Whisky production. Gavin D. Smith writes, "Armstrong has absorbed a great deal of information about Whisky-making from a variety of sources, most significantly from Dr Alan Rutherford, the former UK Production Director of United Distillers, and John Herries, who worked at Bladnoch for 10 years prior to its closure by in June 1993. Herries is central to the project to get Bladnoch

Distilling again, and he describes himself as "stillman, mashman, and the everything else man now, too." Armstrong is fulsome in his praise of Herries and the rest of the workforce, noting: 'their flexibility is marvellous. There's a real eagerness to see the place operating again, not just among the employees, but in the area generally.' Local goodwill towards Armstrong and his plans to resurrect Bladnoch is partly due to the fact that he has a genuine interest in the area and its people, along with a reputation for saying 'yes' to anybody who needs space for an activity. Empty warehouses have played host to line dancing groups, and prior to the re-commencement of Distilling, a full-size wrestling ring was located in the filling store. The Cask store has been converted into a popular venue for musical concerts, wedding receptions, parties and other events, and Bladnoch is the only Distillery in Scotland to boast its own record label, Distilled Records, which produces CDs of concerts held there and showcases local musical talent."

Having gone back into production with Whisky that has been called the missing link between Scotch and Irish Whisky, Bladnoch offers the following Whiskies:

Their Single Malt ranges in age from 9 YO to a rare 20 YO with a 10 YO, 11 YO and 12 YO in between. Raymond also does independent Bottling and so there are Brands such as a 21 YO Glen Spey he has selected and Bottled which you can purchase through the Bladnoch website. Bladnoch was not only rescued, but rescued in style.

REGION FIVE – HIGHLAND

This is the region that gave us the kilt, the clans, the Loch Ness Monster and many a fine Whisky, including the new Loch Ness Single Malt. The Distilleries of the Highlands are as follows: Aberfeldy, Aisla Bay, Ardmore, Auchroisk, Balblair, Ben Nevis, Blair Atholl, Clynelish, Dalmore, Deanston, Edradour, Fettercairn, Glen Albyn, Glencadam, Glen Garioch, Glengoyne, Glenmorangie, Glen Ord, Glenturret, Loch Lomond, Oban, Old Pulteney, Royal Brackla, Royal Lochnagar, Teaninich, The Speyside and Tullibardine. The most confusing of these is The Speyside since there is a whole region called Speyside, but the Distillery is located in Kingussie, Invernessshire which is slap bang in the Highland region. Closed and lost Distilleries include Banff, Ben Wyvis, Glenesk, Glenlochy, Glenugie, Glen Royal, Lochside, Milburn and North Port.

We shall visit four Highland Distilleries and include some honourable mentions.

A MOUNTAIN, TWO COWS AND A WHISKY

The tallest mountain in Scotland – not only in Scotland but the whole of the British Isles - is known as Ben Nevis and it towers over the Highland town of nearby Fort William. Coincidentally, there is a Distillery in Fort William that just happens to be called Ben Nevis as well. What are the chances? Believe it or not, there is another amazing coincidence. Two heavy and shaggy Brand Ambassadors also share the name Ben and Nevis and they wait to greet Distillery visitors from behind a fence. These hippies of the bovine family, with their counter culture, love-child long locks of hair, are the mascots, the symbols of the Distillery. All that is missing from their costume is a tie-dye T- shirt and psychedelic rock music playing in the background. Ben and Nevis have even been trained to answer one question – the most important question that any Brand Ambassador for any Brand has to answer. When Ben and Nevis are asked what Ben Nevis Whisky tastes like they say, "MMMMM!" - Good answer – Someone who has had four years at university studying marketing and public relations could not top that answer. Arguably the tallest Whisky Distiller in the world at the time started the Distillery.

Nearly two hundred years ago, 6 foot 4, Long John MacDonald founded the Ben Nevis Distillery. This is what he said at the time: "There are some who would have you believe that there exists a kind of divine secret, a miraculous ingredient or genius behind the manufacture of Scotch Whisky. I however, acknowledge no miracle other than that which is worked when science and nature combine. The principal ingredients are three, notably water, barley and yeast, with a measure of peat smoke or reek. Of these there can be no doubt that water is the foremost. On Ben Nevis I was fortunate to find a constant and consistent source of pure clean water in two small lochans. In order of importance, the second ingredient is barley. This must be clean and plump, fully rounded and quite dry, containing exactly the right amount of protein. Special Distiller's yeast is the third ingredient.

This has the texture of dough or putty and is vital to the process of fermentation. And fourthly there is peat, which comes to the Whisky through the water passing over peat bogs on its way down the mountain and from the 'reek' from the fire lit during the manufacturing process. Once again, we are fully fortunate in that nature in her magnificence, has created on the hill behind us, an ample supply of peat in our own banks to fuel the fires drying the barley. John MacDonald- 14th June 1827.

Inheriting John MacDonald's role as the man behind the Ben Nevis Distillery is Colin Ross and we spoke to him about all things Ben Nevis. Colin's first job in a Distillery was to wax the floor of Strathisla. From Strathisla, Colin went to Tormore, Ben Nevis, Laphroaig and then back to Ben Nevis as the Distillery manager. The award winning 10 YO came under his watch. In an article for Whisky Magazine, Ian Buxton wrote, "The Ben Nevis 10 YO holds the distinction of Grand Gold medals in 1999 and 2000 from the Monde Selection contest, followed by a further Gold medal in 2001. For this remarkable treble, Ben Nevis was awarded a special trophy by the Monde Selection. One sip tells you that this is an unusual and distinctive dram. Smooth, full-bodied and slightly sweet on the palate its rich colour owes something to caramel but more to a careful Cask policy. The Distillery uses a combination of Sherry, fresh Bourbon wood and some first refills to ensure a consistent colour and uniformly reliable taste. Gold medals three years running in major international competitions are no fluke. This is a Whisky that should be better known." Speaking with Colin, you can sense a pride in the Whisky and also a longing to do so much more for the many visitors that come each year. Nikka in Japan owns the Distillery so ultimately it will be up to them to make the needed improvements for 30,000 plus visitors. Yes, they have a Visitor Centre, a film, good Tour Guides, their own line of Ben Nevis Whisky chocolates, trained superstar highland cows and even converted warehouses that have been used to film scenes in Highlander, Local Hero, Rob Roy and Braveheart! Despite all this, the common complaints that visitors make is that the place needs a bit of sprucing up and no one would like that more than Colin.

Various expressions of Dew of Ben Nevis Special Reserve Blends, McDonald's Glencoe Vatted Malt, and the Single Malt 10 YO and 25 YO are part of the core range of products produced by the Distillery.

SAY HELLO TO TULLIBARDINE

The sun rises with a smile on its face, giggles and sips a dram. Four primary coloured Whisky Bottles jump out of holes in the grassy ground before dancing about and singing, "Tullibardine! Tullibardine! Say Hellooooo!" I do believe the preceding marketing strategy was rejected for many good reasons and never really happened. Re-Branding and a new strategy was needed however and that is exactly what happened.

James Robertson is enthusiastic about the newly revitalised Tullibardine Distillery. He is their Global Brand Ambassador and told C. Ask Whisky that they had just announced a complete re-Branding of the whole product line. The presentation was made at a company meeting and there was palpable excitement by all those in attendance at the new direction and marketing plans.

As a Distillery and a Brand, Tullibardine has been a contender. The champ had been knocked down. The fight looked like it was all but over. The ref was doing the final countdown when the fighter got back on his feet, ready to go a few more rounds. That is essentially the story of the Tullibardine Distillery as far as the 20th century and early 21st century goes. There has been some sort of Brewing on the location since the 1100s. The water near the edge of the Perthshire Village of Blackford is used to fill Bottles of Highland Spring Mineral Water to head out to supermarkets around the UK. The water is also the source of Tullibardine's Whisky and it was the source of water for Scotland's first Beer Brewery. King James the IV ordered Beer from the Brewery for his coronation in Scone Palace, Perth in 1488. The buildings of the old Beer Brewery that had been erected in the 1600s were in a run down, dilapidated state. In the year 1949, a Welshman named William Delme-Evans took over the site, and rebuilt the place making it the first new, 20th century Distillery in Scotland. From then on Tullibardine changed many hands and was a punch bag during some tough economic times. Many people believed in Tullibardine however and saw what it could be. It was in a prime location with many thousands of cars passing each day on the route from Stirling to Perth. It was near the world famous Gleneagles Golf Course. Smartly the owners have developed the site to include an upmarket retail park with a gift shop and Visitor Centre and restaurant. Tullibardine is back on its feet with a re-born zeal, a new lease of life that it is taking full advantage of.

Tullibardine produces a Single Malt with ages such as a 16 YO and a 20 YO. They do Single Cask Bottlings, a personalised Whisky Bottle and they also sell 1488 Cream Liqueur and 1488 Ales.

THE LITTLE BIG DISTILLERY

One of Dustin Hoffman's early films was a western called "Little Big Man," which has been described as a comedy about a white boy raised by the Cheyenne Indians. Dustin Hoffman is one of the few short in stature lead actors who has had such a big career and that Spirit was what was needed in that particular film. Edradour Distillery is proud to be the smallest Distillery in Scotland. It is the little big Distillery - if its stills were any smaller they would be of the illegal sort used to make illicit, unlicensed Spirit...And yet, the Distillery has made a big noise in Distillery tourism and has been having an impact since 1825. Edradour found many an American customer for its Whiskies during the American Prohibition for instance. There was a rumoured Mafia connection to the Distillery during this time – although anyone who can confirm this allegation is probably entombed in the nearby Pitlochry dam. The famous film, 'Whisky Galore' portrayed what happened when the S. S. Politician ran aground the Western Isles. As you may recall, thousands of cases of Whisky were rescued by the islanders who then had to cleverly hide what they had taken – What is not as well known is that much of that Whisky had been produced at Edradour. Since the co-operative ownership of farmers in the area set up Edradour early in the 19th century, the Distillery has been in numerous hands, finally coming into the hands of the man behind the independent Bottlers, Signatory.

Des McCagherty, a partner in Signatory and Edradour told us about the two merged enterprises. When Andrew Symington started Signatory in the 1980s, his original intent was to market his wares by getting the signature of a well known celebrity to sign off on the Cask. It was said that Sean Connery almost became one of these signatories. The problem Andrew had though was that his specially selected Casks would sell out before he could get the signature of a celebrity. The enormous success of Signatory provided the millions needed to purchase Edradour. In a Whisky Magazine article at the turn of the century, we see the following interaction between Andrew Symington and Tom Bruce-Gardyne: "If I'm honest, independent Bottling won't go on forever, a lot of what we specialise in comes from Distilleries that fell under the axe in the 1980s," Andrew admits. With real gems like the '65 Glen Grant growing increasingly rare, he has clearly no interest in abandoning Single Casks to Bottle a standard 12 YO for example. His real desire it transpires, is to have his very own Distillery "and I'm getting quite close," he says with a glint in his eye. He won't say which one, and it's clearly a drawn-out affair. "You have to have all the owners in the right place at the right time. It's not like buying a house, it's like buying a whole street."

Andrew Symington did buy Edradour. He has invested heavily in the little Distillery to build warehouses, a Visitor Centre and an onsite Bottling facility. The range of Edradour Whiskies on offer range in ages and different types of Cask finishes. Rare vintage Bottles of Single Malts from existing Distilleries and closed Distilleries are available as well. The little Distillery is much bigger than it appears.

DR. LUMSDEN'S LABORATORY

If you heard that Dr. Bill Lumsden was going to be at a dinner party, you would probably ask the question, "So what's he like?" The reply would probably be along the lines, "Well, he's a scientist. He studied biology and then Brewing and probably knows more about wood maturation of Whisky than anyone." Instead of being excited, you might think, "Great, this guy is going to be the dullest person at the party. Wood maturation? Pull-Leeeeease!" The socially awkward stereotypical nerd comes to your mind; you think he'll have thick bifocals, the pocket full of pencils, a rumpled shirt that's not tucked in, greasy hair and he'll want to tell everyone about his fungal spore collection - And then Bill shows up and like his Whisky creations, he surprises you and subverts all expectations.

He is actually one of the most exciting personalities in Whisky today – a rock star on the Whisky stage with boundless enthusiasm, passion and humour. When he speaks, even if it's about experimenting with different types of wood and Wine Casks, it is engaging and fascinating. It's exciting to hear how he pushes the science of Whisky making to the limit. Becoming a Distillery manager and overseeing production in the time honoured tradition, with the same recipe that has worked since 1740 might be a prestigious honour that many a Distillery manager would be content with as their lot in life while faithfully carrying out their duties. With Bill Lumsden, you get a sense that he needs to shake things up and strive for the new. Gavin D Smith wrote the following about Bill Lumsden and his creation, Glenmorangie Signet: "Signet is probably the biggest product innovation apart from wood finishes in Scotch Whisky for many years," he (Bill Lumsden) declares. "I was looking for two things, really. Firstly, something that was genuinely innovative, and secondly, when I came to think more about what sort of Glenmorangie I wanted to make, I had something altogether deeper and richer in mind, and something that would work well on ice. On its own, the Whisky made with chocolate malt was too full-on, too spicy and not refined enough.

As it is, you can definitely taste the mocha in Signet, and Whisky Distilled from chocolate malt only makes up around 30 per cent of the total." That total also includes Whisky of varying ages matured in a range of wood types, including ex-Sherry, new-charred Oak and ex-Wine Casks. "I've described Signet as my 'magnum opus,'" says Lumsden with a smile, "but I'm a big Michael Jackson fan and I hope it won't become my Thriller moment! I don't think he ever did anything quite as good again. Let's hope Signet is my 'magnum opus' so far. Watch this space..."

Bill Lumsden told C. Ask Whisky about his experimentation with Brazilian cherry wood Barrels. Like a bloodhound on the path of a fugitive, the Scottish Malt Whisky Society tracked Bill down and said "You can't do that!" Bill replied that he wasn't pursuing it as the Whisky produced was bowfin!" That means disgusting, wretched, horrid and makes you want to throw up. Bill does agree that there needs to be a set of parameters in which to make Whisky and he does follow those rules, although he is endlessly curious as to how much flavour he can infuse into Whisky with the strict rules that are in place. It is under Bill's leadership that Glenmorangie became Distiller of the year and the Brand has gone from strength to strength. He also has his hand in everything going on with Ardbeg and his fingerprints are all over Glen Moray as well.

The first Whisky Bill ever had in his college days was a Glemorangie 10 YO and he loved it. Little did he know then that someday he would be responsible for all of Glemorangie's output. That output includes: The original Single Malt 10 Y0, 12 YO, 15 YO, 18 YO, Quintan Ruban, Lasanta, Nectar D'Or, Astar, Ealanta, Artein, Sonnalta PX, Finealta and Signet.

HONORARY MENTIONS

C. Ask Whisky would like to make special mention of the following Highland Distilleries and encourage you to find out more about their Whiskies. There are further details about some of these Whiskies elsewhere in this book as well. We value the input we have had from Aberfeldy, Ardmore, Dalmore, Fettercairn, Glencadam, Glengoyne, Glenturret and Loch Lomond.

REGION SIX - SPEYSIDE

Speyside is the area of Scotland that no dog wants to go to if it still wants to have puppies. It is also the Whisky producing region along the River Spey in North East Scotland and it contains the largest number of Distilleries. Here is the list: Aberlour, Allt A'Bhainne, Aultmore, Balmenach, Balvenie, Benriach, Benrinnes, Benromach, Cardhu, Gragganmore, Craigellachie, Dailuaine, Dramguish, Dufftown, Glenallachie, Glenburgie, Glendronach, Glendullan, Glen Elgin, Glenfarclas, Glenfiddich,Glenglassaugh, Glen Grant, Glen Keith, The Glenlivet, Glenlossie, Glen Moray, Glenrothes, Glen Spey, Glentauchers, Imperial, Inchgower, Kininvie, Knockando, Linkwood, Longmorn, Macallan, Macduff, Mannochmore, Miltonduff, Mortlach, Roseisle, Speyburn, Strathisla, Strathmil Tamdhu, Tamnavulin, Tomatin,Tomintoul, Tormore.

The closed Distilleries include: Braeval, Caperdonich, Coleburn, Convalmore, Glen Mhor and Pittyvaich.

We will look at five Distilleries and give honourable mention to a few others.

INDEPENDENCE DAY

Many of the people we interviewed throughout the book had no kind words for one of the bigger corporations that had bought up many a Distillery; it seemingly had little or no regard for the people on the ground. It was accused of having no real heart for the Distilleries and no real passion for anything but pleasing the shareholders. All that mattered was the bottom line. The corporation was jokingly referred to as the evil empire with a certain D. Vader wanting to rule the universe (and D doesn't stand for Darth). There is a rebel alliance however of independently minded people that defy the will of the Distillery gobbling empire. The Benriach and Glendronach Distilleries were bought lock, stock and all the Barrels by a consortium of passionate Whisky-makers as opposed to a corporate giant. Now Benriach and Glendronach are not only indepenedent but they are owned by Scots which few of the Distilleries can say.

Stewart Buchanan is one of these independent Scotsmen. He joined Billy Walker in the pursuit of the two Distilleries. He is now a Distillery manager and a Brand Representative. He told us that one of his greatest pleasures as he travelled abroad was to see Benriach and and Glendronach Whiskies treated with the same amount of respect as other Scotch Whiskies. All the politics of who was bigger than who went by the wayside on the shop floors. Benriach and Glendronach had just as prominent a place and display as the Corporate Brands. The shop floor was a great leveller and all Whiskies were treated as equals. As Stewart talked about the work that had gone into the Distilleries, and the care taken to produce such quality Whiskies, there was a real sense of pride conveyed. This was not in any way arrogant or boastful. Rather it was a grateful pride - a humble pride - It was that satisfied good feeling one can have when they built something themselves, created something and owned something. They were not the servants churning out the product for an impersonal corporate master. Rather they were servants only of the customers who liked the Benriach and Glendronach Whiskies.

The two Distilleries both offer customers many choices of age, style and wood finish.

Benriach offers its expressions: Heart of Speyside, 12 YO, 16 YO, 20 YO, 25 YO, 30 YO, 40 YO, Horizons, Solstice, Solstice 17 YO, Benriach Firkin - The peated Benraichs such as Birnie Moss, Curiositas peated 10 YO, Septendecin, Authenticus Peated 21 YO, Autheticus Peated 25 YO.

The Glendronach expressions include the 12 YO, 15 YO, 18 YO, 21 YO, 31 YO, 33 YO with Cask Strength and different wood finishes on offer as well.

THE GLENGLASSAUGH REVIVAL

In that Spirit of independence, the Glenglassaugh Distillery was brought back from the dead and there was no one more qualified to resurrect the Distillery than Stuart Nickerson was. Stuart had worked in Arthur Bell and

Company, Bells, Dufftown, William Grant and Sons and Diageo. He had been in the corporations as well as the independents gaining personal insight into the Whisky biz all along the way. When he had the chance to help revive Glenglassaugh he did not just want to re-institute mechanical production; he wanted to take his many years of experience and bring his creativity and personality into the Whisky Brand. There were stories to tell behind the Whiskies. Stuart told us about the Massandra Cask connection and how the excellent Crimean Casks and Wine had been hidden from the Nazis when they invaded the Crimea. Some expressions of Glenglassaugh are finished in such rare, prized and hard-to-get-a-hold-of Casks. The website reports the following list of accomplishments after its 2008 re-opening: "Since that first mash the new company has continued to grow, winning awards, gaining new friends and advocates. The products can now be found in over 20 countries around the world, in Africa, Australasia, Asia, Europe and North America.

In 2009 three aged Whiskies were released a 21 year old (subsequently replaced by a 26 year old), an "Aged Over 30 Years" and an "Aged Over 40 Years" with the latter two winning Gold Medals (best in class) and individual trophies at the International Wine and Spirit Competition in 2009, while the 21 YO won a double gold medal at the San Francisco International Wine and Spirit Competition in 2010.

In 2009 the Distillery also challenged convention by releasing two Bottled products which were not mature enough to be called Whiskies, "The Spirit Drink that dare not speak its name" and "The Spirit Drink that blushes to speak its name". Both full of character and both very different and which became increasingly popular in mixer drinks. These drinks were followed in 2010 by "Fledgling XB" and "Peated". 2009 also saw the launch of the Octave Cask ownership scheme, where private individuals can own their own Cask of Whisky (50 litres), mature it at the Distillery and then Bottle the contents in a few years time. Over 500 Octaves have now been sold since this scheme was launched."

GRANTS AND GLENS

The independence through Speyside theme carries on with two completely different Grant families. One can imagine being in certain rural counties of the Southern United States and being confused because every other person is named Billy something or Bobby something – Billy Bob, Billy Jo, Billy Jean, Bobby Ray – and the sheer number of Billies, Bobbies and the letter B would drive anyone to distraction. One of the Speyside Grant families has a recurring theme of John and George passed on from father to son – but which John and which George is hard to keep track of. The important thing that the current George Grant would like you to remember is one word and that is Glenfarclas.

The great Tommy Dewar waxed poetic and described Glenfarclas as, "The King of Whiskies and the Whisky of Kings. In its superiority, it is something to drive the skeleton from the feast and paint landscapes in the brain of man. In it is to be found the sunshine and shadow that chase each other over the billowy cornfield, the hum of the bee, the hope of spring, the breath of May, the carol of the lark, the distant purple heather in the mountain mist, the dew of morn and the wealth of autumn's rich content, all golden with imprisoned light."

The other Grant family was headed up by William. When you have 9 sons and daughters you can either start a singing group or you can put all the kids to work building a Distillery. Here's how the story goes: "In the summer of 1886, with the help of his seven sons and two daughters, William set out to fulfil a lifelong ambition. Together they began building his Distillery by hand, stone by stone. After a single year of work it was ready and William named it Glenfiddich, Gaelic for Valley of the Deer. William's passion, determination and pioneering Spirit continues to guide us. Glenfiddich is one of the few Single Malt Distilleries to remain entirely family owned and is now the World's Most Awarded Single Malt Scotch Whisky, a true reflection of our founder's integrity and innovative Spirit, passed down through the generations." On Christmas Day 1887, Glenfiddich began producing Spirit and William was able to say to his nine children, "Look what you're getting for Christmas kids! Just what you've always wanted! A Distillery!"

The company William Grant and Sons (he left out the daughters in the title) now employs 1500 people and Glenfiddich is their world dominating power house of a Distillery and Brand.

The Glenfarclas core range includes: 105 Cask Strength and 105 20 YO, Glenfarclas Single Malt 12 YO, 15 YO, 17 YO, 18 YO ,21 YO,

25 YO , 30 YO, 40 YO, Historic Bottlings and the Family Casks. The Glenfiddich core range includes: 12 YO, 15 YO, 18 YO, 21 YO, 30 YO, 40 YO, 50 YO, 1937 Rare, Master of Malt Edition, Age of Discovery Madeira Cask, Boubon Cask, Rich Oak, Snow Phoenix, Janet Sheed Roberts Reserve, Malt Master Edition, Distillery Edition, Vintage 1974, 1975, 1977 and 1978.

HONORARY MENTIONS:

C. Ask Whisky would like to make special mention of the following Speyside Distilleries and encourage you to find out more about their Whiskies. There are further details about some of these Whiskies elsewhere in this book as well. We value the input we have had from Aberlour, Benromach, Glenlivet, Glen Moray, Glenrothes and Macallan.

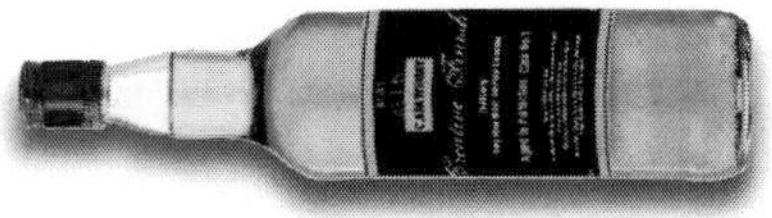

CHAPTER *three*

Whisked around the whirld

We trust you have had your inoculations and all your passports and papers are in order. It is our intention to give you a whirlwind tour of Whisky around the whirld. We shall whisk you away to Ireland, England, Wales, USA, Canada, Mexico, Latin America, the Philippines, Australia, New Zealand, Taiwan, Japan, South Africa and then back to Europe with stops in Denmark, the Netherlands, France, Germany and Sweden. You will need a holiday from your holiday by the time you are through. Like the Six Regions Chapter, we shall break our trip around the world into micro-chapters as follows:

3.1 - IRELAND
3.2 - ENGLAND AND WALES
3.3 - USA
3.4 - CANADA
3.5 - MEXICO AND LATIN AMERICA
3.6 - SOUTH PACIFIC
3.7 - JAPAN, TAIWAN AND ASIA
3.8 - SOUTH AFRICA
3. 9 - EUROPE

3. 1 - IRELAND

As mentioned in the Whisk-tory chapter, the Irish had more than a significant part to play in the genesis of Uisge Beatha (Uisce is the Irish spelling) and when Cask-aged proper Whisky started being produced, Ireland along with Scotland were the two most important players on Planet Earth. In the 1700s there were 2000

Irish stills churning out the Aqua Vitae.

Distillation of one sort or another had been going on in Ireland since just after the first millennium A.D. The art continually being perfected, Irish Whisky came to the attention of important people such as the first Queen Elizabeth who reigned for most of the 1500s. She had Irish Whisky shipped over and available for her court. That was an endorsement money couldn't buy. It is a regular habit of advertising agencies to pay superstars millions to associate themselves with their products, and yet Irish Whisky had the backing of the Queen of England, making the drink quite in vogue and popular with the nobles and aristocracy of Great Britain. Even Peter the Great of Russia gave a big thumbs up to Irish Whisky, saying, "Of all the Wines of the world, Irish Spirit is the best." By the end of the 19th century, Irish Whisky was the most popular Alcoholic beverage in the world.

Irish Whisky then suffered a triple whammy of disasters:

The Industry had some well established manufacturing traditions that were resistant to innovation. As previously noted, Irishman, Aeneas Coffey, offered the two-column Continuous Still to the Irish Whisky Industry of the early 19th century, and they said, "Thanks, but no thanks." When Aeneas took his Continuous Still to the competing Industry in Scotland, one can only imagine the names he was called behind his back - mostly variations of his first name. This efficient and cost effective means of Whisky production gave the Scottish Industry a big advantage. This is Whammy One.

Ireland then won a war of independence with Great Britain in the early 20th century, becoming the Republic of Ireland that we know today. It was an acrimonious divorce however, and Great Britain spitefully made trading in Ireland's former overseas and domestic British markets bloody difficult resulting in economic devastation for the Irish Whisky Industry.

Just when trade was getting going again, Ireland's biggest trading partner in terms of Spirits, America, went dry and instituted Prohibition. This was good for Canadian Whisky producers, good for illegal Moonshine Distilleries, good for gangsters and devastating to Irish Whisky. Most Distilleries were put out of business and only a few Distilleries were left standing when the dust settled.

A café in San Francisco of all places has been credited as helping to revive Ireland's Irish Whisky fortunes in America. As legend would have it, the owner of the Buena Vista Café, a fellow named Jack Koeppler, tried an Irish coffee at the Shannon Airport in 1952 and it was love at first sip. He wanted to re-create the drink in his San Francisco café. Soon it was serving 2000 Irish coffees a day and the popularity of Irish coffee spread across the United States.

The good news is that today, Ireland's Whisky Industry is reinvigorated and producing some world renowned Whiskies.

One of the distinguishing features of Irish Whisky, which explains why it initially rejected the Coffey still, was that it had created some special flavours with the Single Pot Still technique.

What is the Single Pot Still technique? The name says it all. One Single Pot - usually an enormous pot - cooks the fermented mash of malted barley and un-malted green barley and the Distilled beverage that results will be unique to that particular batch of Whisky. The Continuous Still of Aeneas Coffey was more effective at mass producing Alcohol - comparable to a factory conveyor belt that constantly churns out Distilled Spirit, while the Single Pot cooked up its one batch before starting the process all over again.

After all the ups and downs of the Irish Whisky Industry, here are the notable Distilleries that remain:

Bushmills: There is an interesting argument in Ireland about which Whisky Distillery is the oldest. Is it Old Bushmills of County Antrim, Northern Ireland, or the Kilbeggan Distillery n the Republic? If Bushmills wins the argument, they can lay claim to the date of 1608, which would make them the oldest Distillery in the world – but an actual Whisky producing establishment called Bushmills wasn't truly in existence in 1608 so the facts about the date can be misleading. What we do have is a license to Distil given by King James to Sir Thomas Phillips, a governor and landowner of County Antrim in 1608 . The license of 1608 by itself didn't mean Bottles of the famous Bushmills Brands started to be produced in County Antrim. The name Bushmills was not used until 1743 when whatever had been set up as a Distillery was in the hands of smugglers. 1784 is when Bushmills was officially registered by Hugh Anderson and the Pot Still became its trademark.

The word blarney means stretching the truth or evading truth altogether and replacing it with not so much a fib, but more a fanciful tale that sounds slightly plausible. When the Irish say that Santa Clause is buried in Kilkenny (based on the legend that the bones of Saint Nicholas, the Bishop of Myra, were taken to Ireland and buried in a churchyard) you might think "Blarney!" or a stronger word not fit to print. There is some blarney that has not been discouraged about the Bushmills Distillery and the claim that it is the oldest licensed Distillery in the world with a production date beginning in 1608. What was going on in 1608 is very much disputed. The true blarney-less honour of being the oldest licensed Irish Distillery should probably go to Kilbeggan which has had a verifiable license with actual production going on since 1757. What is undisputed is that Bushmills is an old revered Distillery that survived when almost every other Distillery in Ireland died. It even burned down but rose from the ashes, and only closed down for a while during the triple whammy that hit the Irish Whisky Industry.

Part of the Bushmills Distillery is a boutique producer of Ireland's lost Whisky treasures called The Irishman. Irishman Whiskies are all limited editions, re-creations of Single Pot Whiskies of the past from all the Distilleries that went belly-up during all the hardships the Industry faced. The Irishman 70, for instance, claimed many an international Whisky prize such as the International Spirits Challenge and a Double Gold at The San Francisco Spirits competition.

Midleton Distillery: Midleton is the home of world famous Jameson's Irish Whisky, and the Distillery was a result of many Irish Distilleries uniting their efforts during the economic woes that hit the Industry.

John Jameson, a Scots Presbyterian from Alloa, Scotland,

established the Dublin based Jameson Distillery in 1780. His son, also called John, continued the business. In the 20th century, John Jameson and Son Distillers, along with John Power and Son and the Cork Distillers Company joined forces to become the United Distillers and the Whisky production was moved to County Cork and to the Midleton Distillery.

The old and the new are near each other in Midleton. The old is kept as a museum piece that tourists can visit while the new Distillery shows how the Irish Whisky Industry reinvented itself to compete in the world. The old Distillery contains the world's biggest copper Pot Still that can hold nearly 32,000 gallons. It was manufactured in 1825 and instead of being moved into a Distillery, the building was constructed around the pot. What the tourists will see is a replacement pot because the original blew up when it was heated while it was empty - which evidently is a no no! Not anyone was seriously injured in the blast, but one worker had his clothes blown off. They found him in just his hat and shoes – the rest of his clothes had been shredded and fell off him. Happily the fellow survived and is proud that everyone gets to hear the story of the man who found himself bare naked after the BOOM! Speaking only for myself, it would have been a better story if the worker had been a 22-year-old buxom brunette named Felicity!

Dominic Roskow writes, "If the old Distillery is a poignant reminder of where Irish Distillers came from, then the new Distillery a few hundred metres away is a good indicator as to where it's going. Not only does it dwarf the old buildings, and despite the fact it's only 30 years old, part of its vast storage tanks stand redundant due to the need for bigger and better ones. Make no mistake, the new Midleton is huge. More than 500,000 Casks are stored on site. The total Distilling capacity would produce 18 million litres of pure Alcohol every year. They estimate there are 200 million Bottles worth of Whisky maturing here, and that 12,000 Bottles are lost to the angels each day. If you're of the view that the only real difference between an Irish Whisky operation and a Scottish one is triple Distillation, then Midleton will astound from the outset." Describing the various Whisky Brands coming out of the Midleton Distillery, Whisky writer Tim Atkinson says, "The extended Jameson family, as they like to call it in Midleton, includes a number of specialist Whiskies, too. These are generally a lot more interesting than the basic Jameson Blend and include Jameson 1780, Jameson Gold and Redbreast. All three are superbly complex Whiskies. The 1780 is the smoothest and longest of the trio, with pronounced Sherry wood sweetness and rich barley malt characters. The Gold is a more honeyed, toasty Whisky with notes of malt and smoky Bourbon and a powerful grip as it slides past the tonsils. And Redbreast 12 YO is a densely flavoured, pure Pot Still Whisky with the assertiveness of a nightclub bouncer. This is definitely not a Whisky to tangle with on a dark Dublin night."

COOLEY & KILBEGGAN

Just as science opened the door to so many in the Whisky Industry in Scotland, science opened the door for Cooley/ Kilbeggan Master Distiller Noel Sweeney in Ireland. Noel has been a leading light in the renaissance of the Irish Whisky Industry – in fact, Noel Sweeney has been one of those responsible for the revitalized, re-energized, renewed Irish Whisky Industry that exists today. His background was in analytical chemistry. Testing and lab tech work led to working with the neutral Spirit being produced by potatoes. It is hard to imagine today that the Distillery responsible for Greenore, the resurrected Kilbeggan, Connemara and Tyreconnell used to produce Alcohol from fermenting potatoes. That all changed when John Teeling bought the Potato-Alcohol plant in 1987. Noel has had various functions in the Cooley Distillery – he has been a production supervisor and a quality manager but those in the know came to identify talents in Noel that led him into roles more in line with master Distilling and master Blending.

Noel told C. Ask Whisky how he had been with Cooley through the ups and downs of trying to stay afloat in a volatile economy and tempestuous Whisky market. Cooley became the Go-To-Distillery for developing the supermarket Own Brands not only in the UK but in America as well. You name the store – and if you bought that store's name Brand Whisky, it was most likely developed by Noel Sweeney at the Cooley Distillery. Then along came Beam Global and bought Cooley. There was now some corporate muscle and finance to enable Cooley to concentrate on developing its primary Brands without being distracted by the dozens of other Whiskies Noel had been looking after. When asked how he felt about this, Noel told us that it was sweet relief to have the weight of so many Brands lifted off his shoulders.

Yes, he was proud of the babies he had created on behalf of the big supermarkets but Beam Global gave him needed respite when they came riding in. He could now focus solely on making sure the Whiskies he had a big hand in developing for Cooley – the four core ranges of Connemara, Kilbeggan, Greenore and Tyreconnell are the true ambassadors of Irish Whisky they were intended to be.

Cooley goes against some of the Irish Distilling traditions such as triple Distillation and using only the Pot Still. They've had the courage to say, "Why can't Irish Whisky be double Distilled? Why can't we use a Column Still as well? They seem to be asking the right questions since they have won over 300 medals in international Whisky competitions and have been named Distillery Of The Year several times by the IWSC and Malt Advocate Magazine.

Another crowning achievement of Cooley was to re-open the old Kilbeggan Distillery. Despite producing Whisky since the mid 18th century, it closed in the mid 20th century. Some 50 years of gathering cobwebs followed but then thanks to Cooley, Kilbeggan began producing Whisky again. Noel presided over the event, and when the first few drops of Distillate came from the new Kilbeggan stills, there was said to be a few tears shed by the gathered spectators. Kilbeggan is now another arm of Cooley for producing Whisky and also a museum of sorts, providing a tour for those visiting the Distillery.

Here are descriptions of the four major Cooley/Kilbeggan Brands:

Kilbeggan: It is a Blended Whisky. There used to be no age statement, but now there is a 15 YO and coming soon there will be an 18 YO.

Greenore: This is a Single Grain Whisky, the Single Grain being corn. It ranges in age from 6 YO to 18 YO.

Connemara: This is Ireland's only peated Whisky. It is aged in Bourbon Casks. Its range includes single-Cask, Cask-strength, 12 YO, and a steeped in peat version, called, Turf Mór.

The Tyrconnell: This Single Malt Whisky is the resurrection

of a dead Brand. Tyreconnell went extinct in 1925 but Cooley obtained the old Brand in 1988 and began producing it again. It is said to be smooth and creamy.

3.2 - ENGLAND AND WALES

England was undoubtedly too busy ruling the world, or at least the colonies it had established in most of the world, to be too concerned with seriously competing with its neighbours to the north and across the Irish Sea in the Distillation of Whisky. It therefore became a tiny David figure against the Goliath of the Industry in Scotland - only in this case, David died and Goliath triumphed. There were Distilleries operating in London, Liverpool and Bristol but they all ceased production by 1905. England was out of the game for a whole century. Only in the new millennium, has England decided it wants to play with the big boys of Scotland, Ireland, America, Canada and the rest of the world.

In 2006, St. George's Distillery was opened in Roundham, Norfolk in the South East of England and they produced the first English Whisky in over a hundred years. Taking their name, image and logo from the patron saint of England, the Bottles of Whisky feature a medieval type picture of Saint George slaying the mythical dragon. The aim of the Distillery has been to produce the quintessential English Whisky, and now there is a Visitor Centre and Distillery Tour.

We spoke to Andrew Nelstrop about the Distillery he owns and manages. He told us that it was his father James, a barley farmer with a passion for Single Malts that decided to bring Whisky production back to England. They decided to spare no expense in getting the right equipment and hiring a legendary Master Distiller or two from Scotland to help get production going on the right foot. Iain Henderson oversaw the first year of Distillation and Casking. An expert brewer named David Flynn then became the Master Distiller. Some of the first 3 YO Whiskies that came out of the new Distillery went on to be debuted on Chef Gordon Ramsay's TV show. If the famously swearing and outspoken Chef didn't like the taste of the Whisky, he would have spit it out and said how much he hated it to millions of viewers. It was a big risk on Andrew Nelstrop's part to allow the debut on such a show. There was no need to worry. The barley, the climate, the water, the Casks, the equipment, the people on board, even the Visitor Centre and tours have done their part in putting English Whisky back on the map. Andrew told us they have Casks set aside for future Bottling that will be 12 YO, 15 YO, 18 YO – in fact the future is planned ahead up to 2054.

Here is how the St. George's website describes their Whiskies and like us – they have chapters as in a book: "Our Whisky is batch made by hand with no computers, matured in fine Casks, Bottled on site using our own water and is non chill-filtered. We are really proud of these things and believe you will taste the difference too.

Why the Chapters? As a new Distillery we wanted to offer our customers the opportunity to follow the production of a fine Single Malt Whisky, peated and unpeated, from conception through to, well, indefinitely! For this reason we thought it would make easy reading to keep the development in chapters, so at various ages from 1 day old through to 40 YO we will give you the opportunity to taste how the Whisky is maturing. Each new Bottling will be a new chapter to the 'The Book'.

CORNWALL AND ELSEWHERE IN ENGLAND

Another new English Whisky has been produced in Cornwall out of the St. Austell's brewery. St. Austell's had been making Beer and Wine for the most part. It teamed up with Cornish Cider producers Hicks and Healey to Distil Hicks and Healey Cornish Whisky. The united front brought about the first Cornish Whisky in 300 years. By all accounts it was worth the wait and a significant debut and yes there are apple notes in the taste as you would expect from Cider producers. They only make a small amount of Whisky each year and so the advice is to get them while they are hot.

Adnams Copper House Distillery Whisky is to be released in November, 2013 and plans for a Distillery in the Lake District have just been given the go ahead.

It seems that England is getting back into the game in a big way.

THE PENDERYN DISTILLERY

In common with her sister Celtic nations, Ireland and Scotland, Wales had been Distilling Alcohol since the middle ages, and like England, its Whisky production all but stopped toward the end of the 19th century. Some predicted the world would end in 2000, just as it was supposed to end in 2012 and many other prophesied doomsdays, but the year 2000 was actually the re-birth of Welsh Whisky with the opening of the Distillery in the village of Penderyn in the foothills of the Brecon Becons. Four years later, their first Whisky was ready to be partaken of. To quote their website they say: "Penderyn Single Malt Welsh Whisky was first launched on St David's Day, 1st March 2004, in the presence of HRH Prince Charles, to huge critical acclaim from both acknowledged Whisky experts and "ordinary" consumers. At Penderyn we produce just one Cask per day of the finest malted barley Spirit, which, when matured, is recognised worldwide as one of the finest malt Whiskies. The majority of our Spirit goes into Cask for aging in our cellars. Minute quantities are diverted to craft our other award-winning products."

The managing director of Penderyn, Stephen Davies spoke to C. Ask Whisky about the Penderyn Distillery. "The idea for a new Welsh Distillery was birthed in a pub conversation among friends who wondered why there was no Welsh Whisky production," said Davies. One of the friends Davies referred to was Alun Evans and he led the charge to make the dream into a reality. The idea sparked research into Welsh history and Whisky production in the past. Investors were gathered who knew they wouldn't see return on their investment for years to come. The Distillery was built in the Brecon Beacons with a supply of clear water from underground caves and some unique features became part of the Distillery. A relative of the famous scientist Michael Faraday, David Faraday designed a new type of still that no one else in the world has. In our conversation with Davies, he was pleased to announce, that a second such Faraday Still had been given the go ahead and that will mean Penderyn will be able to lay out more than one filled Cask a day. Another unique feature of Penderyn is that its Master Distiller is a young woman in her 20s named Gillian Howell. She did marry a man named McDonald - but Davies and Gillian herself want the world to know that Ms. Howell-McDonald is Welsh through and through.

When asked whether Welsh Whisky was a novelty that would wear out, Davies told Whisky Magazine, "Of course we have benefited from tourists visiting and wanting to take away something unique to the region, and of course we have had many Welsh people buying it because it's Welsh. But that can only work for so long. Eventually it has to come down to the standard of what's in the Bottle, and what's in the Bottle is very good indeed."

3.3 - USA HONEY AND PEPPER WESTERN WHISKY

As an example of the creativity, experimentation and the "Why Not?" innovations in present day American Whisky, we present Western Whisky. We spoke to Art Foss who was backing the new Honey and Pepper Western Whisky Brand. His background was in distribution, importing and retail and when Western Whisky was brought to his attention he thought he was on to a winner. Art was more of a Wine guy than a Whisky guy, but when he took a taste of the Honey Pepper Whisky, he looked at Abe Shrem and Marty Kairey, the two gentlemen behind the creation of the Whisky and thought, "This is delicious!" Before it was packaged and Bottled, they took it out to test on the public, going to a Las Vegas Bar and Restaurant Show. According to Art, the almost universal reaction was a big smile and the question, "Where can I buy it?" That spurred them on to production. Their marketing, their label art and their website are all a lot of fun. The new product is now in 6 states and undoubtedly this will expand across the USA and head overseas.

Already there are plans for new flavours such as the upcoming Peach, Amaretto, Orange, Green Tea, Cappuccino and Maple Bacon flavoured Whiskies. Here is what their sexy cow-girl themed website says about the Whisky: "This remarkable Honey Pepper Whisky starts off caressing your palate with Natural Clove Honey, yet it has a long and teasing chilli pepper finish. Honey Pepper is a hand-crafted artisan Whisky; it is skilfully prepared in small batches to highlight the purity of superior natural ingredients. The initial rich, full bodied Bourbon flavour is softened by smooth natural Honey and followed with a fiery yet subtle pepper finish, dangerously soliciting your palate for another shot. Western Honey Pepper Whisky has an initial rich, full-bodied Bourbon profile with a firm undertone of Oak and vanilla.

This symphony complimented by the medley of clover honey and zesty, savoury chilli pepper make Western Honey Pepper a legend that awaits you. Western Whisky is made with Kentucky Bourbon & Blended Whisky right here in the U.S. of A. ABV: 30% 60 Proof Small Batch Bourbons are Bourbons that Bottled from a small group of specially selected Barrels that are Blended together. Flavour descriptors such as toffee, pralines, vanilla, and dried fruit describe the initial rush of flavours in a good, well-aged Bourbon. The charred white Oak Barrels give Bourbon a distinctive spicy Oak firmness that is unique to American Whiskies.
You can find the award winning product (Sip Awards 2012 Gold) at www.western-Whisky.com/honey-pepper-whisky.html

AMERICA'S THRIVING WHISKY INDUSTRY

The USA and Canada are the second and third biggest Whisky producing countries after Scotland. This should not be surprising since what would become the USA and Canada were colonized by Europeans - many of whom were from Scotland and Ireland. The Irish Potato Famine and the Highland Clearances were but two factors that brought a wave of Distilling knowledge and ready-made customers to North America. This knowledge when combined with that pioneering can-do Spirit and an abundance of new ingredients (such as corn, rye and wheat) with which to produce Distilled Spirits brought about a Whisky revolution to give Scotland and Ireland a run for their Whisky money.

Different local taxes keep North American Whiskies cheaper than their parents across the pond. Rarely will you find an American Whisky that costs over a 100 dollars. Usually the top of the range, Premium Brand of a company is 50 dollars at the most. American Whisky tends to be sweeter than the Whisky of its Scotch-Irish parentage. They don't have the smoky peat flavours of any of the Scotch produced on the island of Islay for instance - which doesn't make them better or worse, but just different. The fermented mash of a North American Whisky tends to be a combination of - yes- barley, like most Scotch, but wheat, corn and rye contribute to the different flavours of the North American Brands. Maturation takes place relatively quickly in Virgin American Oak Casks, and the earlier aging time has a lot to do with the more extremes of temperature between summer and winter. Also, leaving a Spirit too long in a Virgin Cask could ruin the Whisky because of how aggressive the wood influence would be.

The new settlers in Kentucky and Tennessee in America's early history took to Whisky production in a big way. Everything needed to make Whisky was there in abundance, from the wood to make the Barrels, to fields of corn, to clear, fresh water. A very American style of Whisky is affectionately known as Bourbon, and Bourbon is primarily made in the state of Kentucky. To be a Bourbon it has to be made from at least 51 percent corn and aged in a new American Oak Barrel. Most Bourbons are 75 percent corn.

The state next to Kentucky is Tennessee and Tennessee Whisky is essentially Bourbon but after the corn-centric Spirit is Distilled, it is filtered very slowly through a ten foot mound of sugar-maple charcoal. The famous Brand, Jack Daniel's Tennessee Whisky goes through such a process.

The ingredient of rye in North American Whiskies brings a welcome bitter flavour with a hint of something more akin to the spice of pepper without adding actual pepper. The rye gives the Whisky just such a kick.

Then there is the infamous underground Brand of American Whisky called Moonshine, which was made famous during the Prohibition era of the 1920s when illegal stills operated by moonlight so their smoke would not be detected by the powers that be. Of course there had been illegal Moonshine Stills in

Ireland and Scotland long before America's Prohibition, but Moonshine America came to have its own legendary mystique – instead of just one Robin Hood, there were hundreds of Hillbilly versions of the rogue hero who was sticking it to the powers that be. Moonshine had to be made fast and so the slow-aged Cask Whisky process in which the Distilled Spirit took its sweet time to absorb flavours from the Oak Barrels through many a season wasn't going to work for the Moonshiners. The fermentation process took as much time as was allowed before the resulting Spirit went into the jug without any colour and that is why Moonshine is also called White Lightning.

GEORGE WASHINGTON

The story of American Whisky begins almost as soon as the new settlers started arriving and before the USA was the USA. The Europeans brought the technology and the Indians had the corn so even in Jamestown, one of the earliest American colonial towns, Corn Whisky was being made. Shortly after the USA's birth on July 4th, 1776, rye-based Whisky was known to be Distilled in Virginia, Maryland and Pennsylvania. America's first president, George Washington, thought to himself, "Ah ha! A source of revenue for the new federal government. We shall tax Whisky!"

There's a good reason why they decided to put George's picture on the one dollar bill. He was good at making dollars! The only problem was, Whisky tax was about as popular in America as it was back in Scotland and Ireland. There then arose what came to be known as the Whisky Rebellion. When upset Whisky producers thumbed their nose at the same revolutionary soldiers that had thumbed their nose at England's tea tax, they found themselves confronted by George Washington himself, leading a militia of 13000 soldiers - a larger army than Washington had under his command in the War of Revolution. The Whisky Rebels were mad as hell and were not going to take it anymore! The very government that had said, "No taxation without representation and threw the King's tea in the harbour," were now doing what the king of England had done (in their view) and that was slapping on a big tax on top of their Whisky. The huge army of George Washington insured there was no war to speak of, and there were very few casualties. Some 20 men were arrested, and thus the rebellion was quashed and the taxes were made to stick, though they were still very difficult to collect. Ironically, the man who put down the Whisky rebellion, went into the Whisky business himself and became the largest producer of Whisky in his day. The George Washington Distillery has been resurrected to make Whisky now in the old-fashioned still that is part of the Mount Vernon, Virginia estate that tourists can visit to get a Colonial glimpse of all things George and Martha Washington and life in the latter part of the 18th century. Chris Morris, the Master Distiller for Brown-Forman was very much involved in the re-creation of the Washington Distillery. He told C. Ask Whisky how he had had to dress up in uncomfortable Colonial Outfits and brew things the old fashioned way in front of the tourists - and one of those tourists just happened to be Great Britain's Prince Andrew. Everyone had the protocol explained to them about what they could and couldn't do in the presence of a Royal. Chris Morris had been working in the Distillery all day getting things ready for the Prince. Colonial Chris was dirty and sweaty by the time the Prince came a calling. Despite the presence of armed security guards, all protocol went out the window and Colonial Chris put his hand out and said, "Hey Prince, how you doing?" The Prince also broke his own protocol and shook Chris' hand.

"What are you doing?" asked Prince Andrew.

"Making Whisky!" answered Chris. "Put your finger down there and take a taste."

There were drops of Distillate coming out of the still and Chris offered the Prince a taste. This was equivalent to baking a cake and asking the Prince if he wanted to lick the frosting bowl!

" I shan't," said Andrew.

"Come on!" smiled Chris. "Stick your finger down there and take a taste!"

"I shan't," said Andrew before turning awkwardly and leaving the friendly Colonial Distiller to carry on. Obviously there was a culture clash between friendly Southern hospitality and Royal dos and don'ts. Chris felt a little embarrassed, especially when the story of the awkward international incident was printed in the Washington Post. After the opening of the

George Washington Distillery, Chris was able to get back to work overseeing the three Distilleries he is responsible for. We will speak to Chris later when we come to the Distillery Tour Chapter.

MOONSHINE

Whisky carried on happily brewing, Distilling, growing and developing in the USA for many a year, but a negative side effect of everything from Beer to Wine to Whisky was the blight of Alcohol abuse in North America. The same blight and severe social problems had sickened the heart of Scotland and Ireland.

As much as Distilleries profit from those who buy their wares, they purposely distance themselves from the customers who abuse their product and drink irresponsibly. That is why Skid Row Alkies don't appear in the commercials for any Spirit. To compare the marketing of Spirits to the marketing of air travel for instance, airlines will say, "Fly with us" and show you exotic locations, happy people on their planes, pretty stewardesses and handsome pilots. What they won't show you is a plane wreck. No Alcoholic beverage producer wants to talk about the drunks and the tragic domestic abuse that results. They plead with their customers to drink responsibly. The heavy tax duty on Scotch in Scotland has helped to make it a luxury that the typical Scottish Alcoholic is not easily able to afford; it has come to be the drink of the more respectable in society. The American government of the 1920s decided the answer to solving the social ill of Alcohol abuse was to ban Alcohol all together. This was known as Prohibition or the Noble Experiment. What this did however, was create a black market of Liquor production and smuggling that in turn gave birth to many a gangster. Prohibition lasted 11 years from 1922 to 1933 and only then did the American government finally admit that Prohibition was a failure. As has been said, illegal Moonshine was a prominent feature of Prohibition and it was our pleasure to hear some stories from those days from the man behind the now perfectly legal and online - Moonshine.com. His name is Chuck Miller, owner of the Stillhouse Farm and Moonshine Distillery in Virginia.

C. ASK: Hi Chuck. Please tell us how you became a Moonshiner?

CHUCK MILLER: I was hanging out with my grandfather. I had a funny feeling he was up to something because he had all these big old milk containers but only one cow. It took me a while to figure out what my grandfather was doing and that of course was making Moonshine. It wasn't legal, but making Moonshine was the only job he ever had and that's how he supported his wife and kids. The authorities knew he was making Moonshine but never caught him at it. He stored everything under the house and there was a trap door in the floor and a pole he could slide down to where everything was stashed. One time the authorities did come by and my grandmother just parked her rocking chair over the trap door and kept rocking while the authorities searched the house. They didn't find a thing. On another occasion, grandpa had to make a delivery in D.C. - There was a roadblock set up, and Grandpa had to gun the engine and run the roadblock. They shot out his back window, but he still made the delivery and returned to the farm without getting caught.

As a young man, I did a stint in the army, but when I came back, I thought, 'You know, Grandpa had a good thing going. I decided to carry on the family business, although I was going to do it legal. We started up in 1980 and after a couple of years we got our license. They call it a Craft Distillery today, and though I didn't realize it at the time, I was the first licensed Craft Distiller in the United States.

C. ASK: How long does it take to make Moonshine?

CHUCK MILLER: Here' the deal. We make our Moonshine the old fashioned way. We grow our own corn, grind it, cook it - we have a big old Pot Still and our own personalized strain of yeast. We let it ferment for four days and then we Distil it four times - from the grinding of the corn to the Bottling and loading on the truck takes about a week.

C. ASK: Only a week?

CHUCK MILLER: Moonshiners had to work fast, man! They made un-aged Corn Whisky and that's what I make.

C. ASK: How much Moonshine do you sell?

CHUCK MILLER: We can hardly keep up with the demand! We sell thousands of cases all across the States. People come tour the farm all the time wanting to learn about Moonshine. We also have the happiest cows in the USA because we feed them the left over fermented mash. Nothing goes to waste!

C. ASK WHISKY COMMENTARY: If you think Chuck Miller's Moonshine comes in an old jug marked xxx you would be mistaken. Chuck's original Moonshine is presented with style and class in a glass jug that is one of the nicest Bottle presentations that we've seen. We encourage you to check out the website at Moonshine.com, which is a well designed, entertaining website.

WILD TURKEY

Bourbon Whisky is as American as baseball, apple pie and Chevrolet cars and Wild Turkey is an iconic American Bourbon and an iconic American success story. The Austin Nichol Wild Turkey Distillery in Lawrenceburg, Kentucky, existed as a working Distillery long before its present name and its famous Brand came into existence. The Distillery had been in operation since 1869, which is 72 years before the birth of the Wild Turkey Brand in 1941. A Distillery executive took what was in essence Wild Turkey Bourbon on a wild turkey hunting trip with some friends in 1940. Obviously, the friends enjoyed the excursion as well as the Bourbon. The following year, those same friends went with the executive again and asked, "Do you have any of that Wild Turkey Whisky?" Thus, an iconic Brand with an iconic image was born. The image of a grouse didn't hurt a particular Bottle of Blended Scotch either and it is no accident that there are two best selling

Whiskies with an indelible image of a bird printed on the label. The whole purpose of a Brand is to be Branded on the brain, eyes and ears and if it is easy to forget, the Brand has failed in its marketing. The image of the turkey or the grouse on the Bottle is one of the factors that make these two Whiskies so memorable. Note to Whisky Companies – Big Bird is taken and you would get complaints – trying to find an indelible image is good thinking however.

Wikipedia reports a quick summary of the facts about the Brand we are discussing: "Wild Turkey comes in six varieties: 81 proof (formerly 80 proof), 101 proof, Kentucky Spirit, Russell's Reserve, and Rare Breed.

Wild Turkey Kentucky Spirit is a single Barrel version at 101 proof, Russell's Reserve, a 10 YO named for Master Distiller Jimmy Russell, is 90 proof, and the Rare Breed is a Blend of 6, 8 and 12-YO stocks at 108.4 Barrel proof.

Wild Turkey 101 earned an 'Editor's Choice' award from Whisky Magazine

The Wild Turkey Brand has also been extended to a Rye Whisky, made from a mash of roughly 65% rye, 23% corn and 12% barley, and to a Honey Liqueur, called American Honey. International Spirit ratings organizations have consistently given favourable reviews to the Wild Turkey 101 Single Barrel. Proof66.com, aggregator of reviews from various "expert" bodies, places the 101 Single Barrel in the 97th percentile of all rated Bourbons."

What was far more interesting than the above statistics was to hear some of these facts from Bourbon hall-of-famers, the father and son team with 90 years of experience between them, Jimmy and Eddy Russell, the Master Distillers behind the Wild Turkey Brand. We had the great honour of speaking to them both and though we spoke to the father before the son, we thought it appropriate to let the son introduce his dad to everyone and so we will reverse the order of our interview:

C. ASK: Hi Eddie. We had the pleasure of speaking to your father for a good forty minutes. To our surprise we get to speak to the son as well. What's it like to be the son of the great Jimmy Russell?

EDDIE RUSSELL: Well, it's been an honour to follow in his footsteps. When I started working with my dad, everyone said, "Those are some big shoes to fill." I had to laugh and say, "I can't fill those shoes. I can slip them on over my own feet and I've had to find out how to make my own way."

C. ASK: Do you have different ideas and different plans than your dad?

EDDIE RUSSELL: I'm a little bit different than my Dad. I'm willing to try different things to get more people into the Bourbon or Whisky category. I've learned a lot from my Dad. I grew up around Parker Beam and Booker Noe. The attitude was we make this Whisky and you either like it or you don't, where as Ill' try new things to introduce new groups of people to our Whisky. Not every palate is ready for some of the stronger tastes of some of our top shelf Brands such as the 101 or the Rare Breed. I wanted to make a lighter proof version of Wild Turkey – the 81 proof - that still retained the flavour and character – but a version the ladies, the young men in their twenties would be introduced to and also a version the mixologists could use to make cocktails and so keep reaching beyond the happy customers we already have. When their palate is more developed and they're older and their tastes change, the stronger top shelf Brands will be there. I'm not trying to undermine anything Jimmy has done. We only have one recipe for our Bourbon and we want that bolder, spicier taste, so all I'm doing is trying to work with what I've been taught through Jimmy and try to present it to younger males and females, because as I grew up, it seemed like we only promoted to the older gentlemen. Coming up with American Honey Liqueur was about reaching out to those who would like something sweeter while still giving them a taste of Wild Turkey. Even with the 81 proof or American Honey they are still getting that quality 6-8 YO aged Bourbon and that unique Wild Turkey flavour.

C.ASK: Did you always want to go into the family business?

EDDIE RUSSELL: I grew up in it. I went away to college and came back with a business degree and at first, I worked at the Distillery as just a summer job, but then after two weeks it felt like home and I decided that that's what I wanted to do with my life. Now my son might very well end up working here too. He is already a summer tour guide. He would be the fifth generation of Russells working in the Industry if that's what he wants to do.

C. ASK: And it's an Industry you love?

EDDIE RUSSELL: It's been good to me. We're in the entertainment business! We have a good product, a natural product and we represent it well. Growing up, I didn't realize what my Dad meant to this Industry. After a year or two working here, it began to dawn on me what Jimmy meant to this Industry – to Bourbon all together, not just Wild Turkey. And then I got to meet all the other Master Distillers and got a lot of knowledge from them – they would talk about how they were raised in the Industry and that's the good thing about it – its usually passed on from generation to generation. Now I'm taking on some of Jimmy's responsibilities – and that's understandable after 58 years working here – but I don't think Jimmy will ever retire. He still shows up for work every day and still greets as many people as he can that come to visit.

C ASK WHISKY COMMENTARY: We are of the opinion that Eddie Russell has filled his own shoes quite well. We will now meet the man that the son and the whole of the Bourbon Industry – even beyond America, the worldwide Whisky Industry – the man they all hold in such high regard - we will meet Mr. Jimmy Russell!

C. ASK: Jimmy, how did you get started in the Industry?

JIMMY RUSSELL: In my small hometown of Lawrenceburg, Kentucky, there were four Distilleries – and while I was growing up, there were members of my family working at all four Distilleries. My grandfather worked at a Distillery and my father was head of maintenance at a Distillery. I'd been around it all my life so the first thing I thought of was becoming part of the business. I ended up here at Austin Nichol Wild Turkey Distillery. Eventually my Dad came here too and so I got to work with my Dad. Now I get to work with my son and even my grandson works part time at the Distillery.

C. ASK: You've done almost everything there is to do in the

Industry. What keeps you going and what motivates you to go to work everyday?

JIMMY RUSSELL: The motivation is to keep putting out a great product, a consistent product that has a worldwide reputation. Wherever you go in the world, people talk about Wild Turkey. It's not the best selling Bourbon, but it is the best selling Premium Bourbon in the world. What pushes you to keep on putting out a great product is when you meet the people that enjoy Wild Turkey, and they tell you how much they enjoy it and what it means to them. That's why I do what I do.

C. ASK: What Scotch Whisky have you tried?

JIMMY RUSSELL: I've tasted almost all of them and all the Irish Whiskies too. I've been a judge in International Spirit competitions in London, England. I've been fortunate to try all the Scotches, all the Irish, the Japanese Whiskies – many of the Whiskies of the world.,

C. ASK: Do you have any particular favourite Scotches?

JIMMY RUSSELL: I like the light Scotches. I don't care much for the heavy, smoky peated Scotches, say from Islay. A lot of people like those and that's fine. I like the Red Breast Irish Whisky and the John Powers.

C. ASK: Does Wild Turkey do anything like a Single Malt:

JIMMY RUSSELL: By American law, a Bourbon has to be 51% corn. We use corn, rye and malted barley in our product. By law, we can't Distil more than 80% Alcohol. The Spirit has to go into a new Barrel made of American White Oak. No flavouring, no colours, nothing can be added. Its the most heavily restricted product in the world. When the Barrel is charred it carmelizes the sugars, the vanillans and that's where the flavour comes from. The heat of the summer and the cold of the winter- all the expanding and contracting of the wooden Barrels – we call that breathing and that's where the Spirit extracts the flavours from the wood.

C. ASK: What is the Angel's Share in your Bourbon?

JIMMY RUSSELL: After eight years, we lose about a third of the Cask to evaporation. Even though we lose some of the Spirit that way, we still age Wild Turkey. We have our metal storage buildings, seven stories tall, rigged houses where we roll our Barrels in – in the summer time we open the windows to get air circulating and in the winter time we close the windows – we want our Barrels to breathe because that's where they pick up the caramel, the vanilla, the sweetness, the flavour and the colour.

C. ASK: You hear of so many American Whiskies and Bourbons that don't age that long and yet Wild Turkey seems the exception to the rule.

JIMMY RUSSELL: Let me give you my personal taste. I think a 3 YO up to 6 YO is still too young and they are just starting to mature. I think the better tasting Bourbons are 7- 12 YO – any more than that, and because of the virgin wood, it starts to taste bad. It loses the sweetness and you get a woody taste that I don't like. In Scotland, you mature things longer because you're taking Barrels that have already been used and because of the different climate.

C. ASK: Can you talk about some of your range of products such as Russell's Reserve?

JIMMY RUSSELL: Russell's Reserve is a 10 YO small batch limited edition that we came out with about 15 years ago. Actually, when I started with Wild Turkey, we only had the one product, the 50.5% Wild Turkey but now we have the 81 or 40.5%Alcohol Wild Turkey, the single Barrel Russell's Reserve – 55% non-chill filtered, the single Barrel Kentucky Spirit that averages 8 YO and is hand selected one Barrel at a time, and the Rare Breed – which is Barrel proof – I believe in Scotland you say Cask Strength at 52.1% Alcohol.

C. ASK: Do people drink it straight? Do they add water to it in order to tone it down?

JIMMY RUSSELL: People like to drink it straight. They say its smooth. They don't need to add anything to it. They say they can't taste the Alcohol content. That's the way we make Wild Turkey. We want the character, the strong body, the taste. We don't want that strong Alcohol taste and ours doesn't have it.

C. ASK: Who are your biggest overseas customers?

JIMMY RUSSELL: Our biggest export market is Australia and second is Japan. We do good business in Europe too. In Japan, Wild Turkey is considered a prestige drink and in Australia, they drink a lot of Wild Turkey. We're doing well in Taiwan and all of Asia and we've been in Japan for the last 25 years.

C. ASK: Is there a part of you that is experimental and gets the better of you? Do you have any experimental Casks you are working on in the background?

JIMMY RUSSELL: I've been here 58 years and we are still making Wild Turkey the same way as the day I arrived. We do not do a lot of experimenting. In the long run that's paid off for us and the market for our Bourbon has grown all over the world.

C. ASK: A lot of people like to mix Bourbon and Coca-Cola. Do you have any recommendations for mixing?

JIMMY RUSSELL: Speaking personally, I like to drink Wild Turkey straight or on the rocks on a hot summer day. I'm not going to tell you how to drink it. You drink it anyway you want. If you want to mix it, I can recommend Ginger Ale. Bourbon and Ginger Ale marry well and there are nice complimentary flavours if someone wants to try that.

C. ASK: Tell us about American Honey?

JIMMY RUSSELL: That was a sweeter version of Wild Turkey developed for those who thought a straight Bourbon was a bit too strong. Its doing well for us all across the States. Everywhere you go, you find people mixing American Honey and lemonade or American Honey and Ice Tea. It's doing well in Australia and we just started selling it in Germany.

C. ASK: Of the Wild Turkey Brands, which is your favourite?

JIMMY RUSSELL: I drink them all, but I am partial to the stronger taste of the Single Cask Russell's Reserve or the Rare Breed. I am one of these people who likes the stronger Alcohol content. Still the original 50.5 Wild Turkey is doing well all over the world and people like it just fine.

C. ASK WHISKY COMMENTARY: A consistent, recognizable well loved Brand is one way to become a Whisky superstar selling all over Planet Earth, but having ambassadors like Jimmy and Eddie takes Wild Turkey to a whole new level that few other Whiskies can touch.

THE SPIRIT OF TEXAS

"Texas made, Texas proud," boasts the Balcones Distillery. "Balcones Texas Malt Whisky is born of hundreds of years of Distilling tradition transformed by a deep sense of place. Mellow notes of sauteed pears and ripe fruit mixed with a lingering toasty malt character. We are very excited that this Whisky which we have worked so hard to produce is finally ready to release. We hope you enjoy it."

Chip Tate was not kidding about how hard it was to bring Balcones to the world. In a Whisky Magazine article, Chip Tate said, "Balcones isn't one of those cookie-cutter Distilleries, I wanted equipment which would make what I wanted, not one which could make Vodka." The article talks about that do-it-yourself ingenuity in Chip Tate: "After a period touring Scotland, he got his stills and immediately began modifying them. 'The pots were good but they needed adjusting. I learned it's pretty hard to undo someone else's work.'" Chip built the Distillery by hand and that gave him an intimate understanding of the Distillation process. He not only wanted to bring Whisky to Texas but Texas to Whisky. Dominic Roskoe writes, "Equally important for him is making his Spirits Texan. The woodsmoke in Brimstone is from local BBQ woods, Rumble, his homage to rum is based on local honey, while his Baby Blue uses Texan blue corn. 'I love Whiskies from all around the world, but I'm also a Distiller in Texas. We have corn Whiskies in US, but they don't taste of corn. I wondered what would happen if I made a Corn Whisky in the same way as they make malt and use quality grain and make it taste of corn?'

C. Ask Whisky spoke to Chip Tate and asked him about the small Texas Distillery that is making a big noise around the world.

C. ASK: Chip tell us about your background and how you founded Balcones?

CHIP TATE: I have a chequered background. That sounds dodgy, but what I mean is, I did any number of things that unknowingly prepared me to run a Distillery and jump into all this. I've been a technical geek all my life which helps. I've worked in everything from brewing to insurance, statistical analysis, administration and throw into this mix a background in physics and a love for food and cooking. At age 20, the cooking turned to brewing. At one time I wanted to start a brewery, but I turned into more of a Whisky drinker that liked Beer rather than a Beer drinker that liked Whisky. We had next to no money to invest in the Distillery but I was able to build or make much of my own equipment so I could achieve the flavour profiles I was after in a Whisky. We founded Balcones in March, 2008 and had our building by July. We were able to start Distilling in the spring of 2009 and released Texas' first Whisky, Baby Blue in the autumn of 2009. We now have eight products out.

C. ASK: Fantastic. Are you starting to export overseas?

CHIP TATE: Balcones went to the UK recently and got a warm reception. There is a Wizards of Whisky awards and Balcones not only won several medals but was called the best Craft Distillery of the year and also the best Global Distillery. We are just preparing to start getting Balcones into France and into Australia.

C. ASK: How many Bottles are you producing right now?

CHIP TATE: We're putting out 5000-6000 Bottles a month, about 6000 cases a year.

C. ASK: What about aging? In Scotland a Spirit has to stay in a Cask for three years and a day in a used Oak Barrel to be called Scotch.

CHIP TATE: For the American market it is a lot less. We don't put out age statements because I feel they are misleading and people might misjudge the Whisky because of that. There are all these ridiculous laws all over the world, in my country and in your country – The law in Scotland is that the Whisky can't be put into a new Cask and so when John Glaser of Compass Box used a Barrel with new inner French Oak staves, the Scottish Whisky Association had a field day. In this country, you are required by law to use a new Oak Barrel. How absurd is that? As a Distiller the first question I ask is "What the hell right does the SWA or the government have to tell me what kind of Cask to use? Balcones has won 38 international awards, and frankly, I don't need the government's help. I suspect John Glaser feels the same way. He's doing just fine without the Queen's help. Yes, as a businessman I have to work within the rules as we all do, but as an artist, I want to be left alone to create.

C. ASK: What does Balcones mean?

CHIP TATE: It's a geological and geographical reference. We're on the Balcones Fault Line. Basically the Western Tectonic Plate runs into and folds under the Eastern Tectonic Plate and this results in deep springs of water trickling upward through the rock and this is the source of the Balcones Distillery water. I thought it was better than calling the Brand Lonestar or some other overused Texas word.

C. ASK: Of your Whiskies, which is your favourite?

CHIP TATE: I like all of them and don't think one is stronger or weaker than another. If I stopped drinking them, I'd want to discard the Whisky and create something new.

C. ASK: Do you look to Scotch Whisky for influences? What Scotch Whiskies do you like?

CHIP TATE: My first love was Scotch Whisky and they are some of my favourite Whiskies in all the world. It's like walking into an author's library. There are far more books by others than by the author. I am a big fan of Balvenie, Bruichladdich, Ardbeg, Glenmorangie, Glenfiddich and so much more. I can't think of a Distillery over there I dislike.

C. ASK: So how would you compare Balcones to the Scotch Whiskies?

CHIP TATE: In the process of making the Whisky, there are more similarities than differences. The major differences are that we have a longer fermentation time and a more expensive wood program. We can't buy used Casks, and so buying a new Barrel that is custom made, and toasted to my specifications means a greater cost. The new Barrel compared to a used Barrel brings a massive difference to the Whisky that a Scotch doesn't have to deal with. Our environment is different in Texas and all of that has an impact on the Whisky. It's not often in Scotland you'll get 45 degree Celsius weather – but this is not Scotch. It's Texas Whisky!

JACK DANIEL'S

The American Whisky story would not be complete without a visit to Lynchburg, Tennessee, and the Distillery with small beginnings that grew into a global giant. Jack Daniel famously learned his craft from a Lutheran Minister. The preacher Dan Call taught Jack about Distillation and the charcoal mellowing process that would set the Tennessee Whisky apart from its close cousins, the Bourbons. Reverend Dan Call's calling came into conflict with his Whisky making and had to choose between one or the other and choosing to stay in the pulpit, he bequeathed his burgeoning Whisky business to his young assistant, 13 year old Jack Daniel. In many ways, Jack Daniel was ahead of his time.

He was the first to use hot air balloons to promote a Brand and by the early 1900s the Brand had gone global. His death resulted from becoming frustrated with a safe and kicking it. This resulted in a broken toe that wasn't medically treated and so gangrene set in and eventually caused the death of Jack. In the Brand's history there have only been seven Master Distillers overseeing the Whisky Brand starting with Jack himself. There is almost something mystical about the number seven. In folklore the seventh son of a seventh son was supposed to have special powers. There are religious association such as seven days of creation, seven deadly sins and so forth. There are the seven hills of Rome, seven lucky gods of Japanese mythology, the seven sages, seven sisters, seven stars, seven wonders of the world and many think it is a lucky number. We were certainly lucky to talk to the seventh Master Distiller of Jack Daniel's, Jeff Arnett, and we've transcribed part of that conversation here:

C. ASK: It's a pleasure to speak to you Jeff. We've heard a lot about you.

JEFF ARNETT: (laughs) As long as it's good stuff.

C. ASK: Being the seventh Master Distiller - being number seven is pretty significant especially since the Whisky is called number 7.

JEFF ARNETT: Yeah, I feel lucky, that's for sure.

C. ASK: What's it feel like to take on such an important role?

JEFF ARNETT: Before coming to Jack Daniel's, I was already a member of the Jack Daniel's fan club. We were in a group called the Tennessee Squires. I'm a native Tennessean - I grew up two hours away from Lynchburg - so coming to work for Jack Daniel's was a dream come true, and that was long before I was considered for the role of Master Distiller. I feel very fortunate. I work with a great group of people who make our Whiskies everyday - and it's nice to be part of such a strong Brand! When I travel, I meet people who may only know two things about the State of Tennessee and that is Elvis and Jack Daniel's are from there.

C. ASK: Can you talk about the range of Whiskies?

JEFF ARNETT: Let's start with number 7, the Jack Daniel's Black Label, which is what put Lynchburg and Jack Daniel's on the map and is the number one selling Whisky globally. Every drop of that comes from a cave spring in a hollow right here in Lynchburg. That's what brought Jack to the hollow and why after a 147 years we are still here. I always tell people, if you're serious about making a great Whisky you have to start by finding the main ingredient of a great water source. The grain profile across all our products is 80% corn, 12% malted barley and 8% rye. When I describe Jack Daniel's, I say it's sweet to Oaky in character. We run the same grain bill that Jack did when he won his first gold medal under the old number 7 Brand name back in 1904 - but the grain structure made Jack Daniel's unique. If you go through our process, we use Column Stills made of copper that utilize a doubler so all the Spirit is double Distilled. This type of process gives us a very consistent product and so not only is Jack Daniel's unique but it is consistently unique and every Bottle will have the signature Jack Daniel's character and flavour. When the Spirit comes out of the still, it is 140 proof - that's 70% Alcohol and it satisfies the law as to what a Bourbon is - and though we are closely related to Bourbon, it is the charcoal filtering that sets us apart as a Tennessee Whisky. It is the process of dripping every drop of Jack Daniel's through the charcoal mellowing that takes us from being a Bourbon to a Tennessee Whisky. All our products have gone through charcoal mellowing at least one time. That's right after we Distill it and right before we put it into a Barrel. The charcoal mellowing takes away the bitter edge. If you read about the history of Bourbons, you'll find that the reason they introduced the Barrel for maturing was to soften the bitter aftertaste of the corn. If you tasted the Jack Daniel's Spirit before charcoal mellowing there will be a bitter taste. Research has shown that it would take two years in a Barrel before that bitterness starts to be addressed, where as charcoal mellowing does that in days.

C. ASK: What is the aging process of Jack Daniel's?

JEFF ARNETT: After we go through charcoal mellowing, we put our Whisky in a Brand new charred Oak Barrel. There's a big difference in preparing a Scotch which goes into a used Barrel and a Bourbon or Tennessee Whisky. The type of Barrel has a lot to do with how long the Whisky can stay in the Barrel.

Of course, we're making our own Barrels so we know more about our Barrels than most people do. We have chosen not to commoditize - we are not going out and finding somebody who will make us a certain quantity of Barrels for a certain price and have them delivered to our site when we don't know much about those Barrels. We employ a wood buyer who travels the Eastern United States buying American White Oak - we are sawing our logs at three different locations – Jackson, Ohio, Clifton Tennessee and Stevenson Alabama – we then quarter saw our logs, which will help get good grain alignment on the staves for the heading material. The charring process is when you light a fire inside the Barrel. This opens up a colour layer, the Oak finish which will colour the Whisky. If all you do is char the Barrel though you miss out on the chance to carmelize the sugars and that takes time and heat. Before we char the Barrels we go through a heating process to soften the wood sugars, draw them forward and carmelize them and I believe this is where the signature flavours of Jack Daniel's, the vanilla, the butterscotch, the caramel notes come from. After that the Whisky goes into the Barrel and they are stored in one of 83 warehouses we have here in Lynchburg. We have 2,000,000 Barrels stored and all are 200 litres in size. To try to explain the difference in aging between America and Scotland I use the analogy of a tea bag. You want that tea bag to brew in the hot water for just the right amount of time because if you leave it too long, it starts to become too dark and too bitter. A new Barrel is kind of like that tea bag, and if you leave the Spirit too long it will over-do it, and it will lose the sweet notes and start to taste more like the Oak.

C. ASK: So how long does it stay in the Cask?

JEFF ARNETT: For us, it is not a time driven decision, it's a taste decision. Historically, the Spirit stays in the Barrel between 4 and 7 years, but it's not about the time, but about flavour and that's why we don't put out an age statement. It's not like an egg timer rings and then we go dump the Whisky. We have information in the warehouses that indicate when Barrels should be ready, but we will first of all sample them, and even before that, use a machine that can look at the colour. It can see 50 shades of colour where our eyes will only see one shade and we will use technology like that to make sure the Whisky is ready. So if the colour is off it means it isn't ready, but if it looks good, we will then sample it to make sure the character and flavour are there. We sample 1500 to 2000 Barrels a month. Number 7 was our only Brand for a hundred years and it paid off to focus on that for all that time.

C. Ask Whisky asked Jeff about the other Whiskies that Jack Daniel's was making as of late and he told us about the double charcoal mellowing process that made Gentleman Jack a good entry level Whisky for those who want a more gentle finish. Jeff said, "It seems that each generation coming up wants their Whisky sweeter than the generation before so we've tried to address that with our Gentleman Jack and our Tennessee Honey.

Here is a description of Gentleman Jack and the other Jack Daniel's Brands from the official website: "Just like Jack Daniel's Tennessee Whisky and Jack Daniel's Single Barrel, Gentleman Jack is charcoal mellowed before going into the Barrel. Gentleman Jack, however, receives an additional "blessing" when it is charcoal mellowed again after reaching maturity – making it the only Whisky in the world to be charcoal mellowed twice, giving it ultimate smoothness. Gentleman Jack is full-bodied with fruit and spices, and its finish is silky, warm, and pleasant. When you drink Gentleman Jack, you'll always enjoy rich, rewarding taste.

Jack Daniel's Tennessee Honey is a Blend of Jack Daniel's Tennessee Whisky and a unique honey Liqueur of our own making, for a taste that's one-of-a-kind and unmistakably Jack. With hints of honey and a finish that's naturally smooth, Jack Daniel's Tennessee Honey is something special.

Single Barrel is matured in the highest reaches of our Barrelhouse, where the dramatic changes in temperature cause its color and taste to deepen further. We still hand select each Barrel for its robust taste and notes of toasted Oak, vanilla and caramel.

C. Ask Whisky had a chance to speak further to Jeff about the popularity of Jack Daniel's mixed with Coca-Cola. He told us that nearly half of all the number 7 black label that was consumed in the world was mixed with Coke and probably the reason for that was the signature vanilla flavour in the Whisky that was such a compliment to Coca-cola and they were perfectly happy to have their Whisky mixed with the soft drink if that is what made the consumer happy. We asked about what other Whiskies he liked to drink, and Jeff was happy to just drink Jack. He did confess to liking Beer, and when he is on the road meeting the best bartenders and mixologists in the world, he usually asks them for one of their special cocktails that they make with Jack Daniel's. We also had a chance to talk about

Jack Daniel's special edition Sinatra and the Brand"s connection with music, but we have saved that part of the interview for elsewhere in the book. Jeff had to go catch a flight to Bulgaria so we finished the conversation with a big thanks and said, "Please don't kick the safe like Jack did!" Jeff laughed and said, "You know they actually gave me that safe and I would have to agree that it is the most difficult and temperamental safe to open and I can understand why Jack kicked it." We are trusting Jeff will not make the same mistake and if he does, he will go to the hospital and get his toe treated. We are sure the seventh Master Distiller will be looking after the legacy of Jack Daniel's for years to come and C. Ask Whisky is of the opinion that the Brand is in a safe, innovative, creative pair of hands.

3.4 - CANADA

"A baby seal crawls into a bar and the bartender says, 'What'll it be?' The baby seal says, 'Anything but a Canadian Club.' I'm positive it was a Canadian who originally told that joke and no one can say that the Canadians don't have a sense of humour. They don't tend to take themselves as seriously as the Americans and are generally described as culturally more laid back.
Here are some warning signs to keep you on your toes as you explore Canadian Whisky:
"Canadian Liquor manufacturers have accepted the Health Canada's suggestion that the by following warning labels be placed immediately on all varieties of Alcohol containers:

WARNING: The consumption of Alcohol may leave you wondering what the hell happened to your bra and panties!?

WARNING: The consumption of Alcohol may make you think you are whispering when you are not.

WARNING: The consumption of Alcohol is a major factor in dancing like an idiot.

WARNING: The consumption of Alcohol may cause you to tell your friends over and over again that you love them.

WARNING: The consumption of Alcohol may cause you to think you can sing.

WARNING: The consumption of Alcohol may lead you to believe that ex-lovers are really dying for you to telephone them at four in the morning.

WARNING: The consumption of Alcohol may make you think you can logically converse with members of the opposite sex without spitting.

WARNING: The consumption of Alcohol may create the illusion that you are tougher, smarter, faster and better looking than most people.

WARNING: The consumption of Alcohol may lead you to think people are laughing WITH you.

WARNING: The consumption of Alcohol may cause pregnancy.

WARNING: The consumption of Alcohol may be a major factor in getting your ass kicked.

WARNING: the crumsumpten of alchol may Mack you tink you kan type reel gode."

Canadians not only make light of themselves but the distinguishing feature of their Whisky is that it is light and smooth.

Many ask if Canadian Whisky is just a sub-species or a different breed of American Whisky, just as the wolf and the shih tzu are different breeds from the dog family. C. Ask Whisky has no intention of starting a riot or causing an international incident. We are here to set the record straight. Canadian Whisky is its own breed, and is characterized by being one of the lightest of all Whiskies, a Whisky that often sells better south of the Canadian border than the abundance of USA produced Whiskies. Canadian Club for instance will sell more of their Brand in the States than in Canada – but then again there are several hundred million more people living in the USA than Canada. Yes, the Americans and Canadians have the same basic grains - corn, malted barley, wheat and rye - but the Canadians still make a unique product that is neither like Scotch or Bourbon. The emphasis seems to be on the rye grain.

Rye Whiskies from the USA take on a tendency of Americans themselves and can be in your face - exploding over the tongue like 4th of July fireworks, while the Canadian rye in the mix is more gentle. Some prefer the more intense American rye-based flavours, but just as many prefer the lighter style of the Canadian Whiskies, making them a popular mixing Whisky that you can add ice and soda to. You would be burnt at the stake as a Whisky heretic if you mixed 25 YO Glenmorangie with ice and coke but that is not a crime with a Brand like Canadian Club and such mixing is encouraged.

Despite the influx of Scots coming to Canada in the 1780s after the Highland Clearances, (that nasty piece of business where Highlanders were driven off the land by wealthy land owners in favour of sheep) it wasn't the displaced Scots that drove the embryonic Canadian Whisky Industry. Rather, there were Americans who moved to Canada that helped fan the Whisky flames of a thirsty northerly nation. The Americans left for a good reason. They were colonists who liked the King of England and wanted the American Colonies to remain a part of British rule, tea taxes and all. They were not made of the revolutionary stuff of Paul Revere, George Washington, Benjamin Franklin and John Hancock and became as popular among the revolutionaries as Benedict Arnold. Not wanting to have their house toilet papered and nasty things said about them on bathroom walls or something worse, these loyalists to the king of England wisely moved north. It was some of these people who decided, "To hell with it all! I want to Distil something that will help me forget all my troubles!"

Another interesting episode in the history of Canadian Whisky was its role in creating the Canadian Mounties.

After the American civil war south of the border, many a lawless Whisky Fort was set up in the Canadian West, and not by Canadians, but by a Jeremiah Johnson version of the modern day American drug dealer. Put the parasite who pushes drugs to school kids in beaver, bear, and wolf fur and send him to the Native Americans and other settlers of the 19th century and you can imagine what trouble such a nasty piece of work could get up to. These unscrupulous individuals set up centres of human misery and debauchery known as Whisky Forts where the worst kind of Whisky was sold to the Native Americans for ridiculously high prices that robbed those addicted to the drink of the money that should have gone to supporting their wives and children. The social problems created were tragic. The Canadian Mounted Police were created to deal with this cancerous blight.

When America went dry during the Prohibition, it was a boom time for Canadian Whisky and the Moonshiners in the USA. For instance there were faithful, loyal customers such as Al Capone paying 7 bucks for a case of Canadian Whisky and selling it to customers in the USA for 75 bucks after smuggling it across the border. This was the era of curved Whisky flasks that could be hidden or taped to the leg, underneath a dress, or in the boot - hence the bootleg term that came to be associated with smuggled and illicit Spirits. When Prohibition ended, the American customers still had a fond taste for Canadian Whisky and so the Industry went from strength to strength becoming the giant it is today in the Whisky world.

A CONVERSATION WITH DAN TULLIO OF CANADIAN CLUB

While researching Whiskies and companies for the C. Ask Whisky book, a lot of websites were visited, and we spoke to many very impressive people in the Industry around the world representing various Brands. Several of the websites stand out as being especially memorable. You'd expect nothing less than a good website from Jack Daniel's. Chuck Miller's Moonshine.com website is one of our favourites. The writer of the Glengoyne website deserves special recognition and the Dewar's website is very good. A lot more websites could be mentioned but the Canadian Club website is more than good. It is outstanding - as is its Global Ambassador, Dan Tullio.

Dan told us that he started with C.C. just out of college as a computer programmer. Wisely someone saw that he was better suited for marketing and promotion and to the top he rightly floated. He now criss-crosses North America, racks up the frequent flyer miles, and pays annual visits to Australia, Japan, Korea and elsewhere. CC is in 150 countries, 14 more countries than Jack Daniel's and this is a lot of territory to cover for a Global Ambassador. After 30 years at C.C. and telling a story he has presumably told thousands of times, he still has a passion for talking about C.C. The enthusiasm is infectious.

"Hiram Walker was a visionary," says Dan, talking about the founding father of Canadian Club. "Even though he was a patriotic American who loved his country and loved his own community in Detroit Michigan, he could see the signs of Prohibition coming and decided to build his Distillery across the Detroit River in Ontario, Canada rather than in Detroit."

From small beginnings Distilling vinegar in his Detroit grocery store to making Whisky for the prestigious Gentleman's Clubs of his day, he called his Spirit Hiram Walker's Club Whisky. The association with the respectable upper echelons of society in the Clubs gave the Whisky a reputation for elegance and class that worked in the Brand's favour, as did the backlash from American Distilleries – they were angry that the Canadian import was encroaching into their territory and made sure a law was passed that insisted that the country of origin be printed on the label. This was like the Uncle Remus story where Bre'r Rabbit cries, "Don't throw me in the briar patch!" As the foolish fox and bear of the tale debate how to put an end to Bre'r Rabbit, he uses reverse psychology and says "Do anything but throw me in the briar patch!" The fox and bear end up doing the biggest favour for the rabbit when they toss him there. In the same way, by insisting that Canada be printed on the label of the Club Whisky, it gave it even more exclusive prestige, national pride north of the border and it did nothing to halt Canadian Club's march toward's world dominance.

Just as Irish Whisky was esteemed by the court of Elizabeth

the 1st, so Canadian Club was a particular favourite of Queen Victoria and the Brand has received Royal favour ever since.

From Queens and Kings, the Brand then became associated with legendary gangster, Al Capone. He was a regular visitor to the palace that Hiram Walker built during the Prohibition years and in the tasting room, Mr. Capone would conduct his all-legal-and-above-board business of purchasing C.C. He paid his bills, and the Canadian government received their taxes. Legally in Canada, he was just another customer who happened to buy a lot of cases of Canadian Club. His 7 dollar purchase of a case could be sold for 75 dollars in Chicago. Wanting to please their customers and since there was a market for it, flat Bottles were produced that could be stacked in cases without breaking. They could also be stuffed in boots and became known as Bootleg Bottles. Through this time, Canada did nothing illegal. What the customers did in the United States with their legally purchased products was not their concern. They just enjoyed the profits that resulted from America's Noble Experiment. Today, C.C. enjoys some free association with the popular Prohibition set drama series Boardwalk Empire. The opening credits show a sea of Canadian Club Bottles washing up at Steve Buscemi's feet!
The clever marketing of C.C. has also been a factor that makes the Brand a global superstar Whisky. The fun, adventurous ad campaign of hiding cases of C.C. in various parts of the globe such as somewhere above the Arctic Circle, Mount Kilimanjaro, Angel Falls, Mount St. Helens, and the Swiss Alps. The Mount Kilimanjaro case was not discovered for a decade. The polar case has never been found; perhaps the only good thing about global warming will be the discovery of the nearly 50 YO case - or perhaps Coca-Cola got that Christmas commercial wrong that depicts the polar bears drinking ice cold Coca-Cola while watching the Northern Lights. Perhaps they found the case of C.C. and that is what they are drinking during the light show.

The Hide A Case Campaign from the 1960s has been repeated twice since and it is definitely the most fun ad campaign that any Whisky company has ever launched.

Dan talked us through the process of making Canadian Club and it is markedly different than both the Scotch/Irish Whiskies and the American Whiskies/Bourbons in this respect: The Blending takes place before it goes into the Barrel. The general rule of thumb is that Blends are made from fully mature Whiskies all mixed together after they've all come out of their respective Casks. In Canadian Club, Distillates from corn, rye, malted rye and malted barley are produced and then Blended together before the mix goes into the used Bourbon Barrel. It helps that Jim Beam Bourbon and Canadian Club are under the same umbrella. Used Barrels from Jim Beam or other Bourbon's from the company such as Red Stag, Devil's Cut, Maker's Mark, Knob Creek, Basil Hayden's Booker's Baker's, Old Grand-dad and Old Crow are then shipped to Canada. In the maturation process, the Distillates marry and produce the light smooth Whisky that is Canadian Club. At the time of Hiram Walker, Bourbons were usually in the Cask for less than a year, and Walker insisted on aging the Whisky for a decent amount of time. This again set C.C. apart from most of their neighbours to the south. The extremes in temperature from blistering heat in summer to freezing cold in winter do have an effect on the maturation time period and so C.C. tends to be younger than a Scotch or Irish Whisky but generally older than an American Whisky – but as Jeff Arnett put it, it's not about the time, it's about the taste and so C.C. as a rule is left for at least 5 years in the used Bourbon Barrel.

Beam Global says the following: "The award-winning family of Canadian Club Whiskies includes a 6 Year Old/Premium, Classic™ 12 YO, Reserve 10 YO, Sherry Cask, 100 Proof, 20 YO, 30 YO."

Dan didn't just talk about Canadian Club. He also talked about Alberta Premium. The way Canada was described made you want to jump on a plane and go there on your next holiday. He wasn't just flying the flag for his Brand but for his country. He described the rich fields of Alberta and how they naturally produced such great grain for the Alberta Distillers. It was explained that rye was actually harder to work with than corn, but there was rye in abundance and that grain in particular gave the Whiskies much of their flavour. We were told that the problem with rye is that it is like glue in its mashed state and could easily clog up machinery – it was a tough grain to work with. It was very interesting to hear that a scientist at the Alberta Distillery developed an enzyme that could break down the rye and solve some of these problems.

Another great story we were told was about the new Dark

Horse Brand from that Distillery. One of the owners of the Albert Distillers back in the 60s had also been an owner of a champion race horse - one of the most famous race horses in history. Woodford Reserve Bourbon is the official Whisky of the Kentucky Derby but Dark Horse Whisky from the Alberta Distillery is associated with a horse that won the Kentucky Derby. Majestic Prince was the thoroughbred that almost won the Triple Crown after winning the Derby and the Preakness. The great horse was slightly injured and controversially was entered into the Belmont. It lost that race, but still its achievement was huge and the Whisky honours the memory of Majestic Prince; there is a classy picture of a dark horse on the label to commemorate the race horse.

CANADIAN MIST & COLLINGWOOD

There are many other Canadian Whiskies for you to explore. When we spoke to Chris Morris of Brown-Forman, he told us about Canadian Mist and Collingwood. We feature that discussion in the Tipple Tours chapter, but feature some of the facts about the Brands here as described on the official websites:

CANADIAN MIST: Over 25,000 years ago, a glacier driven south by the last Ice Age carved a perfect basin out of the granite Ontario bedrock. Millennia later, as the glacier retreated, it left the granite basin behind, filled with one of the largest sources of pure freshwater in North America. Today, it is known as the Georgian Bay. The lands along the bay were the domains of the Hurons long before the first European settler arrived. It was the happiest of hunting grounds, ringed by abundant fresh water, evergreen forests, fertile fields and the scenic Blue Mountains to the southwest. All of the elements were in place. It was the perfect spot on Earth for Distilling Canada's true Whisky.

By the 1840s, European settlers began to arrive in significant numbers, and the town of Collingwood grew and prospered on the shores of the Georgian Bay. But it wasn't until 1967 that Collingwood fulfilled its great promise for Distilling. That year the Canadian Mist Distillery was built, producing the first Whisky in the world to source its water from the Georgian Bay.

Almost from the very start, Canadian Whisky lovers took note of Canadian Mist, which by 1983, grew to become America's largest-selling Canadian Whisky.* Today, Canadian Mist continues to be one of America's most popular Canadians. Take one sip, and you'll know why.

COLLINGWOOD: Collingwood is an exciting new maple wood mellowed Canadian Whisky that is triple Distilled for maximum smoothness. Very little tannic acid. This reduces the amount of harshness. The wood will impart on any Spirit that mellows with it. Mellowing a mature Blend of Collingwood Whisky with 100% hard maple wood allows the product to extract a degree of natural sweetness without adding the astringent and phenolic components found in Oak. As the maple's chemistry reacts with the Whisky it mellows the finish making it more palatable.

3.5 – MEXICO AND LATIN AMERICA

Moving on from Canada to Mexico is not only what we are doing, but it is what Canadians Larry and Eve Dorwart did. They moved from their home in Canada and opened up the first Mexican Whisky Distillery called Los 2 Compadres. According to the Compadres website, "The Dorwart's story began before the days of Prohibition. Larry Dorwart's family had dabbled in the art of making Moonshine. The tradition had been passed down from generation to generation. Soon, it was Larry's turn to share his family's passion for Spirits, but this time, it would be in another country.

Hailing from Alberta, Canada, Larry and his wife Eve, headed for the sunny shores of Banderas Bay. The plan was to retire, but it wasn't long before they found their calling, Mexican Whisky!

The Dorwarts found a place in the small village of Boca de Tomatlan (just 15 km south of Puerto Vallarta). It was the perfect site for their new Distillery.

Larry set up the small still he had purchased from the States and designed a second still using local materials. What is considered to be the first recognized Whisky production company in Mexico, Destilería Los 2 Compadres boasts of double Distilled, hand-crafted Whisky made from the finest ingredients here in Jalisco.

According to Los 2 Compadres, their Single Cask Sour Mash Whisky is the pride of their Distillery. It is made from 100% Azteca Maize corn Whisky and once aged to perfection. It has 'subtle notes of vanilla, caramel and chocolate with the slightest hint of sweet berries.' Gringo Larry's Shine is a younger version of the Sour Mash Whisky. Aged in toasted Oak Barrels, this traditional style of Corn Whisky offers a sharper flavour that is 'smooth on the palate and pleasing to the senses.'

Both the Single Cask Sour Mash Whisky and Gringo Larry's Shine are carefully crafted on site using a type of corn native to the Sierra Madres. The sun and humidity contribute to the fermentation process. The Whisky is then left to 'rest' in custom-charred White Oak French Barrels for the better part of a year. Once the small Whisky batch is checked for quality, it is hand-filled in special Bottles, capped and ready for purchase."

INTERVIEW WITH LARRY DORWART OF LOS 2 COMPADRES DISTILLERY

C. ASK: So you have established the first Whisky Distillery in Mexico?

LARRY DORWART: That's what Hacienda, the federal tax bureau of Mexico tell us.

C. ASK: So you must be either very courageous or very talented?

LARRY DORWART: (Chuckles) I'm not sure if I'm either one of those. It didn't start off to be such a big venture, but it's now rolling along by itself and we are just following along.

C. ASK: And it's just you and your wife Eve who run the Distillery?

LARRY DORWART: We also have a business partner, Carlos Castille, a Mexican National who helps us get past all the bumps and hurdles of doing business here in Mexico. It's something else! It's not like the States or Canada so the bumps and hurdles come with the territory.

C. ASK: Are people in Mexico excited about having their very first Whisky Distillery?

LARRY DORWART: Yes they are – the locals, the bartenders are all very enthusiastic. We are happy doing what we are doing but we are so far from where we want to be.

C. ASK: Where do you want to be?

LARRY DORWART: We want to have distribution right across Mexico in the next three years. We do have expansion plans and would like to look at exporting but right now we don't have the capacity.

C. ASK: How much Whisky are you making a month?

LARRY DORWART: Right now we are putting out 1500 litres a month. Our expansion in the summer of 2013 wll increase the output to 10,000 litres a month.

C. ASK: Tell us about your Whisky?

LARRY DORWART: We use locally grown corn, rye – we use wild yeast and make a sour mash – we age it in used Wine Barrels from France. Right now we're selling Whisky aged under a year. The heat and high humidity do move the maturation process on quickly. We lose about five inches out of the Barrel in seven months. If we used cool storage, we could age the Whisky a lot longer. Some people who have tried our Whisky say it tastes like a Bourbon and others say it tastes like a Scotch.

C. ASK: What have you done in the way of marketing and promotion?

LARRY DORWART: We had a tasting in Porta Vallarta, and there was also a blind tasting with other Brands such as Jameson's, Jim Beam and Gentleman Jack. Our Whisky scored right in the middle which I was very pleased about. Right now the products we have is our Single Cask and our Gringo Larry Shine – which is a Moonshine, but aged in the Barrel for three weeks. Walmart in Mexico and many bars and Liquor stores are taking the Dos Compadres Whisky. People do come visit and we show them around, but we want to expand our upstairs for more of a Visitor Centre for tasting and to sell products.

C. ASK: Gracias Larry. Thank you for speaking to us.

C. ASK WHISKY COMMENTARY: You now have another destination to visit in your world of Whisky travels and we congratulate the Dorwarts on the opening of their Mexican Distillery.

THE REST OF LATIN AMERICA

Mexico isn't the only Latin American country enjoying Whisky. The Latin Business Chronicle states that business has been booming for Whisky from Mexico to Argentina.

It is viewed as an aspirational product, a status symbol. The more expensive imports from Scotland, Ireland, the States and Canada often do better than the cheaper, local Brands. To quote an article featured in the Latin Business Chronicle, Jim Daly writes, "The momentum gained in the Whisky Industry in Latin America over the past 5 years, 2003 to 2008, has been impressive. Volume sales of Whisky reached 135 million liters in 2008, compared to 84 million liters in 2003. This represents a 61 percent growth in Whisky consumption in that five year period. In many countries, the increased Whisky consumption has taken market share away from more traditional Spirits. Latin American consumers have been shifting from local or less expensive Spirits to Whisky, which is perceived as a Premium product. The Latin American region, along with Asia Pacific countries, is driving the developing world's increase in Whisky sales."

Whiskies are not only imported, but like Los 2 Compadres Distillery in Mexico, there are Distilleries in Guatamala, Brazil, Uruguay, Suriname and Venezuela.

3.6 –SOUTH PACIFIC

Philippines: In our continuing trip around the word, we now leave the western shores of the South American continent and head out over the Pacific Ocean. Our first stop is the Philippines where we encounter a Distillery from the 19th century called Limtuaco. It was founded by a Chinese immigrant to the islands named Lim Tua. Today, the Limtuaco Distillery stands proudly on the world's stage with fine quality Liquors, the result of five generations of skilful Master Blending knowledge. Correct me if I'm wrong, but to the best of my knowledge, there has never been a Distillery in Scotland, Ireland, America, Canada or anywhere else founded by someone trained in the martial arts. Lim Tua could therefore kick you in the head in more ways than one, and one of these ways did not involve feet at all but rather the phrase, "Here, drink this." Perhaps Lim Tua's strategy was to disarm an opponent by giving them one of his Distilled Spirits? I don't know if there is an old Chinese proverb that says, "Why knock out your opponents when they can knock themselves out?" - but it should be a proverb. I am sure the drinkers of Limtuaco's White Castle Whisky would say there's an extra kick that could only have come from someone with one foot in the martial arts and the other foot in the production of Spirits.

Australia: From the Philippines we travel down to the land of Oz, although in this particular Oz there are no flying monkeys, green skinned cackling witches, talking lions, living scarecrows and dancing tin men - that is unless you imbibe too much of the heady brew they make down under. In the last 20 years, Australia has officially become a player on the world Whisky scene. Its island state of Tasmania on its colder southern side is called the Scotland of the south and has more Distilleries than Scotland's famed Isle of Islay. I'm not a natural history expert, but this might explain why the Tasmanian Devil does that whirlwind spinning, growling, spitting slobbering thing it does before grunting, "MORE Whisky!" At one time Tasmania was a penal colony and the prisoners thought using a still was a lot more interesting than standing still. Prisoners and brewing Alcohol was by all accounts like lighting a match inside a dynamite factory and so Distilling was banned for a hundred and fifty years. Only in recent times was the law overturned. Now the President of the United States is going to get a sip of Tasmanian Whisky. The Australian Associated Press reports: "The US Ambassador to Australia is planning to introduce Tasmanian Whisky to President Barack Obama. Ambassador Jeffrey Bleich is so taken with the island state's award-winning Single Malts he was planning to pick up some Bottles for President Obama on a visit to Hobart on Wednesday. "He likes a Whisky," Ambassador Bleich told reporters. "I've already promised I'm going to bring back some Tasmanian Whisky with me."

According to the australianwhisky.com website: "Australian Whiskies can vary greatly in style, but some of the terms used to describe Australian Whiskies include: malt, citrus, vanilla, fruit, smoke, apricot, honey, rainforest and pepper." From the tropical portions of Northern Australia to the southern island of Tasmania, Whisky production carries on. We spoke to Spike Dessert, an American who started a sugar farm and Rum Distillery called the Hoochery in the hot tropical northern climes of Australia near the town of Kununurra in the Ord River Valley. Rum is the mainstay of his production but he does produce Whisky on the side, and whenever he does a Bottling, it sells out. He told us about the challenges of producing Whisky. In his words, "I know when I go to open a Barrel; the angels are going to be happy that day." Evaporation in Scotland is at 4% annually but for Spike it is 20%.

HELLYER'S ROAD DISTILLERY

C. Ask Whisky had a great conversation with Mark Littler of the Hellyer's Road Distillery in Tasmania. We learned that the Distillery was named after a rugged explorer named Henry Hellyer, one of the first Europeans to venture into North West Tasmania. Two hundred years ago the conditions of the lands and forests made getting anywhere tough going and yet Hellyer, along with a bull and a small crew of tough men carved a road through the thick forest of vegetation. The Distillery of present day is on that road. Only a few years ago however, if you were to come to the site for a tour, the only drink you would be sampling is milk. To our knowledge, Hellyer's Road is the only dairy farm in the world that has switched from milking cows to malting barley for Whisky production. To this day, Hellyer's Road Distillery is a wholly-owned subsidiary of Betta Milk Co-operative Ltd.

Hellyer's believes that there a lot of positive advantages to being a former dairy farm. They say: "Our background in dairy processing carries over to our Alcohol production and results in our unique Premium products."

LIMEBURNERS AND TIGER SNAKE

What Australians bring to Whisky making is interesting. For instance, the Great Southern Distilling Company describes the creation of what is essentially an Australian version of Bourbon called Tiger Snake: "With his 'Director's Cut' Single Malt Whisky winning multiple awards, Cameron Syme, turned his attention to where his journey with Whisky began. Long before his palate matured to preferring Single Malts, Cameron enjoyed drinking Bourbon and felt destined to make his own. 'Tiger Snake' is Australia's first legal Sour Mash Whisky. "Our inspiration for Tiger Snake Sour Mash Whisky comes from those great Tennessee Whiskies and Kentucky Bourbons", said Cameron. Like the word 'Champagne', 'Bourbon' is a geographic indicator so is called 'Sour Mash' Whisky in Australia which refers to the type of grain mashing process. The name is taken from the Western Tiger Snake, one of the most venomous snakes in the world which grows up to 2 metres long. These beautiful, albeit dangerous, creatures are native to the area of the Great Southern Distillery, whose Barrel store in Albany is cool, dark and undisturbed. Perhaps that's why on a hot day you may just find a Tiger Snake curled up under a Barrel." Yes, I do think W. C. Fields would have felt right at home in Oz.

C. Ask Whisky spoke to the creator of Tiger Snake and Limeburners Whisky, Cameron Syme.

C. ASK: Tell us about your background and how you got into the Whisky Industry?

CAMERON SYME: I grew up in Western Australia in a small town surrounded by fields of wheat. My grandfather came from Scotland when he was 12 so I grew up with stories about some of the family's history making Whisky, most of it illegally. I know the family had a water driven flour mill. Of course milling grain would have been part of making the Whisky. They also had an illicit still. At the time, the constabulary were offering financial rewards to report such illegal operations.

The family needed to replace the boiler for their still, so they stripped out all the equipment apart from the broken boiler and reported the Still House to the authorities. The old boiler was confiscated, reward money handed over and then the family went out and bought a new boiler and started making Whisky again somewhere else. Hearing stories like that and seeing that Whisky production was in my family planted a seed in me. I had my first drink of Whisky at the legal age of 18 or possibly younger, and it was Johnny Walker Black Label. The sweet taste of Bourbon was next and I started thinking, "You know, Australia is great at making Beer and Wine –why not Whisky? We have all the natural ingredients here. Why don't we start making Whisky ourselves? I had no idea at the time how to go about this or the money but the ideas were there. Over the 16 years that followed I did a lot of research – I got a certificate from the Institute of Brewing and Distilling – I worked with Bill Lark in Tasmania and Gordon Mitchell at Isle of Arran in Scotland. During this time I'd been working as a lawyer, and when I was 32, I had something like a mid-life crisis. I called my wife! I told her I wanted to move out into the countryside and do something else! Opening a Distillery was the result.

THE INDUSTRY TO BE WATCHED

Cameron went on talk about the process they use at the Great Southern Distillery and what comes across is the professionalism and attention to detail. There is a serious ambition behind it all. Cameron wants to make the best Single Malt in the world. The international awards being won by Limeburners are examples of this ambition. With the fierce intelligence that made him a lawyer and the pride that wants to fly the flag for the Australian Whisky Industry, he won't take any perceived slight lying down. When he hears, "Oh, it's not Scotch. It's not aged as long as Scotch," he can counter with, "No, it's Australian and that's something

I'm proud of." Even though the Distillery is 8 years old – as old as a young Scotch – Cameron can point to awards his Whiskies have won even at an age of only two years in the Cask. Like the American Bourbon Industry, he can point to the fact that the different climate aids in the maturation process. He would argue that it matures twice as fast with an increased Angel's Share. A 3 YO Limeburners would be the equivalent of a 6 YO Scotch in maturation. The Australian Industry is one to be watched for they want their Whisky taken seriously.

BILL LARK

One of the most influential names in the Australian Whisky Industry is Bill Lark. Concerning his achievements, he told us, "I'm just a person who liked Single Malt Whiskies from way back and found myself in a position to be able to do something about opening a Distillery here in Australia. I remember enjoying a dram in the Tasmanian highlands after my father-in-law and I caught a trout. We asked the question, "Why can't we make Whisky here? Tasmania has the perfect conditions for making Whisky. It has the water, the climate, the peat, the barley. Everyone I spoke to was enthusiastic about the suggestion of making Whisky in Tasmania and I even got the backing of the government, so much so that the ban on Distilling was overturned."

Bill Lark got his historic license over 20 years ago. Like Cameron Syme, he was a man on a mission. He toured Distilleries in America, Ireland and Scotland. He's taken advice from Scotland and now he comes to Scotland as an adviser. Rob Allanson writes: "These are heady times for Australian Whisky in general and for its Godfather Bill Lark in particular. His presence as a consultant to Scotland's latest Distillery project (Kingsbarns in Fife) caps a remarkable few months that have done much to cement Australia's reputation as a country with a golden Distilling future. Over the last year one of Lark's Whiskies picked up the World Whisky Award for the best malt from a non-traditional Whisky making country, while the highly-respected Malt Maniacs awarded one of Lark's Whiskies the thumbs up award for the most exciting new release in the Premium Malt

Sector."

Rory Nicoll with Greg Ramsay at the launch of New Zealand Whisky in the Old Course Hotel, St. Andrews, Scotland.

New Zealand: Neighbouring New Zealand brings vastly different environments, and you can even share a drink with a hobbit if you so desire in the movie set turned real pub, the Green Dragon from the Hobbit/Lord of the Rings film franchise (located in Matamata on the North Island). The website newzealandWhisky.com says, "The indigenous people of New Zealand, the Maori, call New Zealand 'Aotearoa' - which means 'The Land of the Long White Cloud'.

Famous for its stunning beauty of snow capped mountains, tranquil forest and sweeping green vistas - it comes as no surprise that New Zealand has some of the purest air and water on earth. With the exceptional natural resources and a history of Distillation, New Zealand is the perfect setting for producing world class Whisky.

An island country in the South-Western Pacific Ocean, New Zealand is home to the most southerly Whisky Distilleries in the world. New Zealand Whisky Distilleries are producing both Single Malt Whisky and Blended Whisky; and these unique and wonderful Whiskies are starting to gain attention around the globe."

Because many Scottish settlers immigrated to New Zealand, they brought with them a nostalgia for the Whisky from back home and so Distilling was part of the island nation's heritage. There were problems however that had nothing to do with the pristine conditions of the water and natural resources to produce Whisky and many a Distillery went out of business, putting New Zealand Whisky in the doldrums of stagnation. Talking about this problem and the big turnaround, Dominic Roskrow (writing for Whisky Connosr.com) says, "And while Whisky should run through the people's veins, perhaps it's because of the love of the old country and a respect for the product of Scotland that domestic (New Zealand) Whisky has struggled. Then there are the geographical conditions - perfect for Whisky making. But while there are mountains, plentiful water supplies and great grain growing pastures, there are few people. How can you sustain a Whisky Industry with such a small market and such a long way to go to reach a population of any size?" Roskrow goes on to describe a champion of New Zealand Whisky named Greg Ramsay who took the nation's Distillery Industry by the scruff of the neck, gave it a make-over and went out to fight on the world's stage, winning many a prestigious Whisky prize with products like NZ Doublewood.

C. Ask Whisky had the privilege of speaking to Greg Ramsay at his home in Tasmania and only a few weeks later we were able to meet with him in Scotland where he was hosting tastings of New Zealand Whisky in partnership with Gordon & MacPhail. Here is a portion of our interview with Greg Ramsay:

C. ASK: So how did someone who lives in Tasmania end up promoting New Zealand Whisky?

GREG RAMSAY: I grew up on the Ratho Farm in Tasmania which also has Australia's oldest golf course. In my college gap years, I went to Scotland to study the history of golf and golf tourism. I had jobs being a caddy during the day and working in a Single Malt Whisky bar at night. I learned a lot about golf and I learned a lot about Whisky. After that, I went back to Tasmania and finished up university in Hobart. I then did another year in Scotland working in golf management and at the weekends I was in a Whisky master-class. Upon returning to Tasmania, we developed 7 miles of coastline constructing Australia's number one golf tourist destination and we converted an old mill into a Distillery next to our Ratho Farm. Ever since, I've been involved in various golf or Whisky ventures. The connection to New Zealand was because we were asked to value the stocks of a Whisky company that had gone into receivership in New Zealand. The receiver had taken possession of the stocks from the old Seagram's Distillery – And when we saw the value of the stocks and what they were going for, I put together a syndicate and we bought 75,000 litres of Cask Strength Whisky, 20 years and up. The success story of Tasmania with its nine Distilleries encouraged us to believe that New Zealand could also experience a similar success story. There is no reason why not. It's done well with Beer and all the natural resources are there for Distilling

Whisky. What we've done is take those stocks, and re-Brand them as the New Zealand Whisky collection. Our long term plan is to open Distilleries around New Zealand that will be good for the tourists as they go around the islands.

C. ASK: With the filming of the Hobbit and Lord of the Rings in New Zealand, have you thought about making a Hobbit Whisky?

GREG RAMSAY: (Laughs) Yeah, Middle Earth Malt - or we could have a peaty version made from those bogs of rotting dwarves and elves - No, so far we've resisted the temptation to go that way. All joking aside, we are concentrating on the New Zealand characteristics of the product, honouring the heritage, the culture the great people you find in the country. There are big corporations that own hundreds of Brands, but the individual Whiskies lose some of their personality because some of the corporate types behind the scenes are bean counters who are just interested in maximizing profits from these Brands they have taken over. With New Zealand Whisky, we don't want to just count beans - we want to carry the personal warmth and charm of New Zealand to the rest of the world with quality products made right there in New Zealand!"

C. ASK WHISKY COMMENTARY: We predict that with people like Greg, Bill, Cameron and Mark among those championing the cause of the Australian and New Zealand Whisky Industry, its Whiskies will go from strength to strength and continue to gain prestige around the world. It is already happening. Like America, there is a can-do mentality as demonstrated by the New Zealand film Industry that can compete against the might of Hollywood and win. Already Australia and New Zealand are challenging the Scottish Industry to up their game in passion, zeal and tourism. The competition is good for the whole Industry and in the end benefits those who want the best out of their Whisky companies, wherever they are located in the world.

3.7 - JAPAN, TAIWAN AND ASIA

JAPAN: From New Zealand we fly northward across an expanse of ocean up to the many islands that make up the country of Japan. The two most significant people in the history of Japanese Whisky are Masataka Taketsuru and Shinjiro Torii. Masataka Taketsuru went to Scotland and studied the art of Distilling in the early part of the 20th century. Returning to his native Japan, he came to the attention of entrepreneur, Shinjiro Torii.

Torii started out in the pharmacy business, bringing in medicines from around the world before moving into the business of importing Liquors. Torii then founded the Suntory Distillery which was originally called Kotobukiya. Torii created a port Wine he called Akadama and this gave him a measure of success in his domestic ventures. After the Japanese Port Wine he decided he would make Japanese Whisky rather than just bringing in Whisky from around the world. Torii founded the first ever Japanese Whisky Distillery in a suburb of Kyoto called Yamazaki, which was known for its excellent water. A famous tea room was already in Yamazaki because of the pure water as well. This is where Taketsuru enters the picture. Torii needed the expertise of someone like Taketsuru and he was made an executive in the new Distillery. He helped develop Suntory before going off on his own and founding the Nikka company with the Yoichi Distillery in Hokkaido.

Despite the self-belief of Torrie and Taketsuru, the world needed to be convinced that Japanese Whisky could compete with the rest of the world and hold its own against the Scotland Whiskies that the Japanese modelled their own Whiskies after. Gavin D. Smith wrote, "For many years, Japanese Whisky was considered something of a joke by sophisticated Scotch Whisky drinkers. But then back in the early 1970s, many people in Britain held similar views about Japanese cars - and look what's happened since. Eventually, word began to spread that the Japanese were actually making some pretty decent Whisky, and after decades of concentrating on Blends, they started marketing Single Malts. In 2001 the quality of the malts was confirmed in triumphant style when a Yoichi Whisky from Nikka Distillers was voted 'Best of the Best' by Whisky Magazine. Now it was official, not only could the Japanese make good Whisky, but they could make Whisky that a distinguished international panel of tasters considered the best in the world." Today there are ten major Japanese Distilleries from the north to the south of the nation, and Japan has become a formidable competitor in the world Whisky market. We spoke to Keita Minari, the UK representative for Suntory and he told us that the reason for the Japanese success story was because of the care, the patience, the attention to detail, the water, Japan's seasons and the long years of maturation in the selected Casks. We asked what the best markets were for Suntory outside of Japan. Keita told us the best markets were the USA, Canada, France, Germany and the UK.

There is an interesting philosophical undergirding of what Suntory does. They say, " The Suntory Group's message, 'Suntory, Bringing Water to Life' invites the world to share in Suntory's corporate philosophy, 'In Harmony with People and Nature.' As a corporation that delivers the natural blessing of water through Whisky, Beer, Wine, non-Alcoholic beverages, and healthy foods, we are committed to protecting earth's most precious resource, and supporting an environment that nurtures water. And just as water satisfies the thirst of every living creature, we are devoted to the goal of an abundant society and the active participation of every employee. Water sums up our essence, providing a clear path for our corporation. This is why we are 'Suntory, Bringing Water to Life.' Water expresses our promise to our customers, and our commitment to society's expectation." The marketing of most Whiskies emphasizes flavour, quality and the history where as Suntory also brings philosophy into their marketing and talks about promoting peace and harmony with nature. It is an interesting idea to pair Whisky with peace and harmony. Maybe the pubs in Glasgow should have a Suntory night!

CHINA

After a quick flight from Japan, we arrive in China. The giant of a nation has become one of the most important markets for the worldwide Whisky trade. The wealthy of China like classy products that are relatively exclusive and have history and tradition attached to them, and many a Scotch has these qualities in abundance.

Harpers reported this recent news: "A Scottish Whisky house has opened up a club in Beijing and is successfully selling Whisky at prices ranging from almost £2,000 to a staggering £200,000 a Bottle. Johnnie Walker House is described by Diageo, the company behind the venture, as "the world's largest embassy for luxury Scotch Whisky, providing consumers with bespoke experiences to immerse themselves into the world of Whisky and Johnnie Walker". The opening night of the four-storey emporium to Scotch was an incongruous affair. Bagpipes, kilts and the occasional Scotsman mixing with Beijing's mega-rich and A-list celebrities - a stone's throw from the heart of this Communist country, Tiananmen Square."

Like Japan, China had to overcome its doubts that it could make its own Whisky products that would stand out with the best. Against such doubts, there were those who decided to defiantly open a Distillery on the island of Taiwan and hence the King Car Distillery opened its doors in 1979. So how would the Chinese compete with Scotland? They bought their Distilling equipment in from Scotland and hired Master Blenders from Scotland. Over time the Chinese Whisky developed its own personality and was not just an imitation of Scotch. Their water source was a part of this as were the preferences of style and taste of the Taiwanese people. The Distillery water comes from Green Time Natural Drinking Water which is said to be "famous for its purified natural sweetness. The Distillery team extracts the clean water source from the Central Mountain Range and the Snowy Mountain Range to produce the Whisky that matches Taiwanese tastes." King Car describes their Whisky this way: "The charming part of it is its eccentric and ever-changing personality. It could be as passionate as a Latino woman, or as sweet as the girl next door, and it could be a mature gentleman. A Distillery Blender is like a magician who can transform his Whisky into different personalities which grow on you. How can anyone not be indulged in its multi-personalities?" Scottish, Latino, girl-next-door, a respectable gentleman, magical, Chinese and all in a Bottle. It sounds fun to try and discern which personalities you can detect in their Whisky. The world is a richer place for having so much diversity and the Taiwanese are to be applauded for bringing Kavalan Whisky to the world marketplace. We were able to ask the magician they were talking about a few questions.

INTERVIEW WITH IAN CHANG OF KAVALAN WHISKY

C.ASK: Please tell us about yourself and how you came to work for the

King Car Distillery and the Kavalan Brand of Whisky.
IAN CHANG: My name is Ian Chang, the Master Blender of Kavalan Whisky. I have been working in the Distillery for more than seven years since graduating from college in the UK with a Food Science degree, which is very helpful to me in the Spirits Industry i.e. flavour chemistry.

Basically I carry out all the in-house production controls and Blending operations.

C. ASK: Tell us the story of the King Car Distillery.

IAN CHANG: Kavalan Distillery, located in the north-east of Taiwan, was commissioned by owner King Car Group in March 2006. King Car started producing 1.3 million litres of Alcohol per year. The Distillery is the brainchild of the owner who is also the Chairman of the Group, Mr. TT Lee, who had long wanted his own top-quality Whisky Distillery.

C. ASK: Please tell us about Kavalan Whisky?

IAN CHANG: Kavalan represents sincerity, honesty, and the Spirit of step-by-step cultivation. It is the old name of Yi-Lan County where the Distillery is located. We continue its tradition of passionate commitment to creating the most Premium Whisky that Taiwan can offer.

C. ASK: What are your hopes for the Kavalan Brand?

IAN CHANG: We strive to produce quality and distinctive Taiwanese Whisky and we are confident that it will please the Whisky connoisseurs worldwide. Kavalan Whisky is now available in most European countries and will be launched in the US very soon. Our goal is to make Taiwan visible on the map of Whisky.

C. ASK: What is different about your Whisky compared to other Whiskies around the world?

IAN CHANG: The combination of the Distillery's craftsmanship and great Cask selection contribute to the unique flavour of Kavalan Whisky. It is incredibly smooth, mellow and creamy.

Above all, the Distillery harnesses the heat of the Taiwanese summer to extract the wood and create the magical effect— a natural rich colour. The integration of the new make and Oak in high temperate condition makes Kavalan Classic Single Malt Whisky extraordinary.

C. ASK: What label/Brand of yours do you think will do best overseas and why?

IAN CHANG: Kavalan Classic should do best overseas. It is our first expression, released on the 4th of December 2008 when our Distillery was first open to the public, which is significant for us. It started to attract the attention worldwide after winning the champion in Burn's Night blind tasting (organised by Times newspaper in 2010) and is so far the best selling product in our whole range.

C. ASK: What Brands of Scotch are well known in Taiwan?

IAN CHANG: Glenmorangie and Johnnie Walker are popular Scotch Brands in Taiwan.

C. ASK: How is your Whisky made and what type of Cask do you use? How long is the Whisky aged for?

IAN CHANG: Kavalan Distillery is highly automated but based on a conventional Single Malt plant. Kavalan is the first and only Whisky that is entirely produced in Taiwan. We adopt double Distillation, using Pot Stills to produce a smooth, mellow and complex Single Malt Whisky. The Casks, including ex-Bourbon, refill Barrels, fresh Sherry butts, Wine barriques and Kavalan's own dechar/rechar Casks purposely designed to a special recipe to complement the Spirit's flavour, are stored in a five-storey maturation warehouse building which is also unique in the Industry.

ASIA

People who like to conserve animals, especially endangered species, should look away now. You will recall that one Australian Brand of Whisky was named after a poisonous snake, but in many parts of Asia (predominantly Thailand, Laos, Vietnam), there is literally a snake or scorpion, or frog, or seahorse inside whatever Alcoholic beverage has been Distilled and floats there in the Bottle for all to see. Thailand Unique.com will sell the following to you for about 11 pounds or 20 American dollars: "Real Cobra Snake & VineSnake 74% proof Whisky (Cobra snake with Wine Snake in its mouth) This special Whisky is infused with a real farm raised Cobra snake, Vine Snake, ginseng roots and herbal seed pods. The Whisky is steeped for several months, which then imparts a unique flavour into the Whisky, it is quite an acquired taste." The story is that this is used in S.E. Asia as a very strong aphrodisiac; and it also has many medical uses so they believe, such as the treatment of back and muscle pain. Every Bottle is unique in its own way so therefore the item purchased may differ slightly in looks but not size." I wonder if Jim Murray has ever tried this? These would certainly feature nicely in the Satanic Whisky Bible. It might be a macho challenge, but I'm secure enough in my masculinity to pass as in pass the bucket before I throw up. As one searches the region, there are many more unique Brands of Whisky, many of them rice-based, and mixed up with ideas of magical medicinal properties and ideas that some things will give you more sexual virility such as a reindeer horn Whisky made in China. I don't know if it works like Viagra or not, but I wonder if that's what sent Santa to his grave in Kilkenny, Ireland?

Perhaps we should leave Asia as the Whiskies are becoming increasingly weird here. One last stop however. One of the major markets for Whisky in the world with one of the largest populations is India. Whisky was introduced during the British Raj and Scotch or Whiskies close in style to Scotch are the most popular Alcoholic beverages in India. There is a sizable population that can afford the imports and a sizable population to support the number of Distilleries in the nation. Many domestically produced Indian Whiskies have molasses as one of the main ingredients. According to these sales figures from 2011, 7 of the top selling Whiskies in the world were from India. This isn't a secret in India, but this fact isn't publicized well outside India. Here are the figures:

1. Johnnie Walker, Diageo, Category: Scotch (18 million)
2. Officer's Choice, Allied Blenders & Distillers, Category: Indian

(16.5 million)
3. McDowell's No.1, United Spirits, Category: Indian (16.1 million)
4. Bagpiper, United Spirits, Category: Indian (16 million)
5. Royal Stag, Pernod Ricard, Category: Indian (12.5 million)
6. Old Tavern, United Spirits, Category: Indian (11.1 million)
7. Original Choice, John Distilleries, Category: Indian (10.8 million)
8. Jack Daniel's, Brown-Forman, Category: US-Tennessee (10.6 million)
9. Imperial Blue, Pernod Ricard, Category: Indian (7.2 million)
10. Ballantine's, Pernod Ricard, Category: Scotch (6.5 million)

3.8 – AFRICA

"If you had told me that someday I'd be the only commercial maker of Whisky in Africa and managing a Whisky Distillery, I would have thought what have you been smoking?" Those were the words of Andy Watts, manager, Master Distiller and Blender for the James Sedgwick Distillery in South Africa. Andy Watts was a cricketer from Sheffield in England and playing for Derbyshire County Cricket Club. So how did an English cricketer become the African Continent's top Master Distiller? Here is how the story goes as recounted on the 3 Ships website: "After completing his A Levels at Penistone Grammar School in Sheffield, Andy chose the life of a professional cricketer with Derbyshire CCC. He arrived in South Africa in 1982 to spend six months of each year coaching at schools throughout the Boland and within three years, landed a position at the then Stellenbosch Farmers' Winery (SFW) where he became involved in the Spirits Blending side of the business. He then travelled to Scotland for a six month technical exchange with Morrison Bowmore Distillers and worked at their Bowmore, Auchentoshan and Glen Garioch Distilleries returning to South Africa determined to prove that producing excellent Whisky was not a pursuit reserved exclusively for the Scots! On his return, Andy was transferred to The James Sedgwick Distillery in Wellington where he was appointed Manager in 1991."

Whisky was first introduced to the continent thanks to a ship captain named James Sedgwick. One of the most well known international Brands coming out of the James Sedgwick Distillery is a Whisky called Three Ships. Sedgwick sailed the stormy seas around the cape commanding a clipper, before coming to shore on a new venture and establishing Sedgwick and Co., purveyor of quality Liquor, Tobacco and Cigars. The Distillery website emphasizes the pioneering Spirit of the man himself as it forges ahead in its Whisky production endeavours: "The James Sedgwick Distillery is a pioneer in its own right as it is unusual for a Whisky Distillery to produce both malt and grain Whiskies on the same site. With more than 70 000 Casks of Whisky in maturation any given time, our Distillery handles the entire Whisky making process - from raw material stage through to Blending." Capegrace.com proudly talks up the Three Ships Brand saying: "Three Ships Whisky have brought many 'firsts' to South Africa: the first Whisky Brand, the first Blend of South African and Scotch Whiskies, the first South African Single Malt and the country's first 100% Blended Whisky – definitely worth a taste! The James Sedgwick Distillery has been named Best Brand Innovator in Whisky Magazines' 2011 Icons of Whisky competition."

Andy told us about the explosion of trade that took place when Apartheid was put aside and the country opened up. International Whisky companies such as Jack Daniel's and Canadian Club began selling their wares in the newly free nation. A whole new generation of Whisky drinkers came along in the nation that were proud that their country could stand toe to toe with other nations. The Scottish model that Andy Watts studies is very much in evidence, especially the Cask aging. Despite being in Africa, the Whisky is aged for at least 3 years with a 3% annual Angel Share. A young group of PR reps and Brand marketers have also done much to popularize the Brands. The websites are excellent and an international Whisky Live event has been held in South Africa every year that started out as 300 people and now attracts 20,000 visitors and exhibitors. Whisky writer David Broom said this about going to the Whisky Live South Africa event: "Strangely, people still seem surprised when I tell them that I'm going to South Africa for a Whisky show. 'Whisky?' they say. 'Don't you mean Wine' So I explain (again) that it's one of the fastest-growing markets in the world, that there's a new generation drinking Whisky, that its shows are the biggest, busiest, brashest and craziest of anywhere in the world."

Andy has been responsible for making the following award

winning Whiskies: Bain's Cape Mountain Whisky, Three Ships 10 YO Single Malt, Three Ships 5 YO Blended, Three Ships Bourbon Cask Finish, Three Ships Select Blended.

3.9 – EUROPE

A quick overview of Europe reveals that the days where Scotland and Ireland were the only kids on the Whisky block are long gone. The following countries all have Distilleries making their own Brands of Whisky: Finland (despite a ban on advertising strong Alcoholic beverages), Sweden with a European Whisky champion Distillery in Mackmyra, Norway, Netherlands, Belgium, France, Germany, Spain, Austria, Czeck Republic, Hungary, Denmark, Italy, Poland, Switzerland, Russia, Latvia and the best named country for Alcohol production in the world, Estonia. Even Turkey has a Distillery, which is not to be confused with Wild Turkey in Kentucky.

TURKEY: The country of Turkey straddles the continents of Asia and Europe and the nation has a combination of both European and Asian elements. Despite a secular government, Turkey is predominantly and Islamic nation and Islamic nations are not known for their Alcoholic beverage production or consumption. Ironically, the word 'Alcohol' has its origins in Arabic. Despite some harsh rules against Alcohol in Islamic countries, Turkey has not adopted such strict rules, and there is a giant drink company that nearly has a monopoly on Alcohol beverage production in the country making everything from Beer, to Wine, to Whisky and that is the Mey Trading Company, makers of Ankara Whisky. In an article in the Economist, the subject of Islam and Alcohol was introduced in the following way: "It is Ramadan, Islam's holy month of fasting.

But even now Suleiman, a Muslim hotel worker in the Turkish town of Antakya, sees no reason not to drink Alcohol, widely considered by Muslim believers to be forbidden by the Koran and the Hadith and the sayings of the Prophet Muhammad. "The Koran bans getting drunk, but a Beer or two doesn't hurt," Suleiman says. "This is a matter between me and Allah." The Economist article goes on to say, "Nobody knows exactly when Islamic scholars decided that booze was sinful. In the 1970s political Islam led some countries such as Iran and Pakistan to ban Alcohol although many do not and exceptions are made for non-Muslims. In some countries the punishment for Muslims caught quaffing are severe: 80 lashes in the case of Iran. Things may get more arid yet as Islamist parties from Indonesia to Tunisia moot restrictions on Alcohol. Prohibition has pushed imbibing behind closed doors, but many Muslims still admit to enjoying a tipple. How many people drink varies, but some put the total at 5% of those identifying themselves as Muslim. The black market for Spirits flourishes in Libya. Iranians are adept at producing home brew. And in Pakistan "drinks can be ordered to the door quicker than pizza," says Sadaqat Ali, who runs Willing Ways, a chain of clinics to treat Alcoholics."

GERMANY: The Germans started Whisky production some 30 years ago and now have a number of Distilleries. Their Brands are influenced by Scotch, Irish and American Whisky. Whisky writer, Dominic Roskrow says, "European Whisky pretty much splits in to two parts - the countries based around the Germanic speaking regions which have a long history in Distilling, but mainly of Schnapps and Fruit Liqueurs; and those from elsewhere who have adopted Whisky without any real previous history. Many of the Distilleries in the former category are either very small and don't seek or need external coverage or promotion, or only produce Whisky Spirit for a tiny part of the year. For this reason they are difficult to reach out to and even if I did, you probably wouldn't be able to get their Whiskies anyway. Most of those in the latter are growing in to serious commercial Whisky producers and are either in the frontline of the march of New World Whisky, or will be some time soon."

Competition in the Whisky world is fierce and one of the most daring and outrageous marketing ploys for a Whisky Brand ever was staged by a German company called G-Spirits. They promised their customers that the Whisky they were buying was not only fermented, Distilled and Cask aged, but has been though an extra process that no other Distiller had tried before. Their Whisky was poured over the ample naked breasts of 2012 Playboy Playmate of the year, Alexa Varga. This would certainly liven up the Distillery tour experience. "Here folks are the grains we use, here is how we make the mash, here is how we ferment, we use this particular still, we age the Whisky in these Casks for this number of years and just before we put them in the Bottles we pour them over the naked breasts of our glamour model." There is a video of the G-Spirits showing this further step in action – which was part of our research – honest. A special basin was there to collect the Whisky for Bottling after Alexa Varga's Whisky shower. The Bottles have a picture of a topless Alexa Varga. There are only 5000 Bottles and each numbered Bottle comes with a certificate signed by Ms. Varga to say something to the effect that "Yes, this Whisky was indeed poured over my big perky breasts." G- Spirits says of its limited edition Brand (that will set you back about 140 pounds or 180 dollars), "its unbelievably versatile flavours range from roasted almonds, dried fruit, and toffee, to honey, vanilla, baked apples and cinnamon. Its finish is harmonic, well-balanced, spicy and long-lasting." They didn't mention boob flavour in the list of flavours but every red-blooded male, heterosexual Whisky-drinker knows that flavour is in their someplace, and you have to admit that it is much more appealing than Whisky with a pickled cobra in the bottle.

C. Ask Whisky spoke to Max Goldbach about their Whisky, their ad campaign and German Whisky:

C. ASK: Germany is an important market for Whisky and there are many new German Whisky Distilleries. In your opinion what is the best German Whisky? Who is giving serious competition to the imported Brands from Scotland, Ireland, America and the rest of the world?

MAX: To be honest, I don't know a German Whisky that is really giving serious competition to Scottish Single Malts. I think there is some Japanese competition like Suntory, but no German competition. I would say, we Bavarians are definitively the best brewers of Beer, but we are not the best Whisky Distillers - yet.

C. ASK: Tell us about G-Spirits and how the company was formed?

MAX: G-Spirits is a trademark, which was founded in August 2012 by my brother and I. The idea of founding our own Spirit label was born in our time as barkeepers in a cocktail bar. We quickly noticed that it's not just the taste which makes you enjoy a drink fully. Good flavour is the basis, the feeling conveyed is the highlight. Because of our great interest in the best Spirits, we came across a Vodka filtered over diamonds. A nice idea to convey the feeling. However, for us there is nothing better than the eroticism of a beautiful woman. To create the perfect taste we let every single drop of our Spirits run over the breasts of a special woman, one whose characteristics we saw reflected in the Liquor. Or the short version: We combine what we love, enchantress women and best Liquor. The result is the perfect drug!

C. ASK: Which Distilleries in Scotland do you work with to bring your unique G-Spirits
Whisky? Please tell us about the Whisky, its taste and how it was produced?

MAX: Sorry, but we keep all our suppliers secret, because we want the customer to only combine the Whisky taste, the Whisky, the woman and our design in his head. We offer our customers a test sample before buying the Bottle so they can see and taste for themselves that all of our products have a high quality. If they don't want to buy the Bottle after testing the sample, we will refund them the price of the sample. I think that is a fair deal.

Our G.Whisky No.1 is a sweet one, with mixed flavours between toffee, honey and vanilla without any smoke. So sweet like its representative Alexa.

C. ASK: How successful has your ad campaign been with Alexa Varga and other glamour models?

MAX: We are very delighted with the result and the success of the campaign. But we are also very surprised that there are some people who are very upset about us. Even the German advertising board wrote us an email requesting that we stop our campaign, because it would be too sexy. Paul Skehan,

Director General of the European Spirits Organization called the campaign "outrageous!" To be honest, that amused us deeply. For us it is really outrageous that there are actually such stuffy old men out there. I hope they will never find out what the Playboy Magazine is doing. Probably that would kill them. But the main feedback was very positive and so we will not in the least think about stopping our campaign.

C. ASK: What is the future for G-Spirits and do you have any new Whiskies to come and any new exciting ad campaigns?

MAX: Yes, we plan further Whisky editions, but at the moment I don't want to give too much away. But I can guarantee, it will be damn hot!

THE NETHERLANDS: The inspiration for the Brand of Whisky produced by the Us Heit Distillery in the Netherlands was the Friesian Horse. Friesians are a gallant, sleek, beautiful breed of horse originating from the Netherlands. They were often used to carry knights into battle in times gone by. A picture of a Friesian graces the Bottle of Frysk Hynder Whisky and if there were an award for the Bottle top alone, Frysk Hynder would win such a prize for in the opinion of C. Ask Whisky, they have the best Bottle top in the world.

Forget, a boring cork or screw-cap. Frysk Hynder has an artistically carved horse-head pewter Bottle top. Thankfully, us Heit didn't go the G-Spirits route and pour Whisky over the horse before Bottling. Aart Van Der Linde of the Us Heit Distillery told us that his small, family owned brewery had been producing Beer since 1958, but branched off into Whisky in 2002. Aart did an internship in a Scottish Distillery and was determined to do something with the knowledge he gained. Frysk Hynder Single Malt was the result and the people of the Netherlands are proud to have a Whisky they can call their own. Demand is high and exporting to other countries looks to be in the future of Frysk Hynder. Their malted barley (which they malt themselves) is used to create the Whisky.

DENMARK: There is an avid fan base of Whisky in Denmark and we wanted to hear the story of Danish Whisky. We therefore asked Lasse Vesterby of Stauning Whisky to chronicle the rise of Danish Whisky.

C. ASK: Can you tell us the story of how Stauning Whisky began?

LASSE VESTERBY: It all started in 2005. We were wondering why nobody in Denmark was making Whisky? Why couldn't we make a Whisky of the highest quality in Denmark? Danish farmers have delivered barley to Scottish Whisky production for many years and the quality of the water in Denmark is very good. The climate in the Western part of Denmark, where Stauning Whisky is located, is pretty much the same as in Scotland. It is always windy and there is a lot of salt in the air. So we decided to give Whisky making a go. At first, we thought it would only be a hobby. Our initial plans were to make 2,400 litres of Whisky every year. In other words, it was a small scale production. It was in a former butcher's house where we started the very first Distilling. The hobby idea went by the wayside as we quickly got interested in making Whisky professionally and commercially. We received good feedback on the first batch of Whisky we made and so we decided to build a real Distillery. In 2007 we bought a farm house. We spent a year and a half on rebuilding the place, getting it ready for Whisky production. We installed a 1000 litres Wash Still and a 600 litres Spirit Still. The rest of the equipment ended up being a lot of our own inventions.

We were ready to begin the production in May 2009 and made 6000 litres annual for the first three years. Only one man was working full time at the Distillery.

In May 2012 we hired another man so we now have two full time employees and we are about to increase the production to approximately 14,000 litres annually.

We are an unusual group of people to start a Distillery. We have no professional background that indicates that we should start a Distillery. The only thing we knew about Whisky before we started Stauning Whisky was that most of us liked drinking a fine Whisky. We are four engineers, a butcher, a teacher, a helicopter pilot, a doctor and a chef - yet, despite not having a Whisky Industry background, that could not stop us from trying!

C. ASK: Can you tell us about your Whiskies?

LASSE VESTERBY: We are now making three basic types of Whisky.

We are making a peated Single Malt Whisky. We are also making a non-peated version.

The third type is a rye - a very interesting type of rye. Since we are doing all parts of the production ourselves, we are also doing all the malting ourselves. That gives us the opportunity to malt the rye. It is a lot of work, compared to not malting it, but it is worth the effort. And not only is it made of malted rye, it is also Distilled in Pot Stills.

All the barley and rye, is from local Danish farmers, and even the peat is local. It comes from a museum nearby. That we are using Danish peat is unique. The flavour that it brings to our peated Whisky is different from what you know from Islay Whiskies. It is a sweeter peat.

All three types are benefiting from the fact, that we use very small stills. It gives a very rich and oily Spirit with a lot of flavour. So even very young Spirit from Stauning tastes great and has more complexity to it than other Whiskies at the same age. This is very much because of the small stills. It is a lot of work using these small stills, but as long as that is the way to get the highest quality, that is the way to go for us.

All of these things combined give us three Whiskies that are different from what we know from other Whiskies on the market. The rye is not a type of Whisky, that you see in many other places – if any. The Rye Whisky is also the product that made it possible for us to deliver Bottles to Noma, the Danish restaurant, that three years in a row was awarded the prize for being the best restaurant in the world. We are pleased that they also liked the quality of our two Single Malts, and so much so, they are now serving Stauna Whisky at Noma.

C. ASK: How do you compete with Whisky Brands from Scotland and around the world?

LASSE VESTERBY: We cannot compete directly with the enormous Scottish Whisky Industry. Our production is very small, and therefore the cost of producing each Bottle is very high compared to a mass production Distillery. So our only chance is to make Whisky of the highest quality possible, and give it its own story, so we stand out from the other Whiskies on the market.

That is why we cannot compromise quality any places in our production. But it is not only the production that needs to be of the highest quality. Also the packaging, the design of the Bottle and box have to be well presented so the consumer is completely satisfied with the Stauning experience.

C. ASK: Apart from Denmark, what other countries are your best markets for Stauning Whisky? Are there any markets that you aren't in right now but would like to get into?

LASSE VESTERBY: We have just sent the first Bottles to Norway. Since we are such a young Distillery we have not worked on getting in to other markets besides Denmark because we simply have too few Bottles. So far Stauning is only sold in Denmark and Norway and we are having trouble to keep up with the demand. In the future, we will be able to Bottle a lot more Whisky. We would like to be in the Scandinavian market and then move into Germany, France, UK, Ireland, USA and Canada. We have been contacted by importers from all of these countries, but since we do not have enough Bottles yet, this part of the adventure will have to wait.

C. ASK: Were there any difficulties and hardships in launching Stauning as a Danish Brand of Whisky?

LASSE VESTERBY: In the beginning, people had doubts if Danish Whisky could be any good. People were used to Scotch and did not expect much from a Danish Whisky Distillery. Our biggest task was creating a Brand of Stauning Whisky that people would taste with an open mind; we needed to convince people that Danish Whisky could actually be just as good as Scottish and Japanese Whisky. The good reviews and the fact that Stauning is served in Noma has done a lot to dispel the scepticism.

C. ASK: Has the government of Denmark and the people of Denmark gotten behind Stauning in a big way to support yourselves and endorse the company? Is their national pride that it is a Danish owned and Danish operated Whisky company?

LASSE VESTERBY: There has not been any special help from the government. They have been polite and helpful when we needed the different legal permissions to start a Danish Whisky Distillery. The Danish people however have very much endorsed the project of making a Danish Whisky that in quality would be able to compete with Whiskies around the world in quality. We feel that people are definitely feeling the same pride as we. It is a local and national feeling! One individual compared it to his feeling of pride for the national soccer team.

FRANCE: The French have plenty of grain, water and good conditions for making Whisky and that is indeed what they are doing with a number of Distilleries around the nation. Wine, grapes, Champaign and Cognac may all be as French as escargot, frog legs and the Eifel Tower but the French Whisky producers would love everyone to think Whisky when France is mentioned! One of the reasons that some in France are turning to Whisky production is because of the ups and downs of the Wine Industry. A Frenchman named Thierry Guillon converted to making Whisky instead of Champaign. Complaining about some of the problems in the Champaign Industry and the regulations being imposed by the EU, Guillon worried about a ban on 'chaptalisation' - (a fancy word for putting sugar in the grapes before they ferment). Guillon said, "Without chaptalisation, you have completely unpredictable yields. It would be a disaster for Champagne,' said Guillon. Concerning his decision to turn

Champaign into Whisky, Guillon added, "The French drink 150 million Bottles of Whisky a year. Three billion Bottles are produced worldwide annually, one billion of them in Scotland. There's room for me."
C. Ask Whisky had the privilege of speaking to Jean Donnay, a classy French gentleman who produces his Whisky on the North Brittany Coast. His Glann Ar Mor Distillery means Distillery by the Sea. Jean used to work in advertising and now he runs a Distillery that he designed and built himself. When the Pendaryn Distillery in Wales was established, they brought in David Faraday to design their custom made still. Jean Donnay didn't bring in anybody. He custom built his own still. A unique feature harkens back to Whisky production of the past in that he heats his Pot Stills with a live flame. His education in Whisky production came from two major sources, the French Wine and Cognac Industry and Distilleries like Glenmorangie in Scotland. He did eight years of research before launching Glann Ar Mor.

Here is how the Glann Ar Mor website tells the story: "It is right in the heart of Trégor at the far end of the Presqu'île Sauvage (The Wild Peninsula in French), facing the ocean in the middle of a wild and authentic landscape. It is in this region that Celtic Whisky Compagnie has chosen to build its Distillery Glann Ar Mor (Literally - By the Sea - in the Breton language). The maritime environment is marked by toughness - when the winds blow - as well as by tenderness. A group of seals have chosen to live happily in one of the many groups of small islands which can be seen from the Distillery. The landscape keeps changing with the movements of the tide, which in the area can reach twelve metres of amplitude during the equinox.

In this land of tradition, haunted by Breton and Celtic legends, this peninsula from the Côtes d'Armor represents a very special setting for the implantation of a unique Distillery, and this in the purest of Celtic tradition."

Jean Donnay and his wife Martine also run the Celtic Whisky Compagnie which brings the following Bottlings to France and beyond: Celtique Connexion 16 YO Single Malt, Sauternes Finish, Cloneme Peated Single Malt 8 YO, Clonmel Single Malt, Glen Torness Blended, Glenfinnan Blended 8 YO, Islay Connection Blended. They of course have their peated and unpeated Single Malts produced at the Distillery.

SWEDEN: The Swedish are culturally known for being meticulous and having an attitude that if you are going to do something, do it right! With the Brand Mackmyra, everything has been thought of - from how to mature the Whisky when the freezing temperatures of winter hit to the Visitor Centre and Distillery Tour. Here is their story as they tell it: "Perhaps it sounds too simple, but it all started with a skiing trip. Eight friends met up at a mountain lodge in the spring of 1998. Each had taken along a Bottle of Malt Whisky for the host; the topic of conversation was obvious. How do you make Whisky? And why isn't there a Swedish one? The question led us to start exploring the possibilities of making our own Swedish Whisky. Mackmyra was founded after one year's preparation in March 1999 and started a pilot Distillery the same year. For the first year the business was run by the company's eight founders, with no employees. The first drops of raw Whisky were Distilled on 18 December 1999. We produced 170 different recipes and our ambassadors participated in the challenge to decide which two recipes we were going to use. In spring 2002 we were ready, and the outcome was Mackmyra Elegant and Mackmyra Smoke.

During 2002 we also built the new Distillery and went from being a pilot Distillery to a small-scale producer. 2008 was the year when the first Swedish Whisky produced in large volumes, "The First Edition", was launched. It is produced in our very own way, using Swedish ingredients and no additives whatsoever. 2009 also saw the start of the building process for our own Whisky village deep in the forest of Gävle. In 2010 we launched Mackmyra Bruks Whisky with the aim of becoming established in the Premium range. Mackmyra The Swedish Whisky is made from our soft elegant recipe matured in Bourbon Casks. We then spiced it up with a special combination of large and small Casks: rich Sherry and a touch of our fresh Swedish Oak. For a light hint of juniper smoke, we added some of our smoky variety."

We spoke to Brand ambassador and Master Blender, Angela D'Orazio about Mackmyra and also about herself. Angela went from studying food and beverage to specializing in Whisky. She worked at a Stockholm Whisky bar that had 500 different Brands of Whisky. She helped choose the 500 Brands. She also spent a lot of time in Scotland visiting Distilleries and being mentored by the good folks at Glenmorangie. Angela was the consultant that the eight friends brought in when choosing the two recipes out of a 170 for Mackmyra Whisky. One of the unique features of Mackmyra is that much of the maturation process of their Whisky takes place underground and this helps protect the Whisky from the extreme cold in wintertime and the hot summer temperatures. Another special feature is the Cask ownership scheme.

Owning Casks put out by a Distillery is nothing new, but people have to travel to that Distillery to sample it, where as there are warehouses dotted all over Sweden so that the owners can have their Cask nearby them. Here is a description of this scheme: "Mackmyra Reserve offers customers the opportunity to track their own personal 30-litre Cask from production through maturation to final Bottling, at a time of the customer's own choosing. At present we have several thousand co-owners and/or Cask owners. To a large extent these groups overlap and form a core of ambassadors, people with a deep interest in Mackmyra."

SUMMARY OF OUR TRIP AROUND THE WHIRLD OF WHISKY

The competition might be tough but this is good for Whisky lovers everywhere as the best of the best comes out of this maelstrom of creativity. The variety around the world and the many interesting choices only add to your experience of all things Whisky!

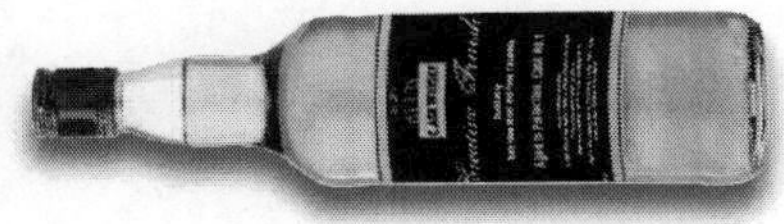

CHAPTER *four*
The nose knows

How can someone tell a good Whisky from a bad one? The reptile staring back at you out of the Bottle you picked up in South East Asia might be one clue. Is there such thing as a bad Whisky? According to William Faulkner, "There is no such thing as bad Whisky. Some Whiskies just happen to be better than others." Evidently, Faulkner never travelled to Thailand, Vietnam and Laos and if he had, he would have shouted variations of his surname...... And then of course there is the urban legend that even in Scotland, with the largest Whisky production in the world, only a small percentage of the Scottish population are able to detect the offending chemicals in cheap Whisky that make it taste like burnt ass.

These musings seemed somehow appropriate as we enter into a chapter about the art of tasting Whisky. One of the early aims of this chapter is to dispel the myth that Whisky Tasting is elitist and for experts only. If you have a nose and a tongue, then you are qualified to taste Whisky. Knowing what you are tasting is just a matter of training the nose, tongue and brain but assuming you have these three essential body parts, you can develop your appreciation of Aqua Vitae.

Another appropriate way to begin this discourse is to reference an old Hans Christian Anderson Fairy Tale.

"The king is naked!" cried the boy.

Admittedly, not as exciting as Alexa Varga naked and advertising G-Spirits Whisky.

Surely you remember the Anderson tale? Con-artists convince the king and everyone in his kingdom that only intelligent people can see the special clothes they have sold to the dufus of a monarch. The king then parades about in the raw and everyone cheers, afraid to admit they can't see the clothes. They remark, "Oh aren't those clothes marvellous! Exquisite! Just look at the seam-work, the expert tailoring!" while secretly thinking, "I've seen stems on apples bigger than his royal crown jewels there?" It takes a cheeky young lad to point out the obvious and to wake up everyone to the honest truth.

The danger of going into a discussion about Whisky Tasting is that sometimes there can be a lot of pretence, a lot of monkey-see tullamore dew, ...er I mean, knockando ......er, I mean, monkey-shoulder, I mean monkey-do. Who knew you could stutter while writing? I digress. The point is, there can be a lot of prancing about in bad Christmas-gift sweaters that you would wear to no other occasion, while sniffing glasses of Spirit and saying things you would get beat up for in other social circles such as, "Isn't that a lovely bouquet!"

Real Whisky Tasting is about honesty and not an Academy Award winning performance. When someone loftily holds their nose up high and proclaims, "I detect spring flowers from a Tyrolean mountain meadow in this Whisky from the Alps," you should be honest enough to say, "I don't smell mountain meadow flowers at all. I smell mountain goats with irritable bowel syndrome."

I am sure there are people who go all hoity-toity, suddenly don a Received Pronunciation, House of Windsor/BBC accent and throw out adjectives, metaphors and analogies that would be thrown out of a high school essay-writing English class....

Writing. That is where we will officially start. Describing Whisky takes just a bit of creative writing skill. It's not that you write down every thought. Some descriptions are just spoken. But whether writing it or saying it, you are searching for the right words and the right comparisons. As tastes and smells need to be translated into words that another human being can understand, we should look at some horrid metaphors/similes/analogies that high school English teachers annually submit as the worst examples of writing they have seen amongst their students. We can learn a thing or two about how not to describe Whisky from these 15 awful but funny attempts at literary greatness, authored by real teenagers in real high school essays. Let the lesson begin:

Bad Metaphor/Simile Example One: "Her artistic sense was exquisitely refined, like someone who can tell butter from I Can't Believe It's Not Butter."

Comment: It starts elegantly and then slips on the butter.

Bad Metaphor/Simile Example Two: "Her face was a perfect oval, like a circle that had its two sides gently compressed by a Thigh Master."

Comment: Sounds like something from 50 Shades of Grey!

Bad Metaphor/Simile Example Three: "She had a deep, throaty, genuine laugh, like that sound a dog makes just before it throws up."

Comment: I'm laughing and making that same sound right now.

Bad Metaphor/Simile Example Four: "The ballerina rose gracefully en pointe and extended one slender leg behind her, like a dog at a fire hydrant."

Comment: Beautifully described until the howler of a comparison at the end.

Bad Metaphor/Simile Example Five: "Her vocabulary was as bad as, like, whatever."

Comment: Some Whisky Tasters are just as limited.

Bad Metaphor/Simile Example Six: "She grew on him like she was a colony of E. coli and he was room-temperature Canadian beef."

Comment: Young love. Cupid. Hearts! Holding hands! Cheap meat that's gone off. One of these images does not belong here.

Bad Metaphor/Simile Example Seven: "The lamp just sat there, like an inanimate object."

Comment: That's like saying "I detect liquid in this Whisky."

Bad Metaphor/Simile Example Eight: "He spoke with the wisdom that can only come from experience, like a guy who went blind because he looked at a solar eclipse without one of those boxes with a pinhole in it and now goes around the country speaking at high schools about the dangers of looking at a solar eclipse without one of those boxes with a pinhole in it."

Comment: Some Whisky descriptions go on this long and are just as repetitive and silly.

Bad Metaphor/Simile Example Nine: "The little boat gently drifted across the pond exactly the way a bowling ball wouldn't."

Comment: Though the teacher pulled this up as a bad metaphor, it is actually good comedy writing. Ridiculous comparisons are comic fodder.

Bad Metaphor/Simile Example Ten: "Her hair glistened in the rain like a nose hair after a sneeze."

Comment: From the sublime to the slime.

Bad Metaphor/Simile Example Eleven: "He fell for her like his heart was a mob informant and she was the East River."

Comment: What synapses in the brain connected falling in love with a mafia hit boggles the mind.

Bad Metaphor/Simile Example Twelve: "She walked into my office like a centipede with 98 missing legs."

Comment: The centipede itself laughing.

Bad Metaphor/Simile Example Thirteen: "Oh, Jason, take me!" she panted, her breasts heaving like a college freshman on $1-a-Beer night."

Comment: Writer with fake ID wrote this after spending too many dollars at dollar a Beer night.

Bad Metaphor/Simile Example Fourteen: "It hurt the way your tongue hurts after you accidentally staple it to the wall."

Comment: As you do. Surely, an experience we can all relate to.

Bad Metaphor/Simile Example Fifteen: "It was an American tradition, like fathers chasing kids around with power tools."

Comment: This kid needs to be taken into care. Call Social Services!

All of these young Shakespeares are reaching for a comparison to help us see in our mind's eye what they are attempting to describe and yet their efforts are unintentionally hilarious. One can detect an element of trying too hard (or not hard enough in some cases); a pretence of being a master wordsmith and yet the absurdity betrays them. When it comes to describing an experience with Whisky, the reach for adjectives, metaphors and similes can be just as unintentionally ridiculous. Like the people in the Anderson fairy tale, we all want to keep up appearances; there is a pretending that one actually knows what they are talking about.

The descriptions can often be a mimicry of someone else that seemed to know a thing or two about Whisky; the attempts to look smart though actually make the person look stupid in the long run. The honest child in the Anderson fairy tale was the only smart one in the story, and if you want to appear truly smart, then honesty is the best policy. Just be yourself and relax. If you taste a Whisky and cannot detect the hints of vanilla, or honey, or fruit that someone else said was in there, it is no good pretending to see, or smell, or taste what you don't see/taste/smell. When you lie, while doing your best Sean Connery impersonation and say, "Oh yesh, I can tashte the frothy, freshness of the sea and lingering cod liver oil in this flotsham and jetsham backwash of a delicious shingle malt," people will begin to see right through the bad poetry, the even worse Connery accent and to the vacuous state of your true knowledge of the subject. There is actually no shame in admitting you can't taste all the elements that someone else says they can. For all you know, they could be spouting as much hogwash as you were spouting. What's wrong with saying, "I like it" or "I don't like it" without feeling the need to wax poetic and recite a sonnet?

Scotland's bard, Robert Burns, had the skill to take a dram and play with words all day long, coming out with whimsical brilliance such as:

" Oh Whisky! soul o' plays and pranks!
Accept a bardie's gratefu' thanks!
When wanting thee, what tuneless cranks
Are my poor verses!
Thou comes - they rattle in their ranks,
At ither's arses!"

If you can pull a Robert Burns, great, but if the words aren't there, don't pretend they are. So no acting. No pressure. You can come to Whisky Tasting as a pure Whisky virgin; you therefore don't have to behave like a worn-out, world-weary Whisky whore, expressing criticism and arrogant opinions no one wants to hear. Come for the pleasure, for the new experience, to increase your appreciation, to have fun with your friends, to taste the art that many a Master Distiller and Blender would love you to love for they cooked up the magic brew for your enjoyment.

When one lacks words, a new vocabulary is in order and you will be glad to know that the moody teenager catchphrase, "Like, whatever!" is not part of the Whisky lexicon you shall acquire.

WHISKY LINGO

There is a Whisky language. Some of the lingo is technical and you will be hated as an insufferable know-it-all smart ass if you throw some of these words around too much, but it won't hurt for you to know some of these smart ass words so you can smugly think, I know what that other smart ass is talking about.

The other type of words are common Whisky descriptive words so you can speak the lingo like a native. This is a balancing act. Overusing these words is tiresome, annoying and nips the head, and yet being too creative, reaching for words never before heard in a Whisky discussion might mean you find something as poetically putrid as E-coli growing on room temperature Canadian beef.

ABV: Is it just me or am I the only one who sees these three letters and thinks The Average White Band? OK that was AWB. ABV means Alcohol By Volume which is the percentage of Alcohol.

Aldehydes: What the ….? Dr. Jekyl's Aunt? It means it smells like grass and leather. This is a nerd word. I swear I will hit anyone who uses this word in my presence.

"Oh yes, I detect the aldehydes in this simply spiffing aroma."

"OY! SHUT IT!"

Angel's Share: The amount of Whisky that evaporates going up into the air in the process of making it, and thus it is said to be given to the angels. There is a movie called the Angel Share set with the Scottish Whisky industry as the background to the story.

Austere: When a hillbilly wants to drive or points at a castrated male cow. In Whisky Tasting austere means it is not sweet and soft. Rather it is harsh, severe, lacking smoothness. it's not fancy. If the Whisky worked at the library, it would frown at you and tell you to shoosh with a face that could curdle a 70 year old Macallan.

Balanced: Not too much of this and not too much of that in the Whisky. Everything is even. No matter how balanced the Whisky is however, if you drink too much of it, you will lose your balance.

Bastard Malt - Like a mongrel of a dog. Not a pure breed and there is almost no telling who the dog's parents were to make such a mutt. Some malts are mutts, their origins suspect. I'd have a bastard malt just because I like the name though. "Bartender, give me a Bastard Malt please - full of aldehydes (that's how to start a bar fight)."

Big: In the context of tasting it means unsubtle. There are flavours that dominate. It's a fun bash-you-over-the-head Whisky."

Blended Whisky: If you think this is like going to the manual soda machine at Burger King and mixing three of four sodas, its not quite that simple or disgusting. Mixing two or more different kinds of Whisky together will turn a Whisky officially into a Blend; usually there is more than one Whisky as well and also neutral Spirits, colourings and flavours. Famous Grouse Whisky is a Blend as are many other well known Brands, and it is a skill and an art by Whisky magicians who work absolute magic.

Body - Alexa Varga. Now that's a body! In Whisky lingo the body of a Whisky is about how it feels in the mouth and how substantial it is. So when someone says, its got a nice body on it, it means the Whisky is the right consistency. Something closer to sticky treacle syrup on one end of the body spectrum and severe diarrhoea on the other end (literally) are the wrong kind of body for a Whisky.

C/S - Cask Strength

Cerealy: Pul-leeeeeese! Instead of saying "The Whisky has got a hint of cereal," must you say "cerealy?" This is adjective/adverb abuse! Spare us!

Cerebral: "Oh this is cerebral!" What the person is really saying is they are stumped and having a hard time figuring out exactly what the Whisky is because they have to think about it. They mean the Whisky is complicated and not easy to figure out. It could also mean the person trying to appear cerebral is anything but.

Complex: A complex Whisky is one the person who said "Cerebral" couldn't figure out.

Creamy: A much better word than 'cerealy'. This reminds the Whisky taster of something that came from a cow.

Dark flavours: The Whisky Taster thinks they detect underlying sweet elements that tend to be dark in colour such as molasses or Liquorice candy although they could be referring to a fermented turd. This is Yoda's favourite Whisky Tasting description. "Mmmmm. Sense dark flavours I do. Drink up I will! Give into the dark side of the froth!"

Dignified: This means the Whisky isn't flamboyant and call too much attention to itself. It is not a show off. It is a good, well made, quality Whisky.

Dram - What a beaver with a speech impediment builds. It is also a Whisky measuring glass.

Dry: Even though it is wet, it seems to somehow take away all the moisture out of your mouth. A dry Whisky tends not to be sweet. Dry can be just right. It can be appropriate. Or it can be too dry and make you lose your will to live.

Estery: As annoying a nerd Whisky word as aldehydes but instead of earthy grass or leather you smell fruits and florals.

I'm really not a violent guy but if someone is sniffing Whisky and saying, "Oh I just love those Estery aromas!" it might make me grab a Bottle and look for an opening somewhere on the offending person to insert the Bottle.

Ethanol: Sounds like a good mother-in-law name as in "Darling, meet my mother, Ethanol." Ethanol is another name for Alcohol, but the kind that comes from grains.

Finish: Ironically, the finish happens after you've actually swallowed the sip of Whisky and is about the taste sensation left on the tongue after the liquid is already down the throat. Some Whiskies you can still taste long after they have been swallowed, and some finish by destroying your sense of taste just as surely as if you'd licked a mousetrap. How a Whisky finishes is described in most Whisky Tasting notes. If you are from Finland, it is what you are.

Firm: Even though there is actually nothing firm, hard or solid about Whisky, a particular Whisky might seem firm in that its body holds together well.

Grain Whisky: Even though barley is a grain, this usually means a Whisky that is made from grains other than malted barley such as corn, wheat, or rye. Calling something a Grain Whisky can be used in a snobbish way by some to refer to Whiskies that are other than Single Malts. Snobbery in the Whisky world? Surely not!

Grassy: Why didn't you just say so instead of laying aldrehydes on us? For whatever reason the Whisky reminds you of your freshly mown lawn. Whatever floats your boat, man.

Harsh: The Whisky pulls your nose hairs, slaps you silly and tortures your tongue.

Heathery: The word heather is thrown around a lot in Whisky circles. Yes there is a lot of heather in Scotland which could very well make it into the flavour of the Scotch, but the isolated smell of heather is not obvious to most people around the world - not even in Scotland. A blogger named Ganga from a Whisky forum said this: "How does one in southern California know what the plant life in the UK smells like? All these descriptions saying, "heather, heather, heather" and I have no reference. However, it smelled like the sweet summer grasses I was familiar with from the US Midwest. Then I spent two weeks driving around Scotland and visiting Distilleries (someone did mention they also have castles there). I was engulfed in heather. Guess what? It smelled quite similar to the grasses across the northern plains in the US." There you go, heather is like sweet grass.

Herbal: The Whisky has taste elements that remind you of the herbs used in cooking.

Hot: Even though the drink is cold, it has the effect of heating you up inside and some Whiskies can have this effect more than others.

Malt: What is malt? Malt is the germinated cereal grains, primarily barley. The grains are soaked in water, start to germinate and then are dried out before the germination gets going. The drying bit is called Malting. These malted grains have the enzymes needed to turn starch into sugars.

Malty: Not the island near Greece. It means there's a lot of malt just like you could look at a triple chocolate cake and say "Chocolatey."

Medicinal: Reminds you of cough syrup and is number one false excuse for taking a dram. "I need this for my rheumatism." No you don't. You just want another dram, dram you!

Mouth-coating: It feels like little people have taken a paint brush and painted the whole inside of your mouth with Whisky paint.

Mouthfeel: What the Whisky feels like in your mouth.

Nose: Instead of saying smell or aroma like normal people, Whisky people say, "What is the nose of the Whisky?" Why can't they just say, "What does the Whisky smell like?" But no, "nose" must sound more posh. Who nose why?

Nutty: You think you taste nuts in the Whisky or you share your drink with an invisible talking unicorn, which means the description is about you.

Oaky: Can mean agreement, especially when paired with dokey, or you think you can taste some of the wood from the Oak Barrel the Whisky sat in for a good few years.

Orangey: Tends to march through Catholic neighbourhoods in Northern Ireland on July 12th, or the Whisky has elements of the citrus fruit orange in its flavouring.

Palate: It is a homonym (same sound but different spelling) of the word palette as in an artist's palette and that means a thin board or slab on which an artist lays and mixes a whole range of colours. Back to the other palate. The boring scientific meaning is the roof of the mouth. To the Whisky Taster, palate is closer to the artist's palette but instead of a range of colours there is a range of tastes. Palate is about everything the whole mouth experiences from the teeth to the tonsils, to the roof of the mouth and beneath the tongue and dominating the event is the tongue and the sense of smell. To have a good palate means you have developed the ability to distinguish different tastes, separate them and identify them. Your tongue is your artistic palette.

Peat: Peat is layers of vegetation from boggy, cold moors. Often there is a lack of wood in places where a lot of peat grows and few trees about, but the people living around peaty areas discovered long ago that dried out peat could burn like a log. Peat fires were used to dry the barley and water for the Distilleries (especially on the Scottish island of Islay) would flow through the peat and so some of the aroma and flavour of the peat would make its way into the Whisky along with the smoke from the peat fires. Peaty and smoky have therefore become common descriptive words in Whisky Tasting. When they double Distill the Whisky they are re-peating the process....

Peppery: Another example of adverb abuse, but yes, pepper is one of the associated flavours that often springs to mind in Whisky Tasting although the Master Distiller wasn't shaking pepper into the mash.

Phenolic: "Ooo! I smell Phenols!" Oh shut up! Stop showing off. Phenols are types of unpleasant scents that smell more industrial and chemical than something fit for human consumption. They usually smell like tar, but it is easier to say, this Whisky smells like roadworks and burning tyres than to say "I smell phenols."

Rich: What some Whisky companies are because of good customers like you. In Whisky Tasting, it means the flavours are strong and the body of the Whisky is substantial

Sherried and Winey: Does the letter 'Y' have to be added to every word to make it an adjective/adverb deformed description? This makes me whiney! Make it stop. If a Whisky was aged in a Barrel first used to make Sherry, the Sherry Cask will influence the flavour of the whisky and some people will taste elements that remind them of Wine.

Single Malt: Malted Barley is the only grain ingredient and it is made using Pot Still Distillation at one single Distillery. It is prized for the same reason pure breed animals are. It is a pure breed drink. Just as a pure breed of Dalmatian, English Bulldog or a Norwegian Elkhound is more valuable than a stray mongrel with who-knows-how many different dog genes in the mix. A Single Cask Malt Whisky means not only is it a Single Malt but it comes from one Single Cask and is therefore very exclusive and prized among Whisky collectors and connoisseurs.

Soft, Sweet, Smooth: The gentler, kinder elements of what a Whisky can offer your taste palate.

Spicy: The sweeter spices like cinnamon or nutmeg are some of the flavours that might come to mind while tasting Whisky with an edge to it.

Subtle: Flavours and elements that don't leap out at you and hit you over the head.

Vegetative: Another way to say you can detect the adelhydes, the grass, heather and peat that entered into the flavour of the Whisky.

Vintage - The year the Whisky was Distilled.

Viscous: Another show off word. It means having a thick, sticky consistency between solid and liquid; having a high viscosity. I'd be tempted to spit in your Whisky and make it even more viscous if you pull that word out.

Youthful: This term may be misleading as the Whisky might be many years old and fully mature and yet, it has an energy, a vitality, a zest that reminds you of a rock star rather than grandpa sitting on the porch with his dram.

These are descriptive Whisky words to get you started, but I am sure you will find a whole host of other appropriate and or inappropriate words with which to talk about your experience with Whisky.

THE FLAVOURING FACTORS

Like a butterfly in the cocoon, or a baby in the womb, there is a whole mysterious process that happens to White Spirit straight from the still when it sits in a Cask Barrel for at least three years. The same thing will not happen in a plastic Barrel or a metal Barrel. To be Whisky it must have been aged in a proper wooden Cask - and not just any kind of wood. Some types of wood will ruin Whisky with their high pitch content and other factors in their make-up that just aren't right for the production of true Whisky.

It was discovered, perhaps accidentally, that sitting in an Oak Barrel over time will create proper Whisky. Why Oak? Oak is tough - but not so tough you can't cut it and bend it into a Barrel shape. The Spirit won't leak out of a properly made Oak Cask and yet the wood lets oxygen in and out almost as if the wood is breathing. Different air can influence the taste of Whisky. Casks breathing in and out salty sea air will produce a different Whisky to Casks breathing in the air of the Western Australian desert, or the foothills of an American mountain range. Back to the wood however. There are oils in the wood called vanillins and slowly over time, these are drawn out of the wood colouring and flavouring the Whisky.

The reason that no one Whisky tastes exactly the same as the other despite aging in the same kind of Barrels (although even here there are variations in size) is because of the different water, air, variation of grains and other ingredients in the recipe. The art of Barrel making (coopering) has to be very exact to meet industry standards. Making the Barrel is just as much a skill as making the Whisky. Different types of Oak (American, European, or Japanese Oak - each slightly different than the other) are used to make the Casks. A smaller Cask means more of the Spirit will be influenced directly by the wood. A lot of Scotch is made in Casks that were first used in America to make Bourbon and so there will be taste factors from left over Bourbon and Sherry that made their way into the wood.

Here are the different Cask sizes and their weird names from smallest to biggest.

Blood tub (40 litres) Sounds like it came from a Transylvanian Distillery. This is a Cask small enough for a horse to carry - which was the idea in its time. This size is mostly used for Beer, but special Whiskies are sometimes made in blood tubs.

The Firkin Quarter Cask (50 litres) Why someone would want to swear at this Cask I don't know. It is exactly a quarter of the size of the American Standard Cask. Because there is so much interaction with the Spirit and the wood, Whisky is aged quickly. Firkin right it is!

The American Standard 200 Litre Barrel (ASB): The ASB. Used for the Bourbon industry and made from American White Oak. These Barrels are then shipped over to Scotland and elsewhere around the Whisky world.

Hogshead: This could mean she looked better last night before you sobered up in the morning, but it is also a Cask size only slightly bigger than the American Standard Barrel. The Hogshead has (225 litres). The old word was Hogges Hede and for some reason it meant 63 gallons back in the 1400s. It was a measurement term. Hogshead Casks are used to mature Bourbon as well, and so the majority of Scotch is aged in Hogshead Casks fresh from the Bourbon trade.

Barrique Cask (300 litres) Casks used for Wine and if Whisky is matured in a used Barrique it will be influenced by the Wine that formerly occupied the Cask.

Puncheon: Like a luncheon but with a mandatory fistfight. It is also a 500 litre Oak Cask that was first used to make Rum or Sherry, and these flavours will of course influence the Whisky.

Butt: I don't know who named this Cask but they should be watched. The Butt is a 500 litres former Sherry Cask used to make Whisky influenced by the Sherry. Sing with me! "I like big butts and I cannot lie…"

Port Pipe: Sound illegal. This is a tall, stretched Barrel, more tubular or pipe-like than the traditional short squat Barrel and it holds 650 litres of port Wine more often than not. But after being used for port, such a Barrel could be used to finish off a port-influenced Whisky.

Madeira Drum: It holds the same 650 litres as the Port Pipe and together they make the Laurel and Hardy of Oak Casks because the Madeira drum is short and fat rather than tall and skinny. It is used for Madeira Wine, and then can be passed on to a Whisky maker desiring the flavourings left behind in the wood from the Madeira Wine.

Gorda: This is the Yo Mama of Oak Casks as in Yo Mama is so fat that when she wears a yellow raincoat, people yell "taxi!" Yo Mama is so fat that when her beeper goes off, people think she's backing up. Yo Mama is so fat that she has to iron her pants on the driveway....You get the idea. The biggest Cask in the industry and holds 700 litres. These are mainly used for Whiskies that will be Blended.

DEVELOPING YOUR SENSE OF SMELL AND TASTE

So we've added to our Whisky vocabulary and common descriptive words, looked at flavouring elements such as Cask aging, and now we will talk about learning how to taste and appreciate the Whisky even more than you already do.

A Master Taster who can identify different Brands, Blends, Single Malts and the ingredients is yes, to be applauded for their skill, but you should not feel intimidated by such an expert. Here is how you can begin to develop your own palate, your sense of smell and taste. I am sure you will recall that the last time your nose was stuffed up, your food was tasteless. Smell and taste are two senses that work together and as far as taste is concerned, is dependent on the sense of smell so the exercises to develop your sense of smell and taste are interlinked.

TIP ONE: Like exercising a muscle, you can exercise your sense of smell. Concentrate and remember the things you smell everyday - I mean the good smells, the natural smells. You will be happy to know that smelling things that stink is not actually good exercise for the nose and should be avoided. That's your nose's way of saying, that's not good for you to be around. You can play games where a friend holds something to your nose where your eyes are closed and you have to identify it. Watch your friends though. All my friends would throw in something stinky for a laugh.

TIP TWO: Back to a bit of creative writing or creative describing; try to find the words to describe what you see or taste. You will find these words in comparisons, memories and associations. There will be elements of the Whisky that remind you of other things and so translating these impressions into words is all part of the skills you are after.

TIP THREE: Dairy products have a tendency to cause mucus build up and this can block your sense of smell so laying off the cream, the yoghurt, the ice cream, the cheese, the milk will be good for your senses of taste and smell. Even too much Whisky and other types of Alcohol can interfere with these senses. And then there is smoking. Among the hundred and one reasons you already know about why you should kick the habit, the fact that it interferes with your sense of smell and taste is one extra reason. Being healthy, exercising and taking vitamins like zinc will improve your sense of smell.

TIP FOUR: Smell your food before you eat it. Savour the different aromas. Remember them. Separate the various smells in your mind. You will bring this identifying and separating skill to Whisky Tasting.

WHISKY TASTING TIPS

WTT1: Remember that Whisky Tasting is as subjective as saying I like toe-maw-toes and you don't like ta-may-toes. It is not an exact science and your opinion is as valid as anyone else's. Someone might have more expertise than you in deciphering what he/she is tasting and identifying ingredients, but your personal reaction to the flavour - whether you like the Whisky or not - is as valid an opinion as the greatest Master Blender who have ever lived.

WTT2: It's not as hard as you think. Whisky Tasting is about associating the tastes and smells with things you have tasted and smelled before. Then it is just a matter of putting those impressions into words.

WTT3: The glass you use for the whisky is important. Paper cup - bad! Plastic cup - bad! Milkshake glass with a crazy straw - bad! Glasses made of actual glass and designed for Whisky are what you are after. A strong cool glass that is wide enough to direct the Whisky aromas up to your nostrils is what you are looking for. An L.A. based Whisky-taster named Tim Read blogs on his Scotch and Ice Cream site, "The first thing I use is a good glass.

I alternate between two primary glasses for tasting: a Crate and Barrel Sipping Glass, which is a nice all-around glass for Spirits, or the Whisky nerd standard Glencairn Whisky Glass. To be honest, I prefer the Glencairn glass because it feels slightly more durable and substantial, but the C&B glass is just fine." Others will recommend that you commence with a tulip shaded glass which will send aromas up your nose like smoke going up a chimney.

WTT4: Nose the Whisky, smell the Whisky, sniff the Whisky. Make the tongue wait. Believe it or not, you will taste most of the Whisky with your nose.

WTT5. Go slow. Take a sip. Let the Whisky paint your tongue and the whole inside of your mouth. Your mind can join in the fun by trying to pick out the various flavours. That's the sport, the hobby, the challenge, the game of Whisky Tasting and all part of the social interaction with others.

WTT5: Now you can change things up by adding a small dash of water. This brings out the oils in the Whisky.

WTT6: Take a larger sip with the intent of analyzing the body of the Whisky and how substantial it is.

WTT7: The next sip is about seeing what other flavours you can pick up in your new favourite sport.

INTERVIEW WITH RICHARD PATERSON

We had the honour and pleasure of speaking with celebrity Whisky Taster/Host/Master Blender Richard Paterson. Elvis is known as the King, Michael Jackson the Prince of Pop, Bruce Springsteen is called the boss and Richard Paterson is called 'The Nose.'

Food and drink writer Michael Calore described Paterson as "a third-generation Whisky man." Calore writes, "His father, a Whisky distributor, gave him his first sip at age 8. Paterson turned pro in the early 1970s. Now in his 60s, his skill at tasting, assessing and Blending Whiskies has become so acute, his nose has been insured by Lloyd's of London for $2.6 million! Employed by Whyte and Mackay of Glasgow, Scotland, his day job takes him around the world. Paterson creates special Blends for Korean and Japanese markets, and travels from the Oak forests of Missouri to the González Byass bodegas in Andalusia in search of wood for Whisky Casks."

C. ASK: You are called "The Nose." Explain "The Nose." How did you get that name and reputation?

RICHARD PATERSON: My grandfather and father had big noses and by extension so did I. It's not like I'm Pinocchio though - and when I became the Master Blender in the company back in '75, I was called the Nose and the name stuck. Really, it's not so much to do with the shape and size of the nose but what it is used for such as working with these rare beautiful Whiskies like the Dalmore 62 or 64 that have brought so much pleasure to people.

C. ASK: You're a celebrity in the Whisky world and bring a lot of entertainment to what you do. Where did the entertainment skills come from?

RICHARD PATERSON: I am passionate about Whisky and the Brands and company I represent. When I started in the Whisky industry - and make no mistake, Whyte and Mackay has always been a reputable company - but compared to Diageo or Pernod Ricard - these giants that own many Distilleries and represent many Brands - Whyte and Mackay doesn't have the same spending power, the same muscle in monetary terms to promote their Brands, and so I believe strongly that when I get up to speak about Whisky, there needs to be passion. I bring the best entertainment I can to the people who come to me. You could say my style is flamboyant - I go out to events wearing a matching tie and handkerchief - that's my style - but the passion and entertainment and flamboyance has to do with making the Whiskies memorable. You cannot be complacent. You are always looking for new angles, whether that's rockets or balloons or squirt guns - Its knowing the client and giving them what they want. Two nights ago I was at an event in London - it was entertaining and exciting - people came up and said, "That was great value for money," which is a terrific response. The more memorable the evening, the more they will remember the Whiskies.

C. ASK: What advice do you have for our readers about how to properly drink Whisky?

RICHARD PATERSON: This is one of my passions. I go to all these Whisky and Wine festivals. I watch the people and how they go about drinking and most do it so badly. What I mean is, they don't get to know the Whisky properly. Just as in meeting a new person, there needs to be an introduction to get to know the person. You need to be introduced to the Whisky. This is the "Hello, and how do you do?" There are no shortcuts in getting to know a person. The more time you spend talking to the other person, the more the personality of that person comes out.

You can then decide whether you like them or loath them. It is the same with Whisky. You say, "Hello" to it and become familiar with the Whisky. You should hold it on the tip of your tongue for a good thirty to forty seconds - hold it underneath the tongue, and then in the middle of the tongue - the longer you keep it in the mouth, the more flavours you will extract from it. It's the same with food. People don't just swallow. They chew and get all the flavour they can before swallowing. Whisky should be no different - And it's not just the first taste - take a similar amount of time the second taste. The longer you take, the more pleasure and flavour you will take from the Whisky.

In the Michael Calore article, Richard Paterson goes into greater depth about the art of tasting:

In summary he says: "Despite what you may have learned in college or seen in John Wayne movies, Whisky isn't supposed to be tossed down your throat like a cowboy's breakfast. Instead, a fine Whisky should be treated like a fine Cognac or Bordeaux. You don't slug it back in one go. You sip it and savour it.

Choose a glass: You'll need a proper glass for nosing and tasting the Whisky. A Sherry glass (also called a copita) is perfect. It has a stem and is tulip shaped -- if you can't find one, use something similar like a snifter. A Wine glass will do, as long as it has a stem.

Don't use a highball, a shot glass or a so-called 'Whisky glass.'

You want to capture the whole aroma. The shape of the glass, the way it's shaped like a tulip, will force the bouquet into one area -- your nostrils. How you approach the Whisky will greatly affect how accurately you are able to assess it.

Prepare the glass: Pour a tiny bit of Whisky into the room-temperature glass. Swirl and tilt the Whisky around in every direction to coat the inside of the glass, then toss it out. It's important to add a swirl as you toss it. You want to make sure the lip of the glass is absolutely clean. Then grab hold at the bottom, at the stem. This prevents your body heat from transferring to the drink during tasting, which is very important.

Pour: One ounce or so is enough for a taste. Remember, only hold onto the stem from now on.

Sniff: This is called 'nosing' the Whisky.

Step 1: Stick your whole nose in the glass and gently sniff it. You'll get a big hit of Alcohol vapour. Now pull it away and have a look at the Whisky. Roll it around and take note of the colour.

Step 2: Wait two seconds, then go back and repeat the process.

Step 3: Go back a third time. This time, bury your nose into the lip of the glass, and roll the glass from one nostril to the other. You need to get to know the Whisky, communicate with it, learn about its character. Look at it, talk to it, really try to experience it.

Add Water: Add a dash of Distilled water and reduce the Whisky down to about 35 percent Alcohol. Adding the water opens it up and makes it more 'approachable.'

For younger Whiskies (12 years or younger) water is always advisable. For Whiskies 15 years and up, don't add water before you first taste it. But no matter what the age of the Whisky is, if it still bites you when you take a sip, it's too strong for you and you should add water a little bit at a time. Don't use sparkling water. Any good still water will do, but Distilled water is best. Don't use ice - it will only mask the flavours.

Taste it: Take a small amount of Whisky -- just a sip -- into your mouth and move it around. Start by putting the Whisky on the tip of the tongue, then under the tongue, then back in the middle of the tongue. Keep it there a few seconds and assess the flavours, then let it go down. As it goes down, the tongue will reveal more interesting flavours. Let the flavours linger for a good 20 or 30 seconds at least. Whisky has an inner world, and you must give it time to show itself. Always take a second taste. Little different layers will start to open up to you with the second taste.

Finish it: OK, cowboy. After you've taken two or three slow tastes, giving yourself plenty of time to get to know the Whisky, go ahead and tip it back."

MORE WATER PLEASE

We wanted to get some more details about adding water to Whisky and asked Richard questions about this subject.

C. ASK: One thing I don't understand is how someone can buy a really expensive Whisky, a 400 pound, or even a 10,000 pound Bottle, take it home and mix it with tap water with all its chemicals or fluoride or chalk. When do you add water and what kind of water should you use?

RICHARD PATERSON: Good quality still Bottled water should be the answer. Don't use sparkling water because that splits the Whisky up. Some mix Whisky and Coca-Cola. That's fine if you personally want to do that and the vanilla in Coke hangs in there well with Whisky - but I get really angry, especially in America - I see them putting rocks and rocks and more rocks of ice in the Whisky and that masks everything the Whisky is! It's like putting sugar or milk into great coffee! I can understand milk and sugar in cheap or bitter coffee to make a bad coffee taste better - but great coffee doesn't need anything and neither does great Whisky - maybe a swirl in the glass and just holding it in the mouth is key. If I took you to a Distillery and gave you Cask strength Alcohol at 56%, you would probably say, "That is pretty strong." Then you should be looking at using water in that strong Whisky. It's important you take the Whisky right down to a palatable level. I'm working on an expensive range of Whiskies right now - and we Bottled them at the perfect strength for drinking - 41 - 45 % Alcohol. There was one Bottle at 46% and one at 49% as well. The strength makes a big impact on your palate."

LORNE MACKILLOP'S TAKE ON THE WATER AND WHISKY QUESTION

Whisky and Wine expert, Lorne Mackillop of Mackillop's Choice told us that because of his background in Wine where Alcohol content was on average 12-14% of the Wine, he was of the opinion that strong Alcohol needed to be watered down. He said, "I don't like strong Alcohol on my palate such as what you can experience with Cask strength Whisky. It can anesthetize or numb the palate. It might seem strange to say, but you need to remove the Alcohol to look at the Whisky. When analyzing a Whisky you are analyzing the Whisky part and not the Alcohol part. After adding a few drops of water, there will be an immediate change. Whisky is hydroscopic - meaning it wants to dilute itself with water. Aging whisking in the Cask will absorb water from the atmosphere so while some of the aging Whisky evaporates in what is called the angel share, there is also a diluting going on from any moisture the Whisky can gather to itself. Carefully adding the right amount of water - every Whisky is different and every Whisky drinker has their own personal preference - will enhance the Whisky and bring out more of the aroma. Tap water with chlorine in it however is not good for Whisky - Bottled spring water and preferably from Scotland is what I would use ideally."

TIME FOR TASTING

So... you have heard the tasting tips from a master and those in the know and from the Nose. You too can stand in the grandest of circles and espouse the glorious virtues of the noble dram. All you have to do is... GO PRACTICE!

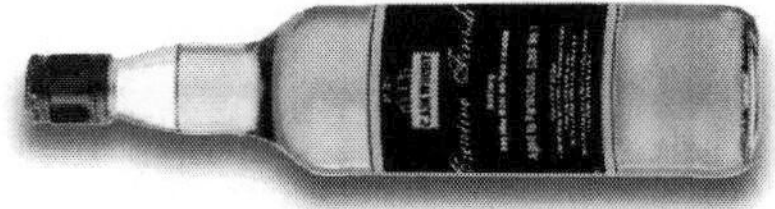

CHAPTER *five*

Mad scientists of malt

Scotland is a land known for its scientific inventions and innovations. From Dolly the cloned sheep to the pedal bicycle - the telephone, hypodermic syringe, insulin, penicillin, radar and much, much more all came from creators with a Scottish connection. James Watt was instrumental in bringing us the steam engine and John Logie Baird the television - and when Baird invented the television, it was very much like today in that there was F*%^ all on! This culture that spawned such an amazing list of accomplishments and breakthroughs, has also spawned some amazing Mad Scientists of Malt.

If you looked at the laboratory of your average Master Blender in the Whisky Industry, your eyes would glaze over by how many glass beakers, Bottles, flasks and samples of Whisky there are for the Mad Scientists of Malt to play with. They aren't really mad of course in the deranged and dangerous sense of the word. They are skilled, talented and creative craftsmen and craftswomen - perhaps mad in a very good way that benefits those who love the taste of an artistically assembled Whisky. Surely, there must be a little obsession and drive to do what they do! They are Whisky artists with highly attuned senses of smell and taste - like a music conductor who can pick out one wrong note that the fifth clarinet player made in the third row of the orchestra. No one else might hear the bum note but the conductor's sense of hearing is such that he detects the B Flat instead of a B note. The Master Blenders have been trained over many years to detect smells and tastes that you or I might not pick up.

How many lonely days and nights do the Mad Scientists of Malt hover over their mixtures crying, "Give my Blend life!?" I can imagine them having hunchbacked assistants and I can hear them shout, "Igor bring me the Mortlach!" Often there are 15 or more Whiskies involved in the Blend, measured at just the right proportions to get the balance of taste just right. There are often months of mixing involved and that is wonderfully mad if you ask me.

Mixology and Whisky really didn't mix until the year 1860 when a Scottish fellow named Andrew Usher ushered in the age of modern Whisky-Blending, creating tastes more palatable to many people not used to the strong taste of Whisky. New flavours, degrees of sweetness, lightness and other taste sensations reached beyond the regular customers and found a whole new audience. It was the Blend and not the Single Malt alone that helped Whisky conquer the world. The Single Malt is viewed as a prized commodity in that it is an exclusive Whisky that can be traced to one single Distillery. A Blend is a bit of this and bit of that and so some Whisky Connoisseurs look down their noses at Blends as inferior beverages to the Single Malt…And yet, there are good reasons to prize a Blend as much as a Single Malt. A Blend represents the skill of a Master Blender who has learned by trial and error to combine just the right percentage of many a Whisky to create a delicious masterpiece. When you look at a masterpiece painting, you can admire the skill of the artist to blend colours, mix paints and produce an image that touches the soul. Here with another orchestra analogy is the Chivas Brothers Master Blender, Colin Scott, who said, "The art of the Master Blender in understanding the many different flavours in Scotch Whisky is like the work of a composer: not only do you need to completely understand the musical characteristics of every instrument, but you must also understand how to combine them to build an unforgettable, spellbinding symphony."

It is an elite group who do the mixing for the major Distilleries and yet the novice, the amateur the layman now has a chance more than ever to Blend Whisky. There are Whisky mixing kits that anyone can buy, usually sold as Christmas presents, and you can even go online and Blend your own Whisky digitally. You can put a percentage of this and a percentage of that into an onscreen Bottle, name the Bottle, slap a label on and order your creation all from the comfort of your computer.

A Whisky-lover from dramming .com described how he made his own home-made Blend, saying "My recent acquisition of a bottle of the Cameronbridge 29 YO single grain gave birth to the idea of whipping together a Blend of the finest Whiskies my shelf had to offer."

His creation was composed of the following:

30 % Cameronbridge 1978/2008 Duncan Taylor
10 % Highland Park 1981/2006 Mackillop's Choice
10 % St. Magdalene 1982/2009 Dun Bheagan
20 % Mortlach 1991/2008 C & S Dram Collection
30 % Lagavulin 16 YO

The Do-it-yourself Whisky Blender then makes these observation about his Blend: "In this case it was not easy to find the right balance between the strong fruitiness of the Cameronbridge and the peat of the Lagavulin. Highland Park and St. Magdalene are a bit similar in profile, so each of them should not be weighted too highly. The Mortlach adds body to the Blend and acts as 'bridge' between the peat of the Lagavulin, the fruitiness of the grain and the delicate characters of the Highland Park and St. Magdalene. The result was in fact an excellent Whisky with a great wealth of flavours and an endless finish. My first try also included a measure of the Talisker 18 YO, but somehow it tasted better with just Lagavulin providing the peat. I have the highest respect for Blenders who create new Whiskies from scratch. The slightest shift in proportions can make or break a Blend. The real art of Blending is to find the set of proportions where the whole really becomes more than the sum of its parts."

By blending himself, he gained a new respect for those who make their living as Blenders. Let us now meet some of these madly talented individuals!

THE DEWAR'S LEGACY

The man and woman were out of breath. They had had to run in order to make it on to the airplane before it took off. They just made it in the nick of time. Both were hurriedly escorted by the stewardess to the last two empty seats of the aircraft. The plane took off and when the food and beverage service was started, the flustered man ordered a Whisky. The Whisky on sale aboard the plane was a Dewar's Blend and so the man said, "Good, I like Dewar's. I'll take that." Moments later he was sipping the Whisky with satisfaction. It had a calming effect after the stress of almost missing his flight. He struck up a conversation with the woman sitting next to him - the woman who like himself had almost missed her flight. "What do you do?" asked the man. "Oh, I work for Dewar's" said the woman modestly. "I created that Blend you are sipping." The story would have ended perfectly if they had fallen in love and lived happily ever after, but that only happens in the movies. Stephanie Macleod didn't need a mushy Hollywood ending to make her story any better. She had achieved what very few ever achieve and became a Master Blender for the prestigious company Dewar's - a company with a legacy dating back to 1846 when John Dewar founded the Whisky Brand bearing his surname. Later his sons John Jr. and Tommy would join him in the family business and the company became John Dewar and Sons.

Stephanie spent 4 years at Strathclyde University in Glasgow trying to unlock the mysteries of Whisky, studying the Cask aging process and trying to scientifically understand why Whisky tasted the way it did. She also studied the smell and taste of Wine from Northern Italy, chocolate, olive oil, cheese, even raspberry jam - almost anything you could taste or smell was studied but there was a particular emphasis on Whisky. Technically she was called a 'Sensory Analyst' and published scientific papers on her research. She was hired by Dewar's just as the Bacardi company took over the Brand. Under Bacardi, Stephanie saw the company expand from one to five Distilleries and one million to five million cases of products sold.

Stephanie describes the process of rising to the position of Master Blender as being in the right place at the right time. There are very few such jobs and the position is usually occupied until the current occupant retires. These Master Blenders take protégé's under their wings, and Stephanie was very fortunate to be trained up by Tommy Aitken, the previous Dewar's Master Blender. When he retired, Stephanie became the new Master Blender for the company. Writing about this achievement for Forbes, Larry Olmstead said: "Few industries remain as traditionally masculine as the Scotch Whisky business, where those at the highest levels of Whisky making are almost exclusively male. If you don't believe me, just Google "Scotch-women-master-Distiller." I did and found exactly one candidate for the highest position available in the creation of Single Malt Whisky - Kristy Lark - except she's making Whisky in Tasmania, about as far as you can get from Scotland. But the glass-bottle ceiling is not completely hopeless. After all, Scotch Whisky is not just about Single Malt Distillation – we drink far more Blended Scotch than Single Malt or Single Barrel, and few Brands sell more Scotch than John Dewar's & Sons, better known simply as Dewar's. To say Dewar's is a woman's Whisky is both accurate and an anomaly, since the person in charge of making the stuff, since 2006, has been Master Blender Stephanie Macleod, only the seventh person in the 160-year history of the venerable house to hold that title, and the first female to do so."

Once in the role, Stephanie created the first of her own Blends, Dewar's 15. This was an exciting and proud moment of her life, and when they were Bottling the Blend she told us that she wept like a mother for a new baby. One of the big marketplaces for Dewar's 15 has been Taiwan. Stephanie also was in charge of the very popular Single Cask releases out of Casks like Madeira and Sherry. She married a 12 YO Dewar's in a Sherry Cask - wondering what would happen, and it turned out exceptionally well. She feels that such experimentation was in the Spirits of Tommy Dewar who was always trying new things.

Tommy was largely responsible for getting the word out about Dewar's across the globe and there was something of the character of master showman P. T. Barnum in Tommy Dewar. He would out-exhibit other Whisky exhibitors in trade shows across the globe by pulling off stunts such as showing up with a piper in highland dress who would drown out the noise of the competition with the bagpipes; such a stunt would make the papers as well. "Advertise or fossilize!" was his philosophy and to show that he meant what he said, he even displayed a giant neon sign on Waterloo Bridge in London that depicted a piper that would take a sip of Dewar's once or twice a minute.

Tommy's father, John Dewar was also a character. There is a story that he and his Whisky rival Arthur Bell met at a pub before a church service they were both supposed to attend. At the bar, Arthur Bell said to John, "What will you have?" John proceeded to order a Bell's. Bell was surprised at this and wondered why he didn't order a Dewar's. John explained, "It wouldn't do to go into the church service smelling of Whisky."

Now looking after the Blending legacy of John Dewar and his sons, Stephanie Macleod has to make sure the 40 different Whiskies from all over Scotland that go into the Dewar's Blend are all in the right proportion, constantly making sure the Blends are to the highest standards, and like Tommy Dewar, she is out and about representing the Dewar name and its Whiskies.

Dewar's makes the following Blends and Single Malts:

DEWAR'S WHITE LABEL
DEWAR'S 12 YO
DEWAR'S Signature
DEWAR'S 18 YO
WILLIAM LAWSON'S Finest Blended
WILLIAM LAWSON'S SCOTTISH GOLD
ABERFELDY 12 YO
ABERFELDY 21 YO
GLEN DEVERON 10 YO
ROYAL BRACKLA
CRAIGALLACHIE
AULTMORE

A ROYAL BLEND

There were 16 months that went into the planning for the one day event - the first coronation of a monarch in the modern era, the first such event in history to be broadcast on television. It was even filmed in 3D back in 1953. Elizabeth the 2nd was all of 26 years of age. The event culminated in the Queen being invested with bracelets called Armills, a Robe Royal and the Sovereign's Orb, followed by the Queen's Ring, the Sceptre with the Cross, and the Sceptre with the Dove. Holding the sceptres, Queen Elizabeth was crowned by the Archbishop of Canterbury. The crowd shouted "God save the Queen!" and at the exact moment the crown touched her head, there was the sound of coronets and a 21-gun salute was fired from the Tower of London.

Chivas Brothers also celebrated Elizabeth's ascension to the throne by releasing Chivas Royal Salute on the day of the coronation, using Whiskies in the Blend that are all 21 YO - 21 to match the number of shots fired in the high military honour. For a mere 20,000 pounds or so you can purchase a Bottle of Royal Salute that dates back to the time of the Coronation although there are far more affordable Bottles of Royal Salute for sale along with the flagship Brand of the Chivas Brothers, Chivas Regal.

Cms.asia-city.com interviewed the Master Blender for Chivas Brothers, Colin Scott and asked him to explain what his job was. He replied "There are two arts to Blending. First, there's selecting the malts, the different grains and harmonizing them, bringing them together. When I created Chivas 18, I used Chivas 12 as a reference. It's blended in a tradition, a style that came from the Chivas brothers in the 1800s. It's similar in style but different in taste. And the second part is maintaining the taste. The Whiskies were put into Casks 20 years ago. Since then, some Distilleries may have stopped producing. That means those Single Malts come out of the Blend, and that changes the harmony, the experience. So we look at what other Whiskies we could bring in, change the percentages and keep the same taste."

PERPETUAL MOTION

Late in the 19th century, a Scottish grocer and his family decided to branch out into Spirits and took up Blending Whisky. The family name was Gloag. We would not be talking about their Famous Blend over a hundred years later if they had named their Whisky the Famous Gloag. There would be no iconic image indelibly Branded on our minds if there was a picture-less label from a Famous Gloag Bottle? Wisely the Gloags chose another name based on the national game bird of Scotland, and thus the Famous Grouse was hatched. The daughter of Matthew Gloag then painted the iconic image of the bird that made the Whisky one of the most recognizable Brands in all the world.

Gordon Motion told us about having the current custodial responsibility over the Blend among other products being released by the Edrington Group.

Gordon wasn't exactly following in the footsteps of anyone in his family. His own grandfather was in the Temperance Movement so for the grandson to go into the Whisky Industry was a reversal of the family tradition. Initially Gordon was studying computer science at Edinburgh's Heriot Watt University. A trip with friends to visit some Distilleries inspired Gordon to change his career plan. He did finish his computing degree but then continued with a post graduate brewing and Distilling degree. Eventually he was hired by the Edrington Group and worked for a decade with Edrington's longtime Master Blender, John Ramsay. When Ramsay retired after 43 years, Gordon stepped into the Master Blender role and now works in a lab with 11,000 Whisky samples at his beckon call. He told Whisky Magazine, "We've had to produce more new Whiskies in the last 10 years than were ever produced in the previous 90 years, and this is a constant challenge for Blenders."

The peated Black Grouse, which was developed for the Scandinavian market, and the Snow Grouse are but some of the Blends Gordon has had a hand in. Commenting on the Snow Grouse Blend, Susan Dick writes, "Among the Bottles and jars crammed into his sampling room at the plant near Drumchapel in Glasgow sits a frosted glass litre Bottle of Scotch, distinct from its more traditional neighbours thanks to the cleverly designed grouse etched on its front and the Skye mountain scene shining through from the back, creating a quirky 3D effect. The Bottle is clearly from the Famous Grouse stable, but its contents are a new concept of Blended Grain Whiskies - Blends are typically created using varieties of malts - resulting in a sweeter, perhaps more female-friendly brew. It's called Snow Grouse and, as the Whisky Industry jostles to attract a new generation of Scotch drinkers, it's about to propel the traditional "comfy slippers beside a roaring fire" image of Whisky straight into the 21st century. 'You can shove this in the freezer,' explains Gordon, "and drink it ice cold. One of the comments from consumers is that they don't drink Whisky because they don't like the smell of it. But when you take the temperature to -18, you can't smell it. When you taste it, it still warms you up and you still have all the flavours in your mouth."

With all the work Gordon has to do, it sounds like he is in a state of perpetual motion.

THE SHIP NAMED AFTER A SHIRT

Cutty Sark was a short shirt before it was a ship and before it was yet another iconic Brand and Blend of Whisky. When ship owner, John Willis, sought to name the new clipper ship, he looked to the literature of his native Scotland and chose the name Cutty Sark from the famous Burns poem, Tam O' Shanter. One explanation touted as to why the name was chosen was because the scantily clad cutty sark witch in the poem was the fastest of

the witches chasing Tam O'Shanter and almost caught him and so it was an appropriate name for a ship built for speed. That same witch was carved into the figurehead of the ship.

Walter and Francis Berry and Hugh Rudd of the Berry Brothers and Rudd, together with the artist James McBey wanted a light, smooth, easy to drink Whisky Blend designed to be exported to the rest of the world and specifically America, despite the onset of Prohibition. The Cutty Sark came to symbolize that transatlantic crossing, that spirit of adventure.

Brand Controller Jason R. Craig wrote, "The creators of the Cutty Sark – both the ship and the Whisky – were brave and pioneering; these original traits still run deep within the Brand's DNA. We have embraced these qualities in the Brand's philosophy and look forward to new adventures on our voyage to faraway horizons."

Climbing aboard the ship recently was its new Master Blender, Kirsteen Campbell, who like Gordon Motion, was mentored by John Ramsay. Kirsteen studied food science and was looking for a job in a laboratory. She did analysis and testing at the Cameron Bridge Distillery in Fife, before working at the Scotch Whisky Research Institute in Edinburgh. She then was hired by Edrington and when John Ramsay retired, she became the Master Blender for the Brand that Edrington had acquired from Berry Brothers and Rudd.

She has the responsibility of making sure the original Blend is consistent. Kirsteen told us that it was a fun Blend to work with. In the 1920s, the Blend had purposely gone light while heavy bodied Whiskies were in vogue at the time. To this day, it retains those vanilla and apple tastes.

Despite being fun to work with, Kirsteen has to make sure the million Bottles of the original Blend all taste the same and are of the same quality. In the book about the Brand, Kirsteen explains that "Cutty is based around a core of the Macallan, Highland Park, Glenrothes, Tamdhu, Bunnahabbain and Glengoyne malts. "Each Blend is a 103 butt equivalents of malt and grain and I do a 120 Blends a year."

Commenting on the task, Whisky writer David Broom writes, "I did a quick calculation – that's up to 25,000 Casks a year depending on size, all of them different, all of them to be checked, all of which somehow have to be marshalled to make a consistent product. Use a computer you say? You could, were it not for the fact that every case is different and, what's more, the Casks available may vary for each Blend of Bottling because of stock issues."

That is just some of the work involved in maintaining the original Blend, but Kirsteen has had to work on other Blends such as the limited release Tam O' Shanter and the Blend she created herself, Cutty Storm.

Cutty Storm was Kirsteen's first opportunity to develop a Whisky Blend from scratch and she used more mature aged Whiskies and came up with a spicy Blend- she was delighted with the achievement and right she should be.

The range of Cutty Sark includes the original Blend, the 12 YO, the 18 YO, Cutty Storm and the 25 YO Tam O Shanter.

COMPASS BOX WHISKY AND ISLE OF MULL BLENDED WHISKY:

John Glaser of Compass Box Whisky had a thing or two to say about the perception of Blended Whisky and challenging tradition. We had a good conversation about these topics. Before we get to that conversation, some background of Compass Box, its history and the traditions it is challenging should be discussed with a detour to talk about Isle of Mull Blended Whisky along the way.

Compared to many other Whisky companies that have been around for hundreds of years, Compass Box Whisky is recently new to the scene, and is only a 13 YO company at the time this book was written. That is younger than many Whiskies! Though there are many challenges that come with being new, Compass Box also have the advantages of youthfulness, energy, innovation and they don't have hundred year old traditions that they have to uphold. In the Whisky Industry there are some traditions that have past there sell-by date. When traditions start they are ironically not traditional but Brand new ideas that may even be considered radical for their day. Time then marches on while the tradition stays in the past becoming as old fashioned as kerosene lamps became after the light bulb was invented or the VHS player after DVD and Blu Ray.

Here is an example of how a tradition gets started and quickly becomes useless: It is said that Catherine the Great of Russia entered into what is now Red Square in Moscow; she saw a beautiful flower coming up through the ground in the Russian Spring and said, "Guard stand here and make sure no one steps on this flower." For the next two hundred years - through sun, wind, rain, snow night and day 24/7 there was a guard standing in that spot out in the middle of Red Square. Most guards were in useful places such as entrance ways, but one lone guard was always standing in uniform, stiff and straight in an obscure spot in the middle of the square. Finally a high ranking officer reviewed the situation, went to the guard in the middle of the square and asked, "Soldier, why are you standing in this spot?"

"I have no idea, Sir!" replied the soldier.

They traced the order back to Catherine the Great and decided to change the outdated rule. Some Whisky companies are resistant to change. Other Whisky companies are trying to change their approach to marketing, to labelling, to competing. They are trying to think ahead in order to reach a new generation of consumers. Dan Tullio of Canadian Club told us that they were purposely marketing their Brand to 26 YO males and using social media and advertising that would associate Canadian Club with everything that an upwardly mobile 26 YO in today's world would want to aspire to. Some Whisky Brands are trying to change what can be a fuddy-duddy image of Whisky and an association as a drink for grandfathers and elderly gentlemen who are set in their ways.

Neil Morrison and Paul Mclean are the young men behind the new Blend Isle of Mull Whisky and they are very much of the new generation of Whisky makers who are trying to reach their own generation in the marketing and packaging of the newly launched Brand. Neil runs a pub on the Isle of Mull called MacGochan's and he organizes music festivals on the isle. He also promotes the Brand he launched. Neil and Paul used a local island artist in the labelling and packaging - they wanted it to appeal to the young generation and not look like their grandfather's Whisky. The Bottle art is shiny red against black and depicts a stormy sea. They wanted to capture that storm in a Bottle look which was energetic and exciting! The press release said, " — two local boys taking the Whisky world by storm!" They describe the Blend as a "Perfect Storm" and say it is an "ideal Blend of the finest Malt and Grain Whiskies from around Scotland, and that means an amazingly smooth and palatable Whisky."

John Glaser of Compass Box Whisky, is a decade or two more experienced than the young men on the Isle of Mull, but he has given his company a youthful zest and he is an example of the upwardly mobile sophistication of a new generation of entrepreneurial Whisky-makers and innovators. He was quite happy to challenge the status quo. He was a marketing director for Johnnie Walker and then began his own London based company. The Compass Box site says, "American ex-pat John Glaser entered the world of Scotch Whisky, learning his art through one of the Industry's largest companies. In 2000, he started Compass Box Whisky Company, based on his commitment to evolving practices in the Industry to make great Scotch Whisky more approachable and relevant to more people. From the beginning, his vision has been to create one of Scotland's finest and most exciting Whisky companies, re-establishing the standards for quality and style in the Industry. Today, John Glaser is considered one of the most respected Whisky-makers of his generation."

Some have unfairly criticised Compass Box and called them

gimmicky with Brand names such as Hedonism, Peat Monster, Flaming Heart, Morpheus, Orangerie Great King Street, The Spice Tree, Oak Cross, Asyla, and Optimism but Richard Paterson thinks that what they are doing is innovative and clever. He says that they are exciting today's consumer. "Packaging is so important," he told us. The Nose knows something about packaging. The Shackleton (the re-created Whisky Blend based on the actual Whisky Ernest Shackleton took to the Antarctic) won an award for its packaging. Mr. Paterson despairs of some of the Whisky companies who think the Whisky -even quality Whisky - will sell itself all by itself and that Brand labelling and presentation are an afterthought. "Why change the old label because if it ain't broke, don't fix it?" is the attitude. Those with foresight can see the tweaks and fixes that are needed. Many saw that re-branding for the Japanese market was important and had no qualms about making changes to the packaging for Japan but changing up at home was much harder to make happen.

JOHN GLASER AND THE SINGLE MALT MYTH

John Glaser told us that his background was in Wine and that he had no intention of going into Whisky. Through university and through literature he decided to enter the Wine Industry and had experience working in California, France and the North East of the U.S. He was then offered a job by a Wine and Spirits marketing company in New York - although the job was in Whisky rather than Wine. Though he didn't consider himself a Whisky person, he took the job anyway, thinking that he would do this for a while and then go back to Wine. Instead he was sent on a two week trip to Scotland and in his words, "hasn't look back since." He has remained working with Whisky to this day and after a time marketing Johnnie Walker, he decided to strike out on his own. "I thought I could make more of a mark on the world and could do more good for Scotch Whisky by starting my own company." His view was that people would more likely listen to the individual with real passion than the impersonal big Brands and big companies with all their corporate interest in the bottom line ahead of Whisky-making art and integrity. According to the official website, "Glaser established Compass Box out of a desire to make great Scotch Whisky more approachable and relevant to more people: evolving traditional Whisky-making, innovating, inspiring, discovering, all in the name of making

Whisky better, without compromise. Part Whisky negociant, part perfume-maker in approach, John first creates every Whisky in his head, as an idea, a style he wants to bring to life. He then seeks out and hand-selects the individual Casks to make it happen. He typically uses three or four different Distillery Whiskies in his recipes; an approach that allows him to showcase the distinct character of particular Whiskies, while skilfully complementing their personalities." Working with Blended Whisky was a platform for creativity and to make Whiskies no single Distillery could make. John acknowledged that Blending is misunderstood and there is a perception that the Single Malt is superior to any Blend. He calls this the Single Malt Myth. "Single Malts can be some of the best Whiskies on the planet," said John, "Not all, but some. Blends are perceived as a cheap way to make Whisky and that is because some Blends are mass produced at the lowest possible cost - there is a heavy emphasis on Grain Whisky with only a little Malt Whisky Blended in - and this is uninteresting to the Whisky Connoisseur. Some 60 Bottlings later, we're known around the world for changing the way people think about Blends."

John spoke to us about the Great King Street Blended Whisky that Compass Box produces. They were asked to come up with a Blend for a New York Whisky Festival and decided to harken back to the way Blends were first approached in the early pioneer days of Blending. Here is how Compass Box describes the Great King Street: "In a world where Malt Whiskies get all the attention, people often overlook the pleasures of good Blended Scotch Whisky. We believe it is time for the world to take a fresh look at this style, and that is why we have created Great King Street. More than just a new Brand, Great King Street is a mission, a mission dedicated to reviving interest in one style of Whisky only: Blended Scotch Whisky. This is the style of Scotch Whisky that combines flavourful Single Malt Whiskies with delicate, elegant Single Grain Whiskies.

There are good reasons why the Blending of Grain Whisky and Malt Whisky has been the mainstay of the Scotch business for well over 150 years." Unlike Colonel Sanders of KFC, John doesn't keep the Great King Street Blend recipe all that secret. Proud of their process, they claim that they do things differently to everyone else, although the other Master Blenders we've spoken to also strive for perfection in the mix of grain to malt

Whiskies and for choosing Casks. How different their approach is could be argued about but the striving for a quality product is beyond debate.
One controversy should be talked about before we move on and this relates to the hullabaloo John Glaser caused when experimenting with a Cask maturation technique. This storm in a tea cup (or should I say Whisky glass?) illustrates two important matters that can sometimes crash into each other. On the one hand you have very stringent laws that police what can be called Scotch and you have Whisky makers pushing their art to the limit in their striving to create a new flavour, a new recipe a new Brand. Compass Box was creating a new Blend called the Spice Tree in which their Blend of Single Malt Distillates were undergoing a second maturation stage in Casks containing new French Oak inserts or inner staves. "So what?" most would argue. "You're supposed to use Oak Casks in the aging so why make such a fuss about new French Oak inner staves?"

The Scotch Whisky Association does make such a fuss and told Compass Box it was against the regulations and threatened legal action unless Compass Box halted production. Compass Box went on to produce Spice Tree but without the inner staves.
To John, Stephanie, Colin, Gordon, Kirsteen, Richard and all the other wonderfully mad scientists of malt, C. Ask Whisky would cheer you on to keep striving, perfecting, being creative and giving the Scotch Whisky Association sleepless nights of worry. Your experiments benefit all those partial to the taste of Uisge Beatha.

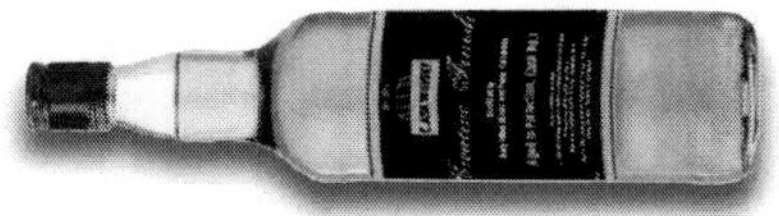

CHAPTER *six*

Whisky go hoard

He was Brazilian. His name was Claive Vidiz. He Collected Whisky from around the world amassing a record breaking Collection of 3,384 Bottles of everything from the common easy to obtain Whisky for the masses - to the rare, old and hard to find Whisky from a mothballed Distillery. Diageo paid 2 million pounds for the Vidiz Collection and it is now on display in the Scotch Whisky Experience that tourists can find on the Royal Mile in Edinburgh.

Perhaps you have the same bug as Vidiz? Let's talk. Pull up a couch! Lie back. Tell me about your mother - Are you ready for some psychoanalysis as we analyze your Whisky Collecting-mania, Whisky-chosis, your hoarding obsession, your drive, your hobby - whatever you want to call it? From one Collector to another, let me share with you my own Collecting quirks: I have been Collecting things since I was a child and toys were the kick-start to my own personal Collector-mania. I was a normal kid in that I liked to play with all these things, but I was just as happy to leave collectable toys in their own original packaging.

They were moments frozen in time, my own personal museum, part of my identity. Keeping the menagerie of untouched toys - every Star Wars figure, spaceship, light sabre anything to do with Star Wars or Matchbox toy cars - keeping them in pristine condition was just as fun as playing with the other toys. There was sentimental value attached. Many were special gifts from my parents on birthdays or Christmas. The thought of ripping them out of the package, getting them dirty and breaking them horrified me. I wanted to treasure these moments and my emotional connection to the gifts forever and so these many years later they are in the same exact condition. There were many toys played with and destroyed along the way, but as an adult, I found these again, and paid a dearer price than they had been all those years ago. Still, it wasn't about the money or the thought of making money from my Collections. It was about capturing those moments in time like a photograph and the nostalgic happy emotion that connected me to the toy and the time in my life. Toys led to other Collections. I gathered the complete Collection of the Scottish comic books, OOR Wullie and the Broons. I've been in the Music Industrysince my youth and so I Collected thousands of records, vinyl LPs, CDs, synthesizers and other musical equipment. I love football and so there is football memorabilia as well that I've Collected. The Collecting bug then moved on to great Bottles of Whisky. You open a nice Bottle and share a dram with friends and then that Bottle has a story, a night to remember and when these magic moments happen, there is a very good chance that Whisky will end up in my Collection and be as valuable to me as a 70 year old Glenlivet is to someone who Collects the oldest and priciest Whiskies.

I've had many a conversation with friends about retro-sweets. "Oh, do you remember that old sweet we used to get as a kid? Whatever happened to it? When did the company go out of business?" Just talking about it, makes you want it to magically come back. I've overheard many a similar conversation in Whisky circles. People talk about a 40 YO such and such a Whisky and it's the romance, the nostalgia, the pleasant memory combined with the fact that it is hard to find or there are only two or three Bottles of it left in the entire world - and it makes you want it that much more! Believe me fellow Collector, I get it!

Let me tell you about one Bottle in my growing Collection. This is also an opportunity to continue our conversation with Richard Paterson as he was the man behind it's re-creation. Here is the tale reproduced from the website about the Shackleton Whisky! "The Mackinlay's Rare Old Highland Malts are re-creations of the original Malt Whisky shipped to Antarctica in 1907 by the explorer Ernest Shackleton to fortify his 'Nimrod' Expedition. The story of how several wooden crates of this precious Whisky were abandoned to the Antarctic winter in early 1909, then rediscovered over a century later, is one that celebrates the enduring Spirit of both man and malt. Mackinlay's Rare Old Highland Malt was originally Distilled at Glen Mhor Distillery in Inverness, Scotland. It was a Whisky much enjoyed throughout the late 19th century, and was personally selected by Ernest Shackleton to help sustain his British Antarctic Expedition of 1907. The original Bottles were labelled the 'Endurance expedition', but the expedition actually sailed South onboard the Nimrod. Having set up a base camp at Cape Royds, Shackleton and his men ultimately failed to reach the South Pole, but they did return safely, and sailed for home in March 1909, leaving three crates of the malt buried in the ice. In 2007, whilst carrying out conservation work on the Shackleton's expedition hut, members of the New Zealand Antarctic Heritage Trust discovered the crates of Mackinlay's Rare Old Highland Malt. One was flown to Canterbury Museum in New Zealand for careful thawing. The conservation team recovered ten Bottles intact, and the Whisky they contained, now well over 100 years old, was described as 'a gift from Heaven' by Richard Paterson, the Master Blender at Whyte & Mackay, owners of the Mackinlay Brand. In 2011, three of the Bottles were flown back to home to Scotland for detailed scientific analysis. Analysis of the original Mackinlay's malt revealed the taste profile of the Whisky. The team also established the strength of the Whisky at 47.3% alc/vol, the fact that Orkney peat was used in the malting, and that the Spirit had been matured in American white Oak Sherry Casks. Inspired by this analysis, efforts to re-create the Whisky begun. Malts from Glen Mhor and Dalmore Distilleries were combined with others from Speyside and beyond. The result is a malt light honey in colour with an aroma that is soft, elegant and refined, and a taste that is both harmonious and exhilarating. This is a meticulous re-creation. It is the enduring Spirit of another time.

With the launch of the Shackleton Epic Expedition, and continued correspondence with Shackleton's granddaughter Alexandra and the Antarctic Heritage Trust, Richard Paterson was inspired to create a second edition of the Mackinlay's Rare Old Highland Malt - The JOURNEY. The Epic Expedition will attempt to replicate Shackle ton's "Double": his journey from Elephant Island to South Georgia, a distance of 800 miles over sea and ice. This will be done with the same kinds of equipment used in the 1916 expedition, including the Alexandra Shackleton, a replica of the 23ft open lifeboat used on the original voyage. The Journey Edition of Mackinlay's takes the same base of Single Malts used to create the original Discovery Edition and, still inspired by the original recipe, builds on them to create a noticeably different dram - a more elegant and refined interpretation." What a story! I have one of these Shackleton re-creations and it is special to me.

Richard Paterson told us the story of the Shackleton Blend this way and gave us additional details:

RICHARD PATERSON: There have been many special Whiskies in my life - The Dalmore, the Jura - but the Shackleton was one of the highlights of my career. We got a call about the 3 cases of Shackleton Whisky left behind in Antarctica in 2007. We decided we had to somehow obtain the Whisky. There were negotiations over the years which resulted in a plane trip to New Zealand in 2011 and the permission to bring back 3 Bottles of the original Shackleton Whisky back to Scotland. The container with the Whisky kept the Bottles frozen and in the same temperature as they had been in the Antarctic for a 103 years. The case was handcuffed and watched over. We had to sign legal documents to say we wouldn't do anything but analyze the Whisky and keep the Bottle in the same condition it was found in. That meant going to Invergordon and keeping the Bottle in the same freezing temperatures. It took a lot of time and care but we managed to insert a syringe into the cork of the Bottles and extract the Whisky. National Geographic was there filming this historic event. The Whisky then warmed in the glass. I began to nose it and the Whisky began to reveal itself. There was that whisper of peat - pear, apple, peaches - all these floral notes began to open up. I nosed it, one hour later, two hours, three, four - twenty-four - fifty six hours until I was absolutely satisfied that I got into every nook, cranny and crevice of the Whisky. The analysis revealed the American White Oak, The Sherry wood, Chivali barley, peat from Orkney, the 6 or 7 year age and the distillation from the Glen Mhor Distillery. From this information I Blended the Whisky, re-creating the Mackinlay Whisky that Ernest Shackleton had taken with him. We produced a 100,000 Bottles. Just last week the original Shackleton Bottles were repatriated back to Antarctica.

C. ASK: Do you have any upcoming special projects like the Shackleton that you are working on at the moment - are there any more special surprises in store?

RICHARD PATERSON: There's always a number of these special projects going on. Obviously, there are the Single Malts, Dalmore, Jura, Fettercairn, Tamnavulin. Oh we got some big ones, some exciting ones coming in - in regard to Blending or creating a vatted malt again, we got a few things in the wings, but they're not for general release for sometime. You have to remember that all these so called expressions, these enhancements using different Casks are literally going on all the time. I mean, I just did a two hour tasting out on Jura and we're looking to see the development of some of these Casks we have out there. There are always some surprises and some disappointments, but that is what goes on in the Whisky Industry. Many of my fellow Master Blenders, my counterparts in other companies and Distilleries might look to a Cask and think they are going to get something - but they get something different that takes them in a different direction, or they'll let the Cask sleep for another few years. Suddenly in the third or fourth year the Whisky in that Cask begins to shine! That's exciting and then we excite our consumers.

C. ASK: Willie Cochrane at Isle of Jura was telling me that one of your favourite Isle of Jura's in the range is the 16 YO. That might surprise some people who think you would always opt for the oldest Bottle such as the 30 or 40 YO Jura?

RICHARD PATERSON: Every time I'm out on Jura, I take a Bottle of the 16 YO, walk out to the pier, sit there, smoke a cigar, sip the 16 YO Jura and enjoy the beauty and tranquillity of Small Isle Bay. Sometimes the bay is covered in mist, or perhaps there is wind on my face or a bit of rain. The peace, the isolation, the loneliness and loveliness are all epitomised in that 16 YO Jura. I won't drink Jura Superstition there. I'll drink that elsewhere such as on top of the mountain of gold on one of the paths - sensational! There is the 30 YO and the 40 YO, which are wonderful, but to me the 16 YO Jura on that spot on the pier is Jura to me.

C. ASK: Stories that go with Whiskies like Shackleton or Jura make the Whisky so much more meaningful. Do you have any particularly humorous stories that go with your adventures around the world with Whisky?

RICHARD PATERSON: I was in Japan at a Whisky event. I was put up in a very nice hotel room, and alone in my hotel room, I was stark naked. I had been given a meal via room service earlier and decided to put the tray out in the hallway so someone could pick it up. I peeked out. The hallway was completely vacant and so I stepped into the hallway, put the tray down and just as I turned to go back in, the door closed and locked behind me. There I am in Japan, naked in a hotel hallway with no way to get back in my room. I feared that any minute a maid or another guest would appear. I was worried that my nickname 'The Nose' would be replaced by the name of the body part I was trying to hide. I knocked on the doorway across the hall and woke one of the Japanese participants in the Whisky event. He opened the door, looked at me and must have thought, "Richard, I really don't know you that well." Eventually my Japanese colleague came to understand what had happened and helped me to get back in my room with what little dignity I had left."

YOUR KIND OF COLLECTION

You will have your own angle on a Collection. Some of you will want to Collect re-creations of Whiskies they don't make any more from Distilleries that went out of business. Some of you will Collect all the Whiskies made in Islay or from every working Distillery in Scotland. Some will want a Whisky Collection from around the world featuring many of the Whiskies talked about in this book. Some will Collect American-made Bourbons and Moonshine. Some will Collect the most far-out, outrageous kinds of Whisky they can find, even the ones with pickled snakes from South East Asia for your scary Halloween Collection. Some of the people who can afford it will go after the rare, old hundred thousand dollar Bottles of Whisky. But why do we do it? Why do I like to Collect? Why do you like to Collect? Let's get some more in depth psychological analysis.

"We use keepsakes to stimulate memory, especially to trigger fond memories," says psychiatrist Terry Shortage in an article entitled, 'Why Do We Like Old Things? Some Ruminations on History and Memory'." "But even if memory cannot be relied upon to faithfully reproduce a record of the past, it remains vital to our understanding of the past." He nailed me. Guilty as charged. Just to hammer home the point, Diane Fricke, writing about Collecting for horizononlines.org comments, "As an anthropologist from the University of California, Marjorie Akin is an expert on the subject of why people Collect. Her essay, "Passionate Possession: The Formation of Private Collections," shares Shoptaugh's idea that people Collect for a connection to the past and memories. "Objects can connect the Collector to the historic, valued past," Akin writes. Akin also includes four other reasons why people Collect. "The first is to satisfy a sense of personal aesthetics. Some Collect to please personal tastes. Others Collect items that are weird or unusual to show individualism. Another reason is for the Collector's need to be complete. Akin said she has seen people cry out in relief once their Collection is complete." Several of these reasons apply to me and to you I suspect. They've figured us out!

The psychology of Collecting is closely related to the more disturbing psychology of hunting and why people feel the need or enjoy the sport of going out and shooting an animal. Talking about the reasons some people like to hunt, Dr. David Samuel says, "Study anthropological literature and you will find that for hundreds of years, if not more, high social status went to early hunters who were the most fit and who killed the most and biggest animals. For example, male members of the King Bushman could only marry after they killed a large herbivore. Most early peoples advertised their hunting success by displaying trophies. Most primitive peoples still do today. Many tribes wore hair bracelets. Mbuti Pygmies killed large antelopes and gave them to the parents of the bride-to-be before the parents allowed a marriage. Males became chiefs of the Sciriono peoples of the Amazon based on their hunting abilities. In many early tribes the best hunters became the leaders and chiefs. The examples go on and on. There was selective advantage in being a good hunter."

Is that what we Whisky hunters are? Is this just some kind of primitive ritual in our lives, but instead of bagging a lion, we bagged an exclusive, rare and valuable Whisky? Any type of Collecting can of course go over the top and underneath it could be a more disturbing need than connecting to a good memory. Gareth Patterson, AKA 'The Lion Man' and an anti-hunting activist, equates the darker side of hunting with serial killing which can be the most extreme and disturbing form of this Collector-mania and he makes the assertions that trophy hunting and serial killing can be shown by science to be related. The disorder DMGDS (Diminutive Male Genitalia Disorder Syndrome) and the serial murderers addiction to killing and the trophy hunters addiction to killing animals have a connection is what the Lion Man says. If I understand this idea correctly, the twisted person has some kind of need to compensate, to dominate, to capture and one of the reasons for this is that he has a small penis? That might be your reason for Collecting the most Whisky, but not mine. If you're having a friendly competition with a fellow Collector, you can always play the DMGDS card and say, "I understand your Whisky Collecting obsession. I Collect for fun, for interest, for nostalgia, but I think you Collect because you have DMGDS." You can then have a lot of fun explaining what DMGDS is in whatever terms you wish to use to your rival.

A COLLECTION OF WISE COUNSEL

We've Collected some advice about Collecting and here is what the Whisky Emporium recommends that you should look out for. They start with limited special editions and say, "Many Distilleries occasionally produce limited editions, anniversary or annual Bottling and commemorative Bottlings for special events. These are often highly Collectible as they are by nature, limited in their production. But how do we know they are limited? What do we look for?" They answer by saying, "Individual Bottle numbers and number produced. Preferably less than 2000 and Single Cask Bottlings also individually numbered."

Stephen Davies of Welsh Whisky told us they would have special Bottlings on special occasion in Wales such as when the rugby team won the Six Nations Tournament or to commemorate important events in the history of Wales such as: The Icons of Wales series consists of special Bottlings, each one celebrating a person, milestone or event from Welsh history with international significance. The Penderyn website says, "The Distillery plans to release 50 editions in total, each one strictly limited in number and containing Penderyn's award-winning Welsh Spirit. The series seeks to celebrate the finest moments from Welsh history that showcase independence, innovation and individuality, raising the profile of these moments both in Wales and abroad. The first edition is Penderyn Red Flag, commemorating the first time that a red flag was raised as a symbol of social protest: during the 1831 Merthyr Rising which ended in the execution of miner Dic Penderyn."

After Limited Editions, Whisky Emporium advises the Collector to go look for the remaining Bottles left over from closed Distilleries. They say, "Many once thriving Scottish Distilleries have in recent years been closed. Some were totally demolished and then the sites redeveloped. However, as the Whisky takes many years to mature in Oak Casks, their products may still be available at the moment, but in some cases, not for too much longer. Typical examples which can still be found and which should be considered for your Collections whilst they are still available, include: Rosebank, Dallas Dhu and Port Ellen."

After Limited Editions, and remaining product from closed Distilleries, it's the older Bottles of Brands still in production before the Brand had a make-over and label change. Whisky Emporium says, "Over time, Distilleries choose to re-market and re-label their products. Although not originally considered 'Collectable', these once standard Bottlings may become more Collectable as they are discontinued or even replaced by new Bottles, labels and packaging. Some good examples are the old Ardbeg 10 years (Black Label), the now discontinued Ardbeg 17, 1975 & 1977 and an old Dufftown Glenlivet from the 1980's."

Whisky-news.com offers some further common sense do and don't type tips. Most are obvious, "Duh, no kidding," type tips which your mother might have given you, but there is the occasional surprise of "Good advice that I didn't think about that before." Here are some of the less obvious tips from their list:

Tip 3: Ensure that you always have readily available budget in case of immediate opportunities. Sellers do not wait and first come first serve is the rule.

Tip 6: Be aware of fakes. For very old Bottles, it is preferable to work with renowned retailers.

Tip 10: Store you Bottles in an upright position, preferably protected from light. You might consider wrapping the cap with Parafilm to reduce evaporation.

Tip 12: Maintain an up to date list of your Collection to avoid buying Bottles that you already own.

Tip 13: Keep your receipts and invoice to document the history of your Bottles.

Patrick Brossard of the site Whisky-news.com offers some personal opinions about Whiskies he thinks Collectors should think about. You might have different opinions based on your angle, your interest and what you are after, but it is interesting to here Mr. Brossards reasons. The list is long, but we quote three of his choices:

"Karuizawa: This is the current blue chip in the Whiskies and the only non-Scottish on my list. The 1971 and 1968 were superb Whiskies, as well as the most recent 1975 and 1976 Single Casks. Single Casks of this Distillery are very sought after and selling out within a few hours. The Distillery is closed, had a small production and used only golden promise barley and top quality Sherry Casks. All the factors contributing to a high Collectability.

Ardbeg: All the Ardbeg Single Casks and regular Bottles Distilled until mid 1970s are very sought after by the Collectors and enthusiasts. This corresponds to the period of production, when floor maltings were still in use (partially). Products were very good, but some versions from the 1960 were of lesser quality, due to some poor quality Cask management. Independent Bottling of this period from Signatory, Cadenhead's, Kingsbury, Douglas Laing, Samaroli and other Independent Bottlers are sought after too. Whiskies Distilled in the 1990s and afterwards are still Collectable, but their prices include a rather hefty "Collectible" value. These will be also the first victims of a decrease in popularity in Islay and peated Whiskies.

Ardmore: A very good Distillery, not much sought after by the Collectors, with the notable exception of the excellent 12 YO Centenary Bottling and the very rare Ardmore 15 and 16 years old Bottled a few decades ago for the Managers."

MEET THE INDEPENDENT BOTTLERS

We will be here all day if we introduced you to every Independent Bottler in the world so we'll stick to the Bottlers at the Hart of the Scotch Whisky Industry- one of these Bottlers does have Hart in the title by the way, as in the Hart Brothers. We will meet Alistair Hart shortly, but also Stewart Lang of Douglas Laing, Euan Shand of Duncan Taylor, Michael Urquhart of Gordon and MacPhail and Ronnie Cox of Berry Brothers and Rudd - all of whom could point you in the direction of great Collectables.

What is an Independent Bottler you might ask? Think about the Distillery for a second. They are always planning for the future. Even if they have massive amounts of space to store Casks, there is still a limit to how many Casks they can store. Each Cask is an investment that will mature overtime and reap financial benefits in the future, but not right now and possibly not for many years. Perhaps the Distillery is cash strapped or about to go under because of the tumultuous economic times. Along comes an Independent Bottler with cash in hand. They'll buy that excess Distilled Spirit produced at your Distillery, take it away for maturing and to use in their own Blends and for their own special Bottlings of a Single Malt from that Distillery. They have provided a great service by rescuing many a Cask from a Distillery being mothballed, keeping alive what is left of say Port Ellen or Rosebank Whisky from the now defunct Distilleries. That is why the Independent Bottlers are an advisable place to shop if you are looking for rare, old and hard to obtain Whiskies for your Collection.

Scottishwhisky.net explains their role in this way: "It has become customary for Distilleries to sell Barrels of Whisky to Blenders and Independent Bottlers as a means of making additional income. In fact, some Distilleries exist solely to serve Independent Bottlers, and do not market any Brands themselves. Distilleries also pass on Barrels of Whisky to ensure consistency. When Blending Whisky, they ensure consistency by using Barrels with similar flavours. If a particular flavour is notably different, it may be deemed uncharacteristic of the Distillery and as such cannot be used in "official" product Bottling. Whiskies Bottled by Independent Bottlers may or may not be labelled with the Distillery of origin, but tend not to use the Distillery's trademarks such as logos, fonts and images as they may not have the authorization to do so."

Here is a fairly comprehensive list of UK based Independent Bottlers who specialise in Scotch Whisky:

1. Adelphi, 2. Alchemist, 3. Berry Brothers and Rudd, 4. Blackadder, 5. Brands Development Worldwide, 6. Cadenhead, 7. Clydesdale, 8. Compass Box Whisky 9. Douglas Laing, 10. Douglas Murdoch 11. Duncan Taylor 12. Gordon & MacPhail 13. Hart Brothers 14. Lorne Mackillop - Mackillop's Choice 15. Ian Macleod 16. James McArthur 17. Meadowside Blending Co 18. Praban Na Linne Ltd. 19. Scottish Malt Whisky Society 20. Scott's Selection, 21. Signatory, 22. The Vintage Malt Whisky Company,

23. The Queen of the Moorland, 24. Whiskies of the World 25. Whisky Castle.

You Collectors will have to go treasure hunting through the online shops of each Independent Bottler on your own. We have space to introduce you to six of these companies and the people behind them.

THE MASTER OF WINE

If I had told my parents I wanted to go to Wine University to study Wine, they would have slapped me on the side of the head. Most students major in Wine anyway with minors in Beer-ology, but Surprise! Surprise! - There is actually a very rigorous and demanding academic Institute of Wine with the pedigree of Oxford, Cambridge, Harvard or Princeton in the Wine world.

Only a few in the 50 year history of the Institute of Masters of Wine have attained the high position of a true Master of Wine and yet, at a relatively young age, Lorne Mackillop attained this lofty title. Writing about Lorne Mackillop for Whisky Magazine, Tom Bruce-Gardyne said: "On leaving London University with a degree in comparative physiology and zoology in the mid-70s, Lorne Mackillop hardly intended a career in the booze trade, let alone Whisky. But when the original plan of becoming a doctor fell through, he found his old holiday job, delivering Wine by bicycle round Belgravia for André Simon, a useful stop-gap. Soon he was hooked, the bike gave way to a van, and by clambering up the ladder of Wine trade exams found himself aged 28, the youngest Master of Wine in 1984." It should also be noted that Lorne is a clan chief of the Mackillop Clan - a clan almost all wiped out in the battle of Culloden apart from two teen-aged boys who carried on the name. The ups and downs of Wine led Lorne to turn his talents to Whisky. He now looks after the exports for much of the world on behalf of Angus Dundee. The Glencadam and Tomintoul Distilleries are all part of the Angus Dundee Company along with Blends such as Parkers, Smokey Joe, Big Ben, Old Ballantruan, Scottish Royal and their own Angus Dundee label Blend. Then there is Mackillop's Choice where he uses all the science of Wine and Whisky he knows to select the Casks and Bottles he can proudly put his name to.

www.askwhisky.co.uk

Collector's take note: a Mackillop's Choice is always about Single Cask Bottling. Like fingerprints, snowflakes and blades of grass, no two wooden Casks are alike even if they are made from the same type of wood to the strict Industry standards that a Cask must adhere to.

No inner stave of wood is like the other, the point being, that no Whisky coming from a Cask will be exactly like the Whisky in the Cask next to it - even if the Spirit came from the same recipe and from the same Distillery. Bruce-Gardyne writes, "...Mackillop's Choice was launched in New York, offering mainly Speysides, all over 28 years of age including Glen Keith, Miltonduff and Tamdhu. This has grown to a current range of 'cased stock' with 22 Bottlings – from a Tomintoul '66 to Caol Ila '89, and a larger selection of 80 'whole Casks' Bottled on demand for the company's importers outside Europe. Some Distilleries are mothballed and some gone for good like Glenesk and Millburn. The philosophy behind it reflects fine Wine which revels in the way one vintage can be poor and the next sublime. In the same spirit, Mackillop's Choice swims against the mainstream where Whisky Brands have to be consistent year in year out. "I want the variation," declares Lorne. "No two Casks are the same and I delight in that difference. Also, a Single Cask is finite – it contains perhaps 300 Bottles, and that's what makes it so unique." Lorne is very particular, rejecting 80 percent of the Casks he looks at. He has been quoted as saying, "When you get a really nice Cask in amongst a batch of others, it just shines out like sun from behind a cloud. It is my name on the Bottle, my signature and therefore I have to be happy with it myself."

A COMPANY NAMED IN HONOUR OF A CLAN CHIEF

The year was 1933. The founder of the company was Leonard J. Russell, which begs the question why the company was not called Leonard J. Russell Distillers? Instead, the company was named in honour of the chieftain of the Clan Macleod and so many of the Ian Macleod Brands have a tie in to the rich history of the clan and their island home on Skye. The Fairy Flag novel of the authors released just prior to C. Ask Whisky, also features that legendary clan chief that the company was named after. The Talisker Distillery is based on Skye but Ian Macleod Distillers are with the island in spirit. Here is how Ian Macleod Distillers introduce themselves: "Leonard J Russell, our company's founder, believed strongly in the value of independence. Beholden to no single Distiller, he bought only those Whiskies that met his own and his customers' exacting standards. Success reinforced his beliefs, and within the space of a few years, he established for the company an enviable reputation within the Scotch Whisky trade.

Ian Macleod Distillers Ltd are the Brand proprietors of Glengoyne Highland Single Malt Scotch Whisky, Tamdhu Speyside Single Malt Scotch Whisky, Isle of Skye Blended Scotch Whisky, Lang's Blended Scotch Whisky, Hedges & Butler, King Robert II, London Hill Gin, The Chieftain's and Dun Bheagan Ranges, Smokehead Islay Single Malt, Six Isles Island Blended Malt Scotch Whisky, Wincarnis Tonic Wines and Macleod's Single Malt Whiskies. We currently produce and sell over 15 million Bottles of Spirits per year."

In 2003, Ian Macleod acquired the nearly two hundred year old Glengoyne Distillery in the heart of what could be called Rob Roy country. Evidently, the real Rob Roy evaded the law by hiding in an oak tree close to the present day Distillery. Some Collectors are known for Collecting core ranges of a particular Whisky and Glengoyne has a range from a 10 YO to a 21 YO with a 12 YO, a 15 YO and a Cask strength as well. They claim that the special taste of Glegoyne comes from being the slowest Distillers in Scotland. They also dry their malt by air and not using peat in the drying process. Humorously, the Glengoyne website remarks: "There is of course absolutely nothing wrong with peat burning, it just is not the Glengoyne way. We do not fully understand it, but we imagine that the process of adding peat smoke to your barley must be akin to that famous scene from The Wicker Man, but with less screaming." Their website is very clever by the way and worth checking out. The 10 YO is said to have hints of toffee and apples while the 21 YO has that Christmas cake, honey, fruit taste with a "long cinnamon finish."

Another range in Macleod stable is the Isle of Skye Blend. There is an 8 YO, a 12 YO, and very Collectable 21 YO's and individually numbered 50 YO's, Blended with Single Malts from Speyside and the Islands.

THE 315 YEAR OLD SHOP

Imagine being in the same shop and in the same premises for 315 years! Berry Brothers and Rudd opened for business in 1698 in number 3 James Street in London and they are still there today - not the original Mr. Berry, Mr. Berry and Mr. Rudd of course - I mean the business that was started. Famous historical customers have included Lord Byron and William Pitt the younger - oh, and the Royal family since George the Third. BBR specialises in both Wine and Spirits and in regard to Whisky - they created the famous Blend Cutty Sark in 1923. In 2010 BBR and the Edrington Group made a trade and Cutty Sark went to Edrington and the Glenrothes Distillery went to BBR. Being such an old company, they ventured into Independent Bottling early on and had an 1887 Macallan and an 1885 Talisker for sale in 1909. Talk about Collector items! Recently, they won Independent Bottler of the year for two years running.

It was the privilege of C. Ask Whisky to speak to Ronnie Cox of BBR. His official title is Brands Heritage Manager. Mr. Cox came uniquely equipped to take on this role when he joined BBR in 1989, for like Lorne Mackillop, he had extensive knowledge of Wine and there was a heritage of Whisky that went back to the late 1700s in his family. As a young man, he ended up going to Germany and while studying sales and marketing from the Germans, he learned to speak Deutsch; he also took in a great deal of knowledge about Wine during this time. A German man named Adolph (not the one you're thinking of) took Ronnie under his wing, becoming a mentor of sorts. Adolph would travel with Ronnie every weekend to teach him about the vineyards along the Rhine. From Germany, he moved to Spain and continued learning the business skills of sales and marketing, while learning yet another language and also learning about the Spanish Wine Industry and the Sherry made in Spain. Distillers Co Ltd in the UK came calling, offering him a position. He accepted the job and shortly thereafter, he was sent globetrotting from India to Latin America. From Distillers Co. he moved on to Berry Brothers and Rudd. Having been at BBR for over 24 years, Ronnie Cox is not only their Brand's Heritage Ambassador, but he oversees the development of the Glenrothes

Single Malt and looks after the Latin America sales territory. It was a privilege to speak to Ronnie about Glenrothes and other BBR Whiskies - many of which are very Collectable.

Speaking about his relationship to the Glenrothes, Ronnie Cox said, "Born the 7th generation in a Whisky Distilling family I soon realised that Distilling was fun but selling a delight. It was about sharing with like minded souls what I thought as the Spirit of God's Own Country. The discovery of The Glenrothes changed my life as it epitomised the elite of Single Malts - the Premier Cru. My favourite Glenrothes expressions are definitely the elegance of the 1987 before dinner, and a 1972 - post dinner delight. They've both gone and I don't really want to tell you my current favourite Vintages for fear of the same thing happening! Though the fruity, butterscotch flavours of the 1991 with pudding is always a great joy. I have never thought it unusual to sample the wonders of a Single Malt alone nor do I think it vital to see an art exhibition with others. These are pleasures in life which can be enhanced with the right people who share and appreciate the greater things in life but if it's just you and your alter ego then so be it. In my book, a Single Malt is best enjoyed outside in summer on a Scottish riverbank discussing a day's fishing, or as an appetiser to a Brazilian barbecue or after dinner in a leather chair in a baronial castle enjoying conversation and music. These moments are as magical to me as an eclipse of the sun. Now go and try surprising a friend with a Bottle from the deep freeze, or, just try surprising a Bottle when it's least expecting you. It will always taste delicious and give pleasure unselfishly."

The website for Glenrothes lists 7 special vintage years going back to 1978, 5 special reserves, 6 Single Casks and the same number of extinct vintages - as in "Get 'em while they're hot, because when all the Bottles go, they'll be gone forever!" The website seems to have you Collectors in mind as it tempts you with such words as: "The Glenrothes has always been universally acclaimed by Blenders as an exceptional Speyside Malt. Only a small number of vintages have been released, such is the exceptional quality required. Each vintage is, by definition, rare and finite. Each has its own unique personality. Of the Vintages produced to date, many are no longer available. They've been sold, imbibed and greatly enjoyed."

In addition to Glenrothes, BBR have a range of Own-Label

Bottlings of Single Malt Whiskies from most Distilleries in Scotland and a number of Blends. Some of the Whiskies they offer you can get nowhere else in the world.

AULD LAING TIME

To quote the Douglas Laing Website: "Glasgow-based Douglas Laing & Co are Independent Bottlers and Blenders headed by brothers, Fred and Stewart Laing, who proved the value of nepotism when they succeeded their father, Douglas Laing, who founded the company in 1948. And, in truth, they've not let their Dad down over the past 25 years in charge. Indeed, they've grafted to uphold the traditions of the family - apart from the sheep stealing and cattle rustling."

Stewart Laing told us the story of the company this way: "Our father came from a humble background and had a dream of working in the Scotch Whisky Industry. He accomplished this shortly after leaving the RAF in 1948. Whisky was in short supply because all the Distilleries had been closed during World War II. When they were re-opened, my father would beg, borrow or steal from the Distilleries. He used his Glasgow humour to work with the Distillery managers who in those days were little gods in control of their own empires. In 1950, he went off to South America, to Columbia, to Venezuela and other South American countries that historically had liked Scotch Whisky but had not been serviced very well since the war.

Through his new business, he bought a Brand, King of Scots, that had been established in 1884 - and this Brand became the vehicle in his Blending. He developed other Brands such as House of Peers and Drury's - Drury's became a famous Brand that he eventually sold on to Brazil and made other people a lot of money. I always wanted to join my father. I did my training with Ballantines as a commercial apprentice. I worked in every department learning a little bit about everything and all for the princely sum of five pounds a week. I then went to work for my uncle who owned two Distilleries - Bladnoch and Bruichladdich. In 1966, I did my Distiller training with Bruichladdich and was out on Islay for six months. It was a great time of life. I didn't learn much about Whisky but I sure learned about life. I joined my father later that year. He had wanted me to work with others and make my mistakes at their expense before I came to work with him. Fred joined us a year later after working with Whyte and Mackay and White Horse. We worked with our father till his death in 1984.

In 1978 we began to wonder why we weren't selling much Whisky in the Far East. That was when I went on my first trip to Japan and had a look around Korea and Taiwan. I was taken quietly aside by the importer in a nightclub out there and it was pointed out that if people were drinking any kind of Spirit, it was most likely to be Cognac. It was explained to me that there were some very clever French marketeers who spread the word that Cognac had properties that made it an aphrodisiac while spreading the rumour that Whisky had the opposite affect. In the 90s, the World Health Organization was able to dispel these misconceptions and Whisky was considered to be the purest of the Spirits. Things were turned on their head. Where there had been ten cases of Cognac for every case of Whisky, there was now ten cases of Whisky for every case of Cognac. While business was booming in Asia, I had the great fortune of meeting a legend in business - I still think he's a legend - a man named Chuck Feeney. He and Bob Miller were behind the Duty Free Shops in the airports and King of Scots became the house Whisky Brand for the DFS. We met British American Tobacco and Imperial Tobacco and the people behind John Player Special.

They were into trademarked Brands such as aftershave, clothes, sunglasses and they wanted a JPS Whisky, which we supplied. Those were great days and business was good. Then in the 90s, the Asian market collapsed at the bank in Thailand went under. Harsh economic times meant people weren't buying the expensive Whiskies in wedgewood and crystal decanters, the 30 YO and 40 YO Whiskies. We were left with lots of expensive Whisky in stock but not a market to sell it to. In 1996, we decided to do 5 special Bottlings under an old Cask label we invented and we were surprised by the reaction and demand. Today in our portfolio an any given month there will be 200 Single Cask Bottlings, all carefully selected for quality. If our father's signature (Douglas Laing) is on the Bottle or our signatures (Stewart or Fred Laing) it is a sign of quality. Still you can't please all the people all the time and so if there are any complaints, I blame the problem on Fred."

Stewart told us that his father had had the foresight to purchase a large quantity of Port Ellen Whisky when the Islay Distillery was shut down in 1983. If you are looking for the rare, the old or the Douglas Laing Brand Rare and Old, one merely needs to shop online at the official website or at many of the Whisky shops in the UK or in the Duty Free Shops in the airports to find what treasures you can dig up. The brands and ranges include their Old Malt Cask, Directors Cut, Provenance, The Premier Barrel, Douglas of Drumlanrig, Clan Denny, The Epicurean Blend - Oh and - Stewart and Fred are behind our friend who did the forward, Big Peat.

"What advice do you have for Collectors?" we asked Stewart. He said, "Get to know your Bottler, stick with them and let them help you find what you are looking for." Good advice!

A TAYLOR MADE TREASURE TROVE

The genre of pirate stories almost always features men with eye-patches, parrots on the shoulder, hook-hands, peg-legs, the Jolly Roger flag and more often than not, there is a map and a buried treasure. In Whisky terms, an American businessman named Abe Rosenburg was like the older pirate in the stories who acquired the treasures and then buried them for others to find. I doubt Abe had an eye-patch, a parrot or walked on a pegged leg and said "ARRRRRR" and "Shiver me Timbers." He may not have even liked sailing. It's the treasure bit that we can associate with Mr. Rosenburg. Abe came out of the American debacle that was Prohibition as the Whisky broker to contend with and built the Brand J&B into the conquering Whisky it came to be. Abe also bought out a Glasgow based Whisky brokerage called Duncan Taylor, buying up Casks all over Scotland and leaving them in the warehouses until their value increased into the liquid gold he had the foresight to see coming down the road.

Euan Shand was like the person in the stories uniquely prepared to find the treasure. In the 70s, he entered the Whisky trade making the Barrels, before doing all the other jobs, the warehousing, the mashing and so forth. He then studied accounting and went into oil and engineering before returning to the business of Whisky. He had already been investing in Casks on a small scale but then he came across the portfolio left behind by Abe Rosenburg and was able to purchase the company Duncan Taylor with an eye-watering amount of Whisky treasure to share with fellow Whisky buccaneers like you – the avid Whisky Collector.

Euan told us he felt like a kid in a sweet shop when he discovered what the Duncan Taylor Company actually owned.

Speaking to Whisky Magazine, Euan described some of the treasures he had found:

Bowmore 1966: This is an unbelievable Whisky. What can you say? I can't think of any other Whisky to touch it. It has lost its peatiness over the years but it has left a kaleidoscope of flavours and tastes that change all the time. This is a second or third fill Bourbon Cask and the 40 years have allowed everything to breathe. As near to perfection as you can get.

Glendronach: Glendronach was where I was brought up. I used to get up on a spring morning and the warmth would release the aromas of Bourbon and Sherry and it was wonderful. I used to play among the empty Casks, hide with the other children among the peat, ride over the coal. I remember when I started work there we used to take a taste from one Cask of Glendronach from a 1932 Sherry Cask. The Alcohol had reduced and it was probably under-strength but the taste had condensed and I remember the honey, then Sherry and then strawberry. I think the current 15 YO is very good. This is a Distillery that means a great deal to me.

Highland Park 1966: I've enjoyed Highland Park ever since I was a young man. This is another great all-rounder but it has more of an earthy feel to it. I like going to the Distillery and being somewhere where they make Whisky in the old way, with the peat from nearby. Also when I smell it I'm taken back to when I went to see Led Zeppelin in Aberdeen and we went with some Beer cans and a Bottle of Highland Park because that's what we thought rock stars did. It was a very long time ago. Robert Plant threw his plastic cup in to the crowd and I got it – and you could tell he had been drinking Whisky and honey from it. It's a very happy and clear memory.

Imperial 1965: We were close to buying it but then the whole Allied deal happened. I think it's terribly misunderstood. Someone described it as a third rate Distillery and that's just plain wrong. And other people have picked up on that and it's stuck. It's just laziness and ignorance. It's another Whisky used for Blending but in fact it's a beautifully sweet, mellow and drinkable Whisky that can be enjoyed at lunchtime or in the afternoon. It's not overpowering at all."

We asked Euan about the range of Whiskies that Duncan Taylor had an offer and he said that they tried to cover all bases, tastes and budgets and their range included affordable Blends to some of the most expensive Whiskies on the planet. Their range includes the Rarest of the Rare featuring choice Bottlings of Macallan from the 60s for instance or Bowmore from the 60s or Bottling from many a mothballed Distillery. These are presented in a crystal decanter and wooden box.

The Dimensions range features 12 YO to 38 YO whiskies. The Battlehill Blend is named after the battle in Huntly Scotland (Duncan Taylor is located in Huntly) where Robert the Bruce fought. Auld Reekie is a Blend of Islay Malts. Big Smoke is a Blend of the smoky Whiskies as is the Brand new range called Smoking, which features the smokier Whiskies from Speyside. Their popular Blend Black Bull is 50% malt and 50% grain and rages from 12 YO to 40 YO. Black Bull won blind tasting prizes three years running and this infuriated one of the empire building corporate giants who thought it was unfair to pit a so-called small Brand against an earth dominating Goliath of a Brand – but Goliaths have never done well against superior so called little guys. After Black Bull there is Scottish Glory and Loch Ness – Yes, Loch Ness does feature a picture of Nessy on the Bottle and that is the type of interesting Whisky that will go in my collection. Duncan Taylor also runs the Whisky Galore festival.

"Where can people get Duncan Taylor Whiskies?" we asked. "You don't see them in the supermarkets."

"Supermarkets don't care what Whiskies they take. It's all about the bottom line and they don't know one Whisky from another," said Euan Shand. "There's no real interest or passion. We prefer to deal with specialist Whisky shops that know their Whiskies. We also do business with the Total Wine chain in the United States as they work hard to learn about the Whiskies. We are happy to work with a company like that. We are re-doing the

Duncan Taylor website and people can buy online directly from us if they so desire."

C. ASK: What Whiskies should we be watching? What common Whiskies today will be the ones that increase in value and turn into the Collector items in the future.

EUAN SHAND: 25 years ago, there was a lot of Glen Livet that was dumped on the market – a very unwise move on the part of the marketing people as Glen Livet was devalued in many people's eyes. I still think Glen Livet is a special Whisky and one to watch.

C. ASK: What will happen when your stocks of the rare Whiskies are depleted? What does the future hold for Duncan Taylor?

EUAN SHAND: We are constantly investing in Casks. Last year we spent 2,500,000 pounds on Casks and 400,000 in the first few months of 2013. We are constantly laying out Casks for the future.

C. ASK WHISKY COMMENTARY: Like Abe Rosenburg before him, Euan Shand is burying treasure that someone just like you might discover!

Rory Nicoll with Alistair Hart

HAVE A HART

Speaking with Alistair Hart of the Hart Brothers, one gets the feeling that he is to Whisky what Willy Wonka is to chocolate. No, he doesn't wear a top hat and have the odd eccentricities of the Roald Dahl character from the children's book, Charlie and the Chocolate Factory. He has a gregarious, charming personality and a passion for his craft that shines through. He cares as much for the customer as he does for the Whisky and like the Wonka

character, he would like to take you on a journey into the magical world of Whisky with all its delights and surprises. Listening to him describe a Whisky is reminiscent of the Dahl description of the three-course meal gum devised by Wonka. His eyes light up as he explains, "First you taste this, and then this happens, and then there is this explosion of taste you finish up with!"

A food scientist that coincidentally shares the same Hart surname but is no relation - a fellow named Dave Hart - thinks he can create the fictional gum in reality that featured in the Chocolate Factory book. In an article that appeared in several UK newspapers, Niall Firth writes: "Food scientist Dave Hart believes that recent advances in nanotechnology, which deals with structures just millionths of a millimetre in size, could capture and release flavours in a precisely controlled manner. The flavours are separated with a tasteless gelatine that stops them from overlapping, with a final dessert taste at the centre, encapsulated in a high-tech gel called Gellan. In Roald Dahl's book Charlie and the Chocolate Factory, Willy Wonka proudly displays a stick of Three-Course Dinner Chewing Gum, which he claims can reproduce the flavours of every individual course of a full meal. The gum is able to convey the flavours of 'tomato soup, roast beef and baked potato, and blueberry pie and ice cream', he claims." Listening to Alistair Hart's description of a special Whisky, one almost expects the same experience, a three course series of flavours in the Whisky. He says he is often asked what his favourite Whisky is and though he thinks there are too many to choose from, he does recall a special experience with a 16 YO Bow more. He would share the experience and get others to taste the Bowmore saying, "OK, now count to 4 .... 1, 2, 3, 4 and then BOOM! A volcanic eruption of flavours! Alistair then compares the experience to a classic love story like Romeo and Juliet. "Imagine you're Romeo trying to seduce Juliet. You express your interest to the girl like you express your interest in the Whisky. At first there's no response. The girl is unmoved to begin with and none of your chat-up lines are working. In like manner, the Whisky is not giving you anything back at the start. But then the Earth moves. Juliet falls for Romeo and he has his way with her. In the same way, the Whisky starts to give back and there is an explosive, satisfying climax of taste." Damn Alistair! We're seduced. To Alistair Hart, it's not just the Whisky Business.

It's the Entertainment Business. It's about being with people and enjoying their company. Alistair considers it part of his job to educate people about Whisky, and to point them in the right direction of the Whiskies they are looking for. The Brothers Hart pride themselves on customer satisfaction and so it was a shock one day to get a complaint from a fellow in Australia who said, "Somebody gave me a Bottle of your Whisky and it was crap!" On the rant went with insult after insult. Alistair could see a tsunami coming down the River Clyde to wipe out their business all because one Australian fellow had complained. Alistair called the fellow up and said, "What you said was very serious and I'm not happy about it. Could you tell me what Whiskies you usually drink?" The fellow said, "I never drink Whisky. I'm a Beer drinker." After a pause, Alistair said, "I'm not psychic but I'm guessing you were given a 14 YO Laphroaig?"

"Mate, how did you know?"

"There's nothing wrong with a Laphroaig, but it's not a Whisky for beginners because of its smoky and heavily peated taste. I recommend that you read up on your Whiskies before you buy them, or buy a book, or talk to me and I'd help you choose the right Whisky for you."

C. Ask Whisky asked about some of the hard to get Whiskies from the mothballed Distilleries. Alistair told us that it was his job to encourage the customer to be adventurous and try something new. For instance, if the customer couldn't get a rare Isla Whisky because of the disappearing stock or increasing expense, then he would say, "Why not try a maritime Whisky like a Pultney or a Clynelish."

In a Previews of Coming Attractions, Alistair told us about a series of upcoming Bottlings called the Whisky Legends that would feature a legendary Macallan, a legendary Highland Park, a legendary St. Magdalene and they would be artistically packaged and yet, for all that, they would be reasonably priced. "Only certain Whiskies are legends," said Alistair.

We brought up a particular trend among Collectors, which is to buy two of the special Bottles they were after - one to save and not touch for a keepsake - and one to drink. Alistair thought it would be an even better idea to buy three, so the third could be shared with special company. In the beginning of our discussion of the Brothers Hart, we referenced Charlie and the Chocolate Factory, but there is another chocolate reference in popular culture we should quote: In the words of the lovable movie simpleton, Forrest Gump, "Momma always said, 'Life was like a box of chocolates. You never know what you're gonna get'." Alistair and Donald Hart do know exactly what you're going to get when you uncork one of their specially selected Bottled Whiskies but they want it to be a surprise to you like that box of chocolates Forrest Gump's mother was talking about. "If you want continuity, go back to the Distillery and buy the Whisky from them," said Alistair, "but the reason you left that Distillery is because they didn't excite you anymore. It would be the same old Bottle that you had before. There was no special tickle, no kiss, no thrill, where as an Independent Bottler can point you to a Single Cask that they and they alone have access to." Alistair and Donald look forward to seeing the surprise of delight on your face!

GORDON & MACPHAIL

Whisky writer Charlie Maclean is quoted as saying, ""It's the oldest Cask of Whisky that, in my knowledge, has ever been Bottled." He was referring to the 70 YO Mortlach Bottled by Gordon & MacPhail on October 15th 1938. On March 12th, 2010 the Telegraph printed an article about the world's oldest Whisky. Warning. If you have un-controllable Collector-mania, look away now or call your sponsor at Collectors Anonymous. Here is what the Telegraph reported: "The Mortlach 70-year-old Speyside was sampled by a select group of tasters at a ceremony in Edinburgh Castle. Bottles of the rare piece of Scotland's 'liquid history' have now hit the market. Only 54 full-size Bottles, costing £10,000 each, and 162 smaller Bottles at £2,500, have been made available. The Whisky has been released under Gordon and MacPhail's Generations Brand." The article goes on to say: "The rare Whisky was matured in a former Sherry Cask made from Spanish Oak. It has been Bottled in a teardrop-shaped hand-blown crystal decanter with a silver stopper."

We will come back to the 70 YO Mortlach, but first we should address the question: "Who exactly are Gordon and MacPhail that had the honour of Bottling the world's oldest Whisky back in 2010?" Here is an attempt to answer that question: They've been in business for over a hundred years. They now own and have revived the Benromach Distillery and they do special Bottlings from Casks they have long held from working and closed Distilleries all over Scotland. Perhaps there is a name missing from the company title Gordon & MacPhail? Let us explain. Yes, the company began in the Highland town of Elgin in 1895 as a combined Wine/Spirit merchant and grocery store venture by James Gordon and John MacPhail, but right from the beginning there was a third name that became more and more prominent, especially when James Gordon and John MacPhail passed away.

The third name - which has never been reflected in the company title - is Urquhart. It was our sincere pleasure to speak to Michael Urquhart of Gordon & MacPhail. Michael's grandfather John was the original Urquhart that joined the company as a fifteen year old lad serving an apprenticeship under J. Gordon and J. MacPhail. Here is his story: "He was an able learner, and before long was helping James Gordon to select and buy Casks of Malt Whisky from local Distilleries, and assisting with the creation of House Blends for the firm's customers around the north of Scotland. When J.A. MacPhail retired in March 1915, Urquhart became a partner in the business, and when James Gordon died suddenly only two weeks later, he became senior partner. In parallel with the grocery side of the enterprise, John Urquhart developed the Whisky broking business begun by James Gordon, and in particular began to specialise in Single Malt Whiskies - Bottling under license for famous Distilleries such as Macallan, Glenlivet, Glen Grant, Linkwood and Mortlach. As part of this business he began to select and fill his own Casks - almost always Spanish Oak, ex-Sherry Casks - at these and other Distilleries, and to mature his Whiskies for much longer than was customary at the time.

John Urquhart was joined by his son, George, and daughter, Betty, in 1933, and by another son, Gordon, in 1950. By this time the family firm held the largest range of Bottled Malt Whiskies in the world. Most makes were unavailable elsewhere, since very few Distillery owners Bottled their own malts as singles - indeed, it is no overstatement to say that Gordon & MacPhail single-handedly kept the amber lamp of aged Malt Whisky burning during the post-war decades!

In the mid-1960s George Urquhart took the unprecedented step of launching a range of Single Malts from different Distilleries under the Brand name 'Connoisseur's Choice', and offered the range for sale in the rapidly expanding Italian, French, American and Dutch markets. This move laid the foundations for the significant interest in Malt Whisky in these countries that remains to this day.

Just as his father had introduced him to the firm, so George brought in his own children. The oldest, Ian, joined in 1967, after having been trained in the Wine and Spirit trade in London and France. He was followed by David in 1972 and Michael in 1981. The former had studied business in Aberdeen; Michael is a Chartered Accountant. George's daughter, Rosemary joined in 1981."

Michael informed us that the next generation of Urquharts are working for Gordon & MacPhail already. There have now been four generations of Urquharts prominent in this prestigious company that boasts one of the largest Whisky Collections on display anywhere in the world and all on display in their shop in Elgin, the very same premises that James Gordon and John MacPhail opened in the late 19th century. Whisky Collectors can go there and salivate, drool and steam up the glass that some Whiskies are kept behind.

C. Ask Whisky asked Michael Urquhart about some of the details about Independent Bottling:
C. ASK: So an Independent Bottler doesn't necessarily buy Cask-aged Whisky from a Distillery?"

MICHAEL URQUHART: No, more often than not it is the White Spirit produced fresh from the stills of that Distillery, Spirit that normally would go into Casks for aging and maturing at the Distillery. Instead we take the Spirit away for aging and maturing in Casks we have selected.

C. ASK: So even if it's called a Mortlach Single Malt, or Glenlivet or Glen Grant it will be slightly different from the Bottles produced directly from the Distillery?

MICHAEL URQUHART: We prefer to look at it as an alternative interpretation of the same thing - as in a phrase in English that can be worded with a slight difference but has an identical meaning - it is a translation. We take great care in choosing Casks that compliment the original Distillery so that the resulting expression is recognizable as having come from there, and yet it is our own special Bottling of that Whisky. The DNA of the Distillery is there in the Whisky and our aim is to bring out the best in that Distilled Spirit in the Cask aging process that we oversee for our customers.

THE PROCESS

Here are the details of the Gordon and MacPhail process: "Gordon & MacPhail Bottles over 300 expressions of Single Malt Scotch Whisky from Distilleries throughout Scotland. Our long established relationships with Distillery owners throughout the country allows us to send our Oak Casks to the majority of Scotland's working Distilleries to be filled with 'new make' Spirit, which then mature for many years at the Distillery of origin or in our bonded warehouses in Elgin. The Oak Casks are carefully stowed and regularly checked until they finally achieve our highest quality standards. Only then are they Bottled and presented for sale. Our philosophy for maturing, selecting and Bottling, ensures that we strive to produce the highest quality Whiskies. Our filling policy allows us to specially select Casks to complement the unique character of Whisky we fill into them. Our Sherry Casks are made in Spain, seasoned for a number of years and finally when they are ready, are brought to Scotland. We source ex-Bourbon Casks from selected Distilleries in Kentucky, and other specialist Wine Casks from throughout the world. Loving care in every aspect of bringing our products to market ensures that every Bottle carrying the G&M mark is simply as good as it can be."

THE OLDEST WHISKY IN THE WORLD

We spoke to Michael about the launch of the oldest Whisky in the world, the 70 YO Mortlach from a Cask of Mortlach his grandfather John filled from the Distillery in 1938.

MICHAEL URQUHART: "It was a momentous occasion - very exciting for us! It was a ceremony, a proud moment in our history. The taste of the Whisky was beautiful. You would think that being in a Cask for 70 years and all the interaction with the wood would leave a wooden taste, but not at all. It was alive, vibrant, youthful - dare I say, a Whisky that had been on Weight Watchers. Not heavy at all and it had light fruit sensations. Marvellous! All of the Whiskies have gone now. Some will be drunk. Others will never be opened. We have kept one back for ourselves.

C. ASK: Do you have any other Special Bottlings coming up you can tell us about?

MICHAEL URQUHART: Another special occasion arose in which we released the 70 YO Glenlivet but as far as upcoming releases (Michael pauses and chuckles) - Watch this space!

We will all be watching Michael – And the same goes for you Euan, Alistair, Donald, Stewart, Fred, Ronnie, Lorne – the Ian Macleod Company, Andrew and Des at Signatory and all the rest of you – we are watching you! Always watching!

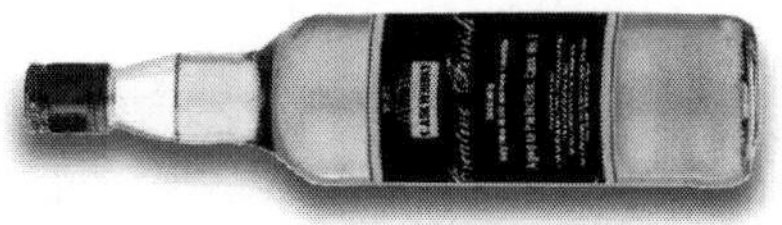

CHAPTER *seven*

Tipple Tours

One of the stereotypes of the Scots is that they are dour. Dour means relentlessly severe, stern, austere - rigid - grim - strict - hard or gloomy in manner or appearance. Since there are so many Distilleries in Scotland, some Tourists wonder if they'll get the Stingy and Dour Tour. No one wants the Dour Tour. The Dour Tour should not be confused with the Dewar's Distillery Tour at Dewar's World of Whisky in Perthshire. They advertise their Tour this way: "Discover Dewar's authentic Scotch experience in the heart of the Highlands and hear the extraordinary tale of John Dewar & Sons.

Just two miles from the birth place of John himself, discover the inspiring story of America's top selling Scotch with a unique Heritage Centre offering interactive challenges and fascinating company archives." Dewar's does a lot to engage the public. There is an award winning Heritage Centre and a movie; there are tasting opportunities, private Tours and an opportunity to fill your own Bottle. The day I went, and very strangely, there was a Peruvian band playing near the Distillery. This had nothing to do with the Distillery but it points to many a missed opportunity for Scotland's Tourism Industry across the board. I have nothing against Peruvian musicians playing in Scotland but I think the 1.2 million Tourists who come to Scotland every year want to taste more of Scottish culture, which is definitely not all stingy and dour. I would have liked to have seen Scottish musicians outside the Distillery. I want my nation's Distillery Tours to be the best in the world - but the competition is tough. Arguably, we are the world leader in making Whisky but we have a long way to go to compete with America when it comes to pleasing Tourists. So how can Distilleries around the world up their game?

The popular animated sitcom the Simpson's features an episode where ten year-old Bart Simpson and his younger sister Lisa travel with their Aunt Selma to what in essence is a Distillery/ brewery type Tour combined with elements similar to Florida's Busch Gardens and the Disney theme parks - It is a Disney-esque amusement park centred around Duff Beer. The summary of the plot and in-jokes even made it into the following Wikipedia entry: "In the gift shop, Bart spots 'Beer-goggles', spectacles that mimic what drunks see: they make Aunt Selma appear young, feminine, and beautiful to Bart - and also, somehow, alter her voice. Later, they see the mascots of Duff Beer, the Seven Duffs. In the same episode, there is also a direct parody of the 'It's a Small

World' attraction at Disney parks. In the cartoon, the boats float on a brown liquid as animatronic children sing 'Duff Beer for me, Duff Beer for you, I'll have a Duff, You have one, too,' over and over again. Lisa drinks the liquid in the ride on a dare from Bart, and she freaks out from its hallucinogenic properties. Other Duff Gardens attractions include the Beeramid, the Beerquarium (Home of the world's happiest fish), the Beer Hall of Presidents, the Washing Machine ride, the Whiplash rollercoaster, singing group Hooray for Everything (who sing a politically correct version of Lou Reed's 'Walk on the Wild Side' and are based on Up with People), and a direct parody of Disneyland's Main Street Electrical Parade." The mascots of the park are the Seven Duffs, grizzled actors wearing Beer Bottle Costumes. "The Seven Duffs are named Sleazy, Queazy, Surly, Edgy, Tipsy, Dizzy, and Remorseful."

Even though this is a send-up of what a Beer-themed amusement park might be like, the same type of interjection of creativity that went into the cartoon is the same kind of creativity needed to create a world class experience for the Tourist wanting to visit the Distillery. C. Ask Whisky is not suggesting going to an over-the-top extreme with actors dressed up in Whisky Bottles or a still-themed rollercoaster where the tracks come dangerously close to what looks like hot, bubbling brew and then travels up, up, up like evaporating Spirit and out a spout, plunging downward into a massive Cask where the coaster loop-to-loops around the Cask before the ride ends inside a giant jug. There is an old Show Biz maxim and that is "Give the people what they want!" If they want clowns dressed up as Whisky Bottles then give it to them, but fortunately, I don't think anybody does want that. So what do they want? Do they just want to see malted barley being dried out, Distillation machinery or Barrels in a warehouse or do they want something more? If in Scotland, Ireland, England Wales, Kentucky, Tennessee, Utah, Montana, New York, Canada, Mexico, Australia, Japan, Taiwan, South Africa or wherever the Distillery is, I would want to taste more than Whisky. I want a taste of the culture. I want to meet the people, hear the stories, see the sights and sounds. I want more than "Here is how we ferment. Here is how we Distil our Spirit. Here is how we age our Whisky." Yes, that is always part of it and with an injection of imagination, enthusiasm, a little ham, a lot of humour that can be made into a rewarding, interesting, entertaining and engaging experience that is unlike any other Distillery's experience.

There are two types of Distillery-visiting Tourists and we will use Scotland again as an example of what these two types of Tourists come to see. Change the nation to Ireland, America or any other nation and the same principles apply. There are those who come to Scotland to see this nation they have heard about from afar and not just the plethora of Distilleries. Since Whisky production is part of the national heritage of the nation, this type of Tourist will want to see at least one Distillery as well as one or two castles, men in kilts playing bagpipes, the Loch Ness Monster and take in a couple historic sights and national beauty spots. If the Distillery Tour is not great, this type of Tourist could easily come away thinking, "Is that it?" or "Seen one Distillery, seen them all." This reaction is a pity and a lost opportunity for a Distillery and the whole Industry, not too mention Scottish Tourism. There must be a better way to interest and entertain the casual Tourist that has only a minor curiosity about Whisky production. These people should come out far more interested than they had been when they went in and they should either want to go again to the same Distillery, recommend it to others or they should want to visit ten other Distilleries in the hopes of getting a different experience from each.

The other type of Distillery Tourist is much more serious about Whisky and some of the Distilleries in Scotland cater well to the true Whisky-enthusiast on a Distillery Tour - though even the best of these Tours could be so much better.

Imagine this dating scenario and compare it to the Tourist experience: The guy finally works up the courage to ask his dream girl out. She says, "Yes!" He picks her up. "Where are we going?" she asks. She is expecting dinner at a swanky restaurant with elegance, class, atmosphere, music, candlelight. Perhaps a show will follow. Instead of such a perfect evening, the guy says, "I'm going to show you my tool shed where I make really cool stuff." She starts to get worried. Reluctantly, she follows the guy in to his woodworking shop. "This is the on and off switch to turn the lights off and on," he says proudly while flicking the switch up and down several times. "This is a saw. It is there to cut wood. Let me demonstrate." He turns it on and cuts a board in half. "Pretty cool, huh?" he laughs. She starts to think, "I've gone on a date with an imbecile!" The guy proceeds to demonstrate how to use a hammer, a screwdriver, a sander and then shows the girl the table he made. What the guy failed to realize was that dream girl wasn't that interested in how he made the chair and all the tools. She wanted an experience, good food, nice drink, conversation, music, fun and yes romance. Such a date could have led to a more intimate encounter of showing off his tools but the idiot missed the opportunity. In the same way, the Distillery Tour has to be much more than "Here is the on and off switch and now you can see the machines running." If watching machines working were truly that interesting, people would be lining up at Laundromats to "OO!" and "AWE!" as they watched clothes go round and round.

The Tourist has travelled a long way to get to your doorstep and your Distillery should give the guest an immersive experience that makes them go "WOW!" You don't want to be the guy who just takes the girl to the workshop. You want to be the guy who knows how to show a girl a good time. The Tourists are your date and it is up to you to impress them. On a real date, you would spruce yourself up, put on the expensive aftershave and you wouldn't take the girl out to a truck stop café. You would take her to the best place you could afford. She's a keeper and worth making an effort for. The Distillery that makes the big effort to engage their guests will reap lifetime customers and financial rewards. The Jack Daniel's and Wild Turkey Tour are even free of charge which seems daft from a business point of view, until you see how many Branded hats, T-shirts, shot glasses, taster glasses, mugs and special souvenir Bottles of JD or Wild Turkey are bought after such Tours. Ralph Erenzo of the Tuthilltown Distillery in Gardiner, New York told us that the revenue in one week from their gift shop paid the monthly wages for all their staff.

TUTHILLTOWN DISTILLERY

Speaking of Ralph Erenzo, allow us to take you to the lovely Hudson Valley in New York State and to the Tuthilltown Distillery. This comes up in recommended Distillery Tour lists. Its origin tale is also one of the most fascinating of any tale we have heard thus far. That's one of the things the Tourists want - they want to hear good stories. If I were visiting the Famous Grouse Experience and Glenturret Distillery in Crieff, Scotland for instance, I would want to hear the story of Towser the Distillery cat that held the Guiness Book of World Records for catching mice - 28, 899 kills in all. I don't know who counted, but I would not only come away wanting a Bottle of Glenturret or Famous Grouse, but I would want a Towser the Killer Cat T-Shirt. I celebrated New Year or Hogmanay as we say in Scotland with a dram of Glenturret. A very tasty Whisky in my opinion. But I still want more than the Whisky. I want to hear the stories that come with the Whisky and Glenturret will forever be associated in my mind with Towser the terrible, the bane of rodents everywhere. The very name Towser should make mice tremble from the tip of their nose to the tip of their tail. I would name a Whisky after Towser. I'd try to make Towser as big as Mickey Mouse.

In fact Towser would probably eat Mickey Mouse. If visiting the Kilbeggan Distillery in Ireland or Glenlivet or Glenrothes or Glen Scotia Distilleries, I would want to hear the spooky tales of ghostly goings on in these reputedly haunted Distilleries. The Glen Livet website tantalises us with this hint that there are more Spirits than the kind they are producing: "Glenlivet is one of the remotest glens in Scotland and is also one of the most haunted. There are many local tales of ghosts, spectres, witches, warlocks, kelpies (evil Spirit horses that drown travellers!) and fairies that hunt and kill babies! There is said to be a grey lady that resided in Minmore House that adjoins the Glenlivet Distillery. She has not been seen since the house was recently exorcised." It may all be bunk but what a lot of fun could be had in relating such tales. Yes, stories add so much to the Distillery Tour experience and that is why we are in Gardiner New York. Talk about the American dream and climbing out of adversity. Here is a classic case of "if life gives you lemons you make lemonade - or Whisky in Ralph's case!" You see, the Distillery became a Distillery by accident. It was never supposed to be a Distillery at all. The land and the building that was purchased was intended to be a Climbing Centre. Ralph Erenzo had no intention of getting into the Spirits business. Some are born into the Whisky Industry and go into the family business following in the footsteps of their father and grandfather. Some get into the Industry through science, through engineering or because they have a business/ marketing background. Not so Ralph, although he was good at business. His business just happened to be rock climbing. He had a rock climbing career with many a mountain he had ascended literally and figuratively. Little did he know he was about to face another figurative mountain, bigger than all the others. "His business ExtraVertical Inc. provided technical services to corporate and media clients for projects that required technical skills developed over his 25 year rock climbing career. Ralph built and managed New York City's first public climbing gyms including The ExtraVertical Climbing Centre on Broadway. His dream of a climbers ranch near the largest rock climbing area in the East were set aside in favour of producing high quality Spirits." The official website quickly mentions this fact but there was a bigger story behind it. On the phone, Ralph went into more detail about why the dream of the Climbing Ranch was set aside to make way for the Distillery. The location was a dream. It was far from the concrete jungle of Manhattan in the picturesque landscape of the Hudson Valley.

Gardiner, New York was picture postcard small town America. It was beautiful to look at - but there was also small town politics, status-quo and "We don't think we want all these hippy climbers coming into town from here, there and everywhere to climb in this strange idea of a Climbing Ranch - I mean ranches are supposed to be for cows - and we don't want none of them either 'cause they smell!" Ralph's great investment of money, blood, sweat and tears into one particular American dream was shot down and became an American nightmare. He had climbed mountains before however, and he set one American dream aside for another. He thought about using his property to make Wine and go into the Wine business but the idea of one more Wine amongst the thousands of other Wines clamouring for attention was too daunting to take seriously. He then came to think about Whisky and realized that nobody in New York State had made Whisky since the Prohibition. Thus the embryonic idea of starting a new Distillery was born. This was still the bottom of another mountain and still without a still as of yet. There were legal hurdles to climb over, more small town politics to climb over and increasingly difficult financial hurdles. They converted an old Grain Mill into a Distillery and did get the still. Churning out Whisky as quickly as possible so they could see a return on the investment was only wishful thinking. The word quick, doesn't come into it when making Whisky. They did make a Brand of White Spirit Corn Moonshine in the beginning that could be produced without a long aging process. They still sell the product today. It is called Hudson New York Corn Whisky. It is described this way: "It is Distilled the old fashioned way, one batch at a time from 100% New York corn. No sugar is added. This un-aged sipping Whisky is clear and soft to the tongue, with the faint aroma of corn fields at harvest. Corn Whisky is known by a variety of nicknames: White Dog, White Light'ng and Moonshine. New York Corn Whisky is traditional American corn. It is Bottled at 40% Alcohol by volume. It is also the foundation for Tuthilltown's popular and unique Hudson Baby Bourbon." The Tuthilltown Distillery has been around long enough to make Cask-aged Single Malts but in the early days, there were fewer products to sell, and not a proper outlet to sell them. Ralph told us that they would sell Whisky from the boot of the car and take it around to restaurants in Manhattan to see if any of these fine dining establishments would take the Hudson Whisky. Many a well-to-do restaurant did take the Whisky and the climb from rock bottom began in earnest.

Today, Scotland's William Grant and Sons helps with international distribution of the Hudson New York Whisky products - many of which have won awards - and there are now many full time staff. Ralph has also helped change laws in favour of Spirit producers and he has had a few well known New York politicians through the Distillery. To quote the Tuthilltown website: "His work at the State level has resulted in the passage of the Farm Distillery Act which permits New York farms to establish Distilleries on site and sell their agricultural Spirits at the farm." Ralph told us that when this law was passed, 28 other Micro-Distilleries opened in the state virtually overnight.

The Tour of the Distillery has become one of the must-see stops when visiting the Hudson Valley. Ralph's approach is to tell it like it is and he wants a no-hype-zone.
There are many reviews online and the general comments are that it is an intimate, fun and very informative Tour with friendly, knowledgeable Tour Guides and a nice gift shop.

Another unique feature of Tuthilltown is the use of sound in the Cask-aging process. I am aware of no other Distillery that purposely uses the vibrations coming from speakers and their subwoofers as music plays. The Distilled Spirit will have that much more interaction with the wooden Casks as sound makes the wood and liquid vibrate. Coming from a Music Industry background, I find this musical version of Cask-aging fascinating.

Tuthilltown produces these Whiskies which any Connoisseur of American Whisky or Bourbon should check out: Hudson Single Malt, Four Grain Bourbon, Baby Bourbon, Manhattan Rye and Corn Whisky.

HIGH WEST DISTILLERY AND SALOON

As mentioned, stories are an important part of the Distillery Tour, but so is the location, the scenery, the setting, the visuals inside and out. People don't want to just look at industrial technology. The grounds, the trees, flowers, gardens, brooks, streams, hills, beaches and the varied different environments are a vital part of the over-all experience. If the romance of a thousand western films and television shows permeates your brain, then saddle up, get on your horse and ride with us to Park City Utah. Listen to the twang of the guitar and picture this. "Big skies. Snow-fed waterways running clear as crystal. Majestic Mountains. This is the High West, a place so legendary you can almost taste it, " says a narrator at the beginning of a short film about the Distillery.

The Distillery is indeed high, as in 7000 feet above sea level and located in the Utah resort town. Three ski resorts in the surrounding mountains are part of the Park City attraction. The setting is stunning. It truly becomes more than a town and an actual city when the Tourists descend. Park City is home to Robert Redford's Sundance Film Festival; every year, Hollywood comes riding in and it is not unusual to see A-list movie stars. The Distillery and Saloon benefit from the location that draws so many people in. High West is more than just a Distillery. It is a working restaurant or as they call it, "Utah's first Distillery since the 1870's, and the only ski-in gastro-Distillery in the world." They invite you to ski in for some victuals, which is handy since they are located at the bottom of a ski run. They'll serve you Western fare and though Wine and other Spirits are available, they also have Whisky they could serve you that they made themselves in their very own Distillery. Two restored historic buildings comprise the operation. One is period Victorian house with five dining rooms. The other is an open spaced Livery-Saloon where there is likely to be country or rock-a-billy band playing and singing.

From the outside this Livery looks like an old Saloon that you would see in almost any cowboy movie you have ever seen. They say, "We wanted to call High West a Saloon to pay homage to the history of Saloons in the old West and the important role they played in each and every town that had one...and almost all did. The Saloon was the epicentre for community gatherings, victuals, and tasty libations." Their Saloon was designed after the pattern they describe here: "Saloons were often elaborately decorated, with oil paintings hanging from the walls and Bohemian stemware to drink from. Most had wooden sidewalks, hitching posts to tie up horses, and a livery stable behind the building. The bars were typically hand-carved oak, mahogany, or walnut, with a brass rail lining the bottom so patrons could put their feet up. Most Saloons were heated by pot belly stoves and dimly lit, with candles or coal oil lamps providing illumination and atmosphere." This is the look they have successfully captured and I know of no other Distillery in the world where you could walk in with your cowboy boots and cowboy hat, bang your fist on the counter and say, "Bartender, give me a Whisky."

We had the pleasure of speaking to David Perkins, the man behind the whole operation. Like Glenmorangie's Dr. Bill Lumsden, Cooley's Noel Sweeney in Ireland and Glen Scotia's John Peterson, David Perkins started off his working life in science. "He moved to Park City in 2004 to pursue his passion to make Whisky. With a background as a biochemist in the biopharmaceutical Industry, a love of Bourbon from being raised in Georgia, and a love of cooking, David knew he was fated to make Whisky. After learning the secrets of making really good Whisky from Distillers in Kentucky and Scotland, David decided to start a Distillery and make Whisky." David thought Park City was a spectacular place and when deciding what to name the new venture he was inspired by the Clint Eastwood film, High Plains Drifter and thus High West was born.

On the Tour, you will step from the past into the future and travel from the 19th century to the 21st across the threshold of a door when you step from the Livery into the working Distillery. There they have a 250 gallon Copper Pot Still where they can make small batches of their Spirit. They also use a Combination Still, which can either operate as a Continuous Still or another Pot Still and this varies the type of Distillates produced.

David and the Tour Guides love to explain the process and the enthusiasm for what they do is contagious. One of the Distilleries early successes was the Rendezvous Rye. David Blended a 16 YO Rye with a 6 YO Rye. This type of Blending is rarely done in the Whisky world. He had heard of mixing such varying ages of Spirit being done with Cognac so David thought, "Why not Whisky?" The Blending paid off and the Whisky won a top prize from Malt Advocate Magazine.

Here is a description of the Rendezvous Rye. "It is a Blend of two exotic straight Rye Whiskies; one old, and one young. It marries the rich aromatic qualities of a 16 YO Rye with the bold spicy properties of 6 YO Rye to create a full flavoured, very complex Whisky. The 6 YO boasts an uncommonly high 95% rye mash bill. Almost every other straight Rye Whisky you can buy today is barely legal, with 51-53% rye in the mash bill. Not Rendezvous Rye. It honours the way Rye Whisky used to be made, with a high rye content and full, uncompromised flavour." High West have produced 12 other Whiskies: Double Rye, 12 YO Rye, Rocky Mountain very rare 16 YO Rye, Rocky Mountain very rare 21 YO Rye, Bourye, Son of Bourye, Valley Tan, New American Prairie Reserve, Silver Oat Whisky, Silver OMG Pure Rye and lastly Campfire. A raised horseshoe is part of all the glass Bottles. Four prominent western artists have contributed artwork, designing colourful western themed pictures for the labels and the whiskies are advertised on WANTED posters just like the legendary outlaws appeared on those yellowed pieces of paper posted around the Wild West.

Describing Campfire, David says, "I was going to write

something cheesy about cowboys, campfires, and Whisky but I figured you might be more interested in how Campfire Whisky came to be. One morning at the Bruichladdich Distillery B&B, my wife and I smelled peat in the air - the great ladies that made our meals were simmering a Bottle of peated Whisky and sugar! Later that night, they brought out dessert of ripe honeydew drizzled with the peated syrup. That was the most unusual, delicious and memorable ending to a dinner I've ever had. The combination of melon and sweet smoke really worked - so (naturally...) I thought why not mix sweet Bourbon and peat? Worked for me! The main flavour (or melody) is sweet honey from a ripe Bourbon. The enhancing flavour (or harmony) is floral fruity spice from a mature rye Whisky. The accent (Satchmo's gravelly voice!) is the smoke from a peated Scotch Whisky. The proportions? Top secret. So...as the sun sinks low and the cold settles in, grab a Bottle of Campfire Whisky and gather round a blazing fire to warm up, wind down your day, share stories, and deepen friendships. One taste of this sweet, spicy and, yes...smoky Whisky, you'll know how it got its name. We like to enjoy Campfire Whisky with s'mores…or good-looking strangers."

Does this sound like a host who wants to show you a good time on a Distillery Tour? We tip our hat to David and the High West Saloon as we ride away from the setting sun.

WILD TURKEY DISTILLERY TOUR IN LAWRENCEBURG KENTUCKY

Heading East, we arrive in the state of Kentucky. Ladies and gentlemen, we are in Bourbon Territory and on the Bourbon trail and our first stop is the Austin Nichol's Wild Turkey Distillery. One of the wisest investments any Distillery can make is in their guest services. The Italian company Campari that owns Wild Turkey are putting in a big investment into the guest services of their well-known Brand to the tune of 4 million dollars to refurbish the Visitor Centre of the Distillery. The official press release says, "The new Wild Turkey Visitor Centre will be a dramatic upgrade over the small, 1,000-square-foot, circa 1800s building that currently hosts tastings for Bourbon fans and serves as the company gift shop. Offering dramatic vistas of Wild Turkey Hill and the Kentucky River, the striking new building will occupy 8,500 square feet and be perched just behind the new Distillery expansion, which opened in 2011. Slated to open in April 2013, the new Wild Turkey Visitor Centre is expected to welcome upwards of 70,000 visitors annually – up significantly from the 35,000 visitors per year of the previous facility. Broad woodwork along the outside of the two-story structure will be reminiscent of the staves that make up Bourbon Barrels. Vast windows will look out over the scenic Kentucky River and an expansive terrace will be perfect for picnics, events, and even musical performances. Inside, Whisky fans can expect to see a thoughtful Blend of the distinctive history of Wild Turkey and the Bourbon Industry presented through modern technology." Many a Tourist in the past has been surprised that their Tour Guide has been none other than Jimmy Russell, the Master Distiller and Brand ambassador - which in Whisky terms, would be like being treated to a guided Tour of Disneyland by Walt Disney himself. Jimmy Russell told us that he likes to drop by as often as he can to say hello to the visitors and in 2012 there were 50,000 visitors. Jimmy says, "I'm a people person and I like the personal touch. I like to hear people tell me their Wild Turkey stories and hear what the Bourbon means to them. When the Tour finishes up in the new Visitor Centre, people will be able to taste our Wild Turkey while looking over the Kentucky River – a perfect finish if you ask me."

JACK DANIEL'S DISTILLERY TOUR

We'll get off the Bourbon trail for the moment, head to the nearby state of Tennessee and look at Tennessee Whisky, and specifically the Distillery built by Mr Daniel. They say that charm will get you everywhere and there is no lack of charm with the Brand Jack Daniel's. You can almost here the relaxed Southern drawl in the open invitation: "Drop by for a firsthand look at our Distillery where one of our guides will accompany you on a Tour and tell you the complete story of our Whisky. And you'll probably hear an interesting story or two about Mr. Jack as well. We hope to see you around Lynchburg sometime soon." Its friendly, personal, relaxed and let's face it - the charm works. Distilleries around the world could learn a thing or two from this secret ingredient that bring 250, 000 visitors a year on the JD Distillery Tour. No one could or should try to duplicate the Tennessee charm - it has to be charm in a Scottish context or Irish, or Japanese or from any other culture the Tourists want to experience. This cannot be manufactured. That's why robots make lousy Tour Guides. "Yep," says the JD website, "I think it's safe to say that Jack Daniel's Whisky & the folks of Lynchburg have successfully merged together as one throughout history to Bottle up one really unique experience & product that depicts the true essence of southern style & charm." One reviewer of the Jack Daniel's' Tour said that it was great even for a teetotaler.

"Our guide was Big John and he was excellent. Big John told us entertaining and informative anecdotes about the history of Jack Daniel's the man and the Jack Daniel's Distillery that he founded. Jack was a very small man and the water flowing through the Distillery property is unique and accounts for the special taste of Jack Daniel's products. Our guide was very knowledgeable and very personable. A lot of the Tour is outdoors so the not-too-cold sunny day that we went made for a pleasant experience. One interesting fact our guide told us is that the Distillery is located in a dry county that has been dry ever since Prohibition. We saw all the phases of producing Jack Daniel's. The Tour involves all the senses, including the sense of smell. The smell of the yeast as the product was fermenting was unforgettable! Big vats, Whisky aging in Barrels and Barrels on floor to ceiling shelves, gauges and dials are all fascinating sights. There was a room where we saw people behind a glass wall monitoring the processes going on in the fermenting rooms and others. Absolutely fascinating Tour even to this teetotaller."

One of our C. Ask Whisky contacts won an all expense trip from Scotland to Lynchburg, Tennessee in order to experience all things Jack Daniel's. JD had put on a UK wide promotional tie in with rock/pop concerts called 'The Jack Daniel's Set.' There were regional competitions around the UK and to make a long story short, our spy ended up on a plane with other winners, flying from the UK out to Nashville. They were put up in a nice Nashville hotel and experienced the Nashville music scene.

The next day, a bus picked up all the winners and took them to Lynchburg. It was our contact's first trip to the USA and he was struck by how friendly the people from Lynchburg were. The Distillery was hard at work, doing what it did day in and day out and it was a treat to watch the process and have it explained. Big John was the Tour Guide and there was a lot of fun banter that went on between the Scot and the good natured guide. There was a friendly argument about which country made the best Whisky and it was pointed out that a lot of the Scotch wouldn't taste the way it did if it wasn't for the virgin Oak Barrels initially filled with Bourbon or Tennessee Whisky. Our contact bought a 1954 limited Edition White Rabbit Bottle of JD and loads of memorabilia. After the Distillery Tour, everyone was bussed out of dry (no Alcohol drinking) Lynchburg to a barn across State lines, where there was a barbecue, free bar and a great rock concert with well known UK acts.

Several years after the JD Tour, our spy went on the Bushmills Tour in Northern Ireland. He said it was good and very interesting but it lacked what Lynchburg had. In Lynchburg, the people who worked at the Distillery were primarily locals including the Tour Guides, where as the Tour Guide they had at Bushmills wasn't even Irish the day he went. It was a university intern from Portugal who had learned the script but the Tour was missing that authenticity that our spy had experienced in Lynchburg. It is the way of the world for big corporations to buy up local Distilleries, but sometimes the impersonal nature of the giant corporation filters on down to the operation at the local level and therefore some of the personal local charm can be the collateral damage of such buy-outs. One Scottish Distillery we talked to wanted to do so much more investment into their guest services but their corporate masters were thousands of miles away and were unwilling to make that investment, leaving the local Distillery frustrated that they couldn't do more for their guests. Tourists should be aware of this problem for many a Distillery and instead of taking out your frustrations on the local Distillery, you should write a letter of complaint to the corporation behind the local Distillery.

WOODFORD RESERVE

We'll go back to Kentucky and take in one more stop on the Bourbon trail.

None other than CNN had a feature article entitled: 10 Tours For Every Kind Of Drinker. They say, "Whichever flavour you like to toss back, somewhere there's a booze Tour with your name on it. From Belgium to Barbados, here are 10 of our favourites." the first on their list was Woodford Reserve: "Kentucky's oldest and smallest Distillery, Woodford Reserve lovingly crafts its Bourbon in small batches. Maybe that's why it's the official Bourbon of the Kentucky Derby. At the Distillery -- also a National Historic Landmark -- visitors take a guided Tour that explains the history of Bourbon, Bottling process and how Woodford Reserve does something special with all five sources of Bourbon flavour. For example, they don't just use water; they use deep limestone well water. Big difference (as they'll explain). Best of all, guests get to linger with the award-winning craft Bourbon. On the Corn to Cork Tour you can dive deeper into the Bourbon-making process. Or you can just start serving up mint juleps." One visitor/ reviewer said, "This has been my favourite Distillery Tour, and I have Toured several. The combination of the beautiful setting, engaging staff and delicious Bourbon made for a relaxing and memorable afternoon that Kentucky natives and visitors alike can enjoy."

Do you see the pattern emerging? Do you see how often the common denominators of Location (especially beauty spots) and great personalities behind the Brands crop up? The personalities behind the products are crucial. The best Tour Guides are those who can explain everything with charm, enthusiasm, warmth and humour. People don't relate well to machines. We relate to people even if the people happen to be talking about machines."

Speaking of the people behind the product, we were able to meet Chris Morris who is not only Woodford Reserve's Master Distiller, but the Master Distiller over three of Brown-Forman's Distilleries.

INTERVIEW WITH CHRIS MORRIS:

C. ASK: Hi Chris. How did you become the Master Distiller for Brown-Forman?

CHRIS MORRIS: I joined Brown-Forman in 1976. My mother and father worked for Brown-Forman and now my daughter and nephew work at Brown-Forman so I'm in the middle of three generations that have all worked for the same company. I worked my way up over 28 years and was trained for 28 years to become the Master Distillery and I took on that role 8 years ago. I now look after three Distilleries – the Canadian Mist Distillery in Ontario that also makes Collingwood Canadian Whisky. The Woodford Reserve Distillery make Woodford Reserve, Woodford Reserve Double Oak, and the Masters Collection. The Brown-Forman Distillery in Louiseville Kentucky makes Old Forrester and Early Times.

C ASK: So how do you look after three Distilleries at once?

CHRIS MORRIS: Each Distillery has a plant manager – they all do a terrific job and even though they answer to me, we are all a team. The Canadian Mist Distillery is in Collingwood, South West Ontario and quite close to Detroit. Each week I get samples shipped down to me, so on a weekly basis, I am reviewing, tasting and approving samples from the products we are putting out from our Canadian Distillery. The Brown-Forman and Woodford Reserve Distilleries are an hour apart and so I'm back and forth, up and down the highway between the two Distilleries.

C ASK: Which of the Brands is doing best overseas?

CHRIS MORRIS: Canadian Mist and Collingwood are really North American specific. Early Times is the largest selling Bourbon in Japan and its doing well in all of Asia and Russia too. Woodford Reserve is in 36 foreign markets and doing well in all of them. That is the product we are continuing to develop on a global scale.

C ASK: Do you think the success of Early Times in Japan is down to packaging and presentation?

CHRIS MORRIS: Much more than that. You know how the Japanese value relationships, integrity and quality? Early Times was truly early getting into Japan after the war and while other Bourbons have changed hands and had different representations, Early Times has always been Brown- Forman, so there has been a consistency in our long good relationship with Japan and that is why Early Times is second only to our big brother in Brown-Forman Jack Daniel's as far as sales go in Japan.

C ASK: What is your opinion of Scotch and Irish Whiskies?

CHRIS MORRIS: I am a big fan of Scotch and Irish Whiskies. I am a member of the Keepers of the Quaich and I hold the Whiskies in the highest regard. Over the history of Brown-Forman we have represented Blended Scotch Whiskies. We at one time had shared ownership of Glenmorangie and Ardbeg, though we no longer do so now. I hold Irish Whiskies in high regard as well. I recognize our distinct differences and I recognize our common heritage.

C ASK: Do any of your products come close to how the Irish and Scotch Whiskies taste or are made?

CHRIS MORRIS: We did a tasting with our executives last week with our Canadian Mist and Jameson's Irish Whisky and it was remarkable how close they were together in taste. They are made practically the same way and our executives couldn't tell the two apart. I haven't run into a Blended Scotch that matches the taste profile of any of our products but I would say our Collingwood compares nicely to a Glenlivet – one that has not been exposed to Sherry wood. Our Woodford Reserve, though very different from a Single Malt, is still enjoyed by Single Malt drinkers. It is the only Bourbon to use some of the features of Single Malt production such as the Copper Pot Still and Triple Distillation. In our Woodford Reserve Masters Collection, we just launched more wood where the Bourbon's have been finished in Port and Sherry Casks and then married and that reminds a lot of people of their favourite Single Malts while still being different. I think our products dovetail nicely with the Irish and Scotch Whiskies that we all love.

C. ASK: Do you hope to make something that is like a Single Malt Scotch Whisky?

CHRIS MORRIS: No, we don't want to be Scotch or Irish. We want to be American and Canadian. What I'm saying is that those who enjoy Irish and Scottish Whiskies could also be just as happy with our Collingwood or Woodford Reserve expressions.

C. ASK: Are your Whiskies good for mixing? Would you advise putting water in the Whisky?

CHRIS MORRIS: We make Whiskies for people to enjoy and if they want to put Coca-Cola, if they want to put water, if they want to put Grandma's dirty socks in – as long as they enjoy it, we are fine with that. Our Whiskies are so well crafted that the addition of anything will not degrade the character and flavour of the Whisky itself.

C. ASK: I know you are in the same corporate family as Jack Daniel's, but would you say Woodford Reserve is more exclusive than Jack Daniel's?

CHRIS MORRIS: Yes, it is. We know from consumer research that Woodford Reserve and Collingwood are generally not used in mixed drinks but are taken straight or on the rocks. In that respect, they are more like a European Whisky. That is not to say that there are not some people that will add Coke, or use them to make a Manhattan or some other kind of cocktail but we know that the Whiskies are heavily skewed toward being consumed in their purest form.

C. ASK: So you would say that the Whiskies are the Connoisseur's choice of American Whiskies?

CHRIS MORRIS: I would say so – in fact, the late great writer for the Los Angeles Times, Larry Apple, said "Woodford Reserve has set the standard by which all other American Whiskies should be judged." High praise indeed. No one had ever done a flavour wheel for North American Whiskies. They've done that for Beer, Wine and European Malts. Brown-Forman had a flavour wheel made to analyze numerous North American Whiskies and Woodford Reserve was well represented in the five categories of flavour – the five spokes of the wheel. The European wheel had six spokes, but we don't have a smoky-peaty side to our Whiskies. The five spokes of the wheel represent the Barrel notes, the fruit and floral notes, spice notes, grain notes and wood characteristics. In all these areas, Woodford Reserve came out strong. There are notes of vanilla, caramel, butterscotch, chocolate both light and dark and marshmallow. Woodford Reserve is very fruity with berry notes such as blueberry and raspberry. There are apple notes, cherry notes, green grape notes. There are tropical fruit notes – hints of pineapple, coconut, orange, banana, mango and dark fruit like figs, dates and raisins. In the floral area there are wonderful hints of rose petals, honeysuckle and orange blossoms. Of wood characteristics there are many expressions of oak, cedar, pine, almond, pecan, hazelnut and walnut. As for grain – and strangely for a Bourbon – corn does not predominate but rather rye and malt. Among the spice notes there is tobacco leaf, coffee bean, cloves, nutmeg, anise, herbs, dill, leather, cinnamon and mint. There is a flavour for everybody. We think we have the most flavourful American Whisky with the science to back it up.

C. ASK: How long is Woodford Reserve aged for and how does that compare to the aging process in Scotland and Ireland?

CHRIS MORRIS: Let's put the aging into its context. Unlike a Scotch or an Irish Whisky, a Bourbon goes into a new charred Oak Barrel and that is an aggressive flavour source. The Barrels then end up in Scotland, Ireland or elsewhere for the maturation and finishing of Whiskies over there have all been used where as we are constrained by law to use a new Barrel. Secondly, the climate is different. Our Barrels are stored in hot warehouses and heat accelerates and drives the maturation process. After 7 years in a Barrel, I lose 50% of what went into the Barrel. If I left it to 12 years like the standard entry level Scotch, I'd have nothing left, and yet our 7 YO is as fully mature as a 12 YO Scotch. We don't put out an age statement because it is unfair to judge our Whisky by age alone. It should be judged by character and flavour. There are a small number of Casks that some hold back and keep in cold storage so it can reach those age numbers approaching Scotch and that is only to market to those who think a number is more important than the flavour and would judge a Whisky on that basis alone.

C. ASK: Don't you think a limited edition 50 YO Jack Daniel's's would sell like hotcakes at a huge price? Couldn't the Casks be held in cold storage for something like that?

CHRIS MORRIS: Even if we did something like that and even in cold storage, the new Barrel would still make the Whisky so tannic, so acidic it would be unpalatable. I've held back Casks of our Old Forrester up to 17 years and went to try it, and it was completely un-drinkable!

C. ASK: What's up ahead for Brown-Forman?

CHRIS MORRIS: There will be special editions of Collingwood that will be exceptional. There will be new Blends and new finishing techniques that have never been done before in Canada. The future is very exciting for Collingwood. In regard to Woodford Reserve, there is the Master's collection - more unique Whiskies that have never been made before in the United States. These are one offs and not to be repeated. The Master Collection releases have already been getting great reviews. In March 2012 we created Woodford Reserve Double Oak that was matured in a toasted, but not charred Barrel. That won best North American Whisky at the International Spirit Awards in Edinburgh. We'll be creating more products along these lines. There is an exciting future ahead and we are picking up new people who like our products everyday!

CANADIAN CLUB BRAND CENTRE TOUR

Heading North from Kentucky, we arrive in Windsor Ontario in Canada, which also just happens to be the home of Canadian Club. Rather than take you to the more industrial Distillery that actually makes the Whisky, Canadian club would rather tell you all about how they make Canadian Club and the extraordinary history of the Brand by inviting you inside an Italian type palace, a copy of a building Canadian Club's creator, Hiram Walker had seen on his world travels. "The elegant exterior features terra cotta ornament and bronze gates and lanterns. The interior boasts mahogany panelling, ornate woodwork and imported marble," says the Windsorkiosk.com. With Canadian Club you get a bit of culture, class, immaculately kept grounds, Renaissance architecture and art. This is what happens once you are guests in the palace: "An hour and a half guided Tour takes a visitor to the CCBC back in history to the height of the Hiram Walker family's success, and his personal friendships with the biggest names in history - (Henry Ford and Thomas Edison). Guests are brought into the basement Speak Easy room, where meetings were held with Al Capone and The Purple Gang, and are told the story of how Canadian Club Whisky quenched the thirst of many U.S. citizens for 13 long years during Prohibition, from 1920-1933. On the second floor, guests are invited into Hiram's Sampling Room, a Canadian Art Gallery and into the theatre where they will watch a short video about the production of Canadian Club. The Tour finishes with a formal Whisky sampling." One of the visitor/reviewers fills in some of the details and the posted review said, "The Tour includes a stop in a Wine cellar once used by Al Capone as a secret meeting room. The gangster, the company's number one customer during Prohibition, commanded his own personal entrance and a windowless private lair insulated from prying eyes. (The number two customer was a Kennedy, we were told). There, he helped the company design flat, thick glass Bottles that resisted breakage ... and that could be literally slipped into a boot and walked back over the border (Coining, apparently, the term bootlegging). As all factory Tours should, this one ends in the tasting room, where we were given small samples of the company's four flagship products. A little sip of each did me just fine, but I have a nephew, I believe, who would have wept over the Whisky we left behind in each sample glass. The guides are knowledgeable, the company has a remarkable sense of humour about the darker side of their business during Prohibition, and everyone in our party seemed to enjoy their hour wandering through the "Palace that Whisky Built."

KILBEGGAN DISTLLERY TOUR

Heading across the pond, we arrive on the Emerald Isle to visit Kilbeggan and Middleton Irish Distilleries. Kilbeggan describes the experience they offer this way: "Start your Tour in 1757 and discover how Irish Whisky was made in the time of the Lockes ownership of the Distillery on one side of the courtyard and then follow on to see how Kilbeggan Irish Whisky is now being made in the traditional manner which includes a 180 year old Pot Still. A visit to Kilbeggan Distillery is a unique experience not to be missed!

Right in the heart of Ireland lies the town of Kilbeggan, home to the world's oldest Distillery, established in 1757. It is the quintessential Irish Whisky Distillery – whitewashed walls, weathered slate roof, brick chimney stack, creaking timber water wheel, even regular ghost sightings. This is no mere "Visitor Centre" but a real working Distillery run by a team of young enthusiastic craftspeople (and a few wise old heads too), skilled in the traditional ways of making Irish Whisky. The Whisky Bar stocks the complete range of Cooley Distillery Whiskies, including the limited edition Kilbeggan Malt Distillery Reserve and Kilbeggan 18 YO. The Gift Shop sells a range of gift ideas including clothing and glasses. We can also personalise a Bottle of Kilbeggan Whisky or Tyrconnell Malt Whisky as gifts."

One visitor wrote: "As a Whisky Enthusiast and Aficionado I've visited countless Distilleries and Distillery museums throughout Scotland, The United States and Ireland, including ALL the Irish Distilleries, and the Kilbeggan Distillery and Locke's Distillery Museum is in my Top 2 Must Visit Distilleries in the World as well as being my Number 1 Must Visit Distillery in Ireland. "

THE JAMESON'S EXPERIENCE IN MIDLETON

Remaining in Ireland, we head to the Midleton Distillery to hear all about Jameson's Irish Whisky. The experience is described this way: "Set on 15 acres and beautifully restored, this is where the true heart of Irish Whisky is born. Our old Distillery is a unique experience with some of the buildings dating back to 1795. Take a journey through history and see the old kilns, mills and malting, water wheel and old warehouses. The Jameson Experience in Midleton is one of the top attractions in Cork, as rated by TripAdvisor." C. Ask Whisky looked at the reviews and it was true that 85 out of the 99 reviews of the Tour were very positive rating it good to excellent. One visitor said: "The Tour starts with a 10 minute audio visual Tour briefing you of the Jameson factory and local area. From here you wander through the factory and mills, learning from a Tour Guide how the Whisky process takes place from when the grains come to the mill to the Bottling of Whisky. afterwards you sit down in the bar and enjoy Whisky tasting session of four Whiskies and a discussion. afterwards you can sit and enjoy your complimentary Whisky. I found inside the fantastic gift store, you can get a Distillary reserve 10 YO Whisky with your name printed on it. It makes for a truly great gift."

It impressed C. Ask Whisky that the manager of the Jameson Experience took the time to write back to this reviewer, saying,

"Thank you for taking the time to review your recent experience , we appreciate getting feedback from our visitors!
It seems you thoroughly enjoyed your visit to the Jameson Experience Midleton, and we are delighted to hear it! Our personalised Bottle of Distillery Reserve truly is a great gift for any Whisky enthusiast. It is said that our founder, John Jameson would always have a special reserve of his Whisky especially for guests to the Distillery and that tradition continues to this day.
We hope you continue to enjoy our Whisky,
Slainte!" To go the extra mile for the guest and follow up with a thanks for coming is commendable.

THE SCOTTISH DISTILLERY TOURS

Taking the ferry across the Irish Sea we arrive in Scotland and our first stop will be Crieff, in Perthshire. Driving up to our first Distillery stop, we see the statue of a bird associated with a well-known Whisky Brand.

THE FAMOUS GROUSE EXPERIENCE: A reviewer for secret-Scotland.com said, "The Famous Grouse Experience and the Glenturret Distillery are the same company. Glenturret is the Malt Whisky produced here, while the Famous Grouse is the Blended Whisky that is based upon the Glenturret Malt. It has the distinction of being the most visited Distillery in Scotland.

The Famous Grouse Experience offers 3 different types of Tour:

1. The Glenturret Distillery Tour, which is like a Tour of any other Distillery in Scotland and shows you the process of making a Malt Whisky.

2. The Experience Tour which is much more interesting and explains the process of making Whisky and creating a Blend (Famous Grouse). There are 2 twists at the end of the Tour: a) the Famous Grouse takes centre stage in an interactive video show, and b) your ability to detect different aromas is tested.

3. The Malt Tasting Tour is like the Experience Tour plus a tasting of 5 different malts.

The Famous Grouse Experience, like Dewar's World of Whisky, is a more modern interpretation of the Distillery visit than you will find in most Distilleries. As a result, it is very good entertainment for the whole family, but maybe a little bit too "theme park" for the Whisky purists."

The reviewer is saying its good, its popular, its family friendly, its imaginative and then gives the niggle, saying it won't please the Whisky purists because it has elements that remind the reviewer of theme parks. In defence of Dewar's and Grouse, they are at least trying to address a major complaint that some of the Distillery Tours get and that is that the Distillery Tour can be lacklustre, boring and not interesting to anyone other than the Whisky purists.

Could it be better? Could Dewar's be better? We have an Entertainment Industry perspective and in the opinion of C. Ask Whisky, there are many ways to improve the entertainment value of the tour and we commend those who make the effort. Is there room for improvement? There is always room for improvement! Since an amusement park comparison has been made, whether fairly or unfairly, there is a lesson to be learned from the amusement parks. They never think, "We're done, that's it ! People love us, like our rides and keep coming back, so we'll just sit still and let the cash roll in." No! They are always thinking, "What new ride can we make for next year? What new rollercoaster?" In a Distilleries case it should be asking, "What else can we do for our guests? Do we need a new script? New stories? New investment into our Visitor Centre? What will make all our guests go "Wow!"

AN INTERVIEW WITH DAVID COX OF MACALLAN

In the 70s David Cox worked in Japan importing Spirits and learned enough Japanese to carry on a conversation. Little did David know then that he would be overseeing the guest relations for a major Brand that would welcome Japanese Tourists and many other Tourists from around the world. This brings up another important matter that Distilleries have to think about. As many Tourists come to Scotland from Japan and elsewhere, foreign guests are always delighted to find someone who can speak to them in their own language. David doesn't always get to meet the guests from Japan or from other places around the globe as his current duties mean overseeing guest relations for

Edrington's Macallan Brand from a base office in Perth; he is up at the Distillery monthly and the Tour Guides of Macallan answer to him but his vital duties are largely behind the scenes. When he does get to meet Tourists from Japan, they are pleasantly surprised to find someone who they can talk to and who can speak to them. I recall being on a Tour on the Spanish Island of Majorca and being very impressed with a Tour Guide who could conduct the Tour around the island in five different languages. "What can we do to improve our service?" asks many a Distillery. Investing in guides who are fluent in several different languages or having translators on speed dial would show that you are bending over backwards for your special guests from another land. C. Ask Whisky thought it important to have this book translated from English into Japanese, Mandarin, Dutch, Swedish, German, French and Danish because the world of Whisky is much bigger than the few countries that speak English.

We've been derailed from David's story so let us return to it. From importing Spirits in Japan, he returned to the UK and worked with Diageo in the 90s, before Edrington hired him to look after guest relations for Macallan.

In David's view, the Distillery Tour of Macallan had always been good; there were enthusiastic, warm, welcoming guides who did a thorough job explaining the Brand Macallan, but it was no different from many other Distillery Tours on offer. A large investment was made to improve the Visitor Centre and the Distillery Tour. Here was an opportunity to tell the story of Macallan with a captive audience and they wanted to do the best job possible. Like and good drama, they dramatically set the scene beginning with the natural history and talking about the geology around the 370 acre estate. They talk about the spring water that feeds the still and the special kind of barley (much of which is grown on the Macallan estate) called Minstrel Barley. Many guests arrive at the Craigellachie location from busy urban areas and even though there is Whisky production happening on an industrial scale - the Industry is dwarfed by the peaceful natural surroundings. Many comment on the beauty and tranquillity of the area which adds to the enjoyable experience of the Tour. Though there are mini science lessons about water and wood, fermentation and so forth - it is fun, entertaining science.

Science? Fun? The two words don't seem to go together, especially if anyone struggled with the subject at school. Way back in the 50s and 60s, Walt Disney pioneered fun educational films using animation to explain, math or science and other topics. The Film Jurassic Park references that style of film making when they tell the animated story of how the Jurassic Park scientists got the dinosaur DNA on the guest Tour for the scientists visiting the dinosaur theme park.

David didn't mention Disney or Jurassic Park - but he did say that the way they explained the biology of the Spanish Oak that they use and other scientific topics that have to do with Whisky production were fun, inter-active and interesting and they do use multimedia to tell their story.

There is even a finale David told us about, but we don't want to spoil that surprise they have waiting for you and that is not the only surprise along the way.

C. Ask Whisky asked about the Guides Macallan hired. David said there were four full time Guides working for the Distillery, which unlike many Scottish Distilleries is open all year round. In the busy seasons of Spring and Summer, university students will join the regular four and shadow the pros until they are ready to take groups on their own. The groups are never big and kept down to around ten in number so there is that more personal touch.

C. ASK: What qualities do you look for in a Guide?

DAVID COX: We look for warmth and a welcoming personality, empathy - someone who is sensitive to the different people and cultures that are in our care while they are with us.

C. ASK: How important is humour and who among your guides would you say is the funniest?

DAVID COX: Margaret Gray has been with us for around 20 years and she has a wonderful, natural bubbly personality. She knows a million stories and people like her the moment they meet her. All four Guides are good, and each is different from the other but I would say Margaret can be the funniest. Humour is very important.

C. ASK: How seriously do you take any complaint that a guest makes?

DAVID COX: Very seriously. Our guests are very important to us. The feedback is by and large very positive, but if there is a problem, we will want to address it immediately.

EVEN MORE MACALLAN

David went on to tell us that for VIP guests flying in from around the world, there was a converted guest house on the estate built originally in 1700 called the East Elchies house and between that and another cottage on the grounds they could entertain special guests, invite them to dinner and not only provide food and lodging - but fishing as the Distillery has the rights to fish along a mile of the River Spey.
Beyond communicating their Brand with invited guests in the Distillery, Macallan has sought to reach out to new consumers around the world through innovative advertising using famous photographers and artists. Their Brand is associated with high culture, sophistication and luxury and so three well known photographers Rankin, Albert Watson and Annie Leibowitz were brought in for a special Masters of Photography series that tells the Macallan story from Speyside to the Casks in Spain, to Leibowitz' four photographs of Scottish actor Kevin McKidd in four different moods and settings in New York City. There are also special Bottlings of Macallan tied to the artist Peter Blake, best known for creating the Beatles' Sergeant Pepper album cover.

IN SUMMARY

Those who make the biggest effort to please their guests will reap the benefits of life long customers. The greatest advertising is word of mouth, and if your guests are happy, they will tell others. The personal human touch, humour, warmth, friendliness combined with great communication skills, stories and anecdotes are vital to make the Distillery Tour experience work. The location, the upkeep, the comfort, the value for money are all winning ingredients in this business of the Distillery Tour.

C. Ask Whisky is pleased to announce the C. Ask Whisky Distillery Tour, a very entertaining Tour of the best Distilleries in Scotland.
Go to www.askwhisky.com for details.

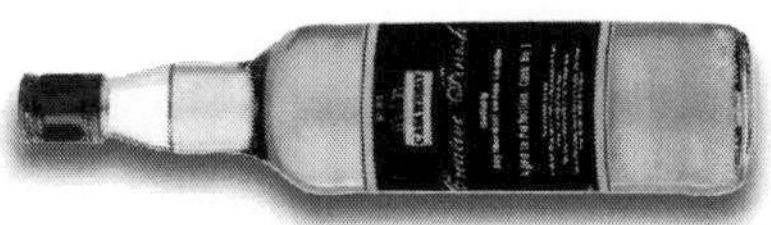

CHAPTER *eight* *Whisky and culture*

Let us now take a brief glimpse at mere snapshots of Whisky's impact on society through books, plays, Cinema, movie stars and well known Musical icons. There are millions of references in Literature alone and a million more in movies and song. Had we the time, we would look to sporting icons and Whisky; that could be a subject all on its own! When C. Ask Whisky interviewed Angela D'Orazeo of the Swedish Whisky brand Mackmyra, she mentioned that the superstar hockey player and hall-of-famer, Borje Salming, who was with the Toronto Maple Leafs for 16 years, was an athlete with a taste for Mackmyra and it is said that Mr. Michael 'Air' Jordan, one of the greatest basketball players who has ever lived is fond of 12 YO Glenlivet.

WHISKY IN LITERATURE

SHAKESPEARE: Whisky was being Distilled in Ireland and Scotland at the time of William Shakespeare but there is no specific mention of Whisky in his works, though there are 360 references to Alcoholic beverages in his 38 plays; Wine, Beer, Ale and Liquor are mentioned many times. Even in the Scottish play, Macbeth, it is not Whisky but Wine and Ale that the characters imbibe. Obviously Will didn't travel much north of the border. He got the women right in the play - but then anyone who has had a disastrous relationship with a Scottish woman would look at Lady Macbeth or the three witches, hold up a dram and say, "Yeah, Will, that's pretty accurate." There is a reference to Distillation in the play, but this refers to a magical witch's brew.
The Wyrd Sisters
Double, double, toil and trouble;
Fire burn, and cauldron bubble.

Second Witch
Fillet of a fenny snake,

In the cauldron boil and bake;
Eye of newt and toe of frog,
Wool of bat and tongue of dog,
Adder's fork and blind-worm's sting,
Lizard's leg and howlet's wing.
For a charm of powerful trouble,
Like a hell-broth boil and bubble.

True, what the Wyrd Sisters are making isn't exactly malted barley that goes through a fermenting and Distillation process, but I don't think it is a coincidence that they are making such a brew in Scotland and after such early experimentation, they probably went on to open a Distillery. Maybe it was called Glen's Liver Distillery or La Hag, Bow-Wow-More or Tomcatintoul. In fact, I think that based on their choice of ingredients, they probably flew on their brooms to Thailand and showed the people how to make Whisky there with eye of newt, toad, batwing and other items that they could pickle and sell to tourists. As we've seen in the Whisked Around The Whirld Chapter, some of the Whiskies in South East Asia are every bit as weird as the brew in Shakespeare's play.

The word Distilled appears later when Hecate, Queen of the Witches gets in on the act, brewing stuff from the moon that will mess up Macbeth's head even further. To be honest, I think the whole subtext of the play is about Whisky.

Hecate
I'll catch it ere it come to ground:
And that Distill'd by magic sleights
Shall raise such artificial sprites
As by the strength of their illusion
Shall draw him on to his confusion.

Just another Saturday night in Glasgow if you ask me.

The word Liquor shows up in many of the plays such as a reference in Romeo and Juliet. As we race toward the cheerful ending of the play, Juliet's dad is going to force her to marry someone she doesn't give a stuff about. She's having none of it. The fact that she is already secretly married to Romeo complicates this matter further. With the help of Friar Lawrence she decides to hit the Bottle and drink some Distilled Liquor that will induce a death-like state - possibly Bruichladdich x 4 quadruple Distilled Whisky, which is reputed to be the strongest Whisky in the world. By faking her own death, she can then wake up later and run away with Romeo, though things don't quite work out how she plans that results in a double suicide of the star crossed lovers and everyone leaves the play on a downer, wanting to go to the nearest bar or pub and order Bruichladdich x 4. If only she had had a mobile phone to text Romeo: "Faking own death. Don't kill yourself. LOL." Here is the reference in the play:

FRIAR LAWRENCE TO JULIET:
Take thou this vial, being then in bed,
And this Distilled Liquor drink thou off;
'Tis Bruichladdich Distilled not the once, nor twice, nor thrice but quadruple times.
When presently through all thy veins shall run
A cold and drowsy humour, for no pulse
Shall keep his native progress, but surcease:
No warmth, no breath, shall testify thou livest;
The roses in thy lips and cheeks shall fade
To paly ashes, thy eyes' windows fall,
Like death, when he shuts up the day of life;

OK, I confess, Shakespeare didn't write one of those lines but if he were alive today, the Bruichladdich x 4 reference would be there!

One more example. You will be such a cultured lot of Whisky enthusiasts by the time you finish this book! In Midsummer Night's Dream, the play with all the fairies - which is almost like saying the football team with all the athletes - Oberon, King of the fairies plays a trick on his wife, Titania. He puts a magic Liquor in her eyes that will make her fall in love with the first thing she sees - which in the play is a guy with the head of a jackass. In other words, it has the same effect that too much Whisky can have!

OBERON
Having once this juice,
I'll watch Titania when she is asleep,
And drop the Liquor of it in her eyes.
The next thing then she waking looks upon,
Be it on lion, bear, or wolf, or bull,
On meddling monkey, or on busy ape,
She shall pursue it with the soul of love.

Come on. Admit it. This kind of thing has happened to some of you before when you've had one dram too many!

Though there is not a specific Whisky named in honour of William Shakespeare, there is a Whisky Liqueur named after the bard, and it comes in one of the most collectable artistic Bottles you can find. We spoke to Roy Lewis, the man behind the William Shakespeare Liqueur at Hebridean Liqueurs. Why Hebridean? Roy's surname, Lewis, is also the name of one of the Hebridean Isles. His many trips to Lewis and Harris were among the reasons he named his Helensburgh-based business after the Hebrides, even though he doesn't operate from the islands. Roy told us that his motive for developing the William Shakespeare Liqueur was that he thought it would sell well to the tourists. His inspiration for the flavour was based on a bit of research that suggested that imported oranges from warmer climates of the world, were just starting to come into Great Britain in the time of the Bard and though the citrus fruit is not the emphasis of any of Will's writings, the flavour of oranges was the emphasis of Mr Lewis's Whisky Liqueur. He could have made a similar concoction in honour of William of Orange, but wisely he chose Shakespeare who is a much less divisive figure in history.

Here is how Mr. Lewis promotes his Whisky Liqueur: "The recipe used harks back to Shakespeare's day when Whisky was mixed with oranges and caramel. This gave the Whisky a unique tangy flavour while retaining the smooth, silky taste of caramel".

The Liqueur is packaged in an antique type Bottle similar to those used in the sixteenth century. A copy of William Shakespeare's Last Will & Testament bearing his signature is wrapped around the Bottle neck. On the reverse of the stylish document is an excerpt from

Macbeth. This, together with the authentic orange and Whisky flavour of 20% Alcohol by volume, provides a unique experience by capturing the spirit of Shakespeare's world.

William Shakespeare, when writing plays such as Macbeth, King Lear and Cymbeline, referred to historical texts, many of which detailed the usage of Whisky and the effects that this potent drink can have. Capturing the spirit of Shakespeare's world, this exquisite combination of Whisky and orange and its stylish packaging is a new production receiving huge applause." Roy produces three other Whisky Liqueurs - Hebridean Liqueur with a caramel flavour, Lakeland Liqueur with a Blending of butterscotch, caramel and Whisky and High Peak Liqueur with a vanilla-centric flavour. All four brands are beautifully packaged and are among the many other Spirit-Liqueurs that Mr. Lewis sells. To Whisky purists, mixing anything with a properly aged Whisky such as Highland Park or a Macallan is tantamount to blasphemy - although a different spirit is being offended in this case. Jack Daniel's, Canadian Club and other North American Whisky and Bourbon brands encourage the mixing as long as people are mixing with their product. The world is a big enough place for proper, luxuriously produced Whisky and also the kind of Whisky that you can mix with coke and sweet Whisky Liqueurs. There is room for all to co-exist peacefully side by side.

THE BIBLE: Hard to read. Small print. Controversial Opinions. That's just the Whisky Bible. For your cultural awareness, we bring up the cornerstone of Western Literature, the Holy Bible. There is no mention of Whisky in the Bible, but what it says about Alcohol is important for the cultured Whisky aficionado to know. "Drink your Wine with a merry heart…." says a verse in Ecclesiastes. I see those sceptical looks. You're waiting for it. What's the rub? What's the catch? When does the guilt trip start? If you had a religious mother, I bet she never quoted 'drink Wine with a merry heart' to you! Surely it means 'drink Wine with a merry heart now, because you're going to pay for that drink for all eternity in Hell so you better enjoy it while you can, you sinner!' The most well known work of Literature in the world is also the most misquoted and misunderstood book. Some have a square imprint on their head from where they were bashed by a wild-eyed angry religious nut. If one can get past those off-putting experiences and look at what is actually written, a very common sense picture emerges. There are positive and negative references to Alcohol in the Bible. The common Alcoholic beverage of the day, Wine, is often found in the context of joyous occasions; it is talked about as a 'gift from God' and a 'sign of God's favour' when the vats overflow and the vineyards yield a great harvest. Drunkenness is described accurately and is frowned upon. Here is a 3000 year old description of a bad a hangover from Proverbs 23:

Who has woe? Who has sorrow?
Who has strife? Who has complaints?
Who has needless bruises? Who has bloodshot eyes?
Those who linger over Wine,
who go to sample bowls of mixed Wine.
Do not gaze at Wine when it is red,
when it sparkles in the cup,
when it goes down smoothly!
In the end it bites like a snake
and poisons like a viper.
Your eyes will see strange sights,
and your mind will imagine confusing things.
You will be like one sleeping on the high seas,
lying on top of the rigging.
"They hit me," you will say, "but I'm not hurt!"
They beat me, but I don't feel it!
When will I wake up so I can find another drink?"

Yes, getting smashed is discouraged as well it should be. But what is so different about that and the message from every Whisky company in the world when they say, "Drink responsibly!" Drunks are not good poster boys and girls for any brand. One of the companies we were dealing with when producing the C. Ask Whisky Book and DVD wanted assurances that any celebrity that appeared with their brand on camera would be reputable and not have a DUI (Driving Under the Influence citation) on their record. We assured them that would be the case. They don't want to be associated with an inebriated fool and nor do we. One of the best speeches ever that argues for this balanced, common sense approach was from a Mississippi U. S. senator back in 1958 when he said: "If you mean Whisky, the devil's brew, the poison scourge, the bloody monster that defiles innocence, dethrones reason, destroys the home, creates misery and poverty, yea, literally takes the bread from the mouths of little children; if you mean that evil drink that topples Christian men and women from the pinnacles of righteous and gracious living into the bottomless pits of degradation, shame, despair, helplessness, and hopelessness, then, my friend, I am opposed to it with every fibre of my being.

However, if by Whisky you mean the oil of conversation, the philosophic Wine, the elixir of life, the Ale that is consumed when good fellows get together, that puts a song in their hearts and the warm glow of contentment in their eyes; if you mean Christmas cheer, the stimulating sip that puts a little spring in the step of an elderly gentleman on a frosty morning; if you mean that drink that enables man to magnify his joy, and to forget life's great tragedies and heartbreaks and sorrow; if you mean that drink the sale of which pours into our treasuries untold millions of dollars each year, that provides tender care for our little crippled children, our blind, our deaf, our dumb, our pitifully aged and infirm, to build the finest highways, hospitals, universities, and community colleges in this nation, then my friend, I am absolutely, unequivocally in favour of it. This is my position, and as always, I refuse to be compromised on matters of principle."

I don't know of a Whisky company in the world that would disagree with anything the senator said. When we were interviewing spokespeople from the companies, the Master Blenders, Distillers and Tasters, PR Reps and so forth, not one person we met was drunk. Everyone was professional, sensible, smart, intelligent and articulate. There was no slurred speech, no glazed eyes, no out-of-control behaviour. In fairness to the Bible, the book that has had the biggest cultural impact on the largest part of the world, it advocates this sensible approach to Alcohol related matters.

ROBERT BURNS: In the teenage movie comedy, Bill and Ted's Excellent Adventure, dim-witted California teens, Bill and Ted, travel through time to kidnap historical figures for their high school history project. They bring

Abraham Lincoln, Billy the Kid, Joan of Arc, Socrates, Genghis Kahn and Sigmund Freud to present day San Dimas High School. There was a missed opportunity. The one historical figure that they would have had more in common with than all the others was Scotland's greatest poet, the handsome, the charming, the affable Robert Burns. Abraham Lincoln tells San Dimas to "Be excellent to each other and party on dudes." This cheerful philosophy was more in keeping with the character of Burns than Abraham Lincoln, although Burns would have undoubtedly been more eloquent. Rabbie did have a way with the historical babes and he did quote them lyrics. Fourteen children resulted, only five of whom were born in wedlock. When not creating children, he created ingenious verse, born out of love, laughter and the celebration of life. With pen and paper in hand he would spend many a merry night in taverns with his friends and many a clever verse was born. Whisky was a friend to Rabbie and many a verse he created reflects this, such as this excerpt from his poem Scotch Drink:

Let other poets raise a fracas
"Bout vines, an' Wines, an' drucken Bacchus,
An' crabbit names an'stories wrack us,
An' grate our lug:
I sing the juice Scotch bear can mak us,
In glass or jug.

O thou, my muse! guid auld Scotch drink!
Whether thro' wimplin worms thou jink,
Or, richly brown, ream owre the brink,
In glorious faem,
Inspire me, till I lisp an' wink,
To sing thy name!

Let husky wheat the haughs adorn,
An' aits set up their awnie horn,
An' pease and beans, at e'en or morn,
Perfume the plain:
Leeze me on thee, John Barleycorn,
Thou king o' grain!

On thee aft Scotland chows her cood,
In souple scones, the wale o'food!
Or tumblin in the boiling flood

Wi' kail an' beef;
But when thou pours thy strong heart's blood,
There thou shines chief....
Party on Rab!

TAM O' SHANTER: If one does the detective work, they can make an educated guess that Burns was drinking Whisky made in the stills in operation in his time from the Ayrshire and Dumfries and Galloway areas of Scotland but there is not a modern brand that can say without a shadow of a doubt, "Ah Ha! We were the brand of Burns!" Isle of Arran have made a Robert Burns Blend and the good people of Edrington's Cutty Sark, and specifically, Master Blender, Kirsteen Campbell have made a special Bottling of 25 YO Cutty Sark that ties in with the Burns Poem Tam O 'Shanter, which uses the phrase Cutty Sark. Long before Cutty Sark was the name of a famous 19th century Clipper Ship, which in turn became the name of a famous brand of Blended Whisky, Cutty Sark meant a shirt or an old garment in 18th century Scotland. To sum up the plot of the 1791 poem, Tam O' Shanter is shellacked and in this drunken state, he rides home late at night on a horse. On this wobbly ride, he happens upon dancing witch's in a Scottish ceilidh. As it happens there is a stunning looking sexy witch named Nannie. She wears a harn (linen) sark (nightshirt) which may have fitted her as a child, but is now too small for a fully grown woman. In other words, she's bulging out all over in this tight, sexy outfit. Burns says:

"Her cutty sark, o' Paisley harn,
That while a lassie she had worn,
In longitude tho' sorely scanty,
It was her best, and she was vauntie.
Ah! little kend thy reverend grannie
That sark she coft for her wee Nannie
Wi' twa pund Scots ('twas a' her riches)
Wad ever graced a dance of witches!

Tam gets an unexpected erotic thrill on his night ride home, and in the equivalent of a wolf whistle, he shouts, "Weel done, Cutty-sark!" Yelling like this was a mistake because now the witches see him. They begin to chase him and he has to ride like the wind to make it across a river, because everyone who knows that witches can't cross running water. He escapes but not before sexy witch babe Nannie pulls the tail off his horse. The metaphorical moral of the story is that thinking about scantily clad young females can conjure up a hellish amount of trouble. "Aye," say all the men with drams in hand.

The Whisky brand, Cutty Sark, promote their Tam O'Shanter tie in this way: "Cutty Sark Tam o' Shanter is a new variant of the existing award-winning Cutty Sark 25 YO Blend with a distinctly darker, wilder side. Limited to 5,000 Bottles, the glass Bottle has been created specifically for this new expression and is based on the oldest in our archive. It features the famous chase scene from the Robert Burns poem Tam o' Shanter, etched around the entire Bottle, as well as a wax closure showing Tam's face in relief. Cutty Sark Tam o' Shanter includes a fantastic book with over 50 illustrated scenes by the late Alexander Goudie, widely considered to be one of Scotland's finest figurative painters. The book and Bottle are presented in a bespoke, Oak Box which has been decorated in the style of Goudie. The colour is: Rich, shadowy dark amber as if glistening from a subterranean Gothic fire. The nose is: Drifting incense held in the evening air, exotic spices, jasmine, anise and sandalwood dance and leap out of the glass - promising something. The palate is: Full bodied, boisterous and sweet with a darkly sinister menace, rich velvet curtains surround dark chocolate, eucalyptus, cracked black pepper and drying mint whilst dancing with rich full Sherry sweetness and toffee. Waves of flavour and texture envelop your tongue, powerfully tantalising and teasing your taste buds. The finish is: Lingering, long, rich, sweet yet spicy. Truly full-bodied Whisky with which to face Auld Nick himself. A maleficent dram!

TINTIN: The Adventures of Tintin, created by Belgian artist Herge in 1929 is a beloved global phenomenon culminating in state of the art performance-capture animation by none other than the world's top directors, Steven Spielberg and Peter Jackson. The official site describes Tintin this way: "Clever and ever-curious, Tintin is a reporter-turned-detective whose pursuit of villains, criminals, treasure and the occasional artefact takes him all over the world, along with a colourful cast of friends. Hergé based his stories on real-world events and cultures that had caught the Belgian national attention — from space exploration to Arab oil wars — and brought them to life for his readers in inspiring and exciting ways."
What is less well known is that the series has an association with

a particular brand of Whisky, said to be the favourite of Tintin's rascal of a friend, Captain Haddock. Again the official Tintin site says, "When Captain Haddock makes his debut in The Crab with the Golden Claws, he makes quite an impression. First, he nearly puts an end to Tintin by burning the oars of their lifeboat to keep warm. As if that weren't enough, he cracks Tintin over the head with a Bottle as he's piloting an aircraft, causing it to crash in the desert. Despite this inauspicious beginning, the captain goes on to become Tintin's closest friend. As the stories progress, Captain Haddock proves himself to be much more than a clumsy, hot-headed sea captain with a colourful vocabulary. He is clearly a highly competent mariner and navigator, and his years of experience on the high seas prove invaluable in numerous adventures, including The Red Sea Sharks. Haddock's favourite Whisky is Loch Lomond. On the Loch Lomond Distillery tour, one can see a framed cover or two from the Herge book series.

WHISKY IN CINEMA

Plays, poems and the novel held up a mirror to society and in their own fictitious way, documented the growing influence of Whisky in society. There are references to Whisky in Dickens, in Twain and in countless other works by the greats and not so greats of Literature. In the advent of Cinema, the cultural mirror and documentation continued in this form of art.

JAMES BOND: From Burns to Bond? There is logic here. We are moving now from Literature to film and the character James Bond began life as a literary creation from the pen of Ian Fleming before becoming the iconic character of over twenty films. James is the ultimate male I-want-to-be-like-this-guy fantasy. He looks good, dresses good, always gets the girl, always takes care of business and can drink the strong stuff and still hold it together. Anything James wears, we men want to wear. If James wears a particular watch, we want that watch. If James drives a particular car, we want that car. If James drinks a particular drink we want it, shaken and not stirred. There have been several kinds of Whisky identified with Bond from the books to the films. The first is Talisker. To quote the brand website: Talisker is "Intense, Smoke, Peat, Balanced, from the Highlands and from the Isle of Skye's only Distillery. In the original Ian Fleming books, Talisker was James Bond's drink of choice, and it's a suitably rugged, explosive, and powerful malt for Bond's original rough-and-tumble persona. Refined, with nice amounts of smoke and peat." This statement by the website is much in dispute, and debated by Bond bloggers on the internet. Allegedly, these Whiskies actually show up in the novels: Black & White (Moon Raker) Haig & Haig (Live and Let Die) Jack Daniel's (On Her Majesties Secret Service and You Only Live Twice) Old Grand-Dad (Live and Let Die and Diamonds Are Forever) I.W. Harper (On Her Majesties Secret Service), Suntory (You Only Live Twice). Canadian Club is said to show up in Bond as well.

In two of the Peirce Brosnan Bond films, The World is Not Enough and Die Another Day, Talisker, finally makes it to the big screen. Other Whisky companies from America and Japan decided that Talisker should not have a monopoly on Bond, and so Jack Daniel's makes an appearance in Goldeneye while Suntory of Japan is featured in the novel You Only Live Twice and in the film of the book, starring Sean Connery as Bond. More recently, Macallan was featured with Daniel Craig in the highest grossing Bond outing to date, Skyfall. The villainous character Silva offers James a 50 YO Macallan (The movie franchise is 50 YO so the 50 YO Macallan was appropriate) while Bond and M have Macallan on two other occasions.

CHARLIE CHAPLIN: A website called Boozemovies.com features excellent write ups and reviews of films with notable elements of Alcoholic beverages that are either visible in the background or influence the plot and feature prominently in the story. Here is but a taste of the site's write up on the legendary little tramp, the amazing Charlie Chaplin: "In the realm of sauced slapstick, no comedian ever surpassed the physical grace and endless invention of Charlie Chaplin. His comic inebriate act initially brought him renown on the British stage, and he carried it over onto film in many of his early one- and two-reelers. That drunkard routine is on glorious display in one of the fastest and funniest of Chaplin's short subjects, The Rounders.

Chaplin portrays Mr. Full, a dapper drunkard in tuxedo and top hat, who arrives at his hotel home after a night of immoderate revelry. Roscoe "Fatty" Arbuckle co-stars as his neighbour, the equally well-dressed and well-oiled Mr. Fuller. Both souses quarrel with their spouses upon returning to their rooms, and before long the two couples are duking it out with each other. While the ladies continue to squabble, the boys discover that they not only share a love of potent liquids, they also belong to the same lodge. That, of course, calls for a drink, so the boozers steal their wives' money and head for the nearest café. Unfortunately, they fall asleep before they have a chance to order a pick-me-up, which also allows the women time to catch up with them. Full and Fuller beat a hasty retreat and find a spot to snooze inside a leaky, stolen rowboat.

It isn't much of a plot, but Chaplin uses every second of screen time to find new ways to display his intoxication--staggering carefully along the pattern in a rug as if walking a tightrope, getting stuck in a hunched position by stepping on the tail of his own coat, and hooking his feet over the top of his headboard after tumbling backwards onto the bed. Arbuckle lends fine support, and it's easy to see why the baby-faced comedian was a close second to Chaplin in audience popularity at the time."

W. C. FIELDS: His real name was William Claude Dukenfield, but he adopted the more user friendly name of W. C. Fields. The comic persona he created liked hard Liquor, especially Whisky; he was an irascible grumpy clown who made contemptuous quips about women, children and animals. He said of the fairer sex, "Women are like elephants to me. I like to look at 'em, but I wouldn't want to own one." Of children he said, "they should neither be seen nor heard from -- ever again" and "I never met a kid I liked." He then contradicts himself and says, "I like children. If they're properly cooked," and "Madam, there's no such thing as a tough child -- if you parboil them first for seven hours, they always come out tender." His quotes about Alcohol are numerous and here we present a small sample:

1. Now don't say you can't swear off drinking; it's easy. I've done it a thousand times.
2. Thou shalt not kill anything less than a fifth.
3. Thou shalt not covet thy neighbour's house unless they have a well-stocked bar.
4. I never drank anything stronger than Beer before I was twelve.
5. A woman drove me to drink, and I'll be a son-of-a-gun but I never even wrote to thank her.
6. During one of my treks through Afghanistan, we lost our corkscrew. We were compelled to live on food and water for several days.

In almost all of his movies he played variations of the same character, perhaps with a different name, but it was always the same surly and sozzled schemer that was never too far away from a flask/bottle of Whisky or at least an allusion to it. We will make mention of one such film: In Never Give a Sucker an Even Break, there is a scene where in Fields jumps from an airplane to recover a fallen Liquor Bottle. He lands in something like a bird's nest of a home where he finds a beautiful girl named Ouliotta Delight. There is only one problem. She has a horrid mother named Mrs. Hemoglobin. Lady Hemoglobin is rich however so W.C. courts her though it takes 100-proof goats milk to find the courage. The whole film was satirical of the Hollywood System and Fields was biting the hand that fed him, but it resulted in one of his funniest films.

CASA BLANCA: Humphrey Bogart plays Rick, and he runs the Café Americain, a drinking hole in Casa Blanca, Morocco. It is also a stop over place for those fleeing from the war in Europe in transition to America. Boozemovies.com describes the plot of Casa Blanca this way, "The bar is owned and managed by Rick Blaine (Bogart), an American expatriate who cynically observes the dealings of the petty thieves, refugees, corrupt police, and Nazis that gather at his watering hole. He doesn't drink with the customers, and he doesn't stick his neck out for nobody. But all of that changes when a resistance leader (Paul Henreid) walks into the bar with a woman from Rick's past (Ingrid Bergman). For the first time in years, Rick takes action--both in terms of his love life and by ingesting large quantities of Bourbon."

JAWS: From a B classic of bad Cinema to a genuine great. The scene depicting the three shark hunting protagonists Hooper (Richard Dreyfuss) Brody (Roy Scheider) and Quint (Robert Shaw) sharing some home-made hooch that Quint has Distilled himself is a masterpiece of writing, acting and filmmaking. From comically comparing scars to a sobering poignant story about a ship going down and men lost to the sharks is Cinematic art at its highest

WHISKY IN MUSIC

One man and a Double Whisky
One man and a single whisky ?
Na. Na thats strayin frae the path
theres nae single whisky - its either a double or a half
An though ye drink for pleasure
Or tae bear the rocky path
if a Scotsman gonna dae the thing
hell never dae the thing be halfs
one man and a Double Whisky
contemplate then that redoutable pair
A template for contemplation , comtemplated
A Double Whisky and one man's fixed stare
into the amber depth of that liquid jewel
slightly effervesing - spitting - hissing
pibroch and heather , claymore and glen
one man and a Double Whisky the history o Scotland
and its there afore a scotsmans in a
Double Whisky
one scot and a double scotch
is Achilles wiithout heel
Mccrimmon wi his pipes playing
the unrelenting reel
A world unto itself - a crystal ball
Mafnificently calm, provoking desire
a Double Whisky for a ithers tae see
tae one man - the kindlin o an inner fire
A man racked in pain.
Pysical or in the mind.
in the whisky finds a freen
O the unnstannin kind.

Good freen - warm me agin the cauld ,
an fill ma mind wi stories o the past
how high in oor highland mountains
ye found yir culloden birth.
gade scottish grain and mountain water
blended an matured wi highland skill
the mind boggles wi oak sherry caskets
an gaurs us drink oor fill.
the first lieutenant o mony a commanding officer aye
the father o mony a bairn
yir spirt cast ma imagination back
therough the centuries again
me thinks me sees a battle field
an proudly stands a tent
inside theres men o rank aroon
a table - whaur a man is bent.
he straightens with a smile - hi pouring task completed
gentlemen - a toast - The scots wha never were
defeated
Yir Royal highness hear oor plea
retreat and save your life
there ten o them tae each o us
the odds are ower risky
spoke up the prince aye ten o them
te wan o us - but we have the whisky
One man and a Double Whisky - Celebrating
One man and a Double Whisky - Mourning
One man and a Double Whisky,
Passiing a pleasant passage
comtemplating a monumental decesion
whiling an hour or indulging
in the self pity or glory o life itsel
One man and a Double Whisky is a scottish love affair

www.askwhisky.co.uk

as old and as passionate and as lasting
as the love of life itsel
One man and a Double Whisky,
is glasgow saturday night

any night of the
week
anywhere in the
world
tae the sick an
ailing - yir a today
tae the troubled in mind - yir escape
yir an ambassaador o scotia colonising the world
last bit no least yer a Double Whisky
yer one man in a big world an never forget it
black yella broon white or dusky
but man jine the scotiish clan the clan o man
One man and a Double Whisky.
Lyrics by Watt Nicoll

TOP TEN WHISKY SONGS FROM ROCK, POP AND COUNTRY

1. Whisky On A Sunday - The Dubliners
2. Whisky River - Willie Nelson
3. Whisky in the Jar - Thin Lizzy
4. Whisky Bent and Hellbound - Hank Williams Jr.
5. Tennessee Whisky - George Jones
6. One Bourbon, One Scotch, One Beer - John Lee Hooker
7. Whisky Lullaby - Brad Paisley with Alison Krauss
8. Streams of Whisky - The Pogues
9. Lace and Whisky - Alice Cooper
10. Snortin' Whisky - Pat Travers

FRANK SINATRA: Most of the Rat Pack were fond of Whisky and Sinatra had a special relationship with Jack Daniel's Tennessee Whisky. So much so that he was even buried with a Bottle. He was a walking advertisement for the brand and so it was natural that Brown-Forman, the company behind Jack Daniel's launched a special Sinatra Edition of their Whisky. Here is how Brown-Forman tells the story of the Sinatra Edition: Following the global launch of Sinatra Select at TFWA Cannes in October, brand owner Brown-Forman is introducing a series of installations at major global airports around the world to "immerse consumers in the Frank & Jack Story". Travellers will be able to taste the limited edition Jack Daniel's Sinatra Select while viewing photos of the famous singer and listening to his Music. Jim Perry, managing director of Brown-Forman travel retail, said: "The Las Vegas Airport was selected to be the first place in the world to receive Jack Daniel's Sinatra Select because Vegas was such an important part of Frank Sinatra's life. Frank and Jack literally spent years flying around the globe together; wherever Frank went, Jack Daniel's was by his side. Along with our retail partner, Nuance, we are very excited about the Las Vegas airport installation.

We feel that our airport installation will engage consumers in the story of the great friendship between Frank and Jack as well as educate them about the unique craftsmanship of this exclusive Whisky. A specially-designed one-litre Bottle of Jack Daniel's Sinatra Select, presented in a gift box complete with a commemorative book, will be available to buy in duty free stores. As one of the most eagerly anticipated launches of the year, fans of Frank Sinatra and Jack Daniel's will be excited to learn that the edition will be available in select cities, including Tennessee, from Spring 2013. Sinatra Select is the first product from Jack Daniel's to feature a high percentage of Whisky aged in special Sinatra Barrels, which have grooves carved into the staves to expose the liquid to more wood. Whisky from the Sinatra Barrels is then Blended with classic Old No. 7 Tennessee Whisky and Bottled at 45% abv." C. ASK Whisky asked Jack Daniel's Master Distiller, Jeff Arnett to explain the Frank Sinatra brand and the connection of the brand with the Music industry as a whole.

JEFF ARNETT: It has the same grain profile as our signature Jack Daniel's. We have the technology to increase the surface inside our Barrels for finishing and that's what we used for the Sinatra. As we thought about Frank we remembered that he would hold up a glass of Jack Daniel's on stage and call it "the nectar of the gods" – and if we were going to create a Whisky that would carry his name, the two words that came to mind were "bold and smooth"- because he was both of those things and we felt like we could create a Whisky that would be that as well – bold and smooth – so we're utilizing a certain percentage of a proprietary Barrel that has an increased surface inside – that creates a lot of Barrel character – but it still maintains that signature sweet note and smooth taste that Jack Daniel's is famous for. I think the Sinatra family and the foundation we worked with to create the Whisky are proud of what is in the Bottle. I know we are and I certainly hope they are as well.

You know, our founder, Jack Daniel, loved Music and Music has been one of the ways we have been able to connect our brand with each new generation and stay relevant. Jack Daniel established the Silver Coronet Band here in Lynchburg. Before radio, the only way to hear Music was to hear it live so he formed this band so people could share his love for Music. We are in a 135 different countries so our support of Music takes many different forms. We've put on concerts on our barbecue hill that above the Distillery – and these have included all styles of Music – We put on a Latin Music concert – we had a British battle of the bands – good Music and good Whisky connect people so it makes sense for us to continue to do that. We sponsor these Studio Number 7s where we help find up and coming Music talent and give them a venue to play their Music. When it comes to Jack Daniel's and Music, it's just a given that we are going to keep on bringing JD and Music together."

Here are some more details about the Musical

and cultural heritage left behind in the wake of super brand JD. Performers who've showed up on the stage with Jack, including Keith Richards, Mick Jagger, Janis Joplin, Robert Plant and Jimmy Paige, Slash from Guns 'n' Roses, Michael Anthony from Van Halen. Slash wrote a piece about Jack Daniel's that appeared in the Rolling Stone's American Icons issue in 2003. Michael Anthony, the bassist for Van Halen, has said of Jack Daniel's: "I know the first time I ever drank Jack Daniel's was during our first tour in 1978. And me, being the kind of guy I am, I'll do a little research on the whole deal. Actually, I really got into the man and the whole thing. Just like Music is the universal language, Jack Daniel's, I think, is the universal Alcohol. [On his Jack Daniel's shaped bass guitars] You drink Jack Daniel's — You play Jack Daniel's. That's my theory. I have three Jack Daniel's guitars. I said let's build it and see if they will come and it totally caught on. Once we built the second bass, it wasn't used so much as a novelty thing because it really wasn't novel. It was part of me. I got a huge poster right behind my bar that's got a picture of Jack Daniel that says 'Our Benevolent Sponsor' because he's the man who watches over my whole bar scene.'

At the 2013 Academy Awards seen by hundreds of millions of people around the world, Jack got even more free advertising when comic host Seth Macfarlane joked that George Clooney was the only sober one in the room before tossing him a small Bottle of Number 7 Black Label.

A cut away of the camera showed George opening the Bottle.

Chivas Regal is another brand that has invested heavily into Music as well as sports sponsorship. Yes, there was Frank Sinatra connection with Jack Daniel's, but also with Chivas Regal. They sponsored him for 45 years and were a sponsor of Frank's Diamond Jubilee Tour. The Rat Pack were known to partake of Chivas Regal backstage and so there were really two Whiskies in Frank's life that were special to him.

THE ROLLING STONES: Keith Richards of the Rolling Stones is reputed to drink a Bottle of Whisky a day (don't try this at home kids) and because Whisky in the presence of one of the Stones is as effective as a 200 foot billboard with flashing lights around it or a prime time TV ad during the Super Bowl it is not surprising that many a Whisky company would like to be associated with the super group - so much so that Suntory have made a Limited Edition - The Rolling Stones 50th Anniversary Whisky - A 150 Bottle run of Blended Whisky with their signature Tongue and Lips logo.

LADY GAGA: As talented as she is outrageous with many a strange outfit (who can forget the meat-dress - which was probably the point? The girl isn't stupid and we're still talking about her, playing right into her publicity stunt manipulative ploy) she is said to play the piano with a glass of Jameson's Irish Whisky close at hand. Speaking of Jameson's and popular culture – they are sponsors of the Empire Magazine Movie Awards.

MORE WELL KNOWN AND WHISKY

Winston Churchill, the man Britain needed to be in charge during World War II, was fond of Johnnie Walker Black Label. One time a lady told him he was drunk to which he replied, "And you're ugly, but in the morning, I will be sober."
The movie director Oliver Stone (Wall Street, Platoon, JFK) collects Single Malt Whiskies.

Scallywag pirate, Captain Jack Sparrow might like his Rum, but the actor who plays him, Johnnie Depp is known to like Bourbon Sour cocktails.

Dashing movie star, heart-throb Errol Flynn said, "I Like my Whisky old and my women young. "

Mark Twain said, "Too much of anything is bad, but too much of good Whisky is barely enough." He also made this comment in his book Life On The Mississippi, "Give an Irishman lager for a month, and he's a dead man. An Irishman is lined with copper, and the

Beer corrodes it. But Whisky polishes the copper and is the saving of him."

Comedian George Burns joked: "I love to sing, and I love to drink Scotch. Most people would rather hear me drink Scotch."

Humphrey Bogart's last words were: "I should never have switched from Scotch to Martini's"

Poet, Dylan Thomas' last words were, "I just had 19 shots of Whisky, I think that's a record."

It's in our songs, our books, our drama. Whisky is a well established part of culture worldwide.

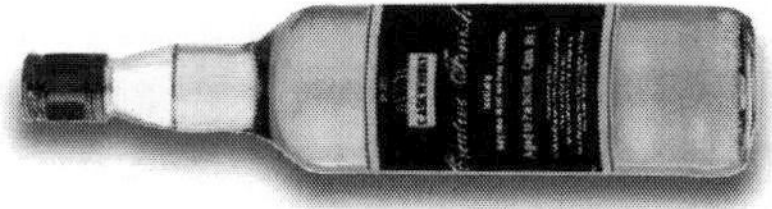

THE END AND A NEW BEGINNING!

This is the end of the C. Ask Whisky stories, anecdotes, topics, interviews and comments. What follows is a helpful reference section of lists. For instance if you want to find every product from Highland Park Distillery you can look that information up in the lists. Happy Studying!

CHAPTER *nine*

Whisk lists

WHISK LIST ONE - RECOMMENDED DISTILLERY TOURS

TOP TEN US DISTILLERIES TO VISIT

In the opinion of Forbes Travel Guide Correspondent Sarah White the top ten US Distilleries to visit are as follows:

1. George Washington's Distillery & Gristmill, Mount Vernon, Va.
2. Jack Daniel's
3. St. George Spirits, Alameda, Calif.
4. Woodinville Whisky Co., Woodinville, Wash.
5. High West Distillery & Saloon, Park City, Utah. Stay:
6. Buffalo Trace, Frankfort, Ky.
7. Woodford Reserve, Versailles, Ky.
8. Balcones Distillery, Waco, Texas
9. RoughStock Distillery, Bozemon, Mont.
10. Tuthilltown Spirits, Gardiner, New York

We are sure Wild Turkey will make this list after April 2013.

RECOMMENDED SCOTTISH DISTILLERY TOURS

So which Scottish Distilleries should get a look in? Opinions always vary; it depends on who you ask. In the opinion of the travel advisory website, Authentic Ireland.com, they recommend the following Scottish Distilleries to those who look to them for advice:

Laphroaig: With their heavy, smoked-peat flavour, the Islay malts are in a class of their own. Try them! This malt is pronounced "lafroyg" but your pronunciation doesn't matter—the taste is famous for instant recognition. A fun, informal Tour with plenty of wit at the ocean. Port Ellen, Islay

Lagavulin: Like its rival Laphroaig, this is a very distinctive malt. It is made in a traditional Distillery with unusual pear-shaped stills. A very personal Tour with no mass-market hustle. Port Ellen, Islay

Glenkinchie: A rare Lowland Distillery, this was founded in 1837 and is 15 miles from Edinburgh. Location makes it a popular place to visit, meaning semi-crowded, but it's prepared. There's a state-of-the-art Visitor Centre.

Edradour: Established in 1825, this is Scotland's smallest Distillery and its cluster of buildings has remained unchanged for 150 years. To witness the process here is great because of the small size. Only 12 Casks a week are produced, making it a rare treat for a rare few. Near Pitlochry.

Glenlivet: One of the first Distilleries to come out of hiding and to be legalized in 1824. Glenlivet has been at the forefront of the Industry ever since. A fluent and comprehensive Tour. We love the musty warehouse where the Whisky sleeps for 12 – 18 years. In Ballindalloch.

Glenfarclas: One of the few independent companies and proud of it. Established in 1836, the Distillery is owned and managed by the fifth generation of the Grant family. Tour the gleaming copper stills and then take a dram in the Ships Room. Terrific. In Ballindalloch.

Macallan: Another of the famous Speyside Brands, and one of the most modern Visitor Centres in the valley. Aside from a guided Tour, you explore Whisky-making using the latest interactive technology. For a fee, you can become a connoisseur by prearranging an individually tutored nosing and tasting Tour. Worth it! In Craigellachie.

Cardow: The only Distillery pioneered by a woman. Beside producing a distinguished Single Malt, it provides the heart of the Johnnie Walker Blend. This is one of the smaller Distilleries and very charming. In Knockando.

Talisker: The only Distillery on Skye, it's been producing a highly-respected malt since 1830. Tours last 40 minutes and are bright and informative. Plus, you're on Skye…

Highland Park: Though definitely among the greats, it's not the most famous Whisky, but it does have the best Tour. They're remote--they try harder. Prepare to be taken through deep piles of malt drying in a delicious reek of peat. In Kirkwall, Orkney.

HONOURABLE MENTIONS

That was the opinion of but one travel advisory. Many other

Distilleries are worthy to be mentioned:

Ann Miller is the Brand ambassador for Chivas Brothers but began her career in Whisky Tourism. She told us that she was looking for a Tour Guide position in Edinburgh and almost all the Tourists she spoke to wanted to go visit a Distillery there in the city. Edinburgh didn't have a Distillery as such but they did have the Scotch Whisky Experience on the Royal Mile. Ann was then offered a Brand spokesperson job for Chivas Brothers. There are three Distilleries associated with Chivas Brothers and Ann would love you to visit all three. Here is what is on offer: The Glenlivet, Aberlour and Strathisla Visitor Centres offer a happy, relaxed atmosphere.

Special Tours have been introduced at the three Visitor Centres, which have proven to be very popular with visitors:
'The Founders Tour' at Aberlour.
'The Spirit of the Malt' at The Glenlivet.
'Straight from the Cask' and 'The Ultimate Chivas Experience' at Strathisla.

Aberlour Distillery
Founded in 1879 by James Fleming at the heart of Speyside, the Aberlour Distillery lies in a beautiful glen, surrounded by glorious scenery dominated by the rugged peaks of Ben Rinnes.

Visitors have the chance to nose and taste new Distillates and five Single Malts from the award-winning Aberlour range and have the unique opportunity to hand-fill and personally register their own Bottle of Aberlour Cask strength Single Malt.

The Founders Tour, introduced in 2010, includes a specialist nosing of Spirit cuts, an in-depth Tour of the Distillery and a tasting that incorporates handmade, specialist chocolates. The Tour ends with a sample drawn straight from the Cask and a gift of a crystal, nosing glass.

The Glenlivet Distillery
The Glenlivet Distillery offers a free, guided Tour of the new Distillery and large bonded warehouse which includes an interactive exhibition area, audio translation and a choice of dram from The Glenlivet range. From August 2013, guests will be able to hand-fill and purchase a Bottle of The Glenlivet

Single Malt Whisky straight from the Cask.

The Spirit Of The Malt Tour is an exclusive offering which takes connoisseurs on a journey following in the footsteps of George Smith, founder of the Distillery, to find out what makes The Glenlivet such an iconic Whisky. This Tour includes a visit to Josie's Well, the Distillery expansion, traditional dunnage warehouse and a tutored tasting of seven different expressions of The Glenlivet.

The Glenlivet Exhibition offer visitors a choice of routes as they embark on a historic journey of The Glenlivet; the path titled "The Spirit of the Glen" allows visitors to learn about the extraordinary chemistry between climate and terrain that produces the perfect conditions for making Malt Whisky. Visitors can also follow "The Glenlivet Legacy" path to see how one man's courage and vision remain an inspiration to this day.

Strathisla Distillery

Strathisla Distillery is the oldest operating and one of the most picturesque Distilleries in the Highlands, with a guided Tour ('Straight from the Cask') which showcases both the Single Malt and Blended Whisky which the Distillery produces. Visitors are welcomed with a dram of Chivas Regal 18 Year Old and the experience ends with a choice of either Strathisla 12 Year Old or a second dram of Chivas Regal 18 Year Old.

'The Ultimate Chivas Experience' Tour begins with a historical overview of the Chivas Brothers range in the luxurious Chivas Regal room, followed by an in-depth Tour of the Distillery and the opportunity to see the warehousing and the exclusive Royal Salute vault. The Tour ends with a tutored Whisky tasting.

Kilchoman and Bruichladdich on Islay are known for being personal and welcoming. Glengoyne, Glentrothes, Ben Nevis and Tullibardine should all get honourable mentions for the efforts they are making to please the guests and they are all in beauty spots.

Two Scottish Distilleries made CNN.Com's list of the ten best Distilleries to go to in the world. They list the Rum Distillery Santa Teresa in Venezuela as one. Maker's Mark, Jim Beam,

George Washington and Heaven Hill make the U.S. cut. Jameson's and Bushmills represent Ireland and Glenfiddich and Macallan represent Scotland - which again, is the opinion of one travel writer contributing an article to the giant news corporation.

CNN.Com says: "Glenfiddich is the world's most awarded single-malt Scotch Whisky, having claimed more big-time international medals since 2000 than any other single-malt Scotch. In the heart of the Scottish Highlands, its Distillery is nearly as decorated. The free Classic Tour runs through 19th-century warehouses and mash rooms and includes three drams of Glenfiddich. For a more in-depth look (and more chest-hair-producing Whisky samples), visitors can opt for the Explorers Tour or even the Pioneers Tour, where they can taste a 30-year-old Whisky and procure a rare, Cask-strength Bottle of Glenfiddich. Glenfiddich stills came on Christmas Day in 1887, which makes this year its 125th.) Three Tours illustrate the stages of Whisky production. The one-hour Classic includes a tutored tasting of 12-, 15- and 18-year-old Whiskies. The Explorers is an in-depth 90 minutes that includes a visit to the Solera Warehouse and a tasting of several Whiskies. The Pioneers is a half-day detailed Tour, with a Whisky master class that showcases Spirits aged for 30 years. Can't get enough? Its sister Distillery, The Balvenie, is located directly across the way."

The Sunday Times is of the opinion that Glengoyne offers the number one Distillery Tour in Scotland.

WHISK LIST TWO - A-Z OF BLENDS

It would be impossible to feature the Blends produced by every Micro-Distillery in the world, but the A-Z list that follows features the more prominent among the Blends being made and marketed in the world today. If you are interested in a particular Blend, we encourage you to do a search on your computer in order to find out more about the Blend, its makers and how you might obtain the Bottle.

1
100 Pipers

A
Aberdour Piper
Abbot's Choice
Abergeldie
Aberlour Centenary Blend
Abraham Bowman
Adams
Addisons
Aden Arms Hotel
Aikman's
Ainslie's
Albany
Alberta Premium
Alibi
Alistair Cunningham's
Ambassador
American Pride
Ancestor
Ancient Age
Ancient Clan
Ancient Memories
Anderson's
Anniversary
Antiquary
Antique
Antique Liqueur
Archer's
Arvedo Zanella
Ascot House
Astor
Asuka
Auld Acquaintance
Auld Curlers
Auld Grey Toon
Auld Lang Syne
Auld Licht
Auld Petrie
Auld Scottie
Averys
Avonside

B
Baird's
Balgownie
Ballantine's
Ballochmyle
Balmoral Castle
Bankers Club
Bank Note
Barrett's
Bartels
Barton's Canadian Supreme Whisky
Barton Reserve
Basil Wood
Baxters
BC
Beam Eight Star
Begbies
Bellows
Bell's

Beltane
Ben Aigen
Ben Alder
Ben Cally
Ben Ledi
Ben Nevis
Bene Vobis
Beneagles
Benmore
Berry's Best
Bertram's
Berwick Blend
Bicentenary
Bickering Brothers
Big Ben
Big Boy
Big T
Biltmore
Bishop's
Bisset's
Black & White
Black Barrel
Black Bear
Black Beard
Black Bottle
Black Bull
Black Bush
Black Cap
Black Cat
Black Cock
Black Dog
Black Douglas
Black Eagle
Bleackheath
Black Horse
Black Jack
Black Knight
Black Prince
Black Ram
Black Rod
Black Shield
Black Swan
Black Velvet
Black Watch
Blair Drummond
Blairathie
Blend 888
Blenders Pride
Blen Garner
Blue Bonnet
Blue Hanger
Bonnie Charlie
Bonnie Lassie
Bonnie Scot
Bonnie Strathyre
Bonnington
Bonny Brig
Bonspiel
Border Blend
Bourye
Bowmore
Braemar
Brave Spiritss First In
Breaking and Entering
Bourbon
Breath of Adelphi
Bridge of Allan
Brigadoon
Bristol Vat
Broadford
Brockford
Browell
Bucanero
Buchanan
Buchanan McKenzie's
Buchanan's
Bulldog
Bulloch Lade's
Burberrys
Burn Stewart
Burrough's
Buvin's Best

C
C & J
Caberfeid

Cairns
Callander 12 YO
Calvert Extra
Camelot
Cameo
Cameron Brig
Cameron Higlander
Cameron's QX
Campbell's
Campbeltown Loch
Campfire
Canadian Mist
Carlton
Carnaby St.
Carnegie's
Carnock Glen
Castle Rock
Catto's
Celtic Football Club
Centenary
Centenary 1974
Century
Chairman's
Chairman's Celebration
Reserve
Challenge
Champion
Champion Club
Charles House
Charles Street
Charlie
Charlie Stuart
Cheers
Chequers
Chieftain
Chivas
Chivas Legend
Chivas Oldest
Chivas Regal
Chopper
Christopher
Churchill
Churchill's
Churtons
Clan Blend
Clan Campbell
Clan Cream
Clan Kennedy
Clan MacGregor
Clan More
Clan Moss
Clan Murdock
Clan Murray
Clann Albhains Choice
Clan Robertson
Clanroy
Clanroyal
Clansman
Clarion
Clark's
Claymore
Clifton Moore
Club
Club 45
Club 99
Clubhouse
Club Imperial
Club Man
Club's Special
Cluny
Clyde Spray
Clydebank
Coachman
Cockburn
Coleraine
Colt
Compass Box
Consul Of Scotland
Consulate
Convent Garden
Cooper's
Courzon
Cousins 93
Crabbie
Craig Athol
Craigburn

Craigpark
Crawford's
Crazy
Crazy Bargain
Crazy Glen
Crazy Horse
Cream of the Barley
Crinan Canal Water
Criterion
Cromwell's
Cromwell's Royal
Crown of Scotland
Crown Seal
Cruachan
Curtis
Custodian
Cutty Sark

D
D&D
D.C.L.
Dalting
Dandie Dinmont
Daniel Crawford's
Daniell's Choice
Davidson's
Davies County
Davison
Dawson
Defender
Demijohn
Derby Club
Desmond & Duff
Dew of Ben Alder
Dew of Ben Lawers
Dew of Ben Varen
Dewar's
Dimple
Diners
Director's Reserve
Director's Special
Doctor's Special
Donald Fischer
Donald Scott
Donal's
Dormy
Double Flag
Double Q
Douglas XO
Drummer
Drury
Duart Castle
Dukes Own
Duncan
Duncan 52
Duncan MacGregor
Duncan Taylor
Duncraig
Dunfife
Dunhill
Dunphy's
Duns Scot
Dunvegan
DYC

E
Eagle's
Earlspark
Eaton's
Edinburgh 1992
Edinburgh Castle
Edinburgh Tattoo
Edward & Edward
Elite
Embassy Club
Embassy Reserve
Evening Express Centenary
Excalibur
Excalibur Excellence
Excalibur Gold
Excelsior
Executive

F
Fair
Falcon's

Famous Grouse
Fauchon
Fifty First
Findlater's
Fine Old Scotch
Finest Scotch Whisky
Five Lords
Flame of Scotland
Fleischmann's Preferred
Flying Scot
Fochabers
Formidable Jock of Bennachie
For You
Fort Glen
Forth Bridge Centenary
Fortification
Fortnum & Mason
Founders
Four Crown
Four Seasons
Francis
Fraser McDonald
Fraser Ross
Fraser's Supreme
Frasers
Fraser's
Fred Hirst
Friar John Cor
Friarroyd
Full Sail

G
G&R
Gaelach
Gaelic Ard
Gamekeeper
Gauscot
Gavin's
Gay Ghost
Gay Higlander
Gentry
George Baxter's
Gibson's
Gilbert J McCaul
Gilbey's
Gillon's
Gilt Crest
Ginkgo Japanese Blended Whisky
Glamis
Glamis Castle
Glasgow Herald
Gleesdale
Glen Alco
Glen Avon
Glen Blair
Glen Brora
Glen Brynth
Glen Burn
Glen Calder
Glen Clova
Glen Cree
Glen Dowan
Glen Eagle
Glen Foster
Glen Fyne
Glen Garry
Glen Gray
Glen Hunter
Glen Kinlay
Glen Laggan
Glen Lion
Glen Lyon
Glen Mavis
Glen Morris
Glen Morven Light
Glen Nevis
Glen Niven
Glen Oykel
Glen Rosa
Glen Ross
Glen Rossie
Glen Royal
Glen Scotia
Glen Shian
Glen Shire

Glen Simon
Glen Stewart
Glen Urquhart
Glen Ythan
Glenaber
Glenalmond
Glenberry
Glenburn
Glenburnie
Glencannon
Glencastle
Glencruach
Glendorris
Glendrostan
Glenesk
Glenfingal
Glenfoyle
Glengrigor
Glenkiltie
Glenleven
Glenlivet Blend
Glenlogie
Glenmark
Glenrosa
Glen's Eagle
Glenshire
Glenside
Glenvar
Glenwood
Gloag's Perth Whisky
Glorious 12th
Gold Award
Gold Bell
Gold Braid
Gold Break
Gold Crown
Gold King
Gold Label
Gold Medal
Gold Seal
Gold Shot
Golden Age
Golden Barret
Golden Crown
Golden Eagle
Golden Glen
Golden Leaf
Golden Life
Golden Lion
Golden Park
Golden Ribbon
Gordon Highlanders
Gordon's
Grand Alastair
Grand Chapter
Grand Duke
Grand Dulky
Grand Macnish
Grand Monarch
Grand Old Liqueur
Grand Sack
Grand Sail
Grand Scot
Gran Legacy
Grant's
Great Macaulay
Great Scott
Green Capsule
Green Plaid
Green Tree
Gregson's
Greyhound
Grey's
Grierson's
Grigor's
Gukenheimer
Gun Club
Gunfighter

H

Haddington House
Haig
Haig & Haig
Haines and Bentley
Halberd Blend
Hamilton

Hankey Bannister
Harmony
Harris & Bowden
Harrods
Harry's
Harts
Harvey Mackay's
Harvey's
Harwood
Hawker's
Hazelwood
HBC
Heather Cream
Heather Dew
Heaven Hill
Hedges & Butler
Heirloom
Heritage
Heritage Centre
Hewitt's
Hi
Hielanman
High Commissioner
Highland 51
Highlands and Islands
Highland Bird
Highland Baron
Highland Black
Highland Blend
Highland Blossom
Highland Brook
Highland Chieftain
Highland Clan
Highland Command
Highland Dream
Highland Earl
Highlander
Highland Farm
Highland Fling
Highland Flock
Highland Gathering
Highland Glen
Highland Gold
Highland Grand
Highland Harvest
Highland Inn
Highland Laird
Highland Mist
Highland Moss
Highland Nectar
Highland Piper
Highland Pride
Highland Queen
Highland Ransom
Highland Reserve
Highland Rose
Highland Warrior
Highland Way
High Liquors
His Excellency
Holland & Sherry
Holt's
Honest John
Horse Guards
Hotel Adolphus
House of Commons
House of Lords
House of MacDonald
House of Peers
House of Stuart
Howard's
Hudson's Bay
Huntly

I
Immortal
Immortal Memory
Imperial
Imperial Federation
Imperial Gold Medal
Imperial Institute
Inish Owen
Inverary
Inver House
Inverlochy Castle
Inverness Cream

Iona
Island Prince
Islay Legend
Islay Mist
Isle of Mull
Isle of Skye

J
J&B
J.G.
J.G. Kinsey
Jaguar
James Douglas
James Ferguson
James King
James Martin
Jameson
Jameson's Special Reserve
Jamie 08
Jamie Stuart
Jamie's
Jas. Gordon & Co.
Jeremiah Weed
Jewel
Jim McEwan's
Jock Fraser
Jock McClure
Johann & Walter
John Barr
John Begg
John Blair
John Brown's Special
John Chappell's
John Crabbie
John Drake
John Haig
John McDuc
John McGeary's
John McKay
John O'Groat's
John Player
John West
Johnnie Walker
Johnny Wright's
Johnstons
Jurgensen's

K
K.C.B.
Kassers
Keith's Glenlivet
Kella
Kelly Brothers
Kelvin Hall
Kenmore
Kennaway's
Kents
Kentshire
Kentucky Beau
Kentucky Deluxe
Kentucky Gentleman
Kentucky Pride
Kessler
Kilbeggan
Kilmally's Favour
Kiltarie
King Arthur
King Charles
King Edgar
King Edmund II
King Edward I
King Edward II
King George IV
King Henry VIII
King John
King Malcolm
King of Kings
King of Scots
King Robert II
King William IV
Kingdom
King's Blended
King's Bin
King's Castle
King's Choice
King's Counsel

Kings Crest
King's Crown
King's Cup
King's Legend
King's Liqueur
Kings Own Scottish Borderers
King's Pride
King's Ransom
King's Rider
King's Royal
Kings Special
Kings Tower
King's Whisky
Kingston
Kinnickinnic
Kinross
Kintore
Kloke's
Knight of the Moor
Knightrider

L
Label 5
Lady Jane
Lady Nicol
Laing's
Laird O' Cockpen's
Lairdshall
Lancer
Langs
Lang's
Langside
Lankester
Largs
Last Drop
Lauder's
Lawson's
Leabank
Legacy
Legendary Scot
Liqueur Cream
Liqueur Harrods
Liqueur Scotch Whisky
Liqueur Scots Whisky
Liqueur Specialite
Lismore
Locheil
Loch Fyne
Loch Imrie
Loch Lomond
Loch Ness
Logan
Logan's
Lombard
London Scottish Whisky
Long John
Longman
Lonsdale
Lord Astor
Lord Douglas
Lord Harold
Lord Hastings
Lord Hynett
Lord Kent
Lord Low
Lord Major
Lord Monty
Lord Nelson
Lord Provost
Lord Richmond
Lord Ronald
Lord Roy
Lord Scott
Loretto
Lorne
Los Angeles Country Club
Love's
LR
Lumsden & Gibson
Lumsden's Travelled Whisky
Lynton

M
M.P.
Mac 8
MacDugan

Macleod
MacQueens
MacAndrew's
MacArthur's
Macbeth
MacDale
Macdonald's
MacDougall's
Macduff
MacGregor's
MacKenzie
MacKenzie's
Mackesack
Mackie's
Mackinlay
Mackinlay's
MacKintosh
Maclachlans
Macleay Duff
MacLennan
MacLeod's Dram
MacNair
Macnish
Macrae's
MacScot
Mactavish's
MacVicar's
Mak' Readie
Malcolm Stuart
Mansion House
Marchants
Mark IV
Mark Royal
Marksman
Marlboro
Marshal
Mars Maltage Satsuma
Japanese Blended Whisky
Marstons
Martin's
Mary Queen of Scots
Match
Matthew Clarks
McDaniel
McHagmoar
McLennan's
McRobie's
McCall's
McCallum's
McCormick's
McCoss
McKechnie's Special
McKenzie
McKirdy
McLane's
McLaren's
McNee Blend
McTryn
Melrose
Metropolitan
Michael Jackson's Memorial
Blend
Millar's Special Reseve
Mitchell
Mitchell's Glengyle Blend
Monarch
Monarch of the Glen
Moncreiffe
Monkey Shoulder
Moorland
Moray Brand
Moray District
Morel's
Morrison
Morton's
Mountain Cream
Mountain Dew
Muirhead's
Munray
Murdoch's Perfection
Murphey's Irish Whisky
Murrayfield
My Fancy

N

N°16 Whisky

N°3
N°8
National Choice
Navy Supreme
NB
Ne Plus Ultra
Neal's Royal
Nelson's
Nikka Super 15 Year Old Single Malt Whisky - 70cl - 43%
Noble Queen
Noble Ryder
North British
Northern Scot
Northwest Blended

O
O.V.H.
Officers
Okay
Old Aberdeen
Old Albert
Old Angus
Old Argyll
Old Arthur
Old Blended Glenlivet
Old Bond
Old Choice
Old Clan
Old Clipper
Old Cobb
Old Court
Old Craig
Old Crofter
Old Cromarty
Old Curio
Old Decanter
Olde Boys Scotch
Old Eight
Olde Smithy
Old Farm
Oldfield's
Oldfield's Blue Label
Old Fisherman
Old George
Old Governor
Old Grans
Old Guns
Old Harmony
Old Harvey
Old Highland Liqueur
Old Highland Williams
Old Inverness
Old Lanark
Old Land
Old Lord
Old Mac
Old Mackay
Old Master Freemason
Old Matthew
Old McDonald
Old Melody
Old Monarch
Old Moor
Old Moore
Old Mull
Old Oban
Old Original
Old Orkney
Old Parr
Old Perth
Old Racy
Old Rarity
Old Regiment
Old Royal
Old Scot
Old Scotch
Old Scots
Old Ship
Old Smuggler
Old Stag
Old St. Andrew's
Old Standard
Old Tom
Old Thompson

Old Troon
Old Whisky
Old Wort
Old Worthy
One on One
Original Mackinlay
Orkney Club
Orson
Our Own
OV
Oxford

P
Paddy
Park Lane
Parkers
Partner's Choice
Partridge
Passport Scotch
Past Ages
Paterson's Best
Peak
Pedigree
Pedlar Brand
Perino's
Perth Royal
Peter Dawson
Peter MacKenzie
Peter Thomson's
Philadelphia
Pig's Nose
Pinch & Pinch
Pinwinnie
Pipe Major
Piper
Pipers
Piper's
Piper's Dram
Plus Four
Potters
Powers
Premier
President
Press Club
Prestige
Preston Field
Pride of Montrose
Prime Vat
Prince
Prince Charlie
Prince Charles Special Reserve
Prince of Wales
Prince O'Scots
Prince Regent
Private Office
Private Stock
Putachieside

Q
QE2
Queen Anne
Queen Eleanor
Queen Elizabeth
Queen Margaret
Queen Mary I
Queen Mary's Seal
Queen of Scotland
Queen Victoria
Queen's
Queen's Bow
Queen's Castle
Queen's Choice
Queen's Own
Queen's Seal
Queen's Tower
Queens's Castle
Quintessential

R
R&B
Rabbie's Dram
Radio Clyde
Rare Old Highland Whisky
Real Antique
Real Mackay
Real Mackenzie

Real McTavish
Rebecca Creek
Red Crown
Red Hackle
Red Hill
Red Lion
Red Seal
Red River
Red Tape
Regal Queen
Regent
Reliance
Richardson
Rixton
Rob Roy
Robbie Burns
Robert Brown
Robert Burns
Robertson's
Robertson's BEB
Roderick Dhu
Rose Royal
Ross
Ross N°1
Rossdhu
Rossmoyne
Rothsay
Royal & Ancient
Royal Abbey
Royal Ages
Royal Arms
Royal Assent
Royal Baron
Royal Blend Thomson
Royal Brook
Royal Burgh of Forres
Royal Cask
Royal Castle
Royal Citadel
Royal Citation
Royal Clan
Royal Club
Royal Deeside
Royal Dornoch
Royal Edinburgh
Royal Findhorn
Royal Gold
Royal Great Glen
Royal Household
Royal Jubilee
Royal Label
Royal Lion
Royal Liqueur
Royal Marshal
Royal Marshall
Royal N°1
Royal Northern Cream
Royal Oak
Royal Pheasant
Royal Salute
Royal Silk
Royal Standard Blend
Royal Stewart
Royal Strathythan
Royal Tradition
Rutherford's
Rutherglen

S
S S
S.S. Politician
Sainte Claire Club
Salisbury's
Saltyre
Sandeman
Sandy Fraser
Sandy MacDonald
Sandy Macnab's
Santa Barbara Club
Santoni
Sauer Special
Saunders'
Savini
Savoy
Scot Royal
Scotch Broom

Scotch Fir
Scotch Guard
Scotch N°10
Scotch Whisky
Scotia Royale
Scotland's Honour
Scotland's Prestige
Scots Bard
Scots Club
Scots Earl
Scots Emblem
Scots Grey
Scots Greys
Scots Guards
Scots Label
Scots Laird
Scots Lord
Scot's Pibroch
Scotsman
Scott & Allan
Scottish Chief
Scottish Collie
Scottish Cream
Scottish Crown
Scottish Dance
Scottish Healt
Scottish Glory
Scottish Leader
Scottish Majesty
Scottish Master
Scottish National
Scottish Peer
Scottish Reel
Scottish Rill
Scottish Royal
Scottish Stag
Scottish Standard
Scottish Star
Scott's Perfection
Screwtop
Seagram's Seven Crowns
Seagram's VO
Sea Gull
Searcy Fauchon
Senator's Club
Seven Eleven
Seven Seven
Seven Stills
Seventy Seven
Seven Star
Sheep Dip
Shooting Lodge
Silver Wedding
Silverburn
Simon Brothers
Sir
Sir Edward's
Sir Frederic
Sir Griffin Pitterson
Sir N°1
Sir Patrick
Sir William
Six Isles
Skinner's Highlander
Skipper
Slaintheva
Slochain Den
Sma' Still
Smith Sinclair
Something Special
Son of Bourye:
Spalding's
Special Brand
Special Regent
Special Reserve
Spencer Club
Spey Cast
Spey Royal
Sportsman
St. Francis Yacht Club
St. James's
St. Leger
Stadium
Standard Selection
Stenhouse
Sterling

Sterlini
Stevenson's
Stewart's
Stewarts Dundee
Still Water I and II Blended Canadian Whisky
Stodart's
Stork Club
Strath Roye
Strathayr
Strathdon
Strathfillan
Strathvegan
Stuart
Stuart Royal
Stuart's
Sullivan
Sunnybrook Kentucky Blended
Suntory Hibiki 12 Year Old Blended Whisky
Suntory Hibiki 17 Years Old Blended Whisky
Suntory Hibiki 30 Years Old Blended Whisky
Sutton Club
Swing
Swords
Symon

T
T.P. Wood
Taggart
Talisman
Tanager
Tangle Ridge
Taplows
Tasters' Choice
Tayside
Tè Bheag
Teacher's
Teith Mill
Teviotdale
The 45
The Antiquary
The Argyll and Sutherland Higlanders
The Berverly Hills Club
The Cabinet Whisky
The Champion
The Dominie
The Hunting Squire
The Kilty
The King's Whisky
The Laird o' Cockpen
The Last Hole
The Master
The Monarch
The Old Shieling
The Perth Royal
The Royal and Ancient Golf Club
The Royal Household
The Scottish Bard
The Society's Special
The Speaker
The Speakers
The Union Club
The Vaults
The Whisky of 1990
The Windsor Blend
Thistle
Thomson's
Thorne's
Three Cheers
Three Fingers
Three Reigns
Thwaites
Toby
Tom Jones
Top Malt
Top Ten
Top Vat
Torrabeg
Torvhaug
Tower Gate

Trader's
Tranquillity
Treasury
Turnberry
Tuxedo
Tweedale
Twelve Pointer
Tymin's

U
Uam Var
Ubique
Uisge Beatha
Ultima
Union Jack
Unique
Usher's
Usquaebach

V
V.C.
V.O.M.
Vat 69
Vat 99
Very Old Choice Whisky
Victoria Club
Victoria Vat
Viscount
Vittoria Clan
VO

W
Wakefield
Wallstreet
W. Coates & Co
W. Turkey
W.R Paterson
W.R. Paterson's Reserve
W5
Wallace
Watson's
Weather Sea
Websters
Westminster
Weston's
Whigham's
Whisky Galore
White 5
White Abbey
White Cat
White Cross
White Hart
White Heather
White Horse
White Label
White River
Whiteley's
Whyte & MacKay
Wild Cat
Wiley'S
William Grant
William Lawson's
William Penn
Williams & Sons
Willie's Choice
Willsher's
Wilson
Winchester
Windsor Blended Canadian
Whisky
Windsor Castle
Woodstone Creek
WP
Wright & Greigs

X
Xlix

Y
Yates's
Ye Auld Toun
Ye Monks'
Yes Sir
Young's

WHISK LIST THREE - DISTILLERIES AROUND THE WORLD

We have listed the Distilleries around the world in bold and a representative list of the products they produce are listed beneath the bold title of the Distillery.

IRELAND
BUSHMILL DISTILLERY
Black Bush Blended
Bushmills 10 YO Single Malt
Bushmills 16 YO Single Malt
Bushmills 1608
Bushmills 21 YO Single Malt
Bushmills 5 YO Single Malt
Bushmills Distillery Reserve
Bushmills Millenium Single Malt
Coleraine Blended
White Bush Blended

MIDLETON DISTILLERY
Crested Ten Blended
Dunphy's Blended
Green Spot Pure Pot Still
Hewitt's Blended
Jameson 15 YO Pure Pot Still Millennium
Jameson 1780 12 YO Blended
Jameson Blended
Jameson Gold Blended
Jameson Master Selection 18 YO
Midleton Very Rare Blended Whisky
Murphy's Blended
Paddy Whisky
Redbreast 12 YO Pure Pot Still
Redbreast 15 YO Pure Pot Still
Tullamore Dew 12 YO Blended
Tullamore Dew Blended

COOLEY/KILBEGGAN BRANDS PAST AND PRESENT
Avoca
Ballygeary
Brennans
Casino
Cassidys
Clanceys
Clonmel Malt
Connemara 12 YO Single Malt
Connemara Cask Strength Single Malt
Connemara Single Malt
Dunlow
Dunville
Eblana Irish Liqueur
Finnegans
Galoway
Golden Irish
Greenfield
Greenore Single Grain 8 YO

Hennessey Na Geanna Single Malt

Highfield

Inishowen Blended

Kavanagh

Kelly's

Ken Dalk

Ken Lough

Kilbeggan 15 YO Blended

Kilbeggan Blended

Lockes Malt Limited Edition

Lockes Rare Malt

MacNamara

Magilligan Single Malt

Michael Collins Blended Whisky

Michael Collins Single Malt

Millars Blended

O'Briens

O'Hara

O'Neills

O'Patricks

Safeway

Sainsburys Malt

Shanagary Single Malt

Slieve nag Cloc

St Patrick

Tesco Irish

Tyrconnell Single Malt

Tyrconnell Single Malt Limited Edition

Waitrose Irish

Locke's Old Kilbeggan

Whisky

Madeira Casks to impart a generous flavour of subtle complexity.

ENGLAND AND WALES
St. George's English Whisky Distillery
Chapter 11 - Heavily Peated Single Malt
Chapter 10 - 3 YO Single Malt Whisky Sherry Finish
Chapter 9 - 3 YO Single Malt Whisky Peated
Chapter 6 - 3 YO Single Malt Whisky
Chapter 5 - 3 YO Single Malt Whisky - Limited edition

Penderyn Welsh Whisky Distillery
Penderyn Madeira Single Malt
Penderyn Peated Single Malt
Penderyn Icons of Wales Series
Penderyn Sherrywood Single Malt
Penderyn Single Cask Whiskies

USA

ALASKA
Alaska Distillery, Wasilla, AK.
Outlaw Whisky

ARIZONA
High Spirits Distillery, Flagstaff, AZ.
Mesquite smoked Single Malt Whisky.
ARKANSAS
Rock Town Distillery, Little

Rock, AR.
Rock Town Arkansas Young Bourbon Whisky
Arkansas Hickory Smoked Whisky.

CALIFORNIA
1512 Spirits, Rohnert Park, CA.
1512 Barbershop Rye

American Craft Whisky Distllery, Ukiah, CA.
Low Gap, un-aged wheat Whisky. (capitals also)

Anchor Distilling, San Francisco, CA.
Old Potrero Single Malt Rye.

Ascendant Spirits, Buellton, CA.
Breaker Bourbon

Ballast Point Spirits, San Diego, CA.
Devil's Share Whisky

Bowen's Spirits, Bakersfield, CA.
Bowen's Whisky

Charbay, St. Helena, CA.
Charbay Double and Twisted Light Whisky

Fog's End Distillery/C&C Shine, Salinas, CA.
Fog's End Monterey Rye

Greenbar Collective, Los Angeles CA.
Slow Hand

Lost Spirits Distillery, Salinas, CA.
Seascape
Leviathan

Old World Spirits, Belmont, CA.
Goldrush Rye Whisky
Goldrun Rye Whisky.

St. George, Alameda, CA.
St. George Single Malt,
Breaking and Entering Bourbon

St. James, Irwindale, CA.
Peregrine Rock Single Malt.

Tahoe Moonshine Distillery, South Lake Tahoe, CA.
Stormin' Whisky

Valley Spirits, Modesto, CA.
Outlaw Moonshine

COLORADO
Colorado Gold, Cedar Ridge, CO.
Colorado Gold Bourbon
Colorado's Own Corn Whisky.

Dancing Pines Distillery, Loveland, CO.
Dancing Pines Bourbon
Wilderness Whisky.

Deerhammer Distilling Co., Buena Vista, CO.
Whitewater Whisky
Down Time.

Downslope Distilling,
Centennial, CO.
Double Diamond Whisky

JF Strothman Distillery, Grand Junction, CO.
Judge's Choice

Peachstreet Distillers,
Palisade, CO.
Colorado Straight Bourbon.

Stranahan's (Proximo Spirits),
Denver, CO.
Stranahan's Colorado Whisky

Syntax Spirits, Greeley, CO.
Class X White Dog
Class X White Cat

Trail Town Distillery,
Ridgeway, CO.
Coyote Light Whisky

Wood's High Mountain Distillery, Salida, CO.
Tenderfoot Whisky

CONNECTICUT
Elm City Distillery, Durham, CT.
Nine Square Rye

FLORIDA
Florida Farm Distillers,
Umatilla, FL.
Palm Ridge Reserve

GEORGIA
Free Spirits Distillery,
Dawsonville, GA.
Dawsonville Moonshine Corn Whisky.

Georgia Distilling Co.,
Milledgeville, GA.
Goodtime Moonshine
Grandaddy Mims Whisky

Moonrise Distillery, Clayton, GA.
Corn Squeezins Georgia Corn Whisky

Thirteenth Colony Distilleries,
Americus, GA.
13th Colony Southern Corn Whisky

ILLINOIS
Koval Distillery, Chicago, IL.
Lion's Pride label

Mastermind Vodka, Pontoon Beach, IL.
LPR Moonshine

Quincy Street Distillery,
Riverside, IL.
Water Tower White Lightning

Southern Sisters Spirits
a.k.a. Grand Rivers Spirits,
Carbondale, IL.
Red Eye Moonshine

IOWA
Broadbent Distillery, Norwalk, IA.
Two Jay's Iowa Corn Whisky.

Cedar Ridge Distillery,
Swisher, IA.
Cedar Ridge Bourbon

Dehner Distillery, Clive, IA.

Red Boot Corn Whisky.

Mississippi River Distilling Co., Le Claire, IA.
Cody Road Bourbon
Windmill Rye
Farmer Brown Whisky

INDIANA
Lawrenceburg Distillers Indiana (LDI)(MGP), Lawrenceburg, IN
4 Spirits Bourbon (4 Spirits)
Backbone Bourbon (Crossroads Vitners/Strong Spirits)
Big Ass Bourbon (Strong Spirits)
Big Bottom Bourbon (Big Bottom)
Bone Snapper Rye (Strong Spirits)

Bulleit Rye (Diageo)

Chattanooga Whisky 1816 Reserve (Chattanooga Whisky Co.)

Cougar Bourbon & Rye (Foster's)

Filibuster Bourbon & Rye (M.S. Trading LP)

George Dickel Rye (George Dickel)

High Liquors Bourbon & Rye (High Liquors)

High West (an element of many of their Whiskys Blends)

Homestead Bourbon

James E. Pepper 1776 Rye (James E. Pepper/Strong Spirits)

Redemption Bourbon & Rye (Dynamic Beverages)
Riverboat Rye (Dynamic Beverages)

Seagram's 7 Blended Whisky (Diageo)

Smooth Ambler Old Scout Bourbon & Rye (Smooth Ambler)

Spring Mill Bourbon (Heartland Distillers)

Templeton Rye (Templeton)

Temptation Bourbon (Dynamic Beverages)

WH Harrison Bourbon (Tipton Spirits)

KANSAS
Dark Horse Distillery, Lenexa, KS.
Long Shot White Whisky
Lewis Redmond Carolina Bourbon
Dark Horse Bourbon and rye.

High Plains Distillery, Atchison, KS.
Most Wanted Kansas Bourbon

KENTUCKY
Alltech Lexington Brewing & Distilling Co. (Lyons Spirits), Lexington, KY.
Pearse Lyons Reserve
Town Branch Bourbon

Barrel House Distilling Co., Lexington, KY.
Woodshed Whisky
Barrel House Bourbon.

Barton 1792 Distillery (Buffalo Trace/Sazerac Co.), Bardstown, KY.

1792 Ridgemont Reserve
Barton Blended Whisky
Bourbon Whisky
Colonel Lee Bourbon and Blended Whisky
Fleischmann's Rye and Blended Whisky
Gran Legacy Blended Whisky
Imperial Blended Whisky
Kentucky Gentleman
Kentucky Tavern
Old Thompson Blended Whisky
Sutton Club Blended Whisky
Ten High
Tom Moore
Trader Joe's Bourbon
Very Old Barton

Brown Forman, Shively, KY.
Old Forester Bourbon
Early Times Bourbon
Kentucky Whisky

Buffalo Trace(Sazerac Co.), Frankfort, KY.
Ancient Age
Benchmark
Black Ridge
Blanton's
Buffalo Trace
Buffalo Trace Experimental Collection
Chestnut Farms

Eagle Rare
E.H. Taylor
Elmer T. Lee
George T. Stagg
Hancock's Reserve
Old Charter
Old Taylor
Rock Hill Farms
Sazerac and Thomas H.
Handy Rye
Single Oak Project
Two Stars
Van Winkle and Pappy Van
Winkle Bourbon and Rye
W.L. Weller
Zackariah Harris

Corsair Distillery, Bowling
Green, KY.
Triple Smoke
Wry Moon
Rasputin
James E. Pepper Bourbon
Graniac 9 Grain Bourbon

Four Roses (Kirin),
Lawrencburg, KY.
Four Roses label
Bulleit Bourbon

Heaven Hill, Bardstown, KY.
Blue State Bourbon
Cabin Still
Echo Spring
Elijah Craig
Evan Williams
Fighting Cock
Heaven Hill
Henry McKenna
JTS Brown
JW Dant
Kentucky Supreme
Larceny
Mattingly & Moore
Old Fitzgerald
Old Whisky River
Parker's Heritage Collection
Pennypacker (export only)
Red State Bourbon
Sam Clay
Tom Sims
William Heavenhill
Virgin
Pikesville Rye
Rittenhouse Rye
Stephen Foster Rye

Wheat Whisky
Bernheim Wheat Whisky
Dixie Dew
Georgia Moon
JW Corn
Mellow Corn
Gukenheimer
Kentucky Beau
Kentucky Deluxe
Philadelphia
TW Samuels
Wilson
Trybox

Jim Beam (Beam Inc.),
Clermont & Boston, KY.
Baker's
Basil Hayden
Booker's
Bourbon de Luxe
Jacob's Ghost White Whisky
Jim Beam Bourbons and Rye
Kessler Blended Whisky
Kirkland Signature (for
Costco)
Knob Creek
Old Bourbon Hollow
Old Crow
Old Grand-Dad

Old Overholt Rye
Old Tub
(r□)[1] (Rye One)

Limestone Branch Distillery, Lebanon, KY.
T.J. Pottinger Corn Whisky.

Maker's Mark (Beam Inc.) Loretto, KY.
Maker's Mark.

MB Roland Distillery, Pembroke, KY.
White Dog
Black Dog
MBR Bourbon.

Wild Turkey (Campari Group), Lawrenceburg, KY.
Wild Turkey 81 Proof
Wild Turkey 101 Proof
Kentucky Spirit
Russell's Reserve
Wild Turkey Rare Breed
Wild Turkey American Honey

Woodford Reserve/Labrot & Graham (Brown Forman), Versailles, KY. Brown
Woodford Reserve
Woodford Reserve Double Oak
Woodford Reserve Master's Collection

MASSACHUSETS
Berkshire Mountain Distillers, Great Barrington, MA.
Berkshire Bourbon
New England Corn Whisky

McMillan Distillery, Worcester, MA.
130 Bourbon.

Nashoba Distillery, Boston, MA.
Stimulus Single Malt Whisky

Triple Eight Distillery, Nantucket, MA.
Notch Single Malt

MICHIGAN
Grand Traverse Distillery, Traverse City, MI.
Ole' George Straight Rye Whisky

Journeyman Distillery, Three Oaks, MI.
Ravenswood Rye
Silver Cross Whisky
Featherbone Bourbon
Buggy Whip Wheat Whisky
Three Oaks Single Malt Whisky

New Holland Brewing Co., Holland, MI.
Zepplin Bend Straight Malt Whisky
Walleye Rye
Malthouse Brewers Whisky
Double Down Barley Whisky
Bill's Wheat Whisky
Black River Bourbon
MINNESOTA
Panther Distillery, Osakis, MN.
White Water Whisky

MISSOURI

Copper Run Distillery, Walnut Shade, MO.
Ozark Mountain Moonshine Corn Whisky.

Mad Buffalo Distillery, St. Charles, MO
Thunderbeast

Pinckney Bend Distilling Co., New Haven, MO.
BootDaddy Moonshine, a corn Whisky. (spacing?)

Square One Distillery, St. Louis, MO.
St. Louis JJ Neukomm Whisky

Still 630, St. Louis, MO.
Big Jake White Dog Whisky
Rally Point Rye.

MONTANA
Glacier Distilling Co., Coram, MT.
Glacier Dew, a light Whisky
North Fork Flood Stage Whisky,
Badrock Rye
Wheatfish Whisky
Belton Point Bourbon.

Headframe Spirits, Butte, MT.
Neversweat Bourbon, a sourced Bourbon
Destroying Angel Whisky

Rough Stock Distillery, Bozeman, MT.
Rough Stock Montana Malt Whisky
Spring Wheat Whisky
Sweet Corn Whisky.

Whistling Andy Inc., Bigfork, MT.
Harvest Select

NEVADA
Las Vegas Distillery, Las Vegas, NV.
Nevada Shine Corn Whisky.

NEW JERSEY
Jersey Artisan Distilling, Fairfield, NJ.
Busted Barrel Bourbon

NEW MEXICO
Don Quixote Distillery, Los Alamos, NM.
Blue Corn Bourbon

KGB Spirits, Alcalde, NM.
Taos Lightning

Santa Fe Spirits, Santa Fe, NM.
Silver Coyote Western Whisky
Glenkeegan Single Malt Whisky.
NEW YORK
Albany Distilling Co., Albany, NY
Half Moon New Make Whisky
Ironweed label

Baron Nahmias, Yonkers, NY.
Legs Diamond Rye Whisky
Legs Diamond label

Black Dirt Distilling Co./ Warwick Valley Winery & Distillery, Warwick & Pine Island, NY.
Black Dirt Bourbon

Breuckelen Distilling, Brooklyn, NY.
Label 77 Whisky

Catskill Distilling Co., Bethel, NY.
Most Righteous Bourbon.

Delaware Phoenix Distillery, Walton, NY.
Rye Dog.

Finger Lakes Distilling, Burdett, NY.
Glen Thunder
Corn Whisky
White Pike Whisky
McKenzie Bourbon

Hidden Marsh Distillery, Seneca Falls, NY.
Judd's Wrecking Ball.

Long Island Spirits, Baiting Hollow, NY.
Pine Barrens Single Malt
Rough Rider Bourbon.

Tuthilltown, Gardiner, NY.
Hudson Baby Bourbon
Hudson Four Grain Bourbon
Hudson Manhattan Rye
Hudson Single Malt
Hudson Corn Whisky

NORTH CAROLINA
Southern Artisan Spirits, Kings Mountain, NC.
Butcher Whisky

Top of the Hill Distillery (aka Topo Distillery), Chapel Hill, NC.
Topo Carolina Whisky

OHIO
Ernest Scarano Distillery, Gibsonburg, OH.
Old Homicide
Whisky Dick

Indian Creek Distillery (Staley Mill Farm & Distillery), New Carlisle, OH.
Staley Rye Whisky.

John McCulloch Distillery, Martinsville, OH.
Green River Whisky.

Middle West Spirits, Columbus, OH.
OYO (O-Why-O) Whisky

OREGON
Cascade Peak Spirits, Ashland, OR.
Cascade Peak Rye
Oldfield Rye

Clear Creek Distillery, Portland, OR.
McCarthy's Oregon Single Malt.

Edgefield Distillery, Troutdale, OR.
Hogshead Single Malt
Devil's Bit rye Whisky.

House Spirits, Portland, OR.
Westward Malt Whisky

Oregon Spirit Distillers, Bend, OR.
CW Irwin Bourbon

Ransom Spirits, Sheridan, OR.
Whipper Snapper Oregon Spirit Whisky

Rogue Spirits, Portland, OR.
Rogue Dead Guy Whisky
Chatoe Rogue Single Malt Whisky.

Stein Distillery, Joseph, OR.
Stein Bourbon
Stein Rye

Stone Barn Brandyworks, Portland, OR.
Hard Eight

PENNSYLVANIA
Mountain Laurel Spirits, Bristol, PA.
Dad's Hat Rye Whisky.

Philadelphia Distilling, Philadelphia, PA.
XXX Shine White Whisky

Pittsburgh Distilling Co., Pittsburgh, PA.
Wigle Whisky

RHODE ISLAND
Sons of Liberty Spirits Co., South Kingstown, RI.
Uprising Whisky
The 1765 Collection

SOUTH CAROLINA
Dark Corner Distillery, Greenville, SC.
Dark Corner Moonshine
Rooster Shine Corn Whisky
Joe-Pye Red wheat Whisky
Obsedian Single Malt Whisky
Independence 1776 Bourbon.

Six & Twenty Distillery, Powdersville, SC.
Six & Twenty Whiksy

SOUTH DAKOTA
Dakota Spirits Distillery, Pierre, SD
Coyote 100 Light Whisky
Bickering Brothers Blended Whisky.

TENNESSEE
Corsair Distillery, Nashville, TN.
Triple Smoke
Wry Moon
Rasputin

Jack Daniel's's (Brown Forman), Lynchburg, TN.
Jack Daniel's No. 7 Black Label
Gentleman Jack
Single Cask Reserve
Tennessee Honey
Sinatra

Ole Smoky Distillery, Gatlinburg, TN.
Ole Smoky Moonshine

TEXAS

Balcones Distillery, Waco, TX.
Baby Blue
True Blue
True Blue 100 Proof
Brimstone
Rumble
Rumble Cask Reserve

Bone Spirits, Smithville, TX.
Fitch's Goat Corn Whisky

Firestone & Robertson, Fort Worth, TX.
TX Whisky.

Garrison Brothers Distillery, Hye, TX.
Garrison Brothers Bourbon.

Ranger Creek Brewing and Distilling, San Antonio, TX.
Ranger Creek .36 Texas Bourbon

Rebecca Creek Distillery, San Antonio, TX.
Rebecca Creek Fine Texas Whisky

Yellow Rose Distilling, Pinehurst, TX.
Outlaw Bourbon

UTAH
High West Distillery, Park City, UT.
Campfire
American Prairie Reserve
Rendezvous Rye
Double Rye
Bourye
Son of Bourye
Silver Whisky Western Oat
Silver Whisky OMG Pure Rye
21 YO Rocky Mountain Rye
16 YO Rocky Mountain Rye
Valley Tan

VIRGINIA
Abraham Smith Bowman (Buffalo Trace/Sazerac Co.), Fredericksburg, VA.
Virginia Gentleman
Bowman Brothers
John J. Bowman
Abraham Bowman

Catoctin Creek Distillery, Purcellville, VA.
Roundstone Rye

Copper Fox Distillery, Sperryville, VA.
Wasmund's Single Malt Whisky
Copper Fox Rye Whisky.

George Washington Distillery Mount Vernon
George Washington Whisky

Stillhouse Distillery (Belmont Farms), Culpeper, VA.
Original Moonshine

Virginia Distilling Co. (Legacy Artisan Distillers), Virgilina, VA.
Four Whitts Virginia Belle Corn Whisky

Virginia Sweetwater Distillery (Appalachian Mountain Spirits), Marion,

VA.
Virginia Sweetwater
Moonshine
War Horn Whisky.

WASHINGTON
Bainbridge Organic Distillers,
Bainbridge Island, WA.
Bainbridge Battle Point
Organic Whisky
Black Heron Spirits, West
Richland, WA.
Desert Lightning Corn
Whisky

Blue Spirits Distilling,
Chelan, WA.
Local Choice

Carbon Glacier Distillery,
Wilkeson, WA.
Stocking Stuffer Whisky

Ellensburg Distillery,
Ellensburg, WA.
Gold Buckle Club
Washington
Frontier Style Whisky
Wildcat White Moonshine

Five O'Clock Somewhere
Distillery, Cashmere, WA.
Block & Tackle Sunshine
Corn Whisky

Fremont Mischief Distillery,
Seattle, WA.
John Jacob Whisky
Fremont Mischief Whisky
Commemorative Soldier
Whisky

Golden Distillery, Bow, WA.
Samish Bay Whisky
White Gold Whisky.

Heritage Distilling, Gig
Harbor, WA.
Elk Rider
Wherskey.
J.P. Trodden Distilling,
Woodinville, WA.
J.P. Trodden Bourbon

Mac Donald Distillery,
Snohomish, WA.
Ty Wolfe Whisky
Headwaters Whisky
Skip Rock Distillers.

Mount Baker Distillery,
Bellingham, WA.
Mt. Baker Moonshine

Oola Distillery, Seattle, WA.
Waitsburg Bourbon.

Parliament Distillery,
Sumner, WA.
Ghost Owl Whisky

Seattle Distilling Co., Vashon,
WA.
Snake Whisky

Second Chance Spirits,
Prosser, WA.
Blue Flame Spirits

Tatoosh Distillery, Seattle,
WA.
Northwest Blended Whisky
Northwest Reserve Whisky
Tatoosh Bourbon

Woodinville Whisky Co., Woodinville, WA.
Headlong White Dog Whisky
Mashbill No. 9 Bourbon
100% Rye.

WEST VIRGINIA
Isaiah Morgan Distillery, summersville, WV.
Southern Moon

Pinch Gut Hollow Distillery (Heston Farm), Fairmont, WV.
Buckwheat Moon
Dixon Corn Whisky.

Smooth Ambler Spirits, Maxwelton, WV.
Exceptional White Whisky
Yearling Bourbon
LDI Distilled Bourbons
Smooth Ambler Old Scout.

West Virginia Distilling Co., Morgantown, WV.
Mountain Moonshine Spirit Whisky.

WISCONSIN
45th Parallel Spirits, New Richmond, WI.
Border Bourbon
New Richmond Rye

Great Lakes Distillery, Miwaukee, WI.
Kinnickinnic Blended Whisky

Old Sugar Distillery, Madison, WI.
Queen Jennie Sorghum Whisky.

Yahara Bay Spirits, Madison, WI.
Yahara Bay Lightning
Yahara Bay Whisky
V Bourbon
Charred Oak Bourbon
Charred Oak Bourbon and rye
Death's Door Whisky
Ugly's Moonshine

CANADA

ALBERTA DISTILLERS
Alberta Premium 5 YO Rye
Alberta Springs 10 YO Rye
Alberta Springs 90 proof Blended
Alberta Springs Sipping Whisky
Canadian Gold 3 YO Rye
Canadian Spirit 7 YO Rye
Carrington 3 YO Rye
Tangle Ridge 10 YO Blended
Windsor 3 YO Rye
Dark Horse
Tangle Ridge Double Casked 10 YO

BLACK VELVET DISTILLING COMPANY
Black Velvet Blended rye

Golden Velvet Blended rye

Red Velvet Blended rye

Regal Velvet Blended rye

Royal Velvet Blended rye

CANADIAN CLUB
DISTILLERY

Burke's Select
C.C. Citrus Blended
Canadian Club 100% Proof
Blended Rye
Canadian Club 15 YO

Canadian Club 20 YO
Blended Rye
Canadian Club 30 YO Ltd.
Edition
Canadian Club 6 YO Blended
Rye
Canadian Club Black
Blended Rye
Canadian Club Classic 12 YO
Canadian Club Reserve 10
YO Blended Rye
Canadian Club Rye
Canadian Club Sherry Cask 8
YO Blended Rye
Corby Royal Reserve Rye

CANADIAN MIST
DISTILLLERY
Canadian Mist

Canadian Mist Black
Diamond

Collingwood Canadian
Whisky

CASCADIA DISTILLERY
Canadian Corn 10 YO Rye

Century Reserve 13 YO Rye

Century Reserve 15 YO Rye

Century Reserve 21 YO Rye

Potter's Old Special Rye

Royal Canadian Whisky

GIMLI DISTILLERY

7 Crowns

Adam's Antique 10 YO

Adam's Private Stock

Canadian Hunter

Royal Crown Cask No. 16

Crown Royal Limited
Reserve

Five Star

Lord Calvert

Melcher's Very Mild

Seagram's 83 5 YO

VO

VO Gold

GLENORA DISTILLERY
Breton Hand and Seal
Blended

Cape Breton Silver

Glen Breton Rare Single Malt

Kenloch

HIGHWOOD DISTILLERY
Highwood Canadian Rye
Whisky

KITTING RIDGE DISTILLERY
Forty Creek Barrel Select Whisky

Forty Creek Three Grain Whisky

Pure Gold Canadian Whisky

SAZERACH FACILITY MONTREAL
McGuiness Silk Tassel Rye

MYRIAD VIEW ARTISAN DISTILLERY
Strait Whisky

VALLEYFIELD DISTILLERY
Canadian Supreme

Colony House Blended Rye

Gibson's Sterling Edition 6 YO

Number Eight Blended Rye
Schenley OFC 8 YO
Schenley's Golden Wedding

Seagram's VO

Triple Crown Blended Rye

VICTORIA SPIRITS
Craigdarroch Whisky

MEXICO AND LATIN AMERICA

BRAZIL

Destilarias Reunidas Lenzi Ltda
The Personal Blend

Destilería Busnello Ltda
Pitt's Blended

Heublein do Brasil Com. Ind
Drury's Special Reserve Blended
Durfee Hall Single Malt
Gold Cup Blended
Old Eight Blended

Vinícola Cordelier Ltda
Malte Barrilete Blended
O Monge Blended
Old Master Blended

GUATAMALA
Industria Licorera Quezalteca De Guatamala

Old Friend Tipo Whisky, Special Reserve

MEXICO
Los Dos Compadres

Single Cask Sour Mash Whisky

Gringo Larry Shine

SURINAME
Sab nv
Lord Parham Blended

URUGUAY

Capurro Distillery

Aged 6 YO Blended

Anejo Blended

Golden King Blended

Mac Pay 6 YO Blended

Mac Pay Blended
The Castle Blended

VENEZUELA
Destilaria Carupano

Scotty's Blended

SOUTH PACIFIC

PHILIPPINES
Consolidated Distillers of the Far East , Inc
APS Whisky Blended
Collector's Whisky Blended
Limtuaco Distillery

White Castle Blended 5 YO

AUSTRALIA
Bakery Hill Distillery

Bakery Hill Classic Single Malt 46%

Bakery Hill Classic Single Malt Cask Strength

Bakery Hill Double Wood Single Malt 46%
Bakery Hill Peated Single Malt 46%

Booie Range Distillery

Booie Range Distillers Single Malt

Cawsey Menck Pty. Ltd.

Great Outback Single Malt

Great Outback Superior Blend

Islay Mist Scotch Whisky Blended

Great Southern Distillery

Limeburners Single Malt

Tiger Snake Sour Mash

Hellyer's Road Distillery

Hellyer's Road Single Malt
Hellyer's Road Single Malt 10 YO

Hellyer's Road Single Malt Peated

Hellyer's Road Single Malt Slightly Peated

Hellyer's Road Single Malt Pinot Noir Finish

Southern Fire Single Malt Whisky

Whisky Cream Liqueur

Hoochery Distillery

Kimberly Corn Liqueur Whisky

Lark Distillery

Lark Single Malt Cask Strength

Lark Single Malt Distiller's Selection

Lark Single Malt Single Cask

Slainte Whisky Liqueur

Southern Coast Distillers

Batch 01

Batch 02

Batch 03

Tasmania Distillery

Franklin River Single Malt

Golden Age Whisky Liqueur

Old Hobart Cask Strength Single Malt

Sullivan's Cove Blended

Sullivan's Cove Bourbon Maturation 60%

Sullivan's Cove Double Cask Single Malt 40%

Sullivan's Cove Port Maturation Single Malt 60%

Sullivan's Cove Singe Malt

Trapper's Hut

NEW ZEALAND
South Pacific Distillery

Roaring Forties Single Malt

Southern Distilleries

Old Hokonui Whisky

The Coaster Single Malt

The Mackenzie Blended Malt

Southern Grain Spirits New Zealand Ld.

Shepherd's Blended Whisky

New Zealand Single Malt Whisky Company

Milford 10 YO Single Malt

Milford 12 YO Single Malt

Milford 15 YO Single Malt

Milford 18 YO Single Malt

Milford 20 YO Single Malt

Preston's Double Wood Blended Whisky

Preston's Single Wood Blended Whisky

1987 Single Malt

Waters of Leith

The South Island Single Malt

Diggers and Ditch Double Malt Whisky

Dunedin Double Wood

1988 Cask Strength

Wilson's Distillery (now

closed)

Lammerlaw 10 YO

Wilson's Whisky

JAPAN, TAIWAN AND ASIA

BANGLADESH
Carew & Co. Ltd.
Carew's Imperial Whisky

BHUTAN
Gelephu Distillery
Bhutan Mist Pure Malt Whisky
Coronation Silver Jubilee CSJ Whisky
Special Courier Whisky

CHINA
Wuliangye Distiller
Ampenas Whisky

INDIA
Shaw Wallace and Company Ltd.
Director Special Whisky
Hayward's Fine Whisky
Mohgul Monarch Deluxe Malt Whisky
Old Tavern Whisky

Amrut Distilleries P Ltd.
Amrut Single Malt
Gold Star Fine Whisky Blended
Maq Scotch Blended Whisky
Maqintosh Blended
Prestige Blended Malt
Prestige Blended Whisky
Prestige Fine Whisky
Prestige Rare Whisky

Silver Cup Blended

Anab – E-Shahi Wines and Distilleries
Golden Fine Whisky
Kay Kay Whiskies

Andhra Winery and Distillery
DSP Back Whisky
Royal Challenge Whisky

Apollo Alcho Bev Ltd.
Club Royal Premium Whisky
MazdoorWhisky
Power Whisky
Royal Shetland Whisky

BDA Ltd.
Officer's Choice

Bharat Distillery Ltd.
Bachelor Deluxe Blended
Bachelor Regal Blended
Double Lion Whisky
Golden Chariot Premium Blended
Nigro Premium Blended
Remembrance Premium Blended

Empee Distillery Ltd.
All Gold Whisky
Empee's Fine Whisky
Empee's Premium Gold Whisky
John Peter Whisky
Royal Club Whisky
Victoria Deluxe Whisky

Herbertson's Ltd.
Bagpiper Blended
Bagpiper Gold Blended

India Brewery & Distillery
Aristocrat Blended Whisky
Aristocrat Premium Whisky
Bonney Scott Special Whisky
Player's Whisky

Kasauli Distillery
Colonel's Special Blended
Solan No 1 Blended
Katra Liquor
3 Soldiers
Royal Crown
Wild Horse
Wild Horse Gold

McDowell & Co.
Bonus Fine Whisky
Derby Special Premium Blended
Gold Ribbon Blended
Keral Malted Whisky
McDowell's Diplomat Blended
McDowell's Premium Blended
McDowell's Signature Premium Blend
McDowell's Single Malt
McDowell's Vintage Classic Blended No. 1
No 1 McDowell's Blended
No. 1 McDowell's Century Blended

Mohan Meakin Breweries & Distilleries
Back Knight Blended
Diplomat Blended
Golden Eagle Deluxe Blended
Highland Chief Blended
London Fine Blended
MMB Blended
Royal Victoria Blended

NV Distillery
Party Special Blended Whisky

Phipson Distillery Ltd.
President's Pride
Regal Crest
Tiger Whisky
United Whisky
Vin Light Whisky

Rampur Distillery
8 PM Blended
Contessa Deluxe Blended
Crown Blended
Genesis Rare Old Premium Whisky
Gold Finger Blended
Whyte Hall Classic Deluxe Whisky
Royal Peg Prestige Blended

Sampson Distillery Ltd.
Deccan Malted Whisky
Fire 'N' Ice Deluxe Whisky
Gold Star Malted Whisky
Harmony Malted Whisky
Hero No. 1 Rich Blend Whisky
Imperial Gold Whisky
Liberty Fine Whisky
Marshall Whisky
Royal Gold Deluxe Whisky
Tractor Fine Whisky
Zoom Fine Whisky

Shiva Distillery Ltd.
Cosmopolitan Whisky
Monitor Whisky
Shiva's Whisky

Sikkim Distillery Ltd.
Red Barrel Noble Malt Whisky
Sikkim Corn Whisky
Sikkim Old Gold Premium Single Malt
Sikkim Shangrila Blended
Sikkim Special Blended

Som Distillery Ltd.
21st Century Pure Malt
Genius Deluxe Blended
Legend Premium Blended

South Sea's Distillery
Gold Rush Blended
Grand National Blended
John Bull Blended
Million Dollar Blended

House of Khoday's
Democrat Blended
Khoday's No. 1 Blended
Peter Scot Blended
Philip's Fine Whisky Blended
Red Knight Blended
Vat 999 Blended

Ugar Distiller
Gentleman's Whisky
Gokak Falls Whisky
Johar'sFine Whisky
Milan Whisky
Old Castle Blended
Sandpiper Whisky
U. S. Whisky
Ugar 2000 Premium Whisky
Ugar's Vatted Malt Rare Whisky

Vinbros & Co
Green Channel Blended
The Warehouse Grain Whisky
Vinbros 7PM Onwards Grain Whisky

LAOS
Inter Spirits (Lao) Co. Ltd.
Champa Blended Whisky

Tiger Whisky Factory
Super Tiger Blend Whisky

JAPAN
Gotemba Distillery
Boston club
Crescent Whisky Supreme Blended
Emblem Blended Whisky
Evermore 2004 21 YO Blended
Fuji-Gotemba 15 YO Single Grain
Fuji-Gotemba 18 YO Single Malt
Gotemba 12 YO Vatted Malt
Gotemba 20 YO Vatted Malt
Gotemba Corn 13 YO
Gotemba Grain 15 YO
Gotemba Vatted Malt
Hips Blended
Robert Brown Deluxe Blended Whisky
Robert Brown Memorial Blend Whisky
Robert Brown Special Blended Whisky
Ten Distilleries Blended Whisky

Hakushu Distillery
Kioke Jikomi Vatted Malt
Kodaru Vatted Malt

Hakushu Higashi Distillery
Hakushu 10 YO Single Malt
Hakushu 12 YO Single Malt
Hakushu 12 YO Single Malt
Sherry Caskk Finish
Hakushu 8 YO Single Malt
Hogshead Cask Finish
Hakushu Hizou-Malt
Mars Whisky Distillery
Mars 3 & 7 Blended
Mars Amber Blended
Mars Extra Blended
Mars Maltage 12 YO Blended
Mars Maltage 8 YO Single
Malt
Mars Maltage Komagatake
10 YO Single Malt
Mars Old Blended
Satsuma 1984 Cask Malt
Whisky Vintage

Miyagikyo Distillery
Miyagikyo 12 YO Single Malt
Miyagikyo 8 YO Single Malt
Nikka Senjai 12 YO Single
Malt

Nikka Distillery
From the Barrel 51.4%
Nikka 10 YO Single Malt
Super Nikka Luxus Blended
10 YO
Super Nikka Luxus Blended
15 YO
Super Nikka Pure Malt
Genshi 10 YO
The Blend of Nikka 17 YO
Tsuru Luxus Blended 21 YO

Nishinomiya Distillery
All Malt Vatted Malt

Yamazaki Distillery
Suntory Hibiki 10 YO
Blended
Suntory Hibiki 12 YO
Blended
Suntory Hibiki 17 YO
Blended
Suntory Hibiki 21 YO
Blended
Suntory White Blended
Yamazaki 10 YO Single Malt
Yamazaki 12 YO Single Malt
Yamazaki 18 YO Single Malt
Yamazaki 25 YO Single Malt
Yamazaki 8 YO Single Malt
Puncheon Cask Finish

Yoichi Distillery
Hokkaido Vatted Malt
Yoichi 8 YO Single Malt
Yoichi 10 YO Single Malt
Yoichi 12 YO Single Malt
Yoichi 15 YO Single Malt
Yoichi 20 YO Single Malt

Hanyu Distillery
Golden Horse
Golden Horse Chichibu 8 YO
Single Malt
Golden Horse Chichibu 10
YO Single Malt
Golden Horse Chichibu 12
YO Single Malt
Golden Horse Chichibu 14
YO Single Malt
Old Halley

Karuizawa Distillery
Karuizawa 10 YO Single Malt
Karuizawa 12 YO Pure Malt
Karuizawa 15 YO Single Malt
Karuizawa 17 YO Single Malt
Karuizawa 21 YO Pure Malt
Karuizawa 8 YO Pure Malt

Master's Blend 10 YO

Shirakawa Distillery
Shirakawa 12 YO Single Malt
Shirakawa 30 YO Single Malt

MYANMAR (BURMA)
Myanmar Brewery & Distillery
Thistle Mandalay Malted Whisky

Peace Myanamar Group Co. Ltd.
Myanmar Whisky

NEPAL
Highland Distillery
Challenger Blended

Shree Distillery Pvt. Ltd.
Mount Everest

Sumy Distillery
Gill Marry Whisky Blended
Old Flame Premium Whisky Blended
Wainscot Whisky Blended

The Nepal Distillery
John Bull Blended
Old Reserve Whisky

PAKISTAN
Murree Distillery
Gymkhana Blended Malt
Millennium Reserve 21 YO Single Malt
Murree's Classic8 YO Single Malt
Muree's Mellenium Reserve 12 YO Single Malt
Muree's Vintage Blended

PALESTINE
Bozwin Distillery
Bozwin No. 24 Palestine Whisky

SOUTH KOREA
Hite Distillery
Lancelot 12 YO Blended
Lancelot 17 YO Blended
Lancelot 21 YO Blended
Lancelot 30 YO Blended

Jinro Distillers
Imperial Classic 12 YO Blended
Imperial Classic 17 YO Blended

TAIWAN
King Car Yuan-Shan Whisky Distillery
Kavalan Single Malt Whisky

Taiwan Tobacco & Liquor Corporation
Jade Supremacy Taiwan Whisky
Wallace Whisky

THAILAND
Kanchanaburi Distillery
Mekhong
Sangthip
Sangsom

Red Bull Distillery
Blend 285 Bended Whisky
Blue Blended Whisky
Crown 99 Blended Whisky

United Winery and Distillery
Black Cat Blended

Sangsom
VO Royal Thai Blended

AFRICA

ANGOLA
Inar Sarl
Black Horse
John Johnston

KENYA
Edermann Company Kenya Ltd.
Tiger Whisky

United Distillers & Vintners Kenya
Bond 7 Whisky

MAURITIUS
Grays & Co. Ltd.
Whisper Green Blended
Whisper Red Blended

SOUTH AFRICA

Drayman's Brewery & Distillery
Drayman's Single Malt Whisky
Drayman's Solera Whisky

James Sedgwick Distillery
Bain's Cape Mountain Whisky
Harrier 3 YO Blended
Knights Blended
Three Ships 10 YO Single Malt
Three Ships 5 YO Blended
Three Ships Bourbon Cask Finish
Three Ships Select Blended

EUROPE

AUSTRIA
Brennerei Weienauer
Waldviertler Hafer Whisky

Bockl Brande
Austrian Barley
Austrian Oak
Austrian Rye

Destillate Siegfried Herzog
Mchagmoar Whisky

Destillerie Reisetbauer
Reisetbauer Single Malt

Destilleries Weutz
Hot Stone Cask Strength Malt
Hot Stone Single Malt

Waldviertler Roggenhof Destillerie
Gersten-MalzWhisky
Gersten-Malzwhsiky (karamell)
Roggen-MalzWhisky
Rogge-MalsWhisky (Nougat)
Roggen Whisky

Wolfram Ortner Destillerie and Cafe Manufactur
Nock-Land Whisky

BELGIUM
Brouwerij Het Anker
Gouden Carolus Single Malt

Graanstokerij Filliers
Filliers Blended Whisky
Goldlys 10 YO
Goldlys Owner's Reserve

Pur. E. Distillerie
The Belgian Pure Malt
The Belgian Whisky

The Owl Distillery
The Belgian Owl 3 YO Single Malt

CZECH REPUBLIC
Fleret Likerka
GWC Blended

Kuba MBC
Gold King Rye Whisky
Hill's Finest Czech
Hill's Finest Moravian

Stock Plzen A. S.
Halberd Smoker Blended Whisky
Printer's Stock Blended

Tesetice Distillery
Goldcock Black 6 YO Malt
Goldcock Red 3 YO Bend
King Barley 12 YO
King Barley 4 YO
King Barley 6 YO

DENMARK
Stauning Distillery
Stauning Peated Reserve
Stauning Traditional Reserve
Stauning Rye Whisky

Vingarden Lille Gadegard
Bornholmsk Whisky
Isle of Fionia Single Malt Whisky
Isle of Fionia Smoked Whisky

C.L.O.C.
CLOC 7 YO Single Malt
CLOC Single Malt

ESTONIA
Onistar A. S.
Old Thomas Blended

FINLAND
10-Vuotias Viski
Kolme Leijonaa
Viski 88

Alko Oy AB

Steak and Whisky House
Galle
Old Buck Single Malt

Teerenpeli Brewery and Malt Whisky Distillery
Teerenpeli Mallasvikit Doublewood Brandy Finish
Teerenpeli Mallasvikit Doublewood Romni Finish
Teerenpeli Mallasvikit Doublewood Sherry Finish

FRANCE
Chevalier Distillery
First Knight Blended
Red Tower Blended

Distillerie Bertrand
Uberach Single Malt Alsace Whisky

Distillerie Claeyssens De Wambrechies
Genievre Vieux Malt 1991 Wambrechies
Genievre Vieux Malt 1992 Wambrechies
La Clef De l'An 2000 Pure

Malt
Old Malt Vintage 5 YO
Pure Malt 42%
Pure Malt 49%
Wambrechies Single Malt

Destillerie Des Menhirs
Eddu Grey Rock Blended
Eddu Silver Single Malt

Distillerie F. Meyer
Blend SuperieurMeyer's
Pure Malt Meyer's

Distillerie Glann Ar Mor
Glann Ar Mor Single Malt
Glann Ar Mor Peated Single Malt

Distillerie Guillon
Guillon Single Malt 40%
Guillon Single Malt 42%
Guillon Single Malt 46%

Distillerie Warenghem
Amorit Single Malt
Whisky Breton Blended

Domaine Mavela
PM 40% Pure Malt
PM 42% Pure Malt

Ferme BrasserieLa Chapelle
Whisky Thor Boyo

Fisselier & Leroyer
Gwenroc Whisky Breton
Whisky De Bretagne

Gilbert Holl Distillery
Lac 'Holl

Kelt Distillery
Kelt Tour Du Monde Pure Malt Whisky

Maison De La Mirabelle
Glenrozeliesres 4 YO

Michel Couvreur
Couvreurs Clearach Single Malt
Michel Couvreur 12 YO Pure Malt Blend 43%
Michel Couvreur 12 YO Pure Malt Blend 56%
Michel Couvreur Bere-Barley 12 YO Single Malt
Michel Couvreur Bere-Barley 14 YO Single Malt
Michel Couvreur Bere-Barley 24 YO Single Malt
Michel Couvreur Bere-Barley 27 YO Single Malt
Michel Couvreur Blossoming Auld Sherried Single Malt
Michel Couvreur Clerach Jura Vin Cask Single Malt
Michel Couvreur Fleeting Single Cask Single Malt
Michel Couvreur Forever Young Prestine 35 YO Single Malt
Michel Couvreur Grain Whisky
Michel Couvreur Pale Single Malt Whisky 12 YO
Michel Couvreur Very Sherried 24 YO 45%
The Aubigny Auld Alliance 12 YO Blend

Whisky Altore
Altore Pure Malt 5 YO Muscat Finish
Altore Pure Malt 8 YO

Altore Pure Malt 8 YO
Reserve Moresca Finish

Distilleries Dikansky
Les Whiskies Insolites

GERMANY
G-Spirits
www.gSpirits.com
Whisky No. 1

A Racke and Co Gmbh
Racke Rauchzart 12 YO
Blended

Bellerhof- Brennerei
Schwabischer Whisky
VonBelerhof 6 YO

Berghof Rabel
Schabischer Whisky Single
Grain

Birkenhof Brennerei
Birkenhof Whisky Blended

Blaue Mause Destillerie
Austrasier Single Cask Grain
Whisky
Blaue Maus (Glen Mouse)
Single Cask Malt Whisky
Blaaue Mause 16 YO Single
Malt
Gruner Hund Single Cask
Single Malt Whisky
Old Fahr Single Cask Malt
Whisky
Schwarzer Pirat Single Cask
Malt Whisky

Brennerei Anton Bischof
Bischof's Rhoner Whisky

Brennerei Brasch
Whisky Aus DerSteigerwald

Brennerei Falckenthal Sohne
GmbH
Der Falckner Malz Whisky
Blend
Endelfalke Blend
Old Masters Single Malt

Brennerei Hohler
Apple Jack Whesskey
Whesskey (Hessischer
Whisky)
Whesskey (Hessischer PMW)

Brennerei Otto Hubner
Frankischer Whisky

Brennerei Scraml
Stonewood 1818 10 YO Grain
Whisky

Brennerei Sigel
Dettinger Whisky
Good Old German Whisky

Brennerei Volke Theurer
Black Horse Original
Ammertal Whisky Blended

Christian Gruel
Schwabisher Whisky Single
Grain 5 YO
Schwabisher Whisky Single
Grain 7 YO
Schwabisher Whisky Single
Grain 9 YO

Hammerschmiede
Spirituosen
Glen Els Single Malt

Krabba Nescht
Blackwood
Obst-Korn Brennerei Zaiser
Zaiser Schwabischen Whisky

Slyers Destillerie GmbH and Co. KG
Slyers 3 YO Single Malt

Weingut Reinermosslein
Frankischer Whisky

Privat Brennerei Sonnenschein
Sonnenschin 15 YO Single Malt

HUNGARY
Pumnondrink es Millenium Kft
Flat Country
George XIX
Windfield

LATVIA
Latvijas Balzams A.S.
LB Viskijs
Viskijs Aleksandrs

NETHERLANDS
Bols Distilleries
Gold Top Whisky

Us Heit Distilleries
Frysk Hinder 3 YO Single Malt

Zuidam Distillers BV
Millstone 5 YO Single Malt

P. J. Vleck
Oude Vleck Blended Whisky

Piet Van Gent Distilleederijen
Gent's Fine Dutch Whisky 70 Proof

NORWAY
Agder Brenneri
Agder Audney Norwegian Single Malt Single Cask 2012

POLAND
Labuska Wytwornia Wodeck Gatuntowych
Dark Whisky Blended
Old Family Whisky Blended

RUSSIA
Praskoveyskoye Distillery
Whisky Praskoveyskoye

SPAIN
Destilerias Del Penedes S. A.
Gold & Black Blended

Destilerias Liber S. L.
Embrujo Pure Malt

Destileria Y Crianza Del Whisky S. A.
Double V Blended
DYC 8 YO Blended
DYC Blended

SWEDEN
Mackmyra Bruk
Mackmyra Den Forsta Utgavan Single Malt
Mackmyra Elegant Single Malt
Mackmyra Preludium: 01 Single Malt
Mackmyra Preludium: 01 Single Malt

Mackmyra Preludium: 02
Single Malt
Mackmyra Preludium: 03
Single Malt
Mackmyra Preludium: 04
Single Malt
Mackmyra Preludium: 05
Single Malt
Mackmyra Preludium: 06
Single Malt
Mackmyra Reserve Single
Malt
Mackmyra Rok Single Malt

Skeppet's
Skeppet's Blended

SWITZERLAND
Brennerei-Zentrum
Bauernhof
St Moritzer Single Malt
Swissky Getreidbrand Single
Malt

Maison Les Vignettes
Glen Vignettes Abred Single
Malt
Glen Vignettes Anouim
Single Malt
Glen Vignettes Gwenwed
Single Malt
Glen Vignettes Keugant
Single Malt
Glen Vignettes Schwisky
Challenge Single Malt
Glen Vignettes Schwisky
Skipper Single Malt

Tawny -Distillation Guy
Amigoni
Tawny Corn Sour Mash Pure
Corn Whisky

Unser Bier
Our Beer Single Malt

Whisky Castle Switzerland
Editon Kaser 71 Vol%
Whisky Castle Hill
Doublewood
Whisky Dinkel
Whisky Full Moon
Whisky Smoke Barley

Whisky Brennerei Holle
Holle Single Malt 3 YO
Holle Single Malt 5 YO Red
Wine Cask
Holle Single Malt 5 YO White
Wine Cask
Holle Single Malt 7 YO
Holle Single Grain Weizen
Whisky

TURKEY
Mey Icki Sanayi Ve Tec A. S.
Ankara Viski

WHISK LIST FOUR - HISTORY OF SCOTTISH DISTILLERIES

IMPORTANT DATES IN THE HISTORY OF SCOTCH WHISKY

Concentrating on historical events at the centre of the whisky-verse in Scotland, the informative whisky website: www.dcs.ed.ac.uk, has provided a list of significant historical events in the history of the Auld Scotch Drink which we have printed in a reduced version:

1494 - Entry in Exchequer Rolls regarding Friar Cor making aqua vitae by order of the King.

1498 - Lord High Treasurer's Account 'To the barbour that brocht aqua vitae to the King in Dundee'.

1505- Barber surgeons in Edinburgh granted right of making aqua vitae.

1506- Treasurer's Accounts in Inverness mention 'aqua vite to the King'.

1527- The vertuose boke of Dstyllacyon by Hieronymous Braunschweig published in English, translated by L. Andrew. First book on the subject, treated aqua vitae as a medicine.

1555 - The Scottish Parliament passed an Act forbidding export of victuals in time of famine, except: 'It sal be leifful to the inhabitants of the burrowis of Air, Irvin, Glasgow, Dumbertane and uthers our Soverane Ladys leigis dwelland at the west setis to have bakin breid, browin aill and aqua vite to the Ilis to bertour with uther merchandice'.

1559 - Treasure of Evonymous published by Peter Morwyng, detailing methods of distilling process.

1578 - Raphael Holinshed's Chroncles of England, Scotland and Ireland mention types of aqua vitae found in Scotland.

1618 - John Taylor in his

Pennyless Pilgrimage visits Earl of Mar and drinks aqua vitae Earliest reference to 'uisge' being drunk at Highland chief's funeral.

1688 - The Revolution An Act referred for first time to single and double proof spirits. The first attempt to charge duty according to strength.

1713 - Attempt to introduce Malt Tax in Scotland, but withdrawn.

1725- Walpole proposed tax on malt in Scotland. Malt Tax riots in Glasgow.

1736 - Porteous Riots in Edinburgh result of capture of smugglers Wilson and Robertson. Escape of Robertson arranged by Wilson, who was hanged. Mob fired on by Porteous in command of troops. Porteous lynched by mob subsequently when about to be reprieved. Smuggling very common and Excise officers mainly English and disliked Magistrates of Middlesex petitioned Parliament regarding gin Gin Act aimed at preventing consumption caused open flouting of law; Scotland specifically exempted from its provisions.

1750 - Final Gin Act reduced the enormous consumption of gin in the south. During the Gin Era consumption had risen from 800,000 gallons in 1694 to over 6 million gallons in 1734. By 1750 over 8 million gallons. By 1758 had dropped to 2 million gallons.

1751 - Act amending laws on spirits specifically ended Scotland's exemption, so that it was no longer advantageous to import from Scotland.

1773 - Johnson on Tour of Highlands with Boswell visited Western Isles. Sampled usquebaugh.

1784 - Wash Act defined Highland Line by Act of Parliament. Forbes's exemption at Ferintosh was finally ended. Riots at Mr. Haig's distillery at Leith. One rioter shot and killed. Colonel Thomas Thornton, Yorkshire sporting squire, toured Scotland.

1786 - Distillery Act. Licensing system introduced. Duty raised in Scotland to English level. No distinction between Highlands and Lowlands. Unfair system gave great impetus to illicit distillation.

1788 - Duty increased. Stein brothers bankrupted. Robert

Burns joined the Excise. Scots distillers still continued to produce more than estimated.

1793 - Tax on whisky trebled to £9. Still the distillers continued to produce more whisky than had been estimated by tax officials. William Hill set up in Rose Street, Edinburgh, as a whisky merchant.

1795 - Tax on whisky doubled to £18. Some stills operating continuously to beat tax at expense of wearing out still. Shape changing for sake of speed.

1797 - Tax trebled to £54.

1800 - Dr. John Leyden's Tour to the Highands. Tax doubled yet again to £108.

1803 - War broke out again and tax raised yet again to £162 Meanwhile whisky was becoming the most important industry. Illicit distilling was accepted by everyone as the only means of paying rent for a farm. The taxation problem had clearly defeated the government in the south.

1805 - The firm of Seager Evans was formed in London as makers of gin.

1814 - The prohibition of stills under 500 gallon capacity in the Highlands according to General Stewart of Garth this amounted to a complete interdict. Matthew Gloag set up as a whisky merchant in Perth.

1815 - The output of the distillery at Drumin in Glenlivet run by George Smith, grandson of John Smith Gow, was already a hogshead a week. Due to the pure water and fine peat available the whisky in Glenlivet was famed as being the finest illicit whisky in the Highlands. It was drunk by many northern lairds, including Grant of Rothiemurchos, M.P. and lawyer. Laphroaig distillery on Islay was built by the Johnstone family.

1817 - Teaninich distillery built by Captain H. Munro in Ross-shire. Sikes's hydrometer superseded the old inaccurate Clarke's hydrometer.

1818 - Bladnoch disti]lery was founded, near Wigtown, by the Maclelland family.

1819 - Clyneleish distillery near Brora was built by the Marquis of Staford, son of the Duke of Sutherland

1820 - John Walker set up as a

licensed grocer in Kilmarnock in Ayrshire. Debates in Parliament on the subject of illicit distilling in Scotland were inconclusive, but the Duke of Gordon addressed the House of Lords urging a more moderate policy Sikes's hydrometer and saccharometer used in conjunction under new Act

1821- Linkwood distillery near Elgin was built

1822 - George IV visited Scotland and was provided with illicit Glenlivet whisky by Grant of Rothiemurchos. He was reported to drink no other

1823 - A new Act was introduced which provided for a £10 annual licence fee and a duty of 2s 3d per gallon Springbank distillery near Campbeltown founded by farmers named Mitchell.

1824 - Under the aegis of his landlord the Duke of Richmond and Gordon, farmer and illicit distiller George Smith was the first to take out a licence under the new Act. The first legal distillery in Glenlivet, his neighbours threatened to burn it down Gillespie made a notable haul of illicit Glenlivet whisky in a desperate battle with smugglers. Gillespie then applied for a less arduous post.

1825 - Consolidation Act introduced uniform measures. T. R. Sandeman founded a whisky merchants business in Perth.

1826 - Robert Stein took out a patent for a single-distillation still.

1827 - Malcolm Gillespie forged a bill, was arrested, tried and hanged, despite pleas for mercy on account of his long service. Christopher North's Noctes Ambrosianae featured James Hogg in Blackwood's Magazine

1830 - Tax per proof gallon raised significantly. Consequent increase in smuggling. Stein built his first still at Kirkliston, a Haig distillery. William Teacher founded his merchant's firm, aged 19. Talisker distillery was founded on the Isle of Skye

1831 - Aeneas Coffey invented his single still, known as the patent Coffey still, providing continuous distillation forgrain whisky. Justerini and Brooks founded their partnership in London.

1832 - The Coffey still was

patented and approved. The Glen Scotia distillery founded in Campbeltown by Stewart Galbrath. Total abstinence was advocated at the Preston Temperance meeting.

1833 - The Parnell Commission of Enquiry into the Liquor Trade started

1836 - The Parnell Commission issued its findings. Mostly ineffectual. The Glenfarclas Glenlivet distillery was founded by Robert Hay

1838 - Hill Thomson granted Royal Warrant

1840 - The Glen Grant distillery was founded at Rothes by James and John Grant. The Glenkinchie distillery in East Lothian founded by farmer J. Gray.

1841 - James Chivas founded his firm of merchants and grocers in Aberdeen.

1842 - Glenmorangie distillery at Tain was founded by William Mathieson.

1846 - John Dewar started as a wine and spirit merchant in Perth. The Repeal of the Corn Laws was to treat grain distilling favourably.

1848 - Queen Victoria and family visited John Begg's distillery at Lochnagar.

1849 - Captain William Grant announced his distillery in conjunction with George Smith's at Drumin the only ones in Glenlivet.

1853 - Andrew Usher was credited with producing the first blended whisky.

1856 - First Trade Arrangement amongst grain distillers.

1857 - W. & A. Gilbey founded as wine and spirit merchants. William Thomson joined William Hill and formed Hill Thomson at 45, Frederick Street, Edinburgh

1865 - New Trade Arrangement formed. Menzies, Barnard & Craig, John Bald & Co., John Haig & Co., MacNab Bros, Robert Mowbray and Macfarlane & Co., who replaced John Crabbie and Co., who had previously been a member. Glenfarclas distillery was bought by John Grant of Blairfindy.

1870 - Phylloxera vastatrix beginning to spread in France.

1874 - The North of Scotland Malt Distillers Association

was formed

1877 - The Distiller's Company Limited was formed by Macfarlane & Co., John Bald & Co. John Haig & Co, MacNab Bros & Co, Robert Mowbray and Stewart & Co. John Haig founded his company at Markinch in Fife

1880 - John Walker opened a London office. Colonel John Gordon Smith, son of George Smith, went to law on the subject of the use of the name Glenlivet. The court held he was the only one entitled to use the label 'The Glenlivet', all others had to use a prefix

1881 - Bruichladdich Islay Malt distillery was founded

1882 - William Sanderson produced his blend 'Vat 69'. James Whyte and Charles Mackay founded Whyte and Mackay, Ltd.

1884 - James Buchanan set up in London and produced the blend 'Black & White'. William Shaw joined Hill Thomson and produced the blend 'Queen Anne'

1887 - The Glenfiddich distillery was built by William Grant. The Dufflown-Glenlivet distillery was founded. Highland Distilleries founded to acquire the Islay distillery of William Grant and the Glenrothes Glenlivet Distillery built in 1878.

1888 - The North British Distillery Co. with productive capacity of three million gallons p.a. founded in opposition to the growing power of the D.C.L.. Mackie & Co. took over Lagavulin distillery on Islay for White Horse.

1891 - Balvenie distillery founded by William Grant of Glenfiddich.

1893 - Cardow was bought by John Walker. The firm of Macdonald and Muir was founded.

1894 - Longmorn-Glenlivet built by Longmorn Co.

1895 - Aultmore founded by Alexander Edward of Sanquhar, Forres. Arthur Bell & Sons formed from Sandeman's of Perth.

1896 - John Dewar built a distillery at Aberfeldy

1898 - The whisky boom came to an abrupt halt with the failure of the Pattison brothers.

1899 - The United Yeast Co. was founded by the D.C.L. as

a subsidiary

1906 - Islington Borough Council brought the 'What is Whisky?' case. Basically a question of malt versus grain. Verdict in magistrate's court in favour of malt, but the D.C.L ressed for Royal Commission

1908 - A Royal Commission on Whisky decided grain and malt blended to make Scotch whisky.

1914- Intoxicating Liquor Act. Scottish Malt Distillers formed as a subsidiary of the D.C.L.

1915 - Central Liquor Control Board formed. Immature Spirits Act required two years' compulsory bonding. Buchanan's and Dewars merged into Buchanan-Dewars.

1917 - Dilution of proof to 30 under proof. Whisky Association formed

1919 - Haig and Haig were taken over by the D.C.L.

1924 - John Haig merged with the D.C.L.

1925 - Buchanan-Dewars and John Walker merged with the D.C.L., with John Ross of the D.C.L. as chairman

1926 - The Pot-Still Malt Distillers Association was formed in place of the North of Scotland Malt Distillers Association to include all malt distillers

1927 - Seager Evans set up Strathclyde distillery for grain whisky. White Horse Distillers was acquired by the D.C.L.

1933 - Arthur Bell & Sons acquired Blair Athol and Dufftown-Glenlivet distilleries.

1936 - Hiram Walker acquired George Ballantine & Go. of Dumbarton, also Milton Duff distillery. Arthur Bell & Sons acquired the Inchgower distillery near Fochabers. Seager Evans acquired John Long.

1937 - Seager Evans took over Glenugie distillery at Peterhead, Aberdeenshire

1938 - Hiram Walker opened a £3,000,000 grain distillery at Inerleven, Dumbarton.

1939 - Start of Second World War. Total whisky stocks lost by enemy action amounted to 4.5 million gallons. Grain distilling halted, limited malt pot-still distilling allowed 194a The Whisky Association dissolved and The Scotch Whisky Association founded in its place.

1945 - End of Second World War

1947 - Distilling still greatly restricted.

1950 - Seagram's took over Strathisla distillery

1952 - George & J. G. Smith, Ltd. and J. & J. Grant Glen Grant, Ltd. formed a public company, The Glenlivet & Glen Grant Distillers, Ltd.

1954 - Hiram Walker took over Glencadam distillery in Brechin and the Scapa distillery in Orkney.

1955 - Hiram Walker took over Pulteney distillery in Wick.

1956 - Seager Evans were bought by Schenley Industries of New York, in turn owned by Glen Alden Corporation.

1957 - Seager Evans built Kinclaith distillery near Glasgow.

1958 - Seager Evans built a new distillery at Tormore on the Spey, north of Grantown.

1959 - Inver House, an American-owned Company, built a new grain distillery by Airdrie and an associated Lowland malt distillery named Glenflagler.

1960 - The Scotch Whisky Association was incorporated to provide legal status in foreign courts. Glenfarclas distillery redoubled in size Ledaig distillery in Tobermory started. Jura distillery started by Scottish & Newcastle Breweries, Ltd. Glenallachie distillery started.

1962 - Laphroaig was acquired by Seager Evans. W. & A. Gilbey, Gilbey Twiss, Justerini & Brooks and United Vintners formed International Distillers and Vintners Ltd.

1965 - Caperdonich and Benriach distilleries were re-built after having been silent for over sixty years. Invergordon Distillers, Ltd., was formed.

1969 - Glen Alden Corporation who owned Schenley Industries

who owned Seager Evans was taken over by Rapid American Incorporated. The name Seager Evans was changed to Long John International, Ltd.

1970 - The Glenlivet & Glen Grant Distilleries, Ltd., merged with Hill Thomson & Co., Ltd., and Longmorn-Glenlivet Distilleries, Ltd. Amalgamated Distiled Products, Ltd., was formed with the Campbeltown Glen Scotia distillery and other interests. The Highland Distillers Co., Ltd., acquired Matthew Gloag Ltd.

1971 - Chivas Bros., the Scots subsidiary of Seagrams, began plans for a distillery in Glenlivet.

1972 - The Glenlivet & Glen Grant Distileries, Ltd., rationalised their name to The Glenlivet Distillers Limited. The Pot-Still Malt Distillers Association of Scotland rationalised their name to The Malt Distillers Association of Scotland

1973 - Britain entered the European Economic Community. With the introduction of V.A.T. the duty on whisky was reduced for the first time since 1896. Dalmore, Whyte & Mackay and Tomintoul distillery taken over by The House of Fraser Braes of Glenlivet distillery operational. The notable feature of the late fifties and sixties has been the influx of foreign, particularly U.S., investment in the industry, taking full advantage of government subsidies but not necessarily with the interests of the industry or of the United Kingdom at heart.

1974 - The Glenlivet Distillers Ltd. celebrate their hundred and fiftieth anniversary since George Smith took out the first licence in 1824 Malt Distillers of Scotland celebrate their centenary.

LIST OF SCOTCH WHISKY DISTILLERIES AND WHEN THEY OPENED FOR BUSINESS

1689 - Ferintosh Distillery (Despite being burnt down during the Jacobite scuffles, it became Scotland's first legal distillery).

1741 - Cambusbarron

1751 - Gilcomston

1752 - Portree

1755 - Dunbeath

1756 - Langholm

1770 - Dundashill, Yoker

1775 - Glenturret

1777 - Littlemill, Kennetpans, Kilbagie

1779 - Bowmore

1780 - Blackhall, Cannonmills, Hattonburn, Kincaple, Lochrin, Underwood

1783 - Glenmavis, Pitheven

1785 - Linton, Stonnywood

1786 - Gorbals, Grange Alloa, St Clement's Wells, Strathisla-Glenlivet

1787 - Portnauld

1788 - Anderston, Cunningham Park, Doghillock, Minamuir

1790 - Aucherachan, Balblair, Ballegreggan, Blackburn, Smithills

1791 - Inchdrewer

1793 - Airdrie, Saucel, Sauchenford

1794 - Ardbeg, Bridge of Don, Craigentinny, Oban

1795 - Ardry, Barnshill, Boggs, Bonnytown, Cannongate, Coblebrae, Cowie, Craigend, Dumfries, Glasgow, Grange Burntisland, Greenock, Hamilton, Highland Park, House of Muir, Inverkeithing, Kepp, Kersebank, Kirkintilloch, Kirkliston, Littlecarse, Loanwells, Maines, Paisley, Richardtown, Shawend, Smallhills, Spynie, Torphichen, Tulliallan, Wallace Paw

1796 - Jacksbank

1798 - Aberfoil, Achlatt, Ardincaple, Ardiseer, Assery, Babute, Ballie, Balnaguard, Balon, Barronepark, Beith, Blackhill, Blair Athol, Blairgowrie, Brabster, Brawlbin, Bught, Cairniehill, Callander, Campbeltown, Cardross, Clathick, Clayock, Cleigh, Clyth, Coultmalindy, Crieff, Culduthel, Cultocheldoch, Dalvey, Daside, Delney, Down, Drumchardney, Drumcuden, Dunblane, Dunverny, Eastertyre, Findon, Gallowhill, Gerston, Gladfield, Glengarioch, Greenhaugh, Greenland, Hartfield, Haugh, Heastigro, Hempriggs, Hopewill, Huntly, Inverness, Inverury, Junich, Killichattan Mill, Ledaig, Leith, Marcasie, Methven, Midfearn, Mill of Alter, Millbank, Millfield, Millifiech, Mucklewartle, Murkle, Nairn, Old Aberdeen, Orlan, Pitcairngreen, Polnach, Port Appin, Portliach, Rhugarve, Rohean, Ryefield, Scoraclet, Skelbo, Souterhill, St Magdalene, Stonefield, Swadale, Tendan, Tornabuiag, Torrich, Tullibardine, Wateresk, West Barns, Wettel

1799 - Carsebridge, Lochend

1800 - Auchentoshan, Portsoy

1803 - Barrowfield

1806 - Cambus

1807 - Millburn

1809 - Croft

1810 - Ballechin, Isle of Jura, Seggie

1811 - Port Dundas, L Brackla

1812 - Glenluig, Old Rome 1812

1813 - Bo'ness, Claypots, Haddington, Poyntsfield, Sunbury, Thurso, Wideford

1814 - Daillm Fintalich, Lochlomond, Overhill, Rockvilla, Taynahinch

1815 - Campbeltown, C Dargall, Provanmill, Achenvoir, Auldtown

1816 - Ballackarse, Balloch, Bankell, Bridgeton, Brownfield, Burnbrae, Cachladow, Corry, Cothall, Denburn, Drummond, Dumbarton Bridge, Dumbrock, Duntanloch, Easdale, Glack, Glenburn, Invernahoyle, Kilbirnie, Lagavulin, Lochside, Lochgilphead, Lynedale, Meldrums Mill, Octomore, Oldhall, Pitleasie, Rountree Bank, Scarinish, Stevenston, Tomdachoill, West Tarbart, Wormyhill, Albion Place, Ballure, Balnakelly, Bladnoch

1817 - Bridgend, Coldwells, Comrie, Cregan, Croftentober, Currylea, Damhead, Drumdowiem, Dudhope, Duntocher, Fintry, Fleemington, Fortrose, Fowlis, Gillybanks, Gorthy, Grange, Kinloch, Kirkapool, Lenereach, Meadow, Milltown, Pollo, Rutherglen Bridge, Scarabuss, Stirling, Stromness, Teaninich, Turrich, Yetts of Muckhart

1818 - Balnaketoch, Bogside, Braes (Brayes) of Dunvorny, Bridgend, Chapeltown, Chartershall, Coulis, Denny, Dingwall, Dundas Castle, Hawick, Kerse Mill, Kinivaugh, Kinture, Littochbeg, Mains of Foss, Maxwell Town, Mill Drummond, Overtown, Pitcastle, Smythyhaugh, West Mill

1819 - Brora

1820 - Laphroaig, Linkwood, Linlithgow, North Port, Stobs, Union Glen, Ballygrant

1821 - Birnam, Camserney, Clackmannan, Frenchmill, Gunsgreen, Hoy, Kirkfield Bank, Kirkwall, Lauriston, Linmill, Luggieside, Middleton, Mile End, Muirheadstone, Olgrin, Olgranmore, Ormiston, Peninich, Perth, Phopochy, Ruthvenbank, Stemster, Strathdee, Tallant, Wolfburn, Polmont, Caledonian

1823 - Dalenamonie, Delnashaugh, Kinloch, Balmenach

1824 - Banff, Benachie, Burnend, Burnside, Blackquarry, Cameronbridge, Cardow, Dalaruan, Drumin, Fettercairn, Finnieston, Huntly Distillery, Lochhead, Longrow, Macallan, Meadowburn, Miltonduff-Glenlivet, Mortlach, Abbeyhill, Abbotshaugh, Arngibbon, Auchtergaven, Baldarroch, Balerno, Ballagort, Ballaird, Ballintomb

!825 - Balnacraig, Bank, Bankside, Bark Mill, Beauly, Bellview, Ben Nevis, Black Middens, Blackburn, Boncloich, Bonhill, Braes of Glenlivat, Broadford, Burnside, Campbeltown, Cairnaget, Calton, Cants Mill, Carinarget, Cashly, Clydesdale, Coltbridge, Corn Cairn, Craigie, Croftbain, Crossburn, Dalkeith, Dandaleith, Devanha, Dobbies, Dores, Dunkeld, Dunmore, Dunning, East Monkland, East Nevay, Ecclefechan, Fortingall, Garnet Well, Garthland, Gill, Tureen Street, Glenalrig, Glenbughty, Glencadam, Glenfinnart, Glenlivat, Glenury, Gollachie, Grandtully, Hazelburn, Helensburgh, Helmsdale, House of Burn, Kelso, Keltneyburn, Killearn, Kilmorich, Kippen, Kirktown, Lagg, Largs, Lasswade, Leith, Lillyburn, Loch Katrine, Adelphi, Loch Laggan, Lumbrane, Mill of Forres, Milton, Mountblairy, New Mill, Newmill, Newton, Northton, Petty, Pitillie, Port Ellen, Prestonpans, Rieclachan, Robert Burns, Rose Well, Sandbank, Seafield, Sheriffmuir, Sibster, South Baloch, Stoneytown, Stornoway, Stralochy, Stranraer, Strathmeldrum, Tain, Tambowie, Taymount, Tegarmuck, Tochineal, Todholes, Town's Mill, Tullibanocher, Tulwmet, West Lochlin, Whitehouse, Wilsontown

1826 - Aberlour-Glenlivet, Auchmedden, Badarrach, Bowertower, Braelangwell, Buck, Camelon, Cashside, Caul, Corgarff Castle, Cromarty, Endrick, Fisherrow, Fort Augustus, Glendronach, Glenfoyle, Glenisland, John O'Groats, Lochnagar, Lossit, Manbeen, Monymusk, Mulen Dry, Newbyth, Pulteney, Rathohall, Tradeston, Tulloch, Union, Argyll

1827 - Avonglen, Ballied, Cabrach, Caldercruix, Carbach, Castle Hill, Crook's Mill, Dumbarton, Enzie, Garchory, Glenavullen, Glendown, Glenramskill, Highland, Holland Bush, Irvine, Kennyhill, Loch, Torryburn, Turret Bank

1828 - Balfron, Bankier, Braes of Tullymet, Broomhill, Camnacumline, Craigwatch, Fairney Glen, Field, Gareloch, Holm, Springbank, Tamnaven, Woodside

1829 - Auchtermuchty, Bankfoot, Coshieville, Dunoon, Glenburgie-Glenlivet, Lochindaal, Logierait, Luncarty, Springfield, Strathbrand

1830 - Aberdeen, Aberfeldy, Albyn, Annandale, Ardtalnaig, Barkmill, Bishop Bridge, Drumblade, Glenlogie, Glenside,

Kintyre, Libster, Pitcarmick, Springside, Wellfield, West Highland

1831 - Bonnymuir, Carnacumline, Glenfyne, Glenside, Glenugie, South Bridge, South Dale, Talisker

1832 - Dalintober, Glen Scotia, Lexwell

1833 - Aldourie, Altduanalt Distillery, Auchnagie, Balmore, Broombrae, Burnside, Cushwell, Eastertown of Dunlappy, Glencarrick, Glenfarr, Glengoyne, Glenpatrick, Lesmurdie, Lochtayside, Manacher, New Seat, North Dale

1834 - Benrinnes, Camlachie, Drumore, Mossfield, Mountain Dew, Toberanrigh,

1835 - Lochruan

1837 - Ardenistle, Damhead, Edradour, Glen Noth, Glenkinchie, Glenmore, Haghill, Inverness, Ord

1839 - Dalmore, Netherton of Fonab, Tourchulan

1840 - Glen Grant-Glenlivet, Rosebank

1842 - Barrelwell, Haughend, Longside,

1843 - Bogroy, Glenforth, Glenmorangie,

1844 - Glenfarclas-Glenlivet, Teabeggan, Woodfoot

1845 - Auchtertool, Lyne of Rutherie,

1846 - Caol Ila, Glen Albyn, Glenochil,

1847 - Drumore, Freeport,

1849 - Delnabo, Edinburgh, Kildalton

1851 - Dalguise, Dron, Dufftown, Eden Bank, Geise, Glenavon, Isla, Rechlerich

1852 - Glentarras, Islay

1854 - Dailuaine

1855 - Bon Accord, Caledonian, Glen Newton

1858 - Glentarff, The Glenlivet

1863 - Benmore

1868 - Cragganmore

1872 - Inchgower,

1873 - Glengyle

1875 - Glenglassaugh

1876 - Glenlossie

1877 - Glen Nevis

1878 - Glenrothes-Glenlivet, Nevis

1879 - Ardlussa

1880 - Bunnahabhain

1881 - Bruichladdich, Dean

1882 - Glenaden,

1885 - Scapa

1886 - Glenfiddich, North British

1891 - Craigellachie, Strathmill

1892 - Balvenie, Glen Mhor

1893 - Knockdhu

1894 - Convalmorem Longmorn-Glenlivet, Parkmore

1895 - Bellefield, Speyside

1896 - Ardgowan, Auchinblae, Aultmore, Drumcaldie, Dufftown-Glenlivet, Glenskiach, Dufftown-Glenlivet, Glenskiach, Tamdhu, Towiemore

1897 - Coleburn, Dalwhinnie, Gartloch, Glencoull, Glenesk, Glenmoray-Glenlivet, Glenspey, Imperial, Speyburn, Tomatin

1898 - Ardmore, Benriach-Glenlivet, Benromach, Caperdonich, Glen Elgin, Glencawdor, Glenlochy, Glentauchers, Knockando

1899 - Dallas Dhu

1900 - Stronachie

1908 - Malt Mill

1927 - Strathclyde

1929 - Tay

1938 - Inverleven, Montrose

1957 - Glenkeith-Glenlivet, Kinlaith, Strathmore

1958 - Tormore

1959 - Invergordon

1963 - Girvan

1964 - Tomintoul-Glenlivet

1965 - Deanston, Glen Flagler, Inver House, Loch Lomond, Tamnavulin-Glenlivet

1966 - Ladyburn

1967 - Glenallachie

1971 - Mannochmore

1973 - Braes of Glenlivet

1974 - Braes of Glenlivet

1975 - Allt a Bhainne, Pittyvaich

1990 - Kininvie

2004 - Glengyle

2005 - Daftmill

2007 - Ailsa Bay

2008 - Roseisle

2009 - Abhainn Dearg

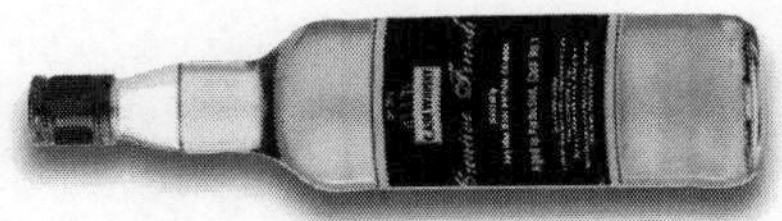

We have listed every distillery in Scotland and the many products they produce. Some of these products will come directly from the Distillery and others will have been bottled and packaged by Independent Bottlers. We have tried to list everything that was available in 2013. As products sell out, the list will go out of date, but it is a historic representation of what is and what was available. The descriptions of the products are by the marketing people behind the various products and bottlings. You can find and purchase the products you are looking for through many of the online retailers such as Whisky Exchange or Masters of Malt. The Distilleries and Independent Bottlers will all go out of their way to help you find what you are looking for.

GRAIN DISTILLERIES OF SCOTLAND

CAMERON BRIDGE
DUMBARTON
GIRVAN
INVERGORDON
NORTH BRITISH
PORT DUNDAS
STRATHCLYDE

ISLAY REGION

ARDBEG RANGE

Ardbeg 10 YO
70cl / 46%

Distillery Bottling
For peat-lovers, Ardbeg 10 YO is probably the highest-quality 'entry-level' Single Malt on the market, and the Distillery many Islay connoisseurs would choose as their favourite. A whirlwind of peat and complex malty flavours.

Ardbeg 10 YO / Bot.1960s
75cl / 40%
Distillery Bottling

A black labelled 10 YO Distillery Bottling of Ardbeg from back in the 1960s.

Ardbeg 10 YO / Bot.1980s
75cl / 40% - Distillery Bottling - A very special old Ardbeg 10 YO, unusually Bottled in clear glass in the 1980s by former owners Hiram Walker. A whopping 95 points from Whiskyfun's Serge Valentin only enhanced this release's legendary status.

Ardbeg 10 YO / Bot.1990s
70cl / 40% - Distillery Bottling - A rare Bottle of 10 YO Ardbeg Bottled some time in the 1990s. This is especially rare as the Distillery was closed for almost the entire preceding decade.

Ardbeg 10 YO Glass Pack
70cl / 46% - Distillery Bottling - A very snazzy gift pack featuring a full-size Bottle of Ardbeg's superb 10 YO Islay Single Malt, plus a rather stylish large green branded glass from which to drink it.

Ardbeg 10 YO 'MOR'
450cl / 46% - Distillery Bottling - A second edition of Ardbeg 'MOR', but unlike 2007's Cask-strength version, this has been Bottled at 46%, as per the normal 10 YO. The Bottle will look pretty impressive in your living room and, when empty, will hold an awful lot of 2ps and a very big candle.

Ardbeg 10 YO 'MOR' / Full Proof
450cl / 57.3% - Distillery Bottling - A massive 4.5 litre Bottle of Cask strength 10 YO Ardbeg, Bottled as 'MOR' (this was the original MOR Bottling). A serious bit of kit that will take up a chunk of space and provide a talking point at Whisky related gatherings for years to come. Lifting it to pour a dram may require help.

Ardbeg 17 YO
70cl / 40% - Distillery Bottling - A tad less peaty than early Bottlings, the classic Ardbeg 17 YO is still a great Whisky, but is sadly becoming very thin on the ground as demand increases and supply runs low - it's now a good few years since owners Glenmorangie discontinued it. The first Bottling of this sparked the revival of Ardbeg's fortunes after the takeover by Glenmorangie.

Ardbeg 1964 / Bot.1995 / Connoisseurs Choice
70cl / 40% - Gordon & Macphail - A very, very rare Ardbeg from

Gordon & Macphail's Connoisseurs Choice series. This was Bottled over 15 years ago in 1995 and Distilled nearly five decades ago back in 1964 when the Distillery was still very old-fashioned, using direct fired stills and its own floor maltings. A slice of history.

Ardbeg 1965 / 39 YO / NO MINI
70cl / 42.1% - Distillery Bottling - A very very special Bottling, this is a vatting of the two oldest Casks that were left at Ardbeg and comes in a suitably hefty 'museum piece' box. you even get some soft white gloves to caress it with.

Ardbeg 1966 / 32 YO
70cl / 42.6% - Cadenhead's - A very very rare 1960s Ardbeg, Bottled at natural strength (42.6%) by distinguished Edinburgh Bottlers Cadenhead's at the end of the 1990s.

Ardbeg 1967 / 30 YO / Sherry Cask
70cl / 49.8% - Signatory - A very special Bottle of Ardbeg Whisky. Distilled in 1967 and matured in a Sherry Cask for 30 years. This single Cask release was limited to just 536 Bottles when it was released 1997 and there are sure to be far fewer Bottles in circulation now.

Ardbeg 1967 / 30 YO / Sherry Cask #1138 / Signatory
70cl / 52.2% - Signatory - A stunning old Ardbeg Bottled by Signatory in March 1997. This Whisky has was Distilled in 1967 and has been matured for 30 years in an Oloroso Sherry butt. Limited to just 580 Bottles, this is a real collectors piece.

Ardbeg 1967 / 30 YO / Sherry Cask / Signatory
70cl / 52% - Signatory - A very special Bottle of 1967 vintage Whisky from Ardbeg Distillery. This Whisky has been matured for 30 years in an Oloroso Sherry Cask, giving it a beautifully dark colour.

Ardbeg 1967 / 32 YO / Douglas Laing
70cl / 49% - Douglas Laing - A single Cask Ardbeg, Distilled in 1967. This has been aged for 32 years and bottled at the beginning of the new millennium for Douglas Laing's Old Malt Cask range.

Ardbeg 1972 / 28 YO
70cl / 49.5% - Douglas Laing - One of a clutch of legendary Old Malt Cask Bottlings of Ardbeg released around the turn of the century. This expression is from 1972.

Ardbeg 1972 / 28 YO

70cl / 48.8% - Douglas Laing - A single Cask release of 1972 Ardbeg, specially selected for Alambic Classique in Germany. This Whisky has been aged for 28 years and Bottled by Douglas Laing as part of their Old Malt Cask range.

Ardbeg 1972 / 28 YO
70cl / 50.1% - Douglas Laing - An old single Cask release, specially selected for Alambic Classique in Germany. These Whisky was Distilled in 1972 and has spent 28 years maturing in an oak Cask. Bottled by Douglas Laing as part of the Old Malt Cask range.

Ardbeg 1972 / 28 YO
70cl / 49.5% - Douglas Laing - An old single Cask release of 1972 Whisky from Ardbeg Distillery. Bottled by Douglas Laing at the age of 28 years, for their Old Malt Cask range.

Ardbeg 1972 / 28 YO / Douglas Laing
70cl / 50% - Douglas Laing - A very rare Ardbeg 1972 Bottled over a decade ago as a 28 year-old for Douglas Laing's Old Malt Cask series.

Ardbeg 1972 / 29 YO
70cl / 50% - Douglas Laing - A 1972 Whisky from Ardbeg. This has been matured for 29 years including a minimum 6 month finishing period in a Sherry Cask. Bottled in November 2001 by Douglas Laing for their Old Malt Cask range.

Ardbeg 1972 / 29 YO / Douglas Laing
70cl / 50% - Douglas Laing - A single Cask Bottling of Ardbeg Whisky, Distilled in 1972 and aged for 29 years. This Whisky has undergone a finishing process of a minimum of 6 months in a sheryy Cask, before being Bottled at Douglas Laing's preferred strength of 50%.

Ardbeg 1972 / Cask 2782
70cl / 49.9% - Distillery Bottling - An old single Cask Ardbeg 1972 Bottled in 2003 for the Italian market in 2003. This was perfectly described as an 'old glory' by Whiskyfun's Serge Valentin, who gave it 95 points.

Ardbeg 1973 / 15 YO
75cl / 43%

Ardbeg 1973 / 15 YO / Moncrieffe

75cl / 46% - Moncrieffe - A very rare 1980s Bottling of Ardbeg 1973, Bottled at 46% by Glasgow's Moncrieffe & Co. for the Italian market.

Ardbeg 1973 / 27 YO
70cl / 50% - Douglas Laing - A 2000 Bottling of 1973 vintage Whisky from Ardbeg. Put in the Bottle by Douglas Laing for their Old Malt Cask label after 27 years of maturation.

Ardbeg 1973 / 27 YO / Douglas Laing
70cl / 50% - Douglas Laing - A single Cask Whisky from Ardbeg Distillery. Distilled in 1973 and aged for 27 years. Bottled by Douglas Laing, without colouring or chill-filtration, for their Old Malt Cask range.

Ardbeg 1973 / 30 YO
70cl / 51.9% - Douglas Laing

Ardbeg 1973 / 30 YO
70cl / 48.9% - Douglas Laing - An old Ardbeg from the days when they still ran their own on-site maltings. Bottled in 2003 by Douglas Laing for their Platinum Selection range. "Top notch again as expected" according to Serge Valentin on Whisky Fun.

Ardbeg 1973 / 36 YO / Platinum
70cl / 44.7% - Douglas Laing - A very, very rare Ardbeg 1973 for Douglas Laing's Platinum Selection - just 78 (!) Bottles were yielded from the Cask. Very elegant and unusual, with threads of Edinburgh rock, clove, cherry and a faint menthol woven through a distinct but not over-powering oak influence.

Ardbeg 1973 / Cask 1143
70cl / 49.3% - Distillery Bottling - An old single Cask Ardbeg 1973 Bottled from a Bourbon hogshead in 2004.

Ardbeg 1973 / Cask 1146
70cl / 49.5% - Distillery Bottling - An old single Cask Ardbeg 1973 Bottled from a Bourbon hogshead for the Italian market in 2004.

Ardbeg 1973 / Kingsbury's
70cl / 47.4% - Kingsbury's - A single Cask 1973 vintage Ardbeg Bottled by Kingsbury at 47.4%. This picked up an incredible 94 point average from the Malt Maniacs, with the lowest score from any of the tasters being an excellent 90/100.

Ardbeg 1974 / 21 YO / Sestante
70cl / 40% - Sestante

Ardbeg 1974 / 26 YO
70cl / 50% - Douglas Laing

Ardbeg 1974 / Bot.1983 / Sherry Wood / Samaroli
75cl / 59% - Samaroli is an Italian independent Bottler, famed for the exceptional quality of their releases and for their arty, innovative labels and packaging. This is a legendary young Ardbeg matured in Sherry Casks and Bottled at full strength in the early 1980s.

Ardbeg 1974 / Cask 2739
70cl / 53.7% - Distillery Bottling - An old Cask-strength Ardbeg 1974 Bottled from a single Cask for the Italian market in 2004.

Ardbeg 1974 / Cask 2743
70cl / 51.7% - Distillery Bottling - An old Cask-strength Ardbeg 1974 Bottled from a single Bourbon Cask for the French market in 2005.

Ardbeg 1974 / Cask 2751
70cl / 51.8% - Distillery Bottling - A single Cask release of Ardbeg 1974 for the UK market, this time a mere 141 Bottles from a Bourbon Cask. We are told there are very few old Casks left at Ardbeg for this kind of Bottling, so this may be one of the last released on these shores.

Ardbeg 1974 / Cask 3309
70cl / 52.5% - Distillery Bottling - An old Cask-strength Ardbeg 1974 Bottled from a single Bourbon Cask for the French market in 2006.

Ardbeg 1974 / Cask 3475
70cl / 44.5% - Distillery Bottling - A Cask-strength Ardbeg 1974 Bottled from a single Cask for Oddbins in 2002. Just 126 Bottles of this were released.

Ardbeg 1974 / Cask 4985
70cl / 46.7% - Distillery Bottling - A single Cask release of Ardbeg 1974 for the UK market, this time a mere 93 Bottles from a Bourbon Cask. We are told there are very few old Casks left at Ardbeg for this kind of Bottling, so this may be one of the last released on these shores.

Ardbeg 1974 / Cask 4989
70cl / 50.7% - Distillery Bottling - A single Cask release of Ardbeg 1974 for the UK market, this time a mere 132 Bottles from a

Bourbon Cask. We are told there are very few old Casks left at Ardbeg for this kind of Bottling, so this may be one of the last released on these shores.

Ardbeg 1974 / Cask 5666
70cl / 51.8% - Distillery Bottling - A Cask-strength release of Ardbeg 1974 for the UK market, Bottled in 2006 from a single bourbon Cask. We are told there are very few old Casks left at Ardbeg for this kind of Bottling, so this may be one of the last released on these shores.

Ardbeg 1974 / Double Barrel
140cl / 50% - Distillery Bottling - Ardbeg Double Barrel is something pretty special. This leather case from Purdey and Sons contains an Omas fountain pen, a leather-bound notebook for you to record your tasting notes and eight sterling silver cups. Oh, and two single cask Ardbegs from 1974 - both Bottled at Cask strength and packaged in hand-blown Bottles with sterling silver labels. Just 250 of these sets are being released worldwide

Ardbeg 1974 Provenance / 23 YO
70cl / 55.6% - Distillery Bottling - A legendary Ardbeg, the 1974 Provenance appeared in 1997 shortly after Glenmorangie's takeover of the Distillery. This version of Provenance was for the European market, other Bottlings were done for the USA and Asia.

Ardbeg 1975 / 15 YO / Cadenhead's
75cl / 46% - Cadenhead's - A 1975 vintage Ardbeg Bottled by the folks at Cadenhead's back in November 1990 after 15 years of maturation.

Ardbeg 1975 / 24 YO
70cl / 50% - Douglas Laing - A 1975 vintage Whisky from Ardbeg. This has been aged for 24 years and Bottled just after the millennium. Bottled at Douglas Laing's preffered strength of 50%.

Ardbeg 1975 / 24 YO
70cl / 50% - Douglas Laing - A single Cask Whisky from Ardbeg Distillery. This Whisky was Distilled in 1975 and aged for 24 years. Bottled at Douglas Laing's preferred strength of 50% and as part of their Old Malt Cask range.

Ardbeg 1975 / 25 YO
70cl / 50% - Douglas Laing - A 1975 vintage Ardbeg released by indie Bottler Douglas Laing in May 2001 after 25 years of

maturation for their Old Malt Cask range.

Ardbeg 1975 / 27 YO / Douglas Laing
70cl / 50% - Douglas Laing

Ardbeg 1975 / 27 YO / Sherry Cask
70cl / 50% - Douglas Laing

Ardbeg 1975 / 29 YO / Douglas Laing
70cl / 47.3% - Douglas Laing - An epic Ardbeg, this is one of Douglas Laing's earlier Platinum series releases from 2004. Some old Ardbegs are sweet and fruity, but here the emphasis is very much on the smoke with the fruit and sweetness in the background. A belter.

Ardbeg 1975 / 29 YO / Douglas Laing
70cl / 58.3% - Douglas Laing

Ardbeg 1975 / 30 YO
70cl / 46.1% - Douglas Laing

Ardbeg 1975 / 30 YO / Douglas Laing
70cl / 47.8% - Douglas Laing - An extra-special Ardbeg from Douglas Laing, Bottled at natural Cask strength to let the juicy peat and sweet spiciness express itself fully.

Ardbeg 1975 / Cask 1378 / Sherry Butt
70cl / 53.7% - Distillery Bottling - A Cask-strength release of Ardbeg 1975 Bottled in 2006 from a single Sherry Cask. There are now almost no Sherry Casks from the 1970s left at Ardbeg for this kind of Bottling.

Ardbeg 1975 / Cask 4699
70cl / 40.9% - Distillery Bottling - Bottled in 2006 for the UK market, this rare Cask-strength Ardbeg 1975 was from a single Bourbon Cask, No. 4699, which yielded 121 Bottles.

Ardbeg 1975 / Cask 4703 / Sherry Cask
70cl / 47.6% - Distillery Bottling - A single Sherry hogshead of Ardbeg 1975 Bottled at Cask strength for the Italian market in 2002.

Ardbeg 1975 / Cask 4704 / Oloroso Sherry Cask Islay Festival
70cl / 47.2% - Distillery Bottling - An ex-Oloroso Sherry Cask of Ardbeg from 1975, this rare Ardbeg was Bottled for the Feis Ile in 2005.

Ardbeg 1975 / Cask 4716 / Sherry Cask
70cl / 44.8% - Distillery Bottling - A single Sherry Cask of Ardbeg 1975 Bottled for the German market in 2002.

Ardbeg 1975 / Cask 4720 / Sherry Cask
70cl / 41.4% - Distillery Bottling - Bottled in 2006 for the Italian market, this rare Ardbeg 1975 was matured in a single ex-Sherry Cask.

Ardbeg 1975 / Natural Strength / Bot.1987 / Samaroli
75cl / 57% - Samaroli - This is a rare Bottling of Cask strength Ardbeg 1975 from the late 1980s and should be outstanding.

Ardbeg 1976 / 25 YO
70cl / 50% - Silver Seal

Ardbeg 1976 / 31 YO / Cask 2397 / Sherry Butt
70cl / 52.4% - Distillery Bottling - A legendary vintage release from Ardbeg in the years after they were acquired by Glenmorangie. Matured for 31 years in a Sherry butt and Bottled at Cask strength in 2008.

Ardbeg 1976 / Bot.1980s
75cl / 40% - Gordon & Macphail - A 1976 vintage Ardbeg Bottled for Gordon & Macphail's Connoisseurs Choice range. This was Bottled in the 1980s, a decade where the Distillery was closed for pretty much the entire time.

Ardbeg 1976 / Bot.1993 / Samaroli
70cl / 46% - Samaroli - An old Samaroli Bottling of Ardbeg 1976, Bottled in 1993.

Ardbeg 1976 / Cask 2391 / Manager's Choice / Sherry Cask
70cl / 56% - Distillery Bottling - The famous Ardbeg 'Manager's Choice' Bottling is a single sherry Cask from 1976 selected by Stuart Thomson for sale at the Distillery in 1999.

Ardbeg 1976 / Cask 2392 / Committee / Sherry Cask
70cl / 55% - Distillery Bottling
Part of the first Bottlings for the Ardbeg Committee in 2000, this single Cask is from a 1976 batch of Sherry Casks that took Ardbeg's reputation into the stratosphere.

Ardbeg 1976 / Cask 2394 / Committee / Sherry Cask
70cl / 53.2% - Distillery Bottling - Part of the first Bottlings for the Ardbeg Committee in 2000, this single Cask is from a 1976

batch of Sherry Casks that took Ardbeg's reputation into the stratosphere.

Ardbeg 1976 / Cask 2395 / Sherry Cask
70cl / 54.5% - Distillery Bottling - Bottled from a Sherry butt for the Japanese market in 2002, this Cask-strength dram is from the 1976 batch of Sherry Casks that took Ardbeg's reputation into the stratosphere.

Ardbeg 1976 / Cask 2396 / Sherry Cask
70cl / 53.5% - Distillery Bottling - A single Sherry Cask release of Ardbeg 1976 Bottled for the Italian market in 2002.

Ardbeg 1976 / Cask 2398 / Sherry Cask / Islay Festival 2004
70cl / 51.4% - Distillery Bottling - A Sherry butt of Ardbeg from the legendary 1976 batch, this rare Ardbeg was Bottled for the Feis Ile in 2004.

Ardbeg 1978 (42.4%)
70cl / 42.4% - Distillery Bottling - Supposedly the product of a mistake when the Bottling strength was reduced to 42.4% instead of 43%, this very rare Ardbeg was Bottled separately from the rest of the 1999 release and sold without a box.

Ardbeg 1990 / 8 YO / MM#2998
70cl / 46% - Murray McDavid

Ardbeg 1990 / Airigh Nam Beist
70cl / 46% - Distillery Bottling - Airigh Nam Beist 1990 is a delicious vintage Bottling from the ongoing success story that is Ardbeg. Sadly now discontinued due to exhausted stocks, 'the Beist' was an extremely popular Ardbeg, with assertive and powerful peatiness and a lovely honeyed edge. Oh, and it's pronounced 'Arry nam Baysht'.

Ardbeg 1990 / Bot.2004
70cl / 55% - Distillery Bottling - A highly sought-after Bottle of 1990 vintage Ardbeg, Bottled at 14 YO and 55% ABV for the Japanese market.

Ardbeg 1991 / 20 YO / Douglas Laing Platinum
70cl / 54.5% - Douglas Laing - A 1991 vintage Ardbeg Bottled by the folks at Douglas Laing as part of their rather shiny Platinum Selection. Matured in a refill hogshead and Bottled in November 2011.

Ardbeg 1991 / 8 YO / Cask #616
70cl / 60.2% - Signatory - A young Ardbeg 1991 Bottled at the end of the 1990s by Signatory at a whopping 60.2% ABV.

Ardbeg 1991 / 8 YO / Casks #611-615
70cl / 43% - Signatory - A young Ardbeg 1991 Bottled at the end of the 1990s by Signatory.

Ardbeg 1991 / 8 YO / Casks# 617 - 620
70cl / 43% - Signatory

Ardbeg 1991 / 9 YO / MM#2999
70cl / 46% - Murray McDavid - A 1991 vintage single Cask Whisky from Ardbeg Bottled at 9 YO in early 2000 by Murray McDavid.

Ardbeg 1992 / 8 YO / Signatory Millennium #416-417
70cl / 43% - Signatory - A young Ardbeg 1992 Bottled for the Millennium by Signatory. This is a vatting of two Casks Bottled at 43%.

Ardbeg 1994 / 15 YO / Cadenhead's
70cl / 58.1%

Ardbeg 1998 - Almost There
70cl / 54.1% - Distillery Bottling - Following on from Very young and Still young, Ardbeg Almost There showed the final stage in the evolution of young Cask-strength Ardbeg 1998 before it blossomed into the Renaissance 10 yr-old. As you would expect, this is a mellower, more rounded, better balanced dram than the younger incarnations.

Ardbeg 1998 - Still young
70cl / 56.2% - Distillery Bottling - The second release in Ardbeg's journey to the new 10 YO, Still young was released in 2006 and continued the successful 'path to peaty maturity' as the marketing types called it. A refreshing dram with great intensity.

Ardbeg 1998 / Renaissance
70cl / 55.9% - Distillery Bottling - Ardbeg Renaissance is the end of the series that began with the 'Very young' 6 YO which now changes hands for silly money on eBay. This is the first 10-YO Ardbeg that is entirely comprised of spirit produced after Glenmorangie's takeover of the Distillery in 1997. A fitting end to the series.

Ardbeg 21 YO / Committee Bottling
70cl / 56.3% - Distillery Bottling - The 2001 Bottling for The Ardbeg Committee, Ardbeg's fan club. This one is part of a limited release matured for at least 21 years at the Distillery, the youngest spirit being Distilled just before its early 80s closure.

Ardbeg 25 YO / Lord of the Isles
70cl / 46% - Distillery Bottling - At 25 YO this Whisky embodies the richness, depth and sweetness of all Ardbegs. Light gold in colour and powerful in character. A phenomenal, much-sought-after Bottling of a really outstanding malt.

Ardbeg 30 YO (Wooden Box)
70cl / 40% - Distillery Bottling - A Bottling of 'Very Old' Ardbeg, matured for at least 30 years, with the old style black label and presented in a dark wooden box.

Ardbeg Alligator / Untamed Release
70cl / 51.2% - Distillery Bottling - The general release of 2011's much anticipated Ardbeg Committee Release - Alligator. It's named for the high level of char on the inside of some of the Casks used for maturation, which makes the wood look like alligator skin.

Ardbeg Blasda
70cl / 40% - One of the most talked-about releases of 2008: Ardbeg Blasda is a lesser-peated version of many people's favourite Islay malt, being just 8ppm in Bottle (as opposed to the standard 10 YO's 23ppm).

Ardbeg Corryvreckan
70cl / 57.1% - Distillery Bottling

Ardbeg Corryvreckan / Committee Reserve
70cl / 57.1% - Distillery Bottling - The limited Committee Reserve Bottling of Ardbeg's popular whirlpool inspired dram. A special edition produced for The Ardbeg Committee in 2008 before it was repackaged for sale to the general public.

Ardbeg Rollercoaster / Committee Bottling
70cl / 57.3% - Distillery Bottling - A special edition Ardbeg released for members of the Ardbeg Committee in celebration of that august institution's 10th Anniversary in 2010. Ten vintages were used in the vatting, ranging from 1997 to 2006.

Ardbeg Supernova 2009
70cl / 58.9% - Distillery Bottling - Ardbeg Supernova has been a

phenomenon since the Advance Committee Release sold out in a matter of hours in January 2009. This is the peatiest Ardbeg ever at over 100ppm.

Ardbeg Supernova 2010
70cl / 60.1% - Distillery Bottling - This is the 2010 version of Ardbeg Supernova, and no doubt will be hoping to follow on from the success of last year's edition.

Ardbeg Uigeadail
70cl / 54.2% - Distillery Bottling - A fine drop of Ardbeg Bottled at Cask strength. A marriage of Ardbeg from Bourbon barrel and Sherry butt which gives a sweet and smokey finish to this malt. Uigeadail is the loch from which all Ardbeg water flows. An absolutely stunning Whisky, and following the demise of the Airigh nam Beist this probably represents the best value in the core range.
IWSC 2012 - Gold Medal - Whisky - Scotch

BOWMORE RANGE

Black Bowmore 1964 / 29 YO / 1st Edition
70cl / 50% - Distillery Bottling -The first edition of the legendary Black Bowmore - Distilled in 1964 and matured in Oloroso Casks for 29 years before being unleashed on the world. Only 2000 Bottles of this were released and there are only few of them left in the wild...

Black Bowmore 1964 / 30 YO / 2nd Edition
70cl / 50% - Distillery Bottling - The second of the three extraordinary Oloroso Cask 1964 Bowmores released in the mid-1990s. An almost unfathomable concentration and intensity of flavour, and with the perfect balance of fruit, peat and power.

Black Bowmore 1964 / 30 YO / 2nd Edition
75cl / 50% - Distillery Bottling - This is the American version of Black Bowmore 2nd edition, the second of the three extraordinary Oloroso Cask 1964 Bowmores released in the mid-1990s. An almost unfathomable concentration and intensity of flavour, and with the perfect balance of fruit, peat and power.

Black Bowmore 1964 / 42 YO / Sherry Cask
75cl / 40.5% - Distillery Bottling - Well, here it is - just over twelve years after the previous release, a legend is reborn: Black Bowmore is back! Selected from the same batch of Oloroso Casks as the previous Bottlings, this is a must-have for wealthy Islayphiles.

Bowmore 10 YO / Provident Mutual 150 yrs Ceramic
75cl / 40% - Distillery Bottling - A rare Bowmore ceramic decanter produced for Provident's 150th anniversary.

Bowmore 12 YO
70cl / 40% - Distillery Bottling - Bowmore 12 YO has a place in many hearts as Islay's 'medium-peated' malt. A pronounced iodine character with plenty of pepper, yet the malt is balanced and smooth as well as smoky.

Bowmore 12 YO / Bot.1980s
75cl / 40% - Distillery Bottling - A dumpy Bottle of 12 YO Bowmore. They were bought by Suntory in 1989 which makes this Morrison's Bottle most likely the product of the 1980s.

Bowmore 12 YO / Bot.1980s
100cl / 43% - Distillery Bottling - A litre Bottle of 12 YO Bowmore in their old-style brown Bottles. Labelled as being from "Morrison's Bowmore Distillery" we think this is from the 1980s, before they were bought by Suntory.

Bowmore 12 YO / Bot.1980s / Morrison Howat
75cl / 54.5% - Distillery Bottling - A Bottle of 12 YO Bowmore Bottled in the 1980s. This Bottle is unusual as it gives the company name as Morrison Howat, rather than the usual Morrison. This makes some sense, as the company was originally founded by Messrs Stanley Morrison and James Howat, and we think this was a shortlived subsidiary.

Bowmore 12 YO / Enigma
100cl / 40% - Distillery Bottling - Bowmore Enigma is a 12 year-old dram originally Bottled for travel retail, and boasts a higher proportion of Sherry-matured malt in its make-up. A full-bodied dram, Enigma's colour is darker and the Whisky itself is sweeter than the standard 12 year-old, with compensating robust smokiness and a hint of brine.

Bowmore 12 YO / Fly Fishing
70cl / 40% - Distillery Bottling - A rare Bottling of Bowmore 12, produced to commemorate the Commonwealth Fly Fishing Championships, held on Islay in June 2009.

Bowmore 12 YO / Half Bottle
35cl / 40% - Distillery Bottling - A half Bottle of Bowmore's 12 YO Whisky, a great place to start your journey through the smoky mystery of Islay's Single Malt Whiskies.

Bowmore 12 YO / Old Presentation
70cl / 40% - Distillery Bottling - In a beautiful inlet of Loch Indall on Islay, Bowmore lies slowly maturing until it reaches perfection. A pronounced iodine character with plenty of pepper, yet the malt is balanced and smooth as well as smoky.

Bowmore 12 YO / Screen Printed Label / Bot.1990s
100cl / 43% - Distillery Bottling - A travel retail-sized Bottle of Bowmore 12 - this screen-printed label is from the late 1990s.

Bowmore 15 YO - Darkest
70cl / 43% - Distillery Bottling - The Bowmore Darkest has flourished since it gained a 15 year-old age statement. The sweet Sherry notes take precedence over the peat here.

Bowmore 15 YO / Carato
75cl / 40% - Sestante - A rare old Bowmore Bottled for Carato at 15 YO by Italian company Sestante Imports.

Bowmore 15 YO / Mariner
100cl / 43% - Distillery Bottling - 1L travel retail version of an old Bowmore favourite.

Bowmore 18 YO
70cl / 43% - Distillery Bottling - A popular expression in Bowmore's ongoing range, this replaced the 17 year-old, which was phased out a few years ago. Fresh, with notes of salty kippers and coalsmoke.

Bowmore 18 YO / Bot.1950s
75cl / 43% - Distillery Bottling - A very rare old Bowmore 18 YO from the 1950s in an unusual pear-shaped Bottle. The original plastic seal was broken and coming off, we replaced it with a new clear plastic seal. A mini of the Bowmore 18 year-old, which replaced the 17 year-old expression in 2007. Probably the most maritime Bowmore we've tried, very kippery.

Bowmore 1955 / 40 YO
70cl / 42% - Distillery Bottling - Bottled in a beautiful crystal decanter, this gorgeous fruity Bowmore has been declared by more than one of our customers to be the best that they have ever tasted. After such a long period of ageing, the malt has taken on a very elegant character and shows restrained peat combined with

ethereal layers of exotic fruit. A serious, subtle malt that demands the drinker's time and full attention.

Bowmore 1955 Ceramic Decanter / Bot.1974 / Half-Bottle
37.5cl / 40% - Distillery Bottling - A ceramic decanter of 1955 vintage Bowmore, specially Bottled for the opening of the Distillery's visitor centre on September 12th 1974. This Bowmore 1955 has become a legendary dram amongst the cognoscenti, and recently picked up an enormous score of 97 points from Whiskyfun - the joint-highest score of any Bowmore on the site. Just 100 of these half-Bottle sized decanters were produced.

Bowmore 1956 / Sherry Cask
75cl / 43% - Distillery Bottling - A beautiful 1956 vintage Bowmore, Bottled sometime in the 1970s or early 1980s. Distilled before the Morrisons took over the business but Bottled rather elegantly by them. A Bottling of this under an Italian label for Soffiantino scooped a staggering 96 points from Serge at Whiskyfun.

Bowmore 1957 / Moon Import
75cl / 40% - Moon Import - A very rare Bowmore 1957, this was Bottled by Moon Imports of Italy in 1990.

Bowmore 1962 / Sherry Cask / Moon Import
75cl / 43% - Moon Import - A very rare Sherry Cask Bowmore from 1962 (just a couple of years before the famous Black Bowmore's were Distilled), this was Bottled by the Italian company Moon Imports in 1990.

Bowmore 1963 / 30 YO / 30th Anniversary
70cl / 50% - Distillery Bottling - A 30 YO Bowmore Bottled in 1963, the year that Stanley Morrison bought the company, and released as a celebration of the 30th year of his ownership.

Bowmore 1963 / Bot.1980s
75cl / 43% - Distillery Bottling - Awesome, ludicrously rare vintage label Bottling (from the 1980s) of long-aged Bowmore.

Bowmore 1964 / 35 YO
70cl / 42.1% - Distillery Bottling - A Bottling of a single Cask, part of the same batch of Oloroso Casks that produced Black Bowmore. This particular Cask yielded just 99 Bottles, of which only 95 went on sale. This was originally earmarked by Bowmore as the very best of these famous Casks and tasting it, you can see why - all the flavours are super-concentrated.

Bowmore 1964 / 46 YO / Fino Sherry Cask
70cl / 42.9% - Distillery Bottling

Bowmore 1964 / Bourbon Cask
70cl / 43.2% - Distillery Bottling

Bowmore 1964 / Fino Sherry Cask
70cl / 49.6% - Distillery Bottling - 1964 seems to be something of a miracle vintage for Bowmore - not only did it produce Black Bowmore and the Oddbins Oloroso Cask, but also this beautiful Fino Sherry expression. Here the peat is restrained and subtle, leaving the way clear for a stunning, incredibly fruity Bowmore.

Bowmore 1964 / Oloroso Sherry Cask
70cl / 42.9% - Distillery Bottling - A Bottling of a single Cask, part of the same batch of Oloroso Casks that produced Black Bowmore. This was released as part of the 'Trilogy' series along with the Fino and Bourbon expressions.

Bowmore 1964 Bicentenary / Unboxed
75cl / 43% - Distillery Bottling - One of the famous Bowmore Bicentenary Bottles from 1979. This Whisky was Distilled in 1964, and has been hailed as one of the finest Bowmores produced to date. Please note that this item does not come with a presentation box.

Bowmore 1965 / Bot.1980s
75cl / 50% - Distillery Bottling - A 1965 vintage Bowmore Bottled in the 1980s with an old style label. This was Distilled in the golden years shortly after the Morrison's takeover and was matured in Sherry Casks.

Bowmore 1966 / 35 YO
70cl / 44%

Bowmore 1966 / 40 YO
70cl / 43.9% - Duncan Taylor - The third of DT's 40yrs old Bowmores appears, almost exactly one year after the first, and at almost exactly twice the price. To be fair, though, a Distillery Bottling of this age would be many times more expensive than this.

Bowmore 1966 / 40 YO / Duncan Taylor
70cl / 43.5% - Duncan Taylor

Bowmore 1966 / 41 YO / Cask #3314
70cl / 44.5% - Duncan Taylor - An old Bottle of Bowmore 1966 vintage Whisky. This Whisky has been matured for 41 years and Bottled without being chill-filtered. Limited to just 162 Bottles.

Bowmore 1966 / Bot.1980s
75cl / 43% - Distillery Bottling - A 1966 vintage Bowmore Bottled in the 1980s by the Distillery with a replica of their old label.

Bowmore 1968 / 31 YO / Signatory
70cl / 43% - Signatory

Bowmore 1968 / 32 YO
75cl / 45.5% - Distillery Bottling - A limited edition 32 YO Bottling of 1968 Bowmore from the turn of the millennium. It was Bottled to celebrate the 50th anniversary of The Stanley P Morrison company, owners of Bowmore since 1963.

Bowmore 1968 / 32 YO / Cask #1422
70cl / 46% - Signatory - A 1968 vintage single Cask Whisky Distilled at Bowmore and then Bottled 32 years later in the August of 2000 by Signatory.

Bowmore 1968 / 34 YO
70cl / 40.2% - Hart Brothers - A 1968 vintage Bowmore, Bottled in the early 2000s by Hart Brothers. The 60s were a time of incredible production from the Distillery, with some legendary drams being produced - hopefully this one lives up to the fearsome reputation.

Bowmore 1968 / 34 YO / Cask #1427
70cl / 41.4% - Duncan Taylor - A single Cask Whisky from Bowmore. This has been aged for 34 years and Bottled at Cask strength by Duncan Taylor for their Peerless range.

Bowmore 1968 / 35 YO
70cl / 40.6% - Celtic Heartlands - A 35 YO Bowmore, Distilled in 1968 and Bottled as part of the Celtic Heartlands range. With Jim McEwan behind the selection you're fairly safe that each Bottle in the series is going to be quite special.

Bowmore 1968 / 37 YO / Bourbon Wood
70cl / 43.4% - Distillery Bottling - A 37 YO release of Bowmore, Distilled in 1968 and Bottled at a Cask strength of 43.4%. A limited edition Bottling that looks to have been the marriage of just 4 or 5 Bourbon Casks, it's gone down as one of the greats from this golden decade of production.

Bowmore 1969 / 32 YO
70cl / 43.4% - Duncan Taylor - A 32 YO peerless Bottling of Bowmore, Distilled in 1969, matured for 32 years and released in the early 2000s.

Bowmore 1969 / 33 YO
70cl / 42.5% - Duncan Taylor - A Peerless release of 1969 Bowmore, aged for 33 years and Bottled at a mellow Cask strength of 42.5%.

Bowmore 1969 / Bot.1978 / Sherry Cask #6636
75cl / 58% - Distillery Bottling - A beautiful rare Distillery Bottling of single Cask Bowmore Whisky. Distilled in 1969 and Bottled in 1978 for Sandra Montanari of Bologna after maturing for a mere 8 or 9 years. It's a sister Cask to the famed #6635 and we expect it to be stunning.

Bowmore 1971 / 18 YO
75cl / 40% - Sestante - An 18 YO Bottling of 1971 vintage Bowmore from Italian independent Sestante.

Bowmore 1971 / 21 YO
70cl / 43% - Distillery Bottling

Bowmore 1972 / 27 YO
70cl / 53.3% - Distillery Bottling

Bowmore 1973 / 50th Anniversary of Morrison Bowmore
70cl / 43% - Distillery Bottling - A very rare Bottling of Bowmore 1973 presented to guests at a banquet held in 2001 to celebrate the 50th anniversary of the original Stanley Morrison company.

Bowmore 1973 / Vintage Label / Cask 5173+74
75cl / 43% - Distillery Bottling - A Bottling of 1972 vintage Bowmore that was matured in Sherry Casks. This is a marriage of only two Casks and it's a rare look into the decade after Morrison's took over the Distillery.

Bowmore 1974 / Artist #2 / Cask #3841
70cl / 51.8% - Signatory - A very limited edition Bottling of 1974 vintage Bowmore for La Maison du Whisky's Artist range, of which this is the second entry. The Whisky was Bottled in 2012 at cask strength and features a label drawn by artist Paola Parés.

Bowmore 1980 / 30 YO / Queen's Visit / Cask #5774
70cl / 46.7% - Distillery Bottling - A very special Bowmore from a

hogshead filled on August 9th 1980, the day that Queen Elizabeth II visited the Distillery. Cask #5774 was acquired by Jim Howat, then Chairman of Morrison Bowmore and was left in his will to the JTH Charitable Trust he created with his wife Christine. Designed and Bottled in 2011 by Morrison Bowmore as a special limited edition for the charitable trust yielding 156 bottles at a natural strength of 46.7%.

Bowmore 1984 / 16 YO
70cl / 58.8% - Distillery Bottling - A classic mid-80s Bowmore, Bottled at 16 YO. Distilled in 1984 and released at a rather pokey 58.8%.

Bowmore 1984 / Cask #M426 / Montgomerie's
70cl / 46% - Montgomery's - An independent Bottling of 1984 vintage Bowmore by the folks at Montgomeries at 23 YO.

Bowmore 1984 / Cask #M427 / Montgomerie's
70cl / 46% - Montgomery's - A 25 YO single Cask Bowmore, Distilled in 1984 and Bottled in July 2009 by indie Bottler Montgomerie's.

Bowmore 1985 / 26 YO
70cl / 52.3% - Distillery Bottling - A limited edition of just 747 Bottles from Bowmore, Distilled in 1985 and Bottled in 2012. A classic mid-80s expression with fruit, chocolate and smoke running through the palate.

Bowmore 1987 / 25 YO / Douglas Laing Platinum
70cl / 56.1% - Douglas Laing - A 1987 vintage single Cask Whisky from Bowmore on Islay, Bottled at 25 YO in April 2012 by the folks at Douglas Laing as part of their Old & Rare Platinum Selection.

Bowmore 1988 / 21 YO / Port Wood Matured
70cl / 51.5% - Distillery Bottling - Released in 2009, this version of Bowmore 21 year-old was Distilled in 1988 and has been full-term matured in Port Wood Casks, giving it a very alluring ruby glow.

Bowmore 1989 / 21 YO / Old Malt Cask #7460
70cl / 50% - Douglas Laing - A lightly coloured single Cask 1989 Bowmore Bottled by Douglas Laing for the Old Malt Cask range. I suspect that this came out of a several-times-refilled Sherry Cask, but with 21 years under its belt it should have a bit of oomph still.

Bowmore 1989 / 22 YO / Liquid Sun
70cl / 50.7% - Liquid Sun - A 1989 vintage Bowmore Bottled

under the Liquid Sun label. Matured for 22 years in an ex-Bourbon Cask and Bottled in 2011.

Bowmore 1989 / 23 YO / The Whisky Agency
70cl / 53.1% - The Whisky Agency - An interesting coloured Whisky from Bowmore, tinged with a bit of olive green. It was Distilled back in 1989 and was Bottled in 2012 by the folks at The Whisky Agency after 23 years in a Sherry butt. Part of the TWA 'Fights' series, this label features an alligator biting a snake.

Bowmore 1989 / Berry Brother's & Rudd
70cl / 50.9% - Berry Bros & Rudd - A Berry's Own Selection release of 1989 vintage Bowmore by Berry Brothers & Rudd. This one has spent about 22 years maturing before being Bottled at Cask strength.

Bowmore 1990 / 16 YO / Sherry Cask
70cl / 53.8% - Distillery Bottling - A 1990 vintage Bowmore Bottled in the mid-2000s after 16 years of maturing in Sherry Casks. A big and rich dram with the traditional Bowmore floral peat and smoke.

Bowmore 1991 / 16 YO / Port Matured
70cl / 53.1% - Distillery Bottling - A Cask-strength Bowmore 16yrs, this time matured in Port Casks. This is a lovely colour and we have high hopes for this Bottling. A 'limited' release - just the 18000 Bottles.

Bowmore 1991 / Scott's Selection
70cl / 54.6% - Scott's Selection - A single Cask Bowmore released by Scott's Selection. Distilled in 1991 and Bottled at a natural Cask strength of 54.6%

Bowmore 1992 / 19 YO / Cask #4192 / Mackillop's Choice
70cl / 43% - Mackillop's - A 1992 vintage Bowmore Bottled at a decent drinking strength of 43% by the folks at Mackillop's Choice after maturing for 19 years.

Bowmore 1995 / 11 YO
70cl / 60.9% - Speciality Drinks Ltd - A potent, yet floral single Cask bottling of Bowmore. A drop of water is advisable to release the full spectrum of peaty, fruity flavours.

Bowmore 1995 / 16 YO / Cask #8 / Adelphi
70cl / 54.4% - Adelphi - A 1995 vintage Bowmore Bottled by the folks at Adelphi. Matured for 16 years in Cask #8 and Bottled

at full Cask strength. Looking at the number of Bottles and the colour, we're guessing this might be from a refill Sherry butt.

Bowmore 1996 / 14 YO / Bourbon / Petrus
70cl / 46% - Murray McDavid - A 1996 vintage Whisky from Bowmore, selected by Bruichladdich/Murray McDavid master Distiller Jim McEwan who worked at Bowmore for a few decades before moving down the road. This was finished in Chateau Petrus wine Casks.

Bowmore 2000 / 11 YO / OMC #7791
70cl / 50% - Douglas Laing - A 2000 vintage Bowmore from Douglas Laing, Bottled for their Old Malt Cask range. Aged for 11 years in a Sherry butt and Bottled in November 2011.

Bowmore 2000 / 12 YO / Cask #1882 / Adelphi
70cl / 56.1% - Adelphi - A 12 YO Bowmore, Distilled in 2000 and Bottled at natural Cask strength for the Adelphi selection range.

Bowmore 2000 / 9 YO / Sherry Cask
70cl / 46% - Murray McDavid - A young 2000 vintage Bowmore matured in Sherry Casks. Despite its young age it's picked up a good chunk of colour from the Cask.

Bowmore 21 YO
70cl / 43% - Distillery Bottling

Bowmore 25 YO
70cl / 43% - Distillery Bottling - A Bottling of 25 YO Bowmore introduced in the early years of the 21st century. Big, fruity and rich with smoke.

Bowmore 25 YO
70cl / 43% - Distillery Bottling - A Bottling of 25 YO Bowmore, most probably released in the mid 1990s. It's a bit more of a peaty beast than the traditional Bowmore style of the 60s, but still has the fruit that you'd expect.

Bowmore 25 YO
70cl / 43% - Distillery Bottling - A long-aged Distillery-Bottled Bowmore, a large proportion of the Casks used to assemble this 25 YO are ex-Sherry, giving sweetness and depth to this complex, fruity Islay malt.

Bowmore 25 YO / Chateau Lagrange
70cl / 43% - Distillery Bottling - One of the rarest Bowmores ever: just 75 of these were made to commemorate the Auld Alliance

Reception held at Chateau Lagrange in 1995.

Bowmore 30 YO / Sea Dragon Ceramic
75cl / 43% - Distillery Bottling

Bowmore Bicentenary
75cl / 43% - Distillery Bottling - A legendary Bottling of Bowmore Bottled in 1979 to celebrate the Distillery's bicentenary. Vatted from some phenomenal 1960s Sherry Casks, this is renowned by aficionados as one of the best Bowmore's ever - at a fraction of the pricetags commanded by the likes of Black Bowmore.

Bowmore Bicentenary
75cl / 56.2% - Distillery Bottling - A very rare version of the famed 1964 vintage bicentenary Whisky from Bowmore. Bottled at Cask strength in 1979 as part of the 200th birthday celebrations this edition was produced for the Italian market and comes in a rather unusual square Bottle.

Bowmore Bicentenary (Unboxed)
75cl / 43% - Distillery Bottling - One of the legendary Bowmore bicentenary releases, Bottled in 1979 as part of their 200th birthday celebrations. Distilled in the 1960s and matured in some rather excellent Sherry Casks this is still considered to be one of the best Bowmores ever produced.

Bowmore Cask Strength / 1L
100cl / 56% - Distillery Bottling - A new 1L presentation of Bowmore's Cask Strength Islay malt.

Bowmore Claret / Bordeaux Wine Cask
75cl / 56% - Distillery Bottling - An uncommon pairing of Bowmore and Claret Casks, using barrels from Suntory owned Bordeaux wineries to finish the Whisky. A strange and uncommon release from Bowmore.

Bowmore Claret / Bordeaux Wine Cask
70cl / 56% - A very interesting release from Bowmore Distillery. Bowmore Whisky matured in Claret casks. Wine finished Bowmores are not something that we see often, which makes this a very interesting release.

Bowmore Darkest / Sherry Cask Finish
70cl / 43% - Distillery Bottling - Easily the most popular of the no-age-statement Bowmores, with a rich Sherry influence calming some of the more fiery attributes of the young spirit. As close in style to the legendary Black Bowmore as most of us mere mortals

will be able to taste.

Bowmore Fly Fishing 2003 Edition
70cl / 40% - Distillery Bottling - A rare commemorative Bottling of Bowmore released to commemorate the 2003 fly fishing championships on Islay. Only a small number of Bottles, with their wooden display case, were produced and this is sought after by collectors.

Bowmore Horse Trials 1996
70cl / 40% - Distillery Bottling - Part of Bowmore's tradition of commemorating Scottish sporting events with limited edition special Bottlings, this one is in honour of the 1996 international horse trials at Blair Castle.

Bowmore Islay
100cl / 56% - Distillery Bottling - A hefty litre Bottle of NAS Cask-strength Bowmore Bottled for Scotch Malt Sales in Japan about 10 years ago.

Bowmore Islay Malt / Bot. 1990's
70cl / 40% - Distillery Bottling - A Bottle of Islay Malt Bottlined in the 1990s for Oddbins. If you look at the small print on the label you can see that it was produced for them by Bowmore.

Bowmore Legend / New Label
70cl / 40% - Distillery Bottling - The new presentation of an old Bowmore favourite, the no-age-statement Legend.

Bowmore Tempest / 10 YO / Batch 3
70cl / 55.6% - Distillery Bottling - The first couple of batches of Bowmore's Tempest, a Cask-strength 10 YO vatted from first-fill Bourbon Casks, have been incredibly popular, and rightly so. This one has a more elegant touch and tantalising tropical fruitiness, especially with a drop of water and a few minutes in the glass. Our favourite batch so far, this is fabulous stuff.

Bowmore Voyage / Port Wood Finish
70cl / 56% - Distillery Bottling - A limited edition, individually numbered, Cask strength Bottling, originally released in 2000. Bowmore Voyage was matured in Bourbon Casks before being finished in port pipes.

Gold Bowmore 1964 / 44 YO
70cl / 42.4% - Distillery Bottling - The final release in the new Bowmore 1964 trilogy, Gold Bowmore is a marriage of three Bourbon Casks plus the last (and supposedly the best) of the

staggeringly good Oloroso Casks from this momentous vintage.

Single Islay Malt (Bowmore) / Morrison Howat / Bot.1980s
75cl / 40% - Islay Single Malt Scotch Whisky - Morrison Howat Single Islay Malt, Bottled and Distilled by Morrison Howat Distillers. We believe this was Bottled during the 1980s.

White Bowmore 1964 / 43 YO
70cl / 42.8% - Distillery Bottling - After 2007's 'new' Black Bowmore, this White Bowmore is the second edition of the Noughties' 1964 Trilogy series, and has spent its life in Bourbon Casks, so should make for a very interesting contrast. Awarded 94 points from John Hansell in Malt Advocate, this was one of the most talked-about releases of 2008.

BRUICHLADDICH RANGE

Bruichladdich / Bot.1970s
75cl / 43% - Distillery Bottling - A no-age-statement Distillery-Bottled Bruichladdich from the 1970s, when the Distillery was owned by Invergordon Distillers.

Bruichladdich 10 YO / Bot.1980s
75cl / 43% - Distillery Bottling - A 1980s Distillery Bottling of 10 YO Bruichladdich, packaged in a rather nice blue ceramic decanter.

Bruichladdich 10 YO / Bot.1980s
75cl / 40% - Distillery Bottling - A Distillery Bottling of 10 YO Bruichladdich from the 1980s. Similar to other Bottlings that we've had, although this one doesn't have a neck label.

Bruichladdich 10 YO / Bot.1990s
70cl / 40% - Distillery Bottling - A Bottling of Bruichladdich 10 YO from the 1990s. This would have been Distilled in the 80s and released around the time of the Distillery's 1995 closure.

Bruichladdich 12 YO / Brown & Tawse 125th Anniversary
70cl / 46% - Distillery Bottling - A very special Bruichladdich 12 YO, Bottled from two Bourbon Casks (with no extra maturation or finishing in wine Casks) for the occasion of Dundee steelmerchant Brown & Tawse's 125th Anniversary.

Bruichladdich 12 YO 1st Edition
70cl / 46% - Distillery Bottling - A cracking dram from the great man, Jim McEwan. Fresh and subtle, with vanilla flavours from the Bourbon Casks, fresh exotic fruit and a well-rounded

maltiness.

Bruichladdich 15 YO / 1st Edition
70cl / 46% - Distillery Bottling - One of the best ongoing Bottlings from this great Distillery. This is more lightly peated, allowing its fresh, coastal maritime character to shine through. This is a real gem.

Bruichladdich 15 YO / 2nd Edition
70cl / 46% - Distillery Bottling - Finished in Chateau d'Yquem Sauternes Casks, this has all the expected Bruichladdich characteristics - seaspray, brine, floral notes - with a deliciously smooth extra veneer of sweetness. A deservedly popular 'Laddie.

Bruichladdich 15 YO / Bot.1980s
75cl / 43% - Distillery Bottling - A Distillery release of 15 YO Bruichladdich, Bottled in a brown glazed ceramic decanter.

Bruichladdich 15 YO / Bot.1990s
70cl / 43% - Distillery Bottling - A 15 YO Distillery Bottling of Bruichladdich from the 1990s, the years before they reopened in their current guise under the watchful eye of Murray McDavid. This is an interesting tall Bottle with a definite maritime air to the design.

Bruichladdich 16 YO First Growth Pauillac Finish 'B'
70cl / 46% - Distillery Bottling - One of a series of 16 YO Bruichladdichs finished in First Growth Bordeaux wine Casks. Unfortunately they've managed to spell Pauillac wrongly for this one, which is probably rather embarrassing for former wine merchant Mark Reynier, Bruichladdich's head honcho.

Bruichladdich 16 YO First Growth Pessac-Leognan Finish
70cl / 46% - Distillery Bottling - One of a series of 16 YO Bruichladdichs finished in First Growth Bordeaux wine Casks. This one has used Casks from Chateau Haut Brion.

Bruichladdich 16 YO First Growth Pomerol Finish
70cl / 46% - Distillery Bottling - One of a series of 16 YO Bruichladdichs finished in First Growth Bordeaux wine Casks. This one is rather controversial, given that the wine Casks come from Chateau Lafleur, which is not actually a first growth claret.

Bruichladdich 17 YO / 1L
100cl / 43% - Distillery Bottling - A Distillery release of 17 YO Bruichladdich, Bottled well before the 2000 Distillery buy-out and reinvention of the brand.

Bruichladdich 17 YO / Bot.1980s
75cl / 40% - Duthies - A rare old Bottle of Bruichladdich 17 YO Bottled by little-seen Scottish independent Bottler Duthies.

Bruichladdich 18 YO / 1st Edition
70cl / 46% - Distillery Bottling - A long-aged Bruichladdich matured for eighteen years in Bourbon Casks and then in Willi Opitz Trocken Beeren Auslese (very sweet) red pinot wine Casks.

Bruichladdich 18 YO / 2nd Edition
70cl / 46% - Distillery Bottling - A second Bruichladdich 18 YO following the successful first edition, which was finished in Willi Opitz Trockenbeerenauslese Casks (that's Austrian pudding wine to you and me). This time the 'Ace-ing' (sigh) has been done with a different sweet wine: Clos Urolat from Jurancon in Southwest France.

Bruichladdich 1965 / 24 YO / Turatello
75cl / 54.2%

A 1965 vintage Whisky from Bruichladdie, Bottled by Gordon & Macphail for Italian distributer Turatello at 24 YO.

Bruichladdich 1966 / 35 YO / Douglas Laing
70cl / 40.5%

Douglas Laing
A release of 35 YO Bruichladdich by Douglas Laing as part of their Old Malt Cask range. This was Distilled in 1966, a few years after the Distillery stopped malting its own barley and switched to buying it in from Port Ellen, and Bottled just in time at a Cask strength of 40.5%.

Bruichladdich 1967 / 32 YO / Cask #967
70cl / 46%

First Cask
A single Cask release of Bruichladdich Whisky Bottled for Direct Wine's First Cask series. Distilled in 1967 and aged for 32 years, this Whisky would have been Bottled around 1999.

Bruichladdich 1967 / 32 YO / Sherry Cask / Signatory
70cl / 48% - Signatory - A high-end release of single Cask Bruichladdich by Signatory. Distilled in 1967 and Bottled after 32 years in a Sherry Cask.

Bruichladdich 1969 / 20 YO / Casks #4928-4932
75cl / 43% - Dun Eideann - A Dun Eideann Bottling of 20 YO Bruichladdich. This is a vatting of 5 Casks Distilled in 1969 and Bottled in 1990.

Bruichladdich 1969 / 20 YO / Casks #4928-4932
75cl / 43% - Signatory - An old Bottling of 20YOBruichladdich 1969, released by Signatory at the beginning of the 1990s.

Bruichladdich 1969 / 22 YO / Stillman's Reserve
70cl / 43% - Distillery Bottling - A rare Bottle of Bruichladdich released as part of the Stillman's Reserve range in the early 1990s - Distilled in 1969 and Bottled 22 years later.

Bruichladdich 1970 Valinch / 31 YO / 45.5%
50cl / 45.5% - Distillery Bottling

Bruichladdich 1988 / Sinnsear
50cl / 50% - Distillery Bottling - A special edition of Bruichladdich Bottled without an age statement and Distilled in 1988. Sinnsear is gaelic for 'Forefathers'.

Bruichladdich 1989 / 14 YO / Cairdean Family
50cl / 46% - Distillery Bottling - A Distillery only Bottling from Bruichladdich, Bottled at 14 YO and showing their habit of dual naming in Gaelic and English. Cairdean means family, or more loosely "friends".

Bruichladdich 1991 / Berry Bros & Rudd
70cl / 50.1% - Berry Bros & Rudd - A 1991 vintage Bruichladdich from Berry Brothers & Rudd. This was Distilled in the Distillery's days of intermittent operation before before it's eventual mothballing in 1995.

Bruichladdich 1991 / Sherry Cask / Gordon & Macphail
70cl / 55.9% - Gordon & Macphail - G&M Bottlings of Bruichladdich are very few and far between, so this Cask-strength Bottling from refill Sherry hoggies is a rare treat.

Bruichladdich 1992 Sherrywood / Cask #1874
70cl / 57.8% - Mackillop's - A 1992 vintage Bruichladdich Sherry Cask produced in 1992 during Invergordon's ownership of the Distillery and Bottled at full strength in March 2012 by Mackillop's Choice.

Bruichladdich 1998 / 10 YO / Sherry Oloroso
70cl / 46% - Distillery Bottling - Part of a pair of 1998 Sherry

Editions from Bruichladdich, this Whisky was Distilled during a six week period in 1998, the only time the Distillery was working between Jan 1995 and May 2001.

Bruichladdich 2001 / 7 YO / Resurrection
70cl / 46% - Distillery Bottling - The Resurrection Dram from Bruichladdich is finally here, its 24000 Bottles constructed entirely from 7 year-old 10ppm Bourbon-matured Distillate made by Jim McEwan in 2001 after the new regime came to power.

Bruichladdich 2006 Islay Barley / 5 YO / Dunlossit
70cl / 50% - Distillery Bottling - The second of Bruichladdich's Islay Barley Bottlings, Distilled in 2006 from a mash of grain grown on nearby Dunlossit Farm.

Bruichladdich 2006 Islay Barley / Small Bottle
20cl / 50% - Distillery Bottling - A small Bottle of Bruichladdich's 2006 vintage Whisky entirely made using unpeated barley from Dunlossit farm, just down the road from the Distillery on Islay.

Bruichladdich 25 YO / Stillman's Dram
70cl / 45% - Distillery Bottling - A Bottling of 25 YO Bruichladdich as part of Whyte & Mackay's now defunct Stillman's Dram range. W&M owned the Distillery between 1993 and it's sale to Murray McDavid in 2000.

Bruichladdich 26 YO / Stillman's Dram
70cl / 45% - Distillery Bottling - An old Bottling of Bruichladdich 26 YO for then-owner Whyte & Mackay's now-defunct Stillman's Dram series.

Bruichladdich 32 YO / Legacy 4
70cl / 47.5% - Distillery Bottling - The fourth of Bruichladdich's 'Legacy' Bottlings of the oldest Whiskies inherited by the Distillery's new owners. This 32 year-old was released in 2005 and was the smallest run of the Legacy series, with a release of just 820 Bottles.

Bruichladdich 34 YO / Legacy 6
70cl / 41% - Distillery Bottling - The last ever Legacy, and we're certain Jim McEwan will have taken pains to ensure it goes out with a bang. A vatting of 1965, 1970 and 1972 vintages, Bottled at a natural strength of 41%.

Bruichladdich 3D3 / Norrie Campbell
70cl / 46% - Distillery Bottling - An excellent Bruichladdich, this 3D3 was produced as a tribute to the well-loved Islay peat-cutter

Norrie Campbell, who passed away in 2006. 3D3 contains three malts - Bruichladdich, Port Charlotte and Octomore - at three different ages, and is the most heavily-peated of the 3D releases.

Bruichladdich Centenary 15 YO
75cl / 43% - Distillery Bottling - A 15 YO Distillery release of Bruichladdich in honour of their 100th birthday in 1981 and packaged in a decanter.

Bruichladdich Cuvee 382 / La Berenice / 21 YO
70cl / 46% - Distillery Bottling - One of the first three Whiskies in Bruichladdich's Cuvee series, with a subtitle of MG41 [L'Age d'Or] (no, us neither), matured in American oak Casks before finishing in Limousin oak Casks previously used to hold Sauternes and Barsac sweet wines.

Bruichladdich Cuvee 407 / PX / 21 YO
70cl / 46% - Distillery Bottling - One of the three initial releases in Bruichladdich's Cuvee range, Cuvee 407 is simply named PX and is subtitled 'La Noche Bocca Arriba', the title of a short story by Julio Cortázar. It's matured in American oak and then finished in PX Casks.

Bruichladdich Cuvee 640 / Eroica / 21 YO
70cl / 46% - Distillery Bottling - The third of the first three Whiskies to appear in Bruichladdich's Cuvee range - Eroica, subtitled 'Oh mensch! Gieb acht! Was spricht die tiefe mitternacht?', the opening line from a song in Nietzsche's Thus Spoke Zarathustra. It's an American oak matured Whisky finished in Limousin oak that once held brandy.

Bruichladdich Laddie 10 YO / Small Bottle
20cl / 46% - A 20cl Bottle of Bruichladdich's first ongoing release since the Distillery's rejuvenation in 2001 - the flagship 10 YO Laddie 10.

Bruichladdich Laddie 22 YO
70cl / 46% - Distillery Bottling - A combination of classic and new Bruichladdich, at release the oldest in the Distillery's revitalised range of unpeated Islay Whiskies.

Bruichladdich Laddie Classic
70cl / 46% - Distillery Bottling - The first of a new series from Bruichladdich, this Laddie Classic is a no-age-statement Bottling intended, as the name would suggest, to showcase the classic 'Laddie style.

Bruichladdich Laddie Classic 16 YO
70cl / 46% - Distillery Bottling - The middle entry in Bruichladdich's revitalised line-up, sitting between the 10 and 22 to provide a Bourbon Cask focused slice of unpeated Islay Whisky.

Bruichladdich MCMLXXXV (1985) / 25 YO / DNA3
70cl / 50.1% - Distillery Bottling - The third edition in Bruichladdich's DNA series, examining the component parts that make the Distillery's Whiskies tick. This one marries together some of their best Casks of the 1980s - their final batch of Sherry butts. Bottled at Cask strength and limited to only 1665 Bottles, this is one for all fans and collectors of Bruichladdich.

Bruichladdich MCMLXXXV (1985) / 27 YO / DNA4
70cl / 49.3% - Distillery Bottling - The 4th edition in Bruichladdich's DNA series, digging into the heart and soul of the Distillery's character. This time it's from 1985 and has been aged for 12 years before Cask selection and bottling.

Bruichladdich Peat
70cl / 46% - Distillery Bottling - A replacement for the highly successful '3D' series, Bruichladdich Peat apparently 'does what it says on the tin' with phenol levels of 35ppm. No age statement, but it is cheaper than the old 3D releases and, shockingly, has escaped from the the Distillery without being finished. Doubly unique 'Laddie!

Bruichladdich Queens Award Valinch 1989
50cl / 53.1% - Distillery Bottling - A Valinch Bottling of Bruichladdich, the name they give to the single Cask 'fill your own Bottle' range that they only sell at the Distillery. This one was selected and named in honour of Bruichladdich receiving a Queen's Award for Enterprise in 2005.

Bruichladdich Rocks
70cl / 46% - Distillery Bottling - Bruichladdich Rocks was introduced to the range in 2007, and is designed to be taken with ice ('Rocks', geddit?).

Bruichladdich The Organic Multi Vintage
70cl / 46% - Distillery Bottling - The second edition of Bruichladdich's Single Malt Whisky made with organically-grown Scottish barley - in this case from the Mid Coul, Coulmore and mains of Tullibardine farms. As with all of Bruichladdich's malts, this has been neither coloured nor unchilfiltered. More unusually for this Distillery, it hasn't been wine-finished either.

Bruichladdich Waves
70cl / 46% - Distillery Bottling - This is the repackaged edition of Bruichladdich Waves, which has now dropped its age statement (and the peating level slightly too, we're told). In this case, the finishing Casks are Madeira.

Bruichladdich X4 - Islay Spirit
70cl / 50% - Bruichladdich X4 has been Distilled four times, reaching 92%, before being Bottled at a reduced 50% without ageing (which is why it can't be called Whisky).

Bruichladdich X4+3 / 3 YO
70cl / 63.5% - Distillery Bottling - X4 is Bruichladdich's quadruple-Distilled experimental revival of usquebaugh-baul, the 'perilous spirit'. Having come off the stills at around 90%, this much-discussed Distillate has now reached three years of age and can be called Whisky. Bottled at an eye-watering 63.5%.

BUNNAHABHAIN RANGE

Bunnahabhain 12 YO
70cl / 46.3% - Distillery Bottling - A giant leap forward for Bunnahabhain 12 YO, this edition was launched in summer 2010 with a jump in strength to 46.3% and a declaration of no chill-filtration and no added colouring. Enormous credit goes to Burn Stewart for giving punters what they want without jacking up the price too much and we earnestly hope that this will be a massive success. Bravo!

Bunnahabhain 12 YO / Old Presentation
70cl / 40% - Distillery Bottling - Bunnahabhain 12 YO is a very lightly-peated malt - probably the mildest introduction to the Islay style. A category winner at the World Whisky Awards 2010..

Bunnahabhain 18 YO
70cl / 46.3% - Distillery Bottling - Introduced in 2010, this is the relaunched version of Bunnahabhain 18 YO, with owners Burn Stewart having ditched the caramel colouring and chill-filtration and upped the strength to 46.3%. A triumph for 'naturalist' Whisky drinkers and a PR triumph for Burn Stewart - Bravo!
IWSC - Gold Medal Winner

Bunnahabhain 1964 / 25 YO
75cl / 46% - Signatory - A very rare old 25 YO Bunnahabhain 1964, bottled in early 1990 by Signatory in their classic dumpy

Bottle.

Bunnahabhain 1965 / 17 YO / Sherry Cask
75cl / 40% - A Bottle of Bunnahabhain 1965 aged for 17 years and Bottled around 1982.

Bunnahabhain 1966 / 35 YO / Sherry Cask
70cl / 46.1% - Distillery Bottling - A limited edition Bunnahabhain Bottled by the Distillery. Distilled in 1966 and released at the turn of the millennium after 35 years in wood.

Bunnahabhain 1966 / 40 YO
70cl / 40% - Duncan Taylor

Bunnahabhain 1967 / 36 YO / Duncan Taylor
70cl / 40.1% - Duncan Taylor - A classic 1967 vintage Bunnahabhain, Bottled in 2003 after 36 years in Cask by Duncan Taylor for their Peerless series.

Bunnahabhain 1968 / 36 YO
70cl / 40.1% - Duncan Taylor - A Duncan Taylor release of 1968 vintage Whisky from Bunnahabhain, aged for 36 years and Bottled at a close-to-the-line 40.1%.

Bunnahabhain 1968 / 38 YO
70cl / 40.5% - Duncan Taylor - A 38 YO Whisky from Bunnahabhain, Distilled in 1968 and Bottled from a single Cask at Cask strength by independent Bottler Duncan Taylor.

Bunnahabhain 1968 / 39 YO
70cl / 40.5% - Duncan Taylor - A well aged Duncan Taylor Bottling of Bunnahabhain. Distilled in 1968 and Bottled just in time at a Cask strength of 40.5%/

Bunnahabhain 1968 / 43 YO / The Whisky Agency
70cl / 47% - The Whisky Agency - A 1968 vintage Whisky from Bunnahabhain, Bottled in 2012 after maturing in a Sherry butt for 43 years by Limburg's The Whisky Agency. It's part of the 'Sea Life' series and its label features a variety of shells, occupied and empty.

Bunnahabhain 1973 / 34 YO
70cl / 46.1% - Celtic Heartlands - A long-aged Bunnahabhain selected by no less than Jim McEwan for the Celtic Heartlands series. At a mouth-watering 46.1%, this should be very drinkable.

Bunnahabhain 1974 / 37 YO / Douglas Laing Platinum
70cl / 57.6% - Douglas Laing - A Sherry matured Whisky from Bunnahabhain, Bottled after 37 years of maturation by Douglas Laing for their Old & Rare Platinum Selection range. Distilled in May 1974 and Bottled in November 2011.

Bunnahabhain 1978 / 32 YO / Sherry Butt
70cl / 54.3% - Douglas Laing - A single Cask Bunnahabhain that you can tell has come from a Sherry Cask as soon as you see it - dark and foreboding, but in a good way. Bottled at Cask strength in January 2011 by Douglas Laing for their Platinum Selection range.

Bunnahabhain 1978 / 33 YO / Douglas Laing Platinum
70cl / 53.9% - Douglas Laing - A 33 YO Whisky from Bunnahabhain, Distilled in December 1979 and Bottled in December 2011 by Douglas Laing for their Platinum Selection range. It's a small outturn of 172 Bottles, despite sitting in a Sherry butt for its entire life.

Bunnahabhain 1979 / 25 YO
70cl / 46% - First Cask - A 25 YO release of 1979 Bunnahabhain Bottled around 2004 by Direct Wines as part of their First Cask series.

Bunnahabhain 1979 / 25 YO / Cask #11910
70cl / 46% - First Cask - A single Cask release of 25 YO Whisky by First Cask. This Whisky has been Distilled at Bunnahabhain Distillery in 1979 and Bottled around 2004.

Bunnahabhain 1980 / 19 YO / First Cask #5643
70cl / 46% - First Cask - A 1980 vintage Whisky from Bunnahabhain, Bottled in the late 1990s by First Cask. This was Distilled on April 17th and matured for 19 years.

Bunnahabhain 1980 / 19 YO / First Cask #5645
70cl / 46% - First Cask - A 19 YO Bottling of 1980 Bunnahabhain by Direct Wines around the turn of the millennium for their First Cask series.

Bunnahabhain 1980 / 31 YO / Cask #604
70cl / 52.5% - Signatory - A single Cask 1980 Bunnahabhain Bottled by Signatory as part of their "Cask Strength Collection". This Whisky was aged for 31 years in a Sherry Butt, and Bottled in January 2012.

Bunnahabhain 1991 / 20 YO / Directors' Cut
70cl / 49.6% - Douglas Laing - A 20 YO single Cask Bunnahabhain Bottled by Douglas Laing as part of their shiny Directors' Cut range. Distilled in December 1991 and Bottled in December 2011 after sitting in a refill hogshead.

Bunnahabhain 1991 / Scott's Selection
70cl / 48.3% - Scott's Selection - A lightly coloured 1991 vintage Bunnahabhain Bottled by Scott's Selection.

Bunnahabhain 1997 / 12 YO / Lafite / Murray McDavid
70cl / 46% - Murray McDavid - A heavily-peated Bunnahabhain from the 1997 vintage, Bottled by Murray McDavid after a period of finishing in wine Casks from Pauillac's first growth claret, Chateau Lafite.

Bunnahabhain 1997 / 14 YO / Cask #5378
70cl / 57.1% - Adelphi - A 1997 vintage Bunnahabhain, Bottled in 2012 at 14 years of age by the folks at Adelphi.

Bunnahabhain 1997 / 14 YO / Cask #5554-6 / Peated
70cl / 46% - Signatory - A 1997 vintage Whisky from Bunnahabhain, vatted from two Casks filled with peated spirit on December 11th and Bottled on November 7th 2012 after almost 15 years of maturation by Signatory for their Un-chillfiltered Collection.

Bunnahabhain 1997 / 14 YO / Peated / Cask #5530+5531
70cl / 53.2% - Signatory - A vatting of two 1997 Casks from Bunnahabhain. This Whisky is 14 YO and has been heavily peated. Bottled by Signatory from their Cask Strength Collection.

Bunnahabhain 2001 / 10 YO / Sherry Butt #1766
70cl / 57% - Signatory - A 2001 vintage Whisky from Bunnahabhain, Distilled on October 17th, matured in a Sherry butt for 10 years and Bottled on September 10th 2012 by Signatory as part of their Cask Strength Collection.

Bunnahabhain 20 YO / Centenary
100cl / 43% - Distillery Bottling - A very special Bottling of 20 YO Bunnahabhain, created in 1983 from some very old Casks to commemorate Bunnahabhain's centenary. Just 600 Bottles of this were originally released.

Bunnahabhain 25 YO
70cl / 43% - Distillery Bottling - A more Sherried style, with the soft, creamy complexity and gentle, sophisticated palate

and mouthfeel that Bunna's aficionados treasure. Handsomely presented, this is a delicious, contemplative dram. Picked up the top prize in its category at the World Whisky Awards 2010.

Bunnahabhain 25 YO
70cl / 46.3% - Distillery Bottling - An update to the much vaunted Bunnhabhain 25 YO, keeping the same age statement and presentation but upping the ABV to 46.3% to bring it line with the rest of the range. A great Whisky at 43% but even better now with a little more oomph.

Bunnahabhain Cruach-Mhona
100cl / 50% - Distillery Bottling - Cruach-Mhona, gaelic for 'peat stack', a pile of drying peat bricks cut for fuel, is a departure from Bunnahabhain's usual style, adding in some peat to their normally unpeated spirit. Originally released solely into travel retail.

Bunnahabhain Darach Ur
100cl / 46.3% - Distillery Bottling - An official 1L Bottling of Bunnahabhain, originally for travel retail. Darach Ur means 'New Oak' in Scots Gaelic - this no-age-statement malt has been matured exclusively in virgin American oak Casks.

Bunnahabhain Toiteach
70cl / 46% - Distillery Bottling - After a string of highly-regarded indie peated Bunnahabhains, the Distillery has finally released an official version of their heavily-peated malt. Toiteach is Gaelic for Smoky, and apparently there's some Sherry influence on this as well. Kudos to Burn Stewart for Bottling this unchilfiltered at 46%.

Caol Ila 12 YO
70cl / 43%

Distillery Bottling
Medium weight, but still packing plenty of potent phenols, this is a refined, powerful dram with a compensating oiliness. A balanced, peaty beauty.
International Wine & Spirits Competition 2010: Gold Medal - Best in Class
IWSC 2012 - Gold Medal - Whisky - Scotch

Caol Ila 12 YO / Bot.1980s
75cl / 43% - Distillery Bottling - A wonderful old Bottling of Caol Ila 12 YO from the 1980s featuring the classic orange Bulloch Lade label with the capital Ls seeming to emphasise the correct 'Co-LEEL-a' pronunciation.

Caol Ila 12 YO / Unpeated / Bot.2011
70cl / 64% - Distillery Bottling - Distilled in 1999, the 2011 release of the unpeated Caol Ila 12 YO is an absolute belter - and amazingly easy to drink, even at its slightly scary full strength of 64%. Bottled from first fill ex-Bourbon American oak Casks, this was one of our favourites in the 2011 Special Releases.

Caol Ila 14 YO / Bot.1980s / Sestante
75cl / 64.7% - Sestante - A 1980s Bottling of 14 YO Caol Ila Bottled by Italian distributor Sestante at a whopping 64.7%.

Caol Ila 14 YO / Unpeated / Sherry Cask
70cl / 59.3% - Distillery Bottling - The latest incarnation of the yearly Cask strength 'unpeated' Caol Ila produced as part of Diageo's Special Releases selection. This time it's been aged for 14 years in ex-Sherry Casks, filled in 1997. There's not a lot of Sherried Caol Ila out there and this might be our pick of this year's range.

Caol Ila 15 YO / 22ct Gold Ceramic Jug
75cl / 43% -Distillery Bottling - A special edition 15 YO Caol Ila - packaged in a 22 carat gold plated ceramic jug.

Caol Ila 15 YO / Flora & Fauna
70cl / 43% - Flora & Fauna - Caol Ila's entry in the Flora & Fauna range - a 15 YO expression. Discontinued in 1982 and replaced by the Distilleries own range of Whiskies.

Caol ila 15 YO / Manager's Dram / Sherry Cask
75cl / 63% - Distillery Bottling

Caol ila 16 YO / Bot.1980s
75cl / 40% - Sestante - A beautiful Bottle of Caol Ila Bottled by Italian distributer Sestante.

Caol Ila 17 YO / TWE Whisky Show
70cl / 58% - The Whisky Show - We're a big fan of 17 YO Caol Ila here at the Whisky Exchange and this special Bottling for the 2011 Whisky Show is right up our street. A crisp and peaty example of the Distillery's output.

Caol Ila 18 YO
70cl / 43% - Distillery Bottling - Extra ageing has calmed the impact of the phenols, with the peat arriving on the palate late, and tempered by smooth oak. A very mellow, mature Islay malt.

Caol Ila 1966 / 29 YO / Centenary Reserve / Gordon & Macphail
70cl / 40% - Gordon & Macphail - An independent Bottling of 1966 Caol Ila from Gordon & Macphail released as part of the Centenary celebrations. Distilled in 1966 and matured for 29 years in a Sherry Cask.

Caol Ila 1969 / Gordon & Macphail
75cl / 40% - Gordon & Macphail

Caol Ila 1974 / 20 YO
70cl / 43% - Hart Brothers - A rare mid-1990s Bottling of 20 YO Caol Ila 1974 from Hart Brothers.

Caol Ila 1974 / 23 YO
70cl / 46% - First Cask - A very rare Bottling of Caol Ila 1974, Bottled in the late 1990s by a now-defunct London retailer under the First Cask imprint.

Caol Ila 1974 / Bot.1993 / Signatory for Velier
70cl / 43% - Signatory - A mid 1990s Bottling of 1974 vintage Caol Ila by Signatory for Italian importer Velier.

Caol Ila 1974 / Map Label / Connoisseurs Choice
75cl / 40% - Gordon & Macphail - A lovely old Bottle of Caol Ila 1974 ,Bottled by Gordon & Macphail for the Connoisseurs Choice series sometime in the late 1980s.

Caol Ila 1975 / 20 YO / Rare Malts
75cl / 61.18% - Distillery Bottling - A 1975 vintage Caol Ila Bottled as part of the Rare Malts series. This edition is 20 YO and was released at a full Cask strength of 61.18%.

Caol Ila 1975 / 20 YO / Rare Malts
75cl / 61.12% - Distillery Bottling - A mid-90s entry into the Rare Malts range with a 20 YO Bottling from Caol Ila. Its Bottled at a big (and pedantically accurate) Cask strength of 61.12% and promises some smoky magic.

Caol Ila 1977 / 21 YO / Rare Malts
70cl / 61.3% - Distillery Bottling - A 21 YO Rare Malts Bottling of Cask strength Caol Ila Distilled in 1977 and released at the end of the last millennium.

Caol Ila 1978 / 23 YO
70cl / 61.7% - Distillery Bottling - A big Cask strength Caol Ila released as part of Diageo's Rare Malts series. Distilled in 1978

and released at the turn of the millennium at a eye-watering 61.7% ABV.

Caol Ila 1979 / 31 YO / Mackillop's
70cl / 46% - Mackillop's - A 1979 Whisky from Caol Ila Distillery on Islay. This Whisky has been aged for approximately 31 years and Bottled in March 2011. This particular single Cask release was specially selected for World of Whiskies.

Caol Ila 1980 / 30 YO / Douglas Laing Platinum
70cl / 59.4% - Douglas Laing - A 1980 vintage Caol Ila released as part of Douglas Laing's always impressive Platinum Selection. It's a single Cask that was Bottled at a Cask strength of 59.4% in the summer of 2011.

Caol Ila 1981 / 21 YO / First Cask #280
70cl / 46% - First Cask - A 1981 Caol Ila Bottled for Direct Wines as part of the "First Cask" range. This single Cask Whisky has been aged for 21 years.

Caol Ila 1981 / 21 YO / First Cask #282
70cl / 46% - First Cask - A 21 YO Whisky from Caol Ila (although they spell it Caol Isla on the Bottle) from First Cask, released in the early 2000s. This was Distilled on 20th January 1980.

Caol Ila 1981 / Bot.1997
70cl / 63.8% - Flora & Fauna - A classic 1981 Caol Ila one of a handful of rare Cask strength Flora & Faunas released in the mid to late 1990s to great acclaim, and which inexplicably were never repeated.

Caol Ila 1981 / Scott's Selection
70cl / 61% - Scott's Selection - A lovely colour (and a massive ABV) on this full-strength 1981 vintage Caol Ila, Bottled without colouring or chill-filtration in 2011 at around 30 YO by renowned independent Bottlers Robert Scott of Rutherglen for their Scott's Selection series.

Caol Ila 1982 / 29 YO / Cask #6484 / Signatory
70cl / 56.3% - Signatory - A long aged single Cask Caol Ila from Signatory, released as part of their Cask Strength Collection. Distilled on December 14th 1982 and Bottled on October 6th 2012 after 29 years of maturation in a hogshead.

Caol Ila 1982 / 29 YO / Cask #6486
70cl / 54.6% - Signatory - A 1982 vintage Whisky from Caol ila Distillery. This Whisky has been aged for 29 years and Bottle at

Cask strength for Signatory's Cask Strength Collection.

Caol Ila 1983 / 28 YO / Cask #1463 / Adelphi
70cl / 54% - Adelphi - A 28 YO single Cask Caol Ila from Adelphi. Distilled in 1983 and bottled in 2012.

Caol Ila 1984 / 18 YO / First Cask #5757
70cl / 46% - First Cask - A 1984 Caol Ila Bottled for Direct Wines as part of the "First Cask" range. This single Cask Whisky has been aged for 18 years.

Caol Ila 1984 / 18 YO / First Cask #5759
70cl / 46% - First Cask - A single Cask Bottling of 1981 Distilled spirit from Caol Ila. Aged for 18 years and Bottled in the late 1990s for Direct Wines as part of their First Cask series.

Caol Ila 1984 / 25 YO / Frisky Whisky
70cl / 54% - John Milroy - A 1984 vintage Caol Ila, selected by industry legend John Milroy for his Frisky Whisky collection. At 25 YO and full of peat and lemony spice, this Cask strength Caol Ila is a steal.

Caol Ila 1990 / 17 YO / Sherry Wood / Mackillop's
70cl / 56.3% - Mackillop's - A 1990 vintage Caol Ila, as selected by Lorne Mackillop for his Mackillop's Choice range. Matured in a Sherry Cask and Bottled after 17 years in 2007.

Caol Ila 1991 / 18 YO / Cask# 194/200
70cl / 56.1% - Speciality Drinks Ltd - A batch of two hogshead Casks vatted together to produce our latest Cask strength Caol Ila 1991 for Single Malts of Scotland.

Caol Ila 1992 / 19 YO / The Whisky Agency
70cl / 50.5% - The Whisky Agency - A 1992 vintage Whisky from Caol Ila Distillery. This has been matured in an Ex-Bourbon barrel for 19 years and Bottled for The Whisky Agency.

Caol Ila 1996 / 16 YO / Old Malt Cask #9057
70cl / 50% - Douglas Laing - A 16 YO Caol Ila Bottled by Douglas Laing from a refill hogshead for their Old Malt Cask range. Distilled in September 1996 and Bottled in September 2012.

Caol Ila 1996 / Feis Ile 2009 / Sherry Cask
70cl / 58% - Distillery Bottling - A very rare Bottling of Caol Ila, originally produced for sale at the Distillery during Feis Ile, the Islay festival of Malt and Music, in 2009. Bottled from a single Sherry Cask at Cask strength after about 13 years in wood.

Caol Ila 1997 / 14 YO / Cask #7813-7815
70cl / 46% - Signatory - A 1997 vintage Whisky from Caol Ila Distillery on Islay. This Whisky is a vatting of 3 Casks and has been aged for a minimum of 14 years. This Whisky has been Bottled without chillfiltration.

Caol Ila 1997 / 15 YO / Cask #7816+7 / Signatory
70cl / 46% - Signatory - A 15 YO Whisky from Clynelish, vatted from a pair of hogsheads and Bottled by Signatory for their Unchillfiltered Collection. The spirit was Distilled on 25th June 1997 and was Bottled on 29th August 2012.

Caol Ila 1997 / Managers' Choice / Sherry Cask
70cl / 58% - Distillery Bottling - A single 1997 European Sherry Oak Cask of Caol Ila chosen to represent the Distillery in the Cask strength Managers' Choice range from Diageo. This is only the second ever single Cask Caol Ila released by Diageo after the wonderful Feis Ile Bottling in 2009 (also a Sherry Cask, coincidentally).

Caol Ila 1998 / Connoisseurs Choice
70cl / 43% - Gordon & Macphail - A 1998 vintage Caol Ila from the fine folks at Gordon & Macphail, Bottlers of the Connoisseurs Choice range of Whiskies. A classic Caol Ila with an edge of fruit thanks to having been matured in first fill Sherry butts.

Caol Ila 1998 / Distillers Edition
70cl / 43% - Distillery Bottling - Caol Ila's 5th release of its Distillers Edition Whisky, finished in Moscatel Casks for some extra richness and spice.

Caol Ila 1999 / The Whisky Trail
70cl / 43% - Speciality Drinks Ltd - A 1999 vintage Caol Ila Bottled by The Whisky Trail in 2011. Briny smoke, like a bonfire on the beach, medium-bodied with a slightly spicy finish - a great session Whisky.

Caol Ila 19 YO / The Whisky Exchange
70cl / 55.9% - The Whisky Exchange - A wonderfully fresh, minerally Caol Ila Bottled by TWE from a single ex-Bourbon Cask. Lots of sea air, seaweed and seashells make this the olfactory equivalent of a picnic on the beach. A big hit at 2012's TWE Whisky Show.

Caol Ila 2000 / Cask #309558-309559

70cl / 61.4% - Gordon & Macphail - A Cask strength release of 2000 vintage Caol Ila. This is a marriage of two Casks which have been matured in first fill Sherry butts. Bottled by Gordon and Macphail.

Caol Ila 20 YO / 150th Anniversary
70cl / 57.86% - Distillery Bottling - A 20 YO Caol Ila Bottled by the Distillery to celebrate their 150th birthday in 1996.

Caol Ila 25 YO
70cl / 43% - Distillery Bottling - Introduced in 2010, after Cask strength versions in 2004 and 2005, this is the first officially-Bottled Caol Ila 25 YO to be Bottled at 43%. It's nice to see growing recognition for this excellent Distillery, and this is a very welcome addition to the official range, with a rich, gentle mouthfeel and restrained, coal-esque phenols.

Caol Ila 8 YO / Unpeated / Bot. 2007
70cl / 64.9% - Distillery Bottling - The second edition of Caol Ila's excellent 8 YO unpeated Single Malt, originally Bottled in 2007 at a whopping 64.9%. That'll put hairs on your chest.

Caol Ila 8 YO / Unpeated / Bot.2008
70cl / 64.2% - Distillery Bottling - The third batch of Caol Ila 8 YO made with unpeated barley - although previous expressions still had an unmistakeably smoky tang about them. Bottled again at extremely high strength.

Caol Ila Cask Strength / 61.3%
70cl / 61.3% - Distillery Bottling - Caol Ila Cask Strength is a Whisky capable of bringing joy to the most jaded peathead - we love its strong, lemony, sooty saltiness. Great on its own or in hardcore Whisky cocktails.

Caol Ila Cask Strength / 61.6%
70cl / 61.6% - Distillery Bottling - A superb, lemony, salty, coal-tar-soapy bonanza, Caol Ila Cask Strength is a Whisky capable of bringing joy to the most jaded peathead. We love this.

Caol Ila Cask Strength / Quarter Bottle
20cl / 58% - Distillery Bottling - A quarter Bottle of Caol Ila's rather popular Cask strength edition. Peaty and punchy, Bottled at 58%, this is a great Whisky and packaged in a useful 'experimentation' size.

Caol Ila Moch
70cl / 43% - Distillery Bottling - Taking its name from the Gaelic

for 'dawn', Moch is a wonderful newcomer from Caol Ila and is a must-try for fans of this outstanding Distillery. Lighter in style than the standard 12 YO expression, Moch is a fantastic easy-drinking dram.

KILCHOMAN RANGE

Kilchoman 100% Islay / 2nd Edition
70cl / 50% - Distillery Bottling - The second edition of Kilchoman's massively popular 100% Islay. From barely to Bottle, everything is from Islay. The Whisky itself is aged for over 3 years in a combination of Bourbon and refill Bourbon barrels.

Kilchoman 100% Islay / Inaugural Release 2011
70cl / 50% - Distillery Bottling - A first for Kilchoman - a Whisky Distilled and matured on Islay as usual, but also only using grain grown on the island. It's only a 3 YO but has a lot to it, as we've come to expect from Kilchoman.

Kilchoman Machir Bay
70cl / 46% - Distillery Bottling - The first ongoing Bottling from Kilchoman, Machir Bay is made up of first fill Bourbon matured Whisky finished in Oloroso Sherry wood before Bottling.
IWSC 2012 - Gold Medal - Whisky - Scotch

LAGAVULIN RANGE

Lagavulin 12 YO / Bot. 2009
70cl / 57.9% - Distillery Bottling - The 2009 release of Cask-strength Lagavulin 12 YO is a simply superb Bottling. One of the highlights of this year's Special Releases, this will delight fans of the Distillery.

Lagavulin 12 YO / Bot.1970s
75cl / 43% - Distillery Bottling

Lagavulin 12 YO / Bot.1980s
75cl / 43% - Distillery Bottling - A 1980s release of Lagavulin, Bottled by the Distillery at 12 YO.

Lagavulin 12 YO / Bot.1980s
75cl / 43% - Distillery Bottling - A wonderful old 1980s Bottle of 12 YO Lagavulin.

Lagavulin 12 YO / Bot.2003 / 3rd Release
70cl / 57.8% - Distillery Bottling

Lagavulin 12 YO / Bot.2004 / 4th Release
70cl / 58.2% - Distillery Bottling - The 4th release of Lagavulin's entry in Diageo's yearly Special Releases collection - the ever reliable 12 YO. Fresher and more feisty than the 16 YO, it's both an excellent Whisky in its own right as well as a way to see how Lagavulin develops over the years.

Lagavulin 12 YO / Bot.2006 / 6th Release
70cl / 57.5% - Distillery Bottling - The 6th edition of Lagavulin's fresh and smoky 12 YO, one of the mainstays of Diageo's yearly Special Releases collection.

Lagavulin 12 YO / Bot.2007 / 7th Release
70cl / 56.4% - Distillery Bottling

Lagavulin 12 YO / Bot.2008 / 8th Release
70cl / 56.4% - Distillery Bottling - At 56.4%, this year's Lagavulin 12 YO is exactly the same strength as last year's - a phenomenon that occurred with the second and third release as well. Do you think they just make up enormous batches and drip-feed them through?

Lagavulin 12 YO / Bot.2010 / 10th Release
70cl / 56.5% - Distillery Bottling Lagavulin 12 YO is always one of the most anticipated Bottlings in Diageo's Special Releases. As before, this is a full strength Bottling from American oak Casks. Malt Maniacs Awards 2011: Best Natural Cask Award (Daily Drams)

Lagavulin 12 YO / Bot.2011 / 11th Release
70cl / 57.5% - Distillery Bottling - As reliably excellent as ever, the 2011 Special Releases Lagavulin 12 YO was Distilled in 1999 and vatted from refill American oak Casks. As you'd expect, this is a very upfront, sooty-sweet Lagavulin in the classic style.
World Whiskies Awards 2012 - Best Islay 12 years and under

Lagavulin 12 YO / Bot.2012 / 12th Release
70cl / 56.1% - Distillery Bottling - The 12th release of 12 YO Lagavulin from Diageo's Special Releases range. A perennial favourite, balancing price against a punchy Cask strength edition of Whisky from one of Islay's most mysterious Distilleries.

Lagavulin 15 YO / Bot.1980s
75cl / 45% - Distillery Bottling - A 15 YO Lagavulin Bottled by the Distillery in the 1980s and presented in a ceramic jug.

Lagavulin 16 YO

70cl / 43% - Distillery Bottling - The Islay representative in the 'Classic Malts' series is a deep, dry and exceptionally peaty bruiser. Probably the most pungent of all Islay malts, Lagavulin is not for the faint-hearted but inspires fanatical devotion in its many followers.

Malt Maniacs Awards 2010 & 2011: Non-Plus-Ultra Award (Daily Drams)
IWSC 2012 - Gold Outstanding Medal - Whisky - Scotch

Lagavulin 1976 / 30 YO
70cl / 52.6% - Distillery Bottling - The oldest official Lagavulin ever released, this caused a storm when it came out a couple of years ago.

Lagavulin 1979 / 23 YO / Murray McDavid
70cl / 46% - Murray McDavid

Lagavulin 1980 / Distillers Edition
70cl / 43% - Distillery Bottling - A 1980 vintage release of Lagavulin's PX Sherry matured Distillers edition. This particular vintage was actually released some years ago and is now a tad difficult to get hold of.

Lagavulin 1990 Distillers Edition
70cl / 43% - Distillery Bottling

Lagavulin 1991 Distillers Edition
70cl / 43% - Distillery Bottling - With all your favourite Lagavulin characteristics, allied to an extra layer of sweetness, this is the most consistently excellent of the highly popular Distiller's Edition series. Winner of a Gold Medal and Best in Class at the IWSC, as well as the 'Best Peated Malt' in the Premium category at the Malt Maniacs Awards 2008.

Lagavulin 1993 / 15 YO / Managers Choice / Sherry Cask
70cl / 54.7% - Distillery Bottling - Lagavulin is probably Diageo's most highly-rated Distillery, with its muscular peaty presence and flashes of honey sending most of the cognoscenti into a swoon. This 15 YO from 1993 is probably the most eagerly-awaited of the Managers Choice series, particularly as it's one of only a handful of Sherried single Cask Lagavulins ever released.

Lagavulin 1993 Double Matured / Distillers Edition
100cl / 43% - Distillery Bottling - Finished in Casks previously

containing Pedro Ximenez Sherry, this Lagavulin is the most popular of the 'Distillers Edition' expressions of the Classic Malts. A delicious layer of Sherry sweetness smooths out the rough edges of the standard Bottling.

Lagavulin 1993 Islay Festival 2007
70cl / 56.5% - Distillery Bottling - A 1993 vintage Lagavulin Bottled as a special release available from the Distillery at the 2007 Islay Festival. A hit with almost all who have tasted it, averaging a score of 90/100 with the Malt Maniacs.

Lagavulin 1994 Distillers Edition
70cl / 43% - Distillery Bottling - By far the most popular of the Distiller's Edition series this double matured Lagavulin has had a finishing period in sweet, sticky Pedro Ximinez Sherry Casks. A Whisky that never disappoints.
IWSC 2012 - Gold Medal - Whisky - Scotch

Lagavulin 1995 / 12 YO / Sherry Cask
70cl / 48% - Distillery Bottling - A special release of Lagavulin 1995 Bottled at 48% for the Friends of the Classic Malts in 2008 from first fill European oak Sherry Casks.

Lagavulin 1995 / Feis Ile 2009
70cl / 54.4%

Lagavulin 1995 Distillers Edition
70cl / 43% - Distillery Bottling - Lagavulin's popular Distiller's Edition, Distilled in 1995 and finished in Pedro Ximinez Sherry Casks. An extra layer of sweetness soothes the rough edges of this much-loved dram.

Lagavulin 1998 / Feis Ile 2011
70cl / 51% - Distillery Bottling - A special edition Bottling of Lagavulin. This Whisky was released for the 2011 Feis Ile festival. Distilled in 1998 and matured in a refill butt, this whisky is atleast 12 YO.

Lagavulin 21 YO / Sherry Cask
70cl / 56.5% - Distillery Bottling - A legendary Lagavulin, originally released in 2007 - and it's to be the last fully Sherried release, we're told. Boasting 95 points on Whiskyfun, this has become incredibly sought-after.

Lagavulin 25 YO
70cl / 57.2% - Distillery Bottling - Rare and highly sought after, this is a 25 YO Lagavulin Bottled at Cask strength.

The Syndicate's Lagavulin 1990 / 14 YO
70cl / 46% - The Syndicate - A rare independent release of Lagavulin, Bottled in 2004 for The Syndicate, which seems from the back label to be a group of five guys, in Bruichladdich's Bottling hall.

LAPHROAIG RANGE

Laphroaig 10 YO
70cl / 40% - Distillery Bottling - Laphroaig 10 YO is a full-bodied, smoky gem, with a residual sweetness and a hint of salt amidst the seaweedy, peaty characters before a long warming finish. A classic dram.
IWSC 2012 - Gold Medal - Whisky - Scotch

Laphroaig 10 YO / Bot.1960s
75cl / 40% - Distillery Bottling - One of the increasingly legendary 1970s Bottling of Laphroaig 10 YO.

Laphroaig 10 YO / Bot.1970s
75cl / 40% - Distillery Bottling

Laphroaig 10 YO / Bot.1980s
75cl / 43% - Distillery Bottling - Very rare to see one of these beautiful old Laphroaigs! One for the collectors, this was imported into Italy by Cinzano in the 1980s.

Laphroaig 10 YO / Cask Strength
70cl / 55.7% - Distillery Bottling - A giant whack of peat, tempered by some toffee-like notes. This is a powerful, uncompromising Whisky, and all the better for it. 'A fine robust dram with lots happening. Laphroaig at its best. 8.75/10' Gavin Smith, Whisky Magazine May 2004

Laphroaig 10 YO Cask Strength / Batch 003 / Bot.2011
70cl / 55.3% - Distillery Bottling - The 3rd batch of Laphroaig's riotously popular small batch editions of their famed 10 YO Cask strength Islay Single Malt. No doubt this will be as big a hit as the previous editions - this is an expression that never disappoints.

Laphroaig 10 YO Royal Warrant
70cl / 40% - Distillery Bottling - A special Bottling of Laphroaig 10 YO, released in 1994 to celebrate the bestowing of a Royal Warrant on the Distillery by Prince Charles.

Laphroaig 15 YO
70cl / 43% - Distillery Bottling - Zesty oak and warm peat smoke top notes, with sweet undertones, reminiscent of fresh nutmeg and toasted almonds. Faintly salty. Laphroaig 15 YO is a smoother and more elegant elder sibling to the robust 10 year-old.

Laphroaig 15 YO / Bot.1980s
75cl / 40% - Distillery Bottling

Laphroaig 15 YO / Bot.1980s
75cl / 43% - Distillery Bottling - A 1980s release of 15 YO Laphroaig, Bottled by the Distillery.

Laphroaig 18 YO
70cl / 48% - Distillery Bottling - Laphroaig 18 YO was introduced in 2009 as a replacement for the old 15 year-old (Prince Chuck's sorely missed favourite Whisky, lest we forget). This is a stronger, altogether gutsier affair at 48%.

Laphroaig 18 YO / Queen's Diamond Jubilee Edition
70cl / 48% - Distillery Bottling - A limited edition of 3000 Bottles of the award-winning Laphroaig 18 YO, released in Summer 2012 in a special commemorative tube celebrating the Queen's Diamond Jubilee. Laphroaig are donating £3000 from the sales of this Bottle to the Queen Elizabeth Scholarship Trust which helps young craftsmen.

Laphroaig 1967 / 27 YO / Cask #2956
70cl / 50.7% - Signatory - A single Cask independent release of Laphroaig Bottled in 1994 for Signatory. It was Distilled in 1967, the same year that the Distillery was sold to Long John International, and Bottled at Cask strength.

Laphroaig 1970 / Samaroli
75cl / 54% - Samaroli - A 1970 vintage Laphroaig, bottled in 1986 for Italian importer Samaroli.

Laphroaig 1973 / 13 YO
75cl / 40% - Gordon & Macphail - A 1973 vintage Laphroaig Bottled by Gordon and Macphail for their Connoisseurs Choice range back in the 1980s.

Laphroaig 1974 / 31 YO / Sherry Cask
70cl / 49.7% - Distillery Bottling - A truly legendary Laphroaig from the 1974 vintage, this heavily-Sherried 31 YO was a limited edition of around 900 Bottles produced for a French retailer and scored a whopping 95 points from Serge Valentin on Whiskyfun

before capping that with a Gold Medal and the Non Plus Ultra award for the highest scoring Whisky out of all the entries at the Malt Maniacs Awards 2005. An acknowledged masterpiece.

Laphroaig 1976
75cl / 43% - Distillery Bottling - A 1976 vintage Laphroaig, Bottled by the Distillery.

Laphroaig 1977
75cl / 43% - Distillery Bottling - A rare and highly sought-after Laphroaig from the 1977 Bottled in the spring of 1995. This Bottle has a very good reputation and is extremely hard to find these days.

Laphroaig 1980 / 27 YO / Sherry Cask
70cl / 57.4% - Distillery Bottling - Gold Medal Winner(The Malt Maniacs Awards 2007)
They say Laphroaig is like Marmite - you either love it or you hate it. That goes double for Sherried Laphroaig, but this Cask-strength vatting of five Oloroso Casks came first in the Malt Maniacs Awards 2007.

Laphroaig 1981 / 27 YO / Oloroso Sherry Cask
70cl / 56.6% - Distillery Bottling - A second batch of 27 year-old Sherried Laphroaig, this time from 1981. Bottled from just five Oloroso Sherry butts - the same as 2007's 1980 vintage which won the top prize at the Malt Maniac Awards.

Laphroaig 1986 / 25 YO / Douglas Laing Platinum
70cl / 55.9% - Douglas Laing - Another impressive Bottling from Douglas Laing's Platinum Selection range. A 25 YO Laphroaig, Distilled in 1986 and Bottled at a solid 55.9%.

Laphroaig 1989 / 17 YO / Islay Fest.2007
70cl / 50.3% - Distillery Bottling

Laphroaig 1989 / Highgrove House
70cl / 43% -Distillery Bottling

Laphroaig 1990 / 18 YO / Cask #M587 / Montgomerie's
70cl / 46% - Montgomery's - A 1990 vintage Laphroaig Bottled by indie Bottler Montgomerie's in July 2009 at 18 years of age. This was Distilled in the early days of legendary former manager Iain Henderson's reign at the Distillery.

Laphroaig 1990 / 19 YO / Cask #11725 / Mackillop's
70cl / 52.5% - Mackillop's - A 1990 vintage Laphroaig Bottled at

Cask strength in 2010 a few months before its 20th birthday by independent Bottler Mackillop's.

Laphroaig 1990 / 21 YO / TWA and TWE Joint Bottling
70cl / 55.9% - The Whisky Agency & The Whisky Exchange - A joint Bottling of 1990 vintage Laphroaig by German independent The Whisky Agency and us, The Whisky Exchange. This is a 21 YO Whisky that matured in a Bourbon Cask until it was Bottled in 2011.

Laphroaig 1990 / 21 YO / Cask #11728 / Mackillop's
70cl / 52.2% - Mackillop's - A 1990 vintage Laphroaig, matured for 21 years and then Bottled in March 2012 by the folks at Mackillop's.

Laphroaig 1991 / Highgrove House
70cl / 43% - Distillery Bottling - A 1991 vintage Laphroaig, Bottled by the Distillery for Highgrove House, the home of the Prince of Wales. Charles likes to ensure he has a ready supply of Laphroaig to hand.

Laphroaig 1992 / 16 YO / Old Malt Cask #4825
70cl / 50% - Douglas Laing - A Laphroaig 1992 Bottled by Douglas Laing from a single refill butt for the Old Malt Cask series.

Laphroaig 1992 / 19 YO / Old Malt Cask #7598
70cl / 50% - Douglas Laing - A 1992 vintage single Cask Laphroaig Bottled by Douglas Laing as part of their Old Malt Cask Range. This one was matured for 19 years before Bottling in the summer of 2011.

Laphroaig 1994 / Highgrove
70cl / 40% - Distillery Bottling - A 1994 vintage Laphroaig Bottled for the official residence of Charles, Prince of Wales, Highgrove House.

Laphroaig 1995 / 16 YO / Cask #45
70cl / 60.9% - Signatory - A single Cask Whisky from Laphroaig Distillery on Islay. After being aged for 16 years in Bourbon Barrels, this has been Bottled by Signatory for their Cask Strength Collection.

Laphroaig 1995 / 16 YO / Cask #50
70cl / 60.3% - Signatory - A 16 YO Cask strength Whisky from Laphroaig, aged for 16 years in a Bourbon Cask and Bottled in early 2012 by Signatory.

Laphroaig 1995 / 17 YO / The Whisky Agency
70cl / 53.9% - The Whisky Agency - A 17 YO Laphroaig Bottled by The Whisky Agency as part of their 'Fights' series (the beautiful label features a tiger catching the tail feathers of a peacock). Distilled in 1995, matured in an ex-Bourbon barrel and Bottled in 2012.

Laphroaig 1996 / 15 YO / Old Malt Cask #7492
70cl / 50% - Douglas Laing - A 1996 vintage Laphroaig Bottled at 50% from a single Cask for Douglas Laing as part of their Old Malt Cask range. A lightly coloured 15 YO Bottled in the summer of 2011.

Laphroaig 1996 / 15 YO / Cask #8512 / Signatory
70cl / 53.1% - Signatory - A 1996 vintage single Cask Whisky from Laphroaig, Distilled on 26th November, matured in a hogshead for 4 days shy of 16 years and then Bottled on 22nd November 2012 by Signatory for their Cask Strength Collection.

Laphroaig 1996 / 15 YO / Liquid Library
70cl / 56.4% - The Whisky Agency - A Bottling of 1996 vintage Laphroaig from The Whisky Agency under their Liquid Library label. Matured for 15 years in a Bourbon Cask and Bottled at a Cask strength of 56.4%.

Laphroaig 1996 / 15 YO / Old Malt Cask #7966
70cl / 50% - Douglas Laing - A 1996 vintage Laphroaig from Douglas Laing's Old Malt Cask range. Distilled in October 1996 and Bottled in December 2011 after 15 years in a refill hoghshead.

Laphroaig 1997 / Highgrove / Cask #136
70cl / 46%

Laphroaig 1997 / Highgrove / Cask #141
70cl / 46% - Distillery Bottling - A special Bottling of vintage Laphroaig Bottled for sale at Highgrove House, home of Prince Charles, who famously loves his 'Froyg. Bottled at a pleasing 46% with a special label showing the Prince's fleur-de-lis Royal Warrant.

Laphroaig 1998 / 14 YO / Cask #5559+60 / Signatory
70cl / 46% - Signatory - A 1998 vintage Laphroaig Bottled by Signatory for their Un-chillfiltered Collection. Distilled on 12th May 1998 and matured in a pair of hogsheads before Bottling on 14th November 2012.

Laphroaig 1998 / 14 YO / Casks #700165+6 / Signatory
70cl / 46% - Signatory - A 14 YO Laphroaig vatted from two Casks and Bottled by Signatory for their Un-Chillfiltered Collection. Distilled on 14th May 1998 and Bottled on 29th August 2012.

Laphroaig 1998 / 14 YO / Old Malt Cask #9222
70cl / 50% - Douglas Laing - An Old Malt Cask Bottling from Douglas Laing of 1998 vintage Whisky Distilled at Laphroaig. Bottled in October 2012 from a refill hogshed.

Laphroaig 1998 / Bot.2011 / Berry Bros & Rudd
70cl / 56.2% - Berry Bros & Rudd - A 1998 vintage Laphroaig Bottled in 2011 by veteran independent wine and spirit merchant Berry Brothers & Rudd.

Laphroaig 1999 / 12 YO / Old Malt Cask #7806
70cl / 50% - Douglas Laing - A 1999 vintage Laproaig from Douglas Laing, matured in refill hogsheads for 12 years and Bottled in 2011 under the Old Malt Cask label.

Laphroaig 20 YO Double Cask
70cl / 46.6% - Distillery Bottling - The travel exclusive Laphroaig 20 YO Double Cask, matured for 18 years in Bourbon hogsheads and finised for 2 years in Laphroaig's bespoke quarter casks.

Laphroaig 25 YO
70cl / 40% - Distillery Bottling - The first edition of Laphroaig 25 YO; this is a very mellow, restrained expression with pretty delicate peat (for 'Froyg anyway), some baked apple notes and a gentle nuttiness. A malt to unwind with.

Laphroaig 25 YO / Cask Strength
70cl / 50.9% - Distillery Bottling - The Cask strength Bottling of Laphroaig 25 YO is a very different beast to the old 25 YO (and in our opinion, upping the strength is a big improvement). Rich and smouldering, with a big coal hit and a lingering seaweed character. We said at the time that this was tremendous stuff, and now it's only gone and won the IWSC Trophy for Best Cask Strength Single Malt.

Laphroaig 30 YO / Wooden Box
75cl / 43% - Distillery Bottling - Originally released around 2000, this great dram is becoming rarer and rarer. Laphroaig 30 YO has garnered many plaudits, including a Double Gold Medal at the San Francisco World Spirits Competition 2005.

Laphroaig Quarter Cask
70cl / 48% - Distillery Bottling - A vibrant young Laphroaig whose maturation has been speeded up by ageing in Quarter Casks. This shows soft sweetness and a velvety feel when first tasted, then the intense peatiness so unique to Laphroaig comes bursting through

PORT ASKAIG RANGE

Port Askaig 12 YO
70cl / 45.8% - Speciality Drinks Ltd - The fresh young addition to the family, Port Askaig 12 YO was introduced at The Whisky Exchange Whisky Show 2012 and is a delightfully vibrant, sooty, salty seaside dram perfect for autumn and winter hipflasks.

Port Askaig 25 YO
70cl / 45.8% - Speciality Drinks Ltd - This Port Askaig 25 YO is a medium-bodied elder statesman, with the oak rounding out delicious citrus flavours. Best appreciated with a drop of water.

Port Askaig 30 YO
70cl / 45.8% - Speciality Drinks Ltd - A splendidly gentle and elegant 30 YO Port Askaig, showing delicious honeysuckle on the nose, then bonfire smoke and leafy oakiness on the palate. One of the most perfectly autumnal Whiskies we've ever tried.

Port Askaig 30 YO / Cask Strength
70cl / 51.1% - Speciality Drinks Ltd - The third release of Port Askaig 30 YO is the first to be Bottled at Cask strength, giving it an unprecedented depth of smoky sweet flavour and a gloriously rich, generous texture. A majestic, magnificent dram.

PORT CHARLOTTE RANGE

Port Charlotte / The Peat Project
70cl / 46% - Distillery Bottling - A statement of intent from Bruichladdich master Distiller Jim McEwan, showing his vivions for Port Charlotte spirit - peated to 44ppm and vatted from various vintages.

Port Charlotte 10 YO
70cl / 46% - Distillery Bottling - The first ongoing release of Bruichladdich's heavily peated Port Charlotte. Aged for 10 years and showing off a mix of Bruichladdich's elegant spirit and big, smoky peat.

Port Charlotte An Turas Mor
70cl / 46% - Distillery Bottling - 2010's release of Port Charlotte is a departure from previous years in two significant ways: as a multi-vintage vatting and being Bottled at 46% rather than the humungous Cask strength of the earlier PC's. An Turas Mor ("The Great Journey", it says here) is intended as a coming-of-age PC, and, it is claimed, fulfils Jim McEwan's original vision for the brand. The journey continues...

PORT ELLEN RANGE

Port Ellen 12 YO / Queen's Visit to Distillery in 1980
75cl / 40% - A very rare 12 YO Port Ellen Bottled when Queen Elizabeth II visited the distillery on 9th August 1980.

Port Ellen 16 YO / Select Hogshead / The Whisky Shop
70cl / 50% - The Whisky Shop - Bottled at 50% for a Whisky retailer at some stage around the turn of the millennium, this rare Port Ellen was selected by Burn Stewart Distillers and has no declared vintage but was Bottled at 16 years of age.

Port Ellen 17 YO Cask Strength / Douglas Murdoch
70cl / 59.5% - Douglas Murdoch - A rather rare 17 YO Port Ellen, Bottled by now-defunct indie Douglas Murdoch around the turn of the millennium. At 59.5% this is pretty sure to be a treat.

Port Ellen 1969 / 15 YO
75cl / 40%

Port Ellen 1969 / 15 YO / Connoisseurs Choice
75cl / 40% - Gordon & Macphail - A very old Connoisseurs Choice 1969 Port Ellen Bottled in the mid-1980s. This little beauty got a hefty 92 points from Malt Maniac Serge Valentin's Whiskyfun website.

Port Ellen 1969 / 31 YO
70cl / 40% - Silver Seal - A historic Port Ellen 1969, this is the first ever Bottling from the Silver Seal company, who have gone on to release some legendary Whiskies (and rums) since this hit the shelves in 2001.

Port Ellen 1970 / 16 YO / Connoisseurs Choice
75cl / 40% - Gordon & Macphail - A 1970 vintage Port Ellen, Bottled at 16 YO by Gordon & Mapchail under their Connoisseurs Choice label.

Port Ellen 1970 / 16 YO / Gordon & Macphail
75cl / 61.1% - Intertrade - A very rare 1980s Bottling of 1970 Port Ellen Bottled by Gordon & Macphail for the little seen but very well respected Intertrade indie Bottler. Bottled at a very high strength for a malt of this age - this should be epic.

Port Ellen 1970 / Connoisseurs Choice
75cl / 40% - Gordon & Macphail - An old 'Map Label' Connoisseurs Choice Bottling.

Port Ellen 1974 / 14 YO
75cl / 43% - Sestante

Port Ellen 1974 / 14 YO / Sestante
75cl / 65.5% - Sestante - An incredibly potent Cask strength Port Ellen 1974 Bottled by Italian importers Sestante at 14 YO in the late 1980s.

Port Ellen 1974 / 30 YO / Signatory
70cl / 46% - Signatory - A 30 YO Port Ellen, Distilled in 1974 and Bottled by Signatory in October 2005.

Port Ellen 1975 / 22 YO / Hart Brothers
70cl / 43% - Hart Brothers - A late 1990s Hart Brothers Bottling of Port Ellen from the 1975 vintage. Nice colour on this - perhaps some Sherry or refill Sherry Casks in the mix?

Port Ellen 1976 / 19 YO / Hart Brothers
70cl / 43% - Hart Brothers - A rare mid-1990s Hart Brothers Bottling of Port Ellen from the 1976 vintage, Bottled at an easy-drinking 43%.

Port Ellen 1976 / 21 YO / Cask #4754
70cl / 57.9% - Signatory - A 21 YO Port Ellen Whisky from a single Cask which was filled in 1976. This Whisky has been Bottled at Cask strength by Signatory for their Vintage series.

Port Ellen 1976 / 22 YO / Cask #4749
70cl / 56.2% - Signatory - A single Cask Bottling of Port Ellen by Signatory. This Whisky was Distilled in 1976 and aged for 22 years before being Bottled.

Port Ellen 1976 / 24 YO / Bot.2000
70cl / 50% - Douglas Laing - A very rare single Cask Bottle of Port Ellen from the 1976 vintage (don't see too many of them these days), Bottled in 2000 at 50% by Douglas Laing for what was then their fledgeling Old Malt Cask series.

Port Ellen 1977 / 16 YO
70cl / 43% - Ultimate

Port Ellen 1977 / 18 YO / Milroys
70cl / 43% - Milroy's - A very rare 18 YO Port Ellen, Bottled in the mid-1990s by famous retailer Milroy's.

Port Ellen 1977 / 35 YO / Douglas Laing Platinum
70cl / 49.3% - Douglas Laing - An incredible 35 YO Port Ellen from Douglas Laing, released as part of their Old & Rare Platinum Selection. One of the oldest, if not the actual oldest, Port Ellens they've ever released, Distilled in August 1977 and Bottled in September 2012.

Port Ellen 1977 / Bot.1992 / Connoisseurs Choice
70cl / 40% - Gordon & Macphail - A Bottle of 1977 vintage Whisky from cult closed Distillery Port Ellen. Independently Bottled in 1992 by Gordon & Macphail as part of their Connoisseurs Choice series.

Port Ellen 1978 / 20 YO
70cl / 60.9% - Distillery Bottling - One of the stellar PE Rare Malts releases that catapulted this obscure Distillery to fame in the late 1990s. A legendary Bottling.

Port Ellen 1978 / 22 YO
70cl / 60.5% - Distillery Bottling - The second sensational OB Port Ellen 1978, Bottled around the turn of the millennium as part of the Rare Malts series. This phenomenal dram was rated at 93 points by Serge Valentin of Whiskyfun, and its popularity and acclaim led to the revivial of interest in this classic closed Distillery and thus to the birth of the annual Special Releases series.

Port Ellen 1978 / 27 YO / 6th Release (2006)
70cl / 54.2% - Distillery Bottling - The 6th release of Diageo's legendary year Special Release Port Ellens. Distilled in 1978 and Bottled at 27 years of age this is an increasingly rare dram as investors and drinkers fight over the remaining Bottles.

Port Ellen 1978 / 29 YO / 8th Release (2008)
70cl / 55.3% - Distillery Bottling - The eighth release of Diageo's Port Ellens is the fourth from 1978 and arrives in slightly tweaked packaging with a new box design, although the label remains largely the same.

Port Ellen 1979 / 14 YO / Signatory
70cl / 43% - Signatory

Port Ellen 1979 / 16 YO / Dun Eideann
70cl / 43% - Dun Eideann - A rare 1979 vintage single Cask Port Ellen, Bottled at 16 YO in August 1995 by Signatory for their Dun Eideann range. Teenage Port Ellens are pretty hard to come by these days, this should be fascinating.

Port Ellen 1979 / 21 YO / Old Malt Cask / Sherry Cask
70cl / 50% - Douglas Laing - A Sherried Port Ellen from the early days of the Old Malt Cask series, this is one of a string of single Cask PE's that really put Douglas Laing on the map as an independent Bottler. The company had vast stocks of Port Ellen after buying it in bulk for their blends, and were able to capitalise on the success of the Rare Malts Bottlings which had made the Distillery hugely sought-after.

Port Ellen 1979 / 23 YO
70cl / 46% - Wilson & Morgan

Port Ellen 1979 / 25 YO / 5th Release (2005)
70cl / 57.4% - Distillery Bottling - The 5th yearly release of Port Ellen from Diageo as part of their 2005 Special Releases. Distilled in 1979 and maintaining the rather excellent quality of the series.

Port Ellen 1979 / 25 YO / Potstill Austria
70cl / 57.1% - Douglas Laing - A 1979 Port Ellen from Douglas Laing. This is an exclusive Bottling for Potstill, a Whisky shop in Vienna, and was put out under the Fine & Rare Platinum Selection label. 25 YO and with a solid Cask strength of 57.1%.

Port Ellen 1979 / 27 YO / Douglas Laing Platinum
70cl / 57.1% - Douglas Laing - A 1979 vintage Port Ellen, chosen by Douglas Laing for their Old & Rare Platinum Selection, and Bottled in early 2007 at natural Cask strength, which in this case just happens to be exactly 57.1% aka 100 UK proof.

Port Ellen 1979 / 28 YO / Douglas Laing PLatinum
70cl / 53.9% - Douglas Laing - A Cask strength 1979 Port Ellen Bottled in 2008 at 28 YO by Douglas Laing for their top-of-the-range Platinum Selection. This was a special release exclusively for travel retail.

Port Ellen 1979 / 30 YO / 9th Release (2009)
70cl / 57.7% - Distillery Bottling - The 9th Port Ellen Annual

Release is the first official 30 YO and a definite return to form after a couple of 'mediocre' releases.

Port Ellen 1979 / 30 YO / Bot. Oct 2009
70cl / 52.1% - Douglas Laing - A truly delicious Port Ellen 1979 Bottled by Douglas Laing for their Platinum Selection. Begins with light sweetness, then takes a phenolic turn, becoming more medicinal before the honey returns at the finish.

Port Ellen 1979 / 30 YO / Douglas Laing Platinum
70cl / 53.3% - Douglas Laing - A thirty year-old Port Ellen 1979, Bottled at full strength from a refill hogshead in August 2010 by Douglas Laing for their Old & Rare Platinum Selection. At a great drinking strength of 53.3%, this should be a fantastic drop from the legendary closed Distillery.

Port Ellen 1979 / 32 YO / 11th Release (2011)
70cl / 53.9% - Distillery Bottling - The eleventh Port Ellen in Diageo's Special Releases series was Distilled in 1979 and Bottled at 32 YO. We reckon it's the best official PE in many years - sadly our allocation was completely pre-booked before the stock arrived.

Port Ellen 1979 / Bot.2012 / Mackillop's Choice
70cl / 43% - Mackillop's - A 1979 vintage Whisky from cult closed Distillery Port Ellen. Distilled in March 1979 and Bottled in March 2012 by Mackillop's.

Port Ellen 1979 / Refill Sherry
70cl / 55.3% - M&H

Port Ellen 1980 / 15 YO
70cl / 46% - Wilson & Morgan

Port Ellen 1980 / 15 YO / Kingsbury
70cl / 46% - Kingsbury's - From the hugely-respected Kingsbury independent Bottler comes this very, very rare Port Ellen 1980, Bottled at 46% in 1995 from a Sherry butt, although the tasting notes say there's very little sign of the Sherry.

Port Ellen 1980 / 16 YO
70cl / 43% - Ultimate

Port Ellen 1980 / 16 YO First Cask #89/589/44
70cl / 46% - First Cask - A mid-1990s independent Bottling of Whisky from this much sought after closed Distillery. It was Distilled a few years before closure and matured for 16 years

before release as part of Direct Wines's First Cask range.

Port Ellen 1980 / Bot.1996
75cl / 40% - Gordon & Macphail - An old Connoisseurs Choice Port Ellen 1980, Bottled by Gordon & Macphail in the mid 1990s. These are becoming increasingly rare.

Port Ellen 1980 / Bot.1997 / Connoisseurs Choice
70cl / 40% - Gordon & Macphail - A lovely old mid-1990s Connoisseurs Choice Bottling of Port Ellen from the not-often-seen 1980 vintage. Anything from Port Ellen Bottled at less than twenty YO is quite rare these days, so this is a bit of a find.

Port Ellen 1980 / Bot.1999 / Connoisseurs Choice
70cl / 40% - Gordon & Macphail - A 19 year-old Port Ellen from the 1980 vintage, Bottled for the Connoisseurs Choice in 1999 by indie legends Gordon & Macphail.

Port Ellen 1980 / Islay Dream / Bot.1997 / Velier
70cl / 43% - Velier - A 1980 vintage Port Ellen, Bottled as 'Islay Dream' in 1997 for Italian importer Velier.

Port Ellen 1981 / 15 YO / Cask Master Selection
70cl / 62.6% - Whisky Connoisseur - A single Cask 15 YO 1981 Port Ellen in the modestly-titled 'Cask Master' series by the equally-modestly-titled The Whisky Connoisseur independent Bottlers. Bottled at its massive full strength of 62.6% in April 1996.

Port Ellen 1981 / Bot.1999 / Connoisseurs Choice
70cl / 40% - Gordon & Macphail - A 1981 vintage Port Ellen, Bottled by Gordon & Macphail for the Connoisseurs Choice range way back in 1999. Quite rare to see a Port Ellen under twenty YO these days.

Port Ellen 1981 / Islay Festival 2008
70cl / 54.7% - Distillery Bottling - A very rare and special Bottle of Port Ellen, Distilled in 1981, Bottled for the 2008 Islay festival and originally only available at the festival. A legendary Bottling currently averaging a score of 92/100 from the Malt Maniacs.

Port Ellen 1982 / 13 YO / Hart Brothers
75cl / 43% - Hart Brothers - One of the few Port Ellens that was Bottled under 15 years of age - this Hart Brothers release of the 1982 vintage appeared in the mid-1990s and is now understandably rare as hen's teeth.

Port Ellen 1982 / 19 YO
70cl / 43% - McGibbon's

Port Ellen 1982 / 19 YO / Sherry Cask / Old Malt Cask
70cl / 50% - Douglas Laing - A 19 YO Port Ellen, Distilled in 1982 (the year before the Distillery closed), matured in Sherry Casks and Bottled in 2001 by Douglas Laing as part of their Old Malt Cask range.

Port Ellen 1982 / 19 YO / Sherry Cask / Old Malt Cask
70cl / 50% - Douglas Laing - A Port Ellen Distilled in 1982 (the year before the Distillery was closed) and then Bottled over a decade ago in 2001 by Douglas Laing under the Old Malt Cask label after 19 years in a Sherry Cask.

Port Ellen 1982 / 23 YO / Douglas of Drumlanrig
70cl / 45% - Douglas of Drumlanrig - Douglas of Drumlanrig is an offshoot label from indie Bottler Douglas Laing. These Bottles are endorsed (and purportedly selected) by the Duke of Buccleuch and Queensberry, the UK's largest private landowner. This single Cask of 23 YO Port Ellen from the 1982 vintage has been Bottled at 45%, and judging by the colour we reckon there's a good chance it was a Sherry Cask.

Port Ellen 1982 / 23 YO / Douglas of Drumlanrig
70cl / 49% - Douglas of Drumlanrig - A single Cask of 23 YO Port Ellen from the 1982 vintage Bottled at 49% by Douglas Laing offshoot Douglas of Drumlanrig for the Italian market. Douglas of Drumlanrig Bottles are endorsed (and purportedly selected) by the Duke of Buccleuch and Queensberry, the UK's largest private landowner.

Port Ellen 1982 / 23 YO / Sherry /
70cl / 51.8% - McGibbon's - Bottled for John Milroy

Port Ellen 1982 / 23 YO / Sherry Cask / John Milroy
70cl / 54.8% - McGibbon's - A 1982 vintage Port Ellen, selected by industry legend John Milroy and Bottled at 23 YO by McGibbon's for their Provenance range.

Port Ellen 1982 / 25 YO
70cl / 57% - Signatory - One of a clutch of new Port Ellen releases from Signatory, this is from a refill Sherry Butt.

Port Ellen 1982 / 25 YO
70cl / 50% - Douglas Laing - A 25 YO Port Ellen of the 1982 vintage, matured full term in a refill butt. Douglas Laing's Old Malt Cask range hit a really sweet spot around 2008 when this was Bottled, and being from a refill butt is unusual as well. We reckon this will be pretty good.

Port Ellen 1982 / 25 YO / Sherry Butt # 3400
70cl / 50% - Douglas Laing - Douglas Laing have released an enormous number of Port Ellens since the Old Malt Cask series was created at the turn of the millennium. This particular example is unusual as it's from a Sherry butt and was Bottled in clear glass so we can all see its lovely colour.

Port Ellen 1982 / 26 YO / Islay Whisky Shop
70cl / 50% - Douglas Laing - A rare Bottle of 1982 Port Ellen, Distilled in 1982 and Bottled from a refill Bourbon Cask at 26 YO exclusively for the Islay Whisky Shop, a legendary institution on everybody's famous Whisky paradise island.

Port Ellen 1982 / 30 YO
70cl / 54.2% - Douglas Laing - A 1982 vintage release of Port Ellen Whisky. This Whisky has been matured for 30 years in a refill hogshead and Bottled at Cask strength. Bottled by Douglas Laing for their Platinum Selection series.

Port Ellen 1982 / 30 YO / Cask #1518 / Chieftain's
70cl / 50.1% - Ian Macleod - A 30 YO Port Ellen from Ian Macleod's Chieftain's range. Distilled in 1982, Bottled in 2012 and released shortly after Diageo unveiled their own Port Ellen Special Release for the year. A few lucky people got to try this at The Whisky Show 2012 leading to some excellent reports.

Port Ellen 1982 / 30 YO / Douglas Laing Platinum
70cl / 51.8% - Douglas Laing - A 30 YO single Cask Whisky from closed Port Ellen released by Douglas Laing as part of their shiny Platinum Old & Rare range. Distilled in 1982 and Bottled in April 2012 at Cask strength.

Port Ellen 1982 / Bourbon Cask
70cl / 55.7%

Port Ellen 1982 / Northern Distillers
70cl / 59.8% - Independent Bottling - A single Cask release of Port Ellen Whisky. This Whisky was Distilled in 1982 and Bottled at

Cask strength in 1996 for Northern Distillers.

Port Ellen 1982 / Parkers Whisky
70cl / 56.8% - Independent Bottling - Another indie Port Ellen with an eccentric label, this time featuring a lovely pair of melons on the front.

Port Ellen 1982 / Royal Wedding Reserve
70cl / 53% - The Whisky Exchange - In celebration of the 2011 Royal Wedding TWE has selected a single Sherry Cask of Port Ellen and Bottled it on 29th April - the wedding day itself. The spirit was Distilled in 1982, the birth year of both bride and groom, and the year before the Distillery closed. It's a big, dark Cask-strength dram with rich, dry Sherrywood flavours.

Port Ellen 1983 / 14 YO
70cl / 43% - Hart Brothers - A 1983 vintage Whisky from closed cult Distillery Port Ellen, Bottled at 14 YO by Hart Brothers.

Port Ellen 1983 / 14 YO / Signatory
75cl / 43% - Signatory

Port Ellen 1983 / 23 YO
70cl / 46% - McGibbon's - A 1983 vintage Port Ellen, Distilled shortly before the Distillery closed and Bottled in Summer 2006 by McGibbon's under their Provenance label.

Port Ellen 1983 / 25 YO / Cask #4465
70cl / 46% - McGibbon's - A new single Cask Port Ellen 1983 from McGibbon's Provenance(aka Douglas Laing).

Port Ellen 1983 / 25 YO / Cask #5008
70cl / 46% - McGibbon's

Port Ellen 1983 / 26 YO / Cask #5133
70cl / 46% - McGibbon's - A rare Port Ellen 1983, originally Bottled for travel retail by Douglas Laing for their McGibbon's Provenance series. this is from a single refill butt and sounds very good from the Bottler's tasting notes.

Port Ellen 1983 / 28 YO / Cask #230 / Old Bothwell
70cl / 55.5% - Old Bothwell - A 28 YO Port Ellen from Old Bothwell, independent Bottlers of Port Ellen Whisky. This was disilled in 1983, the year that the Distillery closed.

Port Ellen 1983 / Cask Strength
70cl / 55% - Jean Boyer - A refill Sherry PE from French independent Bottler Jean Boyer. This is from a single Cask Bottled at Cask strength for JB's modestly-titled 'Best Casks of Scotland' series.

Port Ellen 21 YO / 25th Anniversary Maltings
70cl / 58.4% - Distillery Bottling - A truly legendary Port Ellen, Bottled for the 25th anniversary of the Port Ellen Maltings in 1998. The recipient of an incredible 94 point score from Serge Valentin's Whiskyfun.com, this is one of those rare Port Ellens that really lives up to the hype.

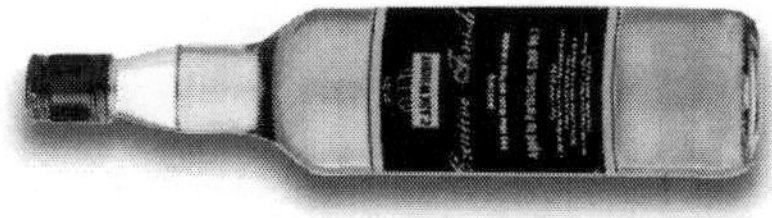

ISLAND REGION

ABHAINN DEARG RANGE

Abhainn Dearg / Spirit of Lewis
50cl / 46%- Distillery Bottling - Spirit of Lewis is Single Malt spirit from the Abhainn Dearg Distillery on the Isle of Lewis. Bottled from a single Cask at 46%, Spirit of Lewis has been aged for less than three years and therefore cannot legally be called Whisky.

Abhainn Dearg 2008 / First Bottling
50cl / 46%
Distillery Bottling - A little piece of Whisky history here - the first legal Single Malt Whisky made at the Abhainn Dearg (Red River) Distillery in Uig on the Outer Hebridean Isle of Lewis. Established in 2008, Abhainn Dearg is the most westerly Distillery in Scotland.

ARRAN RANGE

Arran 10 YO
70cl / 46%
Distillery Bottling
Arran 10 YO is a medium-bodied, citrussy dram that shows an elegance and deftness of touch that belies the Distillery's youth. Tasting the complexity and assurance of this youngster it is difficult to believe that the Distillery only opened in 1995. A great achievement.

Arran 12 YO / Cask Strength
70cl / 54.1% - Distillery Bottling - A Cask strength of Arran's excellent entry level 12 YO Whisky. Spicy with the kick that Cask strength Whisky gives.

Arran 1996 / 15 YO / Sherry Cask #1968
70cl / 53.9% - Distillery Bottling - A 1996 vintage Whisky from Arran, Distilled on December 11th and Bottled on October 1st 2012 after 15 years of maturing in Sherry Cask number 1968.

Arran 1998 / 10 YO / 250th Anniversary Robert Burns
70cl / 43% - Distillery Bottling - A special Bottling of Isle of Arran 1998 released to celebrate the 250th Anniversary of the birth of the Scottish Bard, which was on Burns Night 2009.

Arran 1998 / 12 YO / Sherry Cask #513

70cl / 56.4% - Distillery Bottling - A single Cask release of Arran Whisky, Distilled on 20th April 1998 and Bottled in 2010. This Whisky has been matured in a Sherry Cask Bottled at Cask strength.

Arran 1998 / Bourbon Cask #659
70cl / 57.8% - Distillery Bottling - A single Cask Whisky from the Isle of Arran, Distilled in 1998 and Bottled in February 2010 after maturing in a Bourbon Cask.

Arran 2004 / Orkney Bere
70cl / 46% - Distillery Bottling - A 2004 vintage Whisky from Arran, produced from Bere barley, the oldest cultivated barley strain used in Scotland, as a collaboration with the Agronomy Institute of Orkney College. It hasn't been used for Whisky making since the middle of the 19th century and is not widely grown, with this Whisky's raw materials coming from Orkney.

Arran Machrie Moor / Second Edition / Peated
70cl / 46% - Distillery Bottling - The second batch of Arran's peated 'Machrie Moor', named for the ancient peat bog on the west end of the Isle of Arran and with a picture of Bran on the Bottle, the faithful hound who accompanied legendary giant Fingal around the island when not tethered to a standing stone on Machrie Moor.

HIGHLAND PARK RANGE

Highland Park / Bot.1970s
75cl / 43% - Gordon & Macphail - A beautiful old G&M Bottling of no-age-statement Highland Park from the 1970s, complete with the traditional-style label recently recreated for the Magnus trilogy.

Highland Park 12 YO
70cl / 40% - Distillery Bottling

Highland Park 12 YO
70cl / 40% - Distillery Bottling - Highland Park 12 YO remains one of the gold standard malts for other Distillery Bottlings to aspire to. With a delicious sweetness (heather-honey is their preferred description), a trace of smoke and a warming, silky mouthfeel, this is a Whisky that never lets you down.

World Whiskies Awards 2012 - Best Island 12 years and under

Highland Park 12 YO / Bot.1980s
75cl / 43% - Distillery Bottling

Highland Park 12 YO / Bot.1980s
75cl / 40% - Distillery Bottling

Highland Park 16 YO
100cl / 40% - Distillery Bottling - A litre of Highland Park's discontinued 16 YO Whisky, previously destined for the travel retail market.

Highland Park 18 YO
70cl / 43% - Distillery Bottling - Highland Park 18 YO is one of the all-time greats of the Single Malt world. Delicious sweet Sherry notes alongside the heather-honey Distillery character, rounded with a wisp of dry smoke.

Highland Park 1958 / 40 YO
70cl / 44% - Distillery Bottling

Highland Park 1961 / 22 YO
75cl / 46% - Cadenhead's - An old Cadenhead's Bottling of Highland Park. This Whisky was Distilled in 1961 and Bottled in 1984, making it 22 YO.

Highland Park 1964 / Orcadian Vintage
70cl / 42.2% - Distillery Bottling - Bottled in 2009 from two refill hogsheads, this Highland Park 1964 is the inaugural release in the Distillery's Orcadian Vintage series. The packaging for this series is spectacular, with a heavy oak box featuring Viking design marquetry wood inlays and a handcrafted silver amulet on the front. Just 290 Bottles of this stunning Highland Park have been released.

Highland Park 1967
70cl / 43% - Distillery Bottling - A 1967 vintage Highland Park, Bottled by the Distillery in 1991.

Highland Park 1967 / 36 YO

70cl / 49.7% - Distillery Bottling - A rare single Cask 1967 vintage Highland Park, Bottled at 36 YO and selected for their 'more discerning customers'.

Highland Park 1967 / 38 YO / Split Cask
75cl / 55.5%

Distillery Bottling - Apparently this is the first time ever that someone has had the idea of Bottling half a Cask of Highland Park for release, and then Bottling the rest a few months later for a separate release. Tan Tan Ta-Raaaa!

Highland Park 1968 / Orcadian Vintage
70cl / 45.6% - A mix of seven hogsheads and one butt (all refill Casks), Highland Park 1968 is the second in the Distilery's Orcadian Vintage series. The packaging for this series is spectacular, with a heavy oak box featuring Viking design marquetry wood inlays and a handcrafted silver amulet on the front.

Highland Park 1970 / 19 YO / Gordon & Macphail
75cl / 52.9% - Gordon & Macphail - A very interesting 19 YO Highland Park from the 1970 vintage Bottled by G&M at what they call 100 proof, but which is actually a little higher, at 52.9%.

Highland Park 1970 / Orcadian Vintage
70cl / 48% - Another entry in Highland Park's impressive Orcadian Vintages range - a Whisky made from a marriage of Casks Distilled in 1970. This continues the series incredible presentation, with a heavy dark glass Bottle and hand detailed wooden box.

Highland Park 1974 / 34 YO Ambassador's Cask 5
70cl / 41.5% - Distillery Bottling - The last of the legendary series of Cask strength Bottlings from individual Casks selected by Highland Park's brand ambassador Gerry Tosh. This one is from a refill hogshead and has a relatively low natural strength, allowing the Distillery character to sing with concentrated honey, soft smoke and rancio-esque oak flavours earning it 91 points from Whisky gourmet Serge Valentin at Whiskyfun.

Highland Park 1976 / Orcadian Vintage
70cl / 49.1% - Distillery Bottling - The fifth entry in Highland Park's super-premium Orcadian Vintages range, and one of the highlights of The Whisky Show 2011. Vatted from 13 American oak Casks, a mix of butts and hoghseads, and presented in a box illustrated to celebrate Orkney's Scandinavian heritage.

Highland Park 1977 / 21 YO / Bicentenary
70cl / 40% - Distillery Bottling

Highland Park 1977 / 21 YO / Bicentenary
75cl / 43% - Distillery Bottling - A 21 YO Single Malt Whisky from Highland Park, Distilled in 1977 and Bottled in 1998 in celebration of the Distillery's 200 anniversary.

Highland Park 1977 / 21 YO / Bicentenary/ Repatriation
70cl / 40% - Distillery Bottling - The re-packaged version of the famous Highland Park Bicentenary Bottle. Although the original version was believed to have sold out on release in 1997, hundreds of Bottles were found in a Japanese warehouse in 2008.

Highland Park 1977 / Scott's Selection
70cl / 48.1% - Scott's Selection - A 1977 Highland Park Bottled for the Scott's Selection range. Bottled at its natural Cask strength.

Highland Park 1980 / Sherry Cask #8421
70cl / 50.5% - Distillery Bottling - A single Cask Bottling Sherry Cask matured Highland Park Bottled in commemoration of a visit from Maxxium UK to the Distillery. Distilled on 16th October 1980 and selected on Thursday 31st of May ready for Bottling on its 21st birthday.

Highland Park 1987 / Macphail's / Gordon & Macphail
70cl / 43% - Gordon & Macphail - A 1987 vintage Whisky from Highland Park, Bottled by Gordon & Macphail as part of their Macphail's Collection.

Highland Park 1988 / 23 YO / Cask #716 / Mackillop's
70cl / 50.8% - Mackillop's - A 1988 vintage Highland Park, Bottled in March 2012 after 23 years of maturation by Mackillop's Choice.

Highland Park 1990
70cl / 40% - Highland Park's 1990 vintage Whisky, Bottled in 2010 at about 20 YO. A departure from their usual age statement Bottlings and originally created for distribution through travel retail.

Highland Park 1990 / 21 YO / Sherry Butt #15700
70cl / 53.9% - Signatory - A 21 YO Highland Park Bottled by Signatory. Distilled on December 13th 1990 and Bottled on the August 8th 2012 after maturing in a Sherry butt.

Highland Park 1991 / 20 YO / Cask #8091
70cl / 52.7% - Mackillop's - A 20 YO single Cask Whisky from

Highland Park, Distilled in 1991 and Bottled at Cask strength by Mackillop's in March 2012.

Highland Park 1991 / 21 YO / Sherry Butt #15121
70cl / 46%

Signatory - A 1991 vintage single Cask Whisky from Highland Park, distilled on 17th September and then matured in a Sherry butt for almost 22 years before being Bottled on November 6th 2012 by Signatory for their Un-chillfiltered Collection.

Highland Park 1991 / Sherry Wood / Mackillop's
70cl / 53.9% - Mackillop's - A Sherried Highland Park 1991, Bottled at full strength by Lorne Mackillop for the Mackillop's Choice series in 2007.

Highland Park 1992 / Cask #1233 / Montgomerie's
70cl / 46% - Montgomery's - A 1992 vintage Highland Park Bottled at 15 years of age by indie Bottler Montgomerie's.

Highland Park 1995 / 13 YO / Single Malts of Scotland
70cl / 46% - Speciality Drinks Ltd - Hints of heather, fudge and hazelnuts on the nose of this Single Malts of Scotland Highland Park 1995. The medium-bodied palate shows some hints of marmalade before a peppery finale.

Highland Park 1997 / 13 YO / Adelphi
70cl / 58% - Adelphi - An Adelphi Bottling of single Cask 13 YO Highland Park, Bottled in 2011. It was Distilled in 1997, a couple of years before they transferred into the hands of the current owners.

Highland Park 19 YO / Bot.1970s
75cl / 43% - Distillery Bottling - A glorious old 1970s Bottle of Highland Park in the green glass and dark label that the Distillery used in that era. This should be wonderful.

Highland Park 19 YO / Bot.1980s
75cl / 43% - Distillery Bottling - A very rare Bottling of Highland Park 19 YO from the 1980s. Bottled for the Italian market in the distinctive dumpy Bottle the Distillery was using back then.

Highland Park 2001 / Cask #3006-8
70cl / 57.1% - Gordon & Macphail - A 2001 vintage Highland Park released by Gordon & Macphail as part of their Cask Strength

range. A vatting of three Casks, #3006-8, it has been Bottled at a Cask strength of 57.1%.

Highland Park 21 YO
70cl / 47.5% - Distillery Bottling - A 2012 re-release of Highland Park 21 back at its old strength of 47.5% after a few years of languishing at a lower strength due to stock shortages. This has been much sought after in the travel retail sector and it's good to see it back on our shelves again. Absolutely terrific stuff.

Highland Park 21 YO
70cl / 40% - Distillery Bottling - A shortlived official Bottling of Highland Park 21 YO, this was the second edition launched in duty free and was Bottled at the lower strength of 40%. HP21 was later discontinued altogether to make way for the 1990 vintage Bottling.

Highland Park 25 YO
70cl / 45.7% - Distillery Bottling - A late 2012 release of Highland Park's excellent 25 YO Whisky. A mix of ex-Sherry and Bourbon Cask matured Whisky to balance honey with rich fruit, as well as a lick of the Distilleries trademark Orcadian peatiness.

Highland Park 30 YO
70cl / 48.1% - Distillery Bottling - Until the arrival of the 40YO, this was the ne plus ultra of the standard range of proprietary Bottlings from Highland Park. A Whisky of extraordinary depth and intensity of flavour.

Highland Park 40 YO
70cl / 48.3% - Distillery Bottling - An outstanding Highland Park, Bottled at a remarkable 40 YO. They've done a good job on the presentation, too - extremely heavy box with proper hinges and magnetic closure, with a leather-bound booklet inside extolling the virtues of Distillery and dram.

'WORLD'S BEST NEW RELEASE - World Whiskies Awards 2009'

Highland Park 50 YO
70cl / 44.8% - Distillery Bottling - Another stunning packaging job for this limited release of fifty-year-old Highland Park 1960, featuring a sterling silver abstract 'cage' around the Bottle by Scottish artist Maeve Gillies and a natural-look wooden box. The official tasting notes suggest a Sherry influence on this, with tobacco, raisins and cooked fruit.

Highland Park 8 YO / 100 Proof / Bot.1970s
75.7cl / 57.1% - Gordon & Macphail - An 8 YO Gordon & Macphail release of Highland Park, Bottled in clear glass at 100 proof (57.1% ABV) in the 1970s.

Highland Park 8 YO / Bot.1960s
75cl / 43% - Distillery Bottling - An old release of Highland Park from the 1970s, Bottled younger than today at 8 YO.

Highland Park 8 YO / Bot.1970s
75.7cl / 40% - Distillery Bottling - An 8 YO Whisky from Highland Park, Bottled under their old brown label in the 1970s.

Highland Park 8 YO / Bot.1980s
75cl / 43% - Distillery Bottling - A 1980s Bottling of 8 YO Highland Park, with the old label picturing the Distillery.

Highland Park 8 YO / Bot.1980s
75cl / 40% - Distillery Bottling - An old Bottle of Highland Park 8 YO Whisky. We estimate that this was Bottled sometime in the 1980s.

Highland Park 8 YO / Macphail's Collection
70cl / 40% - Gordon & Macphail - An 8 YO Whisky from Highland Park Bottled by Gordon and Macphail for their Macphail's Collection range.

Highland Park Leif Eriksson
70cl / 40% - Distillery Bottling - Originally released in March 2011, Leif Erikson was originally a travel retail exclusive that we've managed to get a few Bottles of. In celebration of Erikson's trip to the New World it is made up of ex-Bourbon and Sherry Casks, all made from American oak.

Highland Park St. Magnus 12 YO / Edition 2
70cl / 55% - Distillery Bottling - The second edition of Highland Park's Magnus series sees the former Earl elevated to sainthood after his canonisation following his murder by an evil relative.

ISLE OF JURA RANGE

Isle of Jura 10 YO
70cl / 40% - Distillery Bottling - Isle of Jura 10 YO is a very accessible, easy-drinking malt. Medium-bodied with a delicate sweet palate, with a hint of brine developing on the finish. A great introductory malt.

Isle of Jura 16 YO
70cl / 40% - Distillery Bottling - With the smoothness of the 10 year-old allied to extra complexity from more ageing, this is a winner. 'A delicious and sophisticated dram with impressive depth and almost perfect weight.'

Isle of Jura 18 YO
70cl / 40% - Distillery Bottling - Introduced in 2007, this 18 YO Isle of Jura was brought in to replace the discontinued 21 year-old.

Isle of Jura 1965 / 36 YO
70cl / 44% - Distillery Bottling - A 36 YO single Cask Whisky from Isle of Jura, Distilled in 1965 and Bottled in the early years of the new millennium.

Isle of Jura 1966 / 35 YO / Signatory
70cl / 42.7% - A 1966 vintage Signatory Bottling of 35 YO Whisky from the Isle of Jura, presented in a wooden box complete with nosing glass and a miniature sample, so you can have a taste before you crack the big Bottle.

Isle of Jura 1976 / 'Feith A' Chaorainn'
70cl / 46% - Distillery Bottling - A beautifully aged 1976 vintage from the folks at Isle of Jura. Its gaelic name, Feith A' Chaorainn, means 'The lands around the Rowan Tree', an excellent description of Jura and its long traditions and superstitions based around the Rowan. IWSC 2012 - Gold Medal - Whisky - Scotch

Isle of Jura 1993 / Sherry Ji Finish
70cl / 54% - Distillery Bottling - This Isle of Jura 1993 is part of the Distillery's 'Boutique Barrels' series of single Casks, Bottled at full Cask strength. This 'Sherry Ji' edition has been finished in Oloroso Sherry butts.

Isle of Jura Boutique Barrels

Isle of Jura 1995 / Bourbon Jo Finish
70cl / 56.5% - Distillery Bottling - This Isle of Jura 1995 is part of the Distillery's 'Boutique Barrels' series of single Casks, Bottled at full Cask strength. This 'Bourbon Jo' edition has been finished in 'small batch Bourbon Cask', according to the label.

Isle of Jura 1999 / 5 YO
70cl / 61.3% - Distillery Bottling - A five-year-old from a famous experimental peaty batch of Jura Bottled by Matthew Forrest for the Japanese market - boisterous enough to wreak a delightfully

playful havoc on the tastebuds.

Isle of Jura 21 YO
75cl / 43% - Distillery Bottling - An explosion of soft citrus fruits, yet spicy and warm, as the lingering wood tones unfold in perfect harmony. A great Whisky at a great price for this age.

Isle of Jura 21 YO
70cl / 44% - Distillery Bottling - A continuation on from Jura's 200th anniversary edition, well aged for 21 years and presented in a box with built in display plinth.

Isle of Jura 30 YO / Bot. 2010
70cl / 40% - Distillery Bottling - A very snazzy leather box containing a Bottle of Jura's finest 30 year-old Single Malt, in a limited edition of 1200 Bottles. The perfect gift for the Jura fan.

Isle of Jura 8 YO / Bot.1980s
75cl / 40% - Distillery Bottling

Isle of Jura Prophecy / Peated
70cl / 46% - Distillery Bottling - Isle of Jura's 'profoundly peated' Prophecy Bottlings are released in small batches and are drier, stronger and smokier than the standard Superstition peated IOJ.

Isle of Jura Superstition
70cl / 43% - Distillery Bottling - A union of two Jura malt Whisky styles: one bold, strong and peated, the other warm and delicate. Superstition is a unique Whisky created from the marriage of traditional Islay style peated barley and a selection of aged malts.

Isle of Jura Superstition
35cl / 43% - Distillery Bottling - A half Bottle of Jura's Superstition, combining both their hefty almost Islay style Whisky and their more delicate well aged spirit for an interesting and complex mix.

Jura 1976 / 35 YO / Cask #888 / Berry Brothers & Rudd
70cl / 53.5%

Berry Bros & Rudd - A 35 YO single Cask Whisky from the Isle of Jura, Distilled in 1976 and Bottled in 2012 by Berry Brothers & Rudd. This one comes from Cask 888, so we suspect this may be snapped up by fans of lucky numbers.

Jura 1976 / 35 YO / Cask #889 / Berry Brothers & Rudd

70cl / 55.1% - Berry Bros & Rudd - A sister Cask to Berry Bros's lucky numbered #888 single Cask Bottling released at the same time as this, Distilled in 1976 and Bottled in 2012 at 35 YO.

SCAPA RANGE

Scapa 12 YO
70cl / 40% - Distillery Bottling - This is a Bottling that many fans of this underrated Distillery still have a soft spot for - the unpretentious old-style Scapa 12 YO: an easygoing dram, delightfully honeyed and malty. Replaced by the short-lived, unloved 14 YO shortly before owners Allied sold up to Pernod Ricard.

Scapa 12 YO
100cl / 40% - Distillery Bottling - An old litre Bottle presentation of Scapa. This Whisky has been aged for at least 12 years.

Scapa 14 YO
70cl / 40% - Distillery Bottling - From a tiny Distillery in Orkney, Scapa is often overlooked in favour of its more famous neighbour Highland Park. However, under new ownership and back in production after being mothballed for a time, this is a Distillery on the up.

Scapa 16 YO
70cl / 40% - Distillery Bottling - The initially controversial 16 YO official expression of Scapa is now winning people round with a jump in quality after a few wobbly years following the rapid transition from the much-loved 12 YO via the short-lived 14 YO. Orkney's less shouted about (but still lovely in its own way) malt Whisky has found its feet. World Whiskies Awards 2012 - Best Island 13 to 20 years

Scapa 1980 / 25 YO
70cl / 54% - Distillery Bottling - Scapa 1980 is a belter of a malt from a Distillery frequently overlooked in favour of its more famous Orcadian neighbour, Highland Park. Well-presented and Bottled at natural Cask strength for added oomph.

Scapa 2001 / Gordon & Macphail
70cl / 43% - Gordon & Macphail - A 2001 vintage Whisky from Orkney's 'other Distillery' - Scapa. This has been Bottled by independent heroes Gordon & Macphail.

Scapa 8 YO / G&M / Bot.1970s
75cl / 57.1% - Gordon & Macphail - A 1970s release of 8 YO Whis-

ky from Scapa, Bottled by Gordon & Macphail.

TALISKER RANGE

Secret Stills No 1.2 (Talisker) 1986
70cl / 45% - Gordon & Macphail - Another 'secret' release from a Distillery on Skye, ho-hum, who on earth could that be?! Glorious colour from 21 years in first fill Sherry butts - if you want one of these you'll need to be quick as it's unlikely to be hanging around.

Talisker - Isle of Eigg
70cl / 60%

A special release of Talisker Whisky which has been Bottled at a fantastic 60% and released without an age statement or vintage. Bottled to celebrate the historic purchase of the Isle of Eigg by the Isle of Eigg Heritage in 1997.

Talisker / Bot.1980s
75cl / 43% - Gordon & Macphail - An old NAS Bottle of Talisker, Bottled by Gordon & Macphail sometime in the 1980s.

Talisker / Distillery Only
70cl / 60% - Distillery Bottling - A very rare and highly sought-after no-age-statement Talisker special vatting that was only available at the Distillery from around 2004.

Talisker 10 YO
70cl / 45.8% - Distillery Bottling - A massive success as the island representative in Diageo's 'Classic Malts' series, Talisker 10 YO's profile keeps increasing as more fans discover its intense coastal spicy, peaty character. A truly elemental malt.
Malt Maniacs Awards 2010: Best Natural Cask Award 2010 (Daily Drams)

Talisker 12 YO / Bot.1970s
75cl / 43% - Distillery Bottling - A lovely old Bottle of Talisker 12 YO from the 1970s, sporting the 'TD' logo of Scottish Malt Distillers' subsidiary Dailuaine-Talisker Distillers Ltd on the front label.

Talisker 12 YO / Bot.1980s
75cl / 43% - Distillery Bottling - An old Distillery Bottling of Talisker 8 YO from the 1980s, featuring the Johnnie Walker Striding Man at the top of the front label.

Talisker 12 YO / Friends of Classic Malts
70cl / 45.8% - Distillery Bottling - A special Bottling for the Friends of the Classic Malts, this is a 12 year-old Bottled at the classic Talisker strength of 45.8% and is a definite step up in depth and class from the always-terrific 10 year-old. Spicy, peppery and complex - delicious.

Talisker 175th Anniversary
70cl / 45.8% - Distillery Bottling - Commemorating 175 years of Talisker Distillery, this release of the Classic Malt is a complex vatting of Talisker Casks of various ages (many over 20). A sleek, peppery, elegantly muscular celebration of this fabulous Distillery.

Talisker 18 YO
70cl / 45.8% - Distillery Bottling - One of our all-time favourite malts, Talisker 18 YO is a masterpiece from one of Scotland's greatest Distilleries, and was named 'Best Single Malt Whisky in the World' at the World Whiskies Awards in 2007. Stunning balance of peat, spice and sweetness.

Talisker 1947 / 35 YO / Gordon & Macphail
75cl / 40% - Gordon & Macphail

Talisker 1955 / Bot.1980s / Gortdon & Macphail
70cl / 40% - Gordon & Macphail - A very old and rare Bottle of Talisker 1955 Bottled by Gordon & Macphail.

Talisker 1955 / Cask Strength / Gordon & Macphail
70cl / 50.4% - Gordon & Macphail

Talisker 1955 / Cask Strength / Gordon & Macphail
70cl / 53.6% - Gordon & Macphail

Talisker 1956 / Bot.1980s / Gordon & Macphail
75cl / 54.4% - Gordon & Macphail

Talisker 1957 / Bot.1970s / Gordon & Macphail
75cl / 40% - An old Bottling of Talisker Whisky which was Distilled in 1957. We estimate that this was Bottled sometime in the 1970s.

Talisker 1958 / Bot.1980s / Gordon & Macphail
75cl / 40% - Gordon & Macphail - A marvellous old Bottle of 1958 vintage Talisker Bottled by Gordon & Macphail, probably around the early 1980s.

Talisker 1973 / 28 YO
70cl / 43.3% - Distillery Bottling Just 100 Bottles of this famous Talisker were released, yielded from what was at the time the oldest Cask at the Distillery (this was in the days before the superb 30 YO were introduced). Released through Oddbins initially, this extremely rare Bottling of one of Scotland's best malts sold out in a matter of hours and it retains its cachet and desirability to this day.

Talisker 1975 / 25 YO
70cl / 59.9% - Distillery Bottling - One of the great Taliskers, 6000 Bottles of this inaugural Bottling of the now-customary Special Releases Talisker 25 YO appeared in 2001. Talisker 1975 25 YO picked up 90 points from Whiskyfun's Serge Valentin in 2008 and remains the only officially-Bottled 25 YO to date with a specific vintage.

Talisker 1977 / 35 YO / Bot.2012
70cl / 54.6% - Distillery Bottling - A whopping 16th entry for Talisker in the annual Diageo Special Releases, this time the oldest Bottling offered by the Distillery so far - a 35 YO Whisky, Distilled in 1977 and matured in a mixture of refill American and European oak Casks.

Talisker 1981 / 20 YO / Sherry Cask
70cl / 62% - Distillery Bottling - Widely regarded as one of the finest Taliskers ever released. Simply stunning.

Talisker 1994 Managers' Choice / Sherry Cask
70cl / 58.6% - Distillery Bottling - A single Sherry Cask of Talisker 1994 Bottled at full strength as part of Diageo's Managers' Choice series. Bandages and bonfire aromas on the nose give way to a turfy, palate with some citrus also evident before a sweet finish.

Talisker 2000 / Distillers Edition
70cl / 45.8% - Distillery Bottling - The 2000 vintage of Talisker's ever popular and quite excellent Distillers Edition. Double matured, as are all of the range, with the finish being in Amoroso Casks, a sweetened Oloroso Sherry, adding some sweet and juicy fruit to Talisker smoke and maritime edge.

Talisker 25 YO / Bot. 2004
70cl / 57.8% - Distillery Bottling - Released in 2004, this beautifully orchestrated Talisker 25 YO has a full, generous palate, with hot spices balanced by delicious shortbread & syrupy notes. A really

awesome malt from a remarkably reliable Distillery.

Talisker 25 YO / Bot.2005
70cl / 57.2% - Distillery Bottling - Released in 2005, this was the third Talisker 25 YO to be released and was acclaimed at the time as being the best so far. Thankfully the standard has remained at an extraordinarily high level ever since.

Talisker 25 YO / Bot.2006
70cl / 56.9% - Distillery Bottling - There has yet to be a bad version of Talisker 25 yrs - distinguishing between the various releases is just a question of degrees of excellence.

Talisker 25 YO / Bot.2008
70cl / 54.2% - Distillery Bottling - A Talisker 25 YO from Diageo's Special Releases is always a thing to cherish - and this is no exception, with a very clean, citric emphasis when compared to some of the earlier releases. As we've come to expect from Talisker, this is nothing short of superb. Silver Medal Winner (The Malt Maniacs Awards 2009)

Talisker 25 YO / Bot.2009
70cl / 54.8% - Distillery Bottling - The latest Talisker 25 YO is another destined for the pantheon of fantastic expressions of Skye's finest. With a deceptive power hidden in a palate of incredible elegance, this is a classic iron-fist-velvet-glove Talisker par excellence.

Talisker 25 YO / Bot.2011
70cl / 45.8% - Distillery Bottling - Please welcome the 2011 entry into the ranks of superb Talisker 25 YOs. Where previous version of Tally 25 YO been released at fullstrength, 2011's edition is the first to be Bottled from refill Casks at Talisker's traditional strength of 45.8% (80 proof) with a slightly larger outturn than usual to let more people join in on the fun.

Talisker 30 YO / Bot.2006
70cl / 51.9% - Distillery Bottling - The highlight of 2006's super premium releases from Diageo. This was so popular that we sold through our initial allocation within weeks. This starts off as an elegant dram that builds on the palate to a powerful peaty, smoky, salty, peppery beast, it has complex coastal characters with notes of citrus and the most perfectly balanced finish.

Talisker 30 YO / Bot.2008

70cl / 49.5% - Distillery Bottling - A fancier box with a brass catch for 2008's Talisker 30 YO Special Release. The 2007 Bottling of this was magnificent and we've come to expect no less from what is arguably Diageo's most consistent Distillery.
Silver Medal Winner (The Malt Maniacs Awards 2009)

Talisker 30 YO / Bot.2009
70cl / 53.1% - Distillery Bottling - A delicious Talisker 30 YO, one of the highlights of this year's Special Releases. Very, very drinkable, with plenty of character but a restrained, elegant tone after three decades of mellowing in the wood.

Talisker 30 YO / Bot.2010
70cl / 57.3% - Distillery Bottling - One of the most consistently excellent of the super premium releases from Diageo, this Cask strength Talisker 30 YO is vatted from a mix of refill American and European oak Casks and sadly limited to less than 3000 Bottles worldwide.

Talisker 30 YO / Bot.2011
70cl / 45.8% - Distillery Bottling - The 2011 Bottling of Talisker's regularly appearing 30 YO Whisky, Bottled at the Distillery's traditional strength of 45.8%.

Talisker 57' North
70cl / 57% - Distillery Bottling - A Distillery-Bottled Cask strength Talisker, 57' North is deceptively smooth for a Whisky at this strength, but still a muscular presence on the palate, with the pepper and chili Talisker hallmarks very much in evidence.
World Whiskies Awards 2012 - Best Island No Age Statement

Talisker 57' North Bottle Flask
70cl / 57% - Distillery Bottling - A limited edition of Talisker 57' North with a free plastic flask and two stainless steel cups.

Talisker 8 YO / Bot.1960s
75cl / 43% - Distillery Bottling - A glorious old Bottle of 1960s Talisker 8 YO with a beautifully simplistic label design. This museum piece always has the collectors drooling.

Talisker 8 YO / Bot.1970s
75cl / 45.8% - Distillery Bottling

Talisker 8 YO / Clear Glass / Bot.1970s
75cl / 45.8%

A great looking Bottle of 8 YO Talisker, Bottled for the Distillery in the 1970s.

Talisker Pure Malt Whisky / Bot.1960s
75cl / 43% - Distillery Bottling - A wonderful old 1960's Distillery Bottling of Talisker at the more conventional strength of 43%, before they switched to 45.8%.

TOBERMORY RANGE

Ledaig (Tobermory) 2005 / 6 YO / Sherry Butt
70cl / 56% - Speciality Drinks Ltd - Ledaig is the peated spirit made at Tobermory Distillery on the Isle of Mull. This feisty young Cask strength whippersnapper shows plenty of muscle and exhibits flavours of bonfires, honey and fruit cake thanks to maturation in a Sherry Cask. A massive hit at 2012's TWE Whisky Show.

Tobermory / Bot.1980s / 1L
100cl / 43% - Distillery Bottling - A rare 1980s litre Bottle of Tobermory with a screenprinted label.

Tobermory 10 YO
70cl / 40% - Distillery Bottling - The unpeated malt from the producers of Ledaig, Tobermory hails from the Isle of Mull and is a more gentle medium-bodied, accessible malt than its peated sister. A good aperitif malt.

Tobermory 10 YO
70cl / 46.3% - Distillery Bottling - New packaging for Tobermory 10 in 2011 and a modern look for this Mull Distillery that also produces the peaty Ledaig.

Tobermory 15 YO
70cl / 46.3% - Distillery Bottling - Beautifully-presented Bottle of Tobermory. The Whisky is matured in Gonzalez Byass Oloroso Sherry Casks and the Casks mature on the mainland before travelling back to Mull for the final year before Bottling.

Tobermory 1972 / 6 YO / Connoisseurs Choice
75cl / 43% - Gordon & Macphail - A young Tobermory from the 1972 vintage Bottled at 6 YO by Gordon & Macphail for their Connoisseurs Choice series.

Tobermory 1972 / The Animals / Moon Import
75cl / 46% - Moon Import - The Animals is a series of legendary and highly sought-after Bottlings from Italian company Moon Import. This 1972 Tobermory was a vatting of five sister Casks

Bottled in 1990, and comes with a label featuring some nice illustrations of frogs.

Tobermory Bicentenary
70cl / 40% - - Distillery Bottling - A rare screen-printed Bottle of Tobermory, one of only 2500 produced in 1998 to mark the Bicentenary of the Distillery.

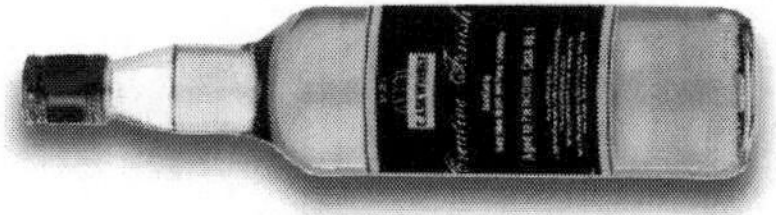

SCOTLAND: Scotland is divided into six Whisky-producing regions, Campbelltown, Highland, Islay, Isles, Lowland and Speyside.

CAMPBELLTOWN REGION

GLEN SCOTIA RANGE

Glen Scotia 1966 / 27 YO
70cl / 51.5% - A rare Signatory release of Glen Scotia 1966, Bottled at twenty-seven YO in the mid-1990s from two sister Casks.

Glen Scotia 1969 / 30 YO / Old Malt Cask
70cl / 50% - Douglas Laing- An Old Malt Cask release of 1969 vintage Glen Scotia, Bottled at the turn of the millennium after 30 years of maturation.

Glen Scotia 1975 / 28 YO
70cl / 46% - - Murray McDavid

Glen Scotia 1977 / 32 YO / Dun Bheagan
70cl / 56% - A Dun Bheagan Bottling of Glen Scotia from Ian Macleod. Distilled in 1977 and Bottled 32 years later.

Glen Scotia 1977 / 35 YO / Cask #2750
70cl / 52.5% - . A 1977 vintage Glen Scotia Bottled by Signatory for French Whisky retailer La Maison du Whisky. We've managed to grab a few Bottles of this distinctively purple labelled Bottle, which was Distilled on September 5th 1977 and Bottled shortly after its 35th birthday on September 17th 2012.

Glen Scotia 1991 / Strawberry Ganache / Wemyss
70cl / 46%- Wemyss Malts are all named after the flavours that have been found within each Bottle. Their 1991 vintage Glen Scotia has been named "Strawberry Ganache" so expect sweet fruity and chocolatey notes throughout.

Glen Scotia 1992 / 16 YO / Cask #4436
70cl / 50% - Douglas Laing - A new Glen Scotia 1992, Bottled from a single refill hogshead by Douglas Laing for their Old Malt Cask series.

Glen Scotia 1992 / 18 YO / Sherry Cask #7017
70cl / 50% - Douglas Laing - A single Cask release of Glen Scotia,

Distilled in 1992. This Whisky has been matured for 18 years in a Sherry Cask and Bottled at 50% for Douglas Laing's Old Malt Cask series.

Glen Scotia 1992 / Cask Strength / Gordon & Macphail
70cl / 59.9% - Gordon & Macphail. A small batch of three refill Hoggies from Glen Scotia, Campbeltown's other distillery, for this new release in G & M's consistently great 'Cask' series. The colour is great and the strength is nudging 60%, so this should be pretty intense.

Glen Scotia 1992 / Macphail's Collection
70cl / 43% - Gordon & Macphail - A Single Malt from Campbeltown Distillery Glen Scotia, this is from the 1992 vintage and has been Bottled by G&M as part of their Macphail's Collection.

Glen Scotia 5 YO / Bot.1960s
75cl / 40% - Distillery Bottling - A marvellous old Distillery-Bottled 5 YO Glen Scotia Bottled for the Italian market in the 1960s.

Glen Scotia 8 YO / Bot.1960s
75cl / 43% - Distillery Bottling - Flat Bottle

Glen Scotia 8 YO / Bot.1980s
75cl / 40% - Distillery Bottling - An old official Bottling of sweet, grassy Glen Scotia 8 YO. This is a Distillery Bottling from the 1980s.

Glen Scotia 5 YO / Bot.1960s
75cl / 40% - Distillery Bottling - A marvellous old Distillery-Bottled 5 YO Glen Scotia Bottled for the Italian market in the 1960s.

Glen Scotia 8 YO / Bot.1960s
75cl / 43% - Distillery Bottling - Flat Bottle

Glen Scotia 8 YO / Bot.1980s
75cl / 40% - Distillery Bottling - An old official Bottling of sweet, grassy Glen Scotia 8 YO. This is a Distillery Bottling from the 1980s.

HAZELBURN RANGE

Hazelburn / Directors Bottling
70cl / 46% - Distillery Bottling - First Bottling, Only 65 Bottles

made for Directors, Staff & Shareholders.

Hazelburn 12 YO / 2010 Release
70cl / 46% - Distillery Bottling - The 2010 official release for Hazelburn, Springbank's triple-Distilled, unpeated Single Malt, which is now fully mature. It's quite a colour too, suggesting some Sherry influence in the final make-up. Well-priced, we expect this to go quickly.

Hazelburn 1997
70cl / 56.2% - Distillery Bottling.

Hazelburn 1998 / 8 YO / Cask Strength
70cl / 58.7% - Distillery Bottling - A Cask strength edition of Hazelburn, Springbanks unpeated triple-Distilled malt. This very rare 8 YO was Bottled for the Springbank Society in 2006.

Hazelburn 2002 / 8 YO / Sauternes Finish
70cl / 55.9% - Distillery Bottling - Amazing colour on this triple-Distilled Hazelburn 2002 from Springbank - the result of a three year second maturation in Sauternes Casks after an initial 5 year period in refill Bourbon wood.

Hazelburn 8 YO
70cl / 46% -Distillery Bottling - A youngish one from Hazelburn, Springbank's triple-Distilled, unpeated Single Malt. A more Lowland-esque dram than its Campbelltown origins might suggest.

Hazelburn 8 YO / 1st Release
70cl / 46% - Distillery Bottling - Hazelburn Whisky is Distilled at Springbank Distillery and is triple Distilled and completely unpeated. This special first release of Whisky has been aged for 8 years and is available in three different presentations. Limited to just 5100 Bottles, this is a definite collectors piece.

Hazelburn CV
70cl / 46% - Hazelburn is the unpeated malt made by Springbank at their Campbeltown Distillery. This 'CV' edition is a blend of different ages designed to act as the perfect introduction to the Hazelburn style.

KILKERRAN

Kilkerran (Glengyle) Work in Progress 4
70cl / 46% - Distillery Bottling - The fourth limited release of Springbank's Glengyle Distillery's Kilkerran "Work in Progress"

Single Malt Whisky, although the tasting notes make it sound like they may be almost there, especially after it won the 'Best Natural Casks' award in the Daily Drams category at the 2012 Malt Maniacs Awards.

LONGROW RANGE

Campbeltown "Fragments of Scotland" (Longrow 1973)
75cl / 50% - Samaroli - A legendary Longrow 1973, Bottled at 50% in 1988 by Samaroli as part of their Fragments of Scotland series. This one is interesting as it's less smoky than the OB's of the same vintage (the first year that Longrow was Distilled at Springbank), though it still scooped a huge 92 point score from Serge on Whiskyfun.

Longrow 14 YO
70cl / 46% - Distillery Bottling - A 14 YO expression of Longrow, Springbank's peated malt, put together from a combination of Bourbon and Sherry Casks. Rich smokey goodness.

Longrow 14 YO / Bot.1980s
75cl / 46% - This rare Longrow from the 1980's does not come up very often. We believe only a small batch was done which was sold only through the Cadenheads shop in Edinburgh.

Longrow 1973 / Bot.1980s
75cl / 46% - Distillery Bottling - A legendary Bottling of Longrow from 1973, the first year that Springbank made this peated malt (and still regarded by many as the best vintage).

Longrow 1973 / First Distillation
70cl / 43.2% - Distillery Bottling - A very rare 1973 vintage Longrow, Bottled from one of the Casks produced as part of the first Distillation of Springbank's heavily peated variant.

Longrow 1973 / The Birds / Moon Import
75cl / 46% - Moon Import - A 1973 Longrow Bottled by Italian import Moon as part of their beautifully labelled 'The Birds' series.

Longrow 1973 Natural Strength / Bot.1985 / Samaroli
75cl / 53% -Samaroli- One of the stupendous Cask strength Longrows Bottled in the 1980s by legendary Italian Bottler Samaroli. These extraordinary Whiskies from Longrow's first vintage sealed the reputation of Springbank's peated malt.

Longrow 1974 / 16 YO / Sherry Cask
75cl / 46% - Distillery Bottling - A 16 YO Whisky from Longrow, Distilled in 1974 and matured entirely in Sherry Casks.

Longrow 1974 / 16 YO / Sherry Cask
75cl / 46% -Distillery Bottling - A Sherry Cask matured 16 YO Longrow from 1974, closed with a cork stopper.

Longrow 1974 / 18 YO
70cl / 54.7% - Cadenhead's - An 18 YO Longrow, the smokier of the drams produced by Springbank, Bottled by Cadenhead's. Both Sprinbank and Cadenhead's have been owned by the same company since the 1970s, making this an intriguing Bottle.

Longrow 1974 / Sherry Cask
75cl / 56% - Samaroli - A quite legendary Sherried Longrow from the batch of stunning Casks secured by the far-sighted Italian firm Samaroli long before Cask-strength bottlings were de rigeur. This was one of the earliest Longrows, Distilled just a year after production started at Springbank in 1973.

Longrow 1987 / 12 YO / Cask #141 / Samaroli Millennium
70cl / 55% - Samaroli - An explosion of peat, herbs, pepper and spices, this is a high-strength Longrow from Samaroli's legendary batch of 1987 vintage Casks. Bottled in 1999 to celebrate the Millennium.

Longrow 1990 / 9 YO
70cl / 46% - Murray McDavid - A rare single Cask ex-Bourbon Longrow Bottled around ten years ago by Murray McDavid.

Longrow 1993 / 13 YO
70cl / 46% -Distillery Bottling - A single Cask Whisky from Longrow. Distilled in 1993, aged for 13 years in Cask #635 and Bottled at 46%.

Longrow 1994 / 11 YO
70cl / 58% - Cadenhead's

Longrow 1995 / 10 YO
70cl / 46% - Distillery Bottling - A limited release 10 YO 1995 vintage of Longrow, the peated Single Malt made by the Springbank Distillery in Campbeltown.

Longrow 1995 / 10 YO / Tokaji Finish
70cl / 55.6% - Distillery Bottling -A Cask strength Longrow from Springbank that spent its last two years in a Tokaji Cask, adding some mouth-watering sweet notes and extra complexity.

Longrow 1996 / 10 YO
70cl / 46% - Distillery Bottling - A 1996 vintage Bottling of Longrow's 10 YO Whisky, the peatier dram Distilled at Springbank. A balanced sweet and smokey dram with a hint of brine.

Longrow 1997 / 14 YO / Burgundy Wood
70cl / 56.1% - Distillery Bottling - A wine Cask finished malt from Longrow, part of their regular series of full proof Bottlings exploring interesting wood. This one was matured for 11 years in refill Bourbon Casks before re-Casking in fresh Burgundy Casks for a 3 year finish.

Longrow Red / 11 YO / Cabernet Sauvignon Finish
70cl / 52.1% - Distillery Bottling - Longrow is the peaty Whisky produced at Springbank Distillery. This Whisky has been aged for 7 years in refill Bourbon barrels and then finished for 4 years in Cabernet Sauvignon hogsheads. Expect a peaty yet fruity experience.

SPRINGBANK RANGE

Springbank 10 YO
70cl / 46% - Distillery Bottling - Springbank 10's relatively light colour belies its richness of character. The nose moves from citrus fruits to pears and a hint of peat, while the palate shows touches of smoke, vanilla essence, nutmeg, cinnamon and the salty tang characteristic of the Distillery. A winner at the World Whisky Awards 2010.

Springbank 10 YO / Bot.1980s
75cl / 46% -Distillery Bottling

Springbank 10 YO / Sherry Cask / Bot.1970s
75cl / 59% - Distillery Bottling - A Sherry Cask matured Springbank 10 YO, Bottled by the Distillery in the 1970s at a hefty 59%.

Springbank 12 YO / 100 Proof
70cl / 57% - Distillery Bottling - A legendary Bottle of high strength Springbank 12 YO Bottled in the 1990s when the company was filling their 'standard' Bottlings with much older stock than was stated on the label. A fabulous Springbank that picked up 94 points from Whiskyfun's Serge.

Springbank 12 YO / Bot.1970s
75cl / 46% - Cadenhead's - A marvellous old Springbank 12 YO from the 1970s in an unusually tall green glass Bottle. One to get the collectors excited.

Springbank 12 YO / Bot.1980s
75cl / 43% - Distillery Bottling - A marvellous old Bottle of Springbank 12 YO from the 1980s, with the simple black label and distinctive Springbank gothic 'S'.

Springbank 12 YO Cask Strength / Batch 4
70cl / 52.2% - Distillery Bottling - The Cask strength release of Sprinbank 12 YO has become more and more popular with each batch. This, the fourth, looks to be just as much of a crowd pleaser as its predecessors.

Springbank 15 YO
70cl / 46% - Distillery Bottling - Another fine malt for a Havana, Springbank 15 YO has an almost bewildering array of flavours: dark chocolate, figs, marzipan, brazil nuts and vanilla are just some of the notes on show. Absolutely top-class.

Springbank 15 YO / Bot.1970s
75cl / 43% - Distillery Bottling

Springbank 15 YO / Bot.1980s
75cl / 46% Distillery Bottling - A beautiful Bottle of Springbank's black labelled 15 YO, released back in the 1980s.

Springbank 15 YO / Bot.1990s
70cl / 46% Distillery Bottling - A Bottling of 15 YO Sprinbank released by the Distillery, probably around the early 1990s. This simply-packaged classic is increasingly difficult to find.

Springbank 175th Anniversay / 12 YO
70cl / 46% - Distillery Bottling - A special edition Springbank 12

YO, released as a batch of 12000 Bottles in 2003 to celebrate the Distillery's 175th anniversary.

Springbank 18 YO
70cl / 46% - Distillery Bottling - This is the second edition of Springbank's 18 YO, with a change of presentation to bring it into line with the rest of the range. The first edition of this was extremely popular, with more than a hint of Sherry amongst the Springbank brine and smoke, and this version has already been named as Best Campbeltown Malt aged 13-20 at the World Whisky Awards 2010..
World Whiskies Awards 2012 - Best Campbeltown and Best Campbeltown 13 to 20 years

Springbank 1919 / 50 YO / Bot.1970
75cl / 46% - Distillery Bottling. One of the rarest Single Malts ever released, This famous Springbank was once in the Guinness Book of Records as the world's most expensive Whisky. Just 24 Bottles of this liquid treasure from the 1919 vintage were Bottled at the Distillery in 1970. A magnificent museum piece of Whisky history.

Springbank 1954 / 25 YO / Cadenhead's
75cl / 45.7% - Cadenhead's - A 1954 vintage Springbank, aged for 25 years and Bottled by Cadenhead.

Springbank 1963 / White Label
70cl / 46% Distillery Bottling - An old Bottle of early 1960s Springbank, probably Bottled some time in the early to mid-1990s.

Springbank 1964
70cl / 46% - Distillery Bottling - An extremely rare Bottle of Springbank from 1964, right in the Distillery's prime. This was probably Bottled in the very early 1990s.

Springbank 1964 / 15 YO / Samaroli
75cl / 45.7% - Samaroli is an Italian independent Bottler, famed for the exceptional quality of their releases and for their arty, innovative labels and packaging.

Springbank 1964 / Distillery Label
70cl / 46% - Distillery Bottling

Springbank 1964 / Lateltin Lanz Ingold 100th Anniversary
70cl / 46% - Distillery Bottling - A 1964 vintage Springbank, Bottled in honour of the 100th anniversary of Swizz drinks importer Lateltin Lanz Ingold (aka Lateltin).

Springbank 1965
70cl / 46% - Distillery Bottling

Springbank 1965
70cl / 46% - Distillery Bottling - A 1965 vintage Whisky from Springbank, Bottled by the Distillery with a picture of the Distillery on the label.

Springbank 1965 / 29 YO
70cl / 46% Distillery Bottling - A very rare old 29 YO Springbank 1965 Bottled by the Distillery in the mid-1990s, this is from the Distillery's golden age and is likely to be a pretty stunning drop.

Springbank 1965 / 36 YO / Cask #8 / Local Barley
70cl / 47.6% - Distillery Bottling - Over the years Springbank Local Barley has become quite the sought-after Whisky, some even say that their finest Whisky is amongst these Bottlings. Each release is made using locally sourced materials, which Springbank claim are all from within an 8 mile radius of the Distillery (except the Casks of course).

Springbank 1965 / 36 YO / Local Barley
70cl / 50.4% - Distillery Bottling

Springbank 1965 / 36 YO / Local Barley
75cl / 51.3% - Distillery Bottling

Springbank 1965 / 36 YO / Local Barley
70cl / 49.1% - Distillery Bottling

Springbank 1965 / 36 YO / Local Barley
70cl / 52.4% - Distillery Bottling

Springbank 1965 / Bot.1980s
75cl / 46% - Distillery Bottling

Springbank 1965 / No.1 "The Golfing Greats"
75cl / 46% - Lombard - A 1965 vintage Whisky from indie retailer Lombard, Distilled on 30th April and Bottled from a vatting of 4 Casks. The tube features a picture of a golfer, hence the subtitle of 'Golfing Greats'.

Springbank 1966
70cl / 46% - Distillery Bottling

Springbank 1966 / 34 YO / Sherry Cask
70cl / 47.1% -Distillery Bottling

Springbank 1966 / Bot.1980s
75cl / 46% - Distillery Bottling - A super-rare Distillery Bottling of Springbank 1966 released in the 1980s before the phenomenal Local Barley Bottlings from the same vintage shot to fame.

Springbank 1966 / Bot.1990 / West Highland/ Sherry Cask #442
75cl / 61.2% - Distillery Bottling - One of a series of staggeringly good 1966 Springbanks Bottled at the beginning of the 1990s from Sherry Casks that have become so famous in Whisky circles as to take on an almost mythic status. The label artwork for this 'West Highland Malt' was to become iconic as well, becoming known as the 'Local Barley' series. An iconic Whisky.

Springbank 1966 / Distillery Label
70cl / 46% - Distillery Bottling

Springbank 1966 / Local Barley / Cask #476
70cl / 52% - Distillery Bottling

Springbank 1966 / Local Barley / Cask #486
70cl / 53% - Distillery Bottling - Cask #504 from Sprinbank, Distilled in 1966 and Bottled as part of the Local Barley series.

Springbank 1966 / Local Barley / Cask #489
70cl / 52% - Distillery Bottling - A 1966 vintage Springbank Bottled from Cask #489 as part of the Local Barley series.

Springbank 1966 / Local Barley / Cask #498
70cl / 55.3% - Distillery Bottling - Cask #498 from Springbank - Distilled in 1966 and Bottled as part of the Local Barley series.

Springbank 1966 / Local Barley / Cask #500
70cl / 54.2% - Distillery Bottling. Another of Springbank's legendary full strength Local Barley single Cask Bottlings from 1966. This particular Bottling has been aged 32 years.

Springbank 1966 / Local Barley / Cask #504
75cl / 55% - Distillery Bottling - A 1966 vintage Springbank, Bottled from Cask #504 as part of the legendary series of Local Barley Bottlings.

Springbank 1966 / Local Barley / Cask# 474
70cl / 51.2% - Distillery Bottling

Springbank 1966 / Local Barley / Cask:477
70cl / 53.6% Another of Springbank's legendary full strength Local Barley single Cask Bottlings from 1966. This particular Bottling has been aged 31 years.

Springbank 1966 / West Highland Malt / Sherry Cask #441
75cl / 60.7% - Distillery Bottling. One of a handful of pre-Local-Barley Cask strength Springbanks of quite stunning intensity. Bottled at the turn of the 1990s, we believe that these heavily-Sherried Springbanks rival Black Bowmore for sheer quality and flavour concentration - yet they are far rarer, being Bottled from single Casks. Amongst the greatest expressions ever Bottled by this legendary Distillery.

Springbank 1966 / West Highland Malt / Sherry Cask #443
75cl / 58.1% Distillery Bottling

Springbank 1966 Local Barley / Cask #478
70cl / 51.9% Distillery Bottling

Springbank 1967 / 20 YO / Sherry Cask
75cl / 46%- Signatory - Another legendary Bottling in the always-impressive Prestonfield, this 20 YO Springbank 1967 received 93-94 points from Malt Maniac Serge Valentin on Whiskyfun and despite being from a multi-Cask batch is now extremely difficult to find, having been Bottled in the late 1980s.

Springbank 1968 / 10 YO
75cl / 59% - Distillery Bottling

Springbank 1968 / 40 YO / Sherry Cask
70cl / 54% - Ian Macleod - A real treat here - a Cask-strength 40 YO Springbank 1968 Bottled for the Chieftain's range from a single Oloroso Sherry butt. This is a phenomenal Whisky - hats off to Ian Macleod for digging this up.

Springbank 1969 / 36 YO / Chieftain's
70cl / 57.3% - Ian Macleod - A Cask strength 1960s Springbank Bottled by Ian Macleod for their Chieftain's Choice series, this is a bargain when you look at how much official Springbanks from the same era go for these days.

Springbank 1969 / 40 YO / Cask #263
70cl / 54.4% - Signatory - A long-aged Cask strength Springbank 1969 Bottled from a single refill Sherry butt by Signatory as part of the Cask Strength Collection. Lovely natural colour on this, not too dark, so there should be plenty of Distillery character

remaining.

Springbank 1970 / 23 YO / Cask #1765
70cl / 46% - Distillery Bottling

Springbank 1970 / 23 YO / Cask 1766
70cl / 46% - Distillery Bottling

Springbank 1970 / 23 YO / Cask:1767
70cl / 46% - Distillery Bottling - A single Cask of Springbank 1970, Bottled by the Distillers in the early 1990s and released with the brilliant 'West Highland Malt' label made famous by the Local Barley series.

Springbank 1970 / 37 YO
70cl / 43% - Ian Macleod - Another of Ian Macleod's excellent single Cask Springbanks, this is from the 1970 vintage, and has been Bottled at 43%.

Springbank 1973 / 18 YO / Rum Butt
75cl / 57.5% - Cadenhead's - This 'Green Springbank' is legendary in collectors circles, not only for its curious colour, presumably the result of a full-term maturation in a rum Cask, but also for its incredible flavours. Serge Valentin rated the sister Bottling of at 93 points on Whiskyfun.

Springbank 1974 / 20 YO
70cl / 46% - Distillery Bottling - A Distillery Bottling of 1974 vintage Whisky from Springbank, one of only 960 Bottles in this batch.

Springbank 1974 / 27 YO
70cl / 56.6% - Ian Macleod

Springbank 1974 / 28 YO
70cl / 56% - Ian Macleod

Springbank 1974 / 29 YO / Cask #1777
70cl / 46% - Distillery Bottling

Springbank 1980 / Samaroli 20th Anniversary
75cl / 45% - Samaroli - A famous Bottling from the much-revered Italian independent Samaroli, for whose 20th anniversary this Sherried Springbank was selected in 1988.

Springbank 1991 / 13 YO
70cl / 54.2% - Campbeltown Single Malt Scotch Whisky
Murray McDavid

Springbank 1991 / 19 YO / Murray McDavid
70cl / 56.1% - Murray McDavid - A 1991 vintage Springbank, Bottled by Murray McDavid at Bruichladdich (their Distillery) in 2011 with no chill-filtering or artificial colour. This was matured for 19 years in a refill Sherry Cask and has picked up a light amber colour over the years.

Springbank 1992 / 15 YO
70cl / 52.6% - The Whisky Society - A Cask-strength Springbank 1992 Bottled froma single hogshead in 2007. Floral and earthy notes and a touch of honey on the nose, and some hot spices and gorgeous cereal notes on the palate.

Springbank 1992 / 7 YO / 'Da Mhile' Limited Edition
70cl / 46% - Distillery Bottling - The first organic Single Malt scotch Whisky, made to celebrate the Millennium. Named 'Da Mhile', meaning 2000 in Gaelic, this fantastic Whisky is a limited release of just 1000 Bottles.

Springbank 1993 / 16 YO / Old Malt Cask #4938
70cl / 50% - Douglas Laing - A single Cask of Springbank 1993, Bottled from refill hogshead by Douglas Laing as part of the Old Malt Cask range.

Springbank 1995 Cask Strength / The Whisky Exchange
70cl / 56.5% - The Whisky Exchange - Something of a curio, this one - a Cask strength Single Malt from Springbank Distillery, with more than a hint of smoke about it, suggesting it might actually be one of the Distillery's other Single Malts. Strong and youthful, this is an assertive dram with notes of flax, wet peat, hay and pear eau de vie.

Springbank 2000 / 12 YO / Calvados Wood
70cl / 52.7% - Distillery Bottling - Very popular at The Whisky Exchange Whisky Show 2012 this is a 12 YO Springbank Distilled in April 2000 and Bottled early in October 2012, matured for half the time in refill Bourbon Casks and half in fresh Calvados Casks.

Springbank 2001 / Rundlets & Kilderkins
70cl / 49.4% - Distillery Bottling - An interesting experimental release from the folks at Springbank - Distilled in November 2001

and Bottled in January 2012 after maturation in Rundlets and Kilderkins, which are small 60 and 80 litre Casks. It's therefore had lots of wood contact over its 10 years and combined with Springbank's regular rustic charm it's a bit good. Noticeable smoke, brine & an oily texture.

Springbank 21 YO / Bot.1990s
70cl / 46% - Distillery Bottling - A legendary dram. Springbank 21 year-old has a place in the heart of every malt-lover for its Sherry-oak charm, velvety mouthfeel and quite bewildering complexity. A malt that approaches perfection.

Springbank 21 YO / First Bottling of 21st Century
70cl / 46% - Distillery Bottling - A very special edition of Springbank 21 YO Bottled only for directors & staff, this was the first Bottling done to commemorate the new millennium, meaning the Whisky in the Bottle would have been Distilled in the 1970s.

Springbank 25 YO / Bot.1970s
75cl / 43% - Distillery Bottling - A very rare 1970s decanter of Springbank 25 YO.

Springbank 25 YO / Bot.1980s
75cl / 43% - Distillery Bottling - A lovely old 25 YO Springbank in an unusual pear-shaped Bottle. Probably Bottled in the 1970s, this should be sensational stuff.

Springbank 25 YO / Bot.1980s
75cl / 46% - Distillery Bottling - A dumpy Bottle of Springbank 25 YO released in the 1980s, meaning the liquid was probably Distilled in the late 1950s or early 1960s. Say no more.

Springbank 25 YO / Bot.1980s
75cl / 46% - Distillery Bottling - A wonderful colour on this 1990s American version of the cracking Springbank 25 YO. Bottled at 46% for your delectation.

Springbank 25 YO / Bot.1990s
70cl / 46% - Distillery Bottling - A dumpy Bottle of rare Springbank 25 YO - Bottled in the 1990s and highly rated by the Malt Maniacs.

Springbank 25 YO / Frank McHardy Bottling

70cl / 46% - Distillery Bottling

Springbank 25 YO / Millennium Edition
70cl / 46% - Distillery Bottling

Springbank 25 YO / Millennium Edition
70cl / 46% - Distillery Bottling

Springbank 25 YO / Millennium Set
75cl / 46% - Distillery Bottling

Springbank 30 YO
70cl / 46% - Distillery Bottling

Springbank 30 YO / Millennium Set
70cl / 46%

Distillery Bottling

Springbank 32 YO
70cl / 46% - Distillery Bottling - A somewhat forgotten Springbank, overlooked by most in favour of the (admittedly great) 21 YO. This is a different kind of special Springbank, Distilled in the early 1970s and matured in refill Sherry Casks - yet despite a 91 point rating from Whiskyfun.com it never really became as well known as perhaps it deserved. Still a great Whisky.

Springbank 33 YO / Bot.1980s
75cl / 43% - Distillery Bottling

Springbank 40 YO / Millennium Set
70cl / 40.1% - Distillery Bottling - A very special Distillery-Bottled Springbank 40 YO released as part of the Millennium Set in 1999.

Springbank 50 YO
75cl / 43% - Distillery Bottling - A real treasure. The malt in this Bottle was Distilled in 1919 and Bottled in 1969, which shows how far ahead of their time the Mitchell family company were. This malt resembles very closely the Whisky Bottled as Campbeltown 1919, of which only 24 Bottles were released. Campbeltown 1919 costs around £50,000 (if you can find it), making this a relative bargain.

Springbank 8 YO / Bot.1980s
75cl / 43% - Distillery Bottling

Springbank 8 YO / Japanese Market
75cl / 43% - Distillery Bottling - A very unusual Bottle of Springbank 8 YO Bottled for the Japanese market in the 1970s.

Springbank 8 YO / Madeira Wood / Bot.Christmas 2004
70cl / 46% - Distillery Bottling - A special Bottling of Madeira-matured Springbank 8 YO presented to directors and staff of Distillery owners J & A Mitchell at Christmas 2004.

Springbank 8 YO / Oval Bottle / Bot.1970s
75cl / 43% - Distillery Bottling - An old skool oval/teardrop shaped Bottle of Springbank from the 1970s - aged for 7 years.

Springbank CV
70cl / 46% -Distillery Bottling - It's taken over a decade, but here we have the second edition of Springbank CV. After the widespread acclaim for the Longrow CV released in 2009, and the Distillery's recent renaissance after a couple of so-so years, we expect this to be one of the hits of 2010.

Springbank Pure Malt 8 YO / Bot.1980s
75cl / 43% - Distillery Bottling - An 8 YO Blended Malt Whisky from Springbank, rather than their usual Single Malt, Bottled back in the 1980s and with light and clean styled label that they used to use back then.

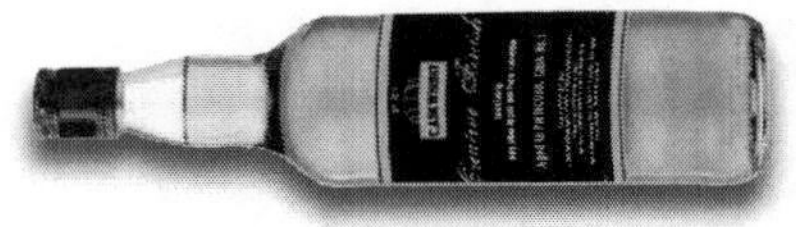

AILSA BAY
Ailsa Bay is a new Distillery constructed by William Grant & Sons. Building started in 2007 and it took just nine months to build. The Distillery is situated next to the Girvan grain Distillery and quite close to the site of the original Ladyburn Distillery, which was closed and dismantled in 1975. William Grant & son felt the need to build a new large Distillery to meet the continued demand for the Grant's blended Scotch Whisky brand. With the Distillery being situated next to the Girvan grain plant it allows for Ailsa Bay to use the resources already available at Girvan, such as its coopers and Distillers. It is not known yet if Ailsa Bay will be available as a Single Malt Whisky.

ANNANDALE
This Distillery is in the process or rebuilding and beginning production again. The re-awakening of Annandale Distillery means that fine Single Malt Scotch Whisky will flow again from the Scottish Borders.

AUCHENTOSHAN RANGE

Auchentoshan / Bot.1970s
75cl / 40% - Distillery Bottling

Auchentoshan 10 YO / Bot.1980s
75cl / 40% - Distillery Bottling
A rare 1980s Bottling of 10 YO Auchentoshan, the triple-Distilled Lowlander.

Auchentoshan 10 YO / Travel Retail / Bot.1980s
100cl / 43% - Distillery Bottling - An old travel retail litre Bottle of 10 YO Auchentoshan that we think was produced in the 1980s.

Auchentoshan 12 YO
70cl / 40% - Distillery Bottling - This Auchentoshan 12 YO expression replaced the old 10 YO a few years ago in 2008, when the range was totally revamped, and has been hailed as a big improvement on the occasionally lacklustre 10 YO.

Auchentoshan 12 YO / Clydebank Ceramic

75cl / 43% - Distillery Bottling

Auchentoshan 16 YO / Bourbon Cask
70cl / 53.7% - A 16 YO Cask-strength Bourbon-matured limited release from Auchentoshan.
Auchentoshan 18 YO
70cl / 43% - Distillery Bottling - After maturation in 100% American oak Casks, this Auchentoshan 18 years is a significant step up in quality and complexity from the Classic and 12 yrs expressions.

Auchentoshan 18 YO / Oloroso Sherry
70cl / 55.8% - Distillery Bottling - A limited edition 18 YO Whisky from Auchentoshan. The Whisky was matured solely in Oloroso Sherry Casks before being Bottled at a quite punchy 55.8% abv.

Auchentoshan 1957 / 50 YO / Sherry Cask #479
70cl / 46.8% - Distillery Bottling - A single Oloroso Sherry Cask of Auchentoshan 1957, Bottled at a full fifty YO. Just 171 Bottles of this were yielded from the Cask after five decades of ageing.

Auchentoshan 1965 / 31 YO
70cl / 45.2% - Distillery Bottling

Auchentoshan 1965 / 31 YO
70cl / 49.3% - Distillery Bottling - An old 1990s single Cask Bottling of Cask strength Auchentoshan 1965.

Auchentoshan 1965 / 31 YO / Cask #2511
70cl / 44.2% - Distillery Bottling - A 31 YO single Cask Whisky from Auchentoshan, Bottled at the full proof 44.2%. It was Distilled in 1965 and then released in the mid-1990s, shortly after Suntory acquired parent company Morrison Bowmore.

Auchentoshan 1965 / 40 YO / Bourbon Cask
70cl / 41.6% - Distillery Bottling - Very handsomely-presented ancient Auchentoshan. This is from a Bourbon Cask and is limited to just 200 Bottles.

Auchentoshan 1966 / 31 YO / Cask #804
70cl / 47.6% - Distillery Bottling - A rare 1990s 31 YO Auchentoshan 1966, Bottled at natural Cask strength from a single hogshead.

Auchentoshan 1966 / 44 YO
70cl / 40.9% - Distillery Bottling - An impressive new release from Auchentoshan, aging their triple Distilled spirit for a whopping

44 years before Bottling in 2011. A 1966 vintage Whisky, great for both good drams and the wonders of English football.

Auchentoshan 1966 / Bot.1980s
75cl / 43% - Distillery Bottling - An old Bottle of Whisky from Lowland Distillery Auchentoshan. This was Distilled in 1966 and Bottled sometime in the 1980s.

Auchentoshan 1998 / Lemon Sorbet / Wemyss
70cl / 46% - Wemyss - A single Cask release of 1998 Auchentoshan by Wemyss. Wemyss have named this "Lemon Sorbet", so expect refreshing citrusy notes.

Auchentoshan 21 YO
70cl / 43% - Distillery Bottling - A deliciously smooth, mellow long-aged Auchentoshan. This 21 YO Lowland Single Malt is a sophisticated and well-balanced dram to savour slowly after a good meal.

Auchentoshan 21 YO
75cl / 43% - Distillery Bottling - The old presentation of Auchentoshan's well-aged 21 YO Whisky. The only Distillery left who produce triple Distilled Lowland Whisky.

Auchentoshan 8 YO / Bot.1980s
75cl / 43% - Distillery Bottling - A 1980s Distillery Bottling of 8 YO Auchentoshan, from the days when there were a few more Lowland Distilleries than there are now.

Auchentoshan Classic / Bourbon Oak Cask
70cl / 40% - Distillery Bottling - A no-age-statement Auchentoshan released in 2008, Classic is aimed at drawing in new drinkers to malt Whisky, and has the easy-going drinkability to do the job. Not only that, but Auchentoshan Classic has now received a Kosher endorsement.

Auchentoshan Select
100cl / 40% - Distillery Bottling - A litre Bottle of Auchentoshan's formerly travel retail exclusive Select, the young and fresh precursor to their ever-popular Classic.

Auchentoshan Three Wood
70cl / 43% - Distillery Bottling - The ever-popular Auchentoshan 3 Wood is matured initially in Bourbon Casks before being finished in Oloroso or Pedro Ximenez Casks for an extra layer of rich, sweet fruitiness.
San Francisco WSC - Double Gold Medal Winner

IWSC 2012 - Gold Medal - Whisky - Scotch

Auchentoshan Valinch / 2012 Release
70cl / 57.2% - Distillery Bottling - The 2012 release of Auchentoshan's no-nonsense, Cask strength, Bourbon Cask matured dram. Built with a similar mix of Casks to the Classic, this is Bottled at full strength for a more concentrated flavour.

Secret Stills 3.5 (Auchentoshan) 1991 / Gordon & Macphail
70cl / 45% - Gordon & Macphail - A very healthy colour on this Auchentoshan 1991, Bottled by Gordon & Macphail from a pair of refill Sherry Casks as part of their Secret Stills collection.

BLADNOCH RANGE

Bladnoch / Bot.1970s
75cl / 43%

Bladnoch / Bot.1970s / White Label
75.7cl / 40% - Distillery Bottling - An old white labelled Bottle of Bladnoch from back in the 1970s.

Bladnoch 10 YO
70cl / 43% - Flora & Fauna - Plucky Lowlander, a bit more weighty than most. The Bladnoch Distillery is now under new ownership - this Flora & Fauna effort was the last Diageo Bottling.

Bladnoch 1964 / 13 YO / Cadenhead's
75cl / 45.7% - Cadenhead's - A great old Springbank Bottled by Cadenhead's. Distilled in September 1964 and Bottled 13 years later in September 1977 after maturing in a Sherry Cask - highly rated by the Malt Maniacs with an average of 92 points.

Bladnoch 1965 / 21 YO / Moncrieffe
75cl / 46% - Lowland Single Malt Scotch Whisky - Moncrieffe - A Moncrieffe Bottling of 21 YO Whisky from Bladnoch, Distilled in 1965. Please note that the level on this Bottle is extremely low and it has a slight leak.

Bladnoch 1966 / 23 YO / Cask #2674-76 / Signatory
75cl / 43% - Signatory - An independent Bottling of Bladnoch made from a vatting of 3 Casks of 1966 Bladnoch after maturing for 23 years.

Bladnoch 1975 / 13 YO / Cask Strength / Intertrade
75cl / 55% - Intertrade - An independent release of 1975 vintage Bladnoch Bottled at 13 YO by Intertrade.

Bladnoch 1980 / 16 YO / First Cask #89/591/14
70cl / 46% - First Cask - A rare independent Bottling of a single Cask of Bladnoch 1980 Bottled in the mid-1990s.

Bladnoch 1990 / 20 YO / Cask #5739
70cl / 51.4% - Distillery Bottling - A 20 YO single Cask Whisky from Bladnoch, Distilled on the 19th of December 1990 and Bottled at a suitably punch strength of 51.4%.

Bladnoch 1990 / Berry Bros & Rudd
70cl / 51.2% - Berry Bros & Rudd - A 1990 vintage Bladnoch from veteran indie Bottler Berry Brothers & Rudd, the oldest family owned spirits and wine merchant in the world. This was Distilled a few years before the then owners United Distillers mothballed the Distillery and a decade before its more recent rebirth.

Bladnoch 1992 / 16 YO / Single Malts of Scotland
70cl / 46% - Speciality Drinks Ltd - The first ever Bladnoch in our Single Malts of Scotland range is a delicate, medium-bodied dram from the 1992 vintage that needs a few minutes to open up and unfurl its citrussy, grassy flavours.

Bladnoch 1992 / 18 YO / Sherry Butt #7162
70cl / 50% - Douglas Laing - A 1992 vintage, single Cask Whisky by Bladnoch. This has been matured for 18 years in a Sherry Butt and then bottled at the standard strength for Douglas Laing's Old Malt Cask series (50%).

Bladnoch 1993 / Connoisseurs Choice
70cl / 43% - Gordon & Macphail - A Connoisseurs Choice Bottling of independent Lowlander Bladnoch. This is from the 1993 vintage and has been Bottled at 43% from refill Sherry hogsheads.

Bladnoch 2001 / 9 YO / Lightly Peated
70cl / 53.4% - Distillery Bottling - A Cask strength peated 9 YO Bladnoch 2001. Peated Lowland Whisky - you don't see a lot of that around, this may be the first one that we've come across. We expect this to be popular. At present we're not sure how 'lightly' peated this is, if anyone knows ppms etc, please post in the comments.

Bladnoch 2002 / Bot.2012
70cl / 55.7% - Distillery Bottling - A 2012 release of 2002 vintage Whisky from indie lowlander Bladnoch.

Bladnoch 9 YO

70cl / 46% - Distillery Bottling - A young 9 YO Whisky from Bladnoch, the most southerly Distillery in Scotland.

Bladnoch 9 YO / Cow Label
70cl / 55% - Distillery Bottling

Bladnoch Distiller's Choice
70cl / 46% - Distillery Bottling - Introduced in 2011, Distiller's Choice is a no-age-statement vatting of selected Bladnoch Casks Bottled at a pleasant drinking strength of 46%.

DAFTMILL DistilLERY

Open since 2005, it it one of the newer Distilleries and is based in a converted barn in Fife. It has not yet produced Whisky for sale though the Distillery can be toured.

GLENKINCHIE RANGE

Glenkinchie 10 YO / Bot.1980s
75cl / 43% - Distillery Bottling

Glenkinchie 12 YO
70cl / 43% - Distillery Bottling - Replacing the 10 YO as the main expression of the Lowland style in the Classic Malts range, this Glenkinchie 12 YO is a bit fuller and more complex.

Glenkinchie 12 YO / 1L
100cl / 43% - Distillery Bottling - A litre-Bottle of Glenkinchie, Diageo's Lowland representative in the Classic Malts series.

Glenkinchie 12 YO / Friends Classic Malt
70cl / 58.7% - Distillery Bottling - A rare Cask-strength Glenkinchie Bottled for the Friends of the Classic Malts a few years ago.

Glenkinchie 1966 / 21 YO
75cl / 46% - Cadenhead's - A very rare 1988 Cadenhead's Bottling of Glenkinchie 1966. 1966 was a difficult year for Scottish football fans, but hopefully a better one for Whisky nuts.

Glenkinchie 1990 / 20 YO
70cl / 55.1% - Distillery Bottling - The second 20 YO Glenkinchie Bottled for Diageo's Special Releases is, like the first, a small batch from refill American oak Casks. This is an equally enjoyable dram,

in our opinion a bit better, although it definitely needs a drop of water to get going.

Glenkinchie 1992 / Distillers Edition
70cl / 43% - Distillery Bottling - The 1992 vintage edition of Glenkinchie's Distillers Edition, finished in Amontillado Sherry Casks and Bottled in 2007.

Glenkinchie 1992 / Managers' Choice
70cl / 58.1% - Distillery Bottling - A single European oak Cask of Glenkinchie 1992, Bottled in 2009 as part of Diageo's Managers' Choice range. Along with the Dalwhinnie, this is one of the oldest Bottles in the series.

Secret Stills 5.1 (Glenkinchie) 1987 / Gordon & Macphail
70cl / 45% - Gordon & Macphail - A small batch of active Lowlander Glenkinchie, Bottled from refill Sherry Casks at 45% by Gordon & Macphail.

GLEN FLAGLER RANGE

Glen Flagler / Bot.1970s
75cl / 40% - Distillery Bottling - A Bottle of no-age-statement Whisky from short-lived Lowland Distillery Glen Flagler. With the Distillery only operating between 1964 and 1985, and not much Single Malt Whisky released under their own label, this is a very rare Bottling.

Glen Flagler 1970 / 23 YO
70cl / 50.1% - Signatory - A rare Bottling of Whisky from short-lived Lowland Distillery Glen Flagler. They closed in 1985 after only 19 years of operation and this is one of a pair of Bottlings that Signatory released in the mid-1990s, one of only a handlful of Bottlings released since the closure.

Glen Flagler 1972 / 24 YO
70cl / 52% - Signatory

Glen Flagler 1973 / 30 YO
70cl / 46% - Distillery Bottling - The 2003 release of 1973 vintage Whisky from short-lived Glen Flagler, Bottled after 30 years of maturation by Inver House. The Distillery only operated between between 1964 and 1985 and this Bottling is some of the last remaining stock known to exist.

Glen Flagler 8 YO
75cl / 40% - Distillery Bottling - A lovely Bottle of 8 YO Single

Malt from extinct Lowlander Glen Flagler, which existed as part of the Moffat complex for a short time between the 1960s and 1980s.

Glen Flagler 8 YO / Bot.1970s
75cl / 40% - Distillery Bottling - A very rare Bottle of Whisky from short-lived Glen Flagler, Bottled in the 1970s with the now classic 'gothic' label after 8 years of maturation. Glen Flagler opened in 1964 and closed in 1985, leaving behind minimal stocks and collectors eagerly awaiting their appearance.

INVERLEVEN RANGE

Inverleven 1973 / 36 YO / Deoch an Doras
70cl / 48.85% - Distillery Bottling - A historic Bottling - the first ever official release of Inverleven, the Lowland Distillery closed in 1991. This is one of the first releases in Chivas Brothers' Deoch an Doras series - the name (roughly pronounced 'Jock an Doris') means 'a drink at the door', the Gaelic equivalent of 'one for the road' - although why the Irish spelling of 'doras' has been used instead of the Scottish 'doruis' or 'dorus' is probably one for the marketing dept to answer.

Inverleven 1973 / 37 YO / Deoch an Doras
70cl / 49% - Distillery Bottling - A 1973 vintage Whisky from Inverleven, a malt Distillery that operated from within the Dumbarton grain Distillery complex until 1991. This is part of Chivas Brothers's Deoch an Doras series, roughly translated as 'One for the road', and was Bottled in 2011 at 37 YO.

Inverleven 1977 / 34 YO / Cask #3605
70cl / 48.7% - Signatory - A 1977 vintage Whisky from Inverleven, which closed in 1991 without having released any official Bottlings. The indies have picked up on it, though, and this is one of a number of releases from Signatory, aged for 34 years in a Bourbon Cask and Bottled at Cask strength.

Inverleven 1991 / Gordon & Macphail
70cl / 40% - Gordon & Macphail - A 1991 vintage Whisky from Inverleven, Distilled in the year that they closed down. There are no official Bottlings from the Distillery, leaving it to people like Gordon & Macphail to get the Whisky out into the world.

KILLYLOCH RANGE

Killyloch 1972 / 22 YO

70cl / 52.6% - Signatory - Killyloch was a very shortlived malt Whisky Distillery based at the Moffat grain Distilling complex. Production began in 1965 and ceased forever in the early 1970s. This is one of only a handful of versions of the Killyloch Single Malt ever released, and was Bottled by Signatory in the mid-1990s.

Killyloch 1967 / 36 YO
70cl / 40% - Distillery Bottling

KINCLAITH RANGE

Kinclaith 1963 / Private Collection / Gordon & Macphail
70cl / 40% - Gordon & Macphail - Extraordinarily rare malt, even by Kinclaith's standards: just 64 (!) Bottles were yielded when G&M Bottled it in 1996 from what must have been, judging by the colour, an exceptional refill Sherry hogshead. Kinclaith was founded in 1957 and closed in 1975. This incredibly scarce Lowlander has never been officially Bottled as most of its output went into parent company Schenley International's Long John blend.

Kinclaith 1966 / 16 YO / Connoisseurs Choice
75cl / 40% - Gordon & Macphail - A lovely old Bottle of the ridiculously rare Kinclaith, this is from the 1966 vintage and was Bottled in the early 1980s at 16 YO for the Connoisseurs Choice series by Gordon & Macphail, who have labelled it as a Highland malt despite the fact that Kinclaith was made in Glasgow at the Strathclyde complex.

Kinclaith 1967 / Connoisseurs Choice
70cl / 40% - Gordon & Macphail - A very rare Connoisseurs Choice Bottling of the even rarer Kinclaith, a Lowland Distillery that was open for just 18 years and was never officially Bottled.

Kinclaith 1967 / Connoisseurs Choice
75cl / 40% - Gordon & Macphail

Kinclaith 1968 / Connoisseurs Choice
70cl / 40% - Gordon & Macphail

Kinclaith 1969 / 35 YO
70cl / 54% - Signatory

Kinclaith 1969 / 35 YO / Cask #301444
70cl / 53.3% - Signatory - A very rare Whisky from a long closed Kinclaith. Built inside the Strathclyde grain Distillery complex

and shut down in 1975 after less than 20 years of production and with no official releases. These 1969 Bottlings may be the last Whiskies that will be seen from the Distillery.

Kinclaith 1969 / 35 YO /Cask #301446
75cl / 51.3% - Signatory - A very rare Bottling of legendarily hard-to-find Whisky from Kinclaith, a malt Distillery incorporated into the Strathclyde complex which ran for just 18 years between 1957 and 1975, with almost all output going into the Long John blend. This 1969 Cask was Bottled by Signatory in 2005.

LADYBURN RANGE

Ladyburn 12 YO / Bot.1980s
75cl / 43% - Distillery Bottling

Rare Ayrshire (Ladyburn) 1975 / 36 YO / Cask #3416
70cl / 44.1% - Signatory - A Signatory Bottling of 1975 vintage Ladyburn Bottled at Cask strength under the mysterious title of 'Rare Ayrshire'.

LITTLEMILL RANGE

Dunglass 1967 + Littlemill 1967
100cl / 43.5% - Signatory - A double pack of Littlemill Whiskies from indie Bottler Signatory. Dunglass was an experimental malt from Littlemill Distilled only in 1967: oily, lightly peated and never made again. In this set it's packaged with a Bottle of the regular 1967 Littlemill for comparison.

Littlemill 12 YO / Bot.1980s
75cl / 54% - Distillery Bottling - A very rare Distillery-Bottled Littlemill released at full strength for the Italian market at some point in the 1980s.

Littlemill 1990 / 21 YO / Cask #18 / Berry Bros & Rudd
70cl / 46% - Berry Bros & Rudd - A 1990 vintage Littlemill Bottled in 2012 at 21 YO by veteran independent Berry Brothers & Rudd from a single Cask.

Littlemill 1990 / 22 YO / The Whisky Agency
70cl / 52.2% - The Whisky Agency - A Sherry matured Whisky from closed Littlemill, Distilled in 1990 and Bottled in 2012 at 22 years of age by The Whisky Agency. This is part of their Sea Life series of Whiskies and has a crab infested label.

Littlemill 1990 / Scott's Selection

70cl / 53.9% - Scott's Selection - A 1990 Whisky from Littlemill, Bottled for the Scott's Selection range.

Littlemill 1991 / 19 YO / Old Malt Cask #6552
70cl / 50% - Douglas Laing - From the sadly-defunct Lowland Distillery Littlemill (demolished in the 1990s) comes this refill hoggie Bottled for the Old Malt Cask collection by Douglas Laing.

Littlemill 1991 / 20 YO / Cask #8481
70cl / 50% - Douglas Laing - A 1991 vintage Whisky from Littlemill. This Whisky has been aged for 20 years and Bottled in 2012. Bottled by Douglas Laing for their Old Malt Cask series.

Littlemill 1992 / 20 YO / Cask #9 / Berry Bros & Rudd
70cl / 54.6% - Berry Bros & Rudd - A 20 YO single Cask Whisky from closed Littlemill, Distilled in 1992 and Bottled in 2012 by independent wine and spirits merchant Berry Brothers & Rudd.

Littlemill 1992 / 20 YO / Liquid Library
70cl / 51.6% - The Whisky Agency - A 1992 vintage Whisky from Littlemill, aged for 20 years in an ex-Bourbon hogshead and Bottled in 2012 by The Whisky Agency for their Liquid Lab series.

Littlemill 20 YO / Royal Marriage Whisky
70cl / 46% - Hart Brothers - A commemorative limited edition from independent Bottlers Hart Brothers of 20 YO Single Malt from the lost Lowland Distillery Littlemill, released in April 2011 to celebrate the Royal Marriage of Prince William and Kate Middleton.

Littlemill 21 YO / Queen's Diamond Jubilee
70cl / 46% - Hart Brothers - Hart Brothers's entry into the Queen's Diamond Jubilee market - a 21 YO Whisky from closed Littlemill.

Littlemill 5 YO / Bot. 1970s / Tall
75cl / 40% - Distillery Bottling - A Bottle of Littlemill from the 1970s. This has been aged for 5 years prior to Bottling. The Littlemill Distillery is now closed, and was dismantled in 1996.

Littlemill 5 YO / Bot.1970s
75cl / 43% - Distillery Bottling

Littlemill 5 YO / Bot.1980s
75cl / 40% - Distillery Bottling - A clear glass Bottled Littlemill, aged for 5 years and released in the 1980s.

ROSEBANK RANGE

Rosebank 1981 / Bot.1997
70cl / 63.9% - Flora & Fauna - The rare 1981 vintage Rosebank Flora & Fauna, Bottled in 1997 as one of the select few Whiskies in the range to get a Cask strength version.

Rosebank 1990 / 22 YO / Sherry Finish / Chieftan's
70cl / 50% - Ian Macleod - A 1990 vintage Rosebank Bottled by Ian Macleod in October 2012 at 22 years of age as part of their Chieftan's range. This was was finished in a Sherry Cask, for an extra kick of fruitiness.

Rosebank / Bot.1970s
75cl / 40% - Distillery Bottling - A 1970s own Bottling of now closed Rosebank, with their old white label.

Rosebank 12 YO / Bot. 1980s
75cl / 43% - Distillery Bottling - A 12 YO Distillery release from closed Rosebank, Bottled in the 1980s.

Rosebank 1979 / Bot.1993 / Connoisseurs Choice
70cl / 40% - Gordon & Macphail - An old Rosebank Connoisseurs Choice. Distilled in 1979 and Bottled in 1993.

Rosebank 1980 / 11 YO
70cl / 60.1% - Cadenhead's - An old Cadenhead's Bottling of Rosebank Distilled in 1980 and Bottled in the (very) early 1990s.

Rosebank 1991 / Cask Strength / Gordon & Macphail
70cl / 55.3% - Gordon & Macphail - A Cask strength Rosebank 1991 from the ever-reliable Gordon & Macphail.

Rosebank 8 YO / Bot.1980s
75cl / 40% - Distillery Bottling - A 1980s release of 8 YO Whisky from closed Lowlander Rosebank, Bottled by the Distillery.

Rosebank 8 YO / Bot.1980s
75cl / 40% - Distillery Bottling - A highly desirable official Bottling of Rosebank 8 YO from the 1980s, shortly before the Distillery's untimely demise.

Rosebank / Bot.1970s
75cl / 40% - Distillery Bottling - This Distillery Bottling of Rosebank comes in a thicker than average Bottle. We estimate that this was Bottled some time in the 1970s.

Rosebank 12 YO

70cl / 43% - Flora & Fauna - An increasingly hard to find Bottling, as it was discontinued a while back, from the closed and now redeveloped Rosebank Distillery. A victim of the early 1990s downturn in the Whisky market and producer of some beautiful Whiskies.

Rosebank 15 YO / Bot.1980s
75cl / 50% - Distillery Bottling - A very rare official Bottling of Rosebank, this high-strength 15 YO dates from the 1980s (when the Distillery was still open) and has a wonderful old-fashioned steely austerity uncharacteristic for such a relatively easy-going spirit. Water reveals a bitter lemon and other tangy citrus notes. A classic of this 'pure' style.

Rosebank 15 YO / Bot.1980s
75cl / 61% - Distillery Bottling - A marvellous old Cask strength Distillery-Bottled Rosebank 15 YO from the 1980s. These OB's are becoming increasingly rare and sought-after.

Rosebank 1989 / Bot.1999 / Jewels of the Lowlands
70cl / 56% - Lombard - A 1989 vintage Whisky from Rosebank. This was specially selected and Bottled by Lombard Scotch Whisky Ltd in 1999, making this approximately 10 YO.

Rosebank 1990 / 21 YO / Cask #8247
70cl / 50% - Douglas Laing - A 1990 vintage Bottling from Rosebank Distillery. This has been aged for 21 years and Bottled in May 2012. Limited to just 116 Bottles.

Rosebank 21 YO / The Whisky Exchange
70cl / 48% - The Whisky Exchange - A single Cask Rosebank 21 YO Bottled by The Whisky Exchange with one of our stylish retro labels inspired by classic Whisky designs from days gone by. This one is from an ex-Bourbon Cask and is delightfully sweet and elegant, even if we do say so ourselves.

Rosebank 1967 / 25 YO
70cl / 54.4% - Signatory

Rosebank 1967 / 26 YO / Cadenhead's
70cl / 43% - Cadenhead's

Rosebank 1981 / 25 YO
70cl / 61.4% - Distillery Bottling - Not at all what you might expect, this is a powerhouse of a malt. Big, full and extremely spicy, with a massive abv for the age and some delicious polished maltiness. A tour de force.

Rosebank 1989 / 11 YO
70cl / 50% - Douglas Laing

Rosebank Ceramic 15 YO / Bot.1970s
75cl / 50% - Distillery Bottling

ST MAGDALENE RANGE

St Magdalene 1965 / Connoisseurs Choice
70cl / 40% - Gordon & Macphail - An early 1990s 'map label' Connoisseurs Choice Bottling of 1965 Single Malt from deceased and highly sought-after Lowland Distillery St. Magadalene (aka Linlithgow).

St Magdalene 1966 / Connoisseurs Choice
70cl / 40% - Gordon & Macphail - A 1966 vintage St Magdalene Bottled by Gordon & Macphail for the Connoisseurs Choice range in 1996.

St Magdalene 1979 / 19 YO
70cl / 63.8% - Distillery Bottling

St Magdalene 1980 / Centenary Reserve / Gordon & Macphail
70cl / 40% - Gordon & Macphail - Released in 1995, this special edition 1980 vintage St. Magdalene was Bottled to celebrate Gordon & Macphail's centenary.

St Magdalene 1981 / Connoisseurs Choice
70cl / 40% - Gordon & Macphail - An old Connoisseurs Choice Bottling from the late 1990s of this much-lamented defunct Lowlander.

St Magdalene 20 YO / Waterloo Street
70cl / 62.7% - Distillery Bottling - A very rare Bottling of St. Magdalene Single Malt (aka Linlithgow). The Waterloo St. Bottling was distributed to Diageo engineering staff and VIPs in 1998 in celebration of 100 years at Ainslie & Heilbron's buildings at 64 Waterloo Street in Glasgow.

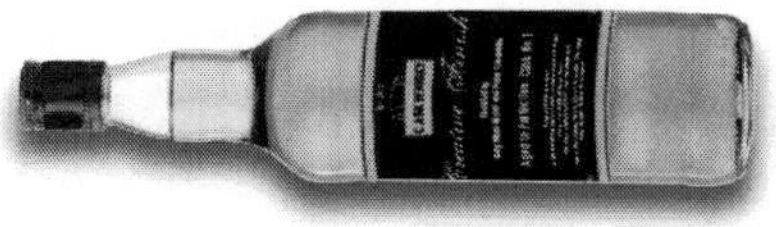

HIGHLAND REGION

ABERFELDY RANGE

Aberfeldy 12 YO
70cl / 40% - Distillery Bottling - An award winning Eastern Highland malt that was almost unknown until it was bought by Bacardi in 1998, Aberfeldy's main claim to fame is as the heart of the excellent Dewar's blend. Clean and polished malt with a touch of honey and spice.

Aberfeldy 1980 / 17 YO
70cl / 62% - Flora & Fauna - A Flora and Fauna Bottling of Aberfeldy from before they were bought by Bacardi. One of a small number of Cask strength expressions in the range.

Aberfeldy 25 YO
70cl / 40% - Distillery Bottling - A 25 YO Bottling of Aberfeldy, Distilled back in the days when they were owned by Diageo. Presented in a dark wooden box.

ARDMORE RANGE

Ardmore 25 YO: Colour: Yellow Gold - Nose: Straight from the Bottle, the initial aroma is of marzipan with just a trace of peat smoke that is overlaid by the morello cherry and blackcurrant fruitiness. A touch of water releases all the multitudes of complex flavours that one expects from this Highland Malt. The peat smoke appears immediately as a touch of leather that fades and allows the creamier fruit and heather flower rich softness that is balanced by the tang of oak. Body: Richness balanced with fruity softness. Palate: At Bottle strength the peat smoke bursts in the mouth and overpowers the softer flavours. With a touch of water the peat concentration is mellowed by vanilla cream and a sweet oakiness. Finish: Crisp and quite long lasting

30 YO Highland Single Malt:
OVERVIEW: In 2008, Ardmore® Traditional Cask redefined the Single Highland Malt Scotch experience in the United States. Masterfully crafted from the only Highland Distillery that consistently peats its barley, Ardmore weaves bold smoky flavour notes historically associated only with Islay malts into the rich Highland malt experience. Expanding on this unique combination of flavours, Ardmore will unveil a limited edition 30 YO in 2009 available only in the United States. Aged in former Bourbon barrels and handmade quarter Casks, the new ultra-premium Scotch bears the same name and pedigree as its predecessor, but reveals a distinctive finish and rich, complex flavor all of its own. Only 230 cases, with each Bottle individually numbered, will be available.
Colour: Bright Gold. Nose: Without water, the peat smoke is not apparent as only the full rich intensity appears. Adding water allows the many layers of complexity to come through. The immediate aroma is fragrant rather than powerful and the scents of roses and violets blend with a slight citrus note that masks the gentle peat smoke.

Body: Full, round and soft
Palate: At Bottle strength, the peat comes through as a dryish liquorice tang. When water is added, the peatiness is smoothed and softened by a cream toffee and flower gentleness. Finish: Quite dry and very long lasting

Ardmore 1990 / 22 YO / Cask #30120+24
70cl / 59.2% - Signatory - A 1990 vintage Whisky from Ardmore. This Whisky is a marriage of two Casks and has been matured in Wine Treated Bourbon barrels for 22 years. Bottled by signatory at Cask strength for their Cask strength collection.

Ardmore 1991 / Cask Strength / Gordon & Macphail
70cl / 57.9% - Gordon & Macphail - It's an independent Cask strength Bottling by Gordon & Macphail and comes in at a fairly hefty 57.9% abv.

Ardmore 1991 / Gordon & Macphail
70cl / 43% - Gordon & Macphail

Ardmore 1992 / 19 YO / Single Malts of Scotland
70cl / 49.3% - Speciality Drinks Ltd - A fruity Ardmore with their traditional whiff of smoke that was a big hit at the 2011 Whisky Exchange Whisky Show. Bourbon matured and Bottled in 2011.

Ardmore 1993 / Gordon & Macphail
70cl / 43% - Gordon & Macphail - Distilled in 1993 and Bottled in 2008.

Ardmore 1994 / 12 YO
70cl / 58.6% - Speciality Drinks Ltd - This 1994 12 YO is a robust, potent dram.

Ardmore 1994 / 12 YO
70cl / 46% - - Speciality Drinks Ltd

Ardmore 1994 / 13 YO / Cask Ref #65
70cl / 56.8% - Speciality Drinks Ltd - Another release from our much-lauded stash of Ardmore 1994, this 13 YO is medium-bodied with intense spices, pepper and soot alongside compensating honeyed fruity hints.

Ardmore 1999 / 12 YO / Un-Chillfiltered Collection
70cl / 46% - Signatory - A batch of two hogsheads of Ardmore, Bottled at 46% by Signatory for their Un-Chillfiltered Collection.

Ardmore 1999 / 13 YO / Cask #800164 / Signatory
70cl / 46% - Signatory - A single Cask Bottling of 1999 vintage

Ardmore. Distilled on July 2nd and Bottled on August 28th 2012 by Signatory for their Un-Chillfiltered Collection.

Ardmore 25 YO / 51.4%
70cl / 51.4% - Distillery Bottling -The most recent extension of the revamped Ardmore brand (sister Distillery to Laphroaig in the Jim Beam portfolio)is a Cask-strength 25 year-old expression. Full and rich, with more than a hint of peat.

Ardmore Centenary 21 YO
70cl / 43% - Distillery Bottling - A 1977 peated Ardmore Bottled exclusively for VIPs & guests at the Distillery's centenary celebrations in 1999.

Ardmore Traditional Cask
70cl / 46% - Distillery Bottling - A young peated Speysider from the excellent Ardmore Distillery, this has been finished in quarter Casks to speed up maturation. Gold Medal in its category at the World Whisky Awards 2010.

BALBLAIR RANGE

Balblair / Bot.1960s
75cl / 40% - A Bottling of Balblair with no age statement that we believe was released in the 1960s, the days when the Distillery was still owned by Robert "Bertie" Cumming.

Balblair 10 YO / Bot.1980s
75cl / 40% - Gordon & Macphail - A 10 YO Balblair Bottled by Gordon & Macphail with the old style Distillery label.

Balblair 10 YO / Bot.1980s / Gordon & Macphail
75cl / 40% - Gordon & Macphail - A Bottle of 10 YO Balblair independently released by Gordon & Macphail. We think this was Bottled in the 1980s.

Balblair 10 YO / Gordon & Macphail
70cl / 43% - Gordon & Macphail - A Gordon & Macphail Bottling of 10 YO Balblair, one of the Highland's finest Distilleries.

Balblair 10 YO / Sherry Cask / Bot.1980s
75cl / 40% - Gordon & Macphail - A 1980s release of 10 YO Balblair Bottle by Gordon & Macphail.

Balblair 15 YO / Bot.1980s
75cl / 40% - Gordon & Macphail - A 1980s Bottling of Balblair 15 YO with the Distillery pictured on the label.

Balblair 16 YO
70cl / 40% - Distillery Bottling - Although Balblair has now gone on to bigger and better things, this discontinued 16 YO still has many admirers.

Balblair 1965
70cl / 52.3% - Distillery Bottling - The oldest and most limited of Balblair's vintage expressions yet released, this 1965 comes from a single American oak ex-Sherry butt that yielded 350 Bottles at natural strength.

Balblair 1966 / Gordon & Macphail
70cl / 43% - Gordon & Macphail - An independent Bottling of 1966 vintage Balblair by Whisky veterans Gordon & Macphail. This one is about 40 YO and should be something quite special.

Balblair 1969 / Gordon & Macphail
70cl / 43% - Gordon & Macphail - An independent Bottling from Balblair, Distilled in 1969 just before the Distillery was sold to Hiram Walker.

Balblair 1975 / 22 YO / First Cask #7283
70cl / 46%

Balblair 1975 / 2nd Release
70cl / 46% - Distillery Bottling

Balblair 1975 / Sherry Cask
70cl / 46% - Distillery Bottling - A follow-up to the wildly successful 1979, this Balblair 1975 is a Bottling of 100% Sherry Casks. We are delighted that this previously-overlooked Distillery is now attracting serious attention. As well as a Gold Medal at the International Spirits Challenge 2008, this also won top prize in its category at the World Whisky Awards 2010.

Balblair 1979 / Gordon & Macphail
70cl / 43% - Gordon & Macphail - A 1979 vintage whisky from Balblair, Bottled from the impressive stocks that Gordon & Macphail keep in their warehouses.

Balblair 1988 / Cask 2248
70cl / 60.7% - Distillery Bottling - A single Cask of Balblair 1988, a welcome addition to the Distillery's range of quality vintage Single Malts. Bottled at its impressively massive full strength of 60.7%

Balblair 1989 / 3rd Release
70cl / 46% - Distillery Bottling - The third release of Balblair's popular

1989 vintage Whisky, sitting in the middle of their range of dated drams. The strength has been upped to 46% from 43% for the previous release, giving this edition a little more oomph and flavour intensity. A very drinkable dram indeed.

Balblair 1991
70cl / 43% - Distillery Bottling - A Distillery-Bottled Balblair from the 1991 vintage. Long known to blenders as a category 'A' malt, Balblair is a terrific malt Whisky worthy of the renewed attention its recent makeover and thrilling vintage releases have bestowed.

Balblair 1991 / 20 YO / Private Collection
70cl / 45% - Gordon & Macphail - A 1991 vintage Balblair which has been finished in Casks which previously held Crozes-Hermitage Wine. The Balblair has been aged for just over 17 years before being transferred for its final 40 months of maturation. This period of maturation has added a fruity side to the Whisky without dulling its original peppery nature.

Balblair 1992 / 12 YO / Peaty Cask
70cl / 61% - Distillery Bottling - An experimental 2005 Bottling of Cask strength Balblair 1992, from a peaty Cask, which we're guessing is another way of saying that this is an Islay finish - unless Balblair have been making peaty spirit that we don't know about...

Balblair 1997 / Bot. 2012 / 2nd Release
70cl / 46% - Distillery Bottling - Bottled in 2012, the second release of Balblair's highly successful 1997 release has had its strength upped to 46% which should increase its popularity even further. A very, very drinkable dram.

Balblair 1997 / First Release
70cl / 43% - Distillery Bottling - Long known to blenders as a category 'A' malt, Balblair is a terrific malt Whisky worthy of far greater exposure than it has previously enjoyed. Relaunched in 2007 as a series of vintage expressions, and repositioned as a premium product, this unsung hero is now finally getting the attention and respect it deserves. This is a young Highland malt from the top drawer.

Balblair 2002 / First Release
70cl / 46% - Distillery Bottling - The first release of Balblair's latest entry level Single Malt, this time from the 2002 vintage. This is a soft and creamy introduction to the world of Balblair, with a nice fruitiness.

Balblair 33 YO
70cl / 44.2% - Distillery Bottling - An excellent Whisky from Balblair that scooped Whisky Magazine's Gold Award for Excellence back in 2003. We've still got a few Bottles of it that are looking for good

homes...

Balblair 5 YO / Bot.1980s
75cl / 40% - Distillery Bottling - A rare young Balblair Bottled in the 1980s in a flat Bottle with a label emphasising the Distillery's (then) connections with Ballantine's blend.

BALLECHIN RANGE

Ballechin / Oloroso Sherry Cask Matured
70cl / 46% - Distillery Bottling - This is the fourth release of Ballechin, the heavily-peated malt from Edradour. The interesting thing here is that while previous releases have been matured in unusual Casks like Burgundy and Madeira, this is a straightforward full-term Sherry maturation - and Oloroso Sherry at that.

Ballechin / Port Cask Matured
70cl / 46% - Distillery Bottling - This is the third Ballechin, a heavily-peated malt made at Edradour. This expression has been matured full-term in port hogsheads.

Ballechin 5th Release / Marsala Matured
70cl / 46% - Distillery Bottling - The fifth release of Edradour's heavily-peated spirit, Ballechin, is comprised of malt that has been fully matured in Casks previously containing sweet Marsala wine. This should be a taste sensation.

Ballechin 6th Release / Bourbon Cask Matured
70cl / 46% - Distillery Bottling - The 6th release of Ballechin, the heavily peated spirit that the folks at Edradour sometimes make. This one eschews the more fancy finishes of the rest of the range and was matured in a Bourbon Cask, for a straight down the line example of their peated malt.

Ballechin 7th Release / Bordeaux Cask Matured
70cl / 46% - Distillery Bottling - Ballechin is the name given to the heavily peated Whisky produced at Edradour Distillery. The barrels used for maturation vary with each release. The seventh release has been fully matured in First Fill Bordeaux hogsheads.

BLAIR ATHOLL RANGE

Blair Athol 10 YO / Dunfermline
70cl / 59.7% - Distillery Bottling - A single Cask "Millennium Malt" edition of Blair Athol Bottled at Cask strength for the Dunfermline Building society in celebration of the new millennium.

Blair Athol 12 YO
70cl / 43% -Flora & Fauna -A great, but sadly neglected, Highlander,

Blair Athol is one of the gems of the Flora & Fauna range. This expression has always tended towards the chunky, Sherried style, with spices and oak adding complexity to rich maltiness. We felt that it was time to remind people about this over-looked dram.

Blair Athol 12 YO Bicentenary
70cl / 43% Distillery Bottling - A rare limited edition Bottling of Blair Athol commemorating the 200th anniversary of the opening of the Distillery in 1998, even if it didn't take the Blair Athol name until 1825.

Blair Athol 15 YO / Manager's Dram
70cl / 59.4% -Distillery Bottling - One of the hallowed Manager's Drams - a single Cask selected by Blair Athol Distillery manager Gordon Donoghue and Bottled at Cask strength in December 1996. A very limited range and much sought after.

Blair Athol 1989 / 22 YO / Cask #2938
70cl / 50% - Signatory - A 1989 vintage single Cask Whisky from Blair Athol, Distilled on 17th May and Bottled on 9th January 2012 by Signatory for their Cask Strength collection after 22 years of maturation.

Blair Athol 1995 / Managers' Choice / Sherry Cask
70cl / 54.7% - Distillery Bottling - A single Sherry Cask of Blair Athol 1995 Bottled for Diageo's Managers' Choice series in 2009. A medium-full biscuity dram, with background notes of syrup and fudge.

Blair Athol 8 YO
75cl / 46% - Distillery Bottling - A rare old Distillery Bottling of Blair Athol 8 YO from the 1970s. Bottled at a palate-friendly 46%, this should be a treat.

Blair Athol 8 YO / Bot. 1970's
75cl / 40% - Distillery Bottling - A 1970s Bottling of 8 YO Blair Atholl Single Malt, the spiritual home of Bell's and a key component of that blend.

Blair Athol 8 YO / Bot.1980s
75cl / 46% - A 75cl 1980s Bottling of Blair Athol from around the time that Arthur Bell & Sons were acquired by the Guinness Group.

Blair Athol 8 YO / Bot.1980s
75.7cl / 40% - Distillery Bottling - A rare old Bottle of Blair Athol 8 YO. We believe this was Bottled in the 1980s.

Blair Athol Bicentenary 18 YO / Sherrywood
70cl / 56.7% - Distillery Bottling - A rare 18 YO Sherried Cask strength Blair Athol Bottled in 1998 to commemorate the Distillery's

bicentenary - a true unsung hero of the Highlands.

BRORA RANGE

Brora 13 YO / Blackadder
70cl / 43% - Blackadder

Brora 1970 / 32 YO / Douglas Laing
70cl / 58.4% - Douglas Laing

Brora 1971 / 29 YO / Old Malt Cask
70cl / 50% - Douglas Laing - A 29 YO Whisky from Brora, Bottled by Douglas Laing for the Old Malt Cask range. Distilled in February 1971 and Bottled in April 2000.

Brora 1971 / 29 YO / Sherry Cask / Douglas Laing
70cl / 50% - Douglas Laing

Brora 1972 / 30 YO / Sherry Cask
70cl / 47.4% - A 1972 Brora Bottled by Douglas Laing for The Whisky Shop in the early 2000s after 30 years of maturing in a Sherry Cask.

Brora 1975 / 20 YO
75cl / 59.1% - Distillery Bottling

Brora 1981 / 18 YO / Sherry Cask
70cl / 43% - Signatory

Brora 1981 / 26 YO / Sherry Butt
70cl / 46% - Dun Bheagan - A Brora 1981 from independent Bottler Dun Bheagan, this 26 YO has been Bottled from a single Sherry butt.

Brora 1982 / 20 YO
70cl / 58.1% - Distillery Bottling - A Cask strength release from the much-missed Brora, this was Distilled in 1982, shortly before the Distillery closed its doors for the last time. These Rare Malt Bottlings are increasingly sought after nowadays.

Brora 1982 / Connoisseurs Choice
70cl / 40% - Gordon & Macphail

Brorageddon 1972 / Sherry Cask
75cl / 50.8%- Douglas Laing - A special Bottling of 1972 Brora for members of the PLOWED Society in the early 2000s after 30 years of maturation. They like their Whiskies big and this doesn't seem to have disappointed.

BEN NEVIS RANGE

Ben Nevis 10 YO
70cl / 46% - Distillery Bottling - A full-bodied malt with a whiff of peat.

Ben Nevis 1965 / 14 YO
75cl / 45.7% - Cadenhead's

Ben Nevis 1965 / 19 YO / Connoisseurs Choice
75cl / 40% - Gordon & Macphail - A release of 1965 vintage Ben Nevis by Gordon & Macphail for their Connoisseurs Choice range, around the end of its late 70s/early 80s closure

Ben Nevis 1966 / 25 YO
75cl / 59% - Distillery Bottling - A 25 YO Distillery Bottling of Ben Nevis, Distilled a couple of years after the death of Canadian Millionaire owner John Hobbs. From the colour on this one I'd guess that some of the Whisky has seen the inside of a Sherry Cask.

Ben Nevis 1992 / 19 YO / Cask #2305 / Signatory
70cl / 55.2% - Signatory - A 1992 vintage Whisky from Ben Nevis, a Distillery who produces a lot of spirit that goes into Japanese blends. This was Bottled at Cask strength after 19 years in a Sherry butt by Signatory as part of their Cask Strength Collection.

Ben Nevis 1992 / 20 YO / Sherry Butt #2524 / Signatory
70cl / 46% - Signatory - A deep amber coloured single Cask Whisky from Ben Nevis, Bottled by Signatory as part of their Un-chillfiltered Collection. This was Distilled on 24th July 1992 and Bottled 20 years later on 12th November 2012 from a single Sherry butt.

Ben Nevis 1996 / 12 YO / TKS / Bourbon Cask Finish
70cl / 56.8% -Distillery Bottling - A Cask strength Distillery Bottling of Ben Nevis 12 YO from the 1996 vintage. This is another single Cask Bottled for Swedish Whisky society TKS and, as with their previous port wood Bottling, this has been re-racked - this time into a fresh Bourbon Cask.

Ben Nevis 1998 / 12 YO / Bot.2010
70cl / 46% - Distillery Bottling - A 12 YO single Cask Ben Nevis Bottled by the Distillery in September 2010. It was Distilled on the 23rd June 1998 and matured in Cask #576, a fresh Sherry Cask.

McDonald's Traditional Ben Nevis
70cl / 46% - Distillery Bottling - A special edition Whisky from Ben Nevis in celebration of their 185th year. It is an attempt at recreating the McDonald's Traditional Ben Nevis which was a popular dram in the 1880s. IWSC 2012 - Gold Outstanding Medal - Whisky - Scotch

BEN WYVIS RANGE

Ben Wyvis 1965 / 37 YO
70cl / 44% - Distillery Bottling - The Ben Wyvis Distillery was closed in 1976, just eleven years after it had opened as part of Whyte & Mackay's Invergordon complex. Only a handful of Bottlings have ever been released, of which this is perhaps the most interesting. Having Bottled what was believed to be the last Casks of Ben Wyvis in 1999 under the name 'The Final Resurrection', Whyte & Mackay were somewhat taken aback to discover that one more Cask did in fact exist in their warehouses.

Ben Wyvis 1968 + Mini / 31 YO / Cask #686
75cl / 50.1% - Signatory - Bottled over a decade ago, this is a very special Signatory edition of Ben Wyvis, the Single Malt made at Whyte & Mackay's Invergordon Distillery for a brief period between 1965 and 1976. Almost all Ben Wyvis went straight for blending so this is rare indeed. Just 84 sets were released, each with a miniature of the spirit included in the box.

Ben Wyvis 1968 / 31 YO / Cask #687
70cl / 50.6% - Signatory - A rare Bottling of Whisky from Ben Wyvis from Signatory's extensive collection of weird and wonderful Whisky. The Distillery opened in 1965 and closed 12 years later, making this one of the rarest obtainable Whiskies out there.

Ben Wyvis 1972 / 27 YO
70cl / 45.9% - Distillery Bottling - A very, very rare Bottling of Ben Wyvis, which closed in 1976 after just 12 years of production. This is from a single Cask of the 1972 vintage, Bottled at full strength for the Japanese market in the late 1990s.

Ben Wyvis 1972 / 27 YO
70cl / 43.1% - Distillery Bottling - A very rare Distillery Bottling of Whisky from short lived Ben Wyvis. They closed in 1977 after a mere 12 years of production and as such Bottlings are rather scarce, especially as time goes by. This is a Cask strength, single Cask Bottling released after 27 years of maturation.

CLYNELISH RANGE

Clynelish 12 YO / Bot.1960s
75cl / 43% - Distillery Bottling - An old Bottling of 12 YO Clynelish from the late 1960s, the days when there were two Distilleries operating on the site - the eponymous Clynelish and the now lost Brora.

Clynelish 12 YO / Bot.1970s

75cl / 56.9% - Distillery Bottling - An old 1970s Cask-strength Bottling of Clynelish. These Cask strength Bottlings were done in the early 1970s, meaning that the spirit was Distilled at the old Clynelish Distillery - now known as Brora.

Clynelish 12 YO / Friends of Classic Malts
70cl / 46% - Distillery Bottling - A very special Distillery-Bottled Clynelish 12 YO from ex-Sherry European Oak Casks, originally Bottled for the Friends of the Classic Malts.

Clynelish 14 YO
70cl / 46% - Distillery Bottling - Clynelish is the successor to the now-silent Brora, built opposite the original Distillery and producing a top-quality rich, smoky dram. One of the best entry-level proprietary Bottlings available from any Distillery.

Clynelish 14 YO / Quarter Bottle
20cl / 46% - Distillery Bottling - A quarter-Bottle of the splendid Clynelish 14 YO. Complex and spicy, this is perfect for hip flasks during long walks in cold weather. If you've never tried the malt from this brilliant Distillery, now's the time to take the plunge.

Clynelish 17 YO / Manager's Dram
70cl / 61.8% - Distillery Bottling - A 17 YO Clynelish 'released' as a Manager's Dram. These Whisky was selected by the manager and Bottles were generally given to workers and friends of the Distillery, meaning that they're rather good and not all that common.

Clynelish 1965 / 29 YO / Sherry Cask
70cl / 52.1% - Signatory - A release of single Cask 1965 vintage Clynelish for Signatory, matured in a Sherry Cask for 29 years and Bottled at 52.1%.

Clynelish 1972 / 30 YO
70cl / 46% - Murray McDavid - An old release of Clynelish from Murray McDavid. This Whisky has been aged for a full 30 years and Bottled as part of the Mission series.

Clynelish 1983 / 20 YO / Murray McDavid / 46% / 70cl
70cl / 46% - Murray McDavid - A 1983 vintage single Cask entry for Clynelish in Murray McDavid's Mission series, aged for 20 years and Bottled in the early 2000s.

Clynelish 1991 / Distillers Edition
70cl / 46% - Distillery Bottling - Another edition of Clynelish for Diageo's yearly vintaged Distiller's Edition range. Clynelish's take on the series's 'Double Maturation' is to finish the Whisky in Oloroso Sherry Casks, to add an extra chunk of rich sweetness.

Clynelish 1992 / Distillers Edition
70cl / 46% - Distillery Bottling - Finished in Oloroso Seco Casks, this

is the second release of Clynelish's Distiller's Edition and looks set to continue on the success of the first.

Clynelish 1994 / Connoisseurs Choice
70cl / 43% - Gordon & Macphail - A 1994 vintage Clynelish from Gordon & Macphail, Bottled as part of their Connoisseurs Choice collection. Expect a classic Clynelish, with some lemon complimenting the normal fruitiness.

Clynelish 1995 / 14 YO
70cl / 46% - Daily Dram - A 1995 Clynelish Bottled for rising indie-Bottling stars Daily Dram for their Nectar range. No details on the label, but from the colour we're guessing that this is from a refill Cask.

Clynelish 1995 / 16 YO / Old Malt Cask #8253
70cl / 50% - Douglas Laing - A 16 YO Clynelish from Douglas Laing's Old Malt Cask range. Distilled in June 1995 and Bottled from a single refill hogshead in March 2012.

Clynelish 1995 / 16 YO / Sherry Butt #12797
70cl / 58.3% - Signatory - A 1995 Clynelish Bottled as part of the "Cask Strength Collection" by Signatory. After being matured in a Sherry butt and aged for 16 years, this single Cask Whisky was Bottled in January 2012.

Clynelish 1997 / Fresh Fruit Sorbet / Wemyss
70cl / 46% -Wemyss - single Cask release from Wemyss. All of Wemyss Malt's are given names to help identify the character of the Whisky. Their 1997 Clynelish has been named "Fresh Fruit Sorbet" so expect some fresh, crisp, fruity flavours.

Clynelish 1997 / 11 YO / Managers' Choice
70cl / 58.5% - Distillery Bottling - An eleven year-old Clynelish 1997 Bottled at Cask strength from a single first-fill Bourbon Cask - something tells us this could be one of the more popular releases from the last batch of Diageo's Managers Choice Bottlings.

Clynelish 1997 / 14 YO / Sherry Cask
70cl / 46% - Murray McDavid - A 1997 vintage Whisky from Clynelish, Bottled by Murray McDavid after 14 years maturing in refill Sherry Casks.

Clynelish 1997 / 15 YO / Cask #12365+6 / Signatory
70cl / 46% - Signatory - A 1997 vintage Whisky from Clynelish, sat on the edge of the town of Brora on the north-east coast of Scotland. This was Distilled on October 29th and bottled from a pair of hogsheads on November 12th 2012 after 15 years of maturation by Signatory for

their Un-chillfiltered Collection.

Clynelish 1997 / 15 YO / Liquid Sun
70cl / 47.9% - Liquid Sun - A 1997 vintage Clynelish by independent Bottlers Liquid Sun. This has been matured for 15 years in a refill hogshead before being Bottled.

Clynelish 1997 / Bot.2012 / Cask #6864 / Berry Brothers
70cl / 46% - Berry Bros & Rudd - A 1997 Clynelish from Berry Brothers & Rudd, released in early 2012 after 14 years of maturation. Textbook, spirit-led flavours from a classic vintage.

THE DALMORE RANGE

Dalmore - Selene 1951 / 58 YO
70cl / 44% - Distillery Bottling - A marriage of two Dalmore Casks filled on the same day in 1951, Selene has been Bottled after nearly six decades of ageing in the darkest of the Distillery's warehouses, and named after the Titan goddess of the moon. Just thirty decanters have been produced, each encased in a solid steel box inlaid with leather.

Dalmore 12 YO
70cl / 40% - Distillery Bottling - A recent batch of Dalmore 12, along with a smart packaging revamp. This new 12 YO is very impressive even by Dalmore's high standards.

Dalmore 12 YO / Bot.1980s
75cl / 43% - Distillery Bottling

Dalmore 12 YO / Bot.1980s
75cl / 40% - Distillery Bottling - An old release of Dalmore 12 YO Whisky. This appears to have been Bottled sometime in the 1980s, before they switched to their current 'dumpy' Bottles.

Dalmore 12 YO / Bot.1980s
100cl / 43% - Distillery Bottling - A litre Bottle of 12 YO Dalmore, Bottled by the Distillery owners in the 1980s.

Dalmore 150th Anniversary Crystal
75cl / 46% - A decanter created in celebration of the 150th anniversary of Dalmore's 1839 founding. Made by Edinburgh Crystal and with a metal medallion engraved with the Dalmore stag crest and Bottle number.

Dalmore 15 YO
70cl / 40% - Distillery Bottling - A favourite expression in the Dalmore stable, this 15-year-old is elegant and smooth, with lipsmacking texture and the flawless balance one would expect from blending

maestro Richard Paterson.

Dalmore 1957 / 23 YO / Cadenhead's
75cl / 46% - Cadenhead's - A 1957 vintage independent release of Whisky from Dalmore, Bottled by Cadenhead's. Distilled in May 1957 and Bottled in December 1980.

Dalmore 1973 / 30 YO / Sherry Finish
70cl / 42% - Distillery Bottling - A very special 1973 vintage Whisky from Dalmore Distillery. This Whisky has been matured for 30 years and has spent time being finished in Sherry Casks which previously held Gonzalez Byass Sherry.

Dalmore 1976 / 33 YO / Old Malt Cask #6632
70cl / 50% - Douglas Laing - A 1976 vintage Dalmore, Bottled from a single Cask by Douglas Laing as part of their Old Malt Cask range. Distilled in December, matured for almost 34 years and Bottled in October 2010 after finishing in a rum Cask.

Dalmore 1980
70cl / 40% - Distillery Bottling - A delicious medium-full Sherried dram from the Dalmore, this 1980 is nutty and chocolatey without being over-heavy. elegant and sophisticated.

Dalmore 1981 / Matusalem Sherry Finesse
70cl / 44% - Distillery Bottling - A very limited 1981 Dalmore, finished in Cask that had previously held the fabulous Matusalem sweet Oloroso Sherry from Gonzalez Byass. There are just 497 Bottles of this, and it should be fabulous.

Dalmore 1986 / 25 YO / Cask #3099
70cl / 43% - Mackillop's - A March 2012 Bottling of 1986 vintage Dalmore from the folks at Mackillop's, aged for 25 years.

Dalmore 1990 / 21 YO / Sherry Butt #9426 / Signatory
70cl / 56% - Signatory - A 21 YO single Cask Whisky from Dalmore, Bottled as part of the Cask Strength Collection by Signatory. Distilled on 11th September 1990, matured in a Sherry butt and Bottled on 12th June 2012.

Dalmore 1990 / Cask #67 / Montgomerie's
70cl / 46% - Montgomery's - A 19 YO Dalmore Distilled in 1990 and released by indie Bottler Montgomerie's.

Dalmore 1995 Castle Leod / Bordeaux Finish
70cl / 46% - Distillery Bottling - A very special wine-finished Dalmore released as a follow-up to 2010's Mackenzie Bottling, and with the same mission - to raise money for the upkeep of Castle Leod, the

Mackenzie clan's ancestral seat.

Dalmore 20 YO / Bot.1960s
75cl / 43% - Distillery Bottling

Dalmore 25 YO / Sherry Cask / Bot.1980s
75cl / 43% - Distillery Bottling - A 1980s release of old (very old for the time) Sherry Cask matured Whisky from Dalmore, Bottled at 25 YO.

Dalmore 26 YO Stillman's Dram
75cl / 45% - A 26 YO Whisky from Dalmore. This has been Bottled as part of Whyte & Mackay's 'Stillman's Dram' series.

Dalmore 32 YO / Rum Finish / Old Malt Cask
70cl / 55.4% - Douglas Laing - This Cask-strength Dalmore 32 YO is part of the range of extra-special Bottlings from Douglas Laing to celebrate their 60th anniversary. Please note that this Bottle has a low fill level - see image - and the price has been reduced accordingly.

Dalmore 50 YO (1926)
75cl / 52% - Distillery Bottling - Very similar in character to the Dalmore 50yrs in the crystal decanter (they are from the same batch of stock), this is an earlier presentation from the 1970s and is packaged in a smart black ceramic decanter within an individual wooden case. Dalmore ages better than perhaps any other Highland Distillery, and gives Macallan a run for its money in the quality stakes, but stocks are always very low.

Dalmore 50 YO Decanter
70cl / 52% - Distillery Bottling - Bottled in 1978 into just sixty beautiful cut crystal decanters, the Casks for Dalmore 50 YO were laid down in the 1920s, and some of the spirit is reputed to have been Distilled in the late 19th century. This is one of the best 50 year-old Whiskies ever produced and is the personal favourite of many connoisseurs worldwide.

Dalmore Cigar Malt
70cl / 44% - Distillery Bottling - The second coming of the Dalmore Cigar Malt, relaunched in a stunning red box. Fans of the previous edition will definitely want to get their hands on this.

Dalmore Gran Reserva + Free Glass
70cl / 40% - Distillery Bottling - A Bottle of Dalmore's rich and elegant Gran Reserva, the replacement for the Cigar Malt in their range - a dram with heather, chocolate and a thick body to match up with strongly flavoured foods, and dare I say it, maybe a cigar. To go along with the Whisky we're also throwing in a chunky, heavy Bottomed

glass to enjoy it from.

Dalmore King Alexander III
70cl / 40% - Distillery Bottling - To make this Dalmore King Alexander III, Master Distiller Richard Paterson has selected a range of differently-aged malts matured in a mixure of French wine Casks, Madeira drums, Sherry butts, Marsala barrels, Port pipes and Bourbon barrels from Kentucky. A remarkable feat of blending.

Dalmore Spey Dram / Rivers Collection
70cl / 40% - Distillery Bottling - Another dram in a good cause, with a sizeable donation being made by the Distillers for each Bottle sold from the Rivers Collection. Like its stablemates, the Spey Dram is a mix of ex-Bourbon & Oloroso Sherry Casks.

Dalmore Tay Dram / Rivers Collection
70cl / 40% - Distillery Bottling - Produced by Dalmore with the object of raising up to £400k for a quartet of beautiful Scottish fishing rivers, like the rest of the Rivers Collection the Tay Dram has been produced from quality Bourbon and Oloroso Sherry casks and at least £4 per Bottle sold will go to the Tay Foundation that protects and conserves the river.

Dalmore Tweed Dram / Rivers Collection
70cl / 40% - Distillery Bottling - Following 2010's hugely successful 'Dee Dram', this is a special Bottling of Dalmore in celebration of the River Tweed, the UK's best salmon river. As with the Distillery's other 'River' drams, a generous donation from the profits will go to the river's conservation foundation.

DALWHINNIE RANGE

Dalwhinnie 15 YO
70cl / 43% - Distillery Bottling - Dalwhinnie 15 YO is a good introduction to the delights of Single Malt Whisky - elegant, smooth and medium-bodied with a light, fruity palate and a whiff of heather on the finish. Part of Diageo's Classic Malt range.

Dalwhinnie 15 YO / Centenary 1898-1998
100cl / 43% - Distillery Bottling - A litre Bottle of 15 YO Whisky from Dalwhinnie, Bottled in 1998, the year of their centenary - 1898-1998.

Dalwhinnie 1973 / 29 YO
70cl / 57.8% - Distillery Bottling - Delicious fruity, honeyed malt from Dalwhinnie, the Highland representative of the Classic Malts. This 29 year-old was released in 2003 and has been a huge hit with punters

and critics alike.

Dalwhinnie 1992 Managers' Choice
70cl / 51% - Distillery Bottling - Bottled for Diageo's Manager's Choice series, this single Cask Dalwhinnie 1992 is a deliciously biscuity dram, with crisp malty notes and hints of cinnamon and lemon curd. A class act.

Dalwhinnie 1995 / Distillers Edition
70cl / 43% - Distillery Bottling - The 1995 vintage of Dalwhinnie's ever reliable Distillers Edition. Finished in Oloroso Sherry Casks for an added layer of rich fruit.

Dalwhinnie 8 YO / Bot.1980s
75cl / 40% - Another 8 YO Dalwhinnie, Bottled by the Distillery in the 1980s and presented in their livery of the time.

DEANSTON RANGE

Deanston 12 YO / Unchillfiltered
70cl / 46.3% - Distillery Bottling - A relaunch in fancy packaging for Burn Stewart's Deanston Single Malt, previously famous as the Whisky used in the much-missed Wallace Whisky liqueur. Trivia snitched from the Malt Whisky Yearbook: Deanston is the only Distillery in Scotland that is self-sustaining for electricity, being equipped with a dam and a turbine.

Deanston 1977 / 35 YO / The Whisky Agency & The Nectar
70cl / 40.4% - The Whisky Agency - A 1977 vintage Whisky from Deanston. This Whisky has been aged for 35 years and is a joint Bottling for The Whisky Agency and The Nectar.

Deanston 25 YO
70cl / 40% - Distillery Bottling - A very rare Distillery-Bottled Deanston 25 YO, probably Bottled in the 1990s. Until recently little was seen of Deanston, as most of its output goes into the Scottish Leader blend.

Deanston 8 YO / Bot.1980s
75cl / 40% - Distillery Bottling - An 8 YO Distillery Bottling from young Highland Distillery Deanston. We think this was Bottled in the 1980s, a decade for much of which the Distillery was mothballed.

Deanston Mill / Bot.1970s
75cl / 40% - Distillery Bottling - A Bottling of Whisky from Deanston under the name Deanston Mill. This is from sometime after 1974, as the Whisky wasn't Bottled under the Distillery's name before then.

Deanston Virgin Oak

70cl / 46.3% - Distillery Bottling - A no-age-statement Whisky from Deanston Bottled at 46.3%. This one is made up of young Whisky which is decanted into new American oak Casks for its final stages of maturation.

Old Bannockburn (Deanston) / Bot.1980s
75cl / 40% - Distillery Bottling

EDRADOUR RANGE

Edradour 10 YO
70cl / 40% - Distillery Bottling - A tiny Distillery in Perthshire is home to Edradour, one of Scotland's most endearingly different malts. Delicious honey notes complimented by an oily mouthfeel and a really stylish finish.

Edradour 10 YO / Bot.1980s
100cl / 43% - Distillery Bottling -An old release of Edradour 10 YO Whisky. This is actually a litre size version which we estimate was Bottled sometime in the 1980s.

Edradour 10 YO / Bot.1980s
75cl / 43%

Edradour 12 YO / Caledonia Selection / Oloroso Cask
70cl / 46%Distillery Bottling - A special Bottling of Edradour 12 YO. Songwriter Dougie Maclean has selected this single Oloroso Cask from 1997 as part of the Homecoming celebrations and named it after his most famous song, Caledonia. This is the first in what will be an ongoing series from Edradour.

Edradour 1998 / 13 YO / Natural Cask #433
70cl / 57.4% - Distillery Bottling - Another of Edradour's outstanding Natural Cask Strength single Cask Bottlings. This is from the 1998 vintage and, judging by the colour and the relatively large number of bottles, it's a pretty safe guess that this was from a Sherry butt. These releases are extremely popular - don't hang around if you fancy one.

Edradour 1999 / 10 YO / Un-chillfiltered
70cl / 46% - Signatory - A curious Edradour 10 YO, Bottled by independent Bottler Signatory - who own Edradour. We're not sure why they've chosen to Bottle this as part of the Un-Chillfiltered collection instead of as an official Bottling (answers on a postcard). Nonetheless, it looks interesting - there's no info on the Cask type, but at this colour for a 10 YO, and with 908 Bottles, we're guessing this might be from a Sherry butt.

Edradour 2000 / 11 YO / Burgundy Finish

50cl / 57.1% - Distillery Bottling - A 2000 vintage Edradour, finished in Chardonnay Casks for almost 3 years. This was distilled on 30th June 2000 and Bottled on 18th July 2011.

Edradour 2000 / 12 YO / Chardonnay Finish
50cl / 56.1% - Distillery Bottling - A 2000 vintage from Edradour, finished in a Chardonnay hogshead for 3 years for a total of 12 years of maturation.

Edradour 2000 / 12 YO / Port Finish
50cl / 56.1% - Distillery Bottling - A 2000 vintage Edradour finished for almost 2 years in a port pipe, for a total of 12 years of maturation

Edradour 2000 / 12 YO / Sauternes Finish
50cl / 55.9% - Distillery Bottling - A sauternes Cask finished 12 YO Edradour. Disilled on June 30th 2000, transferred to the sauternes hogshead on October 29th 2008 and the Botttled on September 17th 2012.

Edradour 2001 / 10 YO / Sherry But #498
50cl / 57.2% - Distillery Bottling - An Edradour single Cask Whisky Distilled on 26th November 2001 and Bottled on 15th September 2012 after almost 11 years of maturation in a Sherry butt.

Edradour 2001 / 10 YO / Sherry Butt #530
50cl / 57.3% - Distillery Bottling - A single Sherry butt matured Whisky from teeny tiny Edradour, Distilled on 6th December 2001 and Bottled on 21st December 2012 from Cask #530.

Edradour 2002 / 10 YO / Chateauneuf Du Pape Finish
50cl / 58.3% - Distillery Bottling - A Cask strength release of Edradour Whisky, specially for their straight from the Cask series. This Whisky was Distilled in 2002 and aged for just over 8 years in Oak Hogsheads, after which it was transferred to a Chateauneuf Du Pape hogshead for just under 2 years. Bottled at a full 10 years of age on 4th July 2012.

Edradour 2002 / 10 YO / Marsala Finish
50cl / 57.6% - Distillery Bottling - A 2002 Whisky from popular Distillers Edradour. This Whisky has been aged for just under 9 years, before being matured for a little over 1 year in a Marsala Cask. Bottled at Cask strength at the age of 10 years.

Edradour 2002 / 10 YO / Marsala Finish
50cl / 57% - Distillery Bottling - A 2002 vintage Edradour, Distilled on 26th March 2002, initially matured in a hogshead until 28th February 2011 and then finished in a Marsala hogshead until 3rd July 2012.

Edradour 2003 / Bourbon Cask / Third Release
70cl / 57.6% - Distillery Bottling - The third release of Edradour's 2003 vintage Bourbon Cask matured Whisky. Previous releases have been

Bottled at Cask strength and this one is no different. At approximately 9 years of age, this edition is limited to 2068 decanters.

Edradour 2003 / Burgundy Cask Matured
70cl / 46% - Distillery Bottling - This Whisky has been matured full-term (not finished) in Pinot Noir hogsheads from France's finest wine region.

Edradour 2003 / Chardonnay Cask
70cl / 46% - Distillery Bottling - A 2003 vintage Edradour which spent the last stage of its maturation in a Cask that used to hold Chardonnay.

Edradour 2003 / Ruby Port Cask Batch 1
70cl / 46% - Distillery Bottling - The first batch of 2003 vintage Ruby Port Cask matured Whisky from Edradour, Distilled in November 2003 and Bottled 8 and a half years later in July 2012.

Edradour 2003 / Sauternes Cask
70cl / 46% - Distillery Bottling - A 2003 vintage Whisky from Edradour, matured for its whole life in Sauternes Casks.

Edradour Cream Liqueur
70cl / 17% - A quality cream liqueur made using Whisky from Edradour, Scotland's smallest Distillery - and one of the most picturesque, located in the beautiful village of Pitlochry.

FETTERCAIRN RANGE

Fettercairn 1995 / 16 YO / Casks #405+6 / Signatory
70cl / 59.9% - Signatory - A 1995 vintage Fettercain Bottled from a pair of Bourbon barrels in July 2011 by Signatory as part of their Cask Strength Collection.

Fettercairn 24 YO (1984)
70cl / 44.4% - Distillery Bottling - A very fancy packaging job for this limited expression of 24 YO Single Malt from the Fettercairn Distillery. Owners Whyte & Mackay clearly have confidence in the RANGE to be spending this sort of marketing money on a Distillery many malt fans had given up on - we wish Fettercairn well with this latest rebirth.

Fettercairn 30 YO (1978)
70cl / 43.3% - Distillery Bottling - A 30 YO Bottling for the latest reincarnation of Fettercairn. This 1978 vintage has a strong Oloroso Sherry influence, and the official tasting notes describe a plethora of fruity flavours including pineapple, grapefruit, cranberries, sweet mango and wild berries.

Fettercairn 40 YO (1969)
70cl / 40% - Distillery Bottling - An ambitious 40 YO for the relaunched Fettercairn Single Malt, just 463 Bottles of this have been produced. Aged in Apostoles palo cortado Sherry Casks, the 1969 'offers thick chunky orange rind, cinnamon and spice...crushed almonds, ginger and bitter chocolate'.

Fettercairn 875 / 8 YO / Bot.1970s
75cl / 43% - Distillery Bottling - A very 1970s Bottle of Fettercairn, this is the mysterious '875' version of the 8 YO. We haven't worked out what the 875 actually means - if anyone has any idea, do let us know in the comments.

Fettercairn Fior
70cl / 42% - Distillery Bottling - Fior means pure or true in Gaelic, and this no-age-statement Bottling launched in summer 2010 is something of a rebirth for the much-maligned Fettercairn Distillery. Described by the producers as tasting of dark chocolate, coffee beans and peat smoke, with nutmeg, mint, citrus fruits and truffle. The finish is said to be of Sherry trifle, marzipan and pineapple.

Old Fettercairn / Bot.1970s
75cl / 40% - Distillery Bottling

Old Fettercairn 8 YO / Bot.1980s / Screwcap
75cl / 43% - Distillery Bottling

GLEN ALBYN RANGE

Glen Albyn 10 YO / Bot. 1970's
75cl / 43% - Distillery Bottling - A very rare 10 YO Whisky from now closed Glen Albyn in the 1970s, one of only a couple released by the Distillery and originally Bottled for the Italian market.

Glen Albyn 10 YO / Bot. 1970's
75cl / 43% - Distillery Bottling - A very rare 1970s Bottling of 10 YO Whisky from Glen Albyn. The Distillery closed in 1983 and was demolished in 1986 and only produced a couple of Distillery Bottlings before it disappeared - this is one of them.

Glen Albyn 10 YO / Bot.1970s
75cl / 56.9% - Distillery Bottling - A very rare 1970s Bottling of 10 YO Whisky from Glen Albyn. The Distillery closed in 1983 and was demolished in 1986 and only produced a couple of Distillery Bottlings before it disappeared - this is one of them.

Glen Albyn 1964 / 23 YO
75cl / 46% - Cadenhead's - A very rare old Cadenhead's Bottling from the 1980s of extinct Distillery Glen Albyn's 1964 vintage.

Glen Albyn 1964 / 27 YO / 150th Anniversary
70cl / 51.4% - Cadenhead's - A special Bottling of Glen Albyn Whisky. Bottled to celebrate Cadenhead's 150th Anniversary in 1992. This 1964 vintage Whisky has been aged for a full 27 years and has been Bottled at Cask strength.

Glen Albyn 1968 / Connoisseurs Choice
75cl / 40% - Gordon & Macphail

GLENCADAM RANGE

Glencadam 10 YO
70cl / 46% - Distillery Bottling - The new Glencadam 10 YO, released at the end of 2008 by (relatively) new owners Angus Dundee. This is styled as 'The Rather Delicate Highland Malt'. Unchilfiltered, with no colouring and Bottled at 46% - this is what we like to see.

Glencadam 12 YO / Bot.1980s
75cl / 40% - Distillery Bottling - A rare Bottling of 10 YO Whisky from Glencadam, a Distillery that's becoming increasingly well known in the 21st century but was almost entirely unknown when this was released in the 1980s.

Glencadam 12 YO Portwood Finish
70cl / 46% - Distillery Bottling - This 12 YO is one of a handful of Glencadam expressions released in late 2010 by (relatively) new owners Angus Dundee, and is the first wood-finished expression from this Distillery.

Glencadam 14 YO / Oloroso Sherry Finish
70cl / 46% - Distillery Bottling - This 14 YO Glencadam has been finished in sweet Oloroso Sherry Casks for a bit of extra depth and complexity. This Distillery has been going great guns since its packaging relaunch in late 2008.

Glencadam 15 YO
70cl / 46% - Distillery Bottling - Fancy new presentation for the Glencadam 15, which has also sensibly been restored to 46% by owners Angus Dundee, who snapped up the Distillery from Allied in 2003.

Glencadam 15 YO / Old Presentation
70cl / 40% - Distillery Bottling - Released in 2005, a couple of years after owners Angus Dundee had bought this little-known Distillery, this landmark 15 YO was the first official Bottling of Glencadam for many years, with most of its previous output going into Cream of the

Barley and Ballantine's.

Glencadam 1964 / 14 YO / Dumpy Bottle
75cl / 45.7% - Cadenhead's - A lovely, and extremely rare Bottle of 1964 vintage Single Malt from the little-seen Glencadam Distillery, Bottled at 80 proof by Cadenhead's in 1979.

Glencadam 1972 / 29 YO
70cl / 52.5% - Signatory

Glencadam 1974 / 13 YO / Gordon & Macphail
75cl / 61.1% - Gordon & Macphail - A very rare Cask-strength indie Glencadam 1974, Bottled in 1988 at 13 YO by Gordon & MacPhail.

Glencadam 1977 / 32 YO / Sherry Cask
70cl / 54.9% - Douglas Laing - A sumptuous (natural) colour on this Glencadam 1977, Bottled from a single Sherry Cask by Douglas Laing for their rarely-less-than-pretty-amazing Platinum Selection. Sweet initially, with plenty of wood as you'd expect and some pleasant savoury notes and burnt toast flavours.

Glencadam 1977 / 34 YO / Sherry Cask
70cl / 56.8% - Douglas Laing - A 1977 vintage Whisky from the increasingly well known Distillery of Glenacadam, revitalised in the early 2000s by Angus Dundee. This has matured for 34 years in a Sherry butt, as you can guess from it's impressive natural colour.

Glencadam 1978 / 32 YO / Sherry Cask
70cl / 46% - Distillery Bottling - A very handsome decanter Bottle filled with Sherried 32 YO Glencadam from the 1978 vintage.

Glencadam 1982 / 30 YO
70cl / 46% - Distillery Bottling - The late 2012 edition of Glencadam's elegant looking 30 YO. Distilled on 10th June 1982, Bottled in September 2012 and limited to just 260 Bottles.

Glencadam 21 YO
70cl / 46% - Distillery Bottling - A 21 YO has been added to Glencadam's rapidly-growing range. Attractively packaged and Bottled at a good drinking strength of 46%, this is a Distillery of great potential and definitely one to watch.

Glencadam 6 YO / Special Reserve / Bot.1960s
75cl / 40% - Distillery Bottling - An incredibly rare 1960s Glencadam 6 YO Special Reserve in excellent condition for its age. A really beautiful Bottle with a springcap, this is a fantastically well-preserved piece with a perfect level.

GLENESK RANGE

Glenesk / Bot.1970s
75cl / 40% - Distillery Bottling - A rare 1970s Distillery Bottling of no-age-statement Whisky from Glenesk, which closed in 1985 and has since been repurposed as a maltings.

Glenesk / Bot.1980s
70cl / 43% - Distillery Bottling - A very, very rare official Bottling of Glenesk, the Distillery also known as Hillside before 1980. This Bottling is by William Sanderson & Sons, the last DCL (now Diageo) subsidiary to run the Distillery before its closure in 1985. The Distillery equipment was removed in 1996 and the site is now used as a maltings.

Glenesk 12 YO / Bottled 1980's
75cl / 40% - Distillery Bottling - An old '80s Bottling of this obscure Highlander.

Glenesk 1982 / Map Label / Connoisseurs Choice
70cl / 40% - Gordon & Macphail

Glenesk 1984 / Connoisseurs Choice
70cl / 43% - Gordon & Macphail - A rare Bottling of Glenesk from Gordon & Macphail as part of their Connoisseurs Choice range. This was Distilled in 1984, the year before the Distillery closed down.

Glenesk 5 YO
75cl / 40% - Distillery Bottling - A very rare Distillery Bottling of whicky now-closed Glenesk. The Distillery closed in 1985 and has since been dismantled, with the buildings now used for malting barley.

Glenesk Maltings 1969 / 25th Anniversary
75cl / 60% - Distillery Bottling - A very rare Bottling of 1969 Glen Esk released to celebrate the 25th anniversary of their onsite maltings in the early 80s. The Distillery closed in 1985, shortly after the release of this Whisky, and now operates purely as a maltings.

GLEN GARIOCH RANGE

Glen Garioch 10 YO / Bot.1980s
75cl / 43% - Distillery Bottling - A charming 1980s Bottling of 10 YO Glen Garioch. The 1970s was a great decade for this Distillery, so this should be good stuff.

Glen Garioch 10 YO / Bot.1980s

75cl / 40% - Distillery Bottling - An old-style Glen Garioch 10 YO, Bottled in the 1980s.

Glen Garioch 10 YO / Bot.1980s
75cl / 40% - Distillery Bottling - A 1980s special Bottling of 10 YO Glen Garioch, numbered and presented in a packing crate style box.

Glen Garioch 12 YO
70cl / 48% - Distillery Bottling - Introduced to Glen Garioch's standard range in late 2010 this 12 YO is a mix of ex-Bourbon and Sherry Casks and, like the other Distillery Bottlings since the revamp, has been Bottled at a feisty 48%. A real charmer.
World Whiskies Awards 2012 - Best Highland 12 years and under

Glen Garioch 15 YO
70cl / 43% - Distillery Bottling - Another subtle, medium-bodied malt, with honey and rich fruity notes on the palate and a long, rounded finish with a trace of peat and spices.

Glen Garioch 15 YO
75cl / 43% - Distillery Bottling - The pre-2009 presentation of Glen Garioch's now-discontinued 15 YO. Complete with pretty deer on the Bottle.

Glen Garioch 1958 / 46 YO
70cl / 43% - Distillery Bottling - Glen Garioch is a Distillery with a comparatively low profile, and quality has varied over its lifetime under a succession of different owners - but real aficionados will tell you that the older expressions are some of the best malts in Scotland. This is a Whisky with fruit and floral notes, but also, crucially, some restrained peat.

Glen Garioch 1965 / 12 YO
75cl / 43% - Distillery Bottling - A 1970s Distillery Bottling of Glen Garioch, Distilled in 1965.

Glen Garioch 1965 / 21 YO / Full Strength
75cl / 50% - Distillery Bottling - A lovely old 1980s Bottling of Glen Garioch 21 YO from the 1965 vintage, Bottled at 50%.

Glen Garioch 1968 / 29 YO
70cl / 56.4% - Distillery Bottling - A Distillery Bottling of 1968 vintage Glen Garioch, Bottled at 29 YO in their old stag livery before their rebranding in the new millennium.

Glen Garioch 1971 / 40 YO / Single Cask for TWE
70cl / 43.9% - Distillery Bottling - A beautiful 40 YO vintage Glen Garioch, Bottled by the folks at Morrison Bowmore for The Whisky

Exchange and released at The Whisky Show in 2011. 1971 Glen Garioch is known for being more peaty than usual, and this delicate, restrained old school dram has a lovely thread of smoke, plus tropical fruit and medicine cabinet aromas. Fabulous.

Glen Garioch 1978 / 18 YO
70cl / 59.4% - Distillery Bottling - A Distillery Bottling of 18 YO Glen Garioch from the 1978 vintage, Bottled at its impressive full strength of 59.4% in 1997.

Glen Garioch 1978 / 30 YO
70cl / 57.8% - Distillery Bottling - A handsomely-presented 30 YO from the revitalised-with-a-new-packaging-design Glen Garioch. We expect great things from this newly-overhauled Distillery - it's great that they're finally getting a bit of marketing attention.

Glen Garioch 1986 / 25 YO / Batch No.11
70cl / 54.6% - Distillery Bottling- A 1986 vintage Whisky from the revitalised Glen Garioch. Bottled at full proof of 54.6% after 25 years of maturation in North American Oak for a powerful and spicy flavour.

Glen Garioch 1986 / 25 YO / Old Malt Cask #7866
70cl / 50% - Douglas Laing - A 1986 vintage Whisky from Glen Garioch, revitalised in the 2000s and now getting the recognition that it deserves. This was aged for 25 years in a refill hogshead before Bottling in late 2011 by Douglas Laing for their Old Malt Cask range - kudos to them for unearthing this little gem, as independent Glen Gariochs are rarer than hen's teeth.

Glen Garioch 1990
70cl / 54.6% - Distillery Bottling - A Cask-strength 1990 vintage release from the previously-overlooked Glen Garioch, which is now turning heads after a successful packaging revamp. Sukhinder was very impressed with this one.

Glen Garioch 1990 / 20 YO / Cask #2750 / Signatory
70cl / 52.6% - Signatory - A 1990 vintage Glen Garioch from Signatory, part of their Cask Strength Collection. Distilled on April 9th and Bottled on December 13th 2010 after 20 years of maturation in a hogshead.

Glen Garioch 1991
70cl / 54.7% - Distillery Bottling - A recently released Cask strength batch from the revitalised Glen Garioch Distillery, this 1991 vintage picked up five stars from Class magazine, who call it "dry...with smoky charred wood/peat and apple fruit". Sounds good to us.

Glen Garioch 1991 / 21 YO / Liquid Library
70cl / 52.5% - The Whisky Agency - A 21 YO Whisky from Glen Garioch Bottled by The Whisky Agency for their Liquid Library range. Distilled in 1991, matured in an ex-Bourbon hogshead and Bottled in 2012.

Glen Garioch 1994
70cl / 53.9% - Single Malt Scotch Whisky - A Cask strength Glen Garioch from the 1994 vintage, Bottled from American oak barrels. This small batch release is said to combine a hint of smoke with classic Highland floral aromas.

Glen Garioch 1995
70cl / 55.3% - Distillery Bottling
A 1995 vintage Whisky from Glen Garioch. Although no age is stated, this has been Bottled in 2012 which makes it roughly 17 YO.
IWSC 2012 - Gold Medal - Whisky - Scotch

Glen Garioch 21 YO
70cl / 43% - Distillery Bottling

Glen Garioch 21 YO
70cl / 43% - Distillery Bottling - A rare version of Glen Garioch's discontinued 21 YO expression, Bottled some time before they revamped their entire range in 2009.

Glen Garioch 8 YO
70cl / 40% - Distillery Bottling - An 8 YO Whisky from Glen Garioch, Bottled before they revamped their entire line-up in 2009.

Glen Garioch 8 YO / Bot.1970s
75cl / 40% - Distillery Bottling - A 1970s edition of Glen Garioch 8 YO. We can't help but like the label of this particular release.

Glen Garioch 8 YO / Bot.1980s
75cl / 43% - Distillery Bottling

Glen Garioch 8 YO / Bot.1980s
75cl / 40% - Distillery Bottling - A rare old official Bottling of Glen Garioch 8 YO Bottled at some point during the early 1980s, meaning that this was probably Distilled pre 1975, when Glen Garioch was still peated more heavily.

Glen Garioch 8 YO / Bot.1990s
70cl / 40% - Distillery Bottling - A screwcap topped Bottle of 8 YO Glen Garioch from before the range's revamping in 2009, complete with stag on the label.

Glen Garioch Bicentenary 37 YO
70cl / 43% - Distillery Bottling - A 37 YO Bottling of Glen Garioch, released in 1997 to celebrate the 200th anniversary of the founding of the Distillery.

Glen Garioch Founders Reserve
70cl / 48% - Distillery Bottling - A top-quality packaging update (farewell, stags!) for this Founders Reserve Glen Garioch which has been Bottled at 48% and priced very sensibly. A very welcome return to form for a Distillery with enormous potential.

Secret Stills 6.6 (Glen Garioch) 1988 / G&M
70cl / 45% - Gordon & Macphail - A Gordon & Macphail release as part of their Secret Stills series, Bottling some 1988 vintage Whisky from Distillery 6. Which is Glen Garioch. Sorry for spoiling the secret.

GLENGOYNE RANGE

Glengoyne 10 YO
70cl / 40% - Distillery Bottling - Glengoyne is one of the only Scottish Whiskies to be Distilled from completely unpeated malt - the malt is allowed to dry naturally before fermentation and Distillation begin, resulting in an elegant, medium-bodied style.

Glengoyne 10 YO / Bot.1980s
100cl / 43% - Distillery Bottling - A litre Bottle of 10 YO Glengoyne from the 1980s.

Glengoyne 12 YO
70cl / 43% - Distillery Bottling - A 12 YO Highlander from Glengoyne, famed for their unpeated Single Malt. Glengoyne is always very pure in style, allowing their high-quality, easy-drinking Whisky to shine in its natural state.

Glengoyne 15 YO
70cl / 43% - Distillery Bottling - A sweet and rounded 15 YO dram from Glengoyne, made using air dried barley and about as unsmoky as a Whisky can get. It's a rich mix of 1st fill Sherry and Bourbon matured Whisky, rounded out with some refill Casks.

Glengoyne 15 YO / Kiln Decanter / Bot.1980s
100cl / 43% - Distillery Bottling - A superbly naff 1980s Bottling of a litre of Glengoyne 15 YO inside a kiln-shaped decanter, complete with pagoda-shaped stopper.

Glengoyne 17 YO
70cl / 43% - Distillery Bottling - Glengoyne 17 YO is a smooth, sophisticated medium-bodied unpeated malt with delicate flavours. A very good match for a mild or medium cigar.

Glengoyne 17 YO / Bot.1980s
75cl / 43% - Distillery Bottling - Classy old dumpy Bottle from the '80s.

Glengoyne 18 YO
70cl / 43% - Distillery Bottling - A replacement for Glengoyne's 17 YO that appeared in their revamped range in late 2012. A mix of refill Sherry Casks and a generous slug of first fill Sherry matured Whisky.

Glengoyne 1968 Vintage / 25 YO
70cl / 50.3% - Distillery Bottling - A rare Bottle of 25 YO Glengoyne from the 1968 vintage, Bottled at its natural Cask strength of 50.3%.

Glengoyne 1969 / The Farewell Dram
70cl / 54.4% - Distillery Bottling - The Farewell Dram is a special release of 1969 Glengoyne to commemorate the 1998 retirement of Distillery manager Ian Taylor. Only 204 Bottles were produced, each packaged in a heavy 'spirit safe' box.

Glengoyne 1986 / 23 YO / Sherry Butt
70cl / 53.6% - Distillery Bottling - A gorgeous colour on this 1986 single Cask Glengoyne, Bottled from a single Sherry butt. Sherried Glengoyne can be particularly sublime, so hopes are high for this.

Glengoyne 1990 / 19 YO / The Whisky Exchange
70cl / 59.6% - Distillery Bottling - A beautiful hogshead of Glengoyne 1990 Bottled for The Whisky Exchange. Creamy melted vanilla ice-cream on thick crust baked apple pie. Glengoyne's lack of peat leads some to regard it as a worthy but dull Whisky, but the truth is that the spirit made here is of remarkable quality, and when it gets into the right Cask the results are magical.

Glengoyne 1990 / Ambassador's Choice / Cask #2850
70cl / 59.9% - Distillery Bottling - A Cask strength 1990 Glengoyne Bottled in 2009. 272 Bottles were yielded from a single Bourbon hogshead.

Glengoyne 1999 / 8 YO / Deek's Choice
70cl / 60.9% - Distillery Bottling - A limited edition 8 YO Glengoyne, Distilled in 1999 and chosen for Bottling by warehouse supervisor Derrick 'Deek' Morrison.

Glengoyne 21 YO / Sherry Cask
70cl / 43% - Distillery Bottling - Glengoyne 21 YO is noticeably deeper than younger expressions, with delicious rich fruity and oaky notes - the darker colour and long finish are testament to the extra years in the Sherrywood.

Glengoyne 8 YO / Bot. 1970s
75cl / 43% - Distillery Bottling - A rare old 1970s Glengoyne 8 YO in green glass with a black and gold label.

Glengoyne 8 YO / Bot.1970s
75cl / 40% - Distillery Bottling - A lovely old Bottle of Glengoyne 8 YO Bottled in the 1970s.

Glengoyne Cask 104 / 12 YO
70cl / 59.1% - Distillery Bottling

Glengoyne Cask Strength / Batch 1
70cl / 58.7% - The first edition of Cask Strength Glengloyne after their 2012 rebranding, labelled with a Batch 1. It's a vatting of 1st fill Sherry matured Whisky tempered by some refill Casks.

Glengoyne Middle Cut 1967 / 30 YO
70cl / 52.5% - Distillery Bottling - A special, very limited edition edition of Glengoyne, Distilled in 1967 and Bottled in 1997. There were only 100 Bottles of this Whisky released, each enclosed in a locked box.

GLENLOCHY RANGE

Glenlochy 1952 / 49 YO / Old Malt Cask
70cl / 43% - Douglas Laing - An old and rare single Cask Bottling of 1952 vintage Whisky from Glenlochy, which closed as part of the wave of shutdowns across Scotland in 1983. It has since been almost demolished and releases are rather rare, making this 49 YO a bit of a find.

Glenlochy 1969 / 26 YO / Rare Malts
75cl / 58.8% - Distillery Bottling

Glenlochy 1980 / 32 YO / Cask #1759
70cl / 60.1% - Signatory - A 1980 vintage Whisky from Glenlochy. This Whisky has been matured for 32 years in a Refill Butt and Bottled by Signatory for their Cask Strength Collection.

GLENMORANGIE RANGE

Glenmorangie / Last Christmas at Leith
70cl / 43% - Distillery Bottling - A very rare old Bottling commemorating the Glenmorangie company's last Christmas at their old Leith headquarters. Please note that the glass button on the front of this old Bottle is damaged.

Glenmorangie 10 YO
35cl / 40% - Distillery Bottling - A half Bottle of Glenmorangie's ever popular 10 YO - a perfect introduction to the world of Single Malt Whisky.

Glenmorangie 10 YO – Original
70cl / 40% - Distillery Bottling - Glenmorangie's 10 YO sets a high standard for Highland Whisky, and has gone from strength to strength as 'The Original' since its slightly controversial packaging redesign a few years ago. Medium-bodied and gently warming, with pleasant spicy notes.

Glenmorangie 10 YO - Original / Jeroboam
300cl / 40% - Distillery Bottling - A whopping three litre Bottle of the splendid Glenmorangie Original. Glenmorangie are getting into large formats in a big way these days (think Ardbeg Mor). It may be gimmicky, but it does look good.

Glenmorangie 10 YO / 100 Proof
100cl / 57.2% - Distillery Bottling - An early version of high-strength Glenmorangie, Bottled at full proof - a potent 57.2% - for the duty-free market, hence the 1L size.

Glenmorangie 10 YO / Bot.1960s
75cl / 40% - Distillery Bottling - A rare old cork-stoppered Glenmorangie 10 YO from the 1960s.

Glenmorangie 10 YO / Bot.1960s
75cl / 43% - Distillery Bottling

Glenmorangie 10 YO / Bot.1970s
75cl / 40% - Distillery Bottling

Glenmorangie 10 YO / Bot.1980s
75cl / 40% - Distillery Bottling

Glenmorangie 10 YO / Bot.1980s
75.7cl / 40% - Distillery Bottling - An old 1980s Bottling of Glenmorangie 10 YO.

Glenmorangie 10 YO / Grand Slam Dram
75cl / 40% - Distillery Bottling - A special Bottling of Glenmorangie 10 YO released in celebration of the Scottish rugby team's Grand Slam win in 1990. The neck label is dated 17th March 1990 - the day of the final match, a still spoken about win against England.

Glenmorangie 10 YO + 2 Tumblers / Gift Pack
70cl / 40% - Distillery Bottling - A Bottle of Glenmorangie's excellent 10 YO Original, perfect for giving as a gift. It comes in a great gift box, along with 2 branded Whisky tumblers.

Glenmorangie 10 YO Cask Strength
70cl / 60% - Distillery Bottling - A great old Distillery Bottling of Glenmorangie's 10 YO, back from their less fancy white label days. Bottled at a whopping natural 60% abv, so be sparing with this one.

Glenmorangie 12 YO / Nectar D'Or / Sauternes Finish
70cl / 46% - Distillery Bottling - Relaunched in 2011, Glenmorangie's sauternes-finished Nectar d'Or is now proudly boasting a prominent age statement that wasn't there before, proclaiming it to be 12 YO. Give it a couple of years and it'll be growing a weedy moustache on its top lip. IWSC 2012 Gold Medal Winner

Glenmorangie 15 YO / Fino Sherry
70cl / 43% - Distillery Bottling

Glenmorangie 18 YO
70cl / 43% - Distillery Bottling - An increasingly hard-to-find old presentation of the splendid Glenmorangie 18 YO.

Glenmorangie 18 YO
70cl / 43% - Distillery Bottling - The 18 year-old has always been one of the best of Glenmorangie's core range and its stylish packaging has ensured its popularity. Picked up the top prize in its category at the World Whisky Awards 2010.
IWSC 2012 - Gold Medal Winner

Glenmorangie 18 YO
70cl / 43% - Distillery Bottling - The 18 year-old has always been one of the best of Glenmorangie's core range and its stylish packaging has ensured its popularity. Picked up the top prize in its category at the World Whisky Awards 2010.
IWSC 2012 - Gold Medal Winner

Glenmorangie 1963 / 22 YO / Sherry Cask
75cl / 43% - Distillery Bottling - Another supremely contemplative malt that demands time and concentration. This Bottling is from Bourbon Casks that were re-racked into Oloroso Sherry Casks for the final stages of maturation. One of the most difficult-to-find Glenmorangies.

Glenmorangie 1974 / Bot.2000
75cl / 43% - Distillery Bottling

Glenmorangie 1975 / Bot 2001

75cl / 43% - Distillery Bottling

Glenmorangie 1975 / Bot.2002
75cl / 43% - Distillery Bottling - A highly rated 1975 vintage Glenmorangie.

Glenmorangie 1975 / Bot.2004
75cl / 43% - Distillery Bottling - A 1975 vintage release of the world's favourite Highlander. This was Bottled in 2004 and has become a bit of a collectors item now.

Glenmorangie 1976 / Concorde
75cl / 60.8% - Distillery Bottling - A 1976 vintage Glenmorangie, Distilled on the 21st of January and Bottled to commemorate the retirement of Concorde, which flew for the last time on 26 November 2003.

Glenmorangie 1976 Concorde Bottling
75cl / 60.4%

Glenmorangie 1978 / Tain L' Hermitage Finish
70cl / 43% - Distillery Bottling

Glenmorangie 1979 / Bot.1996
70cl / 40% - Distillery Bottling

Glenmorangie 1981 / Manager's Choice
70cl / 54.5% - Distillery Bottling - A special Bottling of Glenmorangie consisting of Whisky hand selected by the Distillery manager and Bottled in 1998. 1981 has been a much loved vintage of the Distillery's staff and this looks to have been one of the first Bottlings to start off that affection.

Glenmorangie 1983 / Manager's Choice
70cl / 53.2% - Distillery Bottling - A Cask strength Bottling by Glenmorangie as part of their Manager's Choice range. 1983 vintage Whisky specially selected by the Distillery manager and released in a numbered Bottle.

Glenmorangie 1987 / Margaux Cask Finish
70cl / 46% - Distillery Bottling - A snazzy Bottling of 1987 vintage Glenmorangie with a fancy box and some time finishing in Casks that previously held wine from chateau Margaux. A must for collectors of Glenmorangie.

Glenmorangie 1987 / Margaux Cask Finish
70cl / 46% - Distillery Bottling - A snazzy Bottling of 1987 vintage

Glenmorangie with a fancy box and some time finishing in Casks that previously held wine from chateau Margaux. A must for collectors of Glenmorangie.

Glenmorangie 1991 / Missouri Oak
70cl / 55.7% - Distillery Bottling - A 1991 vintage Glenmorangie produced as part of one of their successful experiments with interesting wood. This was matured in new oak from Missouri in the USA and has a Bourbony tang in addition to the regular Glenmorangie character.

Glenmorangie 1992 / 10 YO
70cl / 57% - Distillery Bottling

Glenmorangie 1993 / Burr Oak
70cl / 56.3% - Distillery Bottling - A full proof Bottling of 1993 vintage Glenmorangie that came from one of their experiments with interesting wood. This was matured in a new Burr Oak Cask, a variety of oak native to the USA and Canadian borders, and has taken on some Bourbon characteristics.

Glenmorangie 1993 / Chinkapin Oak
75cl / 57.3% - Distillery Bottling - A very limited release from Glenmorangie showcasing one of their successful experiments with different woods. This was matured in Casks made from Chinkapin oak, native to North America, and was originally an exclusive Bottling for World of Whiskies at Heathrow.

Glenmorangie 1993 / Post Oak Matured
75cl / 58.2% - Distillery Bottling - One of a series of extremely rare single Cask, Cask-strength releases from Glenmorangie. These releases were matured in a special type of new American oak and released in duty-free shops around the world.

Glenmorangie 21 YO / Claret Wood Finish
70cl / 48% - Distillery Bottling - A 21 YO special edition from Glenmorangie, finished in red wine Casks that previous held Claret. A hard to find and much respected successful red wine finished Whisky.

Glenmorangie 25 YO / Malaga Wood
70cl / 43% - Distillery Bottling - A 25 YO Whisky from Glenmorangie, finished in Casks that once contained sweet fortified wine from Malaga in Spain.

Glenmorangie Artisan Cask
50cl / 46% - Distillery Bottling - One of the best Glenmorangie releases of the last ten years, this has recently been discontinued and replaced by the hugely popular 'Astar' Bottling. A terrific 'Morangie. We have snapped up as much of the remaining stock as we could get our hands on.

Glenmorangie Astar
70cl / 57.1% - Distillery Bottling - The Astar Bottling from Glenmorangie is a second incarnation of the much-loved Artisan Cask Bottling from several years ago. A massive dram, with huge spices - a drop of water is the sensible option.

Glenmorangie Cask Strength 10 YO
75cl / 61.2% - Distillery Bottling - An old Bottle of Glenmorangie's discontinued Cask strength 10 YO, Distilled in 1980 and Bottled in 1991 at a hefty 61.2% from Cask 5562.

Glenmorangie Ceramic 21 YO / 150th Anniversary
70cl / 43% - Distillery Bottling - A 21 YO Whisky Bottled by Glenmorangie in celebration of the 150th anniversary of the founding of the Distillery, presented in a white ceramic Bottle.

Glenmorangie Claret Finish
70cl / 43% - Distillery Bottling - A rare and very sold out expression of Glenmorangie, augmenting the normal maturation with some time finishing in claret Casks. A limited release showing off Glenmorangie's ways with wood.

Glenmorangie Cognac Matured
70cl / 43% - Distillery Bottling - A very limited edition Glenmorangie, matured for 14 years in a Cask that previous held Cognac.

Glenmorangie Finealta / Private Edition
70cl / 46% - Distillery Bottling - The second in Glenmorangie's series of Private Editions (the first being the hugely popular Sonnalta), Finealta is lightly peated barley that has been matured partly in ex-Sherry Casks and partly in plain new American oak Casks. the name means 'Elegance' in Gaelic (it says here).
IWSC 2012 - Gold Medal - Whisky - Scotch

Glenmorangie Lasanta 12 YO / Sherry Finish
70cl / 46% - Distillery Bottling - Updated in summer 2010, Glenmorangie Lasanta now boasts an age statement of 12 YO. Lasanta is a Sherry-finished Glenmorangie and is said to mean 'Warmth & Passion' in Gaelic.

Glenmorangie Millennium 12 YO
70cl / 40% - Distillery Bottling - A special Bottling of Glenmorangie to commemorate our progression into the 21st century, this is made up of only Whisky from first fill Casks, giving a more fuller flavoured Whisky than the regular 12 YO. Highly rated and increasingly rare.

Glenmorangie Quinta Ruban 12 YO / Port Finish

70cl / 46% - Distillery Bottling - Glenmorangie's Quinta Ruban was upgraded in late 2010, and is now sporting a 12 YO age statement where previously there was none.

Glenmorangie Signet
70cl / 46% - Distillery Bottling - A delicious no-age-statement dram from Glenmorangie, some of the spirit in Signet has been made using a unique heavily-roasted Chocolate Malt that really beefs up the rich flavours. The packaging is very impressive too.
World Whiskies Awards 2012 - Best Highland No Age Statement
IWSC 2012 - Gold Outstanding Medal - Whisky - Scotch

Glenmorangie Sonnalta PX
70cl / 46% - Distillery Bottling - Glenmorangie's Sonnalta PX is the second of their Private Collection Bottlings after 2008's release of Astar. Sonnalta PX has been finished in Casks formerly containing Pedro Ximenez. A great success at TWE tastings in Vinopolis.

Glenmorangie Speakeasy 1990
70cl / 60.2% - Distillery Bottling

Glenmorangie Special Reserve
70cl / 43% - Distillery Bottling - A special release of Glenmorangie. This Whisky is made of a vatting of of aged Casks filled between the years of 1980 and 1990.

Glenmorangie Traditional
100cl / 57.2% - Distillery Bottling - A litre Bottle of Glenmorangie Bottled with the minimum amount of fuss - unchillfiltered, undiluted and ready for drinking. A bit of water really helps the flavours on this one, but the higher strength gives you the choice as to how much.

GLEN ORD RANGE

Glen Ord 12 YO
75cl / 43% - Distillery Bottling - An exuberantly spicy malt, with plenty of Sherry influence, Glen Ord is a fine example of the Highland style and very good value for money. This Bottling is now discontinued, to be replaced by Singleton of Glen Ord, so grab one while you can.

Glen Ord 12 YO / Bot.1990s
75cl / 40% - Distillery Bottling - A 1990s Distillery Bottling of 12 YO Glen Ord, more commonly known in the 2000s through its new Asian incarnation as Singleton of Glen Ord.

Glen Ord 1974 / 23 YO
70cl / 60.8% - Distillery Bottling - The Rare Malts are a now-discontinued series of Cask-strength releases designed by Diageo to

showcase some of the hidden treasures in their portfolio. Originally Bottled in 1997, this expression is a brilliant example of what this great Highland Distillery is capable of.

Glen Ord 1990 / 21 YO / Cask #6856
70cl / 50% - Douglas Laing - A single Cask release of 1990 vintage Glen Ord. This Whisky has been aged for 21 years and matured in a Refill butt. Bottled for Douglas Laing's Old Malt Cask series, at their preferred strength of 50%.

Glen Ord 1997 / Managers' Choice
70cl / 59.2% - Distillery Bottling - A single American oak Cask of Glen Ord 1997, Bottled at full strength for the Managers' Choice range. This is only the second ever official vintage bottling of Glen Ord from Diageo.

Glen Ord 25 YO
70cl / 58.3% - Distillery Bottling - A superlative Bottling of Glen Ord, this 25 YO boasts massive fruit with a hint of smoke.

Glen Ord 28 YO
70cl / 58.3% - Distillery Bottling - A top-quality Cask-strength Glen Ord, with typical grassy, heathery and barley-sugar notes alongside summer fruits and well-integrated vanilla oak notes.

Glen Ord 30 YO
70cl / 58.7% - Distillery Bottling - A brilliant malt from a top Highland Distillery. Aged Glen Ord is big and characterful, and this is a terrific price for such a distinguished dram.

Glen Ord Maltings
75cl / 60% - Distillery Bottling

GLENTURRET RANGE

Glenturret (Tayside) 8 YO / Bot.1970s
75cl / 43% - Distillery Bottling - An old Bottling of Glenturret from the 1980s.

Glenturret 1960 / 18 YO / Cadenhead's
75cl / 45.7% - Cadenhead's - An 18 YO Glenturret Bottled by Cadenhead's in the late 1970s after 18 years of maturation.

Glenturret 1965 / 17 YO / Cadenhead's
75cl / 46% - Cadenhead's

Glenturret 1966
70cl / 40% - Distillery Bottling - A rare Bottling of Glenturret 1966, Bottled in 1993 after over 25 years ageing.

Glenturret 1966 / Gold Ceramic Flagon
75cl / 43% - Distillery Bottling - An old release of 1966 vintage Glenturret Whisky, presented in a Gold ceramic flagon. This was actually 'Bottled' sometime in 1987 making the Whisky inside atleast 20 YO.

Glenturret 1976
70cl / 58.7% - Distillery Bottling

Glenturret 1976
75cl / 58.7% - Distillery Bottling - A 1976 vintage Distillery Bottling of Glenturret, Bottled in 1986 at a punchy 58.6%, 102.7 proof.

Glenturret 1977 / 27 YO
70cl / 53.2% - Distillery Bottling - A limited edition Bottling of 1977 vintage Whisky from Glenturret, normally found at the heart of the Famous Grouse blend. This has been aged for 27 years before being Bottled in 2004 to produce a sweet and smooth Whisky with toffee and elegant oak.

Glenturret 1977 / 29 YO / Cask #996
70cl / 55.6% - Distillery Bottling - A rare official Bottling from Glenturret, this is a single Cask from the now much-revered 1977 vintage, released at full strength way back in October 2006 after 29 years in the wood. Just 246 Bottles were yielded from the Cask.

Glenturret 1977 /34 YO/ The Whisky Agency & The Nectar
70cl / 46.7%

The Whisky Agency - A 34 YO Whisky from Glenturret Distillery. This Whisky was Distilled in 1977 and has been Bottled as a join Bottling by The Whisky Agency and The Nectar.

Glenturret 1992 / 14 YO / Sherry Cask
70cl / 59.7% - Distillery Bottling - A single Cask offering from the ancient, picturesque Glenturret Distillery, home of Famous Grouse. This is from a Sherry Cask and has been Bottled at Cask strength

Glenturret 34 YO / Cask #1 / Berry Bros & Rudd
70cl / 46% - Berry Bros & Rudd - A 34 YO single Cask Glenturret, Bottled from Cask number 1 in 2012 by Berry Brothers and Rudd. This is the second 34 YO Glenturret they've released in a short timeframe and we are hoping this is just as fantastic as the previous Bottling.

Glenturret 7 YO / Bot.1970s
75cl / 43% - Distillery Bottling - A very rare Distillery-Bottled Glenturret 7 YO from the 1970s.

Glenturret 8 YO
70cl / 40% - Distillery Bottling - A medium-full honeyed malt with attractive youthful brio from Glenturret, famous as the home of Famous Grouse - and for Towser, the former Distillery cat who caught nearly 30,000 mice.

Glenturret 8 YO / Bot. 1970's
75cl / 43% - Distillery Bottling - A 1970s Distillery Bottling of 8 YO Glenturret Whisky.

Glenturret 8 YO / Bot.1980s
75cl / 43% - Distillery Bottling - A very nice old Bottle of 1980s Glenturret 8 YO, Bottled at 43%.

Glenturret Bicentenary 8 YO
37.5cl / 43% - Distillery Bottling - An 8 YO Glenturret released in a ceramic Bottle to celebrate their 1975 200th anniversary, although back in 1775 it was called Hosh Distillery and was an illicit still hidden on a farm...

GLENUGIE RANGE

Glenugie 1959 / 18 YO / 46% / 75cl / Cadenhead's
75cl / 46% - Cadenhead's - A 1959 vintage Whisky from Glenugie, closed since 1983, Bottled at 18 years of age in the late 1970s by Cadenhead's.

Glenugie 1965 / 23 YO
75cl / 43% - Hart Brothers

Glenugie 1965 / 23 YO / Hart Brothers
70cl / 43% - Hart Brothers - A 1965 vintage Glenugie Bottled by Hart Brothers at 23 YO.

Glenugie 1966 / 15 YO / Connoisseurs Choice
75cl / 40% - Gordon & Macphail - A very old early 1980s Connoisseur's Choice Bottling of Glenugie 1966, this was Bottled at 15 YO.

Glenugie 1966 / 16 YO
75cl / 40% - Gordon & Macphail - An old style Connoisseurs Choice Bottling of Glenugie, Distilled in 1966 and Bottled 16 years later.

Glenugie 1966 / 30 YO / Cask #848
70cl / 58% - Signatory

Glenugie 1967 / Bot. 1997 / Connoisseurs Choice
70cl / 40% - Gordon & Macphail - An old 1990s Connoisseurs Choice Bottling of Glenugie 1967 by Gordon & Macphail.

Glenugie 1967 / Connoisseurs Choice
70cl / 40% - Gordon & Macphail - A 1990s Bottling of Glenugie 1967 for Gordon & Macphail's Connoisseurs Choice series.

Glenugie 1968 / 20 YO / Sherry / Bird Label
75cl / 43% - Sestante - A 1968 Glenugie matured in Sherry Casks for 20 years and Bottled by Sestante as part of their series with birds on the labels.

Glenugie 1970 / Bot.2009
70cl / 43.5% - Gordon & Macphail - A 1970 vintage Whisky from Glenugie, Bottles as part of Gordon & Macphail's beautifully presented Rare Old series. Bottled in 2009 after almost 40 years of maturation.

Glenugie 1976 / 25 YO / Cask #2699
70cl / 51.8% - Signatory - A very rare Signatory Bottling of Glenugie 1976 from a single Cask, Bottled in 2001. The vast majority of Glenugie's spirit went for blending and the Distillery was closed in 1983, so Single Malt expressions are rather rare nowadays.

Glenugie 1977 / 27 YO / Celtic Heartlands
70cl / 46.8% - Celtic Heartlands - A rare 1977 vintage single Cask Glenugie selected and Bottled by Bruichladdich's Jim McEwan for his Celtic Heartlands series. Please note that the box for this Bottle is damaged and will not close properly.

Glenugie 1977 / 32 YO / Deoch an Doras
70cl / 55.48% - Distillery Bottling - The first official Bottling of Glenugie since a near-impossible-to-find 5 YO Grant McDonald Bottling from about twenty years ago, this 1977 was Bottled in 2010, twenty-seven years after the Distillery closed its doors for the last time in 1983. Bottled at its impressive Cask strength of 55% abv.

Glenugie 1977 / 33 YO / Oloroso Finish
70cl / 57.2% - Signatory - A tremedously rich and colourful single Cask of the sought-after Glenugie, this has spent its last 100 months of maturation in an Oloroso Cask, picking up an extremely fetching russet hue en route.

Glenugie 1977 / Murray McDavid
70cl / 46% - Murray McDavid - An old release of 1977 vintage Whisky from Glenugie, Bottled by Murray McDavid and presented in a sturdy wooden presentation case.

Glenugie 1980 / 30 YO / Deoch an Doras

70cl / 52.13% - Distillery Bottling - Only the second official Bottling of Whisky from closed Distillery Glenugie in recent times, following the previous 32 year entry with this 1980 vintage 30 YO. The Distillery closed in 1983 and has since been demolished, and Bottlings in general are quite rare.

Glenugie 1981 / 22 YO / Refill Sherry
70cl / 52.5% - Ian Macleod - Bottled from a refill Sherry Cask, this is stellar malt from a Distillery closed in 1983.

Glenugie 5 YO / Bot.1980s
75cl / 40% - - A rather rare Glenugie 5 YO. We believe this was Bottled around the 1980s.

GLENURY ROYAL RANGE

Glenury 1978 / 14 YO / Cask 9776-79
70cl / 43% - Signatory - A Bottling of 14 YO Whisky from this now closed east highland Distillery. Distilled in 1978 the Whisky is a vatting of 4 Casks, Bottled in 1993.

Glenury Royal 12 YO / Bot.1970s
75.7cl / 40% - Distillery Bottling - A rare 1970s Bottling of Whisky from since demolished Glenury Royal, Bottled at 12 YO under the label of John Gillon and Company.

Glenury Royal 12 YO / John Gillon / Bot.1980s
75cl / 40% - Distillery Bottling - A classic and quite rare old 1980s Distillery Bottling of 12 YO Glenury Royal.

Glenury Royal 1953 / 50 YO / Dark Sherry
70cl / 42.8% - Distillery Bottling - A brilliant richly-Sherried send-off for a sadly now-defunct Distillery. This is another malt that aficionados cherish despite it being relatively obscure, and it is thus extremely collectable.

Glenury Royal 1968 / 36 YO
70cl / 51.2% - Distillery Bottling - A brilliantly-balanced mouth-coating beauty, this Glenury Royal is a very special Whisky from a tragically lost Distillery, and we've always been surprised that it didn't sell out years ago - especially after a 92 point review from Whiskyfun.

Glenury Royal 1970 / 36 YO
70cl / 57.9% - Distillery Bottling - One of only a handful of long-aged Distillery-Bottled releases of Glenury Royal. This 1970 vintage is very special Whisky from a tragically lost Distillery. Impeccable Cask selection has led to perhaps the best of Diageo's recent releases from Glenury.

Glenury Royal 1970 / 40 YO
70cl / 59.4% - Distillery Bottling - A belated entry in Diageo's 2011 Special Releases selection, hitting the market in early 2012. Closed in 1985 and since demolished, Whisky from the Distillery is sought after by collectors and drinkers alike due to the comparatively small number of Bottlings available.

Glenury Royal 1971 / 23 YO
70cl / 61.3% -Distillery Bottling - Unboxed

Glenury Royal 1973 / 24 YO / Silent Stills
70cl / 53.7% - Signatory - A late 1990s Bottling of a single Cask Glenury Royal 1973, Bottled at full strength for Signatory's Silent Stills series.

Glenury Royal 1980 / 20 YO
70cl / 50%

INCHFAD

2001 Heavily Peated / American Oak Cask #665 70cl / 45% Distillery Bottling Inchfad is a heavily-peated Whisky made at the Loch Lomond Distillery. This single Cask expression is from the 2001 vintage and was matured in American Oak.

INCHMURRIN RANGE

Inchmurrin 1993 / 19 YO / Casks #2844+5 / Signatory
70cl / 58.1% - Signatory - A lightly peated Inchmurrin, Distilled at the Loch Lomond Distillery on May 24th 1993, matured in a pair of hogsheads and then Bottled on July 9th 2012 for Signatory.

Inchmurrin 2001 / American Oak
70cl / 45% - Distillery Bottling - A rare Bottling of Loch Lomond's lightly peated Inchmurrin malt matured in American oak Casks.

INVERGORDON RANGE

Invergordon 1964 / Bot.2012 / Scott's Selection
70cl / 42.3% - Scott's Selection - A 1964 Invergordon Grain Whisky Bottled for the Scott's Selection range. This is one of the first grain Whiskies released in 2012.

Invergordon 1964 Single Grain / Scott's Selection

70cl / 43.8% - Single Grain Scotch Whisky - Scott's Selection - An independent Cask strength release of grain Whisky from the Invergordon Distillery. Bottled from a single Cask as part of the Scott's Selection range of Whiskies.

Invergordon 1966 / 45 YO / Bourbon Cask HH7254
70cl / 47.1% - Single Grain Scotch Whisky - Clan Denny
A long aged grain Whisky from Invergordon, Distilled in England's last great year at the World Cup and Bottled in 2011 by Clan Denny.

Invergordon 1966 / 45 YO / Cask HH7864 / Clan Denny
70cl / 47.5% - Single Grain Scotch Whisky - Clan Denny - A 1965 vintage Whisky from the Invergordon grain Distillery, aged for an impressive 45 years before Bottling in 2011 by Clan Denny. Old grain is a style of Whisky that's increasing in popularity and Bottlings such as this show why.

LOCH LOMOND RANGE

Loch Lomond Single Malt
Its exquisite packaging - from the embossed Bottle to the stunning blue labels - is matched by the Whisky within, which has a mellow, slightly peaty nose, with a hint of brandy butter. The taste on the palette is sweet, smokey, with hints of finest Madeira wine and has a long, mellow finish, with echoes of a raisiny Xmas pudding.
All of the Loch Lomond range of Whiskies are double-matured to ensure a perfect marriage of the spirit before Bottling. Launched in the German market in 1999 this malt has enjoyed spectacular success and is now the third best selling malt in Germany (Nielson). It is available with or without a presentation tube, depending on the market.

Loch Lomond 21 YO Black Label Single Malt
The 'big brother' of the blue label, utilising the same embossed Bottle and style of label, but with a black presentation tube, this malt has matured in Cask for a minimum of 21 years. Only a limited quantity is Bottled each year, making it a malt for a special occasion! Similar in style to the Blue Label, but lacking the peaty overtones, as back then we did not use much peated barley.

Distillery Select Scotch Single Malt
This is a range of Single Cask Whiskies that have been Bottled without chill-filtration or colouring so that you can taste them 'straight from the Cask'.

Distillery Select Scotch Single Malt
This is a range of Single Cask Whiskies that have been Bottled without chill-filtration or colouring so that you can taste them 'straight from

the Cask' .

LOCHNAGAR RANGE

Lochnagar 12 YO / Bot.1970s
75cl / 40% - Distillery Bottling - An old 1970s Bottling of Royal Lochnagar 12 YO.

Royal Lochnagar / Selected Reserve
75cl / 43% - Distillery Bottling - A 75cl version of the old wooden box presentation of Royal Lochnagar's prestigious Selected Reserve, which was phased out around 2008. A very drinkable dram.

Royal Lochnagar 10 YO / Manager's Dram
70cl / 57.2% - Distillery Bottling - A youthful Royal Lochnagar, selected by Diageo's Distillery managers as the best of the year and Bottled for staff at full strength in 2006 as part of the Managers Dram series.

Royal Lochnagar 12 YO
70cl / 40% - Distillery Bottling - A favourite of Queen Victoria and Prince Albert, being conveniently situated close by Balmoral Castle. Royal Lochnagar was originally a key ingredient in VAT 69, but most production is now for Single Malts.

Royal Lochnagar 12 YO / 150th Anniversary
70cl / 40% - Distillery Bottling - A special release of Royal Lochnagar 12 YO Bottled for the Distillery's 150th anniversary in 1995.

Royal Lochnagar 12 YO / Bot.1980s
75cl / 40% - Distillery Bottling - A lovely old Bottle of 12 YO Royal Lochnagar - one of only three Distilleries permitted to use the 'Royal' epithet - Bottled in the 1980s.

Royal Lochnagar 12 YO / Bot.1980s
75cl / 43% - Distillery Bottling - A nice old 1980s Distillery Bottling of Royal Lochnagar 12 YO.

Royal Lochnagar 1969 / 14 YO / Brown Label
75cl / 40% - Gordon & Macphail - A 1969 vintage Royal Lochnagar Bottled in the mid 1980s byt Gordon & Macphail for their Connoisseurs Choice range at 14 YO.

Royal Lochnagar 1970 / 14 YO / Connoisseurs Choice
75cl / 40% - Gordon & Macphail - A rare early Connoisseurs Choice Bottling of Royal Lochnagar from the 1980s.

Royal Lochnagar 1972 / 24 YO
75cl / 55.7% - Distillery Bottling - A potent Cask strength Royal Lochnagar 1972 Bottled in the mid-1990s by the Distillers as part of Diageo's Rare Malt selection. The early Rare Malts Bottlings were almost uniformly outstanding.

Royal Lochnagar 1973 / 23 YO
70cl / 59.7% - Distillery Bottling - An early Bottling from the mid-1990s for Diageo's Rare Malt series, this Royal Lochnagar 1983 should be a belter.

Royal Lochnagar 1974 / 30 YO
70cl / 56.2% - Distillery Bottling - A Rare Malts expression of 1974 vintage Royal Lochnagar. Released in the Autumn of 2004 at Cask strength, it's a big Whisky that's definitely one for Lochnagar fans.

Royal Lochnagar 1981 / 25 YO / Roseisle Maltings
70cl / 60% - Distillery Bottling - A very special edition Royal Lochnagar Distilled from the first batch of barley processed at the Roseisle maltings in 1981, and Bottled to celebrate their 25th anniversary.

Royal Lochnagar 1991 / 20 YO / Sherry Butt #374
70cl / 54.8% - Signatory - A single Cask 20 YO Whisky from Royal Lochnagar, Bottled by Signatory as part of their Cask Strength Collection. This was Distilled on April 12th 1991, matured in a refill butt and then Bottled on November 1st 2011.

Royal Lochnagar 1994 / Managers' Choice / Sherry Cask
70cl / 59.3% - Distillery Bottling - A special Royal Lochnagar 1994 Bottled in 2009 at full strength from a single European Sherry Oak Cask for the Managers' Choice range.

Royal Lochnagar 1996 / Distillers Edition
70cl / 40% - Distillery Bottling - The newest addition to Diageo's 'Distiller's Edition' series is Royal Lochnagar - and the packaging's had a facelift too. This has been Double Matured in 'Fine Old Muscat-Wood', so expect more sweetness than the standard-issue 12 YO.

Royal Lochnagar 1998 Distillers Edition
70cl / 40% - Distillery Bottling - The 2010 edition of the Royal Lochnagar entry in Diageo's Distillers Edition range of Whiskies. This one was finished in Casks that previous contained well aged muscat wine, adding a floral richness to the spirit.

Royal Lochnagar Selected Reserve
70cl / 43% - Distillery Bottling - This is the old wooden box

presentation of Royal Lochnagar's prestigious Selected Reserve, which was phased out around 2008. A very drinkable dram.

Royal Lochnagar Selected Reserve
70cl / 43% - Distillery Bottling - A deluxe Royal Lochnagar, with a high proportion of long-aged Sherried malt in the mix. Selected Reserve is a good after-dinner option, especially with a medium-weight cigar.

LOCH NESS MALT Whisky
(70cl, 40%) A Single Malt from the Highlands. Named for the notorious Loch Ness, one of Scotland's most popular tourist attractions and home to the mysterious Loch Ness Monster.
Colour: Full gold.
Nose: Floral hint of jasmine and passion fruit.
Body: Medium and soft.
Palate: Nuts and sweet dried grass notes of great Scotch Whiskies fresh backed biscuits.
Finish: Dry with a little after glow with slight hint of peat coming through.
We have found the Whisky we wanted to but Nessie has still not been found since the first sighting in in 1868 . you never know, you might be the next one to find her. One thing is certain - you will see Nessie on the label and if you look closer inside the Bottle you will see her again. Hopefully, you will be able to visit Scotland and Loch Ness soon to continue the search for Nessie and enjoy all the pleasures of Scotland.

LOCHSIDE RANGE

Lochside / Bot. 1980s
75cl / 40% - Distillery Bottling - An old 1980s Distillery Bottling of extinct Highlander Lochside. We're 99% certain that this is a Bottle of the 10 YO, the age label of which has fallen off.

Lochside 10 YO / Bot. Early 1990s
75cl / 40% - Distillery Bottling - A bit of a historical relic - this 10 YO Lochside was released in 1991 and remains the only official Bottling from the Distillery, which was closed the following year and demolished a short time later.

Lochside 10 YO / Bot.1980s
75cl / 40%

Independent Bottler

Lochside 1966 / Connoisseurs Choice
75cl / 40% - Gordon & Macphail

Lochside 1966 / Map Label / Connoisseurs Choice
70cl / 40% - Gordon & Macphail - An old 1966 vintage Lochside Bottled by Gordon and Macphail for their Connoisseurs Choice series.

Lochside 1979 / 21 YO
70cl / 50% - Douglas Laing

Lochside 1981
70cl / 43% - Gordon & Macphail - This Lochside 1981 was Bottled by Gordon & Macphail for their 'Rare Old' series in 2005.

Lochside 1981 / Bot.1996 / Connoisseurs Choice
70cl / 40% - Gordon & Macphail - A 1981 vintage Whisky from Lochside, closed in 1992 and demolished in 2005, Bottled by Gordon & Macphail for their Connoisseurs Choice range back in the days when they still used their old 'Map Label' livery.

Lochside 1981 / Bot.2011 / Berry Bros & Rudd
70cl / 46% - Berry Bros & Rudd - A 1981 vintage Whisky from Lochside Bottled by Berry Brothers & Rudd. Lochside was closed in 1992 and has begun to pick up a cult following as aged stock has started to come into its prime.

Lochside 1987 / 21 YO
70cl / 59.8% - Dewar Rattray - A Dewar Rattray Bottling of the rarely-seen Lochside, this expression is a single refill hogshead filled in 1987 and Bottled late 2008 at full strength.

Lochside 1991 / Connoisseurs Choice
70cl / 43% - Gordon & Macphail - A 1991 vintage Lochside, closed the year after this was Distilled and demolished in 2005. This has been Bottled by Gordon & Macphail as part of their Connoisseurs Choice collection and is one of the most affordable Whiskies from this closed Distillery.

MACDUFF RANGE

Macduff 12 YO / Bot.1970s / Cadenhead's
75cl / 46% Cadenhead's - A 12 YO Macduff bottled by Cadenheads during the 1970s.

Macduff 1975 / Bot.1995 / Connoisseurs Choice
70cl / 40%

Gordon & Macphail
An old Connoisseurs Choice bottling of Macduff (aka Glen Deveron) from Gordon & Macphail. This was Distilled in 1975 and bottled in 1995.

Macduff 1980 / 30 YO / Old Malt Cask #6624
70cl / 50% Douglas Laing
A 2010 bottling of single Cask Whisky from Macduff, part of Douglas Laing's Old Malt Cask range. Distilled in October 1980 and bottled 30 years later after being finished in a Sherry hogshead.

Macduff 1990 / 21 YO / Old Malt Cask #7149
70cl / 50% - Douglas Laing - A bottling of 1990 vintage Macduff by Douglas Laing for their Old Malt Cask range. Matured in a refill hogshead for 21 years before bottling in early 2011.

Macduff 1995 / 16 YO / Cask #7867 / Signatory
70cl / 56.2% - Signatory - A 1995 vintage Whisky from Macduff, Distilled on March 3rd, matured in a hogshead for 16 years and bottled on January 9th 2012 by Signatory for their Cask Strength Collection.

Macduff 1997 / Connoisseurs Choice
70cl / 43% - Gordon & Macphail - A Connoisseurs Choice bottling of 1997 vintage Whisky from Macduff, a Distillery whose Whisky is normally bottled as Glen Deveron.

Macduff 38 YO / Daily Dram
70cl / 47.8% - Daily Dram - A 38 YO from Macduff, the Distillery whose Whisky is usually known as Glen Deveron, bottled by the Daily Dram in 2011.

MILLBURN RANGE

Millburn 1970 / 11 YO
75cl / 46% - Samaroli

Millburn 1971 / 17 YO / Connisseurs Choice
75cl / 40% - Gordon & Macphail - A very rare 1980s Connoisseurs Choice Bottling of 1971 single Highland malt from the now-defunct Millburn Distillery.

Millburn 1975 / 18 YO
70cl / 58.9% - Distillery Bottling

NORTH PORT BRECHIN RANGE

North Port Brechin 1974 / Connoisseurs Choice
70cl / 40% - Gordon & Macphail - A Bottle of 1974 North Port (aka Brechin) Bottled in 1993 by Gordon & Macphail as part of their Connoisseurs Choice range. North Port closed in 1983 as part of the cull of Distilleries in that year and is now the site of a supermarket.

North Port Brechin 1981 / Connoisseurs Choice / Bot.2002
70cl / 40% - Gordon & Macphail - A 1981 vintage Whisky from North

Port Brechin, which was demolished in 1990.

North Port Brechin 1982 / Connoisseurs Choice
70cl / 43% - Gordon & Macphail - A new Bottling of North Port Brechin from G & M's Connoisseurs Choice series, this was Distilled in 1982, a year before the Distillery closed.

Brechin North Port 1982
70cl / 43% - Private Cellar - independent Bottling from the defunct North Port Distillery (AKA Brechin), which closed its doors for the last time in 1983 and was demolished in 1994 to make way for a supermarket.

North Port-Brechin 1970 / Connoisseurs Choice
75cl / 40% Godon & Macphail - An early 1990s Connoisseurs Choice Bottling of 1970 Single Malt from the defunct North Port Distillery (aka Brechin) by Gordon & Macphail.

OBAN RANGE

Oban 12 YO / Bot.1970s
75cl / 43% - Distillery Bottling - A 12 YO Whisky from Oban, released in their distinct 'diamond' Bottle in the 1970s.

Oban 14 YO
70cl / 43% - Distillery Bottling - The Western Highland representative in Diageo's 'Classic Malt' series, Oban 14 YO is a superb, full-blooded fruity malt with a whiff of heather and more than a hint of smoke.

Oban 14 YO / Small Bottle
20cl / 43% - Distillery Bottling - A great little gift for any malt fan, or a pocket size treat for yourself.

Oban 1968 / 17 YO / Connoisseurs Choice
75cl / 40% - Gordon & Macphail - A very rare Bottle of Oban 1968 Bottled by Gordon & Macphail in the mid-1980s as part of the Connoissuers Choice series.

Oban 1996 / Distillers Edition
70cl / 43% - Distillery Bottling - The 1996 vintage entry for Oban in Diageo's Distillers Edition range, finished in Montilla fortified wine Casks for more depth and a kick of spice.

Oban 1997 / Distillers Edition
70cl / 43% - Distillery Bottling - The 1997 vintage edition of Oban's Distillers Edition, finished in Montilla Casks some extra sweetness and complexity.

Oban Bicentenary / 16 YO / Sherry Cask
70cl / 64% - Distillery Bottling - A legendary Bottling of 16 YO Sherried Oban, Bottled at its remarkable Cask strength of 64% under the Managers Dram label for UDV staff only to celebrate the Distillery's bicentenary in 1994.

OLD PULTENEY RANGE

Old Pulteney 12 YO
70cl / 40% - Distillery Bottling - A very popular highland dram, with a big Sherry presence alongside sweet citrus fruit notes and a faintly detectable whiff of brine. A winner at the World Whisky Awards 2010.

Old Pulteney 12 YO
35cl / 40% - Distillery Bottling - A half Bottle of Old Pulteney's reliable coastal 12 YO Single Malt Whisky.

Old Pulteney 15 YO / Gordon & Macphail
70cl / 40% - Gordon & Macphail - A 15 YO Old Pulteney, Bottled by Gordon & Macphail and presented with a replica of the old Distillery label.

Old Pulteney 1980
70cl / 43% - Gordon & Macphail - A 1980 vintage Whisky from Wick's Pulteney Distillery, released by veteran independent Bottled and rather good grocer Gordon & Macphail.

Old Pulteney 21 YO
70cl / 46% - Distillery Bottling - Pulteney is the most northerly mainland Distillery in Scotland, ensconced in the town of Wick. The 21 YO is a mix of fino Sherry and refill Bourbon Cask matured Whisky and sits at the top of their regular range.

Old Pulteney 30 YO
70cl / 44% - Distillery Bottling - A much-anticipated addition to the Old Pulteney range, this 30 YO has had extremely favourable reviews and, thankfully, this looks like living up to expectations and justifying the pricetag.

Old Pulteney 40 YO
70cl / 51.3% - Distillery Bottling - An impressive and long awaited Bottling from Old Pulteney - their oldest release yet, at a hefty 40 YO. It's presented in a hefty box with a book tracing the history of the Distillery and the hand blown Bottle, capped with a polished stone stopper, is decorated with silver waves, blown across the glass while the metal was molten.

Old Pulteney 8 YO / Gordon & Macphail
70cl / 40% - Gordon & Macphail - A Gordon & Macphail release of

Whisky from Wick's Pulteney Distillery, aged for 8 years.

ROYAL BRACKLA RANGE

Royal Brackla 12 YO / Bot.1980s
75cl / 43% -Distillery Bottling - A rare old Distillery Bottling of Royal Brackla, released in the late 1980s for the Italian market.

Royal Brackla 12 YO / Queen's Diamond Jubilee
70cl / 50% - Single Malt Scotch Whisky - Douglas Laing - A 12 YO Whisky from Royal Brackla, Bottled by the folks at Douglas Laing as the Old Malt Cask celebration of Queen Elizabeth II's Diamond Jubilee, complete with bad puns in the tasting notes.

Royal Brackla 16 YO / Bot.1970s
75cl / 57% - Distillery Bottling - A wonderful old-school Highlander, this UK 100-proof Distillery-Bottled Brackla has plenty of fruit and a grassy undertone. very drinkable at full strength, but really blossoms with a drop of water.

Royal Brackla 1924 / 60 YO
75cl / 40% - Distillery Bottling - A true rarity - as well as being incredibly old, this Bottle was never officially released for general sale. The remains of a batch Bottled in crystal for the Japanese market in 1984, these Bottles were given to staff and guests at an event to commemorate the re-opening of the Distillery in the early '90s.

Royal Brackla 1975 / 22 YO / Cask #5455 / Signatory
70cl / 58.6% - Signatory - A Cask strength single Cask Bottling of Royal Brackla Distilled in 1975 before its mid-80s mothballing and Bottled in 1997 after 22 years in a Sherry Cask.

Royal Brackla 1975 / 27 YO
70cl / 46% - Murray McDavid

Royal Brackla 1976 / 33 YO / Mackillop's
70cl / 43% - Mackillop's - A long-aged 1976 vintage malt from Royal Brackla, Bacardi's little-seen Highland Distillery.

Royal Brackla 1978 / 20 YO
70cl / 59.8% - Distillery Bottling - A 1978 vintage Royal Brackla Bottled at Cask strength at 20 YO as part of the Rare Malts series.

Royal Brackla 1979 / 19 YO / Cooper's Choice
70cl / 50% - Cooper's Choice - An independent release of Royal Brackla as part of the Cooper's Choice range. Distilled before the Distillery was mothballed in the mid-80s this was Bottled in 1997.

Royal Brackla 1991 / 17 YO

70cl / 53.6% - A Murray McDavid Bottling of Royal Brackla 1991.

TEANINICH RANGE

Teaninich 10 YO
70cl / 43% - Flora & Fauna - A very clean, grassy, medium-bodied Highlander with a predominantly malty character. A real charmer, this is a great introductory malt.

Teaninich 12 YO / Reopening of Distillery 1991
70cl / 43% - Distillery Bottling - A special and rare Bottling of Teaninich Single Malt, more usually found these days as part of Johnnie Walker. This was released in 1991 to celebrate the reopening of the Distillery, closed since 1985, and a visit from the Highland Regional Council, Ross & Cromarty Distinct council and the Ross & Cromarty Local Enterprise Company.

Teaninich 17 YO / Manager's Dram
70cl / 58.3% - Distillery Bottling - A rare Teaninich 17 YO selected by the Diageo Distillery managers for staff only. Please note that the Bottle numbers have been removed from the labels on some of these Bottles.

Teaninich 1972 / 23 YO / Rare Malts
75cl / 64.95% - Distillery Bottling - Released in the mid-1990s by owners Diageo as part of the Rare Malts series, this is a rare 1972 Teaninich Bottled at a startling 64.95%.

Teaninich 1973 / Berry Bros & Rudd
70cl / 41.8% - Berry Bros & Rudd - A 1973 Whisky from hidden Highland gem Teaninich, Bottled by the discerning folks at Berry Brothers and Rudd. It's a marriage of two Casks Bottled at a full proof of 41.8%.

Teaninich 1981 / 16 YO / First Cask #89/587/93
70cl / 46% - First Cask - A rare independent Bottling of a single Cask of Teaninich 1981 Bottled in the late 1990s.

Teaninich 1982 / 28 YO / Liquid Sun
70cl / 50.5% - Liquid Sun - A 1982 vintage Whisky from Teaninich, matured for 28 years in a Bourbon Cask and released in 2011 by Liquid Sun.

Teaninich 1983 / 27 YO / Sherry Butt #8074 / Signatory
70cl / 56.9% - Signatory - A 27 YO single Cask Whisky from Teaninich. Distilled on 7th December 1983, matured in a refill butt and then Bottled on 2nd November 2011 by Signatory as part of their Cask Strength Collection.

Teaninich 2001 / Connoisseurs Choice
70cl / 46% - Gordon & Macphail - A 2001 vintage Connoisseurs Choice release of Whisky from Teaninich, Bottled by Gordon &

Macphail.

TULLIBARDINE RANGE

Tullibardine 10 YO / Bot.1970s
75cl / 40% - Distillery Bottling - A simply-labelled Bottle of 10 YO Tullibardine from the 1970s. With the Distillery only having opened in 1949 this ranks as one of the earliest fully-matured OBs from the early days of production.

Tullibardine 10 YO / Bot.1980s
75cl / 40% - Distillery Bottling - A 1980s Distillery release of Tullibardine 10 YO, Bottled in an unusual dumpy Bottle with a gold-edged label proudly boasting of its medal at the 1980 International Wine & Spirit competition.

Tullibardine 10 YO / Bot.1980s
75cl / 40% - Distillery Bottling - An old Distillery Bottling of Tullibardine's entry-level 10 YO. We reckon this is probably from the 1980s or thereabouts.

Tullibardine 1964 / Cask #3359
70cl / 44.6% - Distillery Bottling - A Distillery-Bottled single Cask of Tullibardine 1964, Bottled in September 2004 at full strength from a single hogshead that yielded just 163 Bottles.

Tullibardine 1964 / Cask #3362
70cl / 43.4% - Distillery Bottling - A single Cask Distillery Bottling of Tullibardine from 2006. Just 212 Bottles were yielded from a single Butt, Bottled at natural strength.

Tullibardine 1965 / 18 YO
75cl / 46% - Cadenhead's - An extremely rare Bottling of 1960s Tullibardine from respected Edinburgh indie Bottler Cadenhead's. This is from the 1965 vintage and was Bottled in early 1984.

Tullibardine 1966
70cl / 49.8% - Distillery Bottling - A full-strength single Sherry-butt official Bottling of Tullibardine from 1966.

Tullibardine 5 YO / Bot.1980s
75cl / 40% - Distillery Bottling

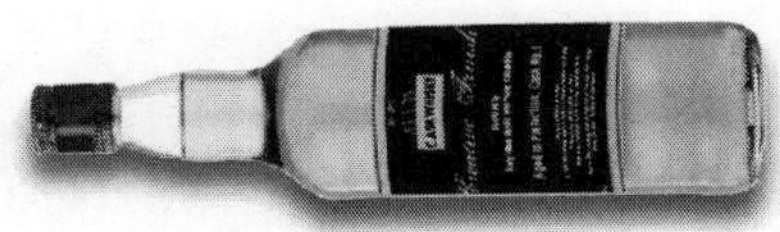

ABERLOUR RANGE

Aberlour 10 YO
70cl / 40% - Distillery Bottling - Aberlour 10 YO is a great entry-level malt, ideal for beginners, with a fine Sherried spiciness. Pound for pound, this is one of the best that Speyside has to offer.

Aberlour 10 YO / Bot.1990s
70cl / 40% - Distillery Bottling - An old 1990s Bottling of Aberlour 10 YO.

Aberlour 10 YO / Sherry Finish
70cl / 43% - Distillery Bottling - A delicious Sherry-finished Aberlour, with just the right amount of Sherry to enhance the profile of the standard 10 YO, without letting the wine take over. Previously only available in France, we think this will be a hit.

Aberlour 10 YO V.O.H.M
75cl / 43% - Distillery Bottling - A 75cl 1980s Bottling of Aberlour 10 YO 'Very Old Highland Malt' in a frosted brandy style Bottle.

Aberlour 10 YO VOHM / 1980s
100cl / 43% - Distillery Bottling - An unusual 1980s frosted glass Bottle of Aberlour VOHM (Very Old Highland Malt) - obviously this is from the days when Cognac was the No.1 sipping spirit in the UK and Whisky was playing catch-up.

Aberlour 12 YO / Double Cask Matured
70cl / 43% - Distillery Bottling - Aberlour is always a good choice - one of the best value Speyside malts around. This double matured version is a mix of traditional oak and Sherry Casks and is rich and fruity with delicious Christmas cake notes.

Aberlour 12 YO VOHM / Bot. 1980's
100cl / 43% - Distillery Bottling - A 1980s release of 12 YO Aberlour "Very Old Highland Malt". A 1 litre frosted glass Bottle with gift tube.

Aberlour 15 YO / Select Cask Reserve
70cl / 43% - Distillery Bottling - A 15 YO Whisky from Aberlour, the Select Cask Reserve was originally a release for the French market but we've managed to grab a few Bottles.

Aberlour 16 YO / Double Cask
70cl / 43% - Distillery Bottling - A recent release from long-time TWE favourite Aberlour, this 16 year-old has been double-matured in traditional oak and Sherry Casks. Deep and complex, with lip-smacking spices - not as Sherry-sweet as the 18 YO.
World Whiskies Awards 2012 - Best Speyside 13 to 20 years
IWSC 2012 - Gold Medal - Whisky - Scotch

Aberlour 18 YO
70cl / 43% - Distillery Bottling - Aberlour is already one of our favourite Distilleries thanks to the excellent a'bunadh. Introduced in 2008, this 18 YO is now one of the stars of the range: rich and fruity, with a great textured mouthfeel. A previous winner of a Gold Medal & Best in Class at the International Wine & Spirit Competition.

Aberlour 1964 / 25 YO
75cl / 43% - Distillery Bottling - A late 1980s Distillery Bottling of 25 YO Whisky from Aberlour. Distilled in 1964, and Bottled at 43%.

Aberlour 1966 / 30 YO / Sherry Cask
70cl / 43% - Distillery Bottling - An old Sherry Cask Aberlour 1966 Bottled in the mid 1990s as a 30 YO.

Aberlour 1970 / 21 YO / Bot.1991
75cl / 43% - Distillery Bottling - A really terrific Aberlour, this 1970 is one of the best ever Bottlings from this much-loved Distillery.

Aberlour 1976 / 22 YO
70cl / 43% - Distillery Bottling

Aberlour 1987 / Scott's Selection
70cl / 54.9% - Scott's Selection - A single Cask 1987 vintage Whisky from Aberlour, Bottled by Scott's Selection at a solid Cask strength of 54.9%.

Aberlour 1989 Millennium
70cl / 40% - Distillery Bottling - A limited edition 10 YO Whisky Bottled in 1999 by Aberlour in celebration of the new millennium.

Aberlour 1992 / 16 YO
70cl / 46% - Speciality Drinks Ltd - A Sherry butt-matured Aberlour 1992 Bottled by Speciality Drinks for the Single Malts of Scotland range. Smooth and tasty, with a bit more lively spice than the standard Bottlings.

Aberlour 1992 / 19 YO / Cask #3919 / Berry Brothers
70cl / 55.5% - Berry Bros & Rudd - Another interesting single Cask Bottling from Indie Bottlers Berry Bros & Rudd. This time it's an Aberlour, Distilled in 1992 and aged for 19 years.

Aberlour 1993 / 14 YO / Sherry Cask #3163
70cl / 59.7% - Distillery Bottling - A single Cask Bottling of Aberlour, Distilled in 1993 and Bottled after 14 years. This Whisky was matured in a Sherry Cask being Bottled at Cask strength.

Aberlour 1993 / Sherry Cask
70cl / 57.6% - Distillery Bottling - A Cask strength Aberlour Bottled by the Distillery as part of their Single Cask Selection. They used a first fill Sherry Cask for the maturation and the 13 years have given this a

rather excellent deep red colour.

Aberlour 2000 / 11 YO / Cask #3070
70cl / 55.8% - Adelphi - A 2000 vintage Whisky from Aberlour Bottled in 2012 by Adelphi, making this Whisky atleast 11 years old.

Aberlour 21 YO Centenary Ceramic
75cl / 43% - Distillery Bottling - A very collectible ceramic decanter of 21 YO Aberlour. Produced from a single Cask to celebrate the Distillery's centenary in 1979.

Aberlour 5 YO / Bot.1980s
75cl / 40% - Distillery Bottling - A young Aberlour Bottled in the 1980s at 5 YO. Light and perfect for summer
drinking.

Aberlour A'Bunadh / Batch 44
70cl / 59.7% - Batch 44 of Aberlour's rightly lauded A'Bunadh - a small batch, Cask strength Sherry monster. After a cracking couple of batches expectations are quite high for this one.

Aberlour A'bunadh 12 YO / Silver Label
70cl / 58.7% - Distillery Bottling - A limited edition release of Aberlour's heavily Sherried A'bunadh. This special edition was aged for a minimum of 12 years and produced in a Bottle with a hallmarked sterling silver label and cloth bag.

Aberlour Antique
70cl / 43% - Distillery Bottling

Aberlour-Glenlivet 12 YO / Bot. 1980's
113cl / 40% - Distillery Bottling - An unusually large square Bottle (1.13L) of 1980s Aberlour, from the days when they were still using the 'Glenlivet' suffix.

Aberlour-Glenlivet 18 YO / Bot.1980s / Cadenhead's
75cl / 46% - Cadenhead's - A marvellous 1980s Bottling of Aberlour 18 YO from Edinburgh independent Bottlers Cadenhead's.

Aberlour-Glenlivet 1965 / 8 YO
75cl / 50% - Distillery Bottling - A collectible square Bottle of 8 YO Aberlour from 1965, Bottled at 50% for the Italian market.

Aberlour-Glenlivet 8 YO / Bot.1970s
75cl / 50% - Distillery Bottling - A 1970s square Bottle of 8 YO Aberlour, Bottled at 50% for the Italian market. These high strength old Aberlour's enjoy a particularly lofty reputation.

Aberlour-Glenlivet 8 YO / Bot.1980s
100cl / 50% - Distillery Bottling - A lovely old 1980s litre Bottle of high-strength Aberlour.

Aberlour-Glenlivet 9 YO / Bot.1970s
75cl / 40% - Distillery Bottling - A collectible 1970s square Bottling of 9 YO Aberlour, complete with original box.

Aberlour-Glenlivet Centenary Crystal
75cl / 46% - Distillery Bottling - A lightly coloured Aberlour (in comparison to the also released dark version) in a heavy crystal decanter, released in 1979 to celebrate the Distillery's 100th anniversary.

ALLT-A-BHAINNE RANGE

Allt-a-Bhainne 1991 / 21 YO / Cask #90114 / Signatory
70cl / 55% - Signatory - A 21 YO Whisky from Allt-a-Bhainne. Distilled on July 9th 1991, matured for 21 years in a hogshead and Bottled on October 6th 2012 by Signatory as part of their Cask Strength Collection.

Allt-a-Bhainne 1996 / Connoisseurs Choice
70cl / 46% - Gordon & Macphail - A Connoisseur's Choice Bottling from Gordon & Macphail of 1996 vintage Whisky distilled at Allt-a-Bhainne

AUCHROISK RANGE

Auchroisk 10 YO
70cl / 43% - Flora & Fauna - The Flora and Fauna release of 10 YO Auchroisk. Until the 2010 release of a 20 year-old, this was the only generally available Distillery Bottling from this young Distillery.

Auchroisk 1990 / 21 YO / Cask #3655+6 / Signatory
70cl / 60% - Signatory - A 1990 vintage Auchroisk, Bottled from two Casks in 2012 at full proof by Signatory for their Cask Strength Collection. Distilled on February 20th and Bottled on January 12th from a pair of hogsheads.

Auchroisk 1991 / Cask #16022 / Berry Bros & Rudd
70cl / 54.6% - Berry Bros & Rudd - A 1991 vintage Whisky from Auchroisk, Bottled by veteran spirits experts Berry Brother's and Rudd. This was Bottled in 2011 at a solid Cask strength of 54.6%.

Auchroisk 1993 / Connoisseurs Choice
70cl / 43% - Gordon & Macphail - Auchroisk (pronounced Athrusk) is a relatively modern Distillery, having begun production in 1974. Most of the production was destined for the J & B blend, however some malt was Bottled as 'The Singleton' due to the perceived difficulty with pronouncing the name.

Auchroisk 1999 / 9 YO / Managers' Choice / Sherry Cask
70cl / 60.6% - Distillery Bottling - Since the demise of the original Singleton range, official Bottlings of Auchroisk are rarer than talented X-Factor wannabes - we reckon that this 1999 Managers' Choice Cask

strength ex-Sherry 9 YO might be only the third OB we've had in recent times, alongside the Flora & Fauna Bottling and a Rare Malts version. At 60.6%, this will be one for the Sherry monsters out there.

Auchroisk 20 YO / Bot.2010
70cl / 58.1% - Distillery Bottling - An exciting release for Diageo's 2010 Super Premium releases - this is the first mainstream officially Bottled Auchroisk since the demise of the original Singleton range at the turn of the century.

Auchroisk 30 YO / Special Releases 2012
70cl / 54.7% - Distillery Bottling - A second entry in Diageo's special releases for Auchroisk, this time the oldest Bottling released to date. It's a vatting of refill European and American oak matured Whisky, Distilled in 1982 and Bottled after 30 years.

AULTMORE RANGE

Aultmore 12 YO
70cl / 43% - Flora & Fauna - This was previously the only generally available official release from Aultmore, launched as one of the earlier entries in the Flora & Fauna range in 1991.

Aultmore 12 YO / 1st Release
70cl / 43% - The first release of Aultmore as part of the Flora & Fauna range. This version was released in 1991, one of the earlier Flora & Fauna Bottlings, and is packaged in a light wood box.

Aultmore 12 YO / Bot.1970s
75cl / 40% - Distillery Bottling - A rare Distillery Bottling of this obscure Speysider from the 1970s.

Aultmore 12 YO / Bot.1970s
75.7cl / 40% - Distillery Bottling - A rare old Bottle of Aultmore from the 1970s.

Aultmore 12 YO / Bot.1980s
75cl / 40% - Distillery Bottling - A screwcap topped Bottle of 12 YO Aultmore from the 1980s. It's got a rather nice subtly coloured label and looks to be the precursor of the more recently released 12 YO expressions.

Aultmore 16 YO / Cask #1 / Square Barrel
70cl / 49% - Square Barrel - One of the first releases from independent Bottler Square Barrel, named for the bespoke square Casks they use to finish their Whisky. This Aultmore spent most of its 16 years in a regular Sherry Cask before being transferred to a square barrel built from a first fill Sherry Cask to finish.

Aultmore 16 YO / Centenary
70cl / 63% - Distillery Bottling - A 16 YO Aultmore Bottled to celebrate the Distillery's 100th anniversary. It's a rare limited edition release and

comes in at an eye-watering 63% abv. From the colour, it's probably safe to assume this was from a Sherry Cask.

Aultmore 1974 / 21 YO / Rare Malts
70cl / 60.9% - Rare Malts - A old Rare Malts Bottling of Aultmore Whisky, Distilled in 1974. This Whisky has been aged for 21 years and Bottled at Cask strength.

Aultmore 1982 / 28 YO / Cask #2233 / Adelphi
70cl / 57.6% - Adelphi - A 28 YO single Cask Aultmore from indie Bottler Adelphi. Distilled in 1982 and Bottled at a punchy Cask strength of 57.6%.

Aultmore 1982 / 29 YO / Adelphi
70cl / 53.9% - Adelphi - A 1982 vintage Aultmore, Bottled from a single Cask by independent Bottler Adelphi. A 29 YO, Bottled at Cask strength in 2011.

Aultmore 1982 / Berry Bros & Rudd
70cl / 57.8% - Berry Bros & Rudd - A 1982 Aultmore from industry veterans Berry Brothers and Rudd. Almost all of the Distillery's output goes into the Dewar's blends, so it's good to see great Bottlings like this one getting out into the wild.

Aultmore 1983 / 14 YO / Cask Strength
70cl / 58.8% - Flora & Fauna - A limited edition 1984 vintage release of Aultmore. This was one of the small number of Cask strength Bottlings that were included in the Flora & Fauna range.

Aultmore 1992 / 15 YO
70cl / 46% - Speciality Drinks Ltd - Another gem from our stash of Aultmore, this 1992 15 YO is a vatting of three ex-Bourbon barrels, and is dry with a fresh, intense maltiness.

Aultmore 1992 / 20 YO / Single Malts of Scotland
70cl / 52.9% - Speciality Drinks Ltd - A 20 YO from the 1992 vintage from Aultmore, a little-seen distillery bought by Bacardi from Diageo in 1998. Most of Aultmore's output goes into the excellent Dewar's blends, but this little gem has been saved. Matured in a Bourbon barrel, which is smaller than the standard hogshead, giving this a rich creamy vanilla character with lipsmacking oaky spices.

BALMENACH RANGE

Balmenach 10 YO / Bot.1990s
70cl / 43% - Signatory - A very rare Bottle of Balmenach 10 YO, this was released by Signatory in the early Nineties as part of their Scottish Wildlife series. The wildlife in question here is the Capercaillie.

Balmenach 1970 / 16 YO / Connoisseurs Choice
75cl / 40% - Gordon & Macphail - A marvellous old Bottling of 1970 Single Malt from the little-seen Balmenach, released as part of the

Connoisseurs Choice series by indie legends Gordon & Macphail.

Balmenach 1973 / Connoisseurs Choice
70cl / 40% - Connoisseurs Choice

Balmenach 1979 / Berry Bros & Rudd
70cl / 56.3% - Berry Bros & Rudd - A 1979 Balmenach Bottled by long running independent Berry Brothers & Rudd as part of their Berry's Own Selection range. One of their Cask strength releases, Bottled at 56.4% after about 32 years in the Cask.

Balmenach 1999 / Connoisseurs Choice
70cl / 43% - Gordon & Macphail - A youthful Conniosseurs Choice vintage Bottling of the little-seen Balmenach, a blend-fodder Speyside Distillery whose owners Inver House have yet to release an official Bottling despite buying the Distillery in 1997 and bringing it out of mothballs the following year. Hopefully that will be rectified soon.

Balmenach 28 YO
70cl / 46% - Distillery Bottling - A very limited edition release of 28 YO Balmenach, Bottled as a follow up to their Highland Selection 27 YO of a few years earlier.

Balmenach-Glenlivet 14 YO / Bot.1980s
75cl / 43% - Sestante - A very rare Bottling of Balmenach 14 YO bottled in the 1980s (when they were still using the '-Glenlivet' suffix) for Italian importers Sestante.

BALVENIE RANGE

Balvenie 10 YO / Bot.1990s
70cl / 40% - Distillery Bottling - An old release of Balvenie 10 YO Founder's Reserve Whisky. This is presented in interestingly shaped Bottle. We usually see this sort of Bottle used for Cognacs, but this is a welcome change. We would estimate that this was Bottled sometime in the 1990s.

Balvenie 10 YO / Founder's Reserve / Bot.1980s
100cl / 43% - Distillery Bottling - An old release of Balvenie 10 YO Founder's Reserve Whisky. This is presented in interestingly shaped, litre-size Bottle. We usually see this sort of Bottle used for Cognacs, but this is a welcome change. We would estimate that this was Bottled sometime in the 1980s.

Balvenie 12 YO / Double Wood
20cl / 43% - Distillery Bottling

Balvenie 12 YO Classic / Bot.1980s
75cl / 43% - Distillery Bottling - A very desirable Bottle of Balvenie Classic, rare because it has a 12 year-old age statement, whereas most Bottles we've seen are either 18 year-old or no-age-statement.

Balvenie 12 YO DoubleWood
70cl / 40% - Distillery Bottling - One of the classic after-dinner malts, Balvenie Doublewood's extra complexity and richness are a result of a second maturation in fresh Sherry Casks. Great stuff.
IWSC 2012 - Gold Medal - Whisky - Scotch

Balvenie 12 YO Signature
70cl / 40% - Distillery Bottling - Balvenie Signature 12 YO replaced the Founders Reserve 10 YO as the staple in the Distillery's range. This is a marriage of Sherry, Bourbon and Refill Casks and, as always with Balvenie, it's a polished, mellow Whisky to relax with.

Balvenie 14 YO / Roasted Malt
70cl / 47.1% - Distillery Bottling - The first Single Malt Scotch Whisky to be made using a batch of dark roasted malted barley, more commonly used in the production of stout, this new Balvenie is wonderfully rich and malty with a silky smooth mouth feel. Hints of toffee, marmalade, honey and oak tannin all enveloped with a spicy, vanilla sweetness.

Balvenie 14 YO / Caribbean Cask
70cl / 43% - Distillery Bottling - A 14 YO limited edition Balvenie which finished its maturation in Casks which had previously held Caribbean Rum. Expect vanilla and toffee notes as the rum contributes extra sweetness to the flavours.

Balvenie 14 YO / Cuban Selection
70cl / 43% - Distillery Bottling - A limited edition Balvenie release, originally produced for the French market. This continues in the tradition of their Golden Cask and uses Cuban rum Casks to finish the Whisky for a total of 14 years of maturation.

Balvenie 14 YO / Golden Cask Rum Finish
70cl / 47.5% - Distillery Bottling - A special Balvenie originally Bottled for the travel retail market, Golden Cask has spent the latter part of its 14 years of maturation in Casks that formerly held golden Caribbean rum.

Balvenie 15 YO Single Barrel
70cl / 47.8% - Distillery Bottling - Balvenie 15 YO Single Barrel is always a complex proposition, the higher alcohol content giving the malt a bit of extra muscle, although the rich, fruity Distillery character is still very evident. This thinker's dram was a winner at the World Whisky Awards 2010.

Balvenie 17 YO / Peated Cask
70cl / 43% - Distillery Bottling - The 2010 release of Balvenie 17 YO is a bit of a curio, having been re-racked after initial normal maturation into Casks that previously held...a peated Balvenie?! So this is a peated finish rather than a peated Whisky. The smoke is there, but not as full-frontal as you'd get if the spirit itself was peated. A very interesting experiment, and we await the peated Balvenie that previously graced

the Casks with eager interest.

Balvenie 17 YO / DoubleWood
70cl / 43% - Distillery Bottling - Another fantastic invention from the workbench of Balvenie Malt Master David Stewart - a 17 YO version of the best selling DoubleWood. Still initially matured in 'Whisky Oak' Casks before being switched to Sherry wood to finish, the extra years give it extra depth without being overpowering.

Balvenie 1967 / 32 YO / Cask #9909
70cl / 49.7% - Distillery Bottling - A very rare Bottling of a single Cask of Balvenie Distilled in 1967. They left it for 32 years before Bottling it at Cask strength as one of their Vintage Cask range.

Balvenie 1967 / 32 YO / Cask #9911
70cl / 49.7% - Distillery Bottling - An old single Cask Bottling of Balvenie 1967, Bottled at the end of the 1990s.

Balvenie 1970 / Sherry Cask #16191
70cl / 52.6% - Distillery Bottling - A very limited Bottling from Balvenie of the 1970 vintage, Bottled at Cask strength from a single Sherry Cask. Just 191 Bottles of this wonderfully dark Single Malt were released.

Balvenie 1973 / 30 YO
70cl / 49.7% - Distillery Bottling - A rare 1973 single Cask Bottling from Balvenie, one of only 309 Bottles released from the Cask. Distilled on 21st May 1973 and Bottled on 28th April 2004, just shy of its 31st birthday.

Balvenie 1993 / Port Wood Finish
70cl / 40% - Distillery Bottling - A long sold out Balvenie that we've got a few Bottles of - a younger version of the ever popular 21 YO port wood.

Balvenie 30 YO
70cl / 47.3% - Distillery Bottling - A highly thought of 30 YO from Balvenie that netted a Gold Medal at the 2010 International Spirits Challenge and a 90 points from Serge Valentin on Whisky fun.

Balvenie 40 YO / Batch 5
70cl / 48.5% - Distillery Bottling - The fifth edition of David Stewart's masterpiece of small batch assemblage, this Balvenie 40 YO is comprised of liquid from three American oak casks and three Sherry butts.

Balvenie 8 YO / Bot. 1970's
75cl / 40% - Distillery Bottling - A 1970s Bottle of Balvenie 8 YO, with a rather grand black leather label on its very Glenfiddich-esque Bottle.

Balvenie Classic / 18 YO / Bot.1980s
75cl / 43% - Distillery Bottling - A flat Bottle of Balvenie Classic from the 1980s. This Bottling states its age of 18 years on the wax seal at the base of the neck. This is one of the rarer versions of these very collectable Balvenies.

Balvenie Classic / Bot.1980s
75cl / 43% - Distillery Bottling - A flat Bottle of Balvenie Classic from the 1980s, with a wax seal at the base of the neck embossed with the year that they started building the Distillery - 1892.

Balvenie Founders Reserve / Bot.1980s
75cl / 43% - Distillery Bottling - A Bottling at 43% of Balvenie's Founders Reserve from the 1980s, packaged in a rare cognac-style Bottle. This Whisky was a key member of the Balvenie range, albeit in less fancy packaging, from the early 80s onwards but was retired a few years ago.

Balvenie Founder's Reserve / Bot.1980s
75cl / 40% - Distillery Bottling - A Bottling at 40% of Balvenie's Founders Reserve from the 1980s, packaged in a rare cognac-style Bottle. Founder's Reserve was a key member of the Balvenie range, albeit in less fancy packaging, from the early 80s onwards but was retired a few years ago.

BANFF RANGE

Banff 18 YO / Bot.1970s
75cl / 45.7% - Cadenhead's - A wonderful old Bottle of 18 YO Single Malt from closed Speyside Distillery Banff. Bottled in the 1970s - check out that hippy font on the label!

Banff 1966 / 31 YO
70cl / 50% - Douglas Laing - A 1966 vintage Bottling of Banff Whisky. This has been aged for 31 years and Bottled at Douglas Laing's preferred strength of 50%.

Banff 1974 / Connoisseurs Choice
70cl / 40% - Gordon & Macphail - An independent Bottling by Gordon & Macphail for their Connoisseurs choice range of 1974 vintage Whisky from this now disappeared Distillery. Closed in 1983 and destroyed by fire in 1991.

Banff 1974 / Map Label / Bot.1994
70cl / 40% - Gordon & Macphail - An old Bottle of Banff 1974 vintage Whisky. Banff Distillery was demolished in 1983, meaning this is one of the few Whiskies released from the remaining Casks.

Banff 1975 / 36 YO / Old & Rare
70cl / 41.8% - Douglas Laing - A 1975 vintage single Cask Whisky from Banff Distillery. This Whisky has been aged for a full 36 years before being Bottled by Douglas Laing for their Old & Rare Platinum selection. Bottled at Cask strength.

Banff 1976 / Connoisseurs Choice
70cl / 43% - Gordon & Macphail - A Bottling of 1976 Whisky from Banff, Bottled by Gordon & Macphail for their Connoisseurs Choice range. The Distillery is now long gone, having closed in 1983 and then destroyed by a fire in 1991.

BENRIACH RANGE

Benriach 10 YO / Bot.1990s
70cl / 43% - Distillery Bottling - This is the discontinued 1990s 10 YO Benriach that was the only Bottling Seagram could be bothered to put out when they owned this fantastic Distillery.

Benriach 12 YO
70cl / 40% - Distillery Bottling - A delicious fruity, honeyed 12 YO from reborn Speysider Benriach. A terrific dram for the money.

Benriach 12 YO Arumaticus Fumosus / Peated / Dark Rum Cask
70cl / 46% - Distillery Bottling - As the name suggests, this is a peated Benriach that's been finished in a rum Cask. Dolium volvitur, if you'll pardon the pun. Apologies for the poor Latin jokes, Mercator aliquantulus dementis.

Benriach 15 YO / Dark Rum Wood Finish
70cl / 46% - Distillery Bottling - After initial maturation in American oak ex-Bourbon barrels, this 15 YO Benriach is transferred for a finishing period in Casks that formerly housed dark Jamaican rum, adding an extra layer of sweet, fruity flavours to the excellent Distillery profile.

Benriach 15 YO / Madeira Wood Finish
70cl / 46% - Distillery Bottling - A new Madeira-finished Benriach 15 YO. Not to be confused with the Maderensis Fumosus, which was more heavily-peated - this is the lighter style of Benriach.

Benriach 15 YO / PX Sherry Wood Finish
70cl / 46% - Distillery Bottling
Part of Benriach's range of wood finished whiskies, this one using Pedro Ximinez Casks to complete the aging of a 15 YO Whisky.

Benriach 15 YO / Tawny Port Wood Finish
70cl / 46% - Distillery Bottling - A 15 YO Whisky from the creatively independent folks at Benriach in Speyside. This time they've finished their Whisky in tawny port Casks, adding some rich vine fruit to their already fruity Whisky.

Benriach 16 YO
70cl / 40% - Distillery Bottling - Benriach is a terrific malt from a Distillery that has really shot up after years of Seagram neglect. This delicious easy-drinking 16 YO is a complex all-rounder - recommended.

Benriach 16 YO
70cl / 43% - Distillery Bottling - Benriach 16 YO is a terrific malt from a Distillery that has really shot up after years of Seagram neglect. A delicious, complex all-rounder.

Benriach 17 YO Burgundy Wood Finish
70cl / 46% - Distillery Bottling - This wine-finished 17 YO Benriach has been finished in what must be red Burgundy (pinot noir) barrels if the description is anything to go by; the nose is described as 'Summer red berries' while the palate evokes 'redcurrant jelly and quince'. Sounds pretty good to us.

Benriach 1966 / 42 YO / Rare Reserve
70cl / 43.9% - Signatory - A very old Benriach Bottled by Signatory for their Cask Strength collection, this 42 year-old is from the 1966 vintage and has been Bottled at natural Cask strength of 43.9%.

Benriach 1966 / 44 YO / Private Collection
70cl / 56.1% - Gordon & Macphail - A single first fill American hogshead of very old Benriach, Distilled in 1966 and Bottled in late 2010 by Gordon & Macphail for their Private Collection series.

Benriach 1968 / 36 YO / Cask #2708
70cl / 51.5% - Distillery Bottling - A 1968 vintage Whisky from Benriach. This limited release has been aged for 36 years, yielding just 111 Bottles. Bottled at Cask strength and without chill filtration.

Benriach 1968 / 37 YO
70cl / 52% - Distillery Bottling - A 1968 vintage Benriach, Bottled in mid 2006 by the Distillery. Back in '68 the Distillery had only been open again for three years, having been previously mothballed in 1903.

Benriach 1976 / 34 YO / Cask #6942
70cl / 57.8% - Distillery Bottling - A 2011 release of a single Cask Benriach 1976. The reputation of this legendary vintage ensures an immediate sell-out.

Benriach 1976 / 35 YO / Cask #6967
70cl / 59% - Distillery Bottling - This Whisky was Distilled in 1976 and has spent 35 long years aging in an oak butt. This limited release is Bottled at Cask strength and is said to taste of "Lashings of raisins and sultanas, dancing with spices, pineapples and cedar wood".

Benriach 1976 / 35 YO / Peated
70cl / 54.9% - Distillery Bottling - A peated release of Benriach Whisky. Distilled in 1976 and aged for 35 years in a Hogshead. Benriach describe the Whisky as having "Mellow peat smoke with a barley and leather front".

Benriach 1976 / 35 YO / Pedro Ximenez Sherry Finish
70cl / 54.1% - Distillery Bottling - A 1976 Benriach which has been aged for 35 years including finishing in a Pedro Ximenez barrel. Expect some fruity notes from this one, it's colour indicates more than a hint of Sherry influence.

Benriach 1977 / 34 YO / Adelphi
70cl / 48.6% - Adelphi - A 1977 vintage single Cask Benriach from independent Bottler Adephi. A deeply coloured 34 YO, suggesting that the single Cask probably used to hold Sherry.

Benriach 1977 / 34 YO / Cask #2588 / Rioja Finish
70cl / 44.1% - Distillery Bottling - An interesting Whisky from Benriach Distillery. Distilled in 1977 and aged for 34 years, this Whisky has been finished in a Rioja Wine barrel. The wine finish has given the Whisky a subtle, grape-y (it's a word!) flavour.

Benriach 1977 / 34 YO / Pedro Ximenez Sherry Finish
70cl / 54.3% - Distillery Bottling - A 1977 vintage Whisky from Benriach, part of their 2011 Limited Release range, the 8th that they've done. Distilled the year before the Distiller was taken over by Seagrams and matured for 34 years, including a period of time finishing in a Pedro Ximenez Sherry Cask. The finish has added a nice bit of a Sherry edge, but without overpowering the flavours from the initial maturation to give a great fruit and nut combination.

Benriach 1977 / 34 YO / Sauternes Finish
70cl / 44.2% - Distillery Bottling - A 1977 vintage Whisky from Benraich Distillery. This has been aged for 34 years, including a term of finishing in a Sauternes Wine barrel. This period of finishing has imparted a number of fruity characteristics, most notably pears and apricots.

Benriach 1978 / 32 YO / Virgin Oak Finish
70cl / 50.9% - Distillery Bottling - A full strength 1978 single Cask Benriach, finished in a brand new virgin American oak hogshead.

Benriach 1983 / 29 YO / Cask #291
70cl / 43.1% - Distillery Bottling - A single Cask Bottling of Benriach which has been Distilled in 1983 and aged for 29 years. Bottled at Cask strength and said to have notes of "Pineapples and bananas". Fruity.

Benriach 1984 / 27 YO / Peated PX Sherry Cask #1052
70cl / 50.7% - Distillery Bottling - Single Cask Whisky Distilled in 1984 at Benriach Distillery. This peated Whisky has been finished in a Pedro Ximenez Sherry Barrel, leading to a character which the Benriach describe as "Huge peat and smoke presence followed by an avalanche of honey and mocha".

Benriach 1985 / 26 YO / Peated PX Sherry Finish
70cl / 48.7% - Distillery Bottling - A peated 1985 single Cask Benriach.

This Whisky has undergone a full 26 years of maturation including finishing in a Pedro Ximenez Sherry Cask. The fact that it this is Bottled at Cask strength just means that there really isn't much of this fantastic Whisky available.

Benriach 1986 / 19 YO / Peated
70cl / 55% - Distillery Bottling - A very pale single Cask Bottling of heavily-peated Benriach from 1986.

Benriach 1990 / 22 YO / Tawny Port Finish
70cl / 53.4% - Distillery Bottling - A single Cask Whisky from Benriach Distilled in 1990. This has been aged for 22 years and has been finished in a Tawny Port Pipe.

Benriach 1996 / Connoisseurs Choice
70cl / 43% - Gordon & Macphail - An independent release of 1996 vintage Benriach Bottled by Gordon & Macphail for their Connoisseurs Choice range.

Benriach 20 YO
70cl / 43% - Distillery Bottling - A very drinkable, fruity 20 YO from Speyside experimenters Benriach.

Benriach 21 YO / Authenticus Peated Malt
70cl / 46% - Distillery Bottling - A continuation of the ideas started in Curiositas, Benriach Authenticus is a big smoky Whisky from this Speyside Distillery that delights ein experimentation.

Benriach 25 YO
70cl / 50% - Distillery Bottling - A 25 YO release from Benriach made from a combination of Whisky finished in new wood and Sherry butts.
IWSC 2012 - Gold Medal - Whisky - Scotch

Benriach 25 YO / Authenticus Peated Malt
70cl / 46% - Distillery Bottling - A 25 YO from Speyside's Benriach, made using their peated spirit and sat at the top end of the age range for their peated Whisky. This is the follow-up to the much-vaunted Authenticus 21 YO and is claimed by the producers to show herb, honey and tropical fruit flavours alongside the smoke.

Benriach 30 YO
70cl / 50% - Distillery Bottling - A mixture of Bourbon, Sherry finished and Sherry matured Benriach Whisky, aged for 30 years and married together to produce an all-round winner, Bottled at a punchy 50%.

Benriach Curiositas 10 YO / Peated
70cl / 40% - Distillery Bottling - Curiositas is the hugely popular 10 year-old peated malt from the recently-revitalised Benriach Distillery. One of the few overtly peated Speyside malts, and definitely one to try for phenol fans.

Benriach Horizons 12 YO/ Triple Distilled / Sherry Finish
70cl / 50% - Distillery Bottling - A potent, high-strength 12 YO Single Malt from Benriach with one extremely unusual feature - it's been triple-Distilled. Horizons has also been finished in Sherry Casks after initial maturation in Bourbon wood, and has been Bottled without colouring or chill-filtration.
IWSC 2011 Gold Medal Winner

BENRINNES RANGE

Benrinnes 1968 / 19 YO
75cl / 57.1% - Sestante - A very old Sestante Bottling of Benrinnes 1968, Bottled at 100 UK proof in the late 1980s.

Benrinnes 1974 / 21 YO
70cl / 60.4% - Distillery Bottling

Benrinnes 1976 / Connoisseurs Choice
70cl / 43% - Gordon & Macphail - A 1976 Whisky from Benrinnes, Bottled in 2010 by Gordon & Macphail for their Connoisseurs Choice range.

Benrinnes 1984 / Berry Bros & Rudd
70cl / 56.5% - Berry Bros & Rudd - A 1984 vintage Benrinnes Bottled in 2011 by veteran independent Berry Brothers after about 27 years of maturation.

Benrinnes 1985 / 23 YO / Sherry Cask
70cl / 58.8% - Distillery Bottling - The first Distillery Bottling of Benrinnes in aeons, this is a heavily-Sherried number, very old-school with dark fruit, crème brulée, a hint of beef gravy and a touch of gun-metal. Released in 2009 as part of Diageo's Special Releases, this is far and away the best official Bottling from this Distillery.

Benrinnes 1992 / 19 YO / Cask #7232 / Old Malt Cask
70cl / 50% - Douglas Laing - A 19 YO single Cask Whisky from Benrinnes Bottled by Douglas Laing as part of their Old Malt Cask range. This was Distilled in 1992, shortly after the Distillery released their first official Bottling, and Bottled in 2011.

Benrinnes 1995 / 16 YO / Cask #5885
70cl / 51.2% - Signatory - A single Cask 16 YO Benrinnes Bottled by Signatory as part of their Cask Strength Collection. Distilled on 6th June 1995, matured in a hogshead and Bottled on 6th January 2012.

Benrinnes 1995 / Connoisseurs Choice
70cl / 43% - Gordon & Macphail - A 1995 vintage Benrinnes Bottling from Gordon & Macphail under their Connoisseurs Choice banner.

Benrinnes 1996 / 12 YO / Managers' Choice
70cl / 59.3% - Distillery Bottling - Benrinnes is another Diageo

Distillery of which very little is seen. Most of the malt produced at Benrinnes is used as blend fodder, so it's great to see a debut single Cask Bottling to sit alongside the Flora & Fauna version and 2009's acclaimed Special Release 23 YO.

BENROMACH RANGE

Benromach 10 YO
70cl / 43% - Distillery Bottling - A smart packaging job for this Distillery-Bottled expression of Benromach 10 YO, which has been a big hit since its introduction in late 2009. Well done to G&M for making the standard release strength 43%.

Benromach 10 YO / Quarter Bottle
20cl / 43% - Distillery Bottling - A 20cl quarter Bottle of the lipsmacking Benromach 10YO, which has been a revelation since its introduction by owners Gordon & Macphail in late 2009, and is really putting this great distillery back on the map.

Benromach 17 YO / Sherry Finish / Centenary Bottling
70cl / 43% - Gordon & Macphail - Released to celebrate the Distillery's centenary, this 17 YO Benromach spent its final two years in Sherry Casks dating from 1886, 1895 and 1901 before Bottling in 1998 by Gordon & Macphail, who had recently taken over and re-invigorated the Distillery after a fifteen year Distilling hiatus.

Benromach 1949 / 55 YO
70cl / 42.4% - Distillery Bottling - Very few malts can stand anything like as much ageing as this Benromach has managed. Which makes it all the more amazing that the Whisky inside the Bottle can still seem so fresh. Of course, over fifty-five years, the angels get to take more than their fair share - only eighty-three Bottles were yielded from the Cask.

Benromach 1965 / 14 YO / Cadenhead's
75cl / 45.7% - Cadenhead's - A rare old Cadenhead's Bottling of this top Speysider. It's great how the fonts on these labels are such a good guide to the tastes of the times - check out the Dallas Dhu '62 or the Macallan 1963 if you don't believe us.

Benromach 1968 / Sherry Cask
70cl / 45.4% - Distillery Bottling - Another release of Benromach 1968, Bottled in 2007 - the two Bottlings are differentiated only by their strength - this Bottling is 45.4% instead of 43%. Incredible colour on this.

Benromach 1969 / 42 YO / Refill Sherry
70cl / 42.6% - Distillery Bottling - A marriage of two Casks of Whisky Distilled at Benromach back in 1969. Matured for 42 years in refill Sherry Casks it's Bottled at 42.6% and is packed full of great Sherry flavour.

Benromach 1978 / 19 YO
70cl / 63.8% - Distillery Bottling - A superb (and hugely potent) expression of Benromach, this 19 YO was Distilled in 1978 and Bottled around 1997 for the Rare Malts series. The Distillery was mothballed at the time of this release but has since re-opened under new owners Gordon & MacPhail.

Benromach 1999 / Origins Batch 1 / Golden Promise Barley
70cl / 50% - Gordon & Macphail - It says here: 'Benromach Origins [are] crafted to highlight how subtle changes to the art of Whisky-making can help shape the character of the final malt'. This first effort is made using Golden Promise barley and matured in Sherry Casks.

Benromach 1999 / Origins Batch 2 / Port Pipes
70cl / 50% - Distillery Bottling - The second batch of Benromach's Origins series has been very lightly peated (4ppm) and matured full term in port pipes, lending a very appealing reddish hue to the Whisky.

Benromach 2000 / Origins 3 / Optic Barley / Sherry Casks
70cl / 50% - Distillery Bottling - The third Bottling of Benromach's Origins series is made exclusively with the Optic barley variety and has been fully-matured in Sherry Casks - this should be delicious.

Benromach 2001 / 9 YO / Cask Strength
70cl / 59.9% - Distillery Bottling - A vatting of seven first-fill Bourbon Casks of 2001 Benromach Bottled at full strength towards the end of 2010. Kudos to owners G&M for Bottling when the Whisky's ready rather than waiting until it was a 10 YO.

Benromach 2002 / Cask #32-34
70cl / 59.9% - Distillery Bottling - A small batch vatting of 2002 vintage Whisky from Benromach, a mix of just three first fill Bourbon barrels Bottled at Cask strength in September 2012 by the Distillery.

Benromach 2002 / Peat Smoke
70cl / 46% - Gordon & Macphail - The second batch of Benromach's peated young Speyside, this has been full-term matured in American oak and peated to a lower level than the previous batch (35ppm as opposed to the previous 55ppm).

Benromach 2004 / Peat Smoke
70cl / 46%

Benromach 2005 / Sassicaia Finish
70cl / 45% - Distillery Bottling - A 2005 vintage Whisky from Gordon & Macphail's Benromach Distillery, finished in "Super Tuscan" Sassicaia wine Casks.

Benromach 25 YO
70cl / 43% - Distillery Bottling - A 25 YO release of Benromach. It

was made part of their core range once production under Gordon & Macphail had settled down in the early 2000s, although the spirit was Distilled during the reign of the previous owners.

Benromach 30 YO
70cl / 43% - Distillery Bottling - A 30 YO Whisky from north Speyside Distillery Benromach. The spirit in this was Distilled back before its 1983 mothballing and subsequent 15 years of silence.

Benromach 8 YO / Sherry Cask / WDCS Longitude 80'
70cl / 45.7% - Distillery Bottling - A very worthy Bottling from Benromach - this is a single Sherry Cask Bottled at 80 proof to represent the longitude of the Whale & Dolphin Conservation Society's project to safeguard the humpback whales of Ecuador.

Benromach Organic
70cl / 43% - Distillery Bottling - A very well-received Benromach with official UK organic status.

Benromach Traditional
70cl / 40% - Distillery Bottling - The first new Bottling since the Distillery began production in 1998 after a 15-year lay-off. The Whisky is young, but has a delicious dollop of peat and plenty of fresh, ripe flavours. A very welcome return.

BRAEVAL

Braeval 1998 / 13 YO / Cask #168871+72
70cl / 56.7% - Signatory - A vatting of two Casks of 1998 Whisky from Braeval Distillery. Matured in a Bourbon Barrel and Bottled at 13 years of age. This has been Bottled by Signatory at Cask strength for their Cask Strength Collection.

CAPERDONICH RANGE

Caperdonich 17 YO / Bot.1980s / Cadenhead's
75cl / 45.7% - Cadenhead's - A great looking 17 YO Bottling of Caperdonich, released by Cadenhead's back in the 1980s. This one shows off Cadenhead's excellent typography choice for the Distillery, assigning them the same font as The Goodies.

Caperdonich 1968 / 17 YO / Connoisseurs Choice
75cl / 40% - Gordon & Macphail

Caperdonich 1992 / 19 YO / Cask #46239 / Signatory
70cl / 57.1% - Signatory - A 1992 vintage Whisky from Caperdonich, Distilled 10 years before the Distillery was closed down. This was Bottled by Signatory after 19 years in a hogshead for their Cask Strength Collection.

Caperdonich 1995 / 17 YO / Cask #95043 / Signatory
70cl / 46% - Signatory - A 17 YO single Cask Whisky from closed and demolished Caperdonich, Distilled on 13th June 1995 and Bottled on 20th November 2012 by Signatory for their Un-chillfiltered collection. after 17 years of maturation in a hogshead.

Caperdonich 1998 / Bot.2011
70cl / 46% - Gordon & Macphail - A 1998 vintage Whisky from closed Caperdonich, mothballed since 2002. This has been Bottled by Gordon & Macphail for their Connoisseurs Choice range.

Caperdonich 5 YO / Bot.1970's
75cl / 40% - Distillery Bottling - A Bottle of young 5 YO Caperdonich from the 1970s, long before the Distillery's mothballing in 2002.

CARDHU RANGE

Cardhu 12 YO / Bot.1970s
75cl / 43% - Distillery Bottling - A Distillery Bottling of 12 YO Cardhu from the 1970s, dressed in their old style white livery.

Cardhu 12 YO / Bot.1980s
75cl / 40% - An old presentation of Cardhu 12 YO which we estimate was Bottled sometime in the 1980s.

Cardhu 12 YO / Bot.1980s
75cl / 43% - Distillery Bottling - An old 1980s Distillery Bottling of Cardhu 12 YO, released at 43% for the Italian market.

Cardhu 12 YO / Bot.1980s
75cl / 43%

Cardhu 12 YO / Bot.1980s
75cl / 40% - Distillery Bottling - An unusual 1980s Bottling of Cardhu 12 YO.

Cardhu 12 YO / Glass Pack
70cl / 40% - Distillery Bottling - A Bottle of Cardhu's popular 12 YO Speyside Single Malt boxed up with a hefty balloon tumbler, for swirling and enjoying your dram.

Cardhu 12 YO / Single Malt
70cl / 40% - Distillery Bottling - A much-loved Single Malt, Cardhu is an easygoing, charming Speysider. With clean, crisp oak and sweet malt evoking flavours of honeyed flapjacks and home-made caramel squares, this is one for the sweet-toothed among you.

Cardhu 15 YO / Manager's Dram / Bot.1980s
75cl / 63% - Distillery Bottling - A very rare Bottling from Cardhu, specially selected by the Distillery manager and originally given to staff and friends of the Distillery as a gift. This was released in the

summer of 1989 at 15 YO and Bottled at Cask strength.

Cardhu 5 YO / Bot.1980's
75cl / 40% - Distillery Bottling - A rare picture-label Distillery Bottling of Cardhu 5 YO from the 1980s.

Cardhu 8 YO / Bot.1970s
75cl / 43% - Distillery Bottling - An old 1970s Bottle of Cardhu, when it was still available as an eight YO in a rather taller, more elegant Bottle than the dumpy thing it hangs around in nowadays.

Cardhu Highland Malt Whisky / Bot.1970s
75cl / 40% - Distillery Bottling - A 1970s Bottling of Cardhu that we're not sure of the age of - its neck label has come off sometime over the years robbing us of that knowledge...

Cardhu Special Cask Reserve
70cl / 40% - Distillery Bottling - Selected from 'very old oak Casks', this new Cardhu Special Cask Reserve is richer and sweeter than the hugely popular 12 YO and has proved very successful since its release.

COLEBURN RANGE

Coleburn 13 YO / Cadenhead
75cl / 46% - Cadenhead's - A 13 YO Coleburn, which has been aged for 13 years prior to being Bottled for Cadenhead. Coleburn Bottlings aren't seen often as the Distillery was closed by Diageo in 1985.

Coleburn 1965 / 17 YO / Connoisseurs Choice
75cl / 40% - Gordon & Macphail

Coleburn 1969 / 12 YO
75cl / 46% - Samaroli

Coleburn 1983 / 16 YO / Silent Stills
70cl / 57.3% - Signatory - An old Bottling of the very rarely seen Coleburn, this 1983 single Cask was released at full strength by Signatory in 2000 as part of their famous Silent Stills series.

CONVALMORE RANGE

Convalmore 1969 / Bot.1992 / Connoisseur's Choice
70cl / 40% - Gordon & Macphail

Convalmore 1977 / 28 YO
70cl / 57.9% - Distillery Bottling - silky and warming dram from the closed Convalmore Distillery that offers a complex mixture of vanilla sweetness along with a pleasant herbal bitterness.

Convalmore 1981 / 16 YO / First Cask #89/604/116

70cl / 46% - First Cask - A rare independent Bottling of a single Cask of Convalmore 1981 Bottled in the late-1990s.

Convalmore 1981 / Connoisseurs Choice
70cl / 40% - Gordon & Macphail - A Bottling of Whisky from rarely seen Distillery Convalmore by Gordon & Macphail for their Connoisseurs Choice range. The Whisky was Distilled in 1981, shortly before its 1985 final closure, and Bottled 17 years later in 1998.

Convalmore 1983 / 15 YO / Chieftan's
70cl / 43% - Ian Macleod - A 1983 Whisky from Convalmore, aged for 15 years and Bottled by Ian Macleod for the Chieftain's Choice range..

Convalmore 1984 / Bot.2010 / Connoisseurs Choice
70cl / 43% - Gordon & Macphail - A recent Bottling from the defunct Convalmore by Connoisseurs Choice. This is from refill Sherry hogsheads.

CRAGGANMORE RANGE

Cragganmore 12 YO
70cl / 40% - Distillery Bottling - The Speyside representative of the Classic Malts series is rich and spicy, with a very satisfying complexity and a well-Sherried backbone.

Cragganmore 14 YO / Friends of Classic Malts/ Bot.2010
70cl / 40% - Distillery Bottling - A special Bottling of Cragganmore for Diageo's Whisky fan club, the Friends of the Classic Malts, released in 2010. This one has been matured for slightly longer than the regular expression, sitting in Casks for at least 14 years.

Cragganmore 14 YO / Friends of the Classic Malts
70cl / 47.5% - Distillery Bottling - A special edition Cragganmore Bottled for Diageo's Whisky fanclub - the Friends of the Classic Malts. A 14 YO Bottled at the stronger than normal ABV of 47.5%.

Cragganmore 1973 / 29 YO
70cl / 52.5% - Distillery Bottling - At 29 YO, this is by some distance the oldest official Bottling of Cragganmore that has ever come to the market. A long-time favourite here at TWE, this is also the top-ranked Cragganmore on Serge Valentin's Whiskyfun.

Cragganmore 1976 Cask Strength / Bot.1989/ Gordon & Macphail
75cl / 56.1% - Gordon & Macphail - An old Gordon & Macphail Bottling of 1976 Cragganmore Bottled in 1989 for their Cask Strength series.

Cragganmore 1985 / 26 YO / Cask #1244+1990
70cl / 50.2% - Signatory - A vatting of two 1985 Cragganmore Casks, which have been matured for 26 full years. Bottled at Cask Strength

for Signatory, for their Cask Strength Collection.

Cragganmore 1989 / 21 YO
70cl / 56% - Distillery Bottling - A special Cragganmore 1989, Bottled at 21 YO for Diageo's 2010 Special Releases. This is from a smallish batch of refill American oak Casks.

Cragganmore 1989 / Bot.2010 / Cask #2880
70cl / 53.5% - Berry Bros & Rudd - A Cask strength Cragganmore 1989 from Whisky Magazine's Independent Bottler of the Year, Berry Bros & Rudd. This is a single Cask Bottled in 2010.

Cragganmore 1993 / 10 YO / Sherry Cask
70cl / 60.1% - Distillery Bottling - Part of Diageo's Super-Premium releases from a few years ago, this is a powerful, richly-fruited expression from the Speyside Classic Malt.

Cragganmore 1993 / Distillers Edition
70cl / 40% - Distillery Bottling - A double-matured Cragganmore finished in port wood pipes for extra complexity and depth. Highly unusual and extremely pleasant drinking Whisky.

Cragganmore 1997 / 14 YO / Cask #1126+1127
70cl / 46% - Signatory - This Whisky is a marriage of two Casks from Cragganmore Distillery. This 1997 Whisky has been matured in oak hogsheads and aged for a minimum of 14 years. Bottled in 2012, without chillfiltration.

Cragganmore 1997 / Distillers Edition
70cl / 40% - Distillery Bottling - One of the more unusual of the Distillers Editions, Cragganmore is finished in Port pipes for extra sweetness and fruity depth.

Cragganmore 1997 / Managers' Choice / Sherry Cask
70cl / 59.7%

Distillery Bottling
A full-strength Cragganmore 1997 Bottled in 2009 from a single Sherry Cask by Diageo for their Manager's Choice series.

Cragganmore 2000 / 11 YO / Cask #3673 / Berry Brothers
70cl / 56.8% - Berry Bros & Rudd - The range of single Cask bottlings from Berry Brothers is something that we are always excited about. This time its a Cragganmore, Distilled in 2000 and Bottled after 11 years of aging.

Secret Stills No: 2.2 (Cragganmore) 1966 / Gordon & Macphail
70cl / 45% - Gordon & Macphail - A Secret Stills release from Gordon & Macphail from Distillery #2 (shh, it's Cragganmore...). A 1966 vintage Whisky Bottled in 2006 at about 40 YO.

Secret Stills No: 2.3 (Cragganmore) 1978

70cl / 45% - Gordon & Macphail - A 1978 vintage Whisky Bottled by Gordon & Macphail in 2011 as part of their Secret Stills series. This is from Distillery number 2, not so secretly known as Cragganmore.

CRAIGELLACHIE RANGE

Craigellachie 1962 / 16 YO / Cadenhead's
75cl / 45.7% - Cadenhead's - A 1970s Bottling of Craigellachie-Glenlivet from Cadenhead's, aged for 16 years and released back in the days when you saw more evidence of the large number of Distilleries in the Livet valley on the labels of Whiskies.

Craigellachie 1980 / 14 YO / Bot.1995 / Milroy's
70cl / 60% - Milroy's - A 1995 release of 1980 vintage Craigellachie, Bottled by independent Whisky pioneers Milroy's.

Craigellachie 1991 / Connoisseurs Choice
70cl / 43% - Gordon & Macphail - A Craigellachie 1991 from refill Sherry hogsheads, Bottled in 2008 by Gordon & Macphail for their Connoisseurs Choice label.

Craigellachie 1993 / Connoisseurs Choice
70cl / 46% - Gordon & Macphail - A 1993 vintage Whisky from Craigellachie, Bottled by Gordon & Macphail under their Connoisseurs Choice label.

Craigellachie 1994 / 15 YO / Single Malts of Scotland
70cl / 46% - Speciality Drinks Ltd - Our first ever Craigellachie for Single Malts of Scotland is a very fudgey, buttery number from the 1994 vintage. Sweet on the nose, with a spicy bite on the medium-bodied palate.

DAILUAINE RANGE

Dailuaine 16 YO
70cl / 43% - Flora & Fauna - A delicious Bottling from a rather obscure Distillery. Big, rich, sweet and smoky, with a very smooth mouthfeel and plenty of fruits and spices.

Dailuaine 17 YO / Manager's Dram
70cl / 59.5% - Distillery Bottling - There aren't many Bottlings from Dailuaine, Distillery or independent, and this sticks out as even rarer due to it being one of the fabled Manager's drams - single Casks chosen by the Distillery managers and originally given to friends of the Distillery.

Dailuaine 1966 / 13 YO / Sherry Cask
75cl / 45.7% - Cadenhead's - A rare 1970s Cadenhead's Bottling of this excellent Sherried Speysider. It's great how the fonts on these labels are such a good guide to the tastes of the times - check out the Caperdonich 1965 or the Macallan 1963 if you don't believe us.

Dailuaine 1975 / 27 YO / First Cask #5521
70cl / 46% - First Cask - A 1975 Dailuaine Bottled by Direct Wines for the "First Cask" range. This single Cask Whisky has been aged for 27 years.

Dailuaine 1975 / 27 YO / First Cask #5527
70cl / 46% - First Cask - A Direct Wines First Cask Bottling of 27 YO Dailuaine, Distilled on the 26th May 1975.

Dailuaine 1979 / 25 YO / Sherry
70cl / 51.4% - Signatory - A 1979 Whisky Distilled at Dailuaine and aged for 25 years. Bottled by Signatory for their Cask Strength range.

Dailuaine 1997 / Managers' Choice / Sherry Cask
70cl / 58.6% - Distillery Bottling A single Sherry Cask of Dailuaine 1997, Bottled at full strength by owners Diageo in 2009 as part of the Managers' Choice range.

Dailuaine 1998 / Connoisseurs Choice
70cl / 46% - Gordon & Macphail - A Connoisseurs Choice Bottling from Gordon & Macphail of 1998 vintage Whisky from Dailuaine Distillery in Speyside.

DALLAS DHU RANGE

Dallas Dhu 1972 / Connoisseurs Choice
75cl / 40% - Gordon & Macphail - An old Bottling of Dallas Dhu Whisky. This Whisky was Distilled in 1972 and Bottled by Gordon & Macphail for their Connoisseurs Choice series.

Dallas Dhu 1977 / 20 YO / First Cask #1117
70cl / 46% - First Cask - A 20 YO Dallas Dhu from First Cask, Bottled in the late 1990s. The Distillery is now closed, and turned into a Distilling museum, but before it went they produced this, Distilled on May 20th 1977.

Dallas Dhu 1979 / 24 YO / First Cask #1383
70cl / 46% - First Cask - A Bottling of 1979 Dallas Dhu, now closed and the site of a Whisky museum. This was released in the early 2000s by Direct Wines as part of their First Cask series.

Dallas Dhu 1983 / 23 YO / Historic Scotland
70cl / 46% - Distillery Bottling - A 1983 vintage Whisky from Dallas Dhu Distillery in Speyside. This Whisky has been aged for 23 years and specially Bottled for Historic Scotland.

Dallas Dhu 1983 / Last Cask Filled
70cl / 48% - Distillery Bottling - A very special Bottle, coming as it

does from the last Cask ever filled at Dallas Dhu Distillery before production stopped in 1983. The Distillery is now a museum.

Dallas Dhu Centenary
70cl / 40% - Distillery Bottling - A special Bottling of Whisky from Dallas Dhu, celebrating their 100th birthday in 1999. The Distillery had been closed for 16 years by then, but it has since been reopened by Historic Scotland as a museum.

DRUMGUISH
Drawing from the wonderful crystal clear waters of the River Tromie, The Speyside Distillery houses some of the smallest, yet most cleverly proportioned stills in Scotland. These two key factors, allied to our Distilling secrets, that have been passed from generation to generation, have earned Speyside the reputation of 'the best Whisky in the world'.

The pure local water coloured and flavoured by the peat of the Cairngorm mountains, together with the fine malted barley from the Moray Firth region, and, of course, our unsurpassed attention to detail.

Nose: Soft and medium-sweet. quite fresh with a slight menthol character, gently peated with a slight earthy touch.

Finish: Of good length, almost dry with a good peaty flavour.

Taste: Medium-dry, minty, with good body and a firm, but gentle dark earthy smokiness.

Colour: Pale mid amber with old gold highlights. (taste notes by Drumguish)

DUFFTOWN RANGE

Dufftown 1982 / 28 YO / Old Malt Cask #7147
70cl / 50% - Douglas Laing - A 1982 vintage Dufftown Bottled at 28 years by Douglas Laing for their Old Malt Cask range. While Dufftown is starting to make an impact as a Single Malt, it's still rare to see independents as most of production goes into blends, mainly Bell's.

Dufftown 1982 / Berry Bros & Rudd
70cl / 53.4% - Berry Bros & Rudd - A 1982 vintage from Dufftown in the heart of Speyside. This was Bottled by Berry Brothers and Rudd at a Cask strength of 53.4% after about 29 years of maturation.

Dufftown 1984 / 27 YO / Signatory
70cl / 55.5% - Signatory - A richly coloured 1984 vintage Dufftown, matured in a Sherry Cask for 27 years before being Bottled by Signatory as part of their Cask Strength Collection in the summer of

2011.

Dufftown 1997 / Managers' Choice
70cl / 59.5% - Distillery Bottling - Bottled as part of Diageo's Managers' Choice series, this 1997 Dufftown is a rare official Bottling from another of the company's Distilleries that rarely sees the light of day.

Dufftown 8 YO / Black & Red Label / Bot.1970s
75cl / 40% - Distillery Bottling - An old Bottle of Dufftown 8 YO from the 1970s. There are several similar versions of this, but this is the one with the red shading on the label.

Dufftown 8 YO / Bot.1960s
75cl / 46% - Distillery Bottling - A 1960s Distillery Bottling of 8 YO Dufftown, complete with the old black, white and red label.

Dufftown 8 YO / Bot.1980s
75cl / 40% - Distillery Bottling - A 1980s Bottling of 8 YO Dufftown Whisky, that looks as if it was destined for the Italian market from the customs seal.

Dufftown Centenary / 20 YO
70cl / 55.8% - Distillery Bottling - A 20 YO Dufftown Whisky Bottled by the Distillery in honour of its 100th anniversary of starting production: 1896-1996.

Dufftown Glenlivet 1969 / Sherry / Bot.1985 / Moon Imports
75cl / 57% - Moon Import - A rare old Bottle of Dufftown (in the Livet valley) Bottled by Italian independent Moon Imports in 1985 as part of their 2nd collection.

Dufftown Glenlivet 8 YO / Bot.1970s
75cl / 40% - Distillery Bottling - A Bottle of 8 YO Whisky from the Dufftown Distillery, released back in the 1970s when you could still call your Whisky "x Glenlivet".

Dufftown-Glenlivet 10 YO / Bot.1980s
75cl / 40% - Distillery Bottling - Another old Bottling from when calling yourself Glenlivet was all the rage.

Dufftown-Glenlivet 8 YO / Bot.1960s
75cl / 46% - Distillery Bottling
A very cool old 1960s Bottle of Dufftown (then still using the Glenlivet suffix) in a brown glass Bottle with a cork stopper. Bottled at 80 proof, also known as 46%.

Dufftown-Glenlivet 8 YO / Bot.1970s
75cl / 46% - Distillery Bottling - A Bottle of 8 YO Whisky from Dufftown, Bottled in the 1970s and hailing itself as being from "The House of Bell's".

Dufftown-Glenlivet 8 YO / Bot.1980s
75cl / 46% - Distillery Bottling - A lovely old 1980s Bottle of the little-seen Dufftown Single Malt, Bottled at a hearty drinking strength of 46%. We love the retro coat of arms label.

Dufftown-Glenlivet 8 YO / Bot.1980s
100cl / 40% - Distillery Bottling - A litre Bottle of Whisky from the Dufftown Distillery Bottled with their black and red coat of arms label. We think this was released in the 1980s.

Singleton of Dufftown 12 YO
70cl / 40% - Distillery Bottling - A relaunched Singleton, this time from Dufftown, to replace the now-defunct Singleton of Auchroisk. This smooth, mellow dram is designed to attract new drinkers to the malt category, while its smart packaging has ensured its popularity as a gift.
World Whiskies Awards 2012 - Best Speyside 12 years and under

Singleton of Dufftown 15 YO
70cl / 40% - Distillery Bottling - A 15 year-old expression of Singleton of Dufftown, Diageo's easy-drinking Speysider. This is a mix of European and American oak Casks, producing a smooth, sweet, approachable style and a spicy, drying finish.

Singleton of Dufftown 18 YO
70cl / 40% - Distillery Bottling - An older 18 YO version of The Singleton of Dufftown, the European entry in the Singleton range. This builds on the massive success of the 12 and 15 YO, bringing more complexity to the spirit.

GLENALLACHIE RANGE

Glenallachie 1969 / 12 YO / Bot.1980s
75cl / 40% - Distillery Bottling - An early 1980s Bottling of Glenallachie, Distilled in 1969 - the year after construction of the Distillery was completed. This was the first vintage Bottling of fully mature Glenallachie.

Glenallachie 1970 / 12 YO
75cl / 40% - Distillery Bottling - A 1980s Bottling of 12 YO Glenallachie, Distilled only 3 years after the Distilleries 1967 founding.

Glenallachie 1973 / 38 YO / The Whisky Agency
70cl / 50.4% - A 38 YO Whisky from Glenallachie, Distilled in 1973 and Bottled in 2011 by The Whisky Agency. This Bottle depicts a lion with a rather poorly trimmed mane and a heron making use of the cuttings as a nest for its chick. Matured in Ex-Bourbon barrels and Bottled at 50.4%

Glenallachie 1992 / Connoisseurs Choice
70cl / 43% - Gordon & Macphail - A Connoisseurs Choice Bottling of the little-seen Glenallachie, one of Pernod Ricard's Speyside workhorses. This is from the 1992 vintage and is a mix of refill Bourbon and Sherry Casks.

Glenallachie 1995 / 14 YO
70cl / 59.7% - Speciality Drinks Ltd - A single hogshead of the little-seen Glenallachie from the 1995 vintage, this has been Bottled at full strength for The Single Malts of Scotland range.

Glenallachie 35 YO / Sherry Cask
70cl / 46.9% - Speciality Drinks Ltd - A full-on first-fill Sherried Glenallachie bursting with spices and fruitcake but balanced with soft leather, tobacco and mocha notes, meaning it never goes over the top into cloying sweetness. Sherryheads will go weak at the knees for this one, which recently topped the overall list on Whisky-Distilleries. info's tasting sessions, where it earned a top score of 93 points.

Glenallachie-Glenlivet 12 YO / Bot.1980s
75cl / 43% - Distillery Bottling - A very rare Distillery Bottling of Glenallachie-Glenlivet Whisky. This is one of the few Single Malt Whiskies Bottled by the Distillery, as most of the Whisky Distilled ends up going into blended Whisky. This Single Malt has been aged for 12 years and was Bottled sometime in the 1980s.

GLENBURGIE RANGE

Glenburgie 10 YO / Gordon & Macphail
70cl / 40% - Gordon & Macphail - A 10 YO Glenburgie, the little seen workhorse malt for the Ballantine's blends.

Glenburgie 15 YO
70cl / 46% - Distillery Bottling - A 15 YO Whisky from Glenburgie, complete with label featuring some of the Distillery workers (or some people dressed up to look like them).

Glenburgie 18 YO
70cl / 43% - Distillery Bottling - A very rare official Bottling of Glenburgie 18 YO. We think this was done for the travel retail market, and that it was probably Bottled around the turn of the 1990s.

Glenburgie 1962 / 16 YO
75cl / 45.7% - Cadenhead's - A 1962 Whisky Distilled at Glenburgie Distillery, aged for 16 years and Bottled by Cadenhead.

Glenburgie 1964 / Gordon & Macphail
70cl / 43% - Gordon & Macphail - An independent release of Whisky from Glenburgie by Gordon & Macphail. Distilled in 1964 and Bottled

in 2005 for an impressive 40+ years in the Cask.

Glenburgie 1966 / Bot.2012
70cl / 43% - Gordon & Macphail - A 1966 vintage Whisky from Glenburgie. Bottled in 2012 by Gordon & Macphail, making this approximately 46 YO.

Glenburgie 1983 / 27 YO / Casks #9817+8 / Signatory
70cl / 55.1% - Signatory - A 27 YO Glenburgie Bottled at Cask strength from two Casks by Signatory. Distilled on 26th October 1983 and Bottled on 11th June 2012.

Glenburgie 1985 / 195th Anniversary
70cl / 57.3% - Distillery Bottling - A special limited edition release of 1985 Glenburgie, Bottled in 2005 to commemorate both the 195th anniversary of the Distillery's opening and the opening of an almost entirely new Distillery on the site.

Glenburgie 1990 / 18 YO
70cl / 62.2% - Speciality Drinks Ltd - A very potent Glenburgie 1990, Bottled at full strength from a single Sherry cask for The Single Malts of Scotland.

Glenburgie 1994 / 15 YO / Cask Strength Edition
50cl / 54.6% - Distillery Bottling - A small batch Glenburgie from the 1994, Bottled at full strength by owners Chivas Brothers for their Cask Strength Edition series, which are normally only available to buy at the Distilleries themselves.

Glenburgie Glenlivet 5 YO . Bot. 1980's
75cl / 40% - Distillery Bottling - A little-seen official Bottling of Glenburgie, this 5 YO dates from the 1980s when the Distillery still used the 'Glenlivet' suffix.

GLENCRAIG

Glencraig 1976 / 35 YO / Cask #4255 / Signatory
70cl / 42.7% - Signatory - A 1976 vintage Whisky Distilled at Glenburgie - the alternative name was used for spirit Distilled with their Lomond stills, removed in 1981 effectively 'closing' Glencraig. This matured for 35 years in a Bourbon barrel before Bottling in late 2011.

GLENDRONACH RANGE

Glendronach / Bot.1930s
75cl / 40% - Distillery Bottling - A wonderful old 1930s Distillery Botttling of Glendronach, with a beautifully simple label in pretty good condition considering its massive age - we believe this Bottle to be from the 1930s.

Glendronach / Bot.1930s

75cl / 40% - Distillery Bottling - An excellently preserved 1930s Distillery Bottling of Glendronach, with an elegant label in impressive condition considering its age.

Glendronach 12 YO - Original / Double Cask
70cl / 43% - Distillery Bottling - A dense, heavily-Sherried dram from a Distillery now producing again after a six-year layoff. A malt best suited to after-dinner sipping.

Glendronach 12 YO / Bot.1970s
75cl / 43% - Distillery Bottling

Glendronach 12 YO / Bot.1980s
75cl / 40% - Distillery Bottling

Glendronach 12 YO / Original / Bot.1980s
75cl / 43% - Distillery Bottling - An old Bottle of Glendronach 12 yrs Original matured in a mix of plain oak and Sherry Casks.

Glendronach 12 YO / Sherry Cask / Bot.1980s
75cl / 40% - Distillery Bottling

Glendronach 14 YO / Virgin Oak Finish
70cl / 46% - Distillery Bottling - A special edition Glendronach, matured initially in re-charred puncheons befroe finishing ina small batch of American virgin oak Casks, which have imparted abundant toasty oak, coconut and tropical fruit aromas and flavours to the final blend.

Glendronach 150th Anniversary (1826-1976)
75cl / 40%

Distillery Bottling - A rare limited Bottling of Glendronach, Bottled to celebrate its 150th anniversary in 1976.

Glendronach 15 YO / Moscatel Finish
70cl / 46% - Distillery Bottling - This 15 YO Glendronach was originally matured in European oak before a finishing period in Moscatel, the (normally) Iberian fortified sweet wine, which has added an extra layer of tropical fruit and marzipan aromas and flavours.

Glendronach 15 YO / Sherry
70cl / 40% - Distillery Bottling - A Bottle of the 15 YO Sherry matured Whisky from Glendronach. This is the old style big Sherried 15 YO which the Distillery's new owners have taken as their inspiration and built upon.

Glendronach 15 YO / Sherry / 1L
100cl / 40% - Distillery Bottling - A litre Bottle of old skool Glendronach, big and Sherried. The 15 YO is the template that the

new owners of the Distillery elaborated on to build their new sherried range.

Glendronach 15 YO Revival / Sherry Cask
70cl / 46% - Distillery Bottling - Glendronach Revival is the culmination of nearly a year's hard work by the Distillery's new owners, replicating their success at Benriach. This Oloroso-matured Revival received a whopping 92 points from the highly-esteemed Whiskyfun website.

Glendronach 15 YO Tawny Port Finish
70cl / 46% - Distillery Bottling - Introduced to the Glendronach range in 2011 the 15 YO Tawny Port finish continued the Distillery's new owner's plans of taking the Bourbon matured Whisky from the old owners and bringing it more into line with their idea of the traditional taste of Glendronach. This one has spent the last few years of its time in Cask in Tawny Port Casks, picking up lovely red fruit flavours.

Glendronach 18 YO / Allardice / Sherry Cask
70cl / 46%

Distillery Bottling - Just like the 15 YO, Glendronach Allardice 18 YO(named after the Distillery's founder) has been 100% matured in Oloroso Sherry Casks. We're delighted to welcome Glendronach back from the wilderness - Billy Walker and his team are doing outstanding work here.

Glendronach 1960 / 25 YO / Connoisseurs Choice
75cl / 40% - Gordon & Macphail - A marvellous mid-1980s Bottling of Glendronach from the 1960 vintage, unearthed by indie heroes Gordon & Macphail for their Connoisseurs Choice series.

Glendronach 1963 / 12 YO
75cl / 43% - Distillery Bottling - A mid-1970s Distillery Bottling of 12 YO Glendronach Distilled in 1963. Bottled at 43% for the Italian market.

Glendronach 1971 / 41 YO / PX Sherry Puncheon #1247
70cl / 47.9% - Distillery Bottling - This Glendronach has been aged for a stunning 41 years in a Pedro Ximenez Sherry Puncheon giving it a beautifully dark colour. A Gold Medal winner at the Malt Manaics Awards 2012.

Glendronach 1971 / Oloroso Sherry Butt #441 / Japan
70cl / 48.1% - Distillery Bottling - A special single-Cask Glendronach 1971 Bottled for the Japanese market, Cask 441 is an Oloroso Sherry butt Bottled in September 201 at the grand old age of 39 YO.

Glendronach 1973 / 18 YO / Sherry Cask
75cl / 43% - Distillery Bottling - An early 1990s Distillery Bottling of Sherried Glendronach 18 YO from the 1973 vintage.

Glendronach 1976 / 18 YO / Sherry Cask
70cl / 43%

Glendronach 1993 / 19 YO / Oloroso Sherry Butt #536
70cl / 59.4% - Distillery Bottling - A 1993 vintage single Cask Whisky from Glendronach Distillery. This Whisky has been aged for over 19 years in an Oloroso Sherry Butt.

Glendronach 1993 / 19 YO / Sherry Cask #487
70cl / 54.2% - Distillery Bottling - A 1993 vintage, single Cask Whisky from Glendronach. This has been matured for 19 years in an a Oloroso Sherry butt and Bottled exclusively for the UK market. Rich, sweet, heavy Sherry aromas and flavours.

Glendronach 21 YO Parliament / Sherry Cask
70cl / 48% - Distillery Bottling - A 2011 release to fill a gap in the rapidly expanding Glendronach range and named for the Parliament of rooks that live in the trees near the Distillery. A tasty combination of Sherry matured Whiskies, both Oloroso and PX, perfect for Sherry-heads.

Glendronach 33 YO / Oloroso Sherry Cask
70cl / 40% - Distillery Bottling - Distilled in 1971 and matured in a small batch of exquisite Oloroso Sherry Casks, this 33 year-old dram appeared in 2004 and at the time was the oldest and quite possibly the best Glendronach ever released.

Glendronach 8 YO / Bot.1980s
75cl / 43% - Distillery Bottling - A terrific old 1980s Distillery-Bottled 'Teacher's' Glendronach 8 YO Bottled for Italian importers Ruffino.

Glendronach 8 YO / Bot.1980s
75cl / 45.4% - Distillery Bottling - A dumpy Bottle of Glendronach Bottled at the higher strength of 45.4% for the Italian importer Ruffino.

Glendronach 8 YO / Dumpy / Bot.1970s
75cl / 43% - Distillery Bottling - An 8 YO Distillery Bottling of Glendronach from the 1970s in a dumpy Bottle.

Glendronach Cask Strength / Batch 1
70cl / 54.8% - Distillery Bottling - The first batch of no-age-statement Cask strength Whisky from Glendronach, Bottled at 54.8% and originally released in December 2012. It's a vatting of Oloroso and Pedro Ximenez matured Whisky, shown in its colour and intense Sherried flavour.

Glendronach Grandeur / 31 YO / Sherry Cask
70cl / 45.8% - Distillery Bottling - A very handsome Bottling of long-aged Glendronach, the malts that went into Grandeur have been aged over three decades in the finest Sherry wood and the Bottling

is described by its proud owners as "a classical representation of the smooth, complex and full-bodied style that the GlenDronach Distillery is famous for." Sounds good to us.

GLENDULLAN RANGE

Glendullan 12 YO / Bot.1980's
75cl / 47% - Distillery Bottling - A 1980s Bottling of Glendullan's old standard expression, pretty much the only Distillery Bottling they've released - a 12 YO.

Glendullan 18 YO / Manager's Dram / Sherry Cask
75cl / 64% - Distillery Bottling - A richly coloured Whisky from Glendullan, selected by the Distillery manager and originally given as a present to the friends and employees of the Distillery. This one went out into the world in November 1989 and only a few remain undrunk.

Glendullan 1972 / 22 YO / Rare Malts
70cl / 62.6% - Rare Malts - A 1972 vintage Rare Malts Bottling of Glendullan. This Whisky has been aged for 22 years and Bottled at Cask strength.

Glendullan 1973 / 23 YO / Rare Malts
75cl / 58.6% - Distillery Bottling - A 23 YO Whisky from Glendullan Bottled as part of the Rare Malts series, showcasing some of UDV's (now Diageo's) lesser known Distilleries. This was Distilled the year after a brand new Distillery was built next to the old one, during which time both were operating simultaneously.

Glendullan 1978 / 26 YO
70cl / 56.6% - Distillery Bottling - The Rare Malts are a now-discontinued series of Cask-strength releases designed by Diageo to showcase some of the hidden treasures in their portfolio.

Glendullan 1995 / 13 YO / Managers' Choice
70cl / 58.7% - Distillery Bottling - A 13 YO single Cask Glendullan Bottled at full strength for the Managers' Choice series. Glendullan is another Distillery we didn't see much of on this side of the pond, but malt from what is one of Diageo's larger Distilleries has recently emerged in the US under the Singleton banner. Interestingly, this is marked as having come from a rejuvenated Cask - kudos to Diageo for this extra snippet of clarity.

Glendullan 1997 / Connoisseurs Choice
70cl / 43% - Gordon & Macphail - A 1997 vintage Bottling from Gordon & Macphail, as part of the Connoisseurs Choice series, of Whisky from seldom seen Glendullan. This was matured in refill Sherry Casks, so expect a bit of fruit.

Glendullan Centenary 16 YO
70cl / 62.6% - Distillery Bottling - Bottled for the Distillery's centenary,

this single Cask 16 YO Glendullan has been kept at its remarkable full strength of 62.6% - so it needs a generous drop of water to tame its elegant, yet firm style and lift the grassy citrus flavours.

GLEN ELGIN RANGE

Glen Elgin / White Horse / Bot.1990s
75cl / 43% - Distillery Bottling - A special no-age-statement Bottling of Glen Elgin for the Japanese market, proudly displaying its status as one of the key ingredients of the iconic White Horse blend.

Glen Elgin 12 YO
70cl / 43% - Distillery Bottling - Glen Elgin 12 YO is a top-quality malt, highly sought-after for blends. This is a little-seen Single Malt expression that represents great value for money.

Glen Elgin 12 YO / Bot. 1970's
75cl / 43% - Distillery Bottling - A very handsome Distillery-Bottled Glen Elgin 12 YO from the 1970s.

Glen Elgin 12 YO / Bot.1980s
75cl / 43% - Distillery Bottling - An old Distillery Bottling of the little-seen Glen Elgin 12 YO, Bottled in the 1980s at 43%.

Glen Elgin 15 YO / Manager's Dram
75cl / 60.2% - Distillery Bottling - A 15 YO Whisky from Glen Elgin, one of the legendary Manager's Drams - a full proof Sherry Cask matured Whisky that was originally produced for staff and friends of the Distillery.

Glen Elgin 1965 / 14 YO / Samaroli
75cl / 45.7% - Samaroli - A 1965 vintage Glen Elgin, Bottled for Italian distributer Samaroli, although with a neck label and Bottle shape that is rather reminiscent of Cadenhead's releases of the time... A 14 YO Whisky matured in Sherry wood.

Glen Elgin 1971 / 32 YO
70cl / 42.3% - Distillery Bottling - Very few expressions of Glen Elgin have been Bottled, so this is a rare treat. Released in 2003, this is a delicious honeyed, fruity dram from an often overlooked Distillery that has long been rated 'First Class' by blenders lists.

Glen Elgin 1991 / 20 YO / Sherry Butt #2325
70cl / 52.7% - Signatory - A single Cask 1991 Whisky from Glen Elgin. This has been fully matured in a Refill Sherry Butt and Bottled at the age of 20 years. Bottled at Cask strength by Signatory for their Cask Strength Collection.

Glen Elgin 1996 / Connoisseurs Choice
70cl / 46% - Gordon & Macphail - A Connoisseurs Choice Bottling of Glen Elgin, one of the key malts in the White Horse blend. Brilliantly, this has been Bottled at 46% - previously unusual for Gordon &

Macphail's CC range, but hopefully a marker of things to come.

Glen Elgin 1998 / Managers' Choice
70cl / 61.1% - Distillery Bottling - A super premium Glen Elgin 1998 Bottled at full Cask strength, this is part of Diageo's Manager's Choice series of single Casks Bottled in 2009.

Glen Elgin 19 YO / Centenary
70cl / 60% - Distillery Bottling - A rare Bottling of Glen Elgin Centenary, released to celebrate the Distillery's first Distillation on the 1st May 1900. This is a 19 YO Whisky with an outturn of only 750 Bottles.

Green Elgin 1976 / 32 YO
70cl / 40.8% - The Whisky Exchange - A very unusual Bottling of Glen Elgin, with a slight (all-natural) green tint. This is a deliciously retro dram, with apples and silky malt on an oak backdrop of the very highest quality.

Old Elgin 1940
75cl / 43% - Gordon & Macphail

GLENFARCLAS RANGE

Glenfarclas 105
70cl / 60% - Distillery Bottling - A full 60% abv, yet the sweet, rich, spicy Distillery character is still very much in evidence. A very small drop of water is recommended to open the flavours.

Glenfarclas 105 / 20 YO
70cl / 60% - Distillery Bottling - Another addition to the 105 family, a series of Whiskies Bottled at a powerful 105 proof. We've already seen the 'No Age Statement' and the 40 YO, and now we have a whole new malt to enjoy. The 20 YO looks absolutely stunning! We'd be surprised if this malt wasn't as popular as its predecessors

Glenfarclas 105' / 40 YO
70cl / 60% - Distillery Bottling - A really incredible Glenfarclas - a forty-YO expression of Cask-strength cult favourite 105, Bottled late in 2008 to celebrate the 40th anniversary of the appearance of the 105 expression. It's astonishing that they managed to maintain the 60% abv over forty years in Sherry Casks - this will be an epic dram.

Glenfarclas 10 YO
70cl / 40% - Distillery Bottling - Glenfarclas 10 YO is a straw-gold , delicately light, sweet and malty dram leaving a long slightly spicy finish. Always impeccably well-made, this is a Whisky that always delivers in quality.

Glenfarclas 10 YO / Sherry Cask / Bot.1980s

75cl / 40% - Distillery Bottling

Glenfarclas 12 YO
70cl / 43% - Distillery Bottling - One up from their standard 10 YO Bottling, the 12 YO has 2 more years in the Cask and is a step closer to the Sherry heavy older expressions.

Glenfarclas 12 YO / Bot.1970s
75cl / 43% - Distillery Bottling - A marvellous old rectangular Bottle of Glenfarclas 12 YO from the 1970s.

Glenfarclas 150th Anniversary
75cl / 43% - Distillery Bottling - A fabulous old Sherried Glenfarclas, the Casks for this were personally selected by John Grant to commemorate the Distillery's 150th anniversary in 1986.

Glenfarclas 15 YO
70cl / 46% - Distillery Bottling - Dark, Sherried 15 YO malt from one of the best Distilleries in Speyside. As always, Glenfarclas remains one of the best value malts on the market, especially compared to Macallan. Top-quality, consistently great Whisky.

Glenfarclas 1952 / The Family Casks
70cl / 47.3% - Distillery Bottling - A single Cask Glenfarclas 1952 Bottled at full strength

Glenfarclas 1952 / The Family Casks II
70cl / 41.9% - Distillery Bottling - The second release of 1952 vintage Whisky as part of the Glenfarclas Family Cask range. This was the oldest Whisky that they have in their warehouse (hopefully they have a few more Casks) and was matured in a plain Cask rather than their more usual Sherry.

Glenfarclas 1954 / Sherry Cask / The Family Casks
70cl / 52.6% - Distillery Bottling - The Glenfarclas Family Casks series is a range of vintage Casks from one of Speyside's best Distilleries. All but three of the range (1952, 1979 & 1984) are from first fill or refill Sherry Casks.

Glenfarclas 1955 / 50 YO / Sherry Cask
70cl / 44.4% - Distillery Bottling - Bottled in 2005 exactly fifty years to the day after it was Distilled, this stunning Glenfarclas was hand-picked by George S. Grant to celebrate the Bicentenary of the birth of his Great-Great-Great-Great-Grandfather John Grant, a farmer and breeder of champion Aberdeen Angus cattle, who bought the Glenfarclas Distillery in 1865. We believe that this could be the best malt ever released by one of our favourite Distilleries.

Glenfarclas 1955 / Sherry Cask / The Family Casks
70cl / 46.1% - Distillery Bottling - The Glenfarclas Family Casks series is a new range of vintage Casks from one of Speyside's best

Distilleries. All but three of the range (1952, 1979 & 1984) are from first fill or refill Sherry Casks.

Glenfarclas 1956 / Sherry Cask / The Family Casks
70cl / 47.3% - Distillery Bottling - The Glenfarclas Family Casks series is a new range of vintage Casks from one of Speyside's best Distilleries. All but three of the range (1952, 1979 & 1984) are from first fill or refill Sherry Casks.

Glenfarclas 1957 Family Cask III / Cask #2 / Sherry Hogshead
70cl / 46.2% - Distillery Bottling - The third release of the 1957 vintage for Glenfarclas's Family Casks series, and this time the Cask in question is a Sherry Hogshead Bottled at a very drinkable natural strength of 46.2%, which is pretty respectable for a Whisky over fifty YO.

Glenfarclas 1959 / 34 YO / Sherry Cask / Signatory
70cl / 50.2% - Signatory - A rare independent release of Glenfarclas, Distilled in 1959, matured in a Sherry Cask and then Bottled 34 years later by Signatory.

Glenfarclas 1959 / 35 YO / Dark Sherry
70cl / 52.6% - Signatory - A fabulous colour on this single Cask full-strength dark Sherried 1950s Glenfarclas, Bottled by Signatory in the mid-1990s.

Glenfarclas 1959 / 42 YO / Sherry Cask
70cl / 46% - Distillery Bottling - A simply stunning refill Sherried Glenfarclas at a phenomenal age. What is amazing about this Whisky is that the oak is not too intrusive and while there is obviously a big fruitcake Sherry character, it isn't overwhelming and the balance is still there. Probably one of the greatest malts ever released from this truly great Distillery.

Glenfarclas 1959 / 50 YO / Family Casks IV
70cl / 48.8% - Distillery Bottling - The perfect gift for any fan of Sherried Whisky born or married in this year, this Glenfarclas 1959 is from a single Sherry Cask Bottled as part of the Distillery's Family Cask range.

Glenfarclas 1959 / Sherry Cask / Family Casks III
70cl / 50.9% - Distillery Bottling - The perfect gift for any fan of Sherried Whisky born or married in this year, this Glenfarclas 1959 is from a single Sherry Cask Bottled as part of the Distillery's Family Cask range.

Glenfarclas 1960 / Bot.2010 / Family Casks VI
70cl / 47% - Distillery Bottling - Bottled in 2010 from a single Sherry hogshead, this vintage Glenfarclas is the perfect gift for anyone born or married in 1960. Majestically rich after five decades of wood

maturation.

Glenfarclas 1960 / The Family Casks III / Cask #1768
70cl / 44.6% - Distillery Bottling - The third 1960 release in Glenfarclas's hugely popular Family Casks series is again from a Sherry hogshead. Just 152 Bottles were yielded from the Cask

Glenfarclas 1962 / Family Casks X / Sherry Hogshead #3247
70cl / 40.9% - Distillery Bottling - A nigh on 50 YO release from Glenfarclas as part of their 10th release of Family Casks. Fully matured in a single Sherry hogshead this is classic old school Whisky from the Distillery.

Glenfarclas 1963 / Family Cask VIII
70cl / 50.4% - Distillery Bottling - A Sherry matured 1960s entry into Glenfarclas's impressive Family Cask range. A single Sherry hogshead laid down in 1963 and then Bottled in 2011 after almost 50 years of maturation.

Glenfarclas 1964 / Family Cask VII / Sherry Butt #4719
70cl / 48.5% - Distillery Bottling - A 1964 vintage from Glenfarclas, Bottled in 2011 after maturing in a Sherry butt.

Glenfarclas 1965 / Family Cask V / Sherry Butt #4362
70cl / 51.9% - Distillery Bottling - A very dark treacle in colour. Light on the nose initially, with some walnuts dipped in chocolate coming through. Similar to the previous 1965 this needs some time to open up in the glass. After forty four years in a Cask this Whisky needs some breathing space, a drop or two of water has the same effect. Distinct heather honey notes emanating after a couple of minutes. An incredibly easy drinking Whisky. Bottled 2010.

Glenfarclas 1966 / Family Cask #4186
70cl / 51.1% - Distillery Bottling - A 1966 single Cask Whisky from Glenfarclas. This Whisky has been aged for an amazing 45 years, Bottled in 2011. This is the 8th release from this vintage that has been used for the Family Casks range.

Glenfarclas 1967 Family Casks V/ Cask #5110/ Sherry Hogshead
70cl / 60.8% - Distillery Bottling - The fifth 1967 release in Glenfarclas's Family Cask series is a Sherry hogshead #5110, and has been Bottled at a frankly astonishing 60.8% after over forty years ageing. That hogshead must have been something pretty special.

Glenfarclas 1968 / Family Casks VI / Cask #534 / Sherry Butt
70cl / 49.5% - Distillery Bottling - The sixth release in the Family Casks series for the 1968 vintage is from a single Sherry butt - this has been another very popular vintage.

Glenfarclas 1969 / 23 YO / Cask #69
70cl / 57.1% - Signatory

Glenfarclas 1969 / Sherry Cask / Family Casks VI
70cl / 56.2% - Distillery Bottling - Another Cask strength vintage Sherry hogshead from Glenfarclas Bottled as part of the Family Casks series. The perfect gift for anyone born in 1969. Speyside's best Distilleries. All but three of the range (1952, 1979 & 1984) are from first fill or refill Sherry Casks.

Glenfarclas 1969 / The Family Casks III
70cl / 55.6% - Distillery Bottling - The third 1969 release from Glenfarclas as part of their Family Casks series.

Glenfarclas 1969 Family Casks IV / Sherry Hogshead #3186
70cl / 53.9% - Distillery Bottling - The fourth release of the 1969 vintage for Glenfarclas's Family Casks is another Sherry hogshead. This should be excellent.

Glenfarclas 1970 / Bot.2011 / Family Casks VII
70cl / 51.7% - Distillery Bottling - Aged over forty years in a Sherry hogshead, 1970 has been one of the most popular vintages in Glenfarclas's Family Cask series. Big Christmas Cask character.

Glenfarclas 1971 / Bot.2011 / Family Casks VII
70cl / 51% - Distillery Bottling - Bottled in 2011 after four decades in a single Sherry butt, this Cask stength 1971 vintage Glenfarclas will make a great gift for any Sherried Speyside fan born in that year.

Glenfarclas 1972 / Sherry Cask / The Family Casks
70cl / 51.1% - Distillery Bottling - The Glenfarclas Family Casks series is a new range of vintage Casks from one of Speyside's best Distilleries. All but three of the range (1952, 1979 & 1984) are from first fill or refill Sherry Casks.

Glenfarclas 1973 / Family Casks VI / Cask #2567/ Sherry Butt
70cl / 51.4% - Distillery Bottling - The sixth release of the 1973 vintage for Glenfarclas's Family Cask series is from a first fill Sherry butt - this should be a cracker.

Glenfarclas 1974 / Sherry Cask / The Family Casks
70cl / 60.8% - Distillery Bottling - The Glenfarclas Family Casks series is a new range of vintage Casks from one of Speyside's best Distilleries. All but three of the range (1952, 1979 & 1984) are from first fill or refill Sherry Casks.

Glenfarclas 1975 / The Family Casks IV
70cl / 45.9% - Distillery Bottling - The Glenfarclas Family Casks series is a range of vintage Casks from one of Speyside's best Distilleries.

Glenfarclas 1976 / The Family Casks

70cl / 49.4% - Distillery Bottling - The Glenfarclas Family Casks series is a new range of vintage Casks from one of Speyside's best Distilleries. All but three of the range (1952, 1979 & 1984) are from first fill or refill Sherry Casks.

Glenfarclas 1977 / The Family Casks
70cl / 59% - Distillery Bottling - The Glenfarclas Family Casks series is a new range of vintage Casks from one of Speyside's best Distilleries. All but three of the range (1952, 1979 & 1984) are from first fill or refill Sherry Casks.

Glenfarclas 1978 / Family Cask VII / Refill Sherry Cask #590
70cl / 46.3% - Distillery Bottling - A 1978 vintage Glenfarclass released as part of the 7th release of family Casks. Matured in a refill Sherry hogshead and Bottled in 2011.

Glenfarclas 1978 / Family Casks III / Cask: 626
70cl / 57.6% - Distillery Bottling - The third edition of Glenfarclas 1978 is, unusually, from a plain hogshead - you might notice the colour is rather less auburn than usual. This, then, will lack the normal overt Sherried qualities normally associated with this Distillery, and has been described by brand ambasasdor George Grant as a floral Whisky, 'almost like camomile tea.'

Glenfarclas 1979 / Family Cask Release IV
70cl / 45.2% - Distillery Bottling - An unusual departure for the Glenfarclas Family Casks - the 1979 fourth release is from a plain hogshead, making quite a contrast to the first-fill and refill Sherry Casks that characterise most of the Distillery's output.

Glenfarclas 1980 / Sherry Cask / The Family Casks I
70cl / 50.1% - Distillery Bottling - This 1980 vintage Cask strength Glenfarclas was the first in the Family Cask series for this vintage and was Bottled in 2007 from a refill Sherry butt.

Glenfarclas 1981 / Family Cask VII / Plain Hogshead #57
70cl / 50.8% - Distillery Bottling - A 1981 vintage Glenfarclass Bottled in 2011 for the Family Casks range.

Glenfarclas 1981 / Family Casks V / Cask #58
70cl / 50.9% - Distillery Bottling - The fifth 1981 released for Glenfarclas's Family Cask series is, unusually, from a plain hogshead - most of the series have been from first fill or refill Sherry Casks, so this is something a bit different and will make an interesting comparison to the rest of the range.

Glenfarclas 1982 / Family Casks V / Cask #633
70cl / 54.2% - Distillery Bottling - The fifth release of Glenfarclas's 1982 vintage Family Cask series is, unusually, from a plain hogshead rather than a first fill or refill Sherry Cask, and will most likely be milder and less sweet than normal Glenfarclas.

Glenfarclas 1983 / The Family Casks
70cl / 56% - Distillery Bottling - The Glenfarclas Family Casks series is a new range of vintage Casks from one of Speyside's best Distilleries. All but three of the range (1952, 1979 & 1984) are from first fill or refill Sherry Casks.

Glenfarclas 1984 / Family Cask VII / Plain Hogshead #6030
70cl / 51% - Distillery Bottling - A 1984 vintage Glenfarclass Bottled as part of the 7th release of Family Casks in 2011.

Glenfarclas 1985 / Sherry Cask / The Family Casks
70cl / 46.3% - Distillery Bottling - The Glenfarclas Family Casks series is a new range of vintage Casks from one of Speyside's best Distilleries. All but three of the range (1952, 1979 & 1984) are from first fill or refill Sherry Casks.

Glenfarclas 1986 / Sherry Cask / The Family Casks
70cl / 56.5% - Distillery Bottling - The Glenfarclas Family Casks series is a new range of vintage Casks from one of Speyside's best Distilleries. All but three of the range (1952, 1979 & 1984) are from first fill or refill Sherry Casks.

Glenfarclas 1987 / Family Casks III / Cask #3826
70cl / 53.2% - Distillery Bottling - A refill Sherry hogshead of 1987 Glenfarclas, this is the third release in the Distillery's hugely popular Family Casks series.

Glenfarclas 1988 / Sherry Cask / The Family Casks
70cl / 56.3% - Distillery Bottling - The Glenfarclas Family Casks series is a new range of vintage Casks from one of Speyside's best Distilleries. All but three of the range (1952, 1979 & 1984) are from first fill or refill Sherry Casks.

Glenfarclas 1989 / Sherry Cask / The Family Casks
70cl / 60% - Distillery Bottling - The Glenfarclas Family Casks series is a new range of vintage Casks from one of Speyside's best Distilleries. All but three of the range (1952, 1979 & 1984) are from first fill or refill Sherry Casks.

Glenfarclas 1990 / Family Cask VIII
70cl / 56.9% - Distillery Bottling - A rich Sherried release of 1990 vintage Whisky from Glenfarclas, part of their Family Cask range of single Casks. This was Bottled in 2011 from a Sherry butt at Cask strength.

Glenfarclas 1991 / Sherry Cask / The Family Casks
70cl / 57.9% - Distillery Bottling - The Glenfarclas Family Casks series is a new range of vintage Casks from one of Speyside's best Distilleries. All but three of the range (1952, 1979 & 1984) are from first fill or refill Sherry Casks.

Glenfarclas 1993 / Family Casks V / Cask #3942 / Sherry Butt
70cl / 59.7% - Distillery Bottling - A first fill Sherry butt of the 1993 vintage from Glenfarclas, this is the fifth release in The Family Casks series for this vintage and at nearly 60% is likely to benefit from a drop of water.

Glenfarclas 1994 / Family Cask #2950 / Release IX
70cl / 57.9% - Distillery Bottling - A 1994 vintage Glenfarclas released as part of the 9th batch of Family Casks. Matured in a Sherry butt and Bottled in 2012.

Glenfarclas 1995 / Family Casks IX / Sherry #6612
70cl / 52.5% - Distillery Bottling - A 1995 vintage Glenfarclas, Bottled in 2012 as part of the 9th release of Family Casks. This has spent about 17 years in a Sherry butt, and has a twist on the regular Glenfarclas Sherried character.

Glenfarclas 1996 / Family Cask VII / Sherry Butt #1306
70cl / 55.6% - Distillery Bottling - A 1996 vintage Glenfarclas Bottled in 2011 for the Family Casks range after maturing in a Sherry butt.

Glenfarclas 21 YO
70cl / 43% - Distillery Bottling - A dark amber-gold, full sweet vanilla delicately smoked with a rich and long lasting finish. Glenfarclas 21 YO is delicious stuff, and a bargain at this price.

Glenfarclas 21 YO / Bot.1970s
75cl / 43% - Distillery Bottling

Glenfarclas 21 YO / Bot.1980s
75cl / 43% - Distillery Bottling - A rare old 21 YO Glenfarclas from the 1980s, when the official Distillery-Bottled editions were done in these rather quaint rectangular Bottles.

Glenfarclas 22 YO / Spirit of the Millennium
70cl / 43% - Distillery Bottling - A special 22 YO Glenfarclas chosen by John Grant in 1999 to celebrate the turn of the Millennium.

Glenfarclas 25 YO
70cl / 43% - Distillery Bottling - An all-time classic, Glenfarclas 25 YO is the epitome of long-aged Sherried Speyside, gorgeously smooth and silkily-textured, with rich, generous flavours of fruitcake, hazelnuts, dried fruit and a hint of dark chocolate and coffee. A thoroughly delightful dram.

Glenfarclas 25 YO / Bot. 1970's
75cl / 43% - Distillery Bottling

Glenfarclas 30 YO
70cl / 43% - Distillery Bottling - With a full complex aroma combining fruit and spices similar to a fruit cake, Glenfarclas 30 YO is an

extraordinarily deep spirit, warm and rich leaving a lingering fruit and nut chocolate feel on the palate.

Glenfarclas 40 YO
70cl / 46% - A remarkably well-priced 40 YO from Glenfarclas range; simply-packaged just like the Distillery's standard Bottlings, and Bottled at a perfect drinking strength of 46%. A 40 YO Sherried Speyside designed for drinking rather than sitting on a mantlepiece or in a display cabinet - bravo. Awarded a very well-merited Gold Medal at the Malt Maniacs Awards 2010.

Glenfarclas 43 YO Cognac Cask
70cl / 40.7% - Distillery Bottling - Glenfarclas are perhaps best known for their heavily Sherried Bottlings. This time, however, we have been graced with something quite special... a 43 YO Glenfarclas matured in Cognac Casks. As far as we know, there have been only a small handful of Whiskies matured in Cognac Casks (and from what we have been hearing, this one is absolutely gorgeous).

Glenfarclas 50 YO / Crystal Decanter
70cl / 50% - Distillery Bottling - A stunning new Distillery Bottling of Glenfarclas 50 YO for The Whisky Exchange. Aged over 50 years in a single refill Sherry Cask, and Bottled at a remarkable 50% abv, just 87 Bottles were yielded from the Cask. This incredibly rare Glenfarclas has been packaged in a gorgeous crystal decanter.

Glenfarclas 8 YO / 105' / Bot.1980s
75cl / 60% - Distillery Bottling - An early Bottling of Glenfarclas 105' from the 1980s, rare in that it has an age statement (from the days when 8 years was pretty old for a Single Malt).

Glenfarclas 8 YO / Bot.1960's
75cl / 40% - Distillery Bottling - A Bottling of 8 YO Glenfarclas from the 1960s, complete with the '-Glenlivet' suffix and an unusual screeprinted label.

Glenfarclas 8 YO / Bot.1970s
75cl / 60% - Distillery Bottling - A Bottling of 8 YO Glenfarclas from the 1970s, the days when they still suffixed their name with a "-Glenlivet".

Glenfarclas Morgan 18 YO
75cl / 43% - Distillery Bottling - An 18 YO Bottling of Glenfarclas Bottled for the Morgan Sports Car Club in celebration of their June 1989 Scottish gathering.

Glenfarclas-Glenlivet 105 / 8 YO / Bot.1970s
75cl / 60% - Distillery Bottling - A really beautiful old 1970s Bottling of Cask-strength Glenfarclas, one of the earliest examples we've seen of the Distillery's pioneering 105-proof expression. Originally an 8 YO,

the 105's age statement was dropped sometime around the late 1980s or early 1990s to keep up with demand.

Glenfarclas-Glenlivet 7 YO / Bot.1970s
75cl / 40% - Distillery Bottling - A 7 YO Whisky from Livet valley resident Glenfarclas, Bottled sometime back in the 1970s.

Glenfarclas-Glenlivet 8 YO / Bot.1970s
75cl / 40% - Distillery Bottling

Glenfarclas-Glenlivet 8 YO / Bot.1970s
75cl / 43% - Distillery Bottling - A 1970s Bottling of Glenfarclas 8 YO, back from the days when they still honoured the location in the Livet valley on their labels.

Glenfarclas-Glenlivet 8 YO / Bot.1980's
75cl / 43% - Distillery Bottling

Glenfarclas-Glenlivet 8 YO / Sherry Cask / Bot.1970s
75cl / 40% - Distillery Bottling - A great looking Bottle of 8 YO Glenfarclas from the 1970s, when they still used to append -Glenlivet to the name.

J. & G. Grant (Glenfarclas) / 12 YO / Bot.1980s
75cl / 43% - Distillery Bottling - A Sherry Cask matured Whisky from John and George Grant (the two names that all of the company managers have had) made at Glenfarclas, aged for 12 years and Bottled in the 1980s.

GLENFIDDICH RANGE

Glenfiddich 12 YO
70cl / 40% - Distillery Bottling - One of the world's best-selling malts, Glenfiddich 12 YO's famous triangular Bottle is a fixture in practically every bar on the globe. Light and easy-drinking stuff loved by millions.

Glenfiddich 14 YO / Rich Oak
70cl / 40% - Distillery Bottling - Released in Spring 2010, this Glenfiddich Rich Oak has spent 14 years in ex-Bourbon Casks in the traditional way, before two separate finishes of 12 weeks in new European oak and six weeks in new American oak before Bottling. We like the sound of this.

Glenfiddich 15 YO Distillery Edition
70cl / 51% - Distillery Bottling - A higher-strength Glenfiddich aged 15 years, this Distillery Edition has been Bottled at 51%.

Glenfiddich 15 YO Solera
70cl / 40% - Distillery Bottling - Immensely popular Glenfiddich

variant. Using a Solera system common in the maturation of quality Sherry, 15 YO malt from three different types of Casks is married together in a wooden vat, which is constantly topped up to ensure the quality is maintained.
IWSC 2012 - Gold Outstanding Medal - Whisky - Scotch

Glenfiddich 18 YO
70cl / 40% - Distillery Bottling - An elegant nose, faintly sweet, scented with apple and wood. Glenfiddich 18 YO is a robust and full-bodied single malt Whisky, yet remains remarkably soft, rounded and long lasting.

Glenfiddich 18 YO / Ancient Reserve / Black
75cl / 43% - Distillery Bottling - Glenfiddich's "Ancient Reserve" 18 YO Whisky, packaged in a black ceramic Spode decanter.

Glenfiddich 1958 Private Vintage / Cask #8642
70cl / 46.3% - Distillery Bottling - An incredibly rare single Cask Glenfiddich, Distilled in 1958 and aged for over 47 years. Each Private Vintage Bottling is selected from a shortlist of 4-6 Casks, selected by the malt master, and then hand Bottled. Each Bottle comes with in a sturdy cherry wood presentation box.

Glenfiddich 1959 Private Vintage / Cask #3934
70cl / 48.1% - Distillery Bottling - An incredibly rare single Cask Glenfiddich, Distilled in 1959 and aged for over 46 years. Each Private Vintage Bottling is selected from a shortlist of 4-6 Casks, selected by the malt master, and then hand Bottled. Each Bottle comes with in a sturdy cherry wood presentation box.

Glenfiddich 1961 / 35 YO / Cask #9015
70cl / 43.2% - Distillery Bottling - A 1961 Vintage Reserve from Glenfiddich. A single Cask aged for 35 years and Bottled on 13th October 2000.

Glenfiddich 1961 / 47 YO / Cask #9016
70cl / 43.8% - Distillery Bottling - A very small release of 1961 vintage from Glenfiddich, with an outturn of just 56 Bottles, packaged in a solid but elegant wooden box. Cask 9016, filled in the year that the farthing ceased to be legal tender in the UK, was selected by Glenfiddich Malt Master Brian Kinsman after 47 years of maturation.

Glenfiddich 1963
70cl / 46.5% - Distillery Bottling - A special edition of Glenfiddich Vintage Reserve. This 1963 vintage Whisky was released exclusively for Scotland and limited to just 219 Bottles.

Glenfiddich 1963 / 24 YO
75cl / 46% - Cadenhead's - It's very rare to see an independently-Bottled Glenfiddich - even more so when it's a Cadenhead's Bottling from the late 1980s (and still carries the 'Glenlivet' suffix on the

Bottle!).

Glenfiddich 1964 Private Vintage / Cask #13430
70cl / 45.6% - Distillery Bottling - An incredibly rare single Cask Glenfiddich, Distilled in 1964 and aged for over 41 years. Each Private Vintage Bottling is selected from a shortlist of 4-6 Casks, selected by the malt master, and then hand Bottled. Each Bottle comes with in a sturdy cherry wood presentation box.

Glenfiddich 1965 / 18 YO / Cadenhead's
75cl / 46% - Cadenhead's - A 1984 Bottling of 1965 Glenfiddich from veteran independent Cadenhead's. A bit of a rare treat this, as you don't often see independent Bottlings of Whiskies from the Wm Grant stable these days.

Glenfiddich 1965 / 35 YO / Cadenhead's
70cl / 49.1% - Cadenhead's - A 35 YO Whisky from Cadenhead's, presented in their gloriously blingy gold livery. This was Distilled in 1965 and Bottled in February 2001.

Glenfiddich 1965 / Republic of Singapore 40th / Cask #10836
70cl / 47.3% - Distillery Bottling - special limited edition Glenfiddich, celebrating the 40th anniversary of the creation of the Republic of Singapore in 1965. This was Bottled from the last remaining Cask of 1965 vintage Whisky and has suitably exclusive small outturn of only 180 Bottles.

Glenfiddich 1965 Vintage Reserve / Cask #10837
70cl / 47.8% - Distillery Bottling - An entry in Glenfiddich's Vintage Reserve range from 2001, chosen by a panel of experts, including the late Michael Jackson. This is different from the Vintage Reserves before it due to coming from a European oak Sherry butt, rather than the usual Bourbon Casks.

Glenfiddich 1966 / 13 YO / Cadenhead's
75cl / 45.7% - Cadenhead's - An old 1966 Whisky from Glenfiddich. Bottled by Cadenhead in 1979, this Whisky has been aged for 13 years.

Glenfiddich 1967 Vintage Reserve / 30 YO
70cl / 43.6% - Distillery Bottling

Glenfiddich 1968 / 30 YO / Cask #13142
70cl / 49.2% - Distillery Bottling - A very rare single Cask Glenfiddich from the 1968 vintage, Bottled at its natural Cask strength of 49.2% some time around the late 1990s at over 30 years of age.

Glenfiddich 1973 / 25 YO
70cl / 49.2% - Distillery Bottling - A 25 YO Glenfiddich Distilled in 1973 and released in the late 2000s as part of their Vintage Reserve range of single Casks Bottlings.

Glenfiddich 1973 / 33 YO / Cask 9874
70cl / 46.5% - Distillery Bottling - The most recent of Glenfiddich's Single Cask expressions.

Glenfiddich 1974 / Queen's Coronation
70cl / 48.9% - The Whisky Exchange - A special limited edition Glenfiddich single Cask Bottled at full strength in 2003 to celebrate the 50th anniversary of Queen Elizabeth's Coronation.

Glenfiddich 1983 / 25 YO/ Dubai Duty Free/ Sherry Cask
75cl / 53.4% - Distillery Bottling - A special Private Vintage Bottling of a 25 year-old single European oak Sherry Cask of Glenfiddich 1983, released to celebrate the 25th anniversary of luxury travel retail in Dubai.

Glenfiddich 21 YO / Gran Reserva
70cl / 40% - Distillery Bottling - A terrific and hugely successful new Glenfiddich, aged for 21 years before being filled into Casks previously containing Cuban rum for a second maturation.

Glenfiddich 21 YO / Gran Reserva / Rum Cask Finish
70cl / 40% - Distillery Bottling - The return of the name Gran Reserva to Glenfiddich's 21 YO after a few years under different titles is also accompanied by an upgrade to its packaging. It is still finished in rum Casks for 4 months, but it now has a more elegant presentation, as befits its position towards the top of the Distillery's regular range.

Glenfiddich 21 YO / Wedgewood Decanter
75cl / 43% - Distillery Bottling - A blue wedgewood decanter of Glenfiddich's 21 YO Whisky. Please note - this is the 75cl version of the decanter.

Glenfiddich 30 YO / Bot. 2010
70cl / 43% - Distillery Bottling - The 2010 release of Glenfiddich 30 year-old has a very classy new look, with a dumpier Bottle and a handsome wooden box. Malt fans will also be very pleased that the Bottling strength of this marriage of Oloroso Sherry and Bourbon Casks has risen to 43% as well.

Glenfiddich 30 YO / Bot.2009
70cl / 40% - Distillery Bottling - Seductively woody, with substantial oakiness and lush notes of Sherry, Glenfiddich 30 YO is an evening Whisky, with sweet floral top notes and a long honeyed finish. This is the last edition of Glenfiddich 30 YO before its 2010 relaunch, and it celebrates the 40th anniversary of the opening of the Distillery's visitor centre in 1969.

Glenfiddich 40 YO / Bot. 2007
70cl / 43.5% - Distillery Bottling - An excellent example of old Glenfiddich, showcasing their spirit's ability to improve in the Cask for a long time without going too far. An elegant and impressive

Whisky.

Glenfiddich 40 YO / Bot.2002
75cl / 45.4% - Distillery Bottling - A very limited-edition official Bottling of Glenfiddich 40 YO, originally released in 2002.

Glenfiddich 40 YO / Bot.2002
70cl / 45.4% - Distillery Bottling - The 2002 edition of Glenfiddich's excellent and much sought after 40 YO whisky. Very rarely seen in the wild this a very rare and collectible Bottling.

Glenfiddich 40 YO / Bot.2008
70cl / 45.4% - Distillery Bottling - The product of truly inspired Cask selection and blending, atypically for a Speyside there is little or no Sherry influence here, allowing the elegant, floral, slightly smoky Distillery character to shine through. A masterpiece.

Glenfiddich 40 YO / Bot.2012
70cl / 41.7% - Distillery Bottling - The 9th release of Glenfiddich's series of incredible 40 YO Whiskies, Bottled in 2012. Vatted from a selection of excellent Casks as well as the saved remnants of previous year's vattings.

Glenfiddich 50 YO
70cl / 46.1% - Distillery Bottling - This is only the second ever official Bottling of Glenfiddich 50 YO, and has been created from two Casks (a 1955 and a 1957) married for six months before Bottling. Just 500 Bottles of this extraordinary Whisky have been created. They are released on a strict global allocation of 50 Bottles per year for the next ten years. Each Bottle is decorated with Scottish silver and is housed in a hand-sewn leather box with a leather bound book and signed certificate.

Glenfiddich 8 YO / Bot.1970s
75cl / 40% - Distillery Bottling - The Bottling on which Glenfiddich cemented its reputation in the 1970s, this is a fabulously complex spirit for its age, (although 8 YO was regarded as pretty old back then). A very tropical, fruity dram with Glenfiddich's textbook elegance - this is a winner.

Glenfiddich Centenary
75cl / 43% - Distillery Bottling - A special edition of Glenfiddich released in 1987 to celebrate the Distillery's centenary - the first run of spirit was on Christmas day 1887.

Glenfiddich Collection / 3x20cl
60cl / 40% - A set of three 20cl Bottles showcasing Glenfiddich's most popular releases - the elegant 12, solera aged 15 and classic 18 YO.

Glenfiddich Malt Master's Edition / Sherry Cask Finish
70cl / 43% - Distillery Bottling - Glenfiddich's Malt Master, Brian Kinsman, is the first to double mature a Glenfiddich Whisky in two

different Casks (although shorter finishing periods in more than one kind of Casks has of course been done several times before). This Whisky has been matured for some time in traditional Oak Casks before finishing its maturation in Sherry Casks.
IWSC 2012 - Gold Medal - Whisky - Scotch

Glenfiddich Pure Malt / Bot.1930s
75cl / 40% - Distillery Bottling - A very rare and difficult to find officially-Bottled Glenfiddich from, we believe, the 1930s. This museum-worthy round Bottle (Glenfiddich did not appear in its now-iconic triangular Bottle until 1963) is one of the earliest Glenfiddichs we've found, and represents a significant piece of Whisky history.

GLENGLASSAUGH RANGE

Glenglassaugh 12 YO / Bot.1980s
75cl / 43% - Distillery Bottling - A rare old 1980s Distillery Bottling of Glenglassaugh 12 YO, the recently-revived Distillery on the cusp of Speyside.

Glenglassaugh 12 YO / Bot.1990s
70cl / 43% - Distillery Bottling - A tasty old 1990s Bottling of 12 YO Glenglassaugh with a pleasingly understated label, this easy-going medium-bodied Speysider is hugely drinkable, nutty and chocolatey with prominent tropical fruits.

Glenglassaugh 1967 / 45 YO / Red Port Style Finish
70cl / 50.2% - Distillery Bottling - A 1967 vintage Whisky from Glenglassaugh. This has been finished in a Red Port Style wine barrel. The wine is made from Cabernet Sauvignon grapes, and is affectionately referred to as 'the Tsar's port'. The Whisky itself has been aged for an amazing 45 years so expect to find strong oak notes present with the wine finish adding juicy, sweet fruits to the experience.

Glenglassaugh 1967 Manager's Legacy / Walter Grant
70cl / 40.4% - Distillery Bottling - A fourth entry and final entry in Glenglassaugh's Manager's Legacy series, celebrating the stewardship of the late Walter Grant, who retired in 1986. A Sherry Cask of spirit Distilled in 1968 and matured for 43 years.

Glenglassaugh 1968 / Manager's Legacy / Bert Forsyth
70cl / 44.9% - Distillery Bottling - The third in Glenglassaugh's recent series of very special Casks editions released as the Manager's Legacy series. This is a refill Sherry Cask from 1968, Bottled to commemorate Bert Forsyth's stewardship of the Distillery. A gentle dram with delightful notes of blackberry pie & heather.

Glenglassaugh 1972 / 39 YO / Sherry Style Finish
70cl / 53.3% - Distillery Bottling - A 1972 vintage Whisky from Glenglassaugh for their "The Massandra Connection" series. This

Whisky has been aged for 39 years and finished in "Sherry Style Wines". Sherry style wines are made from a variety of grapes and have a similar flavour profile as Sherry (as the name would suggest). This particular Sherry style wine is a combination of Sercial, Verdelho, and Crimean Albillo grapes.

Glenglassaugh 1973 / 39 YO / Aleatico Finish
70cl / 50.7% - Distillery Bottling - A 1979 vintage Whisky from Glenglassaugh. This Whisky has been aged for 39 years and spent time finishing in a barrel previously used for Aleatico wine. The influence of such a sweet wine, gives the Whisky a sweet, fruity taste.

Glenglassaugh 1973 / 39 YO / Muscat Finish / Massandra
70cl / 44.1% - Distillery Bottling - A 1973 vintage Whisky from Glenglassaugh Distillery. This Whisky has been aged for 39 years and finished in single Cask previously used for Muscat Wine. The Cask itself is from the Massandra winery in Crimea, which has been producing wine for more than 110 years.

Glenglassaugh 1976 / 35 YO / The Chosen Few
70cl / 49.6% - Distillery Bottling - The first of Glenglassaugh's Chosen Few series of single Cask Bottlings, as chosen by the Distillery team. This one is the selection of Customer Account Manager Ronnie Routledge and has the combination of tropical fruit and Sherry character that he loves in a Whisky.

Glenglassaugh 1976 / 36 YO / Aged over 30 Years
70cl / 49.2% - Distillery Bottling - A 1976 vintage Whisky from Glenglassaugh, aged for 36 years and packaged in an elegant decanter as part of their 'Aged over 30 years' range of older Whiskies.

Glenglassaugh 1978 / 33 YO / Chosen Few
70cl / 46.3% - Distillery Bottling - A 1978 Glenglassaugh, matured for 33 years and chosen by production manager Mhairi McDonald as part of the Distillery's Chosen Few range. She went for something a bit different to the other Bottlings, going for a fresh and fruity dram.

Glenglassaugh 1978 / 33 YO / Madeira Style Finish
70cl / 44.8% - Distillery Bottling - A 1978 vintage Whisky from Glenglassaugh. This Whisky has been finished in a Cask previously used for Madeira style wine. A beautifully sweet, fruity 33 YO.

Glenglassaugh 1984 / 25 YO / Sherry Butt #5362
70cl / 50% - Douglas Laing - A sumptuous Sherry Cask from Glenglassaugh, Distilled in 1984 and Bottled by Douglas Laing for the Old Malt Cask series. Classic chocolate and golden syrup Sherry style.

Glenglassaugh 1986 Manager's Legacy / Dod Cameron
70cl / 45.3% - Distillery Bottling - One of a series of Bottlings of old Glenglassaughs dedicated to former Distillery managers. This is a 1986 refill butt Bottled in 2010 to honour Dod Cameron, who was at the helm from 1974-1986.

Glenglassaugh 19 YO
70cl / 40% - Distillery Bottling - One of the last official Bottlings of Glenglassaugh from former owners Edrington Group before the Distillery changed hands, this 19 YO was Distilled in 1986, the year the Distillery was mothballed, and appeared on our shelves in 2006.

Glenglassaugh 21 YO
70cl / 46% - Distillery Bottling - The rebirth of Glenglassaugh after a hibernation that has lasted since 1986. This 21 YO must therefore be slightly older than 21.

Glenglassaugh 26 YO
70cl / 46% - Distillery Bottling - A long-aged official Glenglassaugh 26 YO, added to the Distillery's range in Spring 2010.

Glenglassaugh Evolution
70cl / 57.2% - Distillery Bottling - The follow up to Revival, Glenglassaugh's Evolution is a limited release showcasing their spirit's interaction with ex-Tennessee Whisky Casks, having matured in barrels that used to contain George Dickel.

Glenglassaugh Rare Cask Series / 26, 37 and 43 YO
60cl / 49.8% - Distillery Bottling - A fantastic looking selection set from the folks at Glenglassaugh, presenting their 26, 37 and 43 YO Whiskies in a slick looking presentation case.

Glenglassaugh Revival
70cl / 46% - Distillery Bottling - The Glenglassaugh Distillery was mothballed from 1986 until 2008 and this the first Whisky to be made from spirit Distilled at the Distillery since it reopened. It was matured in a mixture of first and refill Bourbon Casks before a final 6 months finishing in first fill Oloroso Sherry butts.

Glenglassaugh Sloeberry Liqueur
50cl / 26% - Glenglassaugh like playing with their new make spirit in interesting ways and their experiments with 'Spirit Drinks' have now led to this - a liqueur made using sloes, more usually steeped in gin. Here they use the crisp barley spirit and a bit of sugar to great effect, producing a deeply flavoured and fruity liqueur.

GLEN GRANT RANGE

Glen Grant / The Major's Reserve
70cl / 40% - Distillery Bottling - A no-age-statement entry-level Glen Grant, this is a very accessible, approachable malt ideal for beginners.

Glen Grant / Beige Label / Bot.1980s
75cl / 40% - Distillery Bottling - A 1980s Bottling of Glen Grant with their old beige label

Glen Grant 10 YO
70cl / 40% - Distillery Bottling - Very reliable quality Speyside from a Distillery founded in 1840. Glen Grant is one of the world's best-selling Single Malts and is particularly popular in Italy.

Glen Grant 10 YO / Bot.1970s
75cl / 43% - Distillery Bottling - A 10 YO Glen Grant Bottled in the 1970s at 43% ABV.

Glen Grant 10 YO / Bot.1990s
70cl / 40% - Distillery Bottling - An old presentation of the Glen Grant 10 YO. We estimate that this was Bottled some time in the 1990s.

Glen Grant 12 Years / Bot.1970s
75cl / 43% - Distillery Bottling - An old rectangular Distillery Bottling of Speyside stalwart Glen Grant 12 YO.

Glen Grant 12 YO / Bot.1970's
75cl / 40% Distillery Bottling

Glen Grant 14 YO / Bot.1930s
75cl / 45.7% - Berry Bros & Rudd - A very old 1930s Bottle of Glen Grant Bottled by posh London wine merchants Berry Brothers & Rudd.

Glen Grant 15 YO / 100 Proof / Bot.1970s
75cl / 57% - Gordon & Macphail - A high strength Glen Grant 15 YO Bottled by Gordon & Macphail sometime in the 1970s.

Glen Grant 15 YO / Bot.1970s
75.7cl / 40% - Gordon & Macphail - A handsome Bottle of Glen Grant 15 YO Botttled by Gordon & Macphail at some stage in the 1970s.

Glen Grant 170th Anniversary
70cl / 46% - Distillery Bottling - A special edition of Glen Grant, blended from the Distillery's most valuable Casks and Bottled at 46% without chill-filtration in 2010 to celebrate the Distillery's 170th anniversary.

Glen Grant 1936 / 50 YO / Gordon & Macphail
75cl / 40% - Gordon & Macphail - An old Glen Grant, Distilled in 1936 and Bottled in the mid 1980s after 50 years of maturation. Glen Grant ages well so this rare Whisky should be a cracker when opened.

Glen Grant 1936 / Gordon & Macphail
75cl / 40% - Gordon & Macphail - An incredibly rare 1936 Glen Grant, Bottled by Gordon & Macphail.

Glen Grant 1948 / 50 YO / Gordon & Macphail
70cl / 40% - Gordon & Macphail

Glen Grant 1948 / Bot.1980s

75cl / 40% - A well aged Glen Grant Bottled by Gordon & Macphail from their well stocked warehouses. This was released in the 1980s.

Glen Grant 1948 / Gordon & Macphail
70cl / 40% - Gordon & Macphail - An ancient dram aged for nigh on sixty years. Thankfully, Glen Grant is one of those special Speysiders (like Glenfarclas and Macallan) that is capable of withstanding immense oak ageing. An excellent malt.

Glen Grant 1949 / Bot.1980s
75cl / 40%

Glen Grant 1949 / Gordon & Macphail
70cl / 40% - Gordon & Macphail - Glen Grant is one of a handful of Speyside Distilleries that can handle very extended Cask maturation - this Gordon & MacPhail example was aged for nearly sixty years.

Glen Grant 1950 / Gordon & Macphail
70cl / 40% - Gordon & Macphail - Gordon & Macphail have some good stocks of old Glen Grant to draw on, as shown by this incredible 1950 vintage Bottling, released in 2007 at about 57 YO.

Glen Grant 1951 / Gordon & Macphail
70cl / 40% - Gordon & Macphail - A 1951 vintage Glen Grant, Bottled by Gordon & Macphail with the traditional old Distillery label.

Glen Grant 1952 / 60 YO / Queen's Diamond Jubilee
70cl / 42.3% - Gordon & Macphail - A very rare and exclusive release by Gordon & Macphail in honour of Queen Elizabeth II's Diamond Jubilee in 2012. Bottled from a first fill Sherry Cask laid down four days before the Queen's coronation and decanted on its 60th birthday, 2nd February 2012. A beautiful celebratory decanter presented in a handmade wooden box.

Glen Grant 1952 / Bot.1980s / Gordon & Macphail
75cl / 40% - Gordon & Macphail - A 1980s release of Whisky from Glen Grant, Distilled in 1952 and Bottled by Gordon & Macphail.

Glen Grant 1952 / Gordon & Macphail
70cl / 40% - Gordon & Macphail - A grand old Bottling of Glen Grant, Distilled in 1952 and Bottled sometime in the early 2000s by Gordon & Macphail. G&M have some impressive old stock, but this is about as old as it gets.

Glen Grant 1953 / 48 YO / Gordon & Macphail
70cl / 45% - Gordon & Macphail

Glen Grant 1953 / Gordon & Macphail
70cl / 40% - Gordon & Macphail - A 1953 vintage Glen Grant, Bottled at over 50 YO by Gordon & Macphail. This was an important year for

the distillery, as they merged with Glenlivet to form the imaginatively titled Glen Grant and Glenlivet Distillers Ltd and commenced the expansion that led to the latter being the second biggest malt in the world.

Glen Grant 1954 / Gordon & Macphail
70cl / 40% - Gordon & Macphail - A dark and long aged Glen Grant from Gordon & Macphail's scarily extensive archives of their Whisky from the 1950s. This one was Distilled in 1954 and sat maturing for over 50 years.

Glen Grant 1955 / Gordon & Macphail
70cl / 40% - Gordon & Macphail - A 1955 vintage Glen Grant Bottled by Gordon & Macphail, owners of one of the most extensive collections of old Casks, from Glen Grant and elsewhere, in Scotland. This has matured for over 50 years, an impressive feat that very few Distiller's spirits can stand up to - Glen Grant can.

Glen Grant 1956 / Gordon & Macphail
70cl / 40% - Gordon & Macphail - A 1956 vintage Glen Grant Bottled by Gordon & Macphails from there impressive collection of old Casks of Whisky. A long aged spirit Bottled at about 50 YO.

Glen Grant 1957 / Gordon & Macphail
70cl / 40% - Gordon & Macphail - A lip-smacking Sherried Speyside at an amazing 49 years of age. Very few Whiskies can stand this kind of ageing, which is just one of the reasons that Glen Grant is a great malt. The perfect gift for anyone born in 1957.

Glen Grant 1958 / Gordon & Macphail
70cl / 40% - Gordon & Macphail - Bottled in 2011, this 1958 vintage Glen Grant has been aged for well over fifty years in Sherry Casks and has been packaged in fancy upgraded boxes that at last go some way to befitting the majesty of their contents.

Glen Grant 1959 / Gordon & Macphail
70cl / 40% - Gordon & Macphail - Another of Gordon & Macphail's long-aged Glen Grants which, along with Glenfarclas, represent the best-value long-aged Sherried Speysides available. Thankfully, Glen Grant is one of those special Speysiders (like Glenfarclas, Mortlach and Macallan) that is capable of withstanding immense oak ageing without tasting like a pile of wet sawdust.

Glen Grant 1960 / Gordon & Macphail
70cl / 40% - Gordon & Macphail - Another of Gordon & Macphail's long-aged Glen Grants which, along with Glenfarclas, represent the best-value long-aged Sherried Speysides available. Thankfully, Glen Grant is one of those special Speysiders (like Glenfarclas, Mortlach and Macallan) that is capable of withstanding immense oak ageing without tasting like a pile of wet sawdust.

Glen Grant 1963 / Gordon & Macphail
70cl / 40% - Gordon & Macphail - A long-aged sherried Glen Grant 1963 from pioneering indie Bottlers Gordon & Macphail.

Glen Grant 1964 / 5 YO
75cl / 40% - Distillery Bottling - A very rare Bottle of Glen Grant, Distilled in 1964 and Bottled at the turn of the 1970s for the Italian market.

Glen Grant 1964 / Gordon & Macphail
70cl / 40% - Gordon & Macphail - A 1964 vintage Glen Grant, Bottled from their scary warehouses full of old Casks by Gordon & Macphail. Over 40 YO and incredible value for a Whisky of this age.

Glen Grant 1965 / 5 YO
75cl / 40% - Distillery Bottling - A lovely old Bottle of Glen Grant Distilled in 1965 and Bottled at the start of the 1970s for the Italian market.

Glen Grant 1965 / Gordon & Macphail
70cl / 40% - Gordon & Macphail - A Bottling of 1965 vintage Glen Grant from the depths of the Gordon & Macphail warehouses. Bottled at about 40 YO and impressively well-priced for that age.

Glen Grant 1966 / Gordon & Macphail
70cl / 40% - Gordon & Macphail - Another of Gordon & Macphail's long-aged Glen Grants which, along with Glenfarclas, represent the best-value long-aged Speysides available. Thankfully, Glen Grant is one of those special Speysiders (like Glenfarclas, Mortlach and Macallan) that is capable of withstanding immense oak ageing without tasting like a pile of wet sawdust.

Glen Grant 1967 / 5 YO
75cl / 40% - Distillery Bottling - An old Bottle of 1967 Glen Grant Bottled for the Italian market in the early 1970s.

Glen Grant 1967 / Gordon & Macphail
70cl / 40% - Gordon & Macphail - Another of Gordon & Macphail's long-aged Glen Grants which, along with Glenfarclas, represent the best-value long-aged Sherried Speysides available. This was Bottled in 2006 at 39 YO.

Glen Grant 1968 / Gordon & Macphail
70cl / 40% - Gordon & Macphail - Another of Gordon & Macphail's long-aged Glen Grants which, along with Glenfarclas, represent the best-value long-aged Speysides available. Thankfully, Glen Grant is one of those special Speysiders (like Glenfarclas, Mortlach and Macallan) that is capable of withstanding immense oak ageing without tasting like a pile of wet sawdust.

Glen Grant 1969 / Sherry Cask / James MacArthur
70cl / 57.1% - James MacArthur - A 1969 vintage Glen Grant Bottled by respected independent James McArthur. This was Bottled in the year 2000 making it about 31 YO and it looks to have picked up quite a bit of colour in that time.

Glen Grant 1970 / Sherry / Bot.1985 / Moon Import
75cl / 57% - Moon Import - A lightly coloured Sherry matured Glen Grant, Distilled in 1970 and Bottled in 1985 by famed Italian importer Moon.

Glen Grant 1974 / Bot.2012 / Cask #7646 / Berry Brothers
70cl / 49.3% - Berry Bros & Rudd - An excellent Sherried Glen Grant from the 1974 vintage Bottled at full strength by posh booze merchants Berry Bros.

Glen Grant 1975 / 36 YO / Brandy Finish
70cl / 54% - Douglas Laing - A Bottling of 1975 vintage Glen Grant for Douglas Laing as part of their premium Old & Rare Platinum Selection. Matured for 36 years and finished in a brandy Cask, this is an interesting edition to the range.

Glen Grant 1975 / 5 YO
75cl / 40% - Distillery Bottling

Glen Grant 1992 / Cellar Reserve
70cl / 46% - Formerly only available at the Distillery, this Glen Grant Cellar Reserve 1992 has been introduced by new owners Campari and is being acclaimed as a major step forward.

Glen Grant 20 YO / Director's Reserve
75cl / 43% - Distillery Bottling - One of Glen Grant's famous Director's Reserve Bottlings - a Whisky selected from the Distillery director's own special stock. This one is a 20 YO and comes with an elegant glass decanter.

Glen Grant 21 YO / Director's Reserve / Bot.1980s
75cl / 43% - Distillery Bottling.

Glen Grant 25 YO / Bot.1970s / George Strachan
75cl / 40% - George Strachan Ltd - A rare 25 YO Glen Grant Bottled in the 1970s by indie Bottler George Strachan Ltd.

Glen Grant 25 YO / Directors' Reserve / Bot.1980s
75cl / 43%

Glen Grant 25 YO / Royal Marriage
75cl / 40% - Distillery Bottling - A very special Bottling of 25 YO Glen Grant Bottled for the wedding of Charles & Di in 1981. A quality aged Speyside from one of the classic Distilleries.

Glen Grant 30 YO / 150th Anniversary
75cl / 45% - Distillery Bottling - A Bottling of 30 YO Glen Grant released in 1990 to celebrate the 150th anniversary of the Distillery's 1840 opening.

Glen Grant 30 YO / Brandy Butt / Sherry Finish
70cl / 52.5% - Douglas Laing - A 30 YO Glen Grant Bottled for Douglas Laing's 60th anniversary. Rare to see a Brandy butt used to mature Whisky - let alone for it then to be Sherry-finished as well.

Glen Grant 35 YO / Bot.1970s / Gordon & Macphail
75cl / 40% - Gordon & Macphail - A lovely old 1970s Bottle of 35 YO Glen Grant Bottled by Gordon & Macphail.

Glen Grant 38 YO / Bot.1970s / Gordon & Macphail
75cl / 40% - Gordon & Macphail - A 38 YO Glen Grant Bottled by Gordon & Macphail in the 1970s.

Glen Grant 38 YO / Bot.1980s / Gordon & Macphail
75cl / 40% - Gordon & Macphail - A lovely old Bottle of Gordon & Macphail Glen Grant, released in the 1980s (unusually in a green glass Bottle) at the grand old age of 38 YO.

Glen Grant 42 YO / Bot.1970s
75.7cl / 40% - Gordon & Macphail - An old 1970s Bottling of some very old Glen Grant. This should be spectacular.

Glen Grant 45 YO / Bot.1970s / Gordon & Macphail
75cl / 40%

Glen Grant 8 YO / Hall & Bramley / Bot.1970's
75cl / 40% - Independent Bottling - A 1970s Bottling of 8 YO Glen Grant, released by licensed Bottler Hall & Bramley in the Distillery's normal livery.

Glen Grant 9 YO / Robert Watson / Bot.1960s
75cl / 40% - Robert Watson - A 9 YO Glen Grant Bottled back in the 1960s by Robert Watson of Aberdeen.

Macleod's Glen Grant 1954 / 50 YO
70cl / 42.2% - Ian Macleod - An extraordinary Bottling of Glen Grant 1954 by Ian Macleod, owners of the glengoyne Distillery. Just 100 Bottles of this have been produced. A sensation at The Whisky Show 2009, where it was undoubtedly one of the finest Whiskies at the whole show.

GLEN KEITH RANGE

Glen Keith 10 YO
70cl / 43% - Distillery Bottling - The first official Bottling from Glen Keith, a 10 YO Whisky originally released in the 1990s when the

Distillery was owned by dearly departed Seagrams.

Glen Keith 1963 / 17 YO / Connoisseurs Choice
75cl / 40% - Gordon & Macphail - A 1963 vintage Whisky from Glen Keith, Distilled just 6 years after the Distillery opened in 1957. Unfortunately the Distillery is mothballed, as of 2011, but there is hope it may rise again...

Glen Keith 1968 / 31 YO / Old Malt Cask
70cl / 50% - Douglas Laing - A single Cask release of 1968 vintage Glen Keith Whisky. This Whisky has been aged for 31 years and was Bottled in 1999, just before the Distillery was mothballed. Bottled by Douglas Laing for their Old Malt Cask series, at a strength of 50%.

Glen Keith 1968 / Connoisseurs Choice
70cl / 46% - Gordon & Macphail - A 1968 vintage Glen Keith, Bottled by Gordon and Macphail for their Connoisseurs Choice collection.

Glen Keith 1968 / Old Presentation / Connoisseurs Choice
70cl / 46% - Gordon & Macphail - A 1968 vintage Glen Keith from the folks at Gordon & Macphail under their Connoisseurs Choice banner. The Distillery fell silent in 2000 after a mere 43 years of production but hopefully new owners Chivas Brothers will kick it back into life.

Glen Keith 1989 / 22 YO / Single Malts of Scotland
70cl / 50.7% - Speciality Drinks Ltd - A deliciously light and delicate 1989 vintage Glen Keith Bottled at 22 YO by SDL for The Single Malts of Scotland series. Grassy and fruity with a generous touch of oakspice.

Glen Keith 1992 / 19 YO / Bourbon Barrels #120551+2
70cl / 58.6% - Signatory - A 1992 vintage Glen Keith, Bottled on the 23rd of May 2012 by Signatory for their Cask Strength Collection. It's a single Cask Distilled on October 1st and matured in a pair of Bourbon barrels.

Glen Keith 1993 / 18 YO / Old Malt Cask #7671
70cl / 50% - Douglas Laing - A 1993 vintage Whisky from the (as of 2011) mothballed Glen Keith Distillery, Bottled by Douglas Lain in their Old Malt Cask Range at 18 YO. The Distillery closed down in 2000, but there are hopes that it will start up again soon.

Glen Keith 1996 / Connoisseurs Choice
70cl / 46% - Gordon & Macphail - A 1996 vintage Whisky from the little seen Glen Keith, Bottled by Gordon & Macphail for their Connoisseurs Choice collection.

THE GLENLIVET RANGE

Glenlivet 10 YO / Prime Minister's Reserve
75cl / 40% - A very rare special one-off Whisky from the early 1980s, Bottled for the Prime Minister of the time - Margaret Thatcher.

Glenlivet 12 YO
70cl / 40% - Distillery Bottling - One of the most famous malts in the world. Glenlivet 12 YO has a soft smooth balance of sweet summer fruits and the floral notes of spring flowers.

Glenlivet 12 YO / Bot.1930s
75cl / 45.5% - Distillery Bottling - A wonderful rare old 1930s Bottle of Glenlivet 12 year-old, Bottled at the higher-than-today strength of 45.5%.

Glenlivet 12 YO / Bot.1960s
75cl / 45.7% - Distillery Bottling

Glenlivet 12 YO / Bot.1970s
75cl / 43%

Glenlivet 12 YO / Bot.1970s
75cl / 40% - Distillery Bottling - A 1970s release of Glenlivet's best selling 12 YO Single Malt Scotch Whisky.

Glenlivet 12 YO / Bot.1980s
75cl / 43% - Distillery Bottling

Glenlivet 15 YO / 1L
100cl / 43% - Distillery Bottling - A 15 YO Distillery Bottling of The Glenlivet. A litre Bottle of their regular 15 YO expression with no fancy wood finishes or other messing around - a classic.

Glenlivet 15 YO / Bot.1960s
75cl / 45.7% - Distillery Bottling - A 1960s Distillery Bottling of Glenfiddich's 15 YO Whisky. This has a fantastic label, with a great pre-SWA regs description of 'Unblended All-Malt Scotch Whisky'.

Glenlivet 15 YO / Bot.1970s
75cl / 46% - Gordon & Macphail - An old Sherry Cask 15 YO Whisky from Glenlivet. This has been Bottled at 80 proof for Gordon & Macphail. We estimate that this item is from sometime in the 1970s.

Glenlivet 15 YO / French Oak Reserve
70cl / 40% - Distillery Bottling - A cut above the standard-issue 12 YO, Glenlivet 15 YO is finished, as the name suggests, in Limousin French Oak (the same kind that is used for many cognacs).
International Wine & Spirit Competition: Gold Medal; Best in Class

Glenlivet 15 YO / Sherry Cask / Bot.1970s
75cl / 40% Gordon & Macphail

Glenlivet 16 YO Nadurra / Batch 0512T
70cl / 54.3% - Distillery Bottling - A 2012 release of Cask strength Whisky under Glenlivet's Nadurra label. As with previous batches, this has been Bourbon Cask matured for 16 years and shows off the quality of Glenlivet's spirit.

Glenlivet 16 YO Nadurra / Batch 1210M
70cl / 54.5% - Distillery Bottling - Another batch of Glenlivet's rightfully successful Nadurra, their Cask strength, un-chillfiltered, simply matured 'natural' Single Malt. A look at the other, more raw side of Whisky by one of the biggest producers in the world.

Glenlivet 18 YO
70cl / 43% - Distillery Bottling - A malt Whisky of unmistakable honey-rich maturity and depth. Glenlivet 18 YO is the winner of 2 gold medals in the International Wine and Spirit Competition (I.W.S.C.) and remains one of the best-value expressions of Sherried Speyside.

Glenlivet 18 YO / Guardians
70cl / 55.7% - A very special Bottling of Glenlivet, a single Cask chosen by five of members of The Glenlivet Guardians and then Bottled exclusively for The Guardians. It's an 18 YO Whisky matured in a second fill Sherry Cask and Bottled on November 14th 2011.

Glenlivet 18 YO / Minmore / Single Cask #22378
70cl / 57.9% - Distillery Bottling - A TWE exclusive Bottling, this very special Glenlivet was released in late 2012 as part of the Distillery's Single Cask Editions, which are named alphabetically. Minmore is the name of the site of the Glenlivet Distillery and is manifested here by an 18 YO Bourbon Cask, Bottled at its impressive strength of 57.9%.

Glenlivet 18 YO / Old Presentation
70cl / 43% - Distillery Bottling - A malt Whisky of unmistakable honey-rich maturity and depth. Glenlivet 18 YO is the winner of 2 gold medals in the International Wine and Spirit Competition (I.W.S.C.) and remains one of the best-value expressions of Sherried Speyside.

Glenlivet 1938 / Bot.1970s
75cl / 40% - Gordon & Macphail have been storing Casks of Whisky for years which has given them access to gems such as this Glenlivet over the years - Distilled in 1938 and Bottled in the 1980s after over 40 years of maturation.

Glenlivet 1938 / Bot.1980s / Gordon & Macphail
75cl / 40% - Gordon & Macphail

Glenlivet 1940 / 70 YO / Crystal Decanter / G&M
20cl / 45.9% - Gordon & Macphail - The second in Gordon &

Macphail's Generations series, following up the earlier 70 YO Mortlach with an equally impressive 70 YO Glenlivet. Equal as they are in age they are jointly the oldest Whiskies ever commercially Bottled. This Bottling is the smaller 20cl decanter, although still made in the same elegant design as the larger versions.

Glenlivet 1940 / 70 YO / Tear Decanter / 2nd Edition
70cl / 45.9% - Gordon & Macphail - The second release of Gordon & Macphail's incredible 70 YO Glenlivet. This is the remaining Whisky drawn from Cask 339, filled in 1940, and Bottled in a teardrop shaped crystal decanter at full Cask strength of 45.95%. A slice of liquid history.

Glenlivet 1943 / 55 YO / Private Collection / G&M
70cl / 40% - Gordon & Macphail - Along aged Glenlivet from the special bit of Gordon & Macphail's extensive warehouses that they draw the Casks for the Private Collection from. Distilled in 1943 and then matured for a rather long 55 years.

Glenlivet 1943 / Gordon & Macphail
75cl / 40% - Gordon & Macphail - Wartime Distillation

Glenlivet 1946 / Gordon & Macphail
70cl / 40% - Gordon & Macphail - Gordon & Macphail's warehouses are a treasure trove for those looking for old Whisky, and this is a prime example - a Glenlivet Distilled in 1946. Luckily they make spirit that happily ages for many decades.

Glenlivet 1948 / 21 YO
75cl / 45.7% - Distillery Bottling - Bottled nearly 40 years ago around the time of the moon landings - this is a piece of liquid history.

Glenlivet 1948 / Gordon & Macphail
70cl / 43% - Gordon & Macphail - A 1948 vintage Whisky Distilled at Glenlivet before many years of maturation, selection from Gordon & Macphail's incredible warehouses and Bottling.

Glenlivet 1949 / Bot.1980s / Gordon & Macphail
75cl / 40% - Gordon & Macphail - A very rare old 1980s edition of 1949 vintage Glenlivet Bottled at osme point in the 1980s by Gordon & Macphail.

Glenlivet 1951 / 18 YO / Baretto Import
75cl / 45.7% - Distillery Bottling - A marvellous old Bottle of Glenlivet 18 YO Bottled for Italian importers Baretto at the old 80 proof (45.7%). The rear label is numbered saying '1951 Bottle No: ', but it's not clear whether this Whisky was Distilled or Bottled in that year. We reckon Distilled is more likely.

Glenlivet 1954 Private Collection/ 55 YO / Sherry Hogshead

70cl / 50.6% - Gordon & Macphail - Distilled in November 1954, this is a hugely old Glenlivet Bottled from a first fill Sherry hogshead for G&M's Private Collection.

Glenlivet 1955 / Gordon & Macphail
70cl / 40% - Gordon & Macphail - A 1955 vintage Glenlivet, Bottled by Gordon & Macphail.

Glenlivet 1959 / Bot.1980s
70cl / 43% - Distillery Bottling - A very old and rare 1980s Bottling of Glenlivet 1959. Not to be confused with the Cellar Collection edition of which this vintage Bottling was a forerunner.

Glenlivet 1959 / Sherry Cask / Private Collection
70cl / 47.5% - Gordon & Macphail - a very old Glenlivet 1959 Bottled by Gordon & Macphail for their Private Collection series.

Glenlivet 1963 Private Collection / 47 YO / G&M
70cl / 40.6% - Gordon & Macphail - A vintage Glenlivet from two first fill American hogsheads Distilled in March 1963 and Bottled in November 2010 by Gordon & Macphail for their Private Collection series.

Glenlivet 1964 / 40 YO / 2nd Release
70cl / 45.1% - Distillery Bottling - A recent release of the now-legendary Glenlivet 1964 Cellar Collection Bottled in 2004 (one of Sukhinder's all-time favourite Glenlivets). This is now in Glenlivet's smart new packaging with the clear glass and the sliding wooden box.

Glenlivet 1964 / 40 YO / Cellar Collection
70cl / 45.1% - Distillery Bottling - One of Sukhinder's all-time favourite Glenlivets, this is a phenomenal nutty, fruity Bottling - another hit for the 'Cellar Collection', and highly sought-after by Glenlivet enthusiasts.

Glenlivet 1965 / G&M / Smith's Label
70cl / 40% - Gordon & Macphail - A 1965 vintage Glenlivet Bottled by Gordon & Macphail under the famed Smith's label.

Glenlivet 1965 / Gordon & Macphail
70cl / 43% - Gordon & Macphail - A 1965 vintage Glenlivet at a remarkably reasonable price thanks to the folks at Gordon & Macphail and their unfeasibly big collection of old Casks.

Glenlivet 1966 / Bot.2012 / Gordon & Macphail
70cl / 43% - Gordon & Macphail - A 1966 Glenlivet Bottled by Gordon & Macphail with the now traditional retro "Smith's" label.

Glenlivet 1968 / 28 YO / First Cask #1577
70cl / 46% - First Cask - A 1968 vintage Whisky, Distilled on the 23rd

of February of that year at the Glenlivet Distillery. Matured for 28 years and then Bottled in the mid-1990s for the First Cask range.

Glenlivet 1968 Reserve Vintage / 39 YO / Cask #7629
70cl / 50.9% - Distillery Bottling - A very rare Cask strength Glenlivet 1968, this Reserve Vintage was Bottled from Cask 7629 in 2008, just a few months shy of its 40th birthday

Glenlivet 1969 / Sherry / Bot.1985 / Moon Import
75cl / 57% - Distillery Bottling - A 1969 vintage Glenlivet Bottled in 1985, the early days of legendary Italian importer Moon, and matured in a Sherry Cask.

Glenlivet 1973 / Whisky Show 2012 / Berry Bros for TWE
70cl / 48.6% - Berry Bros & Rudd - A very venerable 1973 vintage Glenlivet, Bottled just a year before its 40th birthday by our chums at Berry Bros. & Rudd, especially for TWE to launch at our 2012 Whisky Show. Delicious woodglue and cake spice notes, this is stonking stuff.

Glenlivet 1974 / 24 YO / First Cask #5131
70cl / 46% - First Cask - A 1974 vintage Whisky from Glenlivet, as of writing the second biggest selling Single Malt in the world. This was Distilled on the 27th of March and Bottled 24 years later by First Cask.

Glenlivet 1974 / 24 YO / First Cask #5134
70cl / 46% - First Cask - A rare single Cask Bottling of Glenlivet by Direct Wines for their First Cask series. This was Distilled in 1974 and matured for 24 years before Bottling in the late 1990s.

Glenlivet 1974 / 37 YO / Cask #5247 / Berry Brothers
70cl / 46% - Berry Bros & Rudd - A well-aged 37 YO Whisky from Glenlivet, Distilled in 1974 and released by veteran wine and spirits trader Berry Brothers and Rudd in early 2012.

Glenlivet 1974 / Gordon & Macphail
70cl / 43% - Gordon & Macphail - A 1974 Glenlivet Bottled under the George G Smith label by Gordon & Macphail.

Glenlivet 1974 Private Collection / Sherry Hogshead / G&M
70cl / 50.1% - Gordon & Macphail - A Sherry hogshead of Glenlivet 1974, Bottled at full strength in 2010 for Gordon & Macphail's Private Collection.

Glenlivet 1979 / 32 YO / Cask #6094
70cl / 46.8% - Mackillop's - A Mackillop's Choice Bottling of 32 YO Cask strength Glenlivet, Distilled in 1979 and Bottled in March 2012.

Glenlivet 1980 / 24 YO / First Cask #13737
70cl / 46% - First Cask - A 1980 Glenlivet Bottled by Direct Wines as part of their First Caks series. This single Cask Whisky has been aged

for 24 years prior to Bottling.

Glenlivet 1980 / Gordon & Macphail's Private Collection
70cl / 48.5% - Gordon & Macphail - A single Cask Bottling of 1980 vintage Glenlivet as part of Gordon & Macphail's rather special Private Collection. Matured for 30 years in an American hoghsead and Bottled in late 2011.

Glenlivet 1983 / French Oak Finish / Cellar Collection
70cl / 46% - Distillery Bottling - A frequently-overlooked Bottle in Glenlivet's Cellar Collection, perhaps as it remains one of the youngest of the series (even at 20 YO). This is sterling stuff, nonetheless, described by Jim Murray as 'sophistication and attitude rolled into one'. With the finish adding nuance rather than dominating the palate, this is a minor classic of the genre.

Glenlivet 1991 Nadurra Triumph
70cl / 48% - Distillery Bottling - A vintage edition of the hugely popular Glenlivet Nadurra. This special version has been made with a single barley variety, Triumph (hence the name), and has been composed exclusively using malt from the 1991 vintage, Bottled at 48%. As with other Nadurras, this Glenlivet has been neither coloured nor chill-filtered.

Glenlivet 1991 Private Collection / Gordon & Macphail
70cl / 54.4% - Gordon & Macphail - A refill Sherry hogshead of Glenlivet Bottled in late 2010 as part of the Private Collection from Gordon & Macphail.

Glenlivet 1992 / 17 YO / Cask Strength
50cl / 59.3% - Distillery Bottling - A tasty-looking natural colour on this impressively high-strength 17 YO Glenlivet from the 1992 vintage. Bottled in 2010 for the Distillery gift shop, and it's batch GL 17 011 for all the nerds out there.

Glenlivet 1996 / 14 YO / Cask #163409 / Signatory
70cl / 57.1% - Signatory - A Signatory Bottling of 14 YO Glenlivet, released as part of the Cask Strength Collection. Distilled in October 1996, matured in a Sherry butt and Bottled in October 2011, 6 days shy of its 15th birthday.

Glenlivet 1996 / 16 YO / Sherry Butt #79237
70cl / 46% - Signatory - A 16 YO single first fill Sherry butt matured Whisky from Glenlivet, Bottled by Signatory for their Un-chillfiltered Collection. It was Distilled on 13th May 1996 and Bottled on 13th November 2012.

Glenlivet 1996 / 16 YO / Sherry Butt 79236 / Signatory
70cl / 46% - Signatory - A lightly coloured 16 YO Whisky from Glenlivet, Bottled from a single Cask by Signatory for their Un-Chillfiltered Collection. Distilled on May 13th 1996, matured in a first fill Sherry butt and Bottled on September 27th 2012.

Glenlivet 20 YO / Bot.1960s
75cl / 45.7% - Distillery Bottling - A Bottle of Glenlivet's 'Unblended All-Malt' 20 YO Whisky, Bottled as a limited edition of 2400 Bottles for the company's Italian importer Baretto. We believe this to have been released in the late 1960s, meaning the Whisky would have been Distilled immediately post-war in the 1940s.

Glenlivet 21 YO / 1963 / Chairmans Reserve
75cl / 43% - Distillery Bottling - A special and very rare Bottling of The Glenlivet, Bottled under the auspices of being for the company chairman. Distilled in 1963, Bottled 21 years late and presented in wooden box with a script label.

Glenlivet 21 YO / Bot.1960s
75cl / 45.7% - Distillery Bottling - This Bottle is missing the back label which shows that this Whisky was Distilled in 1948. Slightly damaged label, but good level. A very special old Whisky Bottled in 1969.

Glenlivet 21 YO / Bot.1980s
75cl / 43% - Distillery Bottling - Beautiful old '80s Bottling of this classic Whisky.

Glenlivet 21 YO / Bot.1980s
75cl / 43% - Distillery Bottling - A rare 1980s release from The Glenlivet - their much lauded 21 YO Whisky presented in a heavy crystal decanter and velveteen red box.

Glenlivet 21 YO / Founder's Reserve
70cl / 55.6% - A Distillery Bottling of Glenlivet released to commemorate the 2010 Distillery expansion and honouring the Distillery's founding in 1824. It's a limited edition of 1824 Bottles (see what they did there), Bottled at Cask strength and comes in an impressive box, sealed with magnetic straps.

Glenlivet 21 YO Archive
70cl / 43% - Distillery Bottling - Glenlivet is one of those Distilleries whose malts just keep improving with age. This fantastic 21 YO is an elegant, intricate, sophisticated malt, presented in a very smart wooden box - just don't drop it on your foot.
IWSC 2012 - Gold Outstanding Medal - Whisky - Scotch

Glenlivet 25 YO / Royal Wedding Reserve
75cl / 43% - Distillery Bottling - A very special 25 YO Glenlivet Bottled for the Royal Wedding in 1981 (Charles & Di in case you missed it). They pulled out all the stops for this one - a tremendous Bottling with a generous dollop of Sherry in the mix.

Glenlivet 25 YO / Silver Jubilee
75cl / 43% - Distillery Bottling - A special limited edition 25 YO Glenlivet released in 1977 to celebrate the Silver Jubilee of Queen Elizabeth II. Packaged with a sturdy dark stained wooden box.

Glenlivet 1974 Private Collection / Sherry Hogshead / G&M
70cl / 50.1% - Gordon & Macphail - A Sherry hogshead of Glenlivet 1974, Bottled at full strength in 2010 for Gordon & Macphail's Private Collection.

Glenlivet 1979 / 32 YO / Cask #6094
70cl / 46.8% - Mackillop's - A Mackillop's Choice Bottling of 32 YO Cask strength Glenlivet, Distilled in 1979 and Bottled in March 2012.

Glenlivet 1980 / 24 YO / First Cask #13737
70cl / 46% - First Cask - A 1980 Glenlivet Bottled by Direct Wines as part of their First Caks series. This single Cask Whisky has been aged for 24 years prior to Bottling.

Glenlivet 1980 / Gordon & Macphail's Private Collection
70cl / 48.5% - Gordon & Macphail - A single Cask Bottling of 1980 vintage Glenlivet as part of Gordon & Macphail's rather special Private Collection. Matured for 30 years in an American hoghsead and Bottled in late 2011.

Glenlivet 1983 / French Oak Finish / Cellar Collection
70cl / 46% - Distillery Bottling - A frequently-overlooked Bottle in Glenlivet's Cellar Collection, perhaps as it remains one of the youngest of the series (even at 20 YO). This is sterling stuff. With the finish adding nuance rather than dominating the palate, this is a minor classic of the genre.

Glenlivet 1991 Nadurra Triumph
70cl / 48% - Distillery Bottling - A vintage edition of the hugely popular Glenlivet Nadurra. This special version has been made with a single barley variety, Triumph (hence the name), and has been composed exclusively using malt from the 1991 vintage, Bottled at 48%. As with other Nadurras, this Glenlivet has been neither coloured nor chill-filtered.

Glenlivet 1991 Private Collection / Gordon & Macphail
70cl / 54.4% - Gordon & Macphail - A refill Sherry hogshead of Glenlivet Bottled in late 2010 as part of the Private Collection from Gordon & Macphail.

Glenlivet 1992 / 17 YO / Cask Strength
50cl / 59.3% - Distillery Bottling - A tasty-looking natural colour on this impressively high-strength 17 YO Glenlivet from the 1992 vintage. Bottled in 2010 for the Distillery gift shop, and it's batch GL 17 011 for all the nerds out there.

Glenlivet 1996 / 14 YO / Cask #163409 / Signatory
70cl / 57.1% - Signatory - A Signatory Bottling of 14 YO Glenlivet, released as part of the Cask Strength Collection. Distilled in October 1996, matured in a Sherry butt and Bottled in October 2011, 6 days shy of its 15th birthday.

Glenlivet 1996 / 16 YO / Sherry Butt #79237
70cl / 46% - Signatory - A 16 YO single first fill Sherry butt matured Whisky from Glenlivet, Bottled by Signatory for their Un-chillfiltered Collection. It was Distilled on 13th May 1996 and Bottled on 13th November 2012.

Glenlivet 1996 / 16 YO / Sherry Butt 79236 / Signatory
70cl / 46% - Signatory - A lightly coloured 16 YO Whisky from Glenlivet, Bottled from a single Cask by Signatory for their Un-Chillfiltered Collection. Distilled on May 13th 1996, matured in a first fill Sherry butt and Bottled on September 27th 2012.

Glenlivet 20 YO / Bot.1960s
75cl / 45.7% - Distillery Bottling - A Bottle of Glenlivet's 'Unblended All-Malt' 20 YO Whisky, Bottled as a limited edition of 2400 Bottles for the company's Italian importer Baretto. We believe this to have been released in the late 1960s, meaning the Whisky would have been Distilled immediately post-war in the 1940s.

Glenlivet 21 YO / 1963 / Chairmans Reserve
75cl / 43% - Distillery Bottling - A special and very rare Bottling of The Glenlivet, Bottled under the auspices of being for the company chairman. Distilled in 1963, Bottled 21 years late and presented in wooden box with a script label.

Glenlivet 21 YO / Bot.1960s
75cl / 45.7% - Distillery Bottling - This Bottle is missing the back label which shows that this Whisky was Distilled in 1948. Slightly damaged label, but good level. A very special old Whisky Bottled in 1969.

Glenlivet 21 YO / Bot.1980s
75cl / 43% - Distillery Bottling - Beautiful old '80s Bottling of this classic Whisky.

Glenlivet 21 YO / Bot.1980s
75cl / 43% - Distillery Bottling - A rare 1980s release from The Glenlivet - their much lauded 21 YO Whisky presented in a heavy crystal decanter and velveteen red box.

Glenlivet 21 YO / Founder's Reserve
70cl / 55.6% - A Distillery Bottling of Glenlivet released to commemorate the 2010 Distillery expansion and honouring the Distillery's founding in 1824. It's a limited edition of 1824 Bottles (see what they did there), Bottled at Cask strength and comes in an impressive box, sealed with magnetic straps.

Glenlivet 25 YO / XXV
70cl / 43% - Distillery Bottling

A super-premium entry in Glenlivet's range, this has been finished for a couple of years in Oloroso Casks - so an extra depth of flavour and silky sweetness is the order of the day. IWSC 2012 - Gold Medal - Whisky - Scotch

Glenlivet 34 YO / 150th Anniversary
75cl / 40% - Distillery Bottling - A special 34 YO Whisky from The Glenlivet, released in honour of their 1974 150th anniversary.

Glenlivet 40 YO / Atlantic / Sherry Cask
70cl / 41.6% - Distillery Bottling - Originally a Distillery only Bottling, this is well aged 40 YO Glenlivet Bottled from a single Sherry Cask in late 2005. A rare and hard to find Whisky.

Glenlivet Archive 15 YO
100cl / 43% - Distillery Bottling - A rare Bottling of Glenlivet Archive from when it was a fifteen year-old. We reckon this was probably Bottled around the early 1990s.

Glenlivet Archive 21 YO
70cl / 43% - Distillery Bottling - Awash with the hallmarks of the Glenlivet and offering the depth, multiple layers of flavour and creamy texture that can only be attained over years of patient ageing.

Glenlivet K Pure Malt / 8 YO / Hatch Mansfield
75cl / 43% - Independent Bottler - An interesting Bottling of 8 YO Whisky from Glenlivet. Named 'Glenlivet K' this was Bottled by Hatch Mansfield and imported into Italy by Orlandi.

Glenlivet Special Export Reserve / Bot.1970s
75cl / 43% - Distillery Bottling - A special reserve Glenlivet Bottled at 43% in the 1970s for the Italian market.

GLENLOSSIE RANGE

Glenlossie 10 YO
70cl / 43% - Flora & Fauna - The only Distillery Bottling of Glenlossie, other than a Manager's Dram. Almost all of their Whisky goes into Diageo's blends, which is a shame as this is a classic spicy speysider.

Glenlossie 12 YO / Manager's Dram
70cl / 55.5% - Distillery Bottling - A rare Glenlossie 12 YO selected by the Diageo Distillery managers for staff only. Please note that the Bottle numbers have been removed from the labels on some of these Bottles.

Glenlossie 1968 / 14 YO / Connoisseurs Choice
75cl / 40% - Gordon & Macphail - A 1968 vintage Glenlossie from Gordon & Macphail. Aged for 14 years and Bottled under their Connoisseurs Choice label, in its 1980s brown label incarnation.

Glenlossie 1975 / 36 YO / Liquid Sun
70cl / 48.3% - Liquid Sun - A Liquid Sun Bottling of 36 YO Sherry matured Whisky from Glenlossie. This was Distilled in 1975, a couple of years after sister Distillery Mannochmore was built next door.

Glenlossie 1975 / Bot.2010 / Cask #5951
70cl / 49.7% - Berry Bros & Rudd - A single Cask Glenlossie from Berry Bros, Bottled in 2010 at its natural strength, just shy of 50%.

Glenlossie 1982 / Connoisseurs Choice
70cl / 46% - Gordon & Macphail - A 1982 Glenlossie Bottled by Gordon and Macphail as part of their Connoisseurs Choice range.

Glenlossie 1984 / 24 YO / Sherry Butt
70cl / 59.1% - Signatory - Another gem from Signatory - a single Sherry Cask of the little-seen Glenlossie 1984 Bottled at the impressive full strength of 59.1%.

Glenlossie 1984 / 25 YO / Sherry Butt #2535
70cl / 59% - Signatory - A single Cask 1984 vintage Whisky from Glenlossie. Aged for 25 years and matured in a Sherry Butt. Bottled by Signatory for their Cask Strength Collection.

Glenlossie 1999 / 9 YO / Managers Choice
70cl / 59.1% - Distillery Bottling - In 1974 Glenlossie was one of only 12 Distilleries rated in the highest category by Whisky blenders, and their enthusiasm for the malt has meant that only around 1% of the Distillery's output is kept for Single Malt, so this 9 YO full-strength 1999 Bottled for Diageo's Managers' Choice will likely be highly sought-after, particularly as only 204 Bottles were yielded from the Cask.

Glenlossie-Glenlivet 1957 / 21 YO
75cl / 45.7% - Cadenhead's

Glenlossie-Glenlivet 1966 / 18 YO / Cadenhead's
75cl / 46% - Cadenhead's - An excellent 1966 vintage Whisky from Glenlossie, Bottled at 18 YO by Cadenhead's.

GLEN MHOR RANGE

Glen Mhor 10 YO
75cl / 43% - Distillery Bottling - An interesting Distillery Bottling from Glen Mhor, formerly of Inverness and now closed and demolished. It's a 10 YO Whisky presented in a Bottle that looks alarmingly close to a modern Isle of Jura Bottle...

Glen Mhor 10 YO / Bot.1960s
75cl / 43% - Distillery Bottling - A rare Distillery Bottling of Glen Mhor, who closed down in 1983 and have since disappeared due to the demolishing of the buildings. This was a standard 10 YO Bottling released in the 1950s, when the Distillery was at its height.

Glen Mhor 1965 / 35 YO
70cl / 49.2% - Signatory - An old 1965 vintage Whisky from Glen Mhor Distillery. The Glen Mhor Distillery was closed in 1983, approximately half way through this Whisky's maturation. Bottled in 2001 at a grand 35 YO, this Whisky has been released as one of Signatory's Silent Stills Bottlings.

Glen Mhor 1965 / Gordon & Macphail
70cl / 43% - Gordon & Macphail - A 1965 vintage Whisky from now closed Glen Mhor, a victim of the 1983 spate of Distillery closures and now demolished. Bottled by Gordon & Macphail in 2005, this is about 40 YO.

Glen Mhor 1969 / Cask #1407/1409
70cl / 45% - Independent Bottler - A rare Bottling of Glen Mhor Whisky from 1969. The Distillery closed down in 1983. This Bottling was limited to just 2265 Bottles at the time of release, who knows how many of these are still around today.

Glen Mhor 1974 / 13 YO
75cl / 58.4% - Sestante - A very rare early-teenage Bottling by Sestante of the 1974 vintage from Glen Mhor, the now sadly defunct Speysider which may have contributed to its own downfall by having a name no-one knows how to pronounce (it's 'Glen Vorr', btw).

Glen Mhor 1974 / Gordon & Macphail
75cl / 58.4% - Gordon & Macphail - Rare old Bottling of the little-seen Glen Mhor for Gordon & Macphail's original 'Cask' series. The Distillery closed in 1983.

Glen Mhor 1976 / 28 YO
70cl / 51.9% - Distillery Bottling - The Rare Malts are a now-discontinued series of Cask-strength releases designed by Diageo to showcase some of the hidden treasures in their portfolio. This particular dram is all the more precious for having come from a Distillery dismantled in 1986.

Glen Mhor 1978 / 10 YO
75cl / 65.3% - Gordon & Macphail - A 10 YO Single Malt from the rarely-seen Glen Mhor Distillery, Bottled for Italian Bottlers Intertrade in the late 1980s by Gordon & Macphail at its full Cask strength of 65.3%.

Glen Mhor 1978 / 10 YO
75cl / 65.3% - Intertrade - A 10 YO Whisky from Glen Mhor Bottled by Intertrade a few years after the Distillery closed. This has a hefty ABV of 65.3%, making us wonder what strength it went into the Cask...

Glen Mhor 1979 / 22 YO / Rare Malts
70cl / 61% - Distillery Bottling - A full strength Bottling of the rarely-seen Glen Mhor, this 1979 vintage was released by Diageo in 2001 as

part of the highly sought-after Rare Malts series.

Glen Mhor 1980 / Gordon & Macphail
70cl / 43% - Gordon & Macphail - A welcome Gordon & Macphail Bottling of the little-seen Glen Mhor from the 1980 vintage. The Distillery was demolished over twenty years ago, and the site is now home to a supermarket.

Glen Mhor 1982 / 28 YO / Cask# 1328
70cl / 56.8% - Signatory - A single Cask Bottling of the obscure (and long-defunct) Glen Mhor, whose original site is now famously occupied by a supermarket after the Distillery was demolished in the mid-1980s. Another of Signatory's enigmatic 'Wine Treated' barrels.

Glen Mhor 25 YO
70cl / 45% - Independent Bottling - A rare 25 YO Whisky from Glen Mhor by independent Bottler Campbell & Clark. The Distillery closed down in 1983 and has since been demolished, and there aren't all that many Casks remaining.

Glen Mhor 6 YO / Bot.1960s
75cl / 43% - Distillery Bottling - A young Bottling of Glen Mhor that we believe was Bottled in the 1960s. A rare official release from the Distillery, closed since 1983 and now demolished, and aged for just 6 years.

GLEN MORAY RANGE

Glen Moray 10 YO / Bot.1970s
75cl / 40% - Distillery Bottling - A lovely old 1970s Bottle of Glen Moray 10 YO.

Glen Moray 10 YO / Bot.1970s / Black Label
75.7cl / 40% - Distillery Bottling - A 1970s Bottling of Glen Moray 10 YO.

Glen Moray 10 YO / Chardonnay Cask
70cl / 40% - Distillery Bottling - An interesting spicy dram from Glen Moray - a 10 YO Whisky entirely matured in Chardonnay Casks. The start of what we hope is a continuing line of new Whiskies from this often overlooked Distillery.

Glen Moray 12 YO
70cl / 40% - Distillery Bottling - Glen Moray's 12 YO Single Malt Whisky. A classic Speysider with honey and spice.

Glen Moray 12 YO / Bot.1980s
75cl / 40% - Distillery Bottling - A 12 YO Whisky from Speyside's Glen Moray, Bottled sometime in the 1980s.

Glen Moray 12 YO / Wine Cask Mellowed
70cl / 40% - Distillery Bottling

Glen Moray 1959 / 25 YO / Sherry Butt Cask / Samaroli
75cl / 46% - Samaroli - One of a pair of 25 YO Sherry Casks of Glen Moray 1959 released by Italian maestros Samaroli in 1984. This is from a single Sherry butt that yielded just 240 Bottles. Extraordinary colour for a 46% Whisky.

Glen Moray 1959 / Sherry Hogshead / Bot.1984
75cl / 46% - Samaroli - A very deeply coloured 1959 vintage Glen Moray, matured in a Sherry hogshead and Bottle in 1984 by Italian independent Samaroli.

Glen Moray 1960 / 26 YO
75cl / 43% - Distillery Bottling - A specially selected long-aged Glen Moray from the 1960 vintage, Bottled in the late 1980s at 26 YO.

Glen Moray 1962 / 27 YO
75cl / 43% - Distillery Bottling - A specially selected long-aged single Cask of Glen Moray from the 1962 vintage, Bottled around the turn of the 1990s.

Glen Moray 1966 / 26 YO
70cl / 43% - Distillery Bottling - A very rare officially-Bottled single Cask of Glen Moray 1966 Bottled in the early 1990s. Lovely colour on this.

Glen Moray 1974 / 28 YO / Distillery Manager's Choice
70cl / 53.4% - Distillery Bottling - An old Bottling of Glen Moray 1974, Bottled in 2002. This was from an Oloroso sherry butt selected by Distillery manager Ed Dodson and is a really fantastic expression of this unloved Distillery.

Glen Moray 1981 / 19 YO/ Manager's Choice/ Sherry Cask
70cl / 57.7% - Distillery Bottling - Amazing colour on this 19 YO Glen Moray 1981, Bottled in 2001 at full strength from a single Sherry butt selected by Distillery manager Edwin Dodson.

Glen Moray 1989 Distillery Manager's Choice
70cl / 57.6% - Distillery Bottling

Glen Moray 1991 / 19 YO / Old Malt Cask #6637
70cl / 50% - Douglas Laing - A refill hoggie of Glen Moray, formerly owned by Glenmorangie, of course, and now missing in action after being snapped up by La Martiniquaise, owners of the up-and-coming Label 5 blend.

Glen Moray 30 YO
70cl / 43% - Distillery Bottling

Glen Moray 5 YO / Bot.1980s
75cl / 40% - Distillery Bottling - A 1980s Distillery Bottling of Glen Moray's young-for-modern-Whisky-but-common-for-the-time five

YO Whisky.

Glen Moray 8 YO / Bot.1990s
75cl / 43% - Distillery Bottling - A Distillery Bottling of 8 YO Whisky from Glen Moray, Bottled in the 1990s.

Glen Moray Centenary / Bot.1997 / Port Wood Finish
70cl / 40% - Distillery Bottling - A special Bottle of Glen Moray, released in 1997 to celebrate the Distillery's centenary. The Casks used were from the 1976-1979 vintages and spent the last ten years of their maturation in port pipes after initial maturation in ex-Bourbon hogsheads.

Glen Moray Classic
70cl / 40% - Distillery Bottling - Glen Moray's no age statement entry level Single Malt - easy drinking and honeyed.

Glen Moray-Glenlivet 1964 / 27 YO
70cl / 43% - Distillery Bottling - A rather smart, but simply-presented 1964 vintage Glen Moray Bottled at 27 years of age in the early 1990s when the Distillery was still using the Glenlivet suffix.

Glenrothes 1961 / Bot.1996 / Gordon & Macphail
70cl / 40% - Gordon & Macphail - A very old Bottling of 1961 vintage Whisky from Glenrothes Distillery. This was Bottled in 1996 by Gordon & Macphail, making it around 35 YO.

Glenrothes 1969 / Macphail's Collection
70cl / 43% - Gordon & Macphail - A new Bottling of some pretty old Glenrothes by Gordon & Macphail. This 1969 vintage is pretty dark even at 43% so it's safe to say that this has been pretty well-Sherried. Bottled in 2008, just shy of four full decades in the wood.

Glenrothes 1970 / 41 YO / The Whisky Agency
70cl / 47.7% - The Whisky Agency - A Whisky Agency Bottling of 41 YO Whisky from Glenrothes. Distilled in 1970 and matured in a Bourbon Cask until 2011, when it was Bottled at a relatively mellow Cask strength of 47.7%.

Glenrothes 1972 / Bot.1996
70cl / 43% - Distillery Bottling - An old 1972 vintage Bottling of Glenrothes from the mid-1990s with the official short description 'Rich, Spicy, Fruitiness'. That'll be Sherry, then, from a period during which Glenrothes produced some of their very best Whisky. These early vintage Bottlings are getting pretty scarce these days.

Glenrothes 1975 / 21 YO / First Cask #6046
70cl / 46% - First Cask - A 21 YO release of 1975 Glenrothes by Direct Wines as part of their First Cask series.

Glenrothes 1975 / Bot.2006
70cl / 43% - Distillery Bottling - Another of Glenrothes' terrific long-aged vintage releases, this 1975 expression was Bottled in 2006.

Glenrothes 1978 / Bot.2008
75cl / 43% - Distillery Bottling - Another outstanding Sherried Glenrothes vintage Bottling, this time from 1978.

Glenrothes 1987 / Bot.2005
70cl / 43% - Distillery Bottling - This is one of a series of highly successful vintage Bottlings from Glenrothes, this time from the 1987 vintage, Bottled in 2005.

Glenrothes 1989 / 19 YO
70cl / 46% - Speciality Drinks Ltd - A single hogshead from the popular Speyside Distillery Glenrothes. This 1989 vintage release from The Single Malts of Scotland has been Bottled at 46%. Clean and fresh, with a hint of spices: much less Sherried than most Glenrothes, allowing the Distillery character to really shine.

Glenrothes 1990 / 18 YO / Sherry Cask
70cl / 46% - Speciality Drinks Ltd - Our first Glenrothes for Single Malts of Scotland is a single Cask refill Sherry Cask from the 1990 vintage, Bottled at 46%.

Glenrothes 1990 / 18 YO / Sherry Cask
70cl / 50.5% - Speciality Drinks Ltd - Bottled from a small batch of Sherry hogsheads, this Cask strength Glenrothes 1990 shows less overt Sherried influence than much of the official output, while retaining a naturally sweet, clean Distillery character.

Glenrothes 1990 / 21 YO / Sherry Cask
70cl / 56.1% - Douglas Laing - A relatively young entry in the Douglas Laing Platinum range, with only 21 years on the clock for this Whisky from Glenrothes. However, it has come from a Sherry hogshead with an outturn of only 94 Bottles - a rare dram which probably has a story behind it...

Glenrothes 1995 / 17 YO / Sherry Butt #6975
70cl / 46% - Signatory - A richly coloured 17 YO single Cask Whisky Distilled at Glenrothes on June 5th 1995 and then Bottled on November 13th 2012 by Signatory for their Un-chillfiltered Collection after maturing in a first fill Sherry Cask.

Glenrothes 1995 / Bot.2011
70cl / 43% - Distillery Bottling - Another entry in Glenrothes excellent range of vintages, Distilled in 1995 and Bottled 16 years later in 2011.

Glenrothes 25 YO
70cl / 43% - Distillery Bottling - Previously a travel retail exclusive, Glenrothes 25 is a well aged example of the Distillery's style - rich and fruity.

Glenrothes 30 YO / Bot.2004
70cl / 50.2% - Distillery Bottling - A 30 YO Glenrothes Bottled by age rather than vintage, as is their common practise. They do let us know when it was Distilled though, with August 1974 written on the label.

Glenrothes 40 YO / The Whisky Exchange
70cl / 45.1% - The Whisky Exchange - Another massive hit at 2012's TWE Whisky Show, this single Cask Glenrothes has a classic Bourbon Cask character after four decades in the wood, without ever becoming over-oaked. Delicious vanilla and honey sweetness, with sweet cinnamon & clove on the finish.

Glenrothes 8 YO / Macphail's Collection
70cl / 40% - Gordon & Macphail - A very approachable Glenrothes Bottled at 8 YO by Gordon & Macphail for their Macphail's Collection. Not the most complex Speyside you'll ever encounter, but it's fantastically easy to drink.

Glenrothes John Ramsay Legacy
75cl / 46.7% - Distillery Bottling - Specially selected by retiring Glenrothes malt master John Ramsay after 43 years service, this Bottling came from a vatting of twenty second fill American oak Sherry Casks racked into Sherry butts. The two Casks showing most development were vatted togather and slowly reduced to 46.7%. A fitting tribute to a giant of the Whisky world.

Glenrothes Robur Reserve
100cl / 40% - Distillery Bottling - A travel retail exclusive, Glenrothes Robur Reserve is named for Quercus Robur, the official name for European or Spanish oak, and contains a greater proportion of first-fill Oloroso Sherry Casks.

Glenrothes Select Reserve
70cl / 43% - Distillery Bottling - Glenrothes traditionally Bottle Single Malts from specific vintages, so this no-age-statement example raised a few eyebrows when it first appeared. However, the only thing recent batches have raised is the bar - this is tremendous easy-drinking Speyside.

Glenrothes Three Decades
70cl / 43% - Distillery Bottling - Glenrothes have been releasing vintage Whisky for some time now. Over the past 17 years or so, they have released Whisky from the 1970s, 1980s and 1990s. The earliest of which was 1971 and the most recent being 1998. The Glenrothes Three decades celebrates these releases by combining Whisky from all three decades into one Bottle. Previously exclusive to Travel Retail, we've finally managed to get our hands on some Bottles of this fantastic Whisky.

Glenrothes 1961 / Bot.1996 / Gordon & Macphail
70cl / 40% - Gordon & Macphail - A very old Bottling of 1961 vintage

Whisky from Glenrothes Distillery. This was Bottled in 1996 by Gordon & Macphail, making it around 35 YO.

Glenrothes 1969 / Macphail's Collection
70cl / 43% - Gordon & Macphail - A new Bottling of some pretty old Glenrothes by Gordon & Macphail. This 1969 vintage is pretty dark even at 43% so it's safe to say that this has been pretty well-Sherried. Bottled in 2008, just shy of four full decades in the wood.

Glenrothes 1970 / 41 YO / The Whisky Agency
70cl / 47.7% - The Whisky Agency - A Whisky Agency Bottling of 41 YO Whisky from Glenrothes. Distilled in 1970 and matured in a Bourbon Cask until 2011, when it was Bottled at a relatively mellow Cask strength of 47.7%.

Glenrothes 1972 / Bot.1996
70cl / 43% - Distillery Bottling - An old 1972 vintage Bottling of Glenrothes from the mid-1990s with the official short description 'Rich, Spicy, Fruitiness'. That'll be Sherry, then, from a period during which Glenrothes produced some of their very best Whisky. These early vintage Bottlings are getting pretty scarce these days.

Glenrothes 1975 / 21 YO / First Cask #6046
70cl / 46% - First Cask - A 21 YO release of 1975 Glenrothes by Direct Wines as part of their First Cask series.

Glenrothes 1975 / Bot.2006
70cl / 43% - Distillery Bottling - Another of Glenrothes' terrific long-aged vintage releases, this 1975 expression was Bottled in 2006.

Glenrothes 1978 / Bot.2008
75cl / 43% - Distillery Bottling - Another outstanding Sherried Glenrothes vintage Bottling, this time from 1978.

Glenrothes 1987 / Bot.2005
70cl / 43% - Distillery Bottling - This is one of a series of highly successful vintage Bottlings from Glenrothes, this time from the 1987 vintage, Bottled in 2005.

Glenrothes 1989 / 19 YO
70cl / 46% - Speciality Drinks Ltd - A single hogshead from the popular Speyside Distillery Glenrothes. This 1989 vintage release from The Single Malts of Scotland has been Bottled at 46%. Clean and fresh, with a hint of spices: much less Sherried than most Glenrothes, allowing the Distillery character to really shine.

Glenrothes 1990 / 18 YO / Sherry Cask
70cl / 46% - Speciality Drinks Ltd - Our first Glenrothes for Single Malts of Scotland is a single Cask refill Sherry Cask from the 1990 vintage, Bottled at 46%.

Glenrothes 1990 / 18 YO / Sherry Cask

70cl / 50.5% - Speciality Drinks Ltd - Bottled from a small batch of Sherry hogsheads, this Cask strength Glenrothes 1990 shows less overt Sherried influence than much of the official output, while retaining a naturally sweet, clean Distillery character.

Glenrothes 1990 / 21 YO / Sherry Cask
70cl / 56.1% - Douglas Laing - A relatively young entry in the Douglas Laing Platinum range, with only 21 years on the clock for this Whisky from Glenrothes. However, it has come from a Sherry hogshead with an outturn of only 94 Bottles - a rare dram which probably has a story behind it...

Glenrothes 1995 / 17 YO / Sherry Butt #6975
70cl / 46% - Signatory - A richly coloured 17 YO single Cask Whisky Distilled at Glenrothes on June 5th 1995 and then Bottled on November 13th 2012 by Signatory for their Un-chillfiltered Collection after maturing in a first fill Sherry Cask.

Glenrothes 1995 / Bot.2011
70cl / 43% - Distillery Bottling - Another entry in Glenrothes excellent range of vintages, Distilled in 1995 and Bottled 16 years later in 2011.

Glenrothes 25 YO
70cl / 43% - Distillery Bottling - Previously a travel retail exclusive, Glenrothes 25 is a well aged example of the Distillery's style - rich and fruity.

Glenrothes 30 YO / Bot.2004
70cl / 50.2% - Distillery Bottling - A 30 YO Glenrothes Bottled by age rather than vintage, as is their common practise. They do let us know when it was Distilled though, with August 1974 written on the label.

Glenrothes 40 YO / The Whisky Exchange
70cl / 45.1% - The Whisky Exchange - Another massive hit at 2012's TWE Whisky Show, this single Cask Glenrothes has a classic Bourbon Cask character after four decades in the wood, without ever becoming over-oaked. Delicious vanilla and honey sweetness, with sweet cinnamon & clove on the finish.

Glenrothes 8 YO / Macphail's Collection
70cl / 40% - Gordon & Macphail - A very approachable Glenrothes Bottled at 8 YO by Gordon & Macphail for their Macphail's Collection. Not the most complex Speyside you'll ever encounter, but it's fantastically easy to drink.

Glenrothes John Ramsay Legacy
75cl / 46.7% - Distillery Bottling - Specially selected by retiring Glenrothes malt master John Ramsay after 43 years service, this Bottling came from a vatting of twenty second fill American oak Sherry Casks racked into Sherry butts. The two Casks showing most development were vatted together and slowly reduced to 46.7%. A fitting tribute to a giant of the Whisky world.

Glenrothes Robur Reserve
100cl / 40% - Distillery Bottling - A travel retail exclusive, Glenrothes Robur Reserve is named for Quercus Robur, the official name for European or Spanish oak, and contains a greater proportion of first-fill Oloroso Sherry Casks.

Glenrothes Select Reserve
70cl / 43% - Distillery Bottling - Glenrothes traditionally Bottle Single Malts from specific vintages, so this no-age-statement example raised a few eyebrows when it first appeared. However, the only thing recent batches have raised is the bar - this is tremendous easy-drinking Speyside.

Glenrothes Three Decades
70cl / 43% - Distillery Bottling - Glenrothes have been releasing vintage Whisky for some time now. Over the past 17 years or so, they have released Whisky from the 1970s, 1980s and 1990s. The earliest of which was 1971 and the most recent being 1998. The Glenrothes Three decades celebrates these releases by combining Whisky from all three decades into one Bottle. Previously exclusive to Travel Retail, we've finally managed to get our hands on some Bottles of this fantastic Whisky.

GLEN SPEY RANGE

Glen Spey 12 YO
70cl / 43% - Flora & Fauna - The only official bottling from Glen Spey, with most of the Whisky going into J&B blends.

Glen Spey 12 YO / Manager's Dram
70cl / 53.5% - Distillery Bottling - A very rare bottle from rarely-seen-as-a-single-malt Glen Spey. It's a 12 YO bottled as a "Manager's Dram", given to friends and employees of the Distillery and not often seen up for sale.

Glen Spey 1981 / Berry Bros & Rudd
70cl / 46% - Berry Bros & Rudd - A 1981 vintage Glen Spey from Berry Brothers & Rudd, the oldest family owned independent wine and spirits merchant in the world. This one has matured for about 30 years before being bottled at 46%.

Glen Spey 1986 / 25 YO / Cask #8196
70cl / 50% - Douglas Laing - A 1986 vintage Whisky from Glen Spey, not often seen as a Single Malt, even from independents. This one was matured for 25 years before being bottled in 2012.

Glen Spey 1989 / 21 YO
70cl / 50.4% - Distillery Bottling - One of the most exciting of 2010's Special Releases, this 1989 Glen Spey is the first mainstream bottling of note from this Distillery, and is comfortably the oldest OB Glen Spey ever released. A vatting of new American oak Casks 'that had also

held Sherry'.

Glen Spey 1995 / Connoisseurs Choice
70cl / 43% - Gordon & Macphail - A medium-bodied Glen Spey 1995 bottled for G&M's Connoisseurs Choice range. Glen Spey's pleasant, grassy Single Malt is rather rare as most of it goes into J & B.

Glen Spey 1996 / Managers' Choice
70cl / 52% - Distillery Bottling - Bottled by Diageo as part of their Managers' Choice series of single Cask bottlings from each of their Distilleries, this Glen Spey 1996 is creamy and nutty, with hints of coconut betraying its new American oak maturation. Best consumed neat.

Glen Spey 8 YO / Bot.1980s
70cl / 40% - Distillery Bottling

Glen Spey 8 YO / Bot.1980s / Cork Stopper
75cl / 40% - Distillery Bottling - An extremely rare bottle of Glen Spey 8 YO from the 1980s. This is the more desirable version with a cork stopper rather than a screwcap.

GLENTAUCHERS RANGE

Glentauchers 1976 / 35 YO / Single Malts of Scotland
70cl / 50.9% - Speciality Drinks Ltd - A long-aged 1976 vintage from the very seldom-seen Glentauchers Distillery, this was bottled from a single Bourbon hogshead that yielded just 150 bottles. Glentauchers keeps less than 1% of its spirit back for bottling as Single Malt, with the rest going into owner Pernod Ricard's blends, particularly Ballantine's.

Glentauchers 1979 Centenary / Gordon & Macphail
70cl / 40% - Gordon & Macphail - A special bottling of 1979 Glentauchers released by Gordon & Macphail to celebrate 100 years of production at the Distillery - 1898 to 1998.

Glentauchers 1991 / Gordon & Macphail
70cl / 43% - Gordon & Macphail - A 1991 vintage Glentauchers, bottled by Gordon & Macphail with the traditionally styled Distillery label.

Glentauchers 1996 / 16 YO / Cask #1387 / Signatory
70cl / 47.8% - Signatory - A single Cask Whisky from Glentauchers, bottled for the Cask Strength Collection by Signatory. Distilled on February 6th 1996 and bottled exactly 16 years later on February 6th 2012 after maturing in a Bourbon barrel.

IMPERIAL RANGE

Imperial 16
A beautiful hogshead-matured, Cask-strength malt from the classic

Speyside Distillery Imperial. This was Distilled on the 9th October 1995, it was then aged in hogsheads 50322 and 50323 before bottling on the 29th March 2012. A release of 398 numbered bottles from Signatory.

Imperial 17 1995
This is an Un-Chillfiltered Imperial from Signatory, Distilled in October 1995 and aged for 17 years in a pair of hogsheads. It was bottled in 2012...

Imperial 17 1995
A 17 YO Imperial Distilled in May of 1995 and aged in a refill hogshead before bottling in May of 2012. This is a single Cask release from Douglas Laing's Old Malt Cask range, and there are just 317 bottles.

Imperial 1995
Distilled at Imperial in 1995, this was aged for 16 years before bottling by Duncan Taylor for their fabulous Octave range of Whiskies finished in smaller "octave" Casks for added pep and zing (also vim).

Imperial 17 YO
Distillation Date - May 1995

Imperial - 1995 Bottling Note
Duncan Taylor have bottled this Single Malt Whisky from the Imperial Distillery for their Dimensions range of Cask strength Whiskies.

Imperial 15 Bottling Note
Distilled at the Imperial Distillery in 1995, this was aged for 15 years in two hogsheads. Bottled in 2011, a release of 737 bottles.

INCHGOWER RANGE

Inchgower 12 YO / Bot.1970s
75cl / 40% - Distillery Bottling - A smart looking 1970s bottle of little-seen Speysider Inchgower, with the inscription 'A Deluxe Highland Malt Scotch Whisky From The House of Bell's' on the label. Rare and in its own way rather beautiful.

Inchgower 12 Year Old / Bot.1980s
75cl / 40% - Distillery Bottling - A lovely old 1980s Distillery bottling of Inchgower 'From the House of Bell's' according to the label. They keep a bit quieter about that these days.

Inchgower 12 YO / Bot.1980s
75cl / 40% - Distillery Bottling - A rare old 1980s official bottling of Linkwood 12 YO from the days when it was administered by Bell's.

Inchgower 13 YO / Manager's Dram
70cl / 58.9% - Distillery Bottling - A rare 13 YO Inchgower Manager's

Dram, originally given to friends and employees of the Distillery and not openly sold.

Inchgower 14 YO
70cl / 43% - Flora & Fauna - The only generally available Distillery bottling from Inchgower, usually a key part of the Bell's blend. It's also not one that independents see much of, so this is one of your only chances to try the output from this quietly elegant distillery.

Inchgower 1967 / 16 YO / CD
75cl / 46% - Cadenhead's - A Cadenhead's bottling of 1967 vintage Inchgower. Distilled the year after they doubled their capacity to 4 stills and bottled in the mid-80s after 16 years of maturation.

Inchgower 1967 / Bot.1988 / The Costumes Butt #788
75cl / 46% - Moon Import

Inchgower 1974 / 22 YO
75cl / 55.7% - Distillery Bottling

Inchgower 1974 / 37 YO / The Whisky Agency
70cl / 60.6% - The Whisky Agency

Inchgower 1976 / 27 YO
70cl / 55.6% - Distillery Bottling - The Rare Malts are a now-discontinued series of Cask-strength releases designed by Diageo to showcase some of the hidden treasures in their portfolio. This little beauty was awarded 5 stars and 90/100 by Serge, www.Whiskyfun.com.

Inchgower 1982 / 28 YO / Old Malt Cask #6455
70cl / 50% - Douglas Laing - A 1982 vintage single Cask release of Whisky from Inchgower by the folks at Douglas Laing as part of their Old Malt Cask range. Distilled in June of that year, matured in a refill hogshead and bottled 28 years later in June of 2010.

Inchgower 1982 / 30 YO / Cask 6985 / Berry Bros & Rudd
70cl / 51.9% - Berry Bros & Rudd - A 30 YO Inchgower bottled by Berry Brothers & Rudd in 2012, Distilled back in 1982 and matured in a single Cask.

Inchgower 1986 / 21 YO / Old Malt Cask #3434
70cl / 50% - Douglas Laing - A 1986 vintage Whisky bottled by Douglas Laing for their Old Malt Cask range. Distilled in June at Inchgower, matured in a refill hogshead for 21 years and bottled in December 2007.

Inchgower 1993 / Managers' Choice / Sherry Cask
70cl / 61.9% - Distillery Bottling - A single Cask of Inchgower 1993, bottled in 2009 from European Sherry Oak by owners Diageo for the Managers' Choice series. Amazing colour on this.

Inchgower 1997 / Connoisseurs Choice
70cl / 43% - Gordon & Macphail - A 1997 vintage Whisky from Inchgower, seldom seen as a Single Malt due to the vast majority of its production going into the Bell's family of blended Whiskies. This was bottled by Gordon & Macphail under their Connoisseurs Choice label.

Inchgower 21 YO / Cadenhead's
75cl / 46% - Cadenhead's - A dumpy bottle of 21 YO Inchgower bottled in the 1980s by Cadenhead's.

KNOCKANDO RANGE

Knockando 1964 / 12 YO
75cl / 40% - Distillery Bottling - A very old release of Knockando 12 YO Whisky. This Whisky was Distilled in 1964 and aged for 12 years including maturation in Sherry Casks.

Knockando 1964 Extra Old Reserve / Bot.1980s
75cl / 43% - Distillery Bottling - A wonderful old 1980s bottling of Knockando 1964 in the traditional rectangular decanter. We think the packaging design on this still looks great after all these years.

Knockando 1965 Extra Old Reserve
75cl / 43% - Distillery Bottling - A wonderful old bottling of the increasingly rare Knockando 1965 Extra Old Reserve. This version was bottled in 1990.

Knockando 1967 / Bot.1979
75cl / 43% - Distillery Bottling - An old bottling of Knockando Whisky, Distilled in 1967 and bottled in 1979. Making this Whisky approximately 12 years old.

Knockando 1968 Extra Old Reserve
75cl / 43% - Distillery Bottling - A marvellous old early 1990s bottling of aged Knockando from the 1968 vintage.

Knockando 1968 Extra Old Reserve
70cl / 43% - Distillery Bottling

Knockando 1976 / Bot.1990
75cl / 40% - Distillery Bottling

Knockando 1980 / Bot.1995
70cl / 40% - Distillery Bottling - An old bottle of Knockando Whisky. This was Distilled in 1980 and aged for around 15 years.

Knockando 1980 / Slow Matured
70cl / 43% - Distillery Bottling - An old release of Knockando Slow Matured. This particular bottling is of 1980 vintage Whisky which was bottled in 1998, meaning this Whisky should be around 18 years old.

Knockando 1982 / Bot.1996
70cl / 40% - Distillery Bottling - An old official bottling of Knockando, this 1982 vintage was bottled in the mid-90s.

Knockando 1994 / 17 YO / OMC #7762
70cl / 50% - Douglas Laing - A 1994 vintage Knockando bottled by the folks at Douglas Laing as part of their Old Malt Cask range. Matured for 17 years in a refill hoghead and bottled in late 2011.

Knockando 1994 / 18 YO
70cl / 43% - Distillery Bottling - A 1994 vintage Knockando, known for always bottling their Whiskies with a vintage. This was matured for 18 years and bottled in 2012.

Knockando 1995 / 15 YO
70cl / 43% - Distillery Bottling - Continuing Knockando's habit of marking the vintage of their Whiskies, this 15 YO was Distilled in 1995 and aged in a mixture of Sherry and Bourbon Casks.

Knockando 1996 / 12 YO / Managers Choice / Sherry Cask
70cl / 58.5% - Distillery Bottling - A remarkably dark 12 YO Knockando 1996 bottled at full strength from a Sherry Cask (surely a first-fill) for the Managers' Choice series. It's fair to say that this will likely be somewhat more intense than the standard 12 YO.

Knockando 1997 / 12 YO
70cl / 43% - A 1997 vintage 12 YO from trusty Speysider Knockando. Easy on the palate and the wallet.

Knockando 21 YO Master Reserve
70cl / 43% - Distillery Bottling - An elegant, sophisticated Knockando, Master Reserve 21 YO is made with Casks lying in the coolest part of the warehouse. These Casks take longer to mature and the resulting malt is extremely smooth.

Knockando 25 YO / Special Releases / Bot.2011
70cl / 43% - Distillery Bottling - The first Knockando in Diageo's special releases line-up and a bit of a swerve from normal. Firstly, there's no vintage on the bottle, unlike their other expressions, and secondly it's matured solely in first fill Sherry Casks, for a heavily rich flavour.

KNOCKDHU – AN CNOC RANGE

An Cnoc 12 YO
70cl / 40% - Distillery Bottling - This lip-smacking 12 YO An Cnoc (formerly Knockdhu) is a top-quality proponent of the non-Sherried Speyside style, showing polished malt and a delicious spiciness throughout a warm, complex palate and lasting finish.

An Cnoc 1996
70cl / 46% - Distillery Bottling - Replacing the 1994 in the an Cnoc

range from Knockdhu Distillery, this 1996 vintage has been bottled at 46% without colouring or chill-filtration.

An Cnoc 35 YO
70cl / 44.3% - Distillery Bottling - A fantastic release from An Cnoc, the oldest bottling in their regular range at 35 years old. A combination of a small number of Bourbon and Sherry Casks to produce a balanced, sweet and fruity dram.

An Cnoc Peter Arkle / 2nd Edition
70cl / 46% - Distillery Bottling - A limited edition bottling from An Cnoc, produced in collaboration with Scottish artist and designer Peter Arkle. This second edition has been matured in a combination of American and European oak Casks, as selected by Distillery manager Gordon Bruce.

LINKWOOD RANGE

Linkwood / Burghead Maltings 25th Anniversary
70cl / 43% - Distillery Bottling - A Whisky from Linkwood specially bottled to celebrate the 25th year of the Burghead Maltings, which opened in 1966.

Linkwood 12 YO
70cl / 43% - Flora & Fauna - Rounded yet delicate. Apples again, tingly spiciness. Fills and perfumes the mouth. Delicious...A classic example of a relatively light and fragrant Whisky that has real complexity and a gorgeous feel. 8/10' Dave Broom, Whisky Magazine, Nov 2002

Linkwood 12 YO / Bot.1970s
75cl / 40% - Distillery Bottling

Linkwood 12 YO / Bot.1970s
75cl / 40% - Distillery Bottling - A rare old 1970s Distillery bottling of 12 YO Linkwood.

Linkwood 12 YO / Bot.1980s
75cl / 40% - Distillery Bottling - A 1980s Bottle of Linkwood 12 YO with a decorative woodcut illustration of a castle on the label.

Linkwood 12 YO / Bot.1980's
75cl / 40% - Distillery Bottling - A charming 1980s bottle of Linkwood 12 YO with a simple but elegant plain white label.

Linkwood 14 YO / Bot.1980s
75cl / 60.8% - Sestante - A Cask strength 14 YO Linkwood bottled in the 1980s by Italian indie Sestante.

Linkwood 1939 / 37 YO / Connoisseurs Choice
75cl / 43% - Gordon & Macphail - A fascinating bottle of Linkwood,

Distilled in 1939 at the beginning of WWII, matured in Sherry Casks and bottled in the mid-1970s by Gordon & Macphail at the grand old age of 37 years old.

Linkwood 1939 / Gordon & Macphail
75cl / 40% - Gordon & Macphail - A marvellous old bottle of Linkwood Distilled in 1939 and bottled by Gordon and Macphail quite some time later.

Linkwood 1946 / Gordon & Macphail
70cl / 40% - Gordon & Macphail - A bottle of 1946 vintage Linkwood from veteran independent bottler Gordon & Macphail, one of the only independents who can claim warehouses filled with Whiskies as old as this.

Linkwood 1954 / Gordon & Macphail
70cl / 40% - Gordon & Macphail - A 1954 vintage Linkwood bottled by Gordon & Macphail.

Linkwood 1955 / 23 YO / Cream Label
75cl / 40% - Distillery Bottling - A 1955 vintage Distillery bottling of Linkwood, matured for 23 years and released in the late 1970s.

Linkwood 1958 / 12 YO
75cl / 43% - Distillery Bottling - A 1958 vintage Linkwood, bottled by the Distillery at 12 years old around 1970. The label on this one suggests that it was bottled for the Italian market and distributed by Samaroli.

Linkwood 1972 / 14 YO / Gordon & Macphail
75cl / 61.6% - Gordon & Macphail - A very rare mid-1980s G&M bottling of Diageo's faithful blend-fodder workhorse Linkwood, bottled in 1987 at the slightly scary full strength of 61.6%.

Linkwood 1972 / 22 YO / Rare Malts
70cl / 59.3% - Rare Malts - A 1972 vintage Rare Malt bottling of Linkwood Whisky. This Whisky has been aged for 22 years and bottled at Cask strength.

Linkwood 1973 / Gordon & Macphail
70cl / 43% - Gordon & Macphail - Another well-priced release from Gordon and Macphail - an early 1970s Linkwood bottled with the traditional old school label design.

Linkwood 1974 / 23 YO
75cl / 61.2% - Distillery Bottling

Linkwood 1974 / 30 YO
70cl / 54.9% - Distillery Bottling - This Linkwood 1974 30 YO was released in 2005 and remains the oldest ever official bottling from this Distillery. The Rare Malts are a now-discontinued series of Cask-strength releases designed by Diageo to showcase some of the hidden

treasures in their portfolio.

Linkwood 1981 / 26 YO / Port Finish
50cl / 56.9% - Distillery Bottling - For this Linkwood 1981, 12 YO malt that had been matured in traditional Casks was transferred to port wine Casks for a further 14 years. Something of a departure for Diageo's Special Releases, releasing three malts from the same Distillery in 50cl bottles.

Linkwood 1981 / 26 YO / Red Wine Finish
50cl / 55.5% - Distillery Bottling - For this Linkwood 1981, 12 YO malt that had been matured in traditional Casks was transferred to sweet red wine Casks for a further 14 years. Something of a departure for Diageo's Special Releases, releasing three malts from the same Distillery in 50cl bottles.

Linkwood 1981 / 26 YO / Rum Finish
50cl / 54.5% - Distillery Bottling - For this Linkwood 1981, 12 YO malt that had been matured in traditional Casks was transferred to rum Casks for a further 14 years. Something of a departure for Diageo's Special Releases, releasing three malts from the same Distillery in 50cl bottles.

Linkwood 1983 / 14 YO
70cl / 59.8% - Flora & Fauna

Linkwood 1984 / 27 YO / Liquid Sun
70cl / 53.2% - Liquid Sun - A Whisky Distilled at Linkwood in 1984, shortly before the old still house stopped regular production. This was bottled in 2011 by Liquid Sun after 27 years of maturation in Bourbon Cask.

Linkwood 1991 / Cask Strength / Gordon & Macphail
70cl / 52.5% - Gordon & Macphail - This should be good: single Sherry-Cask Linkwood 1991 bottled at full strength in 2006 for Gordon & MacPhail's 'Cask' series - Yummy.

Linkwood 1991 / Private Collection / Cote Rotie Finish
70cl / 45% - Gordon & Macphail = A bottling of Linkwood as part of Gordon & Macphail's Private Collection series, with an interesting red wine Cask finish. The Casks originally matured Cote Rotie, a red wine from the north of the Rhone region, and the finishing complimented an initial maturation in Bourbon Casks.

Linkwood 1996 / Managers' Choice
70cl / 58.2% - Distillery Bottling - A superpremium Linkwood 1996 bottled at full Cask strength, this is part of Diageo's Manager's Choice series of single Casks bottled in 2009.

Linkwood 1997 / 13 YO / Old Malt Cask #6309
70cl / 50% - Douglas Laing - A 1997 vintage Linkwood bottled by Douglas Laing for their Old Malt Cask range. Bottled in May 2010

after 13 years in an ex-Bourbon Cask.

Linkwood 25 YO / Gordon & Macphail
70cl / 43% - Gordon & Macphail - A splendid bottle of 25 YO Linkwood from indie bottling heroes Gordon & Macphail.

Linkwood 48 YO
75cl / 40% - Sestante - A very rare 1980s Sestante Imports bottling of long-aged Linkwood aged 48 years.

LONGMORN RANGE

Longmorn 10 YO / Rectangular / Bot. 1960's
75cl / 43% - Distillery Bottling - A 1960s bottling of 10 YO Longmorn. Please note the low fill-level in the bottle and contact if you have any questions.

Longmorn 12 YO / Gordon & Macphail
70cl / 40% - Gordon & Macphail - A 12 YO Longmorn bottled by Gordon & Macphail with an old fashioned label.

Longmorn 15 YO
70cl / 45% - Distillery Bottling - A terrific full-blooded Speysider, oozing complexity with plenty of spice, sweet fruits, heather and balanced oak interplaying with the malt. A highly-respected Whisky with a loyal following.

Longmorn 15 YO / Bot.1980s
75cl / 43% - Distillery Bottling - A rare old Longmorn 15 YO from the late 1980s. This should be delicious.

Longmorn 15 YO / Bot.1990s
70cl / 43% - Distillery Bottling - A rare old Longmorn 15 YO from the early 1990s. This should be delicious.

Longmorn 16 YO
70cl / 48% - Distillery Bottling - An extremely fancy relaunch of Longmorn to replace the 15 YO in a bid to turn this great Distillery into a global super-premium brand.

Longmorn 18 YO / The Whisky Show
70cl / 57.8% - The Whisky Show - An elegant 18 YO Longmorn bottled specially for the 2011 Whisky Exchange Whisky Show and rather popular on our Show Bottlings stand over the weekend.

Longmorn 1957 / 25 YO / Connoisseurs Choice
75cl / 40% - Connoisseurs Choice

Longmorn 1964
70cl / 43% - Gordon & Macphail - Another entry in Gordon & Macphail's excellently priced range of old Whisky - this time a 1964 vintage dram from Speyside's Longmorn.

Longmorn 1967 / Gordon & Macphail
70cl / 43% - Gordon & Macphail - Another incredibly priced retro-labeled old Longmorn bottled by Gordon & Macphail from their scarily well stocked warehouses - this one was Distilled in 1967.

Longmorn 1968 / 20 YO
75cl / 45% - A great looking 20 YO Whisky from Longmorn, Distilled on December 10th 1968 and bottled in July 1989 after maturing in Sherry Casks.

Longmorn 1971
70cl / 43% - Gordon & Macphail

Longmorn 1972 / Sherry Cask / Gordon & Macphail
70cl / 45% - Gordon & Macphail

Longmorn 1973 / 21 YO / Sherry Cask
70cl / 46% - First Cask - A rare independent bottling of Longmorn, this expression is a single Sherry Cask from 1973. Darker than the photo suggests, this should be an epic dram for Sherry fans.

Longmorn 1973 / Sherry Cask / Gordon & Macphail
70cl / 54% - Gordon & Macphail - A Cask-strength Longmorn 1973 matured in Sherrywood and bottled by Gordon & Macphail in 2006.

Longmorn 1975 / 36 YO / The Perfect Dram
70cl / 50.6% - The Perfect Dram - An bottling of 1984 vintage Highland Park for German indie The Whisky Agency. Matured in a Bourbon Cask for 27 years and bottled in 2011 at Cask strength.

Longmorn 1975 / Cask #3967 / Montgomerie's
70cl / 46% - Montgomery's - A 1975 vintage Longmorn bottled at healthy 33 years of age by indie bottler Montgomerie's.

Longmorn 1989 / 22 YO / Cask #18768
70cl / 43% - Mackillop's - A Mackillop's Choice release of 22 YO single Cask Longmorn. Distilled in 1989 and bottled in March 2012.

Longmorn 1990 / 18 YO
70cl / 58% - The Whisky Society - A complex Longmorn, this is a marriage of two barrels from the 1990 vintage. A deliciously fruity dram with prominent red apples balanced by lip-smacking oak spices and a damson sponge cake character.

Longmorn 1990 / 18 YO / Single Malts of Scotland
70cl / 51.4% - Speciality Drinks Ltd - We're lucky to have reclaimed this excellent Longmorn for The Single Malts of Scotland series - it was originally bottled in 2009 for an overseas market, but was shelved at the last minute. A nutty, appley Longmorn with a generous dollop of clove and cinnamon spices.

Longmorn 1990 / Greek Label
70cl / 56.4% - Independent Bottler

Longmorn 1991 / 21 YO / 50% / Old Malt Cask #8256
70cl / 50% - Douglas Laing - A 21 YO single Cask Whisky from Longmorn, bottled as part of the Old Malt Cask range by Douglas Laing. Distilled in February 1991 and bottled in March 2012 after maturing in a refill hogshead.

Longmorn 1992 / 20 YO / Cask #48432 / Adelphi
70cl / 55.1% - Adelphi - A 1992 vintage from Longmorn, bottled from a single Cask in 2012 by the folks at Adelphi.

Longmorn 1992 / 20 YO / Cask #48490
70cl / 55.8% - Signatory - A 1992 vintage Longmorn, matured for 20 years in a single hogshead before bottling on October 15th 2012 by Signatory for their Cask Strength Collection.

Longmorn 1992 / Scott's Selection
70cl / 58.1% - Scott's Selection - A Scott's Selection release of single Cask Speyside Whisky from Longmorn. Distilled in 1992 and bottled at a natural Cask strenght of 58.1%.

Longmorn 1996 / 13 YO
70cl / 49% - Daily Dram - A very fetching bottle of Longmorn from the Nectar of the Daily Dram series. The company has an innovative approach to packaging, with each bottling individually labelled using some really imaginative and modern design - this time it's Stonehenge.

Longmorn 1997 / 14 YO / Cask Strength Edition
50cl / 59.6% - Distillery Bottling - A Cask strength release of 1997 vintage Longmorn bottled by Distillery owners Chivas Brothers as one of their Cask Strength Editions. 14 years old and at a natural strength of 59.6%.

Longmorn Centenary 25 Year Old
70cl / 45% - Distillery Bottling - Not the most expensive malt in our Luxury Collection, but this is a class act, and a benchmark malt for Longmorn, one of the very best Distilleries in Speyside. Superb flavour concentration with the Distillery's trademark grapefruit, boiled sweets and a hint of smoke.

Longmorn-Glenlivet 10 YO / Bot 1970's
75cl / 40% - Distillery Bottling - A 1970s release of 10 YO Longmorn-Glenlivet, bottled by the Distillery.

Longmorn-Glenlivet 12 YO / Bot.1930s
75cl / 43% - A fabulous old 1930s Longmorn 12 YO, bottled by and for New York importer Bellows under their own label.

Longmorn-Glenlivet 1971

75cl / 53.5% - Scott's Selection - A 1971 vintage Longmorn bottled by Scott's Selection in 2004 at Cask strength.

Longmorn-Glenlivet 1971 / Scott's Selection
70cl / 57.8% - Scott's Selection

MACALLAN RANGE

Macallan 10 YO / 100 Proof
70cl / 57% - Distillery Bottling

Macallan 10 YO / Bot.1970s
75cl / 40% - Distillery Bottling - A bottle of Macallan 10 YO from the 1970s, back when they still almost exclusively used Sherry Casks to mature their Whisky.

Macallan 10 YO / Bot.1970s / Gordon & Macphail
75cl / 40% - Distillery Bottling - A bottle of Macallan's 10 YO, released in the 1970s. This was produced back in the days when Macallan used almost exclusively Sherry Casks to mature their Whisky, so we'd expect it to be a classic Sherried Speysider.

Macallan 10 YO / Bot.1980s
70cl / 40% - Distillery Bottling

Macallan 10 YO / Cask Strength
100cl / 58.8% - Distillery Bottling

Macallan 10 Year Old / Cask Strength
100cl / 58.1% - Distillery Bottling - The cracking, but unfortunately discontinued, litre sized Cask strength Macallan 10 YO. Big (in bottle size and flavour), rich and punchy, just like they used to be.

Macallan 10 YO / Fine Oak
70cl / 40% - Distillery Bottling - Macallan 10 YO Fine Oak is matured in a combination of Bourbon & Sherry Oak Casks. The Fine Oak range has been around for a few years now and seems to have weathered the storm it caused amongst the faithful when it was initially released.

Macallan 10 YO / Sherry / Bot.1990s
70cl / 40% - Distillery Bottling - A 1990s bottling of Macallan's Sherry rich 10 YO Single Malt Scotch Whisky.

Macallan 10 YO / Sherry Oak
70cl / 40% - Distillery Bottling - Matured exclusively in oak Sherry Casks from Spain, Macallan 10 YO is a deep, rich, deliciously smooth and well-rounded flavour with a slight sweetness and touch of Sherry and wood. Its deep colour is achieved wholly naturally without the addition of any colouring.

Macallan 10 YO / Speaker Martin's

70cl / 40% - Distillery Bottling - A special edition of Macallan 10 YO, selected by disgraced former Speaker of the House of Commons Michael Martin for sale at the tourist shop in the Houses of Parliament. An interesting historical piece, as Martin was forced to resign shortly after this version had appeared, meaning it was only available for a very short time.

Macallan 12 YO / British Aerospace
75cl / 43% - Distillery Bottling

Macallan 12 YO / Robert Burns Semiquincentenary
70cl / 46% - Distillery Bottling - A very elaborately-packaged Macallan released to celebreate the 250th Anniversary of the birth of Robert Burns. A vatting of two Casks from different years that both bore the number 1759 (the year of Burns' birth), this comes in an unusually pretty decanter with an insert containing a map and a Burns poem as well as information about the bottling.

Macallan 12 YO / Sherry Oak
70cl / 40% - Distillery Bottling - Deliciously smooth, with rich dried fruits and Sherry, balanced with wood smoke and spice. Described by Paul Pacult, the renowned international Whisky writer, in his book Kindred Spirits as: "simply the best 12 YO Single Malt around".

Macallan 12 YO Woodland Estate
70cl / 40% - Distillery Bottling - A limited edition 12 YO Sherry matured Macallan originally only available to Distillery visitors in the mid-2000s. Each of the 1000 bottles has a correspondingly numbered tree planted in the Distillery's ground.

Macallan 15 YO / Bot.1970s / Gordon & Macphail
75cl / 40% - Gordon & Macphail - An old G&M bottling of Macallan 15 YO from the 1980s.

Macallan 17 YO Fine Oak
75cl / 43% - Distillery Bottling - Macallan 17 YO Fine Oak was introduced in the US market in 2006 and, like the rest of the Fine Oak range, this has been matured in a mix of Sherry and Bourbon Casks to showcase a lighter style from the famously rich, opulent Sherried norm.

Macallan 1824 Collection / Limited Release Decanter
70cl / 48% - Distillery Bottling
A limited edition Macallan decanter first unveiled at Changi airport in October 2009 and originally a travel retail exclusive. A combination of some of Macallan's finest Sherry Casks, bottled at 48%.

Macallan 1841 Replica
70cl / 41.7% - Distillery Bottling

Macallan 1841 Replica
75cl / 41.7% - Distillery Bottling - The 1841 was the third in a series of controversial replica bottlings of Macallan from the Distillery. Whatever the provenance of the bottles that were replicated, the Whisky is meant to be tremendous (the late great Michael Jackson gave this a 95 point score), ensuring that this is one of the most popular of these famous (notorious?) bottlings.

Macallan 1874 Replica
70cl / 45% - Distillery Bottling - The first edition of Macallan's replicas of their 1874 Whisky, looking like the original and with a style based on some samples of the legendary old dram.

Macallan 1874 Replica
75cl / 45% - Distillery Bottling

Macallan 1876 Replica
70cl / 40.6% - Distillery Bottling
A smart-looking replica Macallan modelled on a bottle from the Victorian era. Rich in summer fruits, both fresh/citric and dried, with traces of spice. Light vanilla fudge, sweet oak and wood spice.

Macallan 1928 / 50 YO
75cl / 38.6% - Distillery Bottling - One of the first ever 50 year-old Single Malt Whiskies ever released, however although the label states 'Over 50 Years Old', this Macallan 1928 was actually bottled in 1983 (making it in fact a 55 year-old).

Macallan 1938 / 65 YO (Speymalt) / Sherry Cask
70cl / 41.4% - Gordon & Macphail - We tried this at the 2009 Whisky Show in London and it was definitely the star of the show. Unbelievably mellow, very complex with elegant fruit and soft oak. No one could believe that this was so old. A real classy Whisky which should have a much higher price tag. If this was bottled by the Distillery we would be looking at tens of thousands of pounds.

Macallan 1940 / Speymalt / G&M
70cl / 40% - Gordon & Macphail - A 1940 vintage Macallan bottled by Gordon & Macphail.

Macallan 1945 / 56 YO / Fine & Rare
70cl / 51.5% - Distillery Bottling - A very rare 1945 vintage Macallan, bottled at 56 years old as part of the Distillery's Fine & Rare series. Cask 262 has retained an impressive abv of 51.5% despite well over five decades in the wood.

Macallan 1946 / 52 YO
70cl / 40% - Distillery Bottling - This Macallan 1946 is rather unusual, in that it was made with peated malt due to the high post-war prices of coal. In our opinion it also happens to be one of the greatest

Macallans ever released. The inital release of this was quite large and took a while for the Distillery to sell, but it is now recognised as a classic.

Macallan 1949 / 50 YO / Millennium
70cl / 43% - Distillery Bottling - The jewel in the crown, this for us is the most special aged Macallan Whisky ever bottled. Christmas cake style fruit with all the complexity of a classy aged malt. This Macallan is in a league of its own and proudly sits alongside the more recent Lalique range.

Macallan 1949 / Crystal Decanter
75cl / 40.25% - Independent Bottling - A VERY rare bottle of 1949 Macallan, made for a private company in Japan around the turn of the millennium. Only around 100 bottles of this precious vintage release were ever made, bottled just before the Whisky went under permitted strength in a simple, elegant Baccarat crystal decanter.

Macallan 1950 / 52 YO / Fine & Rare Cask #600
70cl / 51.7% - Distillery Bottling - A 1950 Macallan, aged for 52 years in Cask #600 and released as part of their Fine & Rare range of vintaged Whiskies.

Macallan 1964 / 25 YO
75cl / 43% - Distillery Bottling - One of the series of 25 YO Macallans, Distilled in 1964 and bottled in the late 80s.

Macallan 1965 / 17 YO
75cl / 43% - Distillery Bottling - A 17 YO Macallan Distilled in 1965 and bottled with a vintage-look label.

Macallan 1965 / 25 YO
75cl / 43% - Distillery Bottling

Macallan 1965 / Fino Sherry Cask #2114 / CRN
70cl / 51.4% - Carn Mor - This Carn Mor Macallan is a sister Cask to the Cream Sherry bottling, and the two Casks were Distilled on the same day in 1965 and bottled on the same day in 2008. A fascinating experiment (for the deep-pocketed) to see how different types of Cask affect identical spirit.

Macallan 1965 / Speymalt
70cl / 43% - Gordon & Macphail

Macallan 1966 / 30 YO
70cl / 50.1% - Signatory

Macallan 1966 / 34 YO / Cask #4182
70cl / 50% - Signatory - A 1966 vintage Whisky from Macallan. This has been aged for 34 years and bottled in the 3rd quarter of the year 2000. Presented in a distinguished wooden presentation box, bottled by Signatory for their Signatory Vintage Rare Reserve range.

Macallan 1966 / 34 YO / Hart Brothers
70cl / 46.2% - Hart Brothers - A Hart Brothers bottling of 1966 vintage Macallan, aged for 34 years before bottling at a Cask strength of 46.2%.

Macallan 1966 / 35 YO
70cl / 55.5% - Distillery Bottling - A 1966 vintage Macallan, released a decade or so ago as part of the Distillery's Fine & Rare series. This amazingly ambitious range was designed to showcase Macallan throughout its history, with initial vintages going back to 1926 - all bottled at full Cask strength.

Macallan 1966 / 35 YO / Hart Brothers
70cl / 45.1% - Hart Brothers - A 1966 vintage Whisky from Macallan Distillery in Speyside. This Whisky has been aged for 35 full years and bottled at a cask strength of 45.1%.

Macallan 1966 / Speymalt / Gordon & Macphail
70cl / 40% - Gordon & Macphail - An old bottle of 1966 vintage Speymalt Whisky from Macallan Distillery. Bottled by Gordon & Macphail and presented in a lovely wooden box.

Macallan 1967 / 35 YO / Hart Brothers
70cl / 41.9% - Hart Brothers - A 1967 vintage Macallan, bottled after 35 years of maturation by Hart Brothers at a Cask strength of 41.9%.

Macallan 1968 / Speymalt / Gordon & Macphail
70cl / 43% - Gordon & Macphail - Another bargain Speymalt Macallan from Gordon & MacPhail. This 1968 vintage has been bottled at 43% and comes in at just over half the price of a miniature of the officially bottled Macallan 1968 at 46.6%. Thank You, G&M.

Macallan 1969 / 32 YO / Fine & Rare Cask #10412
70cl / 59% - Distillery Bottling - A 1969 Macallan from single Cask #10412, released at a hugely impressive 59% after 32 years of Cask ageing. This vintage Macallan is part of the Fine & Rare series, the Distillery's ne plus ultra range.

Macallan 1971 / 18 YO / Vintage Label
75cl / 43% - Distillery Bottling - A vintage labelled Macallan, Distilled in 1971 and bottled at 18 years old by the Distillery.

Macallan 1971 / 25 YO
70cl / 43% - Distillery Bottling

Macallan 1971 / Speymalt
70cl / 43% - Gordon & Macphail - A 1971 vintage release for Gordon & Macphail's spectacularly good value 'Speymalt' bottlings of Macallan. These bottlings are a fraction of cost of the officially-bottled expressions from the same vintages.

Macallan 1972 / 25 YO
75cl / 43% - Distillery Bottling

Macallan 1974 / 25 YO
70cl / 43% - Distillery Bottling - One of the series of legendary Macallan 25 YO's, this time Distilled in 1974, the year the Distillery went from twelve to eighteen stills.

Macallan 1975 / 25 YO / Sherry Cask
70cl / 43% - Distillery Bottling - Bottled in 2000, this Sherry-Cask Macallan 1975 was, we believe, the last Macallan 25 YO Anniversary Malt with a stated vintage. A lovely colour on this Macallan, produced during the Distillery's golden era.

Macallan 1975 / 25 YO / Sherry Cask / 75cl
75cl / 43% - Distillery Bottling - A 75cl version of Macallan's Anniversary Malt (as the 25 YO Sherry Cask version used to be known) bottled in 2000, this edition was Distilled in 1975 and was, as far as we know, the last time that Macallan's 25 YO had a stated vintage.

Macallan 1975 / 30 YO / Fine & Rare Cask #8845
70cl / 51% - Distillery Bottling - A 1975 Macallan, aged for 30 years in Cask #8845 and released as part of their Fine & Rare range of vintaged Whiskies.

Macallan 1979 / 18 YO / Gran Reserva
70cl / 40% - Distillery Bottling - A truly classic Sherried Macallan, this 1979 is regarded as the best of the highly-sought-after Gran Reserva series released in the 1990s to showcase the extreme end of Sherried whisky from the Distillery. Scoring 91 points on Serge Valentin's Whiskyfun.com, this is one of the landmark Macallan releases of the last twenty years.

Macallan 1980 / ESC 2 / Sherry Cask
50cl / 59.3% - Distillery Bottling - A 1980 vintage Sherry Cask matured Macallan from their 'Exceptional Single Cask' range. This Whisky has been aged for around 18 years and bottled at Cask strength.

Macallan 1981 / Gran Reserva
70cl / 40% - Distillery Bottling - Another of the hugely popular Macallan Gran Reserva series, released around the turn of the century. These releases were made in small batches from Casks that were too good to be vatted into the standard 18 YO release and are highly prized by collectors today.

Macallan 1982 / Gran Reserva
70cl / 40% - Distillery Bottling - A 1982 vintage Macallan carefully selected to reflect the high quality of their Sherry matured Whisky from that year and then bottled in 2000.

Macallan 1988 / Speymalt / Gordon & Macphail
70cl / 43% - Gordon & Macphail - A new Macallan 1988 bottled for Gordon & MacPhail's Speymalt series.

Macallan 1989 / The Gallery / Annie Leibowitz
70cl / 56.6% - Distillery Bottling - A 1989 vintage Macallan selected as part of the Masters of Photography series, celebrating the work of Annie Leibowitz. This was matured in a Sherry butt and features a photograph of actor & director Kevin McKidd entitled 'The Gallery'.

Macallan 1989 / The Whisky Trail
70cl / 43% - Speciality Drinks Ltd - A 1989 vintage Macallan bottled For The Whisky Trail in 2011.

Macallan 1990 / 13 YO / ESC 6 / Sherry Cask
50cl / 59.6% - Distillery Bottling - The 6th entry in Macallan's ESC range - Exceptional Single Casks. Filled on 21st December 1990 into a Sherry butt and bottled in November 2004, with only 830 bottles in the release.

Macallan 1990 / 22 YO / Cask #2397 / Mackillop's
70cl / 50.6% - Mackillop's - A 22 YO single Cask Macallan from the folks at Mackillop's - Distilled in February 1990 and bottled at Cask strength in March 2012.

Macallan 1990 / The Whisky Trail
70cl / 43% - Speciality Drinks Ltd - A 1990 vintage Macallan bottled by Speciality Drinks for their The Whisky Trail range in 2011. Rich fruit and oak flavours and amazing value for money.

Macallan 1990 Elegancia / 12 YO
100cl / 40% - Distillery Bottling

Macallan 1991 / 14 YO / Sherry Oak / Season's
70cl / 54% - Distillery Bottling

Macallan 1991 / The Bar / Annie Leibowitz
70cl / 50.8% - Distillery Bottling - Bottle #3 in the Annie Leibowitz collection in Macallan's Masters of Photography series. This 1991 vintage, Sherry puncheon matured Whisky accompanies a photograph entitled The Bar.

Macallan 1993 / 18 YO / Old Malt Cask #9127

70cl / 50% - Douglas Laing - A 1993 vintage Macallan, Distilled in November and bottled in September 2012 from a single refill hogshead by Douglas Laing for their Old Malt Cask range.

Macallan 1994 / 18 YO Sherry
70cl / 43% - Distillery Bottling - The 1994 vintage edition of Macallan's iconic Sherry Cask 18 YO arrives as news sinks in of the discontinuation of age statements across most of the Distillery's standard range. How much longer will these vintage 18 YOs continue to be produced??

Macallan 1996 / The Skyline / Annie Leibowitz
70cl / 55.5% - Distillery Bottling - Part of the Annie Leibowitz collection in Macallan's Masters of Photography series, this 1996 vintage Whisky was matured in an American Oak butt and is paired with a photograph of New York's iconic skyline, appropriately called 'The Skyline'.

Macallan 2000 / Speymalt / Gordon & Macphail
70cl / 43% - Gordon & Macphail - A 2000 vintage from Macallan bottled by Gordon & Macphail, as usual, under their Speymalt banner. Fairly Young in comparison to some of G&Ms expressions, but with character beyond its years.

Macallan 2002 / Speymalt
70cl / 43% - Gordon & Macphail - A 2002 vintage Whisky from Macallan, bottled at a good drinking strength of 43% by Gordon and Macphail in their Speymalt range's handsome updated livery and packaging, featuring an embossed bottle, atylish minimal label and upgraded box.

Macallan 2003 / Speymalt / Gordon & Macphail
70cl / 43% - Gordon & Macphail - A 2003 vintage Whisky from Macallan, bottled by Gordon & Macphail under their Speymalt label.

Macallan 20 YO / Masters of Photography Albert Watson
70cl / 43% - Distillery Bottling - The second of Macallan's Masters of Photography series sensibly avoids the controversies of the first, with a special 20 YO Sherried Whisky and a book of photos by Albert Watson on the journey of the Sherry Cask. The presentation box contains ten of these photos reproduced as special prints.

Macallan 21 YO / Fine Oak
70cl / 43% - Distillery Bottling - Matured in mixture of Sherry and Bourbon Casks. This range has been around for a few years now and seems to have weathered the storm it caused amongst the faithful when it was initially released.

Macallan 25 YO / Sherry Oak
70cl / 43% - Distillery Bottling

Macallan 25 YO / Sherry Oak / Bot.1980s
75cl / 43% - Distillery Bottling

Macallan 25 YO / Silver Jubilee / Large Bottle
150cl / 45.5% - Distillery Bottling - A limited edition release of 25 YO Macallan, produced in honour of the Queen's Silver Jubilee in 1977. On top of that it's also a rather rarely seen magnum size bottle, to make sure you had enough to go around your street party...

Macallan 50 YO / Lalique Crystal
75cl / 46% - Distillery Bottling - This eye-catching 75cl Macallan decanter caused a sensation when it was released a couple of years ago. The Whisky itself isn't too shabby either, with some of the Casks used much older than the stated fifty years. The limited allocation for each market sold out in near-record time, and was so successful that more Lalique Macallans are in the pipeline - we hear that the next release will be a 55 year-old.

Macallan 55 YO Lalique Crystal Decanter
70cl / 40.1% - Distillery Bottling - The second edition of Macallan's Lalique series of staggeringly old Macallan in difficult-to-ignore crystal decanters.

Macallan 57 YO Lalique Crystal
75cl / 48.5% - Distillery Bottling - A 75cl edition of Macallan's third collaboration with French crystal manufacturer Lalique. It's the oldest spirit in the range yet, bottled at a phenomenal 57 years old at natural strength.

Macallan 7 YO / Bot.1990s
70cl / 40% - Distillery Bottling - A rare old Macallan 7 YO for the Italian market.

Macallan 8 YO / Bot.1980s
75cl / 43% - Distillery Bottling - A rare old Macallan 8 YO, bottled in the 1980s for the Italian market.

Macallan 8 YO / Bot.1980s
75cl / 43% - Distillery Bottling - An 8 YO Macallan, bottled in the 1980s for Italian importer Coppo.

Macallan 8 YO / Easter Elchies Summer Bottling
70cl / 45.2% - Distillery Bottling - A special edition Macallan, bottled as part of a seasonal selection for sale at Easter Elchies.

Macallan Cask Strength
75cl / 58.6% - Distillery Bottling - The now discontinued Macallan Cask Strength. A punchy 58.6% with Sherry flavours to match.

Macallan Director's Edition
70cl / 40% - Distillery Bottling - A short-lived special edition no-age-

statement Macallan, discontinued in 2012 as part of the Distillery's rationalisation of their range. The Director's Edition has a handsome deep gold colour that strongly suggests a goodly proportion of well-aged Sherry Casks in the mix.

Macallan Estate Oak
100cl / 40% - Distillery Bottling - Originally launched exclusively into duty free, Macallan Estate Oak is a rare bottling with an environmentally friendly promise - Macallan will plant a tree on their estate for every bottle purchased.

Macallan Fine Oak 18 YO
70cl / 43% - Distillery Bottling - Matured in Bourbon & Sherry Oak Casks.

Macallan Fine Oak Master Edition
70cl / 42.8% - Distillery Bottling - Introduced in 2010, this Macallan Masters Edition is bottled at the slightly higher strength of 42.8%, and like the other Fine Oak expressions is a mix of ex-Sherry and ex-Bourbon Casks.

Macallan Fine Oak Masters' Edition
70cl / 40% - Distillery Bottling - A lighter style of Macallan, like the rest of the Fine Oak range Masters' Edition has been matured using American oak Casks as well as the more familiar Sherry Casks. Smooth and delicate, with medium weight oak and fruit flavours.

Macallan Gold
70cl / 40% - Distillery Bottling - Macallan Gold was released in late 2012 as part of a series of colour-themed bottlings introduced to replace the Distillery's age-statement expressions. Gold has been produced from 9-15 YO first fill and refill Sherry Casks and is designed to sit between the now-defunct 10 YO Sherry Oak and 10 YO Fine Oak bottlings.

Macallan Nicol's Nectar
70cl / 46% - Distillery Bottling - A very rare Macallan - just 120 bottles of this were produced in 1996 for guests at an event to mark the retirement of Peter Nicol from the Macallan Distillery after 43 years service. The malts used were chosen by Mr Nicol himself.

Macallan Oscuro
70cl / 46.5% - Originally a travel retail exclusive, Macallan Oscuro is a combination of Casks of Whisky Distilled between 1987 and 1997. They have combined the collectability of Macallan with their trademark rich Sherried elegance to create a much sought after Whisky.

Macallan Private Eye
70cl / 40% - Distillery Bottling - One of the most collectable ever

Macallans, bottled in 1996 for the 35th anniversary of the famous satirical magazine Private Eye (still essential reading). The vatting produced 5000 bottles and included one Cask from 1961. This special edition is also unique in that it features a superb screenprinted label by the legendary gonzo illustrator Ralph Steadman.

Macallan Select Oak / The 1824 Collection
100cl / 40% - Distillery Bottling - The 1824 Collection is a range of Macallans released for the travel retail market. The Select Oak edition is a complex combination of first-fill European oak Casks seasoned with Oloroso Sherry, and American oak Casks seasoned with either Oloroso Sherry or Bourbon.

Macallan Special Reserve
70cl / 46% - Distillery Bottling - A very limited release of Macallan with no age statement or vintage and only described as being their 'Special Reserve'.

Macallan Travel Series 1940s
50cl / 40% - Distillery Bottling - Part of Macallan's Travel series, each entry titled with a year and with spirit reflecting the type of Whisky produced at that time. 1940s - lean war-time scotch, with more peat and less Sherry wood.

Macallan Travel Series 1950s
50cl / 40% - Distillery Bottling - Part of Macallan's Travel series, each entry titled with a year and with spirit reflecting the type of Whisky produced at that time. 1950s - a more modern expression, similar to current day Macallan.

Macallan-Glenlivet 12 YO / Bot.1960s
75cl / 40% - Gordon & Macphail - A 1960s release of Macallan's 12 YO 'liqueur Whisky' bottled by Gordon & Macphail.

Macallan-Glenlivet 15 YO / Bot.1970s
75cl / 43% - Gordon & Macphail

Macallan-Glenlivet 1971 / 27 YO / Sherry Cask
70cl / 54.2% -Signatory

Macallan-Glenlivet 1971 / 27 YO / Sherry Cask
70cl / 53.8% - Signatory - A 1971 Macallan-Glenlivet Sherry Cask Whisky. Bottled by Signatory at 27 years of age.

Macallan-Glenlivet 33 YO / Bot.1970s
75cl / 43% - Gordon & Macphail

Macallan-Glenlivet 40 YO / Gordon & Macphail
75cl / 43% - Gordon & Macphail

MANNOCHMORE RANGE

Mannochmore 12 YO
70cl / 43% - Flora & Fauna - Mannochmore's delicate and fragrant entry into the Flora and Fauna range. One of the only bottlings you'll find with their name on the front.

Mannochmore 18 YO / Manager's Dram
70cl / 66% - Distillery Bottling - A rare Mannochmore 18 YO selected by the Diageo Distillery managers for staff only. Please note that the bottle numbers have been removed from the labels on some of these bottles.

Mannochmore 1982 / 28 YO / Liquid Sun
70cl / 49.4% - Liquid Sun - A 1982 vintage Whisky from Mannochmore, sister Distillery to Glenlossie, matured for 28 years in a Bourbon Cask and bottled in 2011 by Liquid Sun.

Mannochmore 1990 / 18 YO
70cl / 54.9% - Distillery Bottling - This heavily-Sherried Mannochmore 1990 was one of Tim F's favourite drams from 2009's Special Releases. A belter from a previously undistinguished Distillery - we'd like to see much more of this sort of thing.

Mannochmore 1991 / Connoisseurs Choice
70cl / 46% - Gordon & Macphail - A lightly smoky Single Malt from Mannochmore, bottled by Gordon & Macphail in their Connoisseurs Choice range. Filled with ripe fruit and with a nice touch of Sherry influence on the finish.

Mannochmore 1998 / Managers' Choice / Sherry Cask
70cl / 59.1% - Distillery Bottling - A single Sherry Cask of the little-seen Mannochmore, this is from the 1998 vintage and was bottled in 2009 for the Managers' Choice range.

MILTONDUFF RANGE

Miltonduff 10 YO / Gordon & Macphail
70cl / 40% - Gordon & Macphail - Given that Miltonduff is the seventh largest Distillery in Scotland, one would think that it would be more common - however the vast majority of its output goes into the Ballantine's blends. This G&M bottling has an attractive grassy, fruity character.

Miltonduff 12 YO / Bot.1980s
75cl / 43% - Distillery Bottling - An old release of Miltonduff Whisky. Ages for 12 years and bottled at 43%. We estimate that this is from sometime in during the 1980s.

Miltonduff 1965 / Bot.1985 / Sherry Wood / Moon Import
75cl / 57% - Moon Import - A rare 1980s bottling of the little-seen Miltonduff Distillery. This is from the 1965 vintage and was bottled in

the mid-1980s by Italian importer Moon after 20 years maturation in Sherry Casks.

Miltonduff 1969 / Sherry Cask / Gordon & Macphail
70cl / 43% - Gordon & Macphail - A Gordon & Macphail bottling of little-seen Speysider Miltonduff. From the colour, we're hazarding a guess that this is from Sherry wood. Bottled in 2008, just shy of its 40th birthday.

Miltonduff 1990 / 21 YO / Old Malt Cask #7921
70cl / 50% - Douglas Laing - A 1990 vintage Whisky from Miltonduff, Distilled in May, matured for 21 years in a refill hogshead and bottled in November of 2011 by the folks at Douglas Lain for their Old Malt Cask range of Whiskies.

Miltonduff 1997 / 14 YO / Cask Strength Edition
50cl / 58.3% - Distillery Bottling - A 1997 vintage Whisky from Miltonduff. This has been aged for 14 years and bottled at Cask strength.

Miltonduff 5 YO / Bot.1970s
75cl / 40% - Distillery Bottling

Miltonduff-Glenlivet / Bot.1970s / Flat Bottle
75cl / 43% - Distillery Bottling - A flat bottle of Miltonduff-Glenlivet from the 1970s.

MORTLACH RANGE

Mortlach / Bot.~1900s
75cl / 40% - An early 20th century bottle from the estate of Dr Alexander Mitchell Cowie, son of George Cowie who was the Distillery licensee from 1854-1923. The family held a number of Casks of Mortlach which were bottled, as this is, by Wm Sheed of Dufftown.

Mortlach 10 YO / Editor's Nose
70cl / 60.5% - A special Distillery bottling of Mortlach released for Scotland's Insider magazine.

Mortlach 12 YO / Bot.1970s / Gordon & Macphail
75cl / 40% - Gordon & Macphail - A bottle of Mortlach 12 YO from the 1970s, bottled by Gordon & Macphail and presented in their old black labelled livery.

Mortlach 14 YO / Bot.1980s
75cl / 57% - Sestante - A 100-proof Mortlach 14 YO bottled in the 1980s by Italian indie bottlers Sestante.

Mortlach 15 YO / Gordon & Macphail
70cl / 43% - Gordon & Macphail - A 15 YO Mortlach from indie pioneers Gordon & Macphail, bottled at their now-standard strength

of 43%.

Mortlach 16 YO
70cl / 43% - Flora & Fauna - A cracking malt from a great, but criminally under-exposed Distillery, Mortlach has a rich, complex, spicy Sherried character and deserves far wider recognition.

Mortlach 1936 / 36 YO / Connoisseurs Choice
75cl / 43% - Gordon & Macphail - A lovely old bottle of Mortlach Distilled in 1936 and bottled in the early 1970s by Gordon & Macphail for the Italian market under the original black Connoisseurs Choice label.

Mortlach 1938 / 60 YO
70cl / 40% - Gordon & Macphail

Mortlach 1938 / Sherry Cask / Bot.1980s / Gordon & Macphail
75cl / 40% - Gordon & Macphail - An ancient Mortlach 1938 bottled by G & M in the 1980s. This vintage seems to have been something of an annus mirabilis for Mortlach, with Gordon & Macphail having released several stunning bottlings. Fabulous old-school style with abundant tropical fruit and a drying oak edge.

Mortlach 1942 / 50 YO / G&M Private Collection
70cl / 40% - Gordon & Macphail - An incredible old Whisky from the archives of Gordon & Macphail. Distilled on New Year's Eve in 1942 and bottled in January of 1993, this has spent over 50 years maturing in a Sherry Cask. An impressive slice of history.

Mortlach 1949 / Sherry Cask
70cl / 40% - Gordon & Macphail - A Gordon & Macphail bottling of 1949 vintage Mortlach. Long aged and richly coloured from spending its life in a Sherry Cask.

Mortlach 1954 / Sherry Cask / Gordon & Macphail
70cl / 43% - Gordon & Macphail - A vintage Mortlach Distilled in 1954 and bottled by Gordon & Macphail after over fifty years maturing in Sherry Casks.

Mortlach 1957 / Private Collection / Gordon & Macphail
70cl / 43.5% - Gordon & Macphail - Wow - a fifty-year-old Mortlach from first-fill Sherry butts! Mortlach is a quality Distillery, and the G&M Private Collections have been very well-received so far, so this is likely to be very good.

Mortlach 1969 / 16 YO / Intertrade
75cl / 56.5% - Intertrade

Mortlach 1969 / 21 YO / Sherry Wood
75cl / 40% - A lovely old Intertrade bottling of Mortlach 1969, matured in Sherrywood and bottled in the early 1990s at 21 years old.

Mortlach 1971 / 32 YO
70cl / 50.1% - Distillery Bottling - A very rare Distillery bottling of Mortlach, one of the most under-rated Speysides around. This 1971 vintage was released a few years ago as part of Diageo's 'Superpremium' series.

Mortlach 1972 / 23 YO
75cl / 59.4% - Distillery Bottling

Mortlach 1973 / 14 YO / Sherry Cask / Carato
75cl / 57% - Sestante - Bottled at 100-proof (not sure if this was natural strength or not), this is an incredibly rare 1980s bottling of Mortlach 1973 by the hugely-respected Sestante importers for fellow Italians Carato.

Mortlach 1976 / Gordon & Macphail
70cl / 43% - Gordon & Macphail - A 1976 vintage Whisky from the well stocked warehouses of Gordon & Macphail - Distilled at Speyside favourite Mortlach.

Mortlach 1978 / 20 YO
70cl / 62.2% - Distillery Bottling - Bottled at its whopping full strength of 62.2%, this little-seen Mortlach 1978 was released in May 1998 as part of the highly desirable Rare Malts series from UDV (now Diageo).

Mortlach 1984 / Centenary Reserve / Gordon & Macphail
70cl / 40% - Gordon & Macphail - 1984 vintage Mortlach bottled in 1995 by Gordon & Macphail as part of their Centenary Reserve range - a celebration of their 1895 founding.

Mortlach 1988 / 18 YO
70cl / 55.3% - Murray McDavid - A Murray McDavid Mortlach 1988, bottled at full strength after 18 years of ageing.

Mortlach 1989 / 22 YO / Cask #3926 / Mackillop's
70cl / 54.9% - Mackillop's - A Mackillop's Choice bottling of 22 YO single Cask Whisky from Mortlach. Distilled in 1989 and bottled in March 2012 at Cask strength.

Mortlach 1990 / 18 YO / Leroy Vosne-Romanée Finished
70cl / 54.2% - Murray McDavid - An 18 YO Mortlach, Distilled in 1990 and bottled in 2009 by Murray McDavid. Continuing their love of finishing Whisky in interesting Casks, this spent the last part of its time in wood sitting in Premier Cru Domaine Leroy red wine Casks from Vosne-Romanée, one of the top wines from one of the highest quality growing areas in France.

Mortlach 1991 / 20 YO / Sherry Butt #7706
70cl / 56.4% - Signatory - A single Cask Whisky from Mortlach Distillery. Distilled in 1991 and aged for 20 years in a Sherry Butt. This

has been bottled by Signatory for their Cask Strength Collection.

Mortlach 1991 / 21 YO / Sherry Butt #12/943
70cl / 53.8% - Signatory - A 21 YO single Sherry butt matured Whisky from Mortlach, released by Signatory as part of their Cask Strength Collection. Distilled on October 1st 1991 and bottled on November 8th 2012.

Mortlach 1993 / 16 Year Old / Single Malts of Scotland
70cl / 60.2% - Speciality Drinks Ltd. Originally bottled in 2009, this immensely powerful (60.2%) Bourbon-matured Mortlach 1993 was originally destined for the overseas market before being shelved at the last minute, and is now safely back in the SMoS fold. Hurrah!

Mortlach 1996 / 11 YO / Sherry / Premier Barrel
70cl / 46% - Douglas Laing - A Premier Barrel edition of 1996 vintage Mortlach, aged for 11 years before bottling in their rather special looking ceramic decanter.

Mortlach 19 YO / Manager's Dram
70cl / 55.8% - Distillery Bottling

Mortlach 21 Year Old / Gordon & Macphail
70cl / 43% - Gordon & Macphail - A superb value for money bottling of Mortlach 21 YO from Gordon & Macphail.

MOSSTOWIE RANGE

Mosstowie 1979 / Connoisseurs Choice
70cl / 40% - Gordon & Macphail - A 1979 vintage Mosstowie, the rare Lomond still Whisky produced at Miltonduff Distillery between 1964 and 1981. This one was bottled by Gordon & Macphail under their Connoisseurs Choice label.

Mosstowie 1979 / 33 YO / Cask #1307 / Signatory
70cl / 48% - Signatory - A 1979 vintage single Cask Whisky from Miltonduff, Distilled using their Lomond Still and thus bottled under the name of Mosstowie, and bottled by Signatory as part of their Cask Strength Collection.

Mosstowie 17 YO / Bot.1980s
75cl / 66% - Sestante - Mosstowie is hard enough to come by - it was only produced between 1964-1981 in Miltonduff's Lomond stills. But an aged Mosstowie 17 YO from Sestante? Ludicrously rare. And check out the strength!! A collector's wet dream.

Mosstowie 18 YO / Bot.1980s
75cl / 64.8% - Sestante - A very rare 18 YO Mosstowie, which was the Single Malt made briefly on a Lomond still at Miltonduff. Bottled by Sestante at the bafflingly-high-considering-it's-age strength of 64.8% alcohol.

PITTYVAICH RANGE

Pittyvaich 12 YO
70cl / 43% - Flora & Fauna - Pittyvaich was one of the newest and most short lived Distilleries in Scotland, only operating from 1974 until 1993. The Distillery has now been demolished and this is the most easily (for now) available of the very small number of bottlings of their spirit.

Pittyvaich 1989 / 20 YO
70cl / 57.5% - Distillery Bottling - A very pleasant appley, biscuity dram from an unheralded Distillery that closed its doors in 1993 after only eighteen years of existence. We were surprised at the quality of this Pittyvaich, which wears its twenty years very lightly.

Pittyvaich 1993 / Bot.2012 / Connoisseurs Choice
70cl / 46% - Gordon & Macphail - A Connoisseurs Choice bottling of Pittyvaich from 1993, which was the short-lived Distillery's final year of operation before being demolished in 2002. We're absolutely delighted to see Gordon & Macphail bottling some of their CC range at 46% these days.

ROSEISLE DISTILLERY

Diageo opened the new Distillery in October 2010.

SPEYBURN RANGE

Speyburn 10 YO
70cl / 40% - Distillery Bottling - Pretty much the only expression of Speyburn on the market until 2008. It may now have stable mates but it still keeps its place as the easy drinking centre of the range.

Speyburn 1968 / 15 YO
75cl / 40% - Gordon & Macphail

Speyburn 1977 / Connoisseurs Choice
70cl / 43% - Gordon & Macphail - A bottling of overlooked Speysider Speyburn from the 1977 vintage by Gordon & Macphail for their Connoisseurs Choice range.

Speyburn 1980 / 26 YO
70cl / 61.3% - Signatory - A single Cask Cask-strength Refill Butt from Speyburn. Just about everything in this 'Cask' series has been very good and several have been exceptional.

Speyburn 21 YO / Centenary Decanter
70cl / 40% - Distillery Bottling - A special limited edition decanter produced by Inver House to mark the centenary of the Speyburn

Distillery in 1997.

Speyburn Bradan Orach
70cl / 40% - Distillery Bottling - A no-age-statement expression from Speyburn. Bradan Orach means Golden Salmon, according to our exhaustive research.

THE SPEYSIDE RANGE

The Speyside / Crystal Decanter in Tantalus
70cl / 40% - Distillery Bottling

The Speyside 8 YO
75cl / 43% - Distillery Bottling - The now discontinued 8 YO Whisky from one of Scotland's Youngest Distilleries. They started production in 1990 after over 25 years of building (a lot by hand) and have now been around long enough to have a 12 YO as their standard bottling.

'Probably Speyside's Finest' 1965 / 46 YO
70cl / 53.6% - Douglas Laing - A well aged 46 YO Whisky from 'Probably Speyside's Finest' distillery, according to bottlers Douglas Laing. Distilled in 1965 and aged in a Sherry butt this has taken on the beautiful colour that is typical of old Whisky from, for example, Glenfarclas.

Speyside 16 YO / Fragments of Scotland
75cl / 50% - Samaroli

Speyside 1992 / 20 YO / Cask #8472
70cl / 50% - Douglas Laing - A 1992 single Cask Whisky from Speyside Distillery. This Whisky has been matured in a Sherry Butt for 20 years before being bottled by Douglas Laing for their Old Malt Cask range.

Speyside 1993 / Scott's Selection
70cl / 61.5% - Scott's Selection - A 1993 Whisky from Speyside Distillery. This Whisky was bottled at Cask strength for the Scott's Selection range.

STRATHISLA RANGE

Strathisla 10 YO / Bot.1960s
75cl / 43% - Distillery Bottling - A very rare 1960s original bottling of Strathisla 10 year-old dating from the 1960s, complete with the original label still used by Gordon & Macphail for their modern bottlings of the Whisky Distilled in this era.

Strathisla 12 YO
70cl / 43% - Distillery Bottling - An overlooked malt that has passed to Pernod Ricard as part of the Chivas Brothers portfolio, Strathisla

12 YO is highly-regarded by blenders and connoisseurs of its fruity Sherried style.

Strathisla 12 YO / Bot.1990s
75cl / 40% - Distillery Bottling - A marvellous old original bottling of Strathisla 12 YO, probably released around the early 1990s.

Strathisla 15 YO / Bot.1970s
75cl / 40% - Gordon & Macphail - A great 1970s Gordon & Macphail bottle of Strathisla 15 YO.

Strathisla 1937 / 34 YO / Sherry Wood
75cl / 43% - Gordon & Macphail - A richly coloured bottle of 1937 vintage Strathisla, bottled by Gordon & Macphail as part of the Connoisseurs Choice range 34 years later.

Strathisla 1937 / 35 YO / Sherry Wood
75cl / 43% - Gordon & Macphail - A 1937 vintage Strathisla, matured for 35 years and bottled by Gordon & Macphail under their Connoisseurs Choice Label.

Strathisla 1948 / Bot.1980s
75cl / 40% - Gordon & Macphail

Strathisla 1948 / Bot.1980s
75cl / 40% - Gordon & Macphail - A 1948 vintage Gordon & Macphail bottling of Strathisla from the 1980s, presented in their stencilled bottle.

Strathisla 1949 / Bot.1980s
75cl / 40%

Strathisla 1949 / Gordon & Macphail
70cl / 40% - Gordon & Macphail - A long aged Whisky from Gordon & Macphail, Distilled at Strathisla back in 1949 just before the Distillery was bought and rejuvenated by Chivas Brothers.

Strathisla 1953 / Bot.1980s
75cl / 40% - Gordon & Macphail

Strathisla 1954 / Bot.1996 / Gordon & Macphail
70cl / 40% - Gordon & Macphail - A release of 1954 vintage Whisky from Strathisla from Gordon & Macphail, bottled in 1996 using a retro-styled Distillery label.

Strathisla 1954 / Gordon & Macphail
70cl / 40% - Gordon & Macphail - Bottled at over fifty years of age, this is another of Gordon & Macphail's remarkable long-aged Strathisla's at a bargain price for a dram of such antiquity.

Strathisla 1957 / Gordon & Macphail
70cl / 43% - Gordon & Macphail - Strathisla is one of those great

Speyside Distilleries (like Glenfarclas, Macallan, Glen Grant etc) with a spirit capable of immense ageing. This Gordon and Macphail bottling is astonishing value for money for a fifty-year-old malt.

Strathisla 1964 / Gordon & Macphail
70cl / 43% - Gordon & Macphail - An amazing colour on this long-aged Strathisla, Distilled in 1964 and bottled by Gordon & Macphail at over forty years old.

Strathisla 1965 / Gordon & Macphail
70cl / 43% - Gordon & Macphail - A 1965 Whisky from Strathisla Distilery in Speyside. This Whisky was bottled in 2011, by Gordon and Macphail, making it at least 45 years old.

Strathisla 1967 / 40 YO / Cask #2716
70cl / 48.6% - Duncan Taylor - A big, oaky Strathisla 1967 from Duncan Taylor bottled early in 2008 from Cask 2716 at 40 years old.

Strathisla 1967 / Bot.1986 / Sherry Wood
75cl / 57% - Samaroli - A 1967 vintage Strathisla, matured in sherry wood and bottled in 1986 by Italian independent Samaroli.

Strathisla 1967 / Gordon & Macphail
70cl / 43% - Gordon & Macphail - Gordon & Macphail's warehouses continue to impress with this 1967 vintage Strathisla, well matured and with a fantastic colour.

Strathisla 1973 / Bot.1991
70cl / 60.5% - Distillery Bottling

Strathisla 35 YO / Bot.1980s / Gordon & Macphail
75cl / 40% - Gordon & Macphail

Strathisla 8 YO / Bot.1970s
75cl / 57.1% - Gordon & Macphail - A rare old bottling of young high-strength Strathisla by Gordon & MacPhail from the 1970s.

Strathisla 8 YO / Bot.1980s / Gordon & Macphail
75cl / 57% - Gordon & Macphail - An independent bottling of 8 YO Strathisla by Gordon & Macphail. We think this was bottled in the 1980s.

STRATHMILL RANGE

Strathmill 12 YO
70cl / 43% - Flora & Fauna - The only official bottling from Strathmill, more usually known as the producer of the core of the J&B blends.

Strathmill 15 YO / Manager's Dram

70cl / 53.5% - Distillery Bottling - A rare Strathmill 15 YO selected by the Diageo Distillery managers for staff only. Please note that the bottle numbers have been removed from the labels on some of these bottles.

Strathmill 1976 / 35 YO / Cask #7817
70cl / 47.2% - Douglas Laing

Strathmill 1991 / Connoisseurs Choice
70cl / 43% - Gordon & Macphail - An affordable bottle of the little-seen Strathmill. This 1991 vintage was bottled from refill Bourbon Casks by Gordon & Macphail a few years ago for their Connoisseurs Choice series.

Strathmill 1996 / Managers' Choice
70cl / 60.1% - Distillery Bottling - Bottled in 2009 as part of the not-altogether-uncontroversial Manager's Choice series, this Strathmill is one of the more interesting bottlings in the series, as one of only a tiny handful of official bottlings from this very obscure Distillery, most of whose output goes into the J&B blend.

Strathmill Centenary Decanter (1891-1991)
75cl / 43% - Distillery Bottling - A special embossed teardrop decanter of aged Strathmill, bottled for the Distillery's centenary in the early 1990s. Very rare to see an official bottling of Strathmill, this is a real collector's item.

Strathmill Fine Old Scotch Whisky
75cl / 40% - Distillery Bottling - A fine looking bottle of seldom seen Whisky from Speyside's Strathmill, a replica of that bottled in the 1940s and emblazoned with original's price (12/6) and tax (8/5).

TAMDHU RANGE

Tamdhu 10 YO / Bot.1980s
75cl / 43% - Distillery Bottling - An old 1980s bottling of the little-known (and rather underrated) Speysider Tamdhu.

Tamdhu 15 YO / Bot.1960's
75cl / 43% - Distillery Bottling - A marvellous old 1960s bottle of Tamdhu 15 YO, bottled at 43%.

Tamdhu 16 YO / Bot.1960s
75cl / 43% - Distillery Bottling - A very nice, quaint old 1970s bottle of Tamdhu 16 YO, bottled at 43%.

Tamdhu 17 YO / Bot.1970s
75cl / 46% - Cadenhead's - A very rare old bottle of Tamdhu 17 YO, bottled in the 1970s by Cadenhead's.

Tamdhu 1962 / Macphail's Collection / Gordon & Macphail

70cl / 43% - Gordon & Macphail - A very handsome colour on this 1962 Tamdhu, bottled at 43% by G&M for their Macphail collection after well over four decades of Cask ageing.

Tamdhu 1966 / Macphail's Collection / Gordon & Macphail
70cl / 43% - Gordon & Macphail - A very old Tamdhu 1966, bottled by Gordon & Macphail for their Macphail's Collection series.

Tamdhu 1971 / Macphail's Collection
70cl / 43% - Gordon & Macphail - A 1971 vintage from (as of 2011) mothballed Tamdhu, bottled by Gordon & Macphail. It's currently hoped that we'll see the Distillery back up and running in 2012, thanks to it being purchased by Ian Macleod.

Tamdhu 1990 / 21 YO / Liquid Sun
70cl / 48.1% - Liquid Sun

Tamdhu 1990 / 21 YO / Old & Rare
70cl / 53.6% - Douglas Laing - A single Cask Whisky from Tamdhu. Distilled in 1990 and matured for over 21 years in a Sherry hogshead. This has been bottled at Cask strength by Douglas Laing for their platinum selection range.

Tamdhu 30 YO/ Macphail's Collection/ Gordon & Macphail
70cl / 43% - Gordon & Macphail - A great value long-aged Tamdhu 30 bottled at 43% by G&M as part of their Macphail's Collection.

Tamdhu 8 YO / Bot. 1970's
75.7cl / 40% - Distillery Bottling - Lovely old Distillery bottling of young Tamdhu from the 1970s.

Tamdhu 8 YO / Bot.1980s
75cl / 40% - Gordon & Macphail - An old Gordon & Macphail bottling of this unsung Speysider, a key ingredient of the Famous Grouse blend.

TAMNAVULIN RANGE

Tamnavulin 1966 / 10th Anniversary of Moon Import
75cl / 45% - Moon Import - A special 1966 Tamnavulin bottled in 1990 for the 10th anniversary of cult Italian indie bottlers Moon Import.

Tamnavulin 1966 / 35 YO / Sherry Cask
70cl / 52.6% - Distillery Bottling - This Cask was matured full-term in a Sandeman cream Sherry butt and remains the finest expression from this Distillery we have tried. Hugely impressive stuff, with complex fruitcake, leather and cognac-esque rancio characters, with a delicious Sherried sweetness.

Tamnavulin 1968 / The Stillman's Dram

75cl / 40% - Distillery Bottling - A very rare limited bottling of Tamnavulin from 1986.

Tamnavulin 24 YO / Stillman's Dram
70cl / 45% - Distillery Bottling - A 24 YO Tamnavulin bottled by the Distillery as part of the Stillman's Dram series.

Tamnavulin 29 YO / Stillman's Dram
70cl / 45% - Distillery Bottling

Tamnavulin Glenlivet 8 YO / Bot. 1980's
75cl / 40% - Distillery Bottling - An old dumpy bottle of 8 YO Tamnavulin bottled in the 1980s when the Distillery was still using the 'Glenlivet' suffix.

Tamnavulin-Glenlivet / Bot.1970s
75cl / 43% - Distillery Bottling - An old dumpy bottle of Tamnavulin-Glenlivet, probably from the early to mid 1970s.

Tamnavulin-Glenlivet 1966 / The Birds / Moon / Bot.1988
75cl / 45% - Moon Import - A Moon Import bottling of 1966 vintage Tamnavulin, released in 1988 as part of their 'The Birds' series of Whiskies.

Tamnavulin-Glenlivet 1967 / Bot.1980s
75cl / 43% - Distillery Bottling - An 1967 Tamnavulin-Glenlivet btotled at 43%, we reckon this is probably from the mid-to-late late 1980s.

Tamnavulin-Glenlivet 20 YO / Sherry Wood / Bot.1980s
75cl / 46% - Distillery Bottling - A very old Distillery bottling of Sherried Tamnavulin 20 YO, produced for the Italian market at some stage in the 1980s, when they were still using the '-Glenlivet' suffix..

TOMATIN RANGE
Tomatin 10 YO / 1970's
75cl / 40% - Distillery Bottling - A wonderful old 1970s official bottling of Tomatin 10 YO, with an understatedly picturesque black and gold label.

Tomatin 10 YO / 1980s
75cl / 40% - Distillery Bottling - An old bottle of Tomatin 10 YO from the 1980s.

Tomatin 10 YO / Bot.1960s
75cl / 43% - Distillery Bottling - A characterful old bottle of Tomatin 10 YO bottled in the 1970s.

Tomatin 12 YO
75cl / 43% - Distillery Bottling

Tomatin 12 YO / Sherry Finish
70cl / 40% - Distillery Bottling - A polished, mellow, very

approachable Speysider, Tomatin was once the largest Distillery in Scotland with 23 stills and a production capacity of 12 milllion litres of alcohol per year. These days capacity is down to 5 million litres, the majority of which goes into the delicious Antiquary blend.

Tomatin 15 YO
70cl / 43% - Distillery Bottling - A smartly-packaged 15 year-old expression of little-seen Speysider Tomatin, bottled at 43%.

Tomatin 18 YO
70cl / 46% - Distillery Bottling - After spending eighteen years in refill oak, this Tomatin is married in Oloroso Sherry Casks to round it out and add a layer of sweet dried fruit flavours.

Tomatin 1964 / 18 YO
75cl / 40%

Tomatin 1964 / Bot.1990s / Spirit of Scotland
70cl / 40% - Gordon & Macphail

Tomatin 1967 / 40 YO / Bourbon Casks
70cl / 42.9% - Distillery Bottling - For this very special Tomatin, Distillery manager Douglas Campbell has selected seven of the best ex-Bourbon hogsheads Distilled in 1967. Rich, fruity, creamy and complex.

Tomatin 1967 / 40 YO / Refill Butt #17904
70cl / 49.3% - Distillery Bottling - A second release of Tomatin 40 YO, this is from the 1967 vintage. Bottled from a single refill butt for the German market, this looks like another winner.

Tomatin 1967 / 44 YO
70cl / 51.9% - Clan Denny

Tomatin 1970 / 15 YO / Connoisseurs Choice
75cl / 40% - Gordon & Macphail - A 1970 vintage Tomatin from Gordon & Macphail's Connoisseurs Choice range. This was bottled in the mid-1980s after 15 years of maturation, and has their lovely old brown label.

Tomatin 1973 / 36 YO / Single Cask
70cl / 44% - Distillery Bottling - A single Cask bottling of Tomatin, bottled at 36 years old and Distilled back in 1973, the Distillery's powerhouse heydays where they had stills numbering in double figures and produced one of the largest amounts of spirit in the country.

Tomatin 1975 / 32 YO / Bourbon Cask
70cl / 55.7% - Douglas Laing - A Bourbon-matured Tomatin bottled by Douglas Laing for their Platinum Selection.

Tomatin 1982 / 28 YO / Sherry Cask

70cl / 57% - Distillery Bottling - A special release single Cask bottling of Tomatin from 1982, aged for 28 years and bottled in 2011. With 560 57% bottles available we assume it was matured in a Sherry butt and it's picked up a nice colour over the years.

Tomatin 1988 / Connoisseurs Choice
70cl / 43% - Gordon & Macphail - A 1988 vintage Whisky from edge-of-Speyside Distillery Tomatin, bottled by Gordon & Macphail for their Connoisseurs Choice range.

Tomatin 1990 / 18 YO / Cask #7738
70cl / 54% - Distillery Bottling - An offically bottled single Cask of Tomatin 1990, released at Cask strength in its natural state, without chill-filtration or colouring. Tomatin is definitely one to watch over the next couple of years.

Tomatin 1999 / 10 YO / Cask #29457
70cl / 57.1% - Distillery Bottling - A 10 YO Tomatin 1999, finished in a Tempranillo (ie Rioja grape) wine Cask after initial maturation in refill American oak. Like the 1997 released at the same time, this has been bottled at 57.1% (100-proof), although the box says 'Natural Strength'. If they really were both naturally 100 proof on the day they were bottled in November 2009, that's a remarkable coincidence.

Tomatin 21 YO
70cl / 52% - Distillery Bottling - A Cask-strength 21 YO from Tomatin, a Distillery which has really benefited from a bit of brand investment recently, with a packaging facelift and a flurry of highly-regarded new releases. Expect smooth, spicy wood influence and more than a hint of Sherry in the mix.

Tomatin 25 YO
70cl / 43% - Distillery Bottling - A jazzed-up presentation of the delicious Tomatin 25 YO. This is exclusively from American oak Casks.

Tomatin 25 YO / Half Bottle
35cl / 43% - Distillery Bottling - A half bottle of Tomatin's revived 25 YO, an excellent example of American oak matured Speysider.

Tomatin 30 YO
70cl / 46% - Distillery Bottling - The replacement for the 25 YO in the standard Tomatin line-up, the 30 YO is limited to just 2000 bottles a year and came about due to the fantastic reception of their last 30 YO release in 2007. An outstanding Whisky, with beautiful honeysuckle, herby, leafy notes, and some polished oak; this is a dram that wears its great age very lightly.

Tomatin 5 YO / Bot.1980s
75cl / 43% - Distillery Bottling

Tomatin Centenary Decanter
70cl / 43% - Distillery Bottling

Tomatin Decades
70cl / 46% - Distillery Bottling - A special Whisky from Tomatin, created to honour master Distiller Douglas Campbell's 50th year of service with the company. He has created the Whisky by selecting Casks from each of the 5 decades he's been at the Distillery to create a complex Whisky marrying age and youth together.

TOMINTOUL RANGE

Tomintoul 10 YO
70cl / 40% - Distillery Bottling - The first bottling of Tomintoul to be released after it changed hands in 2000, it's a rounded dram with fruit and toffee, and a peppery finish.

Tomintoul 12 YO / Portwood Finish
70cl / 46% - Distillery Bottling - A port-finished edition of Tomintoul, one of Speyside's most approachable and easy-drinking drams.

Tomintoul 12 YO / Sherry Cask
70cl / 40% - A recently-introduced variant from the under-appreciated Tomintoul, this has been finished in an Oloroso Sherry Cask and is soft, sweet and creamy. Great value, as always with this Distillery.

Tomintoul 14 YO
70cl / 46% - Distillery Bottling - Kudos to Tomintoul, who are clearly listening to their customers - this 14 YO has been bottled at 46% at its natural colour without being chill-filtered. A big thumbs-up.

Tomintoul 16 YO
70cl / 40% - Distillery Bottling - Long known as 'the gentle dram' Tomintoul 16 YO is soft and nutty, with a pleasant richness. A Gold Medal winner at the International Wine & Spirits Competition (IWSC), this is a cracking dram for the money.

Tomintoul 1967 / 45 YO / The Whisky Agency
70cl / 44.6% - The Whisky Agency - A long aged Tomintoul bottled by the Whisky Agency as part of their 'Fights' label series (here we have Leopard vs Man on Horseback), Distilled in 1967 and bottled in 2012 at 45 years old.

Tomintoul 21 YO
70cl / 40% - Distillery Bottling - This 21 YO Tomintoul boasts a floral, fruity, spicy character and was introduced in summer 2011 following the demise of 27 YO. As with its illustrious predecessor, this will gladden the hearts of fans of mature easy-drinking Speyside Whiskies that don't cost the earth.

Tomintoul 33 YO
5cl / 43%

Tomintoul 33 YO / Special Reserve
70cl / 43% - Distillery Bottling - A long-aged expression of Tomintoul, this 33 YO replaces the old 27 YO bottling. Another hit for Angus Dundee, who have done great things with this Distillery since their takeover in 2000. Award winner at the WWA 2010:

Tomintoul Peaty Tang
70cl / 40% - Distillery Bottling - We assume that this new no-age-statement peated Tomintoul must be similar to the Old Ballantruan but at a reduced strength. Either way, at this price it must be worth a punt for peatheads.

Tomintoul-Glenlivet / Bot.1970s
75cl / 40% - Distillery Bottling - A very unusual 1970s from the Tomintoul Distillery (still using the Glenlivet suffix at the time) with a round bottle in fluted glass and a large silver screwtop rather than the traditional bottleneck.

Tomintoul-Glenlivet 12 YO / Bot.1980s
75cl / 43% - Distillery Bottling - A 1980s bottling of Tomintoul-Glenlivet, packaged in a very 80s bottle.

TORMORE RANGE

Tormore 10 YO
75cl / 43% - Distillery Bottling - An old Distillery bottling of Tormore 10 YO which, judging by the slightly OTT hexagonal bottle, we're reckoning just might be from the 1980s.

Tormore 10 YO
70cl / 40% - Distillery Bottling - A discontinued old early 1990s bottle of Tormore 10 YO selected for defunct Scottish off-license chain Victoria Wine.

Tormore 10 YO / Bot.1970s
75cl / 40% - Distillery Bottling - A Distillery-bottled 1970s edition of Tormore 10 YO from the 1970s when the company was owned by Long John Distillers, a subsidiary of Allied Domecq plc. The Distillery, reportedly one of the most beautiful in Scotland, is now owned by Pernod Ricard following their acquisition of Allied in 2005.

Tormore 10 YO / Bot.1970s
75cl / 43% - Distillery Bottling - A rare old 1970s bottling of Tormore's entry-level 10 YO.

Tormore 10 YO / Bot.1980s
75cl / 43% - Distillery Bottling - A rather rare bottling of obscure Speysider Tormore under a 'Pure Malt' label from the 1980s.

Tormore 10 YO / Bot.1980s
75cl / 43% - Distillery Bottling

Tormore 10 YO / Bot.1980s
75cl / 43% - Distillery Bottling - A 1980s Distillery bottling of 10 YO Whisky from seldom-seen Tormore.

Tormore 12 YO
70cl / 40% - Distillery Bottling - Launched in 2004 this is the main official bottling of Tormore, part of the Chivas Brothers portfolio of Distilleries.

Tormore 1994 / Cask Strength / Gordon & Macphail
70cl / 59.9% - Gordon & Macphail - A Cask strength Tormore from 1994, bottled in 2007 by G&M for their 'Cask' series after over 12 years in Sherry butts.

Tormore 5 YO / Bot.1980s
75cl / 40% - Distillery Bottling - A heroically naff Tormore 5 YO from the 1980s. The hexagonal bottle and ever-so-slightly OTT retro font and labelling take this to a level of magnificent unfashionability. You couldn't find a better gift for a post modern Whisky collector (if such a thing exists).

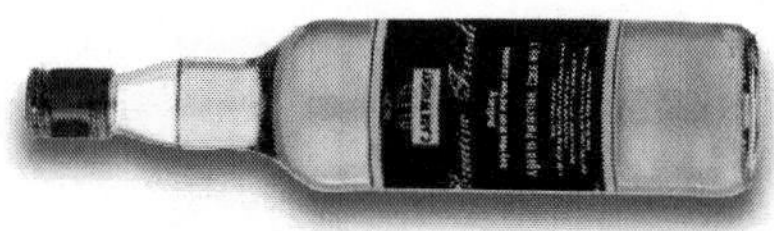

MOST ENTERTAINING WHISKY EITHER BLEND OR MALT WITH THE BEST STORY BEHIND THE BOTTLE

Gold - Shackleton Expedition
Silver – Tam O' Shanter Cutty Sark
Bronze – Highland Park Thor

JAPANESE WHISKY OF THE YEAR

Gold - Hibiki - 17 YO
Silver: Nikka Taketsuru 21 YO
Bronze: Yamazaki 18 YO

NEW WORLD WHISKY OF THE YEAR

1.New Zealand 21 YO
2.Mackmyra Moments
3.Limeburners

SINGLE MALT SCOTCH NO AGE

Gold - Laphroig
Silver - Highland Park 18 YO
Bronze - Glenrothes 1988

SINGLE MALT 30 YO AND OVER

Gold - Glenglassaugh 39 YO Massandra Collection (Aleatico finish)
Silver - Tomintoul 33 YO
Bronze - Port Ellen 1982 / 30 YO / Cask #1518 / Chieftain's - Ian Macleod

www.askwhisky.co.uk

BEST INTRODUCTION SINGLE MALT

Gold - Bladnoch 10 YO
Silver - Glenturret 10 YO
Bronze - Glenmorangie 10 YO

BLENDED SCOTCH

Gold – Whyte and Mackay - 19 YO
Silver – Cutty Sark Storm
Bronze – Loch Lomond

VATTED MALT OF THE YEAR

Gold - Big Peat
Silver – Monkey Shoulder
Bronze – Sheep Dip

BEST NEW SCOTCH BRAND

Gold – Kilchoman Second Edition
Silver – Edradour
Bronze – Abhainn Dearg

BEST PACKAGED WHISKY 2013

Gold - Highland Park Thor
Silver - Shackleton Expedition
Bronze - John Dewar's Signature

BEST PEATED SINGLE MALT

Gold - Port Charlotte Peat Project
Silver – Ardbeg Uigeadail
Bronze - Kilchoman Machir Bay

BEST SMOKY SINGLE MALT

Gold – Smokehead 18 Years Black
Silver – Benromach Peat Smoke
Bronze - The Big Smoke 60

EUROPEAN BLIND TASTE TESTING AWARD

(This features all Whiskies in Europe not including Scotch)
Gold – Penderyn 41 Madeira – Wales
Silver – Mackmyra Bruks Whisky - Sweden
Bronze - Kornnog Peated Single Malt Whisky Brenton (France

NORTH AMERICAN BEST BOURBON

Gold - Woodford Reserve
Silver – Wild Turkey Russell Reserve
Bronze – Bakers 7 YO

NORTH AMERICAN MOONSHINE AWARD

Gold – The Original Moonshine Company
Silver - High West - Silver
Bronze - Hudson New York Corn Whiskey

NORTH AMERICAN WHISKY AWARD

Gold – Jack Daniels Sinatra Edition
Silver – Balcones – Single Malt
Bronze - Canadian Club 9 Years Reserve

WORLD GOLD C. ASK SINGLE MALTS

Gold – Port Ellen Connoisseurs Choice 1982 Gordan and Macphail
Silver – Old Malt Cask Rosebank 19 YO - Douglas Laing
Bronze - Mortlach 14 YO - Hart Brothers

BLIND WORLD WHISKY MALTS

Blind tasting awards by Whisky connoisseur Conny Forsgren from Sweden on behalf of C. Ask Whisky.

Gold - New Zealand 18 YO
Silver - Mccallen 14 YO Hart Brothers Bottling
Bronze - Glengoyne 10 YO

BLIND FUN TESTS - BLENDS VS MALTS

Gold - Kalavan Cask Strength Solo
Silver - Royal Salute
Bronze - Cutty Sark Tam O Shanter

The Blends won on this test 39 Points and Malts 38 Our other awards of our live testing events can be seen at our website www.askwhisky.co.uk

C. Ask Whisky The Directors
Cut due for release in 2014!

Follow C. Ask Whisky on Facebook 

C. Ask Whisky: **http://www.askwhisky.co.uk/**

Printed in Great Britain
by Amazon.co.uk, Ltd.,
Marston Gate.